THE PANTHEON ASIA LIBRARY

NEW APPROACHES TO THE NEW ASIA

No part of the world has changed so much in recent years as Asia, or
awakened such intense American interest. But much of our scholarship,
like much of our public understanding, is based on a previous era. The Asia
Library has been launched to provide the needed information on the new
Asia, and in so doing to develop both the new methods and the new sympathies
needed to understand it. Our purpose is not only to publish new work but to
experiment with a wide variety of approaches which will reflect these new
realities and their perception by those in Asia and the West.

Our books aim at different levels and audiences, from the popular to the
more scholarly, from high schools to the universities, from pictorial to documentary presentations. All books will be available in paperback.

Suggestions for additions to the Asia Library are welcome.

A Political History
of Japanese Capitalism

A Political History
of Japanese Capitalism

JON HALLIDAY

PANTHEON BOOKS
A DIVISION OF RANDOM HOUSE
NEW YORK

Library of Congress Cataloging in Publication Data

Halliday, Jon.
A Political History of Japanese Capitalism.

Includes bibliographical references and index.
1. Japan—Economic conditions—1868– 2. Japan—Economic
policy.   3. Japan—Politics and government—1868–   I. Title.
HC462.7.H25 1975   330.9′52′03   74-4774
ISBN 0-394-48391-X

Grateful acknowledgement is made to the following for permission to reprint previously published material:

AMPO: Four tables from the article "Petroleum and Political Vision: Coming to Crunch" by Yamakawa Akio, *Ampo,* No. 19, Winter 1974.

The Bank of Japan: One table from pages 136–37 of *Hundred-Year Statistics of the Japanese Economy.*

The Economist: Two tables, "Saving and Spending" and "How Bank Reserves Have Been Held Down," from *The Economist,* January 27, 1973.

Editions Calmann-Levy, Paris: Map, "Japan Under the Meiji," from the book *Meiji, 1868* by Akamatsu.

Throgsmorton Publications Ltd.: An adaptation of four tables from an article by Muneo Isshiki, "Keeping Pace With Energy's Demands" from *Investors Chronicle Survey,* September 7, 1973.

The Japan Interpreter: Table showing election results from the article "A Tenuous Victory: The General Election of 1972" by Tosh Lee, *The Japan Interpreter,* Vol. 8, No. 1, Winter 1973.

Pacific Rim Project: Four tables from *Pacific Imperialism Notebook,* Vol. 3, No. 1, December 1971–January 1972, pages 7, 9, 10, 13.

Toyo Keizai Shinposha: Two tables, "Imports and Exports of Machinery in the Mid-Meiji Period" and "Role of Government Operated Factories," from *A History of Industry* (8th Volume of *Gendai Nippon Bunmeishi* by Prof. Takao Tsuchiya, May 1944).

University of California Press: One table entitled "Purgees by Categories" from page 80 of *The Purge of Japanese Leaders Under the Occupation* by Hans Baerwald, University of California Press Publications in Political Science, Vol. 8, published 1959.

Contents

Acknowledgements

Every book is to some extent a collective product, and this one more than most. One of the few pleasant things connected with its production has been the encouragement and assistance from friends who gave of their time and ideas. I would particularly like to thank Luca Baranelli at the Turin publishing company of G. Einaudi, who first suggested I might write such a book and showed patience and enthusiasm about it. I owe a similar debt to André Schiffrin, Susan Gyarmati and the staff at Pantheon Books, who committed themselves to the book at an early stage and provided encouragement and pressure; and especially to Jim Peck, an expert and sensitive editor, who improved the book beyond anything I had a right to expect. A number of people read the manuscript at various stages and made valuable suggestions for restructuring, cuts and additions. My greatest debt is to John Dower and Herb Bix, who read the first draft and commented on it in great detail, providing an optimum combination of criticism and enthusiasm. Without their hard work and kind words this book could not exist in anything like its present form.

Enrica Collotti Pischel, Roger Murray and Gareth Stedman Jones read the bulk of the manuscript at an early stage and were of much assistance with advice on re-organizing the text and avoiding a number of pitfalls. Ben Brewster, Sukie Colegrave, Walter Easey, Peter Wollen and my brother Fred Halliday all read parts of the text and helped me with it in innumerable ways.

I would also like to thank by name a few of the friends who spent time doing the things an author perhaps needs more than anything: talking over problems, signalling texts and lending books. My gratitude on this score especially to Perry Anderson, Don Burton, John Clark, Ishiguro Hidé and Paul Willemen.

I am grateful to the following for permission to quote from manuscripts, theses and copyright material: Herb Bix, Ben Brewster, Don Burton and Martin Collick.

Gavan McCormack, my co-author on an earlier book, *Japanese Impe-*

rialism Today, has been of unfailing assistance in countless ways on this project, too.

It goes without saying that neither the persons mentioned above nor anyone else except myself is responsible for judgements, opinions or errors in the text.

These meagre acknowledgements lamentably fail to express my appreciation of the way those named rejected the traditions of individualistic "scholarship" to help improve the final product, this book.

J.H.

April 1974

Notes on the Text

Currency. From 1949 to December 1971, the Japanese yen was exchanged at ¥ (yen) 360 to U.S. $1. From December 1971 to February 1973, the rate was formally ¥308 to U.S. $1. In February 1973, the yen was floated and, after rising to a high of ¥258 to the dollar, was quoted at about ¥300 to the dollar in spring 1974. The pound sterling (£) was worth roughly U.S. $2.35 or ¥700 as of mid-1974. All references to $ (dollars) are to U.S. dollars.
N.B. Billion=a thousand millions; trillion=a million millions.

Japanese company names. Many Japanese companies have recently adapted their Japanese names and adopted English titles for international usage: the English versions are not always straight translations of the Japanese. Firms are referred to by their official English titles where these were available; otherwise, by translations of the Japanese name.

Japanese proper names. These are given in the Japanese order, i.e., surname first, except where citing non-Japanese language material in which the Japanese order is reversed. Names are cited always in the order given in the original.

Periodicals. The *Economist,* the *Guardian,* the *Observer,* the *Sunday Times,* the *Times* all refer to the London, England, periodicals.

Southeast Asia. In the text this term covers the area from Taiwan to Burma, inclusive. In Japanese government publications the term covers all non-communist Asia from Afghanistan (inclusive) to south Korea and Taiwan, sometimes including Japan itself.

Transliterations of Japanese words. The macron (long sign) is used, where appropriate, on *o* and *u* except: (1) on well-known place names (e.g., Tokyo) and a few other familiar words (e.g., Shinto); (2) in quotes where the sign was not used in the source cited; (3) on names where the source cited did not use the sign in the reference; (4) on names of Japanese companies which have adopted an English name for international usage.

Some Japanese names can be (and are) read in different ways. Persons sometimes also changed their names during their life, or were known by different names. Such alternatives are indicated in parentheses.

Abbreviations

AC	Allied Council
AFL	American Federation of Labor
AMG	Allied Military Government
ASDF	Air Self-Defence Force (post–World War II)
CBI	Confederation of British Industry
CCP	Chinese Communist Party
CEC	Central Education Council
CER	Chinese Eastern Railway
CPSU	Communist Party of the Soviet Union
EEC	European Economic Community
EPA	Economic Planning Agency
FEAC	Far Eastern Advisory Commission
FEC	Far Eastern Commission
FTC	Fair Trade Commission
GSDF	Ground Self-Defence Force (i.e., Army: post–World War II)

ICFTU	International Confederation of Free Trade Unions
ILO	International Labour Office/Organisation
IMF—JC	International Metalworkers' Federation—Japan Chapter
IMTFE	International Military Tribunal for the Far East
INA	Indian National Army
JCP	Japan Communist Party
JETRO	Japan External Trade Organisation
JNR	Japan National Railways
JSP	Japan Socialist Party
KMT	Kuomintang
LDP	Liberal Democratic Party
MITI	Ministry of International Trade and Industry
MSDF	Maritime Self-Defence Force (post–World War II)
NPR	National Police Reserve
NSC	National Security Council (U.S.)
OECD	Organisation for Economic Co-operation and Development
OSS	Office of Strategic Services
PLA	People's Liberation Army (China)
P.N.G.	Papua New Guinea
P.R.C.	People's Republic of China
R.O.K.	Republic of Korea (south Korea)
SCAP	Supreme Commander for the Allied Powers
SDF	Self-Defence Force(s) (post–World War II)
SMR(C)	South Manchuria Railway (Company)
SWNCC	State-War-Navy Coordinating Committee
UNCTAD	United Nations Conference on Trade and Development
WFTU	World Federation of Trade Unions

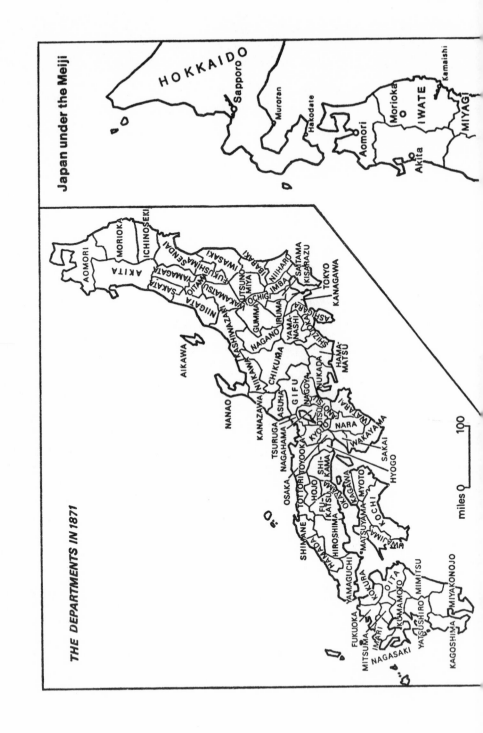

THE DEPARTMENTS IN 1871

Japan under the Meiji

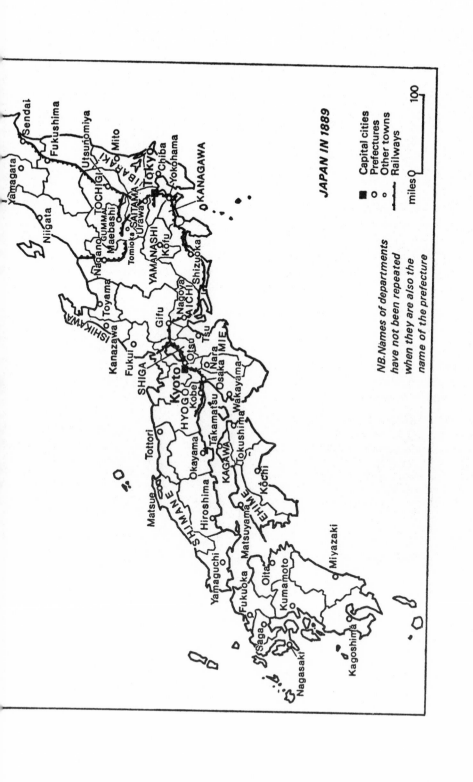

JAPAN IN 1889

■ Capital cities
○ Prefectures
○ Other towns
--- Railways

miles 0 _____ 100

NB. Names of departments have not been repeated when they are also the name of the prefecture

Sendai
Fukushima
Yamagata
Niigata
Utsunomiya
Mito
IBARAKI
TOCHIGI
GUMMA
Maebashi
Tomioka
Urawa
SAITAMA
TOKYO
Chiba
Yokohama
KANAGAWA
Nagano
Toyama
ISHIKAWA
Kanazawa
YAMANASHI
Kofu
Shizuoka
Nagoya
AICHI
Gifu
Fukui
SHIGA
Tsu
Otsu
Nara
MIE
Kyoto
HYOGO
Kobe
Osaka
Wakayama
Tottori
Matsue
SHIMANE
Okayama
Takamatsu
KAGAWA
Tokushima
Hiroshima
Yamaguchi
EHIME
Matsuyama
Kôchi
Fukuoka
Oita
Kumamoto
Miyazaki
Saga
Nagasaki
Kagoshima

Introduction

By John W. Dower

Marxism has played a paradoxical role in the study of modern Japan. Among Japanese intellectuals, its influence has been immense. It stimulated the major historical studies of the prewar period—a burst of provocative research in the late 1920s and early 1930s which was curtailed only by the repression of the state. The influence re-emerged with greater strength and vitality after 1945, drawing partly on the earlier legacy, but fed as well by the extent to which Japan's own recent history seemed to confirm the incisiveness of a Marxist analysis of capitalism. Probably a majority of Japanese historians today work more or less within the Marxist tradition.

Those who rely on English for their understanding of Japan, however, have until now been largely isolated from the insights, even questions, of Marxism, and for various reasons. The scholar's facts, it has been said, are not fish on the carving board but fish in the sea. Men choose the type of net they wish to cast and where they wish to cast it, and certainly there have been impressive catches made without the intricate web of historical materialism or class analysis or dialectical thought. One thinks of the great pioneer Japanologists at the turn of the century, such as W. G. Aston and Basil Hall Chamberlain, whose linguistic and antiquarian studies first introduced Japanese thought and culture to the West. George Sansom continued this tradition, and his pioneer "short cultural history" written in the 1930s still remains the vivid and delightful classic in this field. Sansom's approach was nicely summarized in his preface to a later edition; he saw history, he said, "as a motley procession, with some bright banners but many dingy emblems, marching out of step and not very certain of its destination."

Sansom lived a dual life: scholar of the old tradition by avocation, and by profession the commercial attaché to the British embassy in Japan. And it is interesting to note that in the economic reports he prepared for his government in the mid-1930s, his motley procession marched to a discernible tune of economic determinism, and in the increasingly certain direction of catastrophe. In Western scholarship on Japan, however, such themes have found little voice, although they were implicit in the classic early study of the modern period, E. H. Norman's *Japan's Emergence as a Modern State,* first published in 1940. Economic and class forces assumed an important place in Norman's analysis, although his approach was eclectic and his sense of history carried the strong imprint of the Enlightenment as well as, indirectly, the concerns *and scope* of the Marxist tradition. Be that as it may, in the popular historiographies of Western Japan studies Norman is commonly identified as the first, and last, "Marxist" in the field. This present study by Jon Halliday assumes particular significance in the context of subsequent scholarly trends "away from Norman" in Western writings on Japan.

In the West, postwar scholarship on Japan has been voluminous, varied and useful, as the extended references in this present work amply indicate. It has produced its share of eminent scholars, such as John W. Hall, Ronald Dore and several others. At the same time, however, it must be noted that the profession as a whole has been dominated by Americans, and has been shaped not only by general and disciplinary trends in the American social sciences but also by more overt political and ideological concerns. It is in good part a product of the Cold War, and reflects the biases of this period—overt biases, such as the presentation of Japan as a model of gradual and non-revolutionary development along capitalist lines, or as a "democratic" ally of the "Free World"; and more subtle biases, implicit in the fragmentation and political deradicalization which are integral to the fashionable liberal disciplines. In this milieu, much postwar scholarship on Japan has assumed the specific cast of a counter-analysis or counter-ideology. It has been unmistakably non-Marxist, and often consciously anti-Marxist, without ever actually addressing the Marxist methodology directly. Virtually *a priori,* it rejects the value of attentiveness to such problems as class, mode of production, imperialism, contradictions, etc. Attitudes and cultural values have received exceptional attention, often in isolation from their social and material context; class analysis is replaced by concepts of pluralism or "vertical cleavages"; structural dynamics are overshadowed by studies of decision-making or models of "rationalization" or "dysfunction"; contradictions and recurrent crises of capitalism are approached as problems of "growth"; war (when by capitalist countries and unsuccessful) is analyzed as tactical breakdown, a departure from the norm.

Such trends reached their apogee—or perhaps more accurately, nadir—in the cult of modernization theory which dominated Western Japan studies in the 1960s. In this, the "Marxist formula" was pronounced officially dead, and a new "empiricism" advanced which in practice became condensed into an often repeated litany of remarkable simplicity: "modernization" was characterized by changing attitudes, industrialization and increasing "rationalization." For the prewar period, this led to the conclusion that post-Restoration Japan had been a remarkable success until somehow, after World War I, it went off the track; for post-1945 Japan, this spawned an adulatory preoccupation with the economic "miracle," popularized in Herman Kahn's 1970 book *The Emerging Japanese Superstate*. By the early 1970s, however, even all but the most fervid modernization theorists essentially had conceded that this "value-free" road was leading into rather value-less terrain. To return to the earlier metaphor of the scholar's net, the past several decades of English-language scholarship on Japan brought in mostly bait-fish, frequently tasty, rarely very big or nourishing. It is still difficult to think of a single major piece of original research on modern Japan comparable in conceptual incisiveness and impact to Norman's pioneer volume of 1940.

The field of Western Japan studies now stands at a crossroads. How does one best make sense of the complexity of modern Japan? In 1971, John W. Hall, a mildly reluctant emigrant from the comfortable conservatism of modernization theory, predicted that future scholarship would focus more on "obstructions to modernization," "reverse currents," "tension topics" and possibly even "a partial return to Norman through a renewed concern with class or interest group influence on national policy, a renewed interest in the underprivileged classes, particularly the peasant." The theoretical underpinnings for such "concerned" scholarship, he continued, would come logically from Weber, Parsons, Freud and Durkheim.[1]

Clearly Marx is to remain beyond the pale, and thus this present study by Jon Halliday is of major significance, for it is the only work in English available at present in which the course of modern and contemporary Japanese history is analyzed within a Marxist framework. Briefly put, and over-simply, Halliday is concerned with the interpenetration of class structure (and class conflict), mode of production, politics and ideology within the Japanese state; the relationship between this structure and the global system of imperialism in which Japan of necessity has operated; and the changes within essential structural continuity which have characterized this dynamic configuration over time, through both the prewar and postwar periods. He has attempted to grasp the nettle boldly, and in an undertaking of this scope and nature there inevitably remain some prickly points. The work marshals and reinterprets such a wealth of data that it may be of some use here to try to draw together certain of its central themes and points, and to suggest how these challenge non-Marxist approaches.

The title is significant: this is a *political history* of Japanese capitalism. It does not purport to be a general historical survey, a genre which often overlaps with that of the seed catalogue and retailer's brochure. It is also not an analysis of economic development *per se*, or a simple thesis of "economic determinism," but rather an analysis of the political economy of modern Japan. Unlike liberal social scientists, who commonly compartmentalize the historical experience even while espousing the importance of interdisciplinary study—relegating economics to economic historians, political development to political historians, social and cultural concerns to social and intellectual historians and so on—Halliday argues that a basic feature of modern Japan has been its class and capitalist *structure*. This structure has its own pronounced features, strongly shaped by the Tokugawa legacy and the nature of the early Meiji transition, and to a considerable extent Halliday's revision of prevailing interpretations entails a return to the concept of "absolutism" which has been central to certain schools of Japanese Marxism since the prewar period and can be found also in Norman.

Like Norman, Halliday emphasizes that the Restoration of 1867–1868 was not a popular revolution but rather a multi-class political upheaval in which political control was maintained by elements of the old ruling elite. Specific features of Tokugawa society channelled the Meiji settlement in the direction it took, among them the political hegemony of the samurai class, the weakness of a hamstrung and purely domestic bourgeoisie, and the nature of the existing agrarian system and agrarian surplus. The feudal regime was never overthrown, but selectively and in piecemeal fashion eased out from above, in a manner which brought about changes in the relations of production but not in the essential locus of power. What the early Meiji leaders accomplished was undeniably brilliant in its own terms. It was also a "grafting operation" which implanted critical and enduring distortions in the structure of the modern state, as seen most notably in the nature of the 1873 agrarian settlement, where the peasant remained unliberated, despite institutionalization of private property, and his surplus was expropriated for the state and new industrial sector. Moreover, the political consolidation effected by the early oligarchs *institutionalized* repression, authoritarianism and class rule. By the 1880s, reforms such as the "modernization" of the military, bureaucracy and educational system had ensured, and wittingly, a system virtually impervious to popular influence and thus fundamentally irresponsible.

Several basic themes emerge from this. First, Halliday argues that the Meiji settlement consolidated a ruling class, or ruling bloc, which changed in composition over time but remained integrated as a class, and which has maintained a repressive and antagonistic relationship to the masses throughout the modern period. Property, it should be noted, is not the sole determinant of this ruling class, and the state has not been merely the instrument of the bourgeoisie, but rather the mediator of largely *tactical* differences among the various economic, political and military interests which compose this bloc. One will not find this class thesis as a central concern in most contemporary Western scholarship on Japan; appropriately, for the early period Halliday illustrates the cleavage by quotations from the leaders of the time. *They* drew a sharp and explicit line between themselves and the people. What is more, they and their successors have consistently seen the masses as a threat. These points are worth emphasizing. Since Meiji, the Japanese state has nurtured a potent mystique of "harmony," "paternalism," and social reciprocity within the race. Western as well as many Japanese scholars have perpetuated this, in numerous and often illuminating ways, but all with the ultimate consequence of vitiating the concept of class division and conflict in Japan. Throughout the course of Japan's modern century, however, both the private pronouncements and the actual behaviour of the Japanese elite belie this. They have seen themselves and the masses in essentially class terms; they have been consistently and acutely sensitive to the possibility of class upheaval and even revolution in their country; and they have consolidated their own levers of repression and control accordingly. Halliday does not romanticize the class consciousness of the masses, and although he gives especially close attention to the conditions and organization of the working class and documents the incidence of lower-class protest in impressive detail, at no point does he really strongly suggest that social revolution was, or currently is, possible in Japan. What he does insist is that societal contradictions and class struggle are of greater relevance in comprehending the dynamics of the modern Japanese state than are the staples of Japanese ruling class rhetoric (such as "paternalism," "family-ism," "harmony") or such grab-bag concepts of the liberal orthodoxy as "modernization" and "pluralism."

A second point on which Halliday challenges current interpretations lies in the argument that in fundamental respects the structure of political irresponsibility consolidated in early Meiji has remained intact—even, as will be seen, into the postwar era. The Constitution of 1889 did not create institutionalized repression, but was rather its capstone, and subsequent political developments under the new parliamentary system remained little more than "pseudo-alternatives." The strength of conservative landed interests in the early parties gave parliamentary politics, and the Diet, a reactionary orientation which was never transcended. On the contrary, by the turn of the century the political parties had been fused with government and bureaucracy and absorbed into the ruling apparatus of the state. This trend persisted through the era of "Taishō democracy," which is often presented as a real if aborted turn toward genuine democracy. Where liberal scholarship emphasizes the emergence of party cabinets and "multiple elites" from 1918, Halliday finds more significant the fact that Prime Minister Hara, the "great commoner," carried on Itō's work of tightening the undemocratic relationship of the bureaucracy and political parties. As in Meiji, "liberalization" (such as universal male suffrage in 1925) and repression (*vide* the Peace Preservation Law of the same year) went hand in hand. Even the less elitist interpretation of this period, which emphasizes popular demonstrations and the campaigns for "con-stitutionalism" (rather than formal politics, the cabinets, the new "elites"), does not contravene the basic thesis. Such movements also, Halliday argues, failed to fundamentally challenge either imperialism or the repressive domestic structure, and are most accurately seen as expressions of bourgeois dissidence (over high taxes and the like) rather than as movements which actually reflected the interests of the masses. The new bourgeoisie which assumed a greater political role after World War I represented an "historical compromise-cum-imbrication" with the objectives of the previous ruling strata, both foreign and domestic, and "Taishō democracy" is more notable for its compromises and failures than for its accomplishments either at home or abroad.

As indicated earlier, the anti-Marxist approach lays particularly heavy emphasis upon the basic and causative role of attitudes and cultural values. Robert Bellah, the most influential proponent of this approach, developed this at some length in 1961 when modernization theory was being adopted as *the* methodology for study of Japan: "I do not believe that such value systems are direct reflections of economic or class forces, nor that they change necessarily when economic or class forces change. In fact, I believe that they are more stable and persistent than economic or class forces and, in fact, that change coming from the economic conditions or changes in the system of social stratification will be channeled partly by the structure of values." This is a third area in which Halliday is, by prevailing criteria, heretical. While he would certainly agree with Bellah that the value-system is a dynamic and crucial part of any social analysis, he goes to considerable length to document the manner in which traditional values were *resurrected* and ideology *manipulated* to serve the ends of the state and capital in Japan. Thus he devotes long sections to educational politics in general, and the emperor-system and so-called ideology of the business class in particular.

The emperor-system or concept of the "family state" represented neither an inevitable nor a popular feudal legacy to modern Japan, but rather the conscious, calculated and *belated* popularization by the early Meiji ruling group of a waning and *elite* tradition. Halliday does not merely assert this; he quotes Itō and others to show that the oligarchs were eminently aware of the fragility of old ethics, the potency of new, and the manner in which men of power could shape and impose an orthodoxy by selective use of tradition. Given the tensions and contradictions of the emerging Japanese state and the rulers' own undeniable fear of the populace, ideological obfuscation was the essential cement of authoritarianism. It served to divert popular and potentially progressive and liberating movements from below, and undeniably facilitated the creation of a strong state. But it did so at the expense of the masses, and was callously manipulated in the interests of the ruling class itself. Thus the shrewd use of the emperor-ideology by the political elite had its natural counterpart in the capitalist class, where the allegedly traditional ethics of "paternalism" and "family-ism" were, in Halliday's phrase, *parachuted in* as a deliberate tactic in the oppression of labour. Although the conceit of the patriotic Japanese entrepreneur (presumedly exploiting his workers with tear-filled eyes) has enjoyed a curious vogue in the West, the purportedly traditional ethics of Japanese capitalism served no such abstruse ends: they abetted capital accumulation while simultaneously maximizing profits. In both prewar and postwar Japan, the self-proclaimed "beautiful customs" of big business have functioned to help repress the working class and fragment proletarian solidarity. Like the assiduously propagated mystique of the emperor-system, they are correctly understood, not as a powerful and virtually inevitable "legacy of the past," but rather as a convenient and calculated *use* of the past to serve specific interests. The "beautiful customs" of Japanese capitalism are neither "traditional" *nor irrational;* on the contrary, they represent a high and deliberate level of rationalization *in the interests of capital.*

This argument too deserves careful consideration. Taken at face value, social values indicate, in Bellah's words, "what is a good society, what is good social action, what are good social relations, what is a good person as a member of society." Halliday asks: good *for whom?* and how did these values come into play and who is really pumping the bellows? His analysis indicates—and this is a perception which the anti-Marxist approach almost by definition obscures—that such presumedly quintessential values as the *kokutai* ("national polity") or "family-ism" or "harmony" serve clear class interests, and are recognized as such by those who actively inculate them. This is not, of course, to deny that they have been drilled into the society as a whole. But the fact that from Meiji to the present day the dominant political and economic bloc have deemed it necessary to apply this ideological cement so thickly and painstakingly indicates that they—unlike many of their scholarly admirers—have recognized a real potential for disharmony and unfilial behaviour in their family: a potential, discarding the cant, for social disruption and class conflict.

In his discussion of the Meiji state, Halliday introduces a fourth consideration which remains basic to his entire analysis, namely, the internal-external dialectic. From its very inception, the nature of the modern state has been influenced not only by the direct impact of the West, which has always attracted considerable attention, but also by the nature of the global imperialist system in which Japan was forced to operate. The critical determinant in modern development, Halliday argues, is not "stages" or "take-off," but rather the distinction between dependent and independent development—and in this respect, Japan was *initially* fortunate. For reasons of their own, as Norman also stressed, the imperialist powers did not attempt to colonize Japan; they were preoccupied elsewhere. And for very complex reasons, Japan was able to avoid both heavy initial foreign capital investment and inundation by cheap foreign consumer goods. It was able to separate and control three crucial levers commonly associated with imperialist encroachment: technology, imports and capital.

Foreign pressure and the nature of the global capitalist system nonetheless strongly influenced the structure of capitalist development in Japan and the specific nature of Japanese imperialism. They buttressed the perpetuation of such features of the domestic economic structure as low wages, state intervention, tax and credit priorities, monopolization and specialization. They profoundly distorted the development of the heavy-industrial sector. And they helped to propel the nation on a course of imperialism of its own which was unusual, at least by Leninist theory, in that Japanese expansion preceded attainment of the stage of finance capital —in Halliday's words, "imperialism without capital." The dialectic was inevitably social and political as well as economic. The nature of the Meiji compromise, by which the industrial sector was built upon a semi-feudal agrarian base as well as an impoverished working class, naturally constricted the domestic market in Japan; the quest for external markets thus represented reliance upon development "in width" to compensate for inability to develop "in depth." If overseas expansion was an attempt to resolve internal economic contradictions, however, it also and simultaneously could be used to divert the social tensions resulting from uneven and exploitative capitalist development. Expansionist nationalism, that is, was also promoted to prevent class struggle, and Halliday clearly acknowledges the effectiveness with which the jingoism of the state implanted chauvinism among the populace, even among its purportedly more "enlightened" and "liberal" members. In his view, the Sino-Japanese War of 1894–95, in its visceral fusion of nationalism and imperialism, sounded the real death knell for the popular-rights movement, and signalled the enduring suborning of the bourgeois democratic movement to the ruling bloc and the expansionist goals of the state.

These arguments are not unfamiliar, although as Halliday rather pointedly adds, the wedding of liberalism and expansionism was hardly peculiar to Japan. Nor was it peculiar to any particular period in Japan. The emergence of big business as a political force in the twentieth century certainly entailed no revision of the expansionist goals of the state, just as it offered no challenge to the domestic structures of repression. For reasons of its own, this new bourgeoisie reinforced the expansionist policies of the military, and Halliday characterizes the political oscillations of the interwar period as tactical disagreements over how to resolve the mounting capitalist crisis. He eschews the familiar conspiracy theory of a military take-over in the 1930s, and also rejects the concepts of fascism or totalitarianism for this period. There was no meaningful civilian-military split, no basic change in the political system. Indeed, the years following the depression were characterized by *de facto* political *de*centralization accompanied by the drastically accelerated concentration of economic power by the zaibatsu.

What *was* unprecedented in Japan's actions in the 1930s was its defiance of the Western definition of the imperialist game—its endeavour to break

out of the *subordinate* position to which it had been relegated within the
imperialist camp. There is no controversy over the fact that Japan's
emergence as an imperialist power reflected a need and rather enthusiastic
willingness to play the game of international relations as originally defined
by the West. Bourgeois scholars categorize this, for the early period, as
the "diplomacy of imperialism," and commonly praise the adroitness of
Japan's successful wars and colonial acquisitions during the palmy years
of its imperium; things only began to "go wrong" later, when great-power
co-operation somehow broke down. Halliday is not enchanted by the
trade-offs and "co-operation" of the early decades, for his sympathies lie
with those *against* whom the co-operation was directed; it is a small point
but a great distinction. More challengingly, he argues that the crisis which
culminated in the Pacific War began at the turn of the century, when the
United States and Japan emerged virtually simultaneously as expansionist
powers in Asia, and derived from Japan's relatively backward position
vis-à-vis the other imperialist powers. America played, at this time, a
double game. In the Philippines and Pacific islands, it indulged in the old
imperialism of outright acquisition—the tactic of the military grab, which
Japan might reasonably hope to emulate. At the same time, however, it
introduced for China the new imperialism of the vaunted "Open Door"
notes, which implicitly meant that the spoils of continental Asia were to
go to the economically strong. And Japan, quite simply, could not compete
against the more advanced powers at this level. Within the imperialist
camp, it was a pygmy among giants.

The consequences of this relative weakness in capital were several.
Japan was forced to borrow heavily from the West to finance the first two
decades of its imperialist expansion. Unlike the Western imperialists,
moreover, where expansion had largely followed the development of heavy
industry, Japan—virtually impoverished in basic raw materials—had to
rely on its imperialism *to develop* its industrial base. And inevitably,
Japan was forced to compensate for its economic backwardness by greater
reliance upon military pressure. Its accelerated aggression in China must
thus be seen not only in the context of domestic crisis and a general breakdown of global capitalism but also as an attempt to rectify its structurally
disadvantaged status, even at the expense of the Western powers if
necessary. In this light, the implications of the "economic diplomacy"
espoused at the Washington Conference of 1921–22 and forced upon a
reluctant Japan assume particular significance, and Japan's eventual refusal to join the West in backing Chiang Kai-shek and the Chinese
bourgeoisie—which delivered the deathblow to the always flawed Washington system—appears not a wanton and irrational act of "militarism"
so much as a recognition that support of Chiang furthered the interests of
the West while imperilling Japan's own position on the continent. Anglo-
American barriers against the impressive Japanese export boom which
followed the crash of 1929 similarly were interpreted, not unreasonably,

as indicating that Japan would not be permitted to resolve its own crisis by peaceful economic expansion within the imperilled, Western-dominated world capitalist system. The option of low-posture economic imperialism which became available to Japan under American patronage during the Cold War simply did not exist in the prewar period. What Halliday suggests here is the necessity of a far more economically oriented analysis of prewar imperialism in Asia than is at present available—one which transcends the present almost exclusive focus on "diplomacy" and strategic planning and is attentive not merely to great-power "rivalries" but to fundamental structural differences and contradictions within the imperialist camp.

Throughout his analysis, Halliday is concerned with history's victims, whether they be the workers and peasants ground under the wheels of "progress" or the peoples of those less developed countries on whose backs and corpses the "great powers" rise. This may be taken as a fifth area which distinguishes his work from most other studies in the field. He rejects that "objectivity" which measures gross national product as the true index of progress or "modernity," and which relegates exploitation to a "tension topic." Inevitably, this shapes his methodology: history appears different in the victim's eye. This does not make the writing of history any simpler, for while capitalist Japan has cannibalized its own people in the quest for strength and profit and sacrificed literally millions of other Asians as well, it has at the same time itself been at the mercy of the more powerful Caucasian powers. Such concerns carry throughout the text, and are exemplified by Halliday's treatment of the Pacific War.

Just as Japanese aggression in the 1930s is analytically inseparable from the crisis of global capitalism and eruption of irreconcilable contradictions among the imperialist powers, so also the Pacific War takes on its full meaning against the decadent background of Western colonialism in South and Southeast Asia. Halliday's focus here will be unfamiliar to most English-language readers, for he is scornful of the prevailing Western mythology of the war, as conveyed in both cinema and much scholarship, and eschews conventional partisanship in this clash among thieves. Britain's empire is recognized as no less corrupt than Japan's; perhaps even more so. America's terror bombing of Japan does not appear more civilized than Japan's own atrocities elsewhere. What Halliday captures here, however, is the truly paradoxical nature of the Japanese impact upon southern Asia: its stimulation of anti-Western nationalism among both collaborationists and anti-Japanese resistance movements; and simultaneously, its virtual *interchangeability* with the Caucasian colonialists it displaced.

Thus he recognizes Japan's vast fighting superiority over the Allied powers in Southeast Asia; the unpopularity and dry rot of the Western colonial systems (including a memorable vignette of the final days of British rule in Burma); and the extent to which Japan was actually welcomed as the "light of Asia" by a wide spectrum of indigenous leaders in Malaya, Thailand, Indonesia, Indochina and India. Japan's "co-prosperity sphere," like its policy and polity in general, was riven by contradictions. Although there is no reason to presume that its policy would have been less exploitative and racist than that of its predecessors if Japan had actually succeeded, Halliday does note certain differences between Western and Japanese policy in Southeast Asia—such as its stimulation of local commerce in Thailand and Burma, encouragement of the Tagalog language in the Philippines and of Islam in Indonesia, and support of genuinely nationalist and even progressive regimes in Burma and Indonesia. Japan was both the oppressor and the liberator of the peoples of southern Asia (in ways it only partly intended), and this contradiction is vividly exemplified in its actions during the closing stages of the Pacific War. As defeat became imminent, Japan threw accelerated support behind indigenous nationalist and independence movements; with defeat effected, however, it immediately collaborated with the returning Western colonialists in the callous military suppression of native liberation forces. The legacy, in any case, was enduring. It accounts for both the decline of the white empires and Japan's strength in Southeast Asia today, as well as for much of the nationalistic hatred of Japan which has greeted creation of the new, postwar "co-prosperity sphere."

Many non-radical scholars, while rejecting Halliday's analysis, might more or less agree with the general conclusion that the Japanese regime was repressive and authoritarian prior to 1945; both their appreciation of "gradualism" and their concept of "breakdown" make this not inconsistent. Far fewer would accept his strong argument that the "new Japan" of the postwar era is cut of the same cloth. They face a considerable challenge, however, in refuting his detailed documentation of this thesis. Indeed, while the *elements* of the analysis of pre-1945 Japan are not unfamiliar, this present work is perhaps most original in that it offers, almost for the first time, an extended corrective to the infatuation with Japan's postwar "miracle" and "democratization" which currently characterizes the mainstream in Western literature on the subject. Japan's postwar "democracy," Halliday indicates, has been characterized by *increasing* repression, concentration of power and ideological obfuscation. And impressive as its postwar industrial growth may be, it remains a "bicycle economy," precariously poised and requiring, for its very survival, continued exploitation at home and increasing exploitation abroad.

Halliday's analysis of Japan's post-1945 development is also distinguished by insistence that this has been structured by the nature of postwar American imperialism (rather than just U.S.–Japan "relations," a greatly different conceptualization). While complexity, uncertainty and change did characterize American policy toward Japan, particularly in the early years of the Occupation, the thrust of postwar U.S. policy was consistent: Japan was to be reintegrated into a revised and American-dominated system of global capitalism. Consequently it could not be, and clearly was not, subjected to *basic* change in its mode of production and its ruling class. Unless one is lulled by what Halliday calls the "electoral-constitutional subterfuge," the evidence for this is compelling. It is apparent in the resurgence of the old zaibatsu and the emergence of new structures of immense economic concentration; or stated differently, in the continued gross disparities in wealth and power. It is manifest in the straight continuity of irresponsible bureaucratic influence. The survival of the emperor-system, however modified—and indeed of the same emperor who assumed the throne in 1926—exemplifies this continuity. In social relations, the legacy persists in an intricate web of institutionalized authoritarian relationships. Where personnel, the brokers of real power, are concerned, the résumé of the postwar ruling bloc reads like a listing of the prewar old guard, or of the old guard's disciples.

From the outset, American Occupation policy was formulated within the parameters of capitalism and counter-revolution, although not with a clearly perceived vision of Japan's future role in the global economy. That role became clearer well before the Korean War, when it was recognized that America's own interests were best served by abetting rapid capital growth in Japan and its external expansion. In George Kennan's phrase of 1949, Japan was to be assisted, among other things, in developing an "empire to the south"—not exactly a new idea to Japan's leaders themselves. Thus the parameters of Occupation policy were constricted even further, crushing much of the cautiously defined democratic potential which undeniably had been encouraged in the initial phase, and setting the stage for both the "miracle" and the reconsolidation of the conservative hegemony. Once again, the external-internal dialectic came into play, and again, although with notable differences, Japan entered the world scene in a status Halliday characterizes, for the postwar era, as "subordinate independence." This was effected through a variety of American policies and programs beneficial to Japanese capital: tax credit and budget policies initiated under the "Dodge line" from 1949, designed to promote capital accumulation and concentration; an exchange rate favourable to Japanese exports, maintained from 1949 to 1971; massive U.S. military procurements in Japan, beginning in 1950 and continuing to the present; favoured treatment by "international" lending agencies; integration in a rewarding triangular nexus with the United States and Southeast Asia, welded together by a labyrinthine pattern of U.S. aid and trade policies; access to American technology; etc.

Membership in the "free" world, however, was costly. The contradictions of Japan's postwar status are symbolized by the San Francisco peace conference of 1951—Dulles's "crowning accomplishment" in standard Western sources—where the generous conditions of the peace treaty were conditional upon Japan's acceptance of a bilateral military pact with the United States which revived the best tradition of the unequal treaties of nineteenth-century Western imperialism in Asia. Japan has remained semi-occupied by U.S. forces ever since, with all their familiar accoutrements of the dispossessed peasant and the brothel. Peace for Japan entailed its support of the American war machine and America's wars (brutally costly indeed to Korea and Indochina, if hardly to Japan), as well as Japan's own remilitarization. And economic "self-sufficiency" actually has entailed acquiescence to subtle levers of enforced dependency. Forced until recently to participate in the economic containment of China, Japan has become unnaturally dependent upon trade with the United States. Through the tied loans of the Counterpart Fund program and the subsequent agri-cultural-commodities agreement of 1954, it has become a key importer of the American agricultural surplus, in the process crippling the diversifica-tion of its own production of foodstuffs; the implications of such depend-ence have become vividly apparent with the change in the international food situation in the 1970s. Spurred to impressive heights of industrial production by ready access to American technology, Japan has retarded in the process the development of its own independent capacity for basic scientific research and development. And even while permitting Japan un-common autonomy in its control of foreign capital investment—an im-portant and intriguing dimension of Occupation policy—the United States has maintained strategic control over the raw materials upon which Japan's survival depends. This is particularly evident in petroleum, where Japan is crucially dependent upon the Western cartels—and where, sig-nificantly, the United States "liberalized" Japan as early as 1949 by facilitating major American penetration of the domestic petroleum-refining sector.

Halliday does not argue that American and Japanese ruling-class in-terests invariably coalesced, even during the early period of the postwar interlock, when tensions were certainly not as apparent as they are today. On the contrary, he recognizes the extent to which Japanese acquiescence has often been reluctant, and the manner in which Japan's leaders have successfully manipulated the levers restored to them during the Occupation to impose domestic policies that are even more reactionary than the United States probably envisioned. Similarly, he does not ignore the vastly greater organizational strength of postwar labour and the left, but argues that since Sanbetsu was gutted, neither the union movement nor the estab-lishment left has offered a serious challenge to the fundamentally exploita-tive relations of labour and production—although they have, in some instances, developed an anti-imperialist critique. Sōhyō's unique tactic of the annual *shuntō*, or "spring offensive," has been of undeniable material benefit to *sectors* of the working class. But in the final analysis it is the institutionalized structures imposed by the capitalists which dictate the tune to which labour marches—and marches, moreover, in the direction of increasing disparity of wealth.

These structures, as in the prewar period, have been encrusted with a pernicious and deceptive mythology. Just as the immiseration of the pre-war working class was shrouded in the noxious rhetorical vapours of Japan's "beautiful customs," so also has the nature of postwar exploitation been obscured by images of enterprise "family-ism" and security through guarantees of "lifetime employment." Halliday points out that lifetime employment is privileged and discriminatory; that it benefits only a minority of the labour force and does so by relegating others, particularly in smaller industry, to lifetime insecurity as unprotected or "temporary" workers. Similarly, the vaunted "seniority" system in practice has buttressed a cheap, discriminatory and inequitable wage-system, while the prevailing phenomenon of the enterprise union has served primarily to fragment working class solidarity. Where women are concerned, the image of industrial "family-ism" is indeed accurate, although hardly in the sense intended by those who purvey it. The institutionalized social inferiority of women and their chattel role in the home have been profitably perpetuated in Japanese industry, where women provide over half of all factory labour while receiving an average wage less than half that earned by their male counterparts.

Although postwar Japan has experienced notable, if isolated, instances of popular protest—by students and peasants as well as labour—Halliday's analysis here as earlier emphasizes that the great offensive in the class struggle has been taken by the ruling class *against* the masses, and has entailed the marshalling of a broad arsenal of "ideology, law, physical repression and straight exploitation." The popular argument that basic social cleavages are "vertical" rather than "horizontal" (along class lines), he observes in a telling point, is repudiated by the truly extraordinary integrated power wielded by the postwar business federations. These readily identifiable groups (Keidanren, Keizai Dōyūkai, Nikkeiren, Nisshō and more recently Sanken) are not only more powerful than their Western counterparts but have assumed a *de facto* role as part of the state apparatus. Fragmentation of the working class is thus most correctly seen, not as a cultural phenomenon, but as an exceptionally successful means for controlling the proletariat, maintained by one of the most coherent and co-ordinated ruling blocs in the contemporary capitalist world.

Where pundits such as Herman Kahn have presented Japan as the great emerging superpower of the late twentieth century, Halliday depicts the country as the *Wunderkind* of postwar capitalism, riding toward an uncertain future on a bicycle economy. His perception of vulnerability is not peculiarly radical. In 1972 Zbigniew Brzezinski published a counterargument to Kahn in which he portrayed the condition of state, society and economy in Japan as a "fragile blossom." Halliday, however, accepts neither the metaphor nor the implicit remedy: that a good dose of liberal night-soil will bring about healthy growth. The problem lies in the nature of the organism itself.

Japan's crisis. Halliday argues, is structural on both a national and an international level, and best comprehended by appreciation of the contradictions which have characterized the country's capitalist development to the present day. The metaphor of the bicycle economy is not meant to suggest that Japan's postwar industrial development has been "light," but rather that it has been constructed in such a manner that it cannot slow down without peril. The "contradictions" of the economy, however, which are developed here at some length, are numerous, and raise this very spectre of the end of the era of sustained rapid growth. Japanese industry rests on an extraordinarily large base of financial credits, a paper structure which requires continued high growth to meet interest payments. Industrial growth is also disproportionately dependent upon continued and drastically increasing access to raw materials (the statistical projections are astonishing), in a situation where such access is in fact becoming increasingly costly and difficult; the petroleum crisis is but the most spectacular index of this broader dilemma. Japanese production has been top-heavy, skewed toward heavy industry and the chemical sectors, and can be sustained only by steady expansion of exports. The competitiveness of Japanese exports, however, has rested in considerable part on preservation of cheap labour in Japan, a situation which poses severe political and social threats to the ruling class, and which is in fact undergoing revision as the labour movement increases its effectiveness in wage bargaining. The "miracle" of sustained high growth has also depended on (not merely incidentally resulted in) toleration of immense industrial pollution, the greatest in the world, a situation now past the crisis point and, again for social and political reasons, no longer tolerable. And undergirding the entire precarious structure has been the basic contradiction between the forces of production and the forces of labour. As in the prewar period, the over-riding goal of the "rich country" has required perpetuation of a poor and controlled populace, a sacrifice of genuine social welfare and well-being which obviously cannot be perpetuated indefinitely without dire consequences.

Within itself, the Japanese ruling class is also riven by tightening contradictions. Halliday illustrates this convincingly in the case of the ruling Liberal Democratic Party, whose electoral base has become steadily more constricted as the antagonism between its rural and big-business constituencies becomes more pronounced. As a result, the party of industrial "rationalization" has been driven to intensify the tactics of ideological obfuscation and to tighten the levers of outright repression—in concrete ways described here in some detail.

This mounting crisis, moreover, cannot be separated from the structure of Japan's international involvement and its relationship to U.S. imperialism in particular. Since before the end of the Occupation, the two countries have been interlocked in a mutually beneficial relationship notably different from that of the prewar era. This new imperialism has entailed a convenient division of labour, whereby until recently the military and foreign-investment burdens of empire have been largely undertaken by the United States, while Japan has provided crucial logistic support for American militarism, at the same time pursuing its own "low-posture" economic penetration of Asia. Both sides have a basic interest in supporting the forces of counter-revolution in Asia, and history surely has recorded few conceits more invidious than the so-called "democratic defence" of the "free world" of south Korea, south Vietnam, Taiwan, the Philippines, etc., with which they justify their expansion. The very logic of Japan's mounting crisis indicates that its future relationship with the less-developed countries must necessarily entail transfer of the repression and exploitation upon which sustained economic growth has consistently depended. Japan is hardly in a position to offer, nor are the Third World countries in any position to demand, even that level of "subordinate independence" which Japan itself has enjoyed under the American aegis.

This relationship has been of immense benefit to Japan, and Halliday takes care to note that the United States never desired a Japanese puppet. What it did desire, and succeed in creating, was a dominant class in Japan which has performed the roles of both "comprador" and "national" bourgeoisie. (And as American policy from the latter half of the Occupation makes amply clear, it was recognized and accepted that this class would constitute a *ruling* elite, operating at the expense of true political democratization and equitable distribution of wealth.) At the time the relationship was consummated, however, the United States certainly did not anticipate either the dynamic gross economic expansion Japan was actually able to accomplish or the crisis of American capitalism which became evident around the late 1960s. Consequently, while the collaborative side of the Japanese-American nexus still retains much of its viability, the more *autonomous* growth Japan has accomplished under the relationship poses challenges to America's own economic growth and expansion. Contradictions within the Japanese economy are thus reflected in and exacerbated by contradictions in the "co-operative" imperialism of the two powers. Japan's crisis confronts America's own, and various examples of recent American economic pressure *against* Japan indicate that—much as happened during the great crisis of capitalism in the prewar period—Japan will be hard pressed to find an equal or independent or truly secure place of its own within the international capitalist system. Nor will it be able to solve its problems by further penetration of the less-developed world, whether alone or in the multi-national linkage, in a manner which will benefit the *peoples* of those countries—advocates of the thesis of capitalism's benevolently reciprocal mechanism notwithstanding. The result of such penetration is likely to be increased social ferment in the new imperium.

Domestic and international, or class and imperialist, structures are thus fused for Japan, and in Halliday's view their internal contradictions are coming to a head.

He offers no comforting prospect.

NOTE

1. This summary, as indeed that of Halliday's present work itself which follows, is necessarily grossly simplified, and some further citations of particular historiographic interest are in order. Norman's *Japan's Emergence as a Modern State*, together with the bulk of an unpublished manuscript (*Feudal Background of Japanese Politics*), is currently being reissued by Pantheon, with an introduction, under John W. Dower, ed., *Origins of the Modern Japanese State: Selected Writings of E. H. Norman*. Modernization-theory scholarship on Japan is most aptly represented in six volumes on "Studies in the Modernization of Japan" published by Princeton University Press between 1965 and 1971; volume editors are Marius B. Jansen, William W. Lockwood, Ronald P. Dore, Robert E. Ward, Donald H. Shively and James W. Morley. An especially useful insight into the ethos and objectives of modernization theory as applied to Japan can be found in International Christian University (Tokyo), "Studies on Modernization of Japan by Western Scholars," *Asian Cultural Studies*, 3 (October 1962), particularly in the articles by Marius Jansen and Robert Bellah. Trends in the field are also nicely suggested, both directly and indirectly, in two bibliographic essays by John W. Hall: *Japanese History: New Dimensions of Approach and Understanding*, 2nd ed. (1966), and "Thirty Years of Japanese Studies in America," *Transactions of the International Conference of Orientalists in Japan*, 14 (1971). In addition to the influential and better-known writings of Edwin O. Reischauer, attention should be called to an article entitled "Toward a Definition of 'Modernization,'" originally published in Japanese in the journal *Jiyū* (January 1965), and subsequently reprinted as a bilingual pamphlet. A sense of the re-interpretation by younger scholars within the field is conveyed in T. Najita's thoughtful small volume, *Japan* (1974) and in Harry R. Harootunian's *Toward Restoration* (1970); see also Harootunian's article on the Restoration in *Journal of Asian Studies*, Vol. 93, No. 4 (August 1974). In Japanese, the basic issues and debates are discussed in Tōyama Shigeki, *Sengo no Rekishigaku to Rekishi Ishiki* [Postwar historiography and historical consciousness], first published in 1968. In English, a brief translation of Tōyama's critique of modernization theory appears in "The Meiji Restoration and the Present Day," *Bulletin of Concerned Asian Scholars*, Vol. 2, No. 1 (October 1969).

*A Political History
of Japanese Capitalism*

1.
The Meiji State

Japanese capitalism has been the prodigy of the age of imperialism, the only outsider and late starter to join the leaders of world imperialism. It achieved this in spite of a relatively weak and backward economic base and in spite of engaging almost all the other imperialist powers in war at some point. Thus it is necessary to look not only at the advent of the capitalist mode of production and at the transition from feudalism to capitalism, but also at the construction of the new state machinery which formed the *political* bulwark for capitalism at home and imperialism abroad.[1]

Japan's relatively late entrance into the imperialist group allowed the Meiji oligarchs to model the state on the most advanced and repressive examples available elsewhere in the world. The important government mission, headed by Iwakura Tomomi, which was sent abroad in 1871 greatly admired the British economy—but it was the Prussian state which impressed Japanese politicians.[2] Similarly, some ten years later when Itō Hirobumi, probably the most perceptive of all the Meiji leaders of his day, was scouring Europe for ideas for the new Constitution, it was to Prussia and its theorists that he turned for ideas and for material assistance.[3] This determination to construct a certain kind of state took priority over all other ventures. The Meiji oligarchs put politics firmly in command.

The construction of the new system was not a lightning overnight transformation. The actual "Meiji Restoration" itself (the proclamation of a "return to the old monarchy") can be precisely dated: January 3, 1868. But the political revolution was spread out over a long period, some fifty years—from the reforms in the late Tempō period, through the crucial commercial treaties with foreign powers in 1858 to the installation of the Diet in 1890.[4]

The issues involved in the Meiji Restoration are frequently obscured by placing too much emphasis on subjective intentions (how did the Meiji leaders, who came mainly from the aristocracy, play such an important role in a process which largely promoted the rising forces of capitalism?). The changes were not the result of purely autonomous options on the part of the Meiji leaders. They were caused by developments in the relations of production within Japan and by the irruption of the Western capitalist powers. The key internal question concerns the advent to dominance of the capitalist mode of production.[5]

DOMESTIC PRECONDITIONS: CLASS STRUCTURE

Tokugawa Feudalism

For over two and a half centuries prior to the Restoration of 1868, Japan lived under a regime usually referred to as the Tokugawa shogunate.[6] This regime was formally established in 1603 after the Tokugawa house had led a victorious coalition of feudal lords at the Battle of Sekigahara in 1600. Under the Tokugawa shogunate, the Tokugawa themselves ruled between one-fifth and one-quarter of the country directly, mainly in the central part of Japan, with their capital at Edo (later renamed Tokyo). The area directly controlled by the shogunate also included both Kyoto, the imperial capital, where the powerless Emperor resided, and Osaka, which emerged as the main centre of the merchant class. The rest of Japan was ruled by great lords (daimyō), who were semi-autonomous in their fiefs. The Tokugawa regime can not be characterized as a centralized autocracy, at least in its initial stages. It was more like a nation-wide truce, with a relatively centralized regime ruling about 20 per cent of the country, surrounded by feudal lords of varying degrees of friendliness or hostility to the shogun.[7]

The Tokugawa devised a highly ingenious system for consolidating their grip on the country and ensuring peace. The key elements in the solution were the virtually total isolation of Japan from the outside world and an institutionalized hostage system under which the daimyō had to leave their wives and children permanently in Edo, and also attend the shogun's court there in alternate years (the sankin kōtai system).[8]

In certain ways the Tokugawa system can be seen as an attempt to "refeudalize" Japan.[9] Clearly foreign contact was a prime danger, from the point of view both of ideas and of goods such as armaments. By 1638 the shogunate had enacted a strict seclusion policy, which both prevented Japanese travelling abroad and strictly limited foreign traders' activities in Japan. Prior to the exclusion edicts of 1638 Japan had had a developing merchant class, flourishing, like its counterparts in Europe, on foreign trade. Japanese traders and pirates were operating throughout much of Southeast Asia. The "closure" of the country was a political decision connected with security. It both prevented any anti-Tokugawa han (fiefs) being able to arm themselves well enough to challenge the shogunate for over two centuries and also blocked off the normal avenues of development for the nascent bourgeoisie.

The shogunate also developed a sophisticated system of internal control, of which the core was the *sankin kōtai*. This hostage system forced obedience from the daimyō and, together with other measures of a similar nature, gave the Tokugawa the power to control political appointments and, to some extent, to regulate economic policy. The Tokugawa project was a wholesale driving back of the bourgeoisie, which covered politics, economics and culture. By the end of the seventeenth century, after about one hundred years of Tokugawa rule, Japanese society had been formally immobilized. But though the Tokugawa oppressed the merchant class *politically* with considerable success, they never succeeded in destroying it as an economic force. The *sankin kōtai* system, like Louis XIV's Versailles centralization, encouraged luxury and ostentatious expenditure and forced the aristocracy into heavy indebtedness to the bourgeoisie. All of this encouraged the development of a money economy and strengthened the bourgeois class.[10] At the same time changes in agriculture and among the oppressed peasantry further contributed to the weakening and ultimate collapse of the shogunate.

The Class Structure of Tokugawa Japan

As part of their system of control, the Tokugawa shoguns ritualized and formalized class relations to a very high degree. At the top of the class structure were the Emperor and the shogun, the sovereign and the ruler, respectively. The shoguns sustained the fiction that they ruled because power was delegated to them by the Emperor. In fact the shoguns used the Emperor's spiritual authority, while keeping him virtually powerless for most of the Tokugawa period.[11] Directly beneath the shogun came the great lords or daimyō, of whom there were 266 immediately before the 1868 Restoration.

The rest of the population was formally divided into four classes (the *shi-nō-kō-shō* structure): samurai (or warriors); farmers (or peasants); artisans (or manufacturers); and merchants at the bottom. However, beneath these four groups there were further "sub-human" divisions, people excluded from society to such an extent that they were not even fitted into the formal categorization. These groups included both the *Hinin* (literally "non-people") and outcastes located even lower than the "non-people."[12]

Under the feudal regime *political* power remained firmly in the hands of the shogunate and the aristocracy, while *economic* power moved increasingly into the hands of the bourgeoisie. The formal class system, which placed the merchants below both artisans and peasants, as well as below the samurai, was therefore subjected to growing strains as time went on.

Immediately prior to the Restoration of 1868 some fifteen-sixteenths of the country's wealth was reportedly in the hands of the bourgeoisie.[13]

The size of the population during the Tokugawa period is a subject of some dispute. For some time it was widely thought that the population was virtually stagnant for much of the Tokugawa period. Now it seems more probable that it grew, if rather slowly and unevenly,[14] throughout the period. By 1852 the population was between 29.4 and 32 million.[15] The sectoral distribution of the population in the 1860s was roughly as follows:[16]

Primary industry	80%
Secondary industry	4%
Tertiary industry	9%
Samurai	7%

Immediately after the Restoration, in 1872, the distribution of the gainfully employed (total: 17,319,000) was:[17]

Agriculture and forestry	14,100,000
Mining	6,000
Manufacturing	826,000
Fishery	395,000
Communications	118,000
Commerce	948,000
Public service	502,000
Miscellaneous	179,000

The Tokugawa enforced strict class divisions: "Every social class, and every subdivision within it, had its own regulations covering all the minutiae of clothing, ceremony and behavior, which had to be strictly observed on pain of punishment. The criminal code [was] severe even by feudal standards . . . ; in every conceivable way the Tokugawa administration emphasized the difference, the relative degree of superiority or inferiority of one class to another."[18]

THE ARISTOCRACY

Immediately below the small group of great lords was the class known as the samurai, or warriors. Formally military retainers of the daimyō, they lived on an annual stipend of rice given them by their lord. The imposition of peace by the Tokugawa deprived them of the chance to engage in military activity.

The society was thus encumbered with a huge parasitic class, sitting very close to the apex of the structure. Along with their families, the samurai, on the eve of the Restoration, numbered some two million people, an incomparably larger feudal class than in European feudal societies. Indeed, a single *han* in Japan had a larger number of samurai than the total number of English knights.[19]

The most important feature of the Japanese aristocracy lies in its relationship to the means of production, particularly land. In Japan, unlike Europe, feudal power was based not on direct ownership of the land but on revenue in rice. The daimyō ran his *han* from a castle town, where he and his samurai resided, the samurai accounting for about half the total population of the average castle town.[20] The most important result of this relationship between the feudal class and the land was the commercialization of the economy. The Tokugawa period saw a real "commercial revolution."[21] Thus the ruling class in Japan was fundamentally in a very much *weaker* position than its counterpart in either feudal Europe or China. Whereas in China, the essential class equation of political power and economic wealth held, in Japan, on the whole, it broke down. Samurai status was often extremely out of line with real economic power. This separation of the samurai as a class from the source of wealth, land, made them highly vulnerable.[22]

However, partly as a result of this situation, the aristocracy developed to some extent as a bureaucracy. Feudalism, although essentially *divisive,* also has a strong centralizing tendency in order to try to minimize anarchy. There emerged a distinctive combination of centralization and decentralization, characterized on the one hand by the elaborate bureaucracy of the Tokugawa in Edo and on the other hand by local bureaucracies under the individual daimyō. The latter, emanating from the central castle town in each fief, were sizeable and complex, being responsible for both administration of the entire domain and relations with Edo. This bureaucratization of the aristocracy both contributed to some slight flexibility within the class structure (caused by the need to find competent administrators) and established one of the conditions for the relatively smooth political transition in the latter half of the nineteenth century.[23]

This bureaucratic entrenchment is linked with the position of the samurai as the country's *ruling* class. As a class, the samurai exploited the labour of others and lived off the fruit of their toil. There was no legal redress for the other classes against the samurai, who were frequently cruel and exploitative. "Their social function was chiefly to over-awe the commonalty, to act as the visible agent of the feudal ruling class in its increasingly exploitative policy toward the people and the peasantry in particular."[24] Easy-going samurai were punished if their severity was found lacking.

On the other hand, the samurai set themselves forth as society's cultural leaders. The centuries of peace undermined their martial role. Many of them were not warriors at all. As part of the attempt to preserve feudal rule, the Tokugawa regime discriminated against bourgeois culture: the aristocratic Nō theatre was privileged against the bourgeois Kabuki; Zen culture, integrally associated with militarism and oppression, was turned against the artisans and the merchants. The Japanese ruling class placed a high value on cultural hegemony—as can be seen from their success in imposing, to a very large extent (as in England), repressive cultural standards on the bourgeoisie after the end of feudalism.[25]

Recent scholarship, particularly in the United States, argues that the samurai did not form a social class at all. Much of this recent work has been directed against the Marxist interpretations of Japanese authorities, and against the pioneering work of E. H. Norman. The central thrust has been to detail the proliferation of divisions within the samurai. Albert Craig, an eminent exponent of the anti-Marxist school, notes that: "In Chōshū, for example, there were seventeen ranks or strata within the class of *shi* or knights, and twenty-three of *sotsu* or soldiers. Within each of these two divisions there was a certain limited measure of mobility; between them there was almost none."[26] Such detailed analytical work is extremely valuable; it has shown that previously accepted divisions of samurai simply into "upper" and "lower" are untenable. A highly differentiated analysis is required covering status (*shi* and *sotsu* and distinctions within these two groups), regions (distinctions between the southwest and the northeast, for example) and breakdowns between rural and urban aristocracy within a given *han* (for example, the samurai in Kagoshima, the capital of Satsuma, were quite a different group from those in the Satsuma hinterland). But the detailed work of Craig, Jansen and others has shown only that there were refined internal differentiations within the samurai class; it has not demonstrated that the samurai did not form a class in the Marxist sense.[27] Clearly not only did the samurai see themselves as a separate group, but so did the Tokugawa leaders who endowed them with specific political, legal and economic privileges which differentiated them from the classes below them.

THE BOURGEOISIE

Although formally at the bottom of the class ladder, the *chōnin* (bourgeoisie) actually fared better than the peasantry under the Tokugawa.[28] The internal peace which the Tokugawa imposed after Sekigahara was very stimulating for the economy, in spite of the almost total curtailment of foreign trade. The enforced idleness of the large aristocracy, through whom the country's surplus passed, the construction of castle towns, and the vast expansion of Edo, created conditions for the further enrichment of the *chōnin*.

The most obvious specific feature of the Japanese bourgeoisie was its purely domestic character. Cut off since the early seventeenth century from overseas trade, the lifeblood of all other bourgeoisies, the merchant class was deprived of the base which gave it its relative autonomy in Western societies. By driving the bourgeoisie inwards, seclusion reinforced its social and political subordination.

> Unlike the great merchant bourgeoisie of France and England on the eve of the Industrial Revolution, the merchant class of late Tokugawa Japan was closely tied to the existing political order. The power of the French and English merchants, though certainly not independent of their national political systems, was based firmly upon international commerce and thus gained strength from sources outside any one nation's boundaries. Japanese merchants in contrast grew economically strong wholly through the manipulation of an internal economic structure.[29]

By the end of the eighteenth century Edo was the largest city in the world, and there were many other very large towns dotted around the country.[30] These were not classical "bourgeois" cities, but political-military constructs (as in China), administrative centres with large populations of samurai and hangers-on. This was different from the pattern in the West. The samurai were cut off from the land and barred from engaging in commerce, yet they received much of the agricultural surplus. The *sankin kōtai* system both contributed directly to the expansion of Edo and also forced the daimyō and their retainers into colossal expenses to finance the journeys to and from Edo, and to maintain suitable establishments in the capital and in their own fiefs. Vanity and the ostentation of snobbery accelerated expenditure. Merchants became increasingly attracted to the castle towns and to Edo, and thus attached to the centres of feudal authority. After the mid-seventeenth century, merchants were allowed to organize into guilds and many of them prospered, particularly in the earlier period of Tokugawa rule. The centre of bourgeois prosperity was the city of Osaka, and Osaka merchants came to control about 70 per cent of the entire country's wealth by the time of the Restoration.[31] Osaka's prosperity was largely based on the *sankin kōtai* system: daimyō converted their rice revenues into money to pay for their *sankin* expenses. Elsewhere, merchants prospered both as middlemen between the growing castle towns and the countryside, and from the commercialization of the rice surplus via the samurai. By the end of the Tokugawa period as much as half "and probably nearer two-thirds of [agricultural] output was marketed in one form or another."[32] The merchants and merchant financiers, who controlled the commercialization of the economic surplus, thus came to perform some of the functions of a central bank. "They controlled the credit system not only of Osaka and its environs, but of all the major centers of Japan."[33] In Crawcour's phrase, they became "quasi-samurai,"[34] receiving stipends which could be as much as those of a minor daimyō in some cases. Merchants prospered on the income from interest on loans to the feudal aristocracy.

Politically and legally, Japan remained a feudal society up to the middle of the nineteenth century. The classes below the samurai had no political rights. There were no representative *chōnin* institutions at all, and the classic bourgeois concept of law was totally absent. "Even the most powerful of the merchant houses were without a tradition of legal protection from debt cancellation, forced levies, or even outright confiscation by political authorities."[35] Before the irruption of the West there were no lawyers in Japan at all, an absence indicative of the highly rigid nature of aristocratic rule under the Tokugawa, and the extent to which Tokugawa feudalism succeeded in divorcing political power and "status," on the one hand, from economic power, on the other.[36] Driven inwards into *rural* commerce by the lack of foreign trade, the merchants thus established a position between the oppressed peasantry and the oppressing aristocracy, operating very much as an agent of the latter. Yet even as the more powerful urban merchants were inextricably joined to the feudal regime, rural merchants developed much greater autonomy. The rural merchants were much more aware of, and sympathetic to, peasant discontent. Their objective class interests did not necessarily lie with the preservation of the existing feudal order. In the critical period between the irruption of the West in the 1850s and the Meiji Restoration in 1867–68, a real break became apparent between the urban guild merchants "with their timidity and attachment to the past" and the rural merchants "with their aggressiveness and fresh outlook."[37]

Essentially, the urban bourgeoisie and the aristocracy formed a power bloc well before the Meiji Restoration. "The interests of the feudal ruling class and the big merchants became so closely intertwined that whatever hurt one necessarily injured the other."[38] This imbrication of a large part of the bourgeoisie with the shogunal regime (the Bakufu) and the success of the feudal regime in retaining a monopoly on political and legal power goes a long way towards explaining the general absence of the bourgeoisie, particularly the urban bourgeoisie, from the anti-Bakufu movement.

The Tokugawa period, in short, combined the retention of the feudal mode of production with the rapid expansion of bourgeois control over capital accumulation. It was not a period of struggle between the merchants as a class and the feudal regime. Not only did the bourgeoisie attach itself to the aristocracy, but the shogunate, although officially hostile to the commercialization of the economy, to some degree had to allow commerce to develop, since it was essential to the working of the regime. The shogunate sought only to keep commerce within certain bounds which were *politically* determined by policy considerations relating to internal control.[39]

The system of feudal *political* control directly affected the long-term development of the economy in every aspect. The urban bourgeoisie, almost wholly dependent on domestic trade and finance, and allied with a parasitic aristocracy split from the land, was to play little part in Japan's early and predominantly rural industrialization—a feature which was to mark the whole process of industrialization.[40] At the same time the use by the shoguns and the local daimyō of political power to allocate monopoly contracts to privileged merchants and financiers (the shogunate in the case of the limited foreign trade permitted and the daimyō by manipulating franchises in their own *han*), as Norman stresses, "is of considerable importance in the history of industrialization in Japan since it strengthened the trend toward State subsidy."[41] The calculated restriction of bourgeois activity allowed the state to wield monopolization as an instrument of control throughout the Tokugawa period. This strengthened state-industry ties along monopoly lines; the interests which catered to this monopoly structure also reinforced the ruling bloc in consolidating a system of capital accumulation based on a very high level of exploitation of labour: "perhaps the most significant role which the plateau [i.e., the later Tokugawa] period played was in imprinting the pattern of monopolistic capitalism with its severe income inequality firmly on Japan."[42]

Rural industry in Japan, moreover, unlike that in the countries of Western Europe just before the bourgeois revolutions there, was not strong enough to win independence from the control of commercial capital, because of the burdens imposed by the prevailing Japanese feudal landed property system. "The Japanese rural industrialists," writes Takahashi, "were unable to overwhelm the privileged seigneurial manufacture based on the financial and military requirements of feudal lords (i.e., the coexistence of feudal authority and commercial capital); on the contrary, the country industry was eventually swallowed up by the ruling setup."[43] In other words, the urban bourgeoisie-aristocracy bloc, although impeding the development of industry for political reasons, retained sufficient control over the process of capital accumulation to buy out the more go-ahead rural interests at the time of the political revolution. Behind this lies the crucial fact that the established system of land ownership (the exaction of feudal rent in kind) prevented the growth of free and independent classes of peasants. And it is this feudal agricultural structure which lies behind and beneath the subsequent industrial structure.

Finally, those commercial contacts which did exist during Japan's two and a half centuries of seclusion were in the hands of the aristocracy, an especially important fact in the middle of the nineteenth century when it was the aristocracy in the southwestern *han* who were accumulating foreign techniques and technicians and thus enabling themselves to leap forward in industry after the "opening" of the country as a whole. In Western Europe much of the contact between countries had been in the hands of the bourgeoisie, traders and pirates, which had put that class in the forefront of foreign relations. But in Japan the general absence of commercial relations with foreign nations meant that the process of re-establishing contact was a predominantly political one, and this left the power of discrimination significantly in the hands of the aristocracy.

THE PEASANTRY

At the time of the Restoration over three-quarters of the population were peasants. Their standard of living, although varying considerably from one area of the country to another, was, on the average, extremely low. Their political power was nil. Their status was far worse than was implied by their formal position in the *shi-nō-kō-shō* four-class structure. The basic agricultural product was rice, a large part of which was handed over by the peasants who farmed it as rent and tax.[44] Many aspects of the peasantry's existence are subjects of controversy, but it seems certain that agricultural output rose quite considerably during the Tokugawa period.[45]

However, the role of the peasantry in the political changes which culminated in the Meiji Restoration is strongly disputed. As Barrington Moore puts it, "For a variety of reasons, the present generation of Western historians tends to minimize the importance of peasant discontent."[46] The classic Western position is simply stated by T. C. Smith, the author of *The Agrarian Origins of Modern Japan*. Smith wishes to refute the view "popular in some academic and journalistic circles in Japan, that members of the ruling class succeeded in turning the 'revolutionary energy' of the peasants to their own ends—so distorting what would otherwise have been a genuine class revolution. . . . The Restoration was not a product of class struggle, though its social consequences were nonetheless revolutionary."[47]

There are really two questions here. What was the nature of the peasant struggles which did indisputably occur? And to what extent did they contribute to the political revolution in the nineteenth century, not just to the Restoration of 1868, in the limited sense of the term?

By their very nature, peasant revolts tend to be poorly documented. History is rarely written by poor farmers, particularly under a feudal regime. But the evidence that exists, allowing for ups and downs within the general trend, shows a steady trend upwards in peasant uprisings throughout the Tokugawa period.[48] The curve continues upwards through the Restoration and peaks in 1873.

The original documents assembled by Hugh Borton in his "Peasant Uprisings in Japan of the Tokugawa Period" give a devastating picture of rural life. Time after time groups of peasants rose in revolt against their feudal lords and against the appropriation of their hard-earned "surplus." These revolts occurred in spite of very harsh laws introduced in 1741, what Borton calls an attempt at "tranquilization by intimidation," which included an almost certain death penalty, usually by crucifixion, for the leaders of the revolt irrespective of whether or not the peasants' complaints were acknowledged to be "justified."[49] The documents also show that the feudal ruling class saw the peasantry's opposition as a *general* threat to feudal power. The shogunate was organized on a national level against peasant revolts, and daimyō were enjoined to assist one another where necessary. Borton, too, in stating his opposition to a peasant revolution, strongly implies that the peasantry were viewed *as a class:* "Japan was spared the ordeal of a bloody revolution such as France had endured. It was fortunate, perhaps, that the farmers had been kept subjugated as a class and had never been unified within the whole country ready to forcibly revolt as a mass against the old feudalistic form of government."[50]

The question of whether or not these revolts can be called "anti-feudal" is disputed. Some of the revolts certainly attacked what the feudal administration saw to be *its* power—and *was* its power. Further, a revolt to prevent the alienation of the peasantry's surplus clearly attacked the very base of feudalism as a system. That the uprisings very rarely set about trying to overthrow the *han* administration, much less the shogunate, says more about the shogunate's success in keeping the peasantry in ignorance than about the class *nature* of the uprisings.

In fact, in spite of Borton's disclaimers, his material supports Norman's contention that "the peasant risings of the Tokugawa period . . . played a noteworthy part in overthrowing the Bakufu. Thus the Restoration, to a large degree, can be justly called the harvest of peasant revolt."[51] The peasant uprisings had made it impossible for the feudal administration, depending as it ultimately did on the dominance of the feudal mode of production, to continue.

It was thus the cumulative effect of repeated uprisings, rather than any one single "peasant revolution," which brought about the downfall of the Bakufu. This is hardly surprising, since it was extremely difficult to communicate from one part of the country to another, as movement between *han* was banned, except on special occasions such as a pilgrimage. Poverty and its attendant problems added to the difficulty. The nature of class antagonisms and class alignments under the Tokugawa can perhaps be further elucidated by a glance at the landholding system and the development of a money economy under the Bakufu.

The prevailing system was that of feudal land ownership based on rent in kind. Both before and after the Meiji Restoration, the key distinction in most Japanese villages was between the *jinushi* or large landowners and the *kosaku* or small dependent peasant-farmers who were tied to paying rent in kind (rice). The "classical" division into capitalist farmers and agricultural wage labour did not occur on the same scale as it did in Western Europe, where the polarization into capital and wage labour led to the disintegration of the village "community."[52]

As the money economy expanded, the feudal lords intensified their exactions from the *kosaku*. Many peasants were driven into extreme poverty and were forced, in spite of the legal prohibitions, to raise money on the security of the lands they leased. But, although the larger peasant revolts did bring about some changes in the shogunate's economic policy, there was no change in the mode of production or in production relationships: "the parasitic system formed itself in imitation of, and side by side with, the land ownership sanctioned by the seigneurial system."[53]

The development of a money economy gradually built up new pressures in the countryside, particularly in the southwest where the money economy was most advanced. Many of the revolts in the later Tokugawa period were against both the feudal system of appropriation and against the new, wealthy farmers. As Horie Hideichi argues: "Agrarian revolts which were anti-feudalistic disturbances at first, later became movements against the wealthy farmers who held a strong economic control over the agricultural field. Agrarian revolts developed into 'Yonaoshi ikki' or 'World levelling revolts'."[54] In the more advanced *han* of southwestern Japan the wealthy farmers managed to turn these revolts against feudalism, and under pressure, the feudal class often split, sometimes allowing alliances to be formed between wealthy farmers and "lower-class military." This development was greatly accelerated by the opening of the ports in 1858 under Western pressure, a move which caused prices to rocket upwards "and brought much suffering to the lower classes."[55] In the north of Japan, where a mercantile economy had not yet developed, the military class stood solid behind the feudal regime.

However, the alignments around the time of the Meiji Restoration can not be explained primarily by reference to the economic level. In fact the major common feature of the three key *han* in the Restoration, Satsuma, Chōshū and Hizen, was their political autonomy as *tozama han,* which enabled them to mobilize their economic forces to the best effect.[56]

Yet the Restoration of 1868 did not by any means satisfy the discontented peasant class. Although the original "causes" of these uprisings varied greatly, "somehow the *flames* always spread to the quarter of the richest usurer, the land-grabbing village headman, the tyrannous official of the former feudal lord."[57] Though there were different immediate causes behind the revolts, which did not manage to coalesce, yet, once detonated, the revolts continued to demonstrate clear class characteristics. The new regime soon set about demobilizing this rural potential for revolutionary action.

THE DIALECTIC OF THE INTERNAL AND THE EXTERNAL

The most obvious question about Japan's experience in the nineteenth century in the global context is: why did the competing imperialisms not turn Japan into a colony? And how, after the forcible "opening" of the country, could Japan experience a relatively rapid and unusually "autonomous" economic growth? What, therefore, was the international economic context in which Japan "emerged" from seclusion? By first examining the role of the imperialist powers and their expanding economies in forcing Japan out of seclusion, and then describing which forces inside Japan responded to these external pressures, it will be possible to understand the relationship between this "response to the West" and the domestic forces of production and class struggle.

The Irruption of the West

> What is the "impact of the West"? It is the effort of the Western bourgeoisie, as Marx and Engels said in the *Manifesto of the Communist Party* of 1848, to remould the world after its own image by means of terror.[58]
>
> Mao Tsetung, 1949

Until 1853 the only official contact between Japan and the West was via a small establishment of Dutch traders who had been permitted to maintain a post on an island called Deshima in Nagasaki Bay.[59] Limited official contact was also permitted with Japan's two main Asian neighbours, China and Korea. Some of the *han* carried on unofficial trade with the Asian continent. Satsuma, for example, one of the key *han* in the overthrow of the Bakufu, controlled trade with the Ryukyu Archipelago, where it had a base for trade with China. Satsuma also had unofficial relations with Britain towards the end of the Tokugawa period. Thus, Japan was not completely isolated from the rest of the world, but its contacts were very limited and, mainly, controlled by the shogunate.

The three Western countries which played the main roles in breaking Japan's seclusion were Russia, Britain and the United States. The only Western power actually with a base in Japan, the Dutch, played a negligible role in this process, although they were the conduit for new ideas in the period leading up to the Restoration. Dutch interest was concentrated further south in the East Indies (now Indonesia).

Russia had had intermittent contact with the Japanese in Sakhalin and the Kuriles since the early eighteenth century. Early Russian interest was evident in the establishment of an Institute of Japanese Studies in St. Petersburg in 1736.[60] In 1804–5 a fruitless attempt was made to open official relations, via a mission which stayed six months in Japan, but was rebuffed.[61] After the 1804–5 failure, Russian activity flagged, reviving in the middle of the century when it was decided to pursue an active policy in the Pacific and try to make friends with Japan in order to check American and British influence in East Asia. In August 1853 a Russian embassy, headed by Rear Admiral E. V. Putiatin, reached Nagasaki—one month after the American, Commodore Perry, arrived at another port, Uraga, near Edo. Russia subsequently signed consular and commercial treaties with Japan in 1855 and 1858.

During the seclusion period, Russia's drive across the great Eurasian land mass was Japan's most acute worry. The shogunate seems never to have been quite sure of Russia's intentions, as probings and minor clashes occurred in Sakhalin, the Kuriles and even on Hokkaido (then called Ezo). In the early part of the nineteenth century the shogunate is recorded trying to put pressure on a group of daimyō to meet the encroachments of Russia.[62] It was against the Russian threat that the first major attempts at a defence system were mooted.

However, by the middle of the nineteenth century, when Putiatin's mission arrived, Russia seemed primarily interested in a diplomatic friendship with Japan to protect its Pacific flank. Russia at the time was engaged in a major land-grab on the Asian mainland, which culminated in the Treaty of Aigun of 1858, under which China, exhausted by fighting against Britain and France, was forced to sign away vast territories to the Tsar.[63] With its position on the Pacific coast of North Asia thus consolidated, Russia became extremely interested in controlling Sakhalin, where there was a strong Japanese presence. In 1875 Russia and Japan signed a treaty under which Japan renounced its claims to any part of Sakhalin in return for possession of the Kurile Islands.[64] As Sansom has pointed out, Western historians tend to underrate the effect Russia's trans-Asian encroachment had on Japan over the years.[65] Russia presented a territorial and military threat, more than a commercial, economic one. Russia remained fairly unimportant in Japan's trade.

In the middle of the nineteenth century Britain was the number one imperialist power in the world; it had a strong economy, the most powerful navy in the world, and large colonial possessions in Asia, of which the most important was India. Britain had paid little attention to Japan, and London had refused support for attempts by the leading British pirate and looter in East Asia, Stamford Raffles, to break the Dutch monopoly in 1813–14. However, the possession of India led directly to attempts to open up China as a market for Indian opium (and thus as a means to finance British colonialism in India) and as a market for Lancashire textiles. British attempts to unload their unwanted colonial merchandise on the Chinese people led to the Opium War of 1840–42 which both greatly weakened the central Chinese government and led to Britain acquiring its first colonial possession in China, Hong Kong (formally "acquired" in 1842).

The combination of China's weakness and British ruthlessness in the Opium War galvanized many Japanese into an acute awareness of their predicament.[66] The Opium War, followed shortly by the Taiping Rebellion (1850–65), a mass peasant uprising aimed at overthrowing the Manchu regime which had capitulated to British imperialism, had a stimulating effect on the Japanese. The idea of resistance to imperialist pressures was further strengthened by the great revolt in India in 1857–59 (the so-called Indian Mutiny).[67]

The Opium War had two wider effects which connect closely with why Japan was not turned into a colony. First, the grab for China tied up most of Britain's energies in the area over the ensuing decades. Second, the forcible opening of China for foreign trade and the concomitant weakening of the Manchu regime put penetration of China right at the top of most imperialists' list of priorities.

The effect of the Opium War was almost as great in America as it was in Japan. And it was immediately followed by important developments involving the consolidation of the Union's power on the Pacific coast: in 1846 Britain ceded Oregon to the Union; California was added in 1848. The California gold rush focussed America's attention on the Pacific, just when China was being "opened up." Japan, up to then thought of mainly as a possible port of call for whalers,[68] became attractive as a refuelling point on the route to Shanghai. Right from the start Japan was seen by the United States as subordinate in interest to China, and more a *strategic* than an economic goal.

The story of Commodore Perry's intrusion into Japan is fairly well known.[69] Perry made his first successful landing in Japan in July 1853. Formal diplomatic contacts followed and a first treaty was signed the next year. Though the treaty did not explicitly mention trade, it did open two ports to the Americans who saw it as a tactical preliminary to a full "opening." Agreements similar to Perry's followed in quick succession with other powers, including Britain. The "opening of the ports" came in 1858, when Japan was obliged to sign unequal economic treaties with the United States (in the person of Townsend Harris, on July 29, 1858), followed in rapid order by Holland (August 18), Russia (August 19), Britain (August 26) and France (October 9). These treaties, which "opened" Japan to foreign trade on very harsh terms, were the subject of fierce controversy within Japan. The treaties accelerated the general economic disintegration of the period. Foreign trade, naturally, soared, with huge profits for foreign traders because of the extraordinarily large amounts of gold in Japan.[70] The government had to debase the coinage; there was serious inflation, and violent fluctuations in the price of rice.

Part of the reason why Japan was not turned into a colony was the organized resistance of the Japanese ruling class. It had a long and uninterrupted tradition of rule behind it and enjoyed a very high level of literacy and education. Japan's population was also unusually well-educated; its culture was relatively homogeneous. The Japanese regime was not completely successful in keeping the Western imperialists away, but it certainly made penetration of Japan appear a daunting, and perhaps unrewarding prospect—an aspect which must not be underestimated, when it seemed there were quick killings to be made elsewhere. Japan just did not look very attractive.

Connected with this was the fact that China was being invaded *simultaneously*. Both Britain and America which, in spite of their great power, did not have limitless resources, were much more interested in China than in Japan. The British interest involved not simply prising open markets, but also fighting; and for some of these years, Britain also had the Indian Rebellion to fight. Britain, like France and Russia, was also much preoccupied with the Turkish question: the Crimean War started in 1854, the year of the first Japanese treaties with the Western powers. France was tied down in Mexico for a lot of the time—and then had to prepare for the war with Prussia. Germany had not yet come on the scene, and when it did its main energies were directed further south and towards the China coast. Russia had the Crimean War to worry about and needed Japan as an ally against the British and the French. Russia's poor communications would have made any assault on Japan at this stage impossible. Spain, already in the Philippines for centuries, was a declining power, not keen to get involved any further. Portugal, somnolent in Macao, reacted likewise. The United States, which had led the best-co-ordinated drive on Japan, was soon plunged into the Civil War, which meant there could be no military follow-up to Perry. There was a short period of expansionism under Seward in the 1860s, when Alaska and the Aleutians were acquired from Russia, but no full-scale drive across the Pacific.

REVOLUTION AND COUNTER-REVOLUTION

The Restoration Process, 1853–68

Though Japan was not colonized by any of the Western powers, between 1853 and 1868 various Western powers forced the Bakufu to enter into diplomatic relations and to open major ports to trade under unequal treaties and under unequal trading conditions. The Western powers also landed several thousand troops in Japan and engaged in such sizeable military operations as the opening of the Straits of Shimonoseki in 1864.

The Western powers first attempted to break into Japan by suborning the Bakufu, the central government. The Bakufu made a number of major concessions, including the opening of the ports. These concessions infuriated the aristocracy in many of the *han,* not only those who might be adversely affected economically, but also those who objected politically. This anti-Bakufu feeling at first crystallized around the slogan of *sonnō jōi* ("Revere the Emperor, expel the barbarians"), a negative political position which could hardly be implemented. In this early period it was the Bakufu which was the main supporter of foreigners' rights in Japan, while the *tozama han,* especially in the southwest, were opposed to them. For a time, the Bakufu, under the outstandingly able leadership of Abe Masahiro, the shogunal counsellor, manoeuvred to conciliate the survival of the shogunate with the intrusion of imperialist trade, culture and law, but after a few years of stop-gap measures, Abe's policies were bowled over by the huge socio-economic storm unleashed by the unequal treaties.[71]

Dissatisfaction with the performance of the Bakufu was widespread, and was particularly strong in several of the southwestern *han*, especially in Satsuma, Chōshū and Hizen. These were all *tozama han*, which had a degree of political autonomy from the Bakufu. Their relative economic backwardness meant they had been less integrated economically with the central government. Being in the southwest, they were more in touch with news from abroad, which came through the Dutch at Nagasaki, and thus more alert to the dangers exemplified by the Opium War. They were also involved in illegal foreign trade.

With the increase in internal disorder during the Tempō famine, they turned to Western models for advancement, smuggling *samurai* overseas, setting up schools on the fiefs to teach new learning, and creating Western-style armies in preparation for foreign invasion, or possible conflict with the Bakufu. Meanwhile, the Bakufu, facing the same situation of bank-ruptcy as the *han*, sought to save itself by currency manipulation and cancellation of debts or interest.[72]

In the period 1853–68 the shogunate's control over much of the country weakened. Part of the samurai class in certain *han* stood by the Bakufu; others, especially in the southwest, turned against it. Some of the samurai who turned against the Bakufu were closely connected to the local *han* administrations; others were *rōnin* (masterless samurai), who often oper-ated as free-lance aides to members of the bourgeoisie in activities as varied as fencing teachers and debt collectors. In the Western *han* a new highly educated technical bureaucratic samurai group emerged, brought up with Western military technology and political ideas. This group, while Western-influenced, was also in favour of the *jōi* ("expel the barbarians") policy and can not be easily characterized as "progressive" or "reac-tionary." Some were interested in improving their economic position, in the face of increasing *chōnin* power and prestige; others were more inter-ested in miltary reassertion; some in political anti-feudalism; others in samurai reinstatement. As the showdown came nearer, actual military equipment, as well as martial spirit, became important, and here again it was mainly the southwestern *han* which had been active in importing advanced Western technology.[73]

In the meantime, a new factor emerged: the reassertion of the Emperor as a political force separate from the shogun. The first autonomous political act by the Emperor was in 1846, when he had written to the shogun expressing his concern at foreign encroachment after the abortive visit that year by Commodore Biddle of the United States.[74] But the Emperor became a real force on the political scene in 1858, when the court refused to ratify the treaty with the United States (the "Harris Treaty").[75] Although the court (or rather the forces behind it at the time) failed to impose its will in this case, this open opposition to shogunal policy on a key issue marks a turning point in the whole Restoration process. First, it meant the establishment of a polycentric, and therefore potentially indecisive, executive authority for the traditional autocracy of the shogun, further weakening the central government. Second, the existence of incompatible policy positions within the executive authority made the attraction of appealing to an allegedly outside authority—in this instance, the imperial institution—stronger. It naturally also bolstered the position of those who opposed the shogunate's compromises with the foreign powers.

Such compromises ignited the roundabout process which led to the Restoration. In the years following the opening of Yokohama, the main port (near Edo), in 1858, the Bakufu became increasingly concerned at the negative effects of that decision, and came under growing pressure to reverse it. A move in this direction was adumbrated in 1863, but collapsed before it was implemented. Some of the other *han,* however, were eager to go through with the expulsion of all foreigners. Among these *han* was Satsuma, in southern Kyushu. In the summer of 1863 a British fleet shelled Satsuma, burning about one-third of its capital, Kagoshima, to the ground. The ultimate outcome of this encounter was a settlement reached in December which both brought Satsuma closer to Britain and moved Satsuma out of the "extremist" anti-foreigner group.[76]

The other *han* which was to play the key role in the overthrow of the shogunate was Chōshū, in southwest Honshu. Chōshū guarded the vital Straits of Shimonoseki at the western entrance to the Inland Sea, the natural route for any ship wishing to reach Central Japan from India or China. Chōshū was hostile to the Bakufu, and hostile to the intrusion of the Western powers. In 1864 Chōshū closed the Shimonoseki Straits, which were then forced open by a joint British-Dutch-French-U.S. force, which subjected Chōshū to heavy shelling. Chōshū's decision to close the straits was part of a larger policy of anti-Bakufu activities involving land warfare against the Bakufu. After a major battle at Kyoto in August 1864 and the Shimonoseki Straits episode, the Bakufu launched the first of two major, and unsuccessful, campaigns against Chōshū. As with Satsuma, the effect of having been defeated by Western military might caused certain samurai leaders in Chōshū to advocate a policy of allying with the West against the Bakufu. The Western imperialists, led by Britain, began to realize that the anti-Bakufu fiefs were not simply obscurantist reactionaries, and seized on the chance to encourage internal divisions. From this time on the British gave tacit support to the Western fiefs, and during the Restoration period they persuaded the foreign legations to remain neutral. Only France continued to back the Bakufu.[77]

From 1864 to 1866 Chōshū maintained its military defiance of the Bakufu regime but was unable to defeat the Tokugawa armies on its own.

In March 1866 it made a secret alliance with Satsuma, hitherto its bitter
enemy—an alliance which was largely the diplomatic work of Sakamoto
Ryōma of the minor Tosa *han*—and scored a big victory against the
shogunate in July that year. In August 1866 the shogun died, precipitating
a crisis at Edo. His successor, Tokugawa Yoshinobu, did not take up office
until January 10, 1867, after considerable manoeuvring over much-needed
reforms in the governmental system. Yoshinobu was not entirely happy
about taking the post, but finally agreed. One of the reasons for his acceptance was the fact that he thought he had a good working relationship with
the Emperor Kōmei. Twenty days after Yoshinobu's investiture as shogun,
the Emperor died. Pressure built up on the shogun to surrender the
Bakufu's power to the Emperor, the Tosa *han* again playing a key intermediary role. In November Yoshinobu resigned, surrendering his power to
the court which nonetheless ordered Chōshū and Satsuma to attack the
Bakufu. In January 1868 the "allied" *han* staged a coup, replacing the
Tokugawa troops at Kyoto, the imperial capital, and the Restoration of the
Emperor was announced on January 3. In September 1868 Edo was
proclaimed the capital and renamed Tokyo ("Eastern capital"). By the
end of 1869 the last Tokugawa resistance (on the northern island,
Hokkaido) had been eliminated.

In spite of its title, the "Restoration" was not primarily a move to install
a monarchist regime in the classic sense in which the term "monarchical
absolutism" is usually deployed.[78] It was in many ways a "negative"
process—to remove a regime, the Bakufu, which represented only sectional
interests, and those no longer very efficiently. The upheaval, moreover,
cannot be defined simply in terms of either the class origins or the conscious intentions of the leading participants. Detailed work on the key *han*
which led the overthrow of the Bakufu shows that different social strata
pursued different policies in different *han*;[79] and that some strata were
split inside given *han*. In Chōshū there was virtually no class difference
between the two sides in the Civil War.

The Restoration can perhaps most easily, if loosely, be compared to the
Gaullist "restoration" of 1958—although De Gaulle clearly played a
different role from that of the Japanese Emperor ninety years before. Both
events showed something of the same mix: a multi-class political upheaval,
in which the *declining* classes imprinted their mark, as well as the rising
classes.[80] Moreover, in both cases the political momentum generated went
far beyond the original project of many of the participants—De Gaulle,
far from crushing the Algerian revolution, came to terms with it.

When the Western bourgeoisies broke into Japan by force, they pro-
voked a crisis which was both political and economic. The confrontation
was between two fundamentally unequal forces. The domestic reaction
against the Bakufu was primarily at a political (and military) level; it was
against the shogunal *state*. But this political opposition rested on under-

lying economic changes and a major redistribution of economic power within the society. The aristocracy, however, was the only class whose members could take the required political initiatives against the Bakufu. To talk of an "aristocratic revolution,"[81] however, is to reduce to the class origins of the leading participants a process which involved the construction of a new state system in a *global* context dominated by the imperialist bourgeoisies. This involved, naturally, not simply building defences against the rest of the world, but also mobilizing and transforming the domestic society—which, in turn, meant promoting the capitalist mode of production, and the ascendancy of the bourgeoisie.[82]

Japan was not jarred right off track by external pressures as were most countries subjected to classic colonialism. It continued structurally along its own course, but the pace and timing of its economic development were fundamentally altered by the irruption of the West. International bourgeois terror, as Mao calls it, forced the Japanese ruling coalition to press the country into a mould as similar to imperialist Western societies as possible, as fast as possible. This abrupt acceleration produced two of the most remarkable "distortions" which mark Japanese capitalism—the process of the formation and accumulation of capital, and the specific form of Japanese imperialism which was distinguished by an acute lack of capital ("the highest stage of capitalism" without capital).[83] The problem for the new coalition was not only to construct a state which could deal with the foreign threat and cope with the class struggle at home, but also to use the new state to release the latent surplus in the economy and reallocate it in two ways:[84] investing so as to strengthen Japan *as an independent nation* vis-à-vis the outside world; and redistributing it internally to consolidate the new ruling bloc, whose *political* survival in the new global context depended on economic transformation.

Rollback and Periodicity

The new Meiji state took over twenty years to build—from the time the Bakufu was overthrown in 1867–68 to the enactment of the Constitution in 1889 and the convocation of the first Diet in 1890. The first few years were devoted mainly to the destruction of the basis of feudal power. The central element in this was the remission by the daimyō of their fiefs in 1871; by 1877 the new central government had subdued the last regional feudal revolts. The first decade or so of the new regime was one of relative "liberalization" in many areas. The installation of the network of repressive institutions and ideology sometimes referred to as "the Emperor-system" really starts only in 1881.

The early "liberalization" was to a large extent a forced response to the explosive power released in the society of which the overthrow of the Bakufu was only the most spectacular aspect. The whole system of cultural repression was threatened; the educational system virtually collapsed; the new proletariat challenged industrial relations as envisaged by their employers.[85]

The new regime, not surprisingly, was at first fairly weak and was lucky to be able to deal with only one class enemy at a time. Although the peasantry did not carry off an active revolution, there was a revolutionary situation over much of the country. The new regime launched at once into a vigorous counter-revolution against the class which had made the Restoration possible. Norman stressed the importance of the help given to the Imperial armies by numerous peasant revolts in the war against the Bakufu. For example, in Echigo Province, 60,000 armed peasants forced the local Tokugawa commander to go over to the anti-Tokugawa side with his entire army. This, Norman says, was "a genuine anti-feudal peasant army."[86] There are several examples of autonomous local revolts against the Bakufu resulting in popular democratic governments, such as on the Oki Islands.[87] Usually this breathing space lasted only a few months before these pockets were suppressed by the new army, often with the assistance of former Bakufu officials. Many of the peasant outbreaks after the Restoration can be traced not just to renewed economic pressure against the peasantry, but to this traumatic experience of armed counter-revolution. The regime's power to intervene against the peasantry was greatly enhanced with the introduction of conscription in 1873, the year in which peasant revolts began to decline. Thus, although the regime tended to portray samurai discontent as its main fear, and it was only the samurai who could organize well-armed and trained forces, the regime's initial period of consolidation involved a major bout of class struggle against the peasantry, who constituted the vast majority of the population and the foundation of the society's economy. By the time dissident members of the old feudal aristocracy had geared themselves up to battle, the new regime had managed to suppress the rebellious peasantry with some success.

THE RULING BLOC AND THE NEW STATE

Two preliminary points are necessary to understand the construction of the new state system. First, in spite of the definite rupture in 1868, there was a considerable degree of continuity in personnel through the Restoration. As Horie Yasuzō puts it, "The leadership of the country remained in the hands of the self-same class, before and after the Restoration."[88] Although the Tokugawa family was ousted from power and the shogunate was terminated, there was not a complete destruction of the existing state machinery. Second, although there was considerable continuity of personnel in class terms, there was a real shift of power within the new ruling bloc, especially in the early 1870s. Most of the key figures in the actual Restoration either died very early (like Sakamoto Ryōma) or were removed from power shortly after 1868 (like Saigō Takamori), to be replaced by a new caucus, centred largely on the bureaucracy. One of the first tasks of the new regime was to break the power of the great lords and to provide some satisfaction for the large numbers of idle and disgruntled samurai. With the destruction of the shogunate, Tokugawa lands were taken over by the court and administered by imperial officials. In July 1869, after considerable disagreement, the daimyō were named governors of their fiefs—a transitional step to the abolition of the fiefs in 1871. The remission of fiefs completed the *formal* centralization of power and also strengthened the imperial institution. As expected, not all the feudal lords welcomed giving up their fiefs and a series of samurai uprisings against the new regime broke out in the mid-1870s. As it was, the daimyō were probably persuaded to accede to the central government's request only by a combination of the possibility of being subdued by armed force and a hefty compensation programme.[89] Thus, in Norman's words, "the feudal lord ceased to be a *territorial* magnate drawing his income from the peasant and became instead . . . a *financial* magnate investing his freshly capitalized wealth in banks, stocks, industries, or landed estates, and so joined the small financial oligarchy."[90] The commutation of daimyō pensions took place in two stages: in 1873 (voluntary commutation) and in 1876 (compulsory). The significance of this settlement is well summed up by Norman again:

> The commutation of *daimyo* pensions, while symbolizing the political compromise between a former governing class and the new government resting largely upon merchant and landed interests for its support, represents at the same time a far-reaching social process in which the interests of usurer, landlord, merchant, financier and *ci-devant daimyo* were melted down, transfused and solidified into a homogeneous mass in which the original elements become indistinguishable.[91]

An extensive new land survey and a new land tax were the corollary to the remission of the fiefs and, with associated measures, "constituted the economic machinery that the Meiji leadership employed to destroy the old economic and social system and to create a new one."[92]

In addition to settling with the daimyō, the new regime also had to deal with the much more numerous samurai. The main step came, after some experimentation, in December 1871, when the government passed a law allowing samurai to engage in any occupation they wanted and then moved energetically to create employment for samurai both in the administration and in business.

Samurai became employed in key areas of the new regime. In the central government bureaucracy, samurai totalled 78.3 per cent of all office holders listed in the years immediately after 1868; they accounted for between 77.7 per cent (in 1876, 1877) and 63 per cent (1882) of *all* government officials.[93] In local government, over 70 per cent of all office holders were former samurai between 1872 and 1877; this figure fell to 57 per cent in 1882. The forces of repression were particularly heavily staffed by ex-samurai. The police force was the main locus for unemployed lumpen samurai and was marked by a "complete absence of commoners in the ranks." Kawajō Toshyoshi, one of the first police superintendents of Tokyo, made it his explicit policy to recruit only samurai for the force. When the Tokyo police expanded to 3000 in 1874, 1000 of these were Kagoshima clansmen. In education, 48 of the 67 people enrolled into the faculty by Tokyo University, the central educational institution of the state system, in 1882 were ex-samurai; 32,488 out of 43,467 administrative and teaching positions in the national school system were held by ex-retainers in the same year (72 per cent), though this latter figure fell fairly fast a few years later.

The 1871 law "liberating" the samurai was accompanied by vigorous measures to assist them economically. These took three main forms: government aid to assist migration to and rehabilitation of new areas; setting up branches of the national bank as a safeguard for samurai investments; and the establishment of machinery for loaning money to samurai to go into business. To back up this aid, the government initiated and subsidized major land reclamation schemes to co-ordinate with its pension commutation plans. Samurai, like demobilized Roman soldiers, were encouraged to colonize outlying areas like Hokkaido. With the abolition of the fiefs, and thus of the responsibilities of daimyō for their retainers, the central government took on the maintenance of the samurai class and paid them stipends. Between November 1874 and August 1876 these stipends were progressively commuted, at first voluntarily, and finally compulsorily. About 310,971 ex-samurai received, in exchange for their military pensions, public bonds amounting to ¥113,000,000.[94] From 1876 onwards, especially after the Satsuma Rebellion of 1877, the government, prodded by Ōkubo Toshimichi and Iwakura Tomomi in particular, provided large loans. "From 1876 to 1882 nearly 200 individual samurai business organizations . . . were established as a direct result of government loans and encouragement, and approximately 100,000 samurai participated in the formation of these organizations."[95] The programme continued until 1890, subsidizing ship-building, construction, cement works, fertilizer concerns, salt works, and artisanal projects. One assessment, while surprisingly claiming that it is "dubious" that the programme accomplished what the government intended, admits that "by erasing the dangers of class rebellion and relocating a large social group with no apparent function in an industrialized society, the Meiji government did realise a measure of success. . . . By the late 1880's, the threat of class discontent had been removed, and the government could allow the program of rehabilitation to lapse."[96] The programme not only contributed to demobilizing the threat from the samurai right, but helped to consolidate the political alliance between aristocracy and bourgeoisie at the economic level. Later research confirms the continuing important role of the aristocracy as a class in business and industry.[97]

Political Divisions and the New Army

The overriding concern of the new regime with security led to the rapid development of forces of repression to hold down internal dissidence. In the years 1869–71 the government concentrated the legal military units in Kyoto and Tokyo. By the imperial edict of August 29, 1871 which transformed the former *han* into prefectures, the domain samurai armies were legally disbanded; each prefecture was authorized to maintain only one platoon of troops for "public order." The national government then had only some 9,000 troops—about 3,000 each from Chōshū, Satsuma and Tosa, many of whom still owed allegiance to their old domain leaders.[98]

From 1871 to early 1873 there was a kind of moratorium on political initiatives while half the regime's leaders were abroad assessing the world situation and studying other countries for the applicability of their institutions to Japan. But in January 1873, after bitter disagreement, a first conscription law was introduced and in that spring and summer agrarian riots and general disturbances swept the country. Japan probably came nearer to revolution then than at any other time in the early Meiji years, a result to a great extent of a conscription system which forcibly removed many able-bodied farmers from their work.[99]

As Iwakura and the other members of his mission returned to Japan, major disagreements on such ideas as launching an attack on nearby Korea emerged between the "ambassadors" and the "caretakers" who had stayed behind. These disagreements covered a vast area of both domestic and foreign policy, which became inextricably intertwined. Saigō Takamori of Satsuma, the chief proponent of invading Korea, sought not simply to attack the Koreans, but also to create the conditions for forming a national samurai army which would be a military-political instrument of class rule at home. "The central issue at stake was the traditional monopoly of force by the samurai class."[100]

The idea of invading Korea was squelched, and with it Saigō's projects for a samurai, as opposed to a conscript, army. The tide was largely turned by Ōkubo Toshimichi who wrote a famous "memorial" against an invasion. In particular, Ōkubo warned that if Japan invaded Korea this could upset the delicate balance with the Western imperialists and Britain might turn Japan into "another India." Japan should, therefore, concentrate on internal economic development. An invasion of Korea would only impose strains and diversions at home.[101]

When the invasion proposal was defeated, Saigō and several other top leaders (Itagaki Taisuke, Soejima Taneomi, Gotō Shōjirō and Etō Shimpei) left the government, Saigō's departure precipitated a number of developments. It left the military leadership open once again to Yamagata Aritomo of Chōshū, who was to become the dominant figure until well into the twentieth century. Yamagata reassumed command of the Imperial Guard, a post he had previously held in 1872, and reorganized it with a large grant from the Emperor's private funds.[102] Chōshū dominance in the army was established from this time.

Early in 1874 the first of a series of major revolts broke out against the central government in Hizen, led by Etō Shimpei, an ally of Saigō and the "war party" which favoured invading Korea in 1873.[103] This uprising, like subsequent ones in Haga and Akizuki in 1876, was successfully put down by the new conscript army. In 1876 the government ordered an end to the practice of wearing swords, a traditional samurai privilege, and the main outward sign of samurai status. Coinciding with the compulsory commutation of *shizoku* stipends, this decree further fanned samurai resentment against the government, already high because of conscription and its implications for the former warrior class. In this context the last and greatest of the feudal revolts erupted, the Satsuma Rebellion of 1877 led by the redoubtable Saigō Takamori. This was an outright reactionary feudal rebellion. Satsuma had an unusually high proportion of samurai— just over one-quarter of the population belonged to this class[104]—and Saigō's army was almost entirely a samurai one. Under Yamagata's able leadership, and with superior weapons, the central government's new peasant conscript army subdued Saigō's forces, and Saigō himself committed suicide.

The Satsuma Rebellion was followed almost immediately by an even more worrying episode, the Takebashi (or Takehashi) Mutiny of 1878 by the Imperial Guard.[105] Though the immediate cause of the mutiny was a delay in pay and bonuses for the guard's role in putting down the Satsuma Rebellion, the deeper reasons seem to have been political. The guard was mainly composed of samurai, but many of the soldiers were former peasants. The soldiers killed two of their own officers and tried to attack one of the imperial palaces, and perhaps even the Emperor himself.

This mutiny among the elite troops was highly disturbing, for it raised the possibility that the new army might not function as the instrument of counter-revolution it was intended to be. Fifty-three soldiers were executed by firing-squad, and Yamagata launched a sustained campaign to cut the army off from any contact with democratic movements and to inculcate the old samurai ethic of Bushidō as the ethic of the new, non-samurai army. One month after the mutiny, he issued an order known as the Admonition to Soldiers which set out in extremely oppressive terms the need for unquestioning obedience to the Emperor and the state. The drift of the document was not, as is sometimes alleged, that the army should stay out of politics. Rather, the army was to stay out of "left-wing" or democratic politics, and engage only in reactionary political activity.[106] In January

1881 the *kempei* or military police were set up not only to combat the growing movement for some form of more popular government, but also to give the military a police force which could operate more easily in civilian society, even against the existing, politically less reliable police force.[107] One year after the *kempei* were set up, the Emperor, in an unprecedented ceremony, handed down his Rescript to Soldiers and Sailors. At Yamagata's suggestion, this was done explicitly outside the authority of the Prime Minister and the government, cementing the authoritarian links between Emperor and military and keeping them well away from the limited existing civilian institutions. In the same year sanction was given to expand the army to 73,000 men, with an immediate mobilization potential of 277,000 —an authorized increase of 600 per cent.[108]

In 1883 the conscription law was revised, extending the length of active and reserve service from ten to twelve years. Within the army Yamagata accentuated the diffusion of reactionary ideology. Every effort was made to cut the peasant recruits off from their background among the people and infuse them with a blind subservience ("obedience" and "loyalty") that combined with the arrogance of the old samurai. This ideology can be clearly seen in documents like the 1878 Admonition and the 1882 Rescript. At the same time Yamagata and his group ensured that the army's loyalty was not to anything so abstract as the "nation" or to the people of Japan, but to the Emperor personally. In 1878–79 Yamagata and a young Chōshū assistant, Katsura Tarō, who had been military attaché in Berlin, reorganized the upper administrative echelon of the army so that a new body, the General Staff Headquarters, headed by Yamagata, took over the job of advising the Emperor on matters relating to the supreme command—a job which hitherto had fallen to the Prime Minister. In this way the command function was removed completely from any possible influence by the cabinet.[109] And all these major developments—the revised conscription laws, the enactment of the doctrine of the independence of the supreme command (*tōsuiken*)—took place well before either the Constitution came into force or the Diet convened. (As Norman aptly recalls, Charles I's attempts to assert the right of the Crown to maintain a standing army without Parliament's consent gave rise to one of the bitterest struggles in English constitutional history.) In effect, Yamagata managed to establish this "feudal" position, profoundly inimical to democracy, so well that it survived until the middle of the twentieth century.

The New Institutional Framework of the State

The Japanese constitutional system was "the product of a counter-revolutionary *tour de force*"[110] which embraced a much wider arc of political activity than the constitutional area. For the Constitution and related developments, such as the convocation of a Diet, came rather late in the construction of the overall system. The foundations were built well before the Constitution.

The construction of the new institutional framework proceeded by a combination of public proclamations and largely behind-the-scenes *coups de main,* followed by the gradual promotion of pseudo-democratic constitutional institutions. Woven through the whole process was the gradual, though uneven, advancement of the Emperor. Immediately after the overthrow of the shogunate, the new ruling coalition issued a brief document in the name of the Emperor Meiji, known as the Charter Oath. This was a relatively liberating document, but also contained an only slightly veiled expression of intent to repress political opposition (in clause 3). Clause 5 read: "Knowledge shall be sought throughout the world so as to strengthen the foundations of imperial rule."[111]

Two months later, in June 1868, a first Constitution was issued, to fill out and implement the Charter Oath. It asserted the authority of the central government without directly attacking feudal authority—"lest inferior authorities be confounded with superior and the government be thrown into confusion"[112]—and was grounded on the putative achievements of the Taika Reform of 646 A.D., a pre-feudal reorganization based on the model of a centralized state imported from China.

In the early years the key political decisions were taken by a very small group, without any kind of formal consultation with any segment of the population. The crisis of 1873, for example, produced a decision to concentrate on economic reconstruction at home, rather than engage in premature imperialism abroad. In fact, in spite of internal differences of varying importance, the regime operated on an irresponsible and authoritarian basis without being seriously challenged from within the ruling stratum until 1881.

In that year a major crisis broke out as a result of a conflict between two groups, headed by Ōkuma Shigenobu and Itō Hirobumi.[113] Ōkuma, a member of the government, was the first really powerful politician to come out openly with a call for a form of parliamentary government. This open appeal to the Emperor, combined with Ōkuma's devious manoeuvrings at the time, seriously undermined the position of Itō and his group, then dominant in the government. When a spectacular scandal connected with Hokkaido broke out in 1881, Itō and his group found themselves obliged to compromise in order to stay in power. In return for Ōkuma's resignation, the Itō group conceded the substance of Ōkuma's demands—the convocation of a Diet in 1890. An Imperial Rescript was promulgated, announcing that the Diet would be convened in nine years' time. The Rescript's language sums up the nature of the move as a demobilizing concession:

> We perceive that the tendency of Our people is to advance too rapidly, and without that thought and consideration which alone can make progress

enduring, and We want Our subjects, high and low, to be mindful of Our will, and [of the fact] that those who may advocate sudden and violent changes, thus disturbing the peace of Our realm, will fall under Our displeasure.[114]

A "LEFT" OPPOSITION?

Agitation for democratic rights is usually associated with the "popular rights movement" (*jiyū minken undō*) whose origins can be found in the split which occurred in 1873 when the government decided not to invade Korea. A part of the group, headed by Itagaki Taisuke, left the government and adopted a line which tried to exploit genuine democratic hostility to the regime by capturing this opposition and merging it with an aggressive policy toward Korea.[115] Regardless of the subjective opportunism of the samurai involved in this operation, it must be understood that this manoeuvre was carried out in a context where the regime was severely repressing all genuinely democratic opposition. The *jiyū minken undō,* in effect, was siphoning off the anti-regime feeling which could find no other channel to express itself. On the other hand, the fact that the *jiyū minken undō* was opportunist must not be allowed to obscure the deep mass opposition to the regime.

Itagaki and his chauvinist group, setting out to capture democratic anti-regime sentiment, both locked the drive for (limited) popular rights (*minken*) in with imperialism and at the same time helped to sabotage the development of any autonomous proletarian socialist movement for several decades. The movement for "political democracy" was, in many ways, little more than one wing of the samurai opposition to a *specific* form of oligarchic government. For many of the founders of the movement *jiyū minken* (peoples' rights) actually meant *shizoku minken* (samurai rights).[116]

This coalition of "liberalism" and imperialism is not surprising, since the two also fused in the Western "democracies." Indeed, although the coalition in Japan was largely the result of political opportunism and political repression by the regime, Western experience also played a part. The possibility of travel to the West and the influx of foreign ideas *suddenly* opened up vast new worlds of thought.[117] It is hard now to conjure up the earth-shaking effect produced on Meiji readers by such authors as John Stuart Mill, Guizot, Buckle, Samuel Smiles, or Charles Darwin. One man, Kōno Hironaka, was reportedly converted to bourgeois parliamentary democracy in one lightning flash while out horseback riding one day in March 1872, studying *On Liberty*. At one stage all three tutors to the Emperor were lecturing on Smiles' *Self-Help* (and the original draft of the Imperial Rescript on Education of 1890 was compiled by the translator of Samuel Smiles). Kinoshita Shōkō, the author of a famous left-wing novel, decided to start studying English law after reading about Cromwell and the execution of Charles I to see if it might be possible to get rid of the monarchy.[118]

This veritable torrent of new ideas stimulated a certain degree of cultural reaction in Japan. But much of Western thought was also integrally connected with the menace of colonization. This was particularly the case with Britain, where the Japanese immediately noticed that the ideology which accompanied imperialism was liberalism, and that imperialism was an internationalized form of protectionism.[119] The Japanese leaders rapidly began to synthesize the material available. Along with the "liberating" ideas found in some Western thinkers, they also found useful repressive elements. Thus Darwin, appropriately enough, along with Herbert Spencer,[120] became one of the chief imported theoretical props of the Meiji leadership. Samuel Smiles, although idealized in the West as an ideologue of "free" enterprise, was utilized in Japan as a further prop for the Emperor system (cf. the ambiguity of Saint-Simon, easily transformed by List). On the other hand, where British thinking was found to be inappropriate to Japanese practice, British ideas were soon dropped, especially in economic thought where German ideas quickly became paramount.[121]

Thus the weakness of a "left" opposition is not surprising. There was a strong groundswell for democratic reforms, but it was never able to make itself felt as an autonomous political force. While those in power moved to suppress the opposition, the samurai out of power exploited it, making use of the very narrow limits imposed on political action by the regime. At the same time, for structural and ideological reasons, "liberalism" became intertwined with imperialism. This had an important long-term effect because many of those who later wished to push for "left" reforms at home tended to base themselves on jingoistic opinion.

The Components of the New State Apparatus

The 1880s were the decade of crucial political activity in the construction of the new system. The key objective was to build a machine *before* Constitutional government came in, and to make sure that all the key areas of power would be out of reach of any democratic organizations which might emerge as a result of the introduction of the Constitution. This was a multi-faceted operation which involved: first, the strengthening of the Emperor as an institution and the "legitimizing" of irresponsible government; and second, the consolidation of a bureaucratic system which would *de facto* be running the country before the Constitution, the Diet and functioning political parties were in operation. These two aspects complemented each other, and both were cemented by a major overhaul of the educational system and a massive campaign of ideological and religious mystification.

THE IMPERIAL INSTITUTION

The extremely important place in the state apparatus that the Emperor occupies poses a number of theoretical problems. Japan is the only advanced capitalist society in which the Emperor is an integral element in the state though the real power which accrues to the institution was *allocated* to it after the Meiji Restoration. During the Tokugawa period, the Emperors, immured in Kyoto, were virtually prisoners of the shogunate. The Emperors certainly were the object of a certain amount of religious veneration, especially in times of major unrest.[122] This Emperor "worship" was part of folk Shinto, but, as Webb points out, it is "difficult to draw a line between worship of the imperial institution and religious practices directed more diffusely among the Shinto pantheon."[123] Vast numbers of people apparently made pilgrimages to the major shrines like Ise and Iwashimizu, but it is unclear what part genuine religious fervour played in these pilgrimages and to what extent religious and non-religious feelings rubbed off either on any specific Emperor or on the institution as such. Assessment of this is made even more difficult by the fact that Shinto as a religion did not have what might be called full autonomy, but was merely a part of a syncretic Shinto-Confucian philosophy within a largely Buddhist-dominated context.[124]

The imperial loyalism which emerged under the Tokugawa was not originally directed towards the restitution of ancient political powers of the imperial institution in any practical way. "Restorationism might be used as a moral guideline for the performance of ordinary political acts, it was not intended as a call for some extraordinary political settlement."[125] In time, there emerged the more general objective of trying to establish political "legitimacy" independent of the vicissitudes of military power. Then, as the *sonnō jōi* movement developed, the *national* role of the Emperor grew, the Emperor being the only person to whom *everyone* in the feudal system stood in exactly the same relation.[126] Paradoxically, by being excluded from power by the shoguns, the Emperors became the symbol of resentment against the established order, and the symbol of redemption.[127]

The weakening of the Bakufu in the middle of the nineteenth century allowed the Emperor at Kyoto to make two direct political interventions, in 1846 and 1858, which accelerated and meshed with the loyalists' moves to "restore" the Emperor and oust the shogun. But with the ousting of the shogun, the new regime, as well as the position of the Emperor, remained extremely weak. At first the new regime tried to promote "Restoration Shinto" as the state religion to try to capitalize on the "imperial credentials" and rally popular support for the new order.[128] This campaign failed lamentably, a failure attributable to both political and religious causes. Quite apart from the problem of transferring religious or quasi-religious feelings onto a political object, there was the historical problem of

the fusion of Shinto with both Buddhism and Confucianism. The years
1867–72 saw a virulent persecution of Buddhism by the new regime in an
attempt to extricate Shinto and try to stand it on its own as the new state
religion.[129] This attempt failed, partly because Buddhism was much
stronger than Shinto, partly because the two were inextricably intertwined
in the minds of the people. The regime then tried to institutionalize Shinto
at a formal level, as the cultus of the state, while leaving Buddhism fairly
free as the "unofficial" private religion of the people. Yet, even though the
regime enlisted the assistance of Buddhism in this second stage, the
operation also failed. In 1873 the government abandoned active propa-
gation of Imperial Shinto and cut back on shrine support.[130]

The subsequent development of the imperial institution was closely
linked to educational changes and the promotion of state ideology, which
in turn were also integrally linked to the promotion of the bureaucracy, the
other key element in the consolidation of the authoritarian regime. Education, like everything else, had benefited greatly from the general liberation of the 1860s. In the years immediately after the Restoration, ethics
(*shūshin*), mainly embodying repressive Confucian principles, were considerably downgraded. Men like Fukuzawa Yukichi, the leader of the
Japanese enlightenment, were calling for a new kind of learning.[131] This
plea was surprisingly successful, and the new Fundamental Code of
Education of 1872 was an extremely advanced document for its time.[132]
"Not only was the traditional Confucian ethical learning despised as
narrow and useless, but moral teaching of any kind had been virtually
dropped from the school curriculum, and the textbooks prescribed for its
teaching were a ludicrous collection of translations of obscure foreign
works on ethics and law."[133] The most important of these was a translation of a French Catholic textbook. "Enterprising teachers," Ronald
Dore notes, "were allowed to substitute instruction in contemporary Japanese police regulations."[134] Basically, the curriculum instituted by the
1872 reform was a modification of the French encyclopedic curriculum
(very like the Argentinian and Turkish systems). Although this was a
product of a centralizing and authoritarian regime, in the context of Japan
it represented a moment of enormous liberation, even though the main
ideological shift was the ambiguous one from *oppressive* collectivism to
bourgeois individualism. This was, however, as Dore puts it, only "an
aberrant interlude." Reaction soon counter-attacked.

The 1872 reform was vulnerable on a number of counts, including
problems over administration and finance as well as content. Traditionalists argued it was too much influenced by foreign ideas, both in its
original conception and in its application. This charge was particularly
directed against the Education "Minister,"[135] Tanaka Fujimaro, and his
chief adviser, David Murray, from Rutgers University, New Jersey.

But the counter-attack on the educational reforms was only a part of a more general reactionary movement which built up after about a decade of Meiji rule. By the end of the 1870s the imperial institution, though stronger than it had been ten years before, was still extremely weak; the government had instituted conscription and defeated several feudal revolts, but lacked firm roots in the country as a whole. Increasingly, educational reform was suggested as a means to strengthen the foundations of the state, especially the imperial institution and the bureaucracy.

BUREAUCRACY, EDUCATION AND IDEOLOGY

There are two specific reasons why Meiji Japan developed a very powerful bureaucracy. First, in the four key *han* which overthrew the Tokugawa, a bureaucracy had developed as part of the internal *reforming* movement. But as it was simultaneously turned against the local peasant revolts, it also formed part of the new type of oppression within these *han*. In Chōshū it was the activist bureaucratic clique which decided to push Chōshū as the mediator between the Court and the Bakufu in 1861. Well before the Restoration, the bureaucracies in the leading southwestern *han* were well poised to take over central power.

Second, given the specific combination of interests that had to be reconciled from 1868 onwards (interests of the *han,* of the new business groups, the warding off of democratic institutions), the bureaucracy was the obvious locus of power to act as mediator. By its very nature, it operated in the interstices of these different interests. In the initial stage it was used to pre-empt the Diet and subsequently to circumvent the parties. Ultimately, the bureaucracy came to dominate both Diet and parties, which increasingly functioned as residual front institutions left over from democratic or para-democratic drives in the late nineteenth century.

> Whatever might be said of the civil bureaucracy as an administrative instrument, its political role was crucial in the constitutional history of the empire. In establishing a civil bureaucracy well trained in the state sciences of law and administration and protected against the encroachments of parliamentary politics, the elder statesmen were motivated by a desire to create an efficient and responsive instrument by which the all-inclusive administrative prerogatives would be secured against parliamentary control.[136]

In this they were overwhelmingly successful. "For the most part parliamentary politics never escaped the pattern, early established, by which the major parties did not gain control of the civil service but, instead, became victims of collusive connections between their own leaders and ambitious members of that service."[137]

From a class point of view, the bureaucracy was relatively open in the early years after the Restoration, particularly after 1874 until Ōkuma's ouster from office in 1881. Ōkuma, Itō Hirobumi, and Inoue Kaoru were the most important figures in establishing this early bureaucracy. They concentrated mainly in the Finance Ministry and formed the concrete base on which Ōkuma (and later Ōkubo) built an alternative to the "wild" line of the original Restoration group led by Saigō.

In 1878 Ōkubo, the strongman of the regime, was assassinated. From this point on Itō Hirobumi led the campaign to make the bureaucracy the absolutely unassailable base and centre of political power in the state system. It was Itō's campaign to strengthen the bureaucracy which built the bulwark against democratic government for many decades to come. It was the same concern—for the weakness of the state—which fired this movement for bureaucratic consolidation and for the strengthening of the imperial institution as an "external" legitimating factor.

Towards the end of the 1870s the government felt itself beset by dangerous new ideas and faced with political opposition in the *jiyū minken undō* which it was apparently not as confident of crushing as one might now think it ought to have been. In 1877, as the battle was heating up, Tanaka, the Education "Minister," put through a new Education Ordinance even more liberal than the 1872 Code.[138] In the following summer, the Emperor made a tour of the provinces after which, much alarmed, he instructed his Confucian tutor Motoda Eifu (Nakazane) to draft a statement which embodied the Emperor's views. It was issued in 1879 in the form of an Imperial Rescript—the Great Principles of Education.[139] In the same year, 1879, Motoda published his *Essentials of Learning for the Young (Yōgaku Kōyō)*, a ponderous Confucianist text in highly obscure language. Motoda's concept of "learning" can be appreciated when one realizes that school children could not understand his text; "Motoda suggested that they could memorize it: when they were older its meaning would become clear."[140]

This stage of the rollback was based on a return to Confucianism, necessitated by the earlier failure to promote Shinto and the inability to adapt Buddhism to function on behalf of the state machine. In fact, Confucianism was almost perfectly suited to this repressive objective. In it education, morality and subservience formed a self-contained circle from which it was extremely difficult, if not impossible, to escape. The general principles which Confucianism stood for, particularly those involving unquestioning obedience to higher authority, could be mobilized simultaneously on behalf of the Emperor and on behalf of the bureaucratic apparatus of the state.

In 1878 Murray returned to the United States. In 1879 the Emperor and Motoda produced their conservative Rescript. In 1880 Tanaka resigned, under considerable pressure. In that same year, *shūshin* (ethics) became a compulsory item of instruction in the schools; military drill was introduced into the curriculum, and the Ministry of Education called in all textbooks for vetting.[141] Fukuzawa was deeply upset. "The government," he wrote, "began to advocate in education the queer policy of Confucianism. . . . It also brought together old-fashioned Confucianists to compile readers, and otherwise staged the farce of trying to restore past customs in a civilized world."[142] Motoda, on the contrary, was delighted. "Since the compilation of *Yōgaku Kōyō* by imperial order, the evils produced by American education have steadily been corrected, the nation has again turned to the principles of loyalty to the sovereign and love of the country, and people have come forward who advocate benevolence, duty and morality."[143]

By the time Itō and his group began their sustained rollback in the state administration following the ouster of Ōkuma in 1881, the educational structure for imposing this ideology was largely in place. In 1880 an ordinance had been promulgated forbidding teachers to attend political meetings, and this measure was strengthened in 1881. In the view of Kōno Togama, the new "Minister" of Education who replaced Tanaka in 1880, "Teachers were not independent scholar-educators, . . . but rather public officers, official guardians of morality, responsible to the state."[144]

In 1881, with the morals course established in the curriculum, Tokyo University was reorganized into a school for government bureaucrats. "By this reform the entire staff of the University was placed under government control, subject to all the responsibilities and restrictions of government officials, and given places in the bureaucratic hierarchy."[145] Tokyo University was *part* of the government—as much the Ministry of Education's training school for the government bureaucracy as it was a university in the Western sense of the word. Article 1 of its Ordinance read: "It shall be the purpose of the Imperial University to teach the sciences and the arts and to probe their mysteries in accordance with the needs of the state."[146] The establishment of the Imperial University at Tokyo came only three months after a major statement by Itō outlining the principles of official discipline, and calling for the selection of officials by examination—a proposal which was to be implemented some years later. Such changes were not directed towards a democratization of the regime. In certain cases, they allowed the regime to recruit cadres from a wider area of the population than before, but this was in the interests of consolidation. The initial Meiji reforms were designed by the ruling group more to create opportunities for the aristocracy than to introduce equalization for the *chōnin*.[147]

In 1881 Itō also suggested a reorganization of the upper strata of society in order to consolidate the still fragile position of the Emperor. In September (1881) he wrote to Itō Miyoji:

> I believe that this [the creation of a peerage] is an absolutely indispensable instrument for fortifying the position of the Imperial House. . . . We are both worried about the recent tendency of both the government and the people to slip unknowing into the spirit of republicanism. If we do nothing about it, and it finally reaches an irredeemable situation, no matter how

good a plan we have, it will be useless. Therefore, I hope to find a way to save the situation by taking advantage of the fact that as yet the after glow of the feudalistic pro-Emperor sentiment has not yet completely died down [and create a peerage] even though this is contrary to the spirit of the times and goes against the feelings of the people.[148]

In this private letter, Itō frankly recognizes the weakness of the Emperor's position and outlines the idea of using the Emperor's creation of a peerage in order to strengthen the imperial institution. This peerage, when created, became not only a prop to the Emperor-system, but also a pro-Itō (Hirobumi) clique from which political opponents, like Gotō, Itagaki and Ōkuma, were excluded.

In the early 1880s Itō went on an extended tour of Europe to study its political systems in preparation for his own work on the forthcoming Japanese Constitution. While in Vienna attending the International Exhibition in 1873, he and Iwakura had met the Hegelian constitutionalist expert, Lorenz von Stein, and it was to him and to Prussian ideas in general that Itō now turned for advice. In August 1882 Itō wrote to Iwakura:

By studying under two famous scholars, Gneist and Stein, I have been able to reach a general understanding of the structure of the state. Later I shall discuss the way to achieve the great objective of strengthening the foundations of the imperial sovereignty. Indeed, the trends in our country today erroneously lead to a belief in the works of the extreme liberal radicals of England, America and France and to considering these theories as the supreme norm. In having found principles and means of reversing these trends, I believe I have rendered an important service to my country, and I feel that I can die a happy man.[149]

Stein and Gneist, like Mosse, whose lectures Itō also attended, were not supporters of absolutism. Stein can best be described as a theoretician of what he himself called "bureaucratic constitutionalism"—a far cry from democracy, certainly, but not equivalent to absolutism. Under the influence of these scholars, the Japanese ruling group moved ahead, developing a conservative constitution and a strengthened bureaucracy. A leading German scholar, Carl Friedrich Hermann Roesler, was engaged to work on the Constitution in Japan. Itō, as head of the Bureau for Investigation of Constitutional Systems, set up in 1884, had this body attached to the Imperial Household Department, so that it thereby became "sacrosanct and completely removed from any outside influence."[150] This was of crucial importance subsequently, since it meant that the Constitution could not be questioned at all (which would be treason), and the only issue left open to non-treasonable discussion was the suffrage. The Constitution, when it came, in 1889, was presented as a *gift* of the Emperor.

Having removed the elaboration of the Constitution from the area of open discussion, Itō and his group then saw to it that the cabinet system was instituted prior to the Diet; a move, as was so often the case, justified as a return to ancient Japanese political tradition. The first cabinet, set up in 1885, reflected tight oligarchic power: of the ten cabinet posts, four each went to Satsuma and Chōshū samurai, leaving only two for "outsiders."[151]

The Education Minister in this first cabinet was a man whom Itō had met in Europe in 1882, Mori Arinori.[152] Mori had been greatly influenced by German ideas on education, particularly by the school of the idealist philosopher Herbart. Mori, completely in tune with Itō, was able to build on the reactionary foundations laid down since Tanaka's ouster five years before. Given these five years of heavy Confucian moral indoctrination, Mori was able to impose a more subtle, but nonetheless repressive system which fitted in well with the development of a reactionary constitution and the strengthening of the bureacracy and of authoritarianism, exemplified by the imperial institution.

Essentially, Mori set up a dual system. The lower part was a compulsory sector "heavily indoctrinated in the spirit of morality and nationalism." At the top was a university sector for the elite and "an atmosphere of the greatest possible academic freedom and critical rationalism."[153] The two were to be linked by the normal school, where students would be subjected to heavy nationalistic and militaristic influence, with six hours of military drill per week. This reform of the educational system, which lasted through the Second World War, was specifically linked to the preparations for the Constitution and the opening of the Diet, "setting the supreme objective of education as the making of people who could be useful for the welfare of the state."[154]

In 1887 a basic civil service and entrance apprentice system based on the Prussian model was installed. The main purpose of these changes was to strengthen the power of the state by concentrating all stages of the formation of government cadres under state control.[155] The 1887 reforms were designed to smash the position of the private universities' law schools by exempting graduates of certain government schools from the civil service examinations.[156] In theory, the 1889 Constitution made all offices in the civil service and elsewhere open to all via examination, and there was a partial revision of the 1873 reforms in 1893. But Tokyo University law graduates still had special exemptions in the higher civil service examinations, and the board of examiners was permanently dominated by Tokyo University professors. In addition, *chokunin* (the highest rank of official) were still selected by "free appointment" (patronage).

In 1899 Yamagata, in order to protect the state machinery even more carefully from party politics, introduced a sweeping amendment to the Civil Service Appointment Ordinance simultaneous with two imperial ordinances on the same subject, issued through the Privy Council, to the effect that no changes could be carried out except with the approval of the Privy Council. Any chance of democratic reform in the civil bureaucracy was thus made impossible.[157] The bureaucracy was regulated by ordinance, not law; its members, like the cabinet, were "servants of the Emperor," beyond the control of either the political parties or the Diet—not to mention the people. Once again, a brilliant grafting operation was crowned with success. The bureaucracy, along with the economy, has been the greatest achievement of Japanese capitalism. Confucianism and the combined influence of disciples of Gneist like Karl Rathgen produced an ideology for an apparatus wherein education was at the service of a state completely dominated by the bureaucracy. The measure of the success of the "bureaucratic spirit" is not hard to find in law, where even the meagre participation contained in the German *Schöffengericht* was soon abandoned, but above all in politics, where the bureaucracy successfully first stifled the Diet and then the parties, which it virtually absorbed. In 1937, 73.6 per cent of the Civil Officials and 49.7 per cent of the Judicial Officials came from Tokyo University. Only five of the thirty-five heads of government in the twentieth century up till 1972 had not had a bureaucratic (civilian or military) background.[158] Because of the formal changes since 1945 most ministers now pass via the Diet, whereas prior to 1945 they often moved straight from a bureaucratic post into government—but this is a marginal shift, marking only an even more cohesive integration of bureaucracy, party, Diet and cabinet. It does not denote any increased democratization.

Much of the credit for the success of the system must go to the men who crafted the Constitution, and the behind-the-scenes measures which accompanied it. Inoue Kowashi and Roesler were among the most important agents on this.[159] Roesler's commentaries on the Constitution and other documents show that he grasped with exceptional lucidity the entire range of problems involved: the social and class contradictions which economic change was bringing about and how these contradictions could be demobilized; a conciliatory function for the state without an explicit social role; the function of law as a specific mode of class dominance. Roesler argued brilliantly for the installation of a bourgeois-capitalist state which could handle the problem of class consciousness, deal with the contradictions of property, involve the state in banking and industry, and strengthen the bureaucracy.

In a memorandum drawn up on June 6, 1887, in connection with the draft of the constitution, Roesler develops an over-all plan for setting up the modern Japanese state as a monarchical socialized state. The basic points of this memorandum are as follows: (1) In modern Japan's development of commerce and industry the bourgeois acquisitive class will most certainly emerge as the dominant class. The justifiable demands of this class the state will have to take into account. (2) The tendency of the acquisitive class toward even greater profit will, if left unchecked, undermine the security of the other classes, both that of the land owners and that of those without property. It is the most urgent task of the state to maintain impartially the welfare of the whole and a harmonious social balance by means of social legislation and an active administrative policy that works for the physical and spiritual welfare of the lower classes. The maintenance of a free peasantry, founded upon the institution of inherited property, has to be especially cared for. (3) To overcome class conflict and to maintain an ethical political attitude that places the welfare of the whole above class interests, the institution of hereditary monarchy is necessary.[160]

In 1889, on the day the Constitution was promulgated, Mori was assassinated. The following year, the fruits of Mori's relatively rational and "modern" reforms, combined with the earlier achievements of the re-pressive Confucian period, were capped by the famous Imperial Rescript on Education of 1890, fundamentally the work of Motoda again,. This document is not really about education at all, but rather about obedience, loyalty and class subservience.[161] It was a crucial element in the renewed drive to set the new, post-Constitution, post-inauguration of the Diet system under the sign of the Emperor—remote, untouchable, unques-tionable.

The relationship of the Emperor to the rest of the state apparatus underwent a definite change around the middle of the Meiji period.[162] Previously, the throne's separation from politics tended to identify it with more or less purely ethical values, but with the Meiji Constitution and attendant measures, the throne came to represent state power as such. Along with this, the relationship between the government and the Emperor underwent a subtle change. Hitherto, the tradition had been that the government was responsible to the throne for its actions, but the develop-ments promoted by the Meiji ruling group, while forcing the whole population to revere the Emperor and carry out his (alleged) will, in fact made the government itself very largely *irresponsible*.

The advantage of promoting the imperial institution is obvious, for it allowed the ruling clique to handle many of the contradictions in the tran-sition from the feudal to the capitalist state. Though the formal institutions of bourgeois parliamentary democracy were introduced (largely because of Japan's place in the *world* "bourgeois system")[163] the existence of the imperial institution placed the ultimate moral authority for all the state's acts outside the bourgeois democratic arena. Emperor-ism was the founda-tion of Japanese authoritarianism.

The "how" of the metamorphosis is a bewildering episode.[164] It is even more extraordinary when one considers the complex class and religious basis on which the new ideology had to be built. The mid-Meiji educators made normative for all classes the ethic of emperor-loyalty which had fired the samurai loyalists in the late Tokugawa period, men who had shifted their loyalty from their daimyō to the imperial family. But Japanese commoners had not participated in this elite tradition, and therefore the educational leaders had to devise formulae for focusing their loyalties on imperial symbols. They began with the home, stressing the (real or alleged) feelings of family loyalty and filial piety, and then transmuted these into a larger loyalty to the "national family" with the Emperor as the father figure. The Emperor was the father of the nation, it was argued, because the imperial family was the "national head family" (*kokumin sōka*), and the imperial family was the *kokumin sōka* because it derived from the topmost *kami* (spirits, deities) in the Shinto tradition. In this way, "Confucian familial ethics found their ultimate sanctification in Shinto mythological beliefs regarding the origins of the imperial line."[165] By 1890 the key elements of the system had been set up, although not yet fully integrated into a cohesive unit.

The perfection of the system came only in the late Meiji period, with a two-fronted manoeuvre: Shinto shrines were protected and consolidated, and the school ethics programme moved into high gear after its leisurely start. These two operations were tied in to other socio-ideological enterprises, such as the Local Improvement Movement (from 1909), the Hōtoku Society sponsored by the Home Ministry (from 1906), and the Youth Association, sponsored nationally by the same Ministry (from 1910). "All were geared into a massive movement to extend effective controls down to the grassroots level,"[166] particularly after the end of the Russo-Japanese War in 1905.

What in retrospect has been called the "family-state" (*kazoku kokka*) was referred to by contemporary intellectuals as "national morals" (*kokumin dōtoku*). Though the "family-state" ideology incorporated earlier elements, it cannot be identified with the forms of repression practiced at the start of the Meiji period. Only in the late Meiji period did the system take on its full distinctive form. To simplify somewhat, this familial ideology had three components: a German "state organism" (*kokka yūkitai*) theory of state sovereignty; a Confucian-like familism (*kazoku shugi*); and ancient Shinto mythology "by which the entire complex was ultimately sanctified."[167]

The "state organism" theory essentially held that the state was one big living organism in which transitory individuals were merely component cells subordinate to the whole; there was no sense of individuals in any way "contracting in" to society. The Confucian-type familistic ethic provided the real foundation for the society, and increasingly, from the late Meiji period on, Japanese ideologists spoke of the nation as an "extended family." The nation was not *like* a family, it really *was* a family. This national family, supported from below by the socio-ethical patterns of individual households, was then "sanctified from above by Shinto beliefs which imbued it with a quality of sacredness."[168] The 1889 Constitution contributed to this by declaring the Emperor "sacred and inviolable." In this way, although Confucianism provided powerful repressive force, the essentially secular Confucian familistic ethic was reinforced by locating the ultimate justification for it at the *sacred* level—Shinto.

This ideology was vigorously propagated through ethics textbooks in an expanded state school system.[169] In the late 1890s there was a move towards texts written and produced entirely by the government. The first series, completed in 1903, was judged too feeble and a new committee was set up under the Minister of Education in 1908 to revise not only the ethics texts, but also history and language texts. This new series, completed in 1910, incorporated the "family-state"/"national morals" ideology in simple language, accessible to elementary school children. The emphasis of these texts is on indigenous Confucian and ·Shinto teachings, with "state organism" theory occupying a lesser role. These new 1910 texts demand filial piety and obedience, and seek to transfer familial loyalties upwards to the Emperor by identifying Emperor-loyalty with filial piety. The favourite expression in these texts is *chūkō no taigi* ("the great loyalty-filial principle") in which loyalty (*chū*) and filial piety (*kō*) are fused into a single concept. Emperor-loyalty is then fused with patriotism; the two terms *chūkun* (lord- or Emperor-loyalty) and *aikoku* (patriotism, love of country) are fused into one expression: *chūkun-aikoku* (roughly, "patriotic Emperor-loyalty"). Finally, Shinto mythological tradition is mobilized to infuse Emperor-loyalty and patriotism with sacred absoluteness. Moreover, the 1910 texts present Shinto mythology as believable historical fact, thus further fusing history and myth—and, of course, by debasing "fact," strengthening irrationality, mystification and repression.

The system installed by Itō and the oligarchs might thus be defined not so much as "bureaucratic constitutionalism," since the Constitution as such was not the key to the system, but rather as "bureaucratic Emperor-ism," since the two pillars of the regime were these two arbitrary and irresponsible authoritarian institutions which worked in tandem for over half a century.

THE STATE AND ECONOMIC POLICY

Meiji Agrarian Policy

Since the vast majority of the population lived and worked on the land, and agricultural output had to be the basis of capital accumulation, it was clearly urgent for the new regime to survey the entire country and establish a system which could produce a constant flow of revenue for the state.

Although prior to the Restoration Japan had a feudal political structure, its economy was oriented to and regulated by the market. According to Crawcour's calculations, in the 1860s farmers marketed 20–25 per cent of their rice, after payment of tax in rice.[170] Altogether the percentage of rice marketed (tax + sales) probably came to 70–80 per cent of output, and the average for all agricultural crops was probably 60–70 per cent in the 1860s, a very high rate of commercialization. Thus, by the end of the

Tokugawa period agricultural productivity was well above the subsistence requirements of the peasantry, although the distribution of the surplus left much to be desired.

The new regime set about mobilizing and redirecting this surplus through a reorganization of the land ownership and taxation systems in the 1870s. But this new system was marked by contradiction and compromise: on the one hand, at the political level, the regime had to conciliate the aristocracy and the big landlords, who were not prepared to be dispossessed; on the other hand, it needed to use agriculture as the base for rapid expansion of the economy as a whole.

The new agrarian policy was, therefore, quite different from that of the French Revolution. The Restoration did not offer a general liberation of the peasantry, as the Revolution had done in France. "Far from suppressing the essential relations of feudal property, the Meiji Revolution introduced these relations into the new Japanese capitalist society by giving them juridical endorsement."[171]

In 1873 the regime put through new land tax legislation which "revised the land tax system from a harvest tax assessed as a proportion of the harvest in rice, or its equivalent in money, to a land value tax assessed as a proportion of the land value."[172] In this way the regime guarded itself against the possibility of a fall in revenue as the result of a bad crop. The agrarian settlement was the basis of Meiji economic policy; it caused "a revolutionary transfer of income from the Tokugawa ruling class to the landowners, a transfer made possible because the agricultural sector was producing a substantial surplus above subsistence. This was a transfer to a class with a lower average propensity to consume."[173]

Japan had not been through an experience comparable to either the enclosures in England or the *Bauernlegen* in Germany. The government wanted to modify the existing system rather than transform it radically— the latter being a *political* impossibility given the class interests of the new ruling bloc. It first distributed certificates of landownership, which served to institute the transition from the feudal land system to the concept of private ownership of the land. It was also a necessary prerequisite to both the land tax inaugurated in 1873 (and the subsequent revision of 1876) and to the land survey of the Empire which was carried out in the years 1875–81.

Unlike after the French Revolution, feudal rights were not abolished outright in Japan, but eased out with an indemnity paid for by the poorer classes. There was, in short, a change in the relations of production, but not of power. In addition, common lands were turned over to private ownership, eliminating such essential activities as grazing and wood-gathering in many areas and thus liquidating the possibility of subsistence. This was accompanied by a huge increase in the holdings of both the state and the Emperor personally. Between 1881 and 1890 the Crown and the state owned more than half the land in Japan. The vertiginous increase in the Emperor's holdings can be seen from the following table:

TABLE 1

INCREASE IN EMPEROR'S ESTATES

Year	Size of Emperor's Estates
1882	1,000 *chō*
1886	31,000 *chō*
1889	1,130,000 *chō*
1890	3,650,000 *chō*

* SOURCE: Ikeda Yoshimasa and Sasaki Ryūji, *Kyōyō-jin no Nihon Shi* (Tokyo, Shakai Shisō-sha, 1967), Vol. 4, pp. 174–75.[174]

This increase in the imperial estates had a directly political motive. It was Iwakura Tomomi, one of the leading members of the old court nobility, who proposed, in 1882, that the Emperor should build up a vast personal holding. Iwakura was concerned that a revolution might be imminent. The army was apparently not wholly reliable, and the promulgation the previous year of the plans for a Constitution and Diet (which he supported) did not seem to have blocked popular dissidence completely. Iwakura suggested that the Emperor expand his resources until they matched private resources in order to have enough financial independence to be able to support the entire armed forces and the police out of his own pocket.[175] This not only meant depriving countless farmers of their livelihood by taking over enormous areas of communal grazing land and forests, but this incorporation of large tracts of land into the imperial domain "formed the material base for the absolutist theories of the Tenno."[176] Much of the Emperor's later independence and power which allowed the ruling clique to consolidate the "Emperor-system" rested on this solid material base. The Emperor became the largest parasitical landlord in Japan.[177]

This transfer of land was assisted and promoted by the deflationary policy of the 1880s associated with the name of Finance Minister Matsukata Masayoshi. Landlords exacted exceptionally high rent from their tenants—consistently over 60 per cent of the gross proceeds from the land. Money was being extracted from the economy by Matsukata and highly unjust taxes were being levied (taxation by family rather than size of holding). There was a catastrophic fall in farm income, dispossession and concentration. Between 1883 and 1890 some 368,000 peasant proprietors were dispossessed for failure to pay taxes.[178] These dispossessions were wildly out of proportion to the sums of money involved: the average sum of money owed per person dispossessed was 0.31 yen, while the value of the land sold or confiscated was twenty-seven times the total of the debts. It is virtually certain, too, that an even larger number of people lost their lands through mortgage foreclosure. The results included massive concentration and the collapse of the democratic movement based on the rural areas.

In spite of these wide-scale expropriations, there was no mass exodus to the cities as there was in England with the enclosures. The relative weight of the different factors behind this is a subject of some dispute. Norman emphasized the very high rent which landlords could extort from their tenants, which made it attractive for the landlords to keep the peasants where they were rather than drive them off the land.[179] The landowners, enriched by the Meiji land and tax reforms, transferred most of their new savings out of agriculture.[180]

These events coincided with the rise of the textile industry, which had started on a small scale under the Tokugawa regime. Much of the textile industry was located in rural areas, and most of the labour was recruited from villages. The majority of the workers were women who were simply sold off to labour bosses and forced to send most of their wages back to their families. This constellation of factors contributed to the preservation of "family" relations in industry.[181] It also fortified the landlord-industrialist alliance (unlike in England where the Corn Laws, for example, had the opposite effect). "The reason for this coincidence of landlord and industrialist interest lies in the fact that the burden of the upkeep of the unemployed is largely removed from state and employers, while at the same time the resulting overcrowding of the village bids up the rent rate."[182] This feature of Japanese industrialization has remained to the present day. There are still strong elements of both rural and feudal "spirit" involved, and the state has resolutely refused to take on the "social" role it has developed in Western capitalist countries. Industry did not simply coexist with backward rural areas:

the two were bound together, and supported one another, in a form in which the one considered the other a prior condition for its own persistence—witness the supply of cheap labour from the villages, and the attempts to preserve the traditional social institution which would secure this source of supply—and so it was rather on the foundations provided by the strong persistence of traditional institutions in the agricultural villages that the towering edifice of modern industrial enterprise was raised, and in this way the unique structure of the national economy was produced.[183]

The fact that the government did not carry out expropriation was already fundamental; the regime also did everything it could to consolidate the landlord class. There is no doubt which way the regime was turned:

the government of *samurai* and clan bureaucrats, confronted by mounting peasant revolt, now found it politic to make peace on one front, the front against feudalism, in order to concentrate its full strength upon the other, the agrarian front. Relieved of the one front, the Government could devote its energies to solving the agrarian question, not simply by the use of naked force in suppressing peasant unrest, but by strengthening the machinery of state, by reforming administration, by concessions to the peasant proprietors (notably the reduction of the land tax in 1876), and by the further consolidation of a landlord class which could become the political foundation for the Government on the countryside.[184]

The commutation of daimyō pensions was part of this consolidation. But the government also introduced a system for guaranteeing debts via bonds.

These bonds not only secured the bad debts due the *chonin,* but supplied the bondholders with the funds for investment in industrial projects or in land. This settlement had the effect of converting the greatest landlords and usurers into stockholders and bankers. . . . We see at this early date that interlocking of landlordism, banking and government, which is one of the peculiar characteristics of the modern Japanese political and social organization.[185]

The land settlement was of the greatest importance in building the new political and economic machinery of the Meiji state. The land tax played a crucial role in early capital accumulation. Between 1871 and 1875 it accounted for between 85 and 93.2 per cent of total government tax revenue, and did not drop below 50 per cent of the total until 1896 (see Table 2).[186] The compromise with the landlord class, which was both political and economic, closely affected the process of industrialization— and the specific modes of oppression within industry. The regime, seeing peasant discontent as a major threat, worked out an agrarian settlement under which it would ensure itself a safe base among the landlord class.[187] This was true after 1890 as well as before; big landlords predominated in the Upper House and middle and smaller landlords in the Lower House in the early Diets (after 1890). But being a compromise, this incomplete settlement led to structural bottlenecks (in the 1930s especially); and in many ways it lay at the root of the phenomenon often called "fascism."[188] As the major malfunctioning element in the capitalist system it was the one component which had to be overhauled by U.S. imperialism after 1945. This was because, as Takahashi puts it, "On the one hand, the agrarian reform abolished the seigneurial and shogunal system, i.e., the purely feudal organization of land ownership . . . but at the same time it maintained, in modern society, feudal relations of production in agriculture as constituent elements of Japanese capitalism."[189]

The State and Industrial Policy

The most urgent problem facing the new regime was to protect the economy from the onslaught of the foreign powers, and to strengthen, transform and expand it. Starting in the 1850s the foreign treaties smashed the country's economic as well as political cocoon. A veritable "gold drain" occurred as much of the large amount of gold which had been accumulated in Japan under the Tokugawa was bought by foreign interests at less than half the going world rate.[190]

But Japan did not only lose reserves. Imports shot up. In 1863 only 34 per cent of total trade was accounted for by imports. By 1867 the figure had become 61 per cent, and by 1870 it was 71 per cent. In 1870 exports totalled 14 million yen—while imports came to nearly 34 million. "Cheap English textiles flooded in, destroying domestic industry, narrowing the tax base as cottage industry declined, and creating monetary chaos with the flight of specie from the country."[191] This was on top of the serious inflation stimulated by the civil war. The provisional government, whose only income came from the then limited imperial lands, had issued unbacked paper currency which amounted to 72 per cent of the budget, and most of the rest of the budget came from loans from the big urban merchants.[192]

The Meiji state was the state of a new ruling bloc and was designed to serve the economic and political interests of those in it and represented by it. For a number of reasons—the nature of Tokugawa feudalism, the insistent pressure of imperialism, and the subsequent need for *sudden* political and economic change detonated *from outside*—the state was the mechanism which both reorganized the political and economic (class) situation internally and acted as *overall* intermediary with the outside world. Imperialism determined the context of Japan's economic activity. There was no Japanese bourgeoisie with experience of foreign trade; both diplomatic and economic relations with foreign powers were kept under government control.[193] Indeed many of the features which distinguish Japanese capitalism have their origin in the early Meiji period: vigorous state intervention in the formation, accumulation and investment of capital; concentration in capital goods; state control over banking; state guidance and intervention in foreign trade; tough measures against foreign capital; high savings, relatively independent of the economic condition of the mass of the people; and very low expenditure on consumer goods and virtual absence of many social services.

Ōkubo's memorial against intervention in Korea in 1873 lucidly set out the case for domestic reconstruction. He developed his case in another document he wrote in 1874 immediately after putting down the Saga (Hizen) Rebellion where he argued strongly and persuasively for state planning of the economy. Ōkubo's economic programme can be summarized as follows: (1) land reclamation—particularly important for settling samurai; (2) promoting exports (such as silk) and slowing down imports; (3) improving the quality of exportable craft goods; (4) developing a merchant navy (particularly urgent after the invasion of Taiwan in 1874); (5) building model factories; (6) providing government loans to business.[194] This entire programme had to be developed without benefit of protective tariffs, which were banned under the unequal treaties.

TABLE 2

BREAKDOWN OF TAX REVENUES

1868–1945: thousand yen
1946–1965: million yen

Fiscal Year	Total	Land Tax	Income Tax	Corporation Tax	Business Tax	Inheritance Tax	Liquor Tax	Sugar Excise	Custom Duty	Gasoline Excise
1868	3,157	2,009	—	—	—	—	—	—	720	—
1869	4,399	3,355	—	—	—	—	—	—	502	—
1870	9,323	8,218	—	—	—	—	—	—	648	—
1871	12,852	11,340	—	—	—	—	—	—	1,071	—
1872	21,845	20,051	—	—	—	—	16	—	1,331	—
1873	65,014	60,604	—	—	—	—	961	—	1,685	—
1874	65,303	59,412	—	—	—	—	1,683	—	1,498	—
1875	76,528	67,717	—	—	—	—	1,310	—	1,038	—
1875	59,194	50,345	—	—	—	—	2,555	—	1,718	—
1876	51,730	43,023	—	—	—	—	1,911	—	1,988	—
1877	47,923	39,450	—	—	—	—	3,050	—	2,358	—
1878	51,485	40,454	—	—	—	—	5,100	—	2,351	—
1879	55,579	42,112	—	—	—	—	6,463	—	2,691	—
1880	55,262	42,346	—	—	—	—	5,511	—	2,624	—
1881	61,675	43,274	—	—	—	—	10,646	—	2,569	—
1882	67,738	43,342	—	—	—	—	16,329	—	2,613	—
1883	67,659	43,537	—	—	—	—	13,490	—	2,681	—
1884	67,203	43,425	—	—	—	—	14,068	—	2,750	—
1885	52,581	43,033	—	—	—	—	1,053	—	2,085	—
1886	64,371	43,282	—	—	—	—	11,743	—	2,989	—
1887	66,255	42,152	527	—	—	—	13,069	—	4,135	—
1888	64,727	34,650	1,066	—	—	—	17,063	—	4,615	—
1889	71,294	42,161	1,052	—	—	—	16,439	—	4,728	—
1890	66,114	40,084	1,092	—	—	—	13,912	—	4,392	—
1891	64,423	37,457	1,110	—	—	—	14,686	—	4,539	—
1892	67,167	37,925	1,132	—	—	—	15,812	—	4,991	—

Year									
1893	5,125	—	16,637	—	—	—	1,238	38,808	70,004
1894	5,755	—	16,130	—	—	—	1,353	39,291	71,286
1895	6,785	—	17,748	—	—	—	1,497	38,692	74,697
1896	6,728	—	19,476	—	0	—	1,810	37,640	76,387
1897	8,020	—	31,105	—	4,416	—	2,095	37,964	94,912
1898	9,092	—	32,959	—	5,478	—	2,351	38,440	97,629
1899	15,936	—	48,918	—	5,507	(1,520)	4,837	44,861	126,034
1900	17,009	—	50,293	—	6,051	(2,244)	6,368	46,717	133,926
1901	13,630	612	58,017	—	6,481	(2,176)	6,836	46,666	139,574
1902	15,501	4,145	63,738	—	6,777	(2,267)	7,460	46,505	151,084
1903	17,378	6,942	52,821	—	7,049	(2,355)	8,247	46,873	146,163
1904	23,159	8,362	58,286	—	12,601	(3,753)	14,369	60,939	194,362
1905	36,757	11,348	59,099	629	18,784	(7,945)	23,278	80,473	251,275
1906	41,853	16,156	71,100	1,405	19,770	(9,435)	26,348	84,637	283,468
1907	50,027	16,178	78,406	1,822	20,383	(8,345)	27,291	84,973	315,983
1908	40,067	19,684	83,590	2,446	23,574	(8,918)	32,144	85,418	322,636
1909	36,423	13,270	91,480	2,784	25,112	(8,254)	32,800	85,693	323,407
1910	39,949	17,906	86,701	3,132	25,756	(7,527)	31,722	76,291	317,285
1911	48,518	17,255	86,032	4,061	24,598	(9,713)	34,755	74,936	329,071
1912	68,496	13,517	93,861	3,629	26,021	(11,474)	38,933	75,365	360,969
1913	73,722	21,049	93,223	3,351	27,392	(13,068)	35,591	74,635	369,479
1914	44,228	23,384	95,781	3,317	28,594	(13,222)	37,157	74,925	343,708
1915	32,165	22,675	84,649	3,357	21,455	(14,721)	37,567	73,602	312,744
1916	35,918	27,442	89,837	4,077	22,833	(26,692)	51,284	73,274	348,672
1917	45,186	29,812	106,738	4,597	26,394	(59,391)	94,649	73,478	430,604
1918	68,937	36,353	120,635	4,618	34,375	(61,952)	122,817	73,527	600,882
1919	81,135	46,168	137,626	5,312	44,075	(110,297)	193,148	73,754	834,649
1920	69,371	40,394	163,896	7,032	62,092	(127,944)	190,344	73,944	730,553
1921	100,941	54,966	176,085	9,311	68,453	(95,895)	200,938	74,130	790,938
1922	108,044	72,905	222,585	11,788	77,132	(91,677)	229,132	74,325	897,320
1923	89,309	64,754	221,497	11,150	55,837	(50,508)	163,846	73,134	787,337
1924	119,638	80,200	221,577	14,183	61,943	(66,231)	209,992	71,969	887,364
1925	111,160	76,726	212,638	17,134	65,791	(88,551)	234,971	74,614	894,895

TABLE 2 *(Continued)*
BREAKDOWN OF TAX REVENUES

Fiscal Year	Total	Land Tax	Income Tax	Corporation Tax	Business Tax	Inheritance Tax	Liquor Tax	Sugar Excise	Custom Duty	Gasoline Excise
1926	887,020	68,728	209,577	(64,881)	62,153	18,409	216,583	82,439	150,612	—
1927	898,690	67,576	215,070	(72,369)	48,449	21,081	242,037	79,285	140,600	—
1928	915,937	67,821	206,741	(65,840)	58,065	29,224	235,749	83,216	150,944	—
1929	893,505	67,484	199,851	(55,116)	56,131	29,721	242,562	82,244	136,096	—
1930	835,041	68,035	200,616	(63,632)	54,343	32,904	218,854	77,889	105,379	—
1931	735,512	63,915	144,501	(33,452)	37,931	30,169	188,798	77,386	114,274	—
1932	695,837	58,348	136,131	(37,261)	35,291	30,216	177,395	72,654	105,375	—
1933	748,566	58,137	159,706	(51,677)	40,396	25,594	208,865	72,522	113,962	—
1934	843,183	57,646	196,381	(71,903)	48,649	27,172	218,434	74,967	144,433	—
1935	926,082	58,042	227,339	(93,743)	57,137	30,255	209,327	84,817	151,265	—
1936	1,051,761	58,592	276,555	(125,794)	73,235	31,790	220,099	86,781	174,129	17,334
1937	1,431,891	58,455	478,488	(209,203)	91,261	35,852	241,460	95,229	184,963	13,494
1938	1,984,057	51,531	732,790	(314,315)	105,280	45,482	278,668	145,892	166,422	10,431
1939	2,495,302	48,684	888,849	(376,390)	126,285	58,389	266,694	136,003	147,728	22,218
1940	3,653,064	29,322	1,488,678	182,872	129,332	56,555	285,174	141,467	143,999	—
1941	4,257,311	25,424	1,401,363	534,907	101,675	64,612	359,340	119,836	87,424	11,953
1942	6,633,788	25,627	2,236,191	775,946	114,900	86,137	433,790	143,843	56,042	6,192
1943	8,455,155	25,654	2,604,097	993,616	126,124	117,551	720,176	141,665	44,688	3,270
1944	11,437,365	37,823	4,040,580	1,326,514	166,715	145,612	883,942	70,114	15,468	—
1945	10,337,172	27,648	3,820,426	1,180,834	124,639	176,602	1,130,653	10,356	7,726	—
1946	29,705	38	18,134	1,315	167	359	2,378	109	15	—
1947	146,525	—	84,894	7,290	—	462	27,499	537	86	—
1948	341,047	—	191,454	28,108	—	2,300	54,794	4,383	261	4,354
1949	509,192	—	278,857	61,264	—	3,969	83,329	1,093	901	7,372
1950	447,184	—	220,134	83,790	—	2,694	105,376	748	1,626	—
1951	593,508	—	225,672	183,881	—	2,881	122,830	7,144	12,441	9,016
1952	695,237	—	269,919	186,008	—	2,764	139,290	21,119	21,221	15,120
1953	763,797	—	292,294	198,882	—	3,378	140,252	36,255	30,260	20,478

Year											
1954	—	776,530	285,632	200,252	—	4,255	151,213	47,865	24,407	29,271
1955	—	772,647	278,675	192,121	—	5,563	160,508	47,558	26,973	25,451
1956	—	921,692	304,945	259,808	—	7,083	172,800	54,049	46,181	32,584
1957	—	1,016,257	251,787	364,066	—	8,237	190,378	50,543	51,366	49,777
1958	—	995,463	259,310	308,320	—	8,386	195,581	56,252	51,286	56,731
1959	—	1,170,861	278,033	390,552	—	9,925	217,758	33,755	80,820	82,218
1960	—	1,567,695	390,606	573,353	—	12,285·	248,523	28,106	109,782	103,029
1961	—	1,958,023	495,823	714,265	—	16,109	296,920	30,285	139,119	138,187
1962	—	2,134,610	579,529	780,374	—	21,158	277,600	32,363	148,366	162,786
1963	—	2,459,294	690,671	862,914	—	28,895	315,462	31,159	191,336	186,449
1964	—	2,889,410	839,293	1,002,982	—	36,526	352,021	26,285	224,260	233,709
1965	—	3,197,558	989,134	1,035,721	—	40,956	388,959	27,876	248,728	267,922

SOURCE: Statistics Department, Bank of Japan, *Hundred-Year Statistics of the Japanese Economy* (Tokyo, Bank of Japan, 1966), pp. 136–37.

While the *global* context within which Japan was trying to expand its economy was determined by Western imperialism, much of the impetus towards state predominance was provided by domestic pressures for Japan to engage in imperialism. The argument (rarely challenged) that Japan should have a strong economy frequently came to mean it should have a strong military economy—to resist foreign imperialism if necessary, and engage in its own imperialism if possible. In addition, the specific domestic problems of capital formation and class conciliation within the new ruling bloc (and repression outside it) played a major role.

THE INTERNATIONAL CONTEXT AND
THE UNEQUAL TREATIES

For almost the whole of the Meiji period Japan's economic situation was dominated by the unequal treaties whose revision became the number one feature of foreign relations for at least a quarter of a century. The unequal treaties forced on Japan were much less drastic than those imposed on China some years earlier,[195] but they were, nonetheless, highly restrictive. The treaties had ramifications which went beyond Japan's relations with the Western powers alone. When Hawaii (then still an independent nation) offered Japan an equal treaty in 1881, Tokyo felt obliged to turn it down because acceptance might antagonize the West and delay the signing of equal treaties with the major powers.[196] The first equal treaty which Japan dared to conclude was in 1888, with Mexico.[197]

By their original terms, the treaties with the Western imperialists were due to come up for possible revision in 1872. Yet it was not until 1894 that Japan was able to make a significant break out of the treaty stranglehold. In that year a treaty of commerce and navigation was signed with Britain, to become operative in 1899. Although this did not fully restore Japan's rights, it was a big breakthrough, and in the revised treaties of 1899 Japan recovered its juridical autonomy. Tariff autonomy was not recovered until 1911.[198]

The effect of these "treaties" was two-edged, but on the whole thoroughly negative. They forced Japan into a "third world" relationship with the West on the manufacturing front. Japan was in the position of "an agricultural country which in its relations with the countries of Europe and America was a buyer of the manufactured goods of heavy industry and a seller of raw silk, tea, coal and other raw materials and half- [*sc.* semi-] finished goods."[199] Since industry could not be protected by sufficiently high import duties, Japan was unable to develop an integrated production circuit. This made it highly sensitive to international trading conditions: "roundaboutness in the structure of production [was] spread out in space beyond the national boundary, 'higher' stages being located abroad."[200] However, like liberalism as an ideology (which forced "free"—and therefore unequal—trade on other, weaker, nations but also promoted the transfer of cadres and techniques across frontiers), the unequal treaties had a dual effect. While inflicting colossal pressure on Japan, they also forced it to adopt economic policies which helped Japanese capitalism in the longer run. Lacking protective tariffs, Japan was forced into specialization right from the start. The unequal treaties made the development of many branches of industry unviable from a commercial point of view. This had several important effects. On the one hand, it fostered a climate in which industry, on the grounds of competitivity, based its output on extremely low wages. On the other hand, it stimulated state intervention (in every aspect of the process) as the only means to deal with the internationally-imposed impediments.[201] The need to specialize and the large-scale intervention of the state accentuated the trend towards monopoly already well established in the later Tokugawa period. The constraints on the development of industry greatly affected the formation of the Japanese combines, the zaibatsu. With the development of heavy industry blocked by Western imperialism, Japan became an exporter of the only two vital industrial raw materials it had—coal and copper.[202] In addition, maintenance of low wages justified by reference to the unequal treaties and the lack of "balance" in the economy directly brought about by the treaties helped to create pressures which played their part in Japanese imperialism.

CAPITAL FORMATION AND ACCUMULATION

The new Meiji regime had to devise means both to maximize new accumulation and to release and redirect the capital within the society.

The two main elements in the state's accumulation programme were taxation and credit creation. The statistical data on taxation are set out above in the discussion on the land settlement. The land tax continued to be the main source of government revenue till almost the end of the century, when it was temporarily exceeded by the liquor tax (in 1899).[203] Taxation was wielded as an instrument of both political and economic policy, in conjunction with other fiscal and monetary weapons. Thus, just as the high inflation of the late 1870s was functional to the government's economic programme, so was Matsukata's deflationary policy of the early 1880s. Prices fell, and small and medium enterprises were knocked out of business. The policy, according to G. C. Allen, "biassed the distribution of income in favour of profits."[204] The privileged fiscal position of business and property is shown by the fact that as late as 1913 taxes on business income and property provided less than 15 per cent of national tax collections. Contrary to widespread myth, early Japanese businessmen were highly profit-oriented, and were encouraged in this by the regime's inequitable tax policy. One result was that, since businessmen ploughed very little profit back into their firms, the state, via the banks, was the principal source of funds for industry throughout the period.[205]

Credit expansion was also crucial. For example, in the period December

1867 to June 1875 of total revenues of ¥406.4 million, ¥123.5 million came from "extraordinary" revenue such as credit and loans (the rest coming from "ordinary" revenue such as taxes).[206] Foreign loans were relatively unimportant in Japan's early development, and the government took good care that these loans were made only to itself and not to private concerns. Apart from two loans right at the start of the Meiji era (a railway loan in 1870 and a pension loan in 1873), Japan borrowed no money abroad until 1897—to defray the costs of the war against China. In the 1920s direct foreign investments became of sizeable proportions, but only after the infrastructure had been laid down. The contrast in the location of foreign investment between Japan and China is equally marked. Whereas in 1930 nearly 80 per cent of foreign capital in China was in the form of direct business investment, in Japan it was only 26 per cent.[207] Even as late as 1930, when restrictions had been considerably eased, practically three-quarters of all the foreign money in Japan was in the form of loans to the government.[208] War indemnities paid to Japan from China (¥369 million, payable in sterling [£38 million], after the Sino-Japanese War; and ¥24 million after the so-called Boxer Rebellion) also greatly assisted the expansionist programmes at the time.[209]

This policy of tightly controlling foreign capital naturally necessitated an efficient banking system. The 1870s had been fairly chaotic, and it was not until the early 1880s, with Matsukata's accession to the post of Finance Minister, that Japan stabilized its financial institutions. In June 1882 a central bank was set up for the first time; prior to this, in the quaint formulation of Takahashi (Chōtarō), "some 152 national banks were disorderly organized." Now credit could be systematically centralized, although the government was not able to break the foreign monopoly on foreign exchange dealings until 1887, when it reorganized the Yokohama Specie Bank.[210]

The other key factor in capital accumulation was the oppression and exploitation of the working masses, through very low wages, ideological mystification, the use of violence in recruiting and keeping labour, horrible working conditions in the mines, factories and dormitories, and the legal privileging of the exploiters over the exploited in every way. This exploitation was made easier by the desperate condition of much of the population and the widespread use of female workers, who were markedly more oppressed than the male proletariat. Right from the start the process of the formation, accumulation and investment of capital was, both politically and legally, entirely in the hands of the ruling class, and the working class was able to challenge this control only for fleeting moments. The extent of capitalist control over the labour force is shown both by the severe restrictions on union organization, and by management's ability not just to hold wages down over the decades, but even to lower them at a time of a business boom such as in the 1930s.[211]

There is one further aspect to the Japanese case of capital formation: Japan's success in avoiding being taken over by foreign capital. The critical difference in development is not in "stages" or "take-off" but in the distinction *between dependent and independent development*.[212] It is notable that very little of the "development" literature which portrays Japan as a model for other countries comes to grips with this factor. Japan's success in keeping foreign capital out is particularly remarkable when one considers the competition for investment immediately after the Restoration. A Tokyo-Yokohama Railway, first planned by Britain and France in 1865–68, was contracted with the United States by the new Meiji government as one of its first acts. British pressure then forced revocation of this agreement and a loan was contracted with Britain, only to be cancelled (with heavy compensation) at U.S. instigation. The railway was finally built in 1870 with money raised from the British Oriental Bank.[213]

In the 1870s the Japanese government had a deliberate policy of discouraging foreign investment and of buying back foreign-owned capital equipment and repaying foreign loans—the sort of policy which Bismarck had advised the Iwakura mission to adopt when it visited him. From about 1872 the government tried to push Dutch and British–Hong Kong (Jardines) interests out of the Takashima coal mine, which was eventually repurchased (by Mitsubishi) only in 1881.[214] In 1875, Mitsubishi was granted a government loan to buy out the American Pacific Steam Ship Company's Tokyo-Shanghai route; in 1877 and 1880 the British- and French-owned postal services were nationalized, and by 1874 the reparations for the Shimonoseki Straits incident were repaid in full. Thus, by the beginning of the 1880s Japan had cleared itself of foreign capital.

There were other factors involved. As Lockwood remarks: "Prior to 1897, the deterrents to the flow of Western capital into Japan were found on both sides. The Japanese were wary of financial imperialism, seeing it in operation among their Asiatic neighbors. In any case Japan was not a very inviting opportunity, for either the European *rentier* investor or the European businessman."[215]

This active hostility on the part of the Japanese government to foreign capital was certainly the main domestic reason why so little of it came into the country. In addition, the unequal treaty system forbade foreigners trading in the interior and Japan's economic condition made investment seem rather unattractive. In particular, the depreciation of non-convertible notes, combined with the efflux of specie due to the huge excess of imports over exports, made the inflationary situation unappealing. Besides, the difference in monetary standards complicated things for foreign exploiters: from 1871 to 1878 Japan was *de jure* on the silver standard, and then on the bi-metallic system until October 1899, and only after that on the gold standard.[216] All this made foreigners cautious. Further, the establishment of a central bank in 1882 meant that one critical zone in which foreign capital had always insisted on control was held under Japanese power. The reorganization of the Yokohama Specie Bank in 1887 broke the foreign monopoly of foreign exchange dealings (it eventually became the biggest bank in Japan, with three times the paid-up capital [see Glossary] of the Bank of Japan). All over the world, imperialist traders have disliked doing business except through banks or at least a banking *system* they themselves control.

It was also the *type* of development which Japan went through that kept out foreign capital. Apart from the conjunctural reason that Western capital at the time was predominantly attracted by China, which gave Japan a breathing space, there were specific factors in Japan's growth which deterred foreign capital. The key factor is that it was not just Japan's relationship to foreign *capital* in Japan that was unique; it was the whole relationship with foreign trade and imports. The seclusion of Japan meant there was no Japanese trading group involved in foreign trade of any size—and therefore no imports of the "classic" kind, luxury items or cheap consumer goods. Since the government handled foreign trade, it concentrated exclusively, as soon as it could, on importing what it needed: raw materials and capital goods for industry. This determined the actual trading structures, because such items could easily be handled through a few centralized foreign trading companies and the zaibatsu banks. By contrast, India's imports continued to be mainly consumer goods, and distribution remained highly fragmented. The imperialist bourgeoisies tried to push Japan towards a "consumer society," but Japan cut out both the kind of people who pushed consumer items and the actual items themselves; it kept foreign capital at arm's length until it could handle it, and staved off products which might have had a deleterious effect on domestic consumption patterns.[217]

What Japan managed to do was to split up three factors which imperialism often tries to pretend are inseparable: technical "know-how," actual imports of the products of advanced technology, and foreign capital. The fact that this period coincided with the high tide of liberalism, while hindering Japan in one way (by impeding protectionism), also helped it by fostering a relatively free flow of ideas, apprentices, and industrial techniques: Japan was able to hire large numbers of foreign technicians—at a cost. Between 40 and 50 per cent of the budget of the Ministry of Industry went on foreign technicians' salaries at the end of the nineteenth century.[218] These policies slowly had an effect. Foreign control over Japan's foreign trade fell gradually from about 90 per cent to four-fifths in 1890 and three-fifths in 1900. By 1920 more than half was in Japanese hands. A similar slow improvement took place in shipping. Up till 1880 all trade, even coastal shipping, was in the hands of foreigners. In 1885, 95 per cent of all foreign trade was still carried in foreign ships, but this fell to 70 per cent in 1900 and 50 per cent in 1913. Here again, it was active government policy which made this possible by building, buying and then virtually giving away ships to Mitsubishi;[219] by organizing concentration, mainly through sub-sidies (and in two cases even guaranteeing dividends); by excluding foreign ships from some ports (in 1894) and from coastal trading (in 1911); and by providing regional subsidies such as postal contracts and navigation bounties. Between 1900 and 1914 these accounted for 77 per cent of the total net earnings of all Japanese shipping companies with an authorized capital of more than 300,000 yen.[220]

EARLY INDUSTRY

Japan lacked almost all the raw materials needed for autonomous industrialization, except for coal (its main source of energy) and copper.[221] It did, however, have agricultural raw materials, such as raw silk.[222] This general lack of industrial raw materials, combined with the effects of the unequal treaties (and other causes connected with the historical development of the society), meant that Japan developed mainly light industry, while the society as a whole remained overwhelmingly agricultural right into the 1930s.

In 1900 less than half a million people were employed in factories, and 4,150 of the 7,171 industrial enterprises in the country were in the textile sector. Of these seven thousand plus enterprises only 2,388 were using mechanical power.[223] The textile industry still accounted for over half of all factory employees as late as 1929. Most industry continued to be very small-scale. In 1935, about 95 per cent of the 5,900,000 people employed in factories were in plants with less than thirty workers and there were one and a half times as many people in plants employing five or less workers as in those employing more than five people. The structure of industry was, naturally, reflected in Japan's trading position: textiles accounted for 59 per cent of Japan's exports in the decade 1920–30—a considerably higher figure than in 1870 (49.9 per cent).[224]

The high degree of state intervention in the economy which came out of the *political* compromise at the time of the Restoration was given a further boost by the Western imperialist powers' impediments to Japan developing a heavy industrial base; but Japan, wishing to engage in imperialist ventures of its own, felt obliged to develop a heavy industry. It is this particular combination of factors that shaped both the economy as a whole and the zaibatsu.

Thus, the first burst of industrialization after the Restoration came in *heavy* industry exclusively for military use.[225] This sector was government-controlled, and modern equipment, imported from abroad, was concentrated here. In this first stage there was no generalized expansion of heavy industry. In the second stage came the development of a consumer goods industry, based mainly on textiles. This sector was in private hands, but again the government played a crucial role in organizing the importation of both foreign technicians and the equipment needed for the more advanced

sectors of industry (while at the same time keeping out foreign capital).[226]
This importing was absolutely crucial, since, due to the impossibility of
building up an industrial base, Japan had not produced any textile machinery at all as late as 1910. Japan did not become self-sufficient in
machinery, or in the machine-tool industry as a whole, until the 1930s
(Table 3).

TABLE 3

IMPORTS AND EXPORTS OF MACHINERY
IN THE MID-MEIJI PERIOD

Year	Exports (¥10,000)	Imports (¥10,000)	of which textile machinery (¥10,000)	Imported shipping (¥10,000)
1887	–	220	12	52
1892	6	358	35	43
1897	22	2,297	540	823
1902	86	1,321	70	148

SOURCE: Andō, "The Formation of Heavy Industry," p. 455; from T. Tsuchiya, *Sangyō-shi* [A history of industry] (Tokyo, Tōyōkeizai-shimpō sha, 1944), p. 239.

The third stage came with the general expansion of heavy industry
around the time of the Russo-Japanese War after the end of the unequal
treaties and when Japan was already embarked on its colonial ventures. At
this stage there was a big boom in manufacturing and mining. Development
was very rapid, but it was "inverted" and disproportionate. By 1910 Japan
had completed the largest battleship in the world, the *Satsuma,* but had
built no textile machinery at all.

The extent to which the development of heavy and chemical industry in
Japan was government-led and arms-oriented can hardly be exaggerated.
Professor Andō Yoshio states that military industries had "overwhelming
significance in relation to heavy industry and the chemical industries
among [those] government-run factories and mines . . . it would be no
exaggeration to say that all factory industry was built with a military
significance."[227] The government's early moves to build up a railway
network were connected both to military objectives and towards stimulating commerce.[228] Heavy industry thus took on a special form "in that it
was transplanted at government initiative in advance of the industrial
revolution centred on the cotton industry . . . the transplantation of
industry . . . may . . be described as being of an emergency character."[229] (See Table 4)

This particular order of development naturally affected the internal
structures of the Japanese economy. This can be seen by looking at the
zaibatsu and the position of mining. Mining was the basis of the German

TABLE 4

ROLE OF GOVERNMENT-OPERATED FACTORIES

In 1897 government-operated factories accounted for:

56 per cent of the total number of factories
75 per cent of the total horse-power employed
88 per cent of employees

Among armaments factories, government-operated plants accounted for:

40 per cent of the total number of factories
74 per cent of the horse-power employed
54 per cent of the total number of employees

SOURCE: Andō, "The Formation of Heavy Industry," p. 455.

combines, and since coal was one of Japan's few assets, one could expect it to occupy a roughly similar function here. But in Japan mining developed largely as an *export* industry, due to the fact that Western imperialism was blocking the *generalized* development of heavy industry. This blockage was not definitively overcome until after 1945. Combined with the specific domestic features connected with the role of merchant capital, this produced a phenomenon very different from the kind of combine which appeared in Germany. Instead of a mining-based operation turning into a coal and steel combine (or an oil and petrol combine), the zaibatsu developed around holding companies and, though they owned mines, did not on the whole develop an iron and steel industry. Rather they diversified into multiple light industrial sectors and large distribution and trading networks. The apparently curious structure of mines–holding company–light industry–trading results directly from the forced absence of heavy industry.[230]

But the development of the zaibatsu was, of course, not only determined by the restrictions of the established imperialist powers. It was also interconnected with the role of the state. Early on in the Meiji period, the new government decided to sell off enterprises under its jurisdiction to private interests. Railways, telegraphs, the Yokosuka shipyard, arsenals and ordnance works were excluded.[231] As Andō stresses, "these factories and mines were sold off to the privileged political merchants of the time at prices which were merely nominal and under conditions which were absurdly easy." Moreover, even after they had been sold off, "they were accorded generous protection by means of subsidies and in other ways."[232]

The nature of this state/zaibatsu "division of labour" has been the subject of much controversy. What it boiled down to was that the government retained control over arsenals and military-related activities, while "civilian" industry mainly went to private individuals. Although "ownership" was thus technically split, the state, both directly and indirectly, retained very tight control over the accumulation and distribution of capital. In a way, the zaibatsu functioned as "semi-detached" instances in the state economy and, again partly as a result of the *political* weakness of merchant capital at the time of the Restoration, it was *political* authority which strengthened merchant capital in the 1880s (hence the phenomenon sometimes known as "political merchant capital").[233] It seems hardly plausible to deny that one of the purposes of this was to strengthen the alliance between government and business.[234] The government sales were designed not only to win over people outside the regime, but also to consolidate the power of those *within* the regime itself. This is evident in the major sales to figures like Gotō Shōjirō and Shibusawa Eiichi, who were early members of the Meiji government.[235] Moreover, the sale of enterprises at very low rates to private individuals formed only one part of a more general industrial programme, in which the key element was to establish an economic base which would secure the state. This involved economic measures to consolidate the new aristocratic-bourgeois bloc, but the central element was the construction of a military-oriented heavy industrial base since, as Burton puts it, "In Restoration days and for decades to come, the army would be a much stronger base for the authority of the Imperial Government than any loose association of businessmen."[236]

This peculiar structure of Japanese industry has given rise to considerable theoretical debate. The two Comintern experts, Tanin and Yohan, mainly concerned with examining the causes of Japanese imperialism, insist on the relative backwardness of the economy and the restricted domestic market. They reject the applicability of the term "finance capital" before the Russo-Japanese War (1904–5) since, they argue, at the time the economy was not based on anything like a solid foundation of large-scale industry.[237] Andō, too, dates "financial capitalism" [*sc.* finance capital] from the 1906 nationalization of the railways, "purchased by the government for about twice as much as the amount of their capital."[238] Finance capital *as a system,* however, he argues, only "takes root" after World War I. Another Japanese expert, Shibagaki, defines the zaibatsu as "the special form of finance capital in the Japanese capitalism of the period preceding the Second World War," and singles out two special features: first, that the zaibatsu, unlike most of the combines in the West, were not simple market monopolies, but "monopolies of capital as such"; second, that they were "practically devoid of the organic interconnectedness in production technology which characterizes modern monopolies in general."[239] In other words, the Japanese state promoted (through credit, tax privileges, etc.) a select group of oligopolies, rather than monopolies, each of which operated across much of the industrial, commercial and banking spectrum, but none of which had a monopoly in any one area.

These oligopolies were integrally connected to the central state-controlled core of the economy, the armaments and shipbuilding sectors. Under the impetus of imperialism, these were the only sectors of heavy industry which were developed to the level of other advanced capitalist countries[240] while, overall, industry remained concentrated in light industry right up to the Pacific War. Thus while developing as an imperialist power itself, Japan remained in an essentially "third world" relationship with the West commercially, while holding the position of an "advanced" capitalist country vis-à-vis the rest of Asia[241]—and here the *domestic* structure of Japanese industry forced by the unequal treaties tended to push Japan further along the road of imperialism which its own political and military leaders were backing for other relatively autonomous reasons.

2.
The Beginnings of the Left

> In this country a man as a worker is socially a doomed being,
> whether he be a skilled mechanic or a waste paper picker. When
> we look at the life conditions of the workers, the demarcation-
> line of their trades is completely blotted out; for they lead, one
> and all, a life of hopelessness.
>
> Takano Fusatarō, 1897[1]

There were enormous obstacles in the way of any form of proletarian or socialist organization in Japan, perhaps greater than in any other society. Early industrialization was predominantly rural, and most factories were extremely small. In 1884, 72 per cent of all factories had less than twenty workers and fifty-one years later, in 1935, 95 per cent still employed less than thirty people. At the turn of the century factory workers accounted for less than 1 per cent of the population. The majority were women who suffered from severe extra discriminations and oppression. Of the 422,019 people employed in the 7,284 factories in Japan in 1900, 257,307 were female. This reflects the preponderant role of the textile industry. As late as 1929 the cotton and silk spinning and weaving industries alone accounted for 54.7 per cent of all factory workers.[2]

As in Europe at a comparable stage, there was extremely high mobility of labour. The factory owners' reaction to this was repression. Workers were housed in "dormitories" (usually slum huts) on the factory grounds, and often not allowed off the grounds for several months after arrival. Guards patrolled the dormitories for a period after payday until funds needed to leave had been whittled down.[3]

In addition, the calculated "division of labour" between the state and private industry whereby the state renounced all social activities meant that individual workers were virtually helpless vis-à-vis their employers. Real, if minimum, "security" was proffered in stark contrast to the jungle outside the factory gates. This abdication of responsibility by the state meshed with pre-existing forms of patriarchal oppression to produce particularly brutal exploitation of women. Women were not legally allowed to take part in any political activity and were completely disfranchised socially as well as politically. The bulk of the early proletariat was made up of women who had been sold off by the male members of their family, without consultation.[4] Such sales were frequently made not direct to an employer but to a labour-boss intermediary.[5]

The development of the specifically Japanese system of industrial repression sometimes loosely referred to as the "life employment system"[6] is a subject of considerable dispute.[7] In the early stages of industrialization factory owners and managers had two main concerns: how to get, and how to keep workers. Since industrialization was built on the maximum exploitation of the very poorest and weakest in the country,[8] the mere job of getting even 1 per cent of the population to work in the factories was a major undertaking. The acute shortage of labour in the textile industry in the 1890s strengthened the position of the labour-bosses. As Taira notes, three components of labour cost became clear to employers: direct wages to the worker; additional non-wage expenses to keep the worker; and payments to the recruiter.[9] With the labour shortage, the power of the recruiters grew, and the employers responded by squeezing both direct wages and non-wage expenditure on their work force, leading in turn to such grinding misery that employees simply could not be kept by their employers. Defections rose to an intolerable extent.

Consequently employers began, not entirely successfully, to arrange a system whereby they would not actively buy away each others' employees. A skilled silk-reeler, for example, needed about one year's training, and labour force stability became increasingly necessary. Inter-employer agreements also would somewhat lower labour costs.[10] This system, frequently referred to as "paternalism,"[11] evolved to deal with three specific problems: the day-to-day instability of the work force, seasonal irregularity, and recruitment.[12] The employers' response, although ideologically disguised as "partnership" and serving the nation, was in fact directed exclusively towards securing an adequate and oppressed work force in the interests of maximizing profit.[13]

The system of repression was created before the working class had reached the stage of being able to organize itself; it was not a response to unionization. Yet even *without* the existence of trade unions or other workers' organizations, the Japanese capitalist class had difficulty maintaining the necessary level of exploitation. Without unions to sustain them and mobilize solidarity among other workers, the employed masses were still repeatedly driven to non-cooperation and outright defection. Nothing more graphically suggests how bad conditions must have been.

Attempts by employers to organize schemes for "non-interference" in each others' labour force proved inadequate in times of economic expansion. In the 1890s, during a major boom, the government floated plans for its reintervention directly in the economy,[14] in order, it was argued, to stave off the class struggle which would otherwise erupt because of working conditions. Although individual capitalists complained about the state interfering in business's "beautiful customs," the state was clearly acting as the unifier of the interests of the capitalist class as a whole, transcending the contradictions its individual members had been unable to resolve without it.

The state, in revamping the educational system, had stressed the application of the ideology of "family-ism" both to the nation as a whole, and to each of its elements. State and business together used it to oppose working class demands right across the board, including demands to form unions and to have the right to engage in industrial action or collective bargaining.[15] This all-embracing ideology was heavily fostered around the turn of the century, and parachuted in from above by the ruling class in order to try to tranquillize the turbulent labour scene. It was not, as its supporters claimed, a "traditional" Japanese system at all.

"Family-ism" was also used by certain capitalists against the government's moves towards introducing a Factory Act and similar legislation.[16] These "traditionalists" argued that it was only in the West, where employers had a mercenary relationship with their workers, that legislation or unions were needed.

> [T]he master—the capitalist—is loving toward those below, and takes tender care of them. . . . The capitalists of our country have a warm affection for their workers such as Europeans and Americans are incapable even of imagining. . . . Nothing like these beautiful customs can be found within the capitalist system, or in the labor unions of Europe and America, which have developed from the ancient institution of slavery.[17]

Round the turn of the century, the government began to get quite frightened about poor working conditions and decided to take action, "largely prompted by the fear that the maltreatment of workers would have serious adverse effects on the achievement of the national goal of building a wealthy nation and a strong army."[18] The result was the 1911 Factory Act, a feeble enough measure, strongly opposed by the business community. Yoshino argues that business's campaign against the Act produced the first formal articulation of "paternalistic ideology."

> Thus, the stressing of familial paternalism as the central aspect of the Japanese managerial ideology of this period was not fortuitous. That familial paternalism was used as a deliberate means to solve economic, political, technological, and social problems specific to the era of intense industrialization and urbanization cannot be overemphasized. The ideology of industrial paternalism was articulated only after a desperate search by management for viable ideological appeals to meet these problems. Paternalism proved eminently suited to the prevailing climate of the era.[19]

"Family-ism" (so-called "paternalism") was specifically designed to defuse the class struggle.[20]

Ideology in itself was not enough. More down-to-earth instruments, like the "life employment system," were needed in order to obtain and retain skilled labour. In 1900 the Public Peace Police Law, while not formally banning unions or even strikes, gave the government powers to intervene against a union or any action by workers under such catch-all rubrics as "instigation" and "temptation."[21] With this law enacted, the government moved towards introducing its Factory Act, designed more to *outline* than enforce the minimum conditions needed to keep workers, many of whom were the future mothers of the country's soldiers, alive.[22] Yet the government refused to accept the idea of a minimum wage, and passed the Factory Act without a date for its implementation.[23]

Business made tentative moves to construct a system involving both entry into employment and remuneration in order to stabilize the work force before the First World War, but the wartime boom created a new labour shortage like that in the 1890s and delayed the consolidation of the system until the mid-1920s. In theory, no company would take on an employee from another company *directly,* either during the industrial year or immediately after a worker had left the company with which he or she had been working.[24] The cement for this agreement was provided by a new wage system.

The rickety agreement about not "poaching" was given some real consistency by a pay system known as *nenkō joretsu* (ranking by years of experience).[25] Ideally, pay rises were fixed at regular intervals for men and based mainly on length of service in a company. A worker who wanted to move from one firm to another, whatever his level of skills, would be heavily discriminated against in the second company, where he would be paid the lowest wage, which could not be accelerated later. The discouragement to moving was, therefore, very powerful, and it is best to see the "life employment system" as basically a *discriminatory wage system,* enveloped in the mist of "family-ism." While any precise estimate of the net effect of the institution of *nenkō joretsu* is hard to make, available data indicate labour turnover probably slowed somewhat, though labour mobility continued at a high rate.[26]

The terms "paternalism" and "life employment system" suggest a real commitment by employers to their employees. On the whole, this is false. Factory owners and managers naturally wanted to keep their skilled labour, but their outlook was purely instrumental. The system was fundamentally *negative and discriminatory:* by refusing to guarantee a minimum wage, what it said, in effect, was not, "you will be better off with me," but "you will be even worse off anywhere else." Accounts by Japanese business, still circulated in the West, also suggest a cast-iron job guarantee by employers. Despite incomplete data, this is clearly not true. During the late 1920s in the steel industry, for example, when the *nenkō* system was already well institutionalized, a worker achieved really permanent status only after the age of about forty. "Until then, on the basis of his lack of loyalty or his failure to obtain the requisite skill level, he could be forced to leave the firm."[27] While plugging the myth of the "happy family" and its "beautiful customs," firms held out the *prospect* of permanent job security (only between the ages of forty and fifty-five—and only for men) as a lure. The real insecurity for the workers was actually accentuated since, along with the permanent employees, business instituted the category of "temporary" workers, who were paid lower wages, given no job guarantees, and excluded from whatever fringe benefits the company provided.[28] This practice became institutionalized in the early 1930s. An incomplete 1934 government survey showed that in factories in the engineering industry which acknowledged the use of "temporary" employees, 26 per cent were "temporary." The huge Yawata Iron and Steel Works, with 21,000 workers, had nearly 70 per cent of its employees under "temporary" status, though some of these 70 per cent had been continuously with the company for fifteen years.[29] These were simple devices to allow firms to pay lower wages and to keep them low. While holding out the carrot of job security, companies could thus easily fire workers when they wanted to. Under this system, employers kept a high degree of flexibility as regards layoffs, while the workers had little prospect of a guaranteed job and were certain of being discriminated against for the rest of their lives if they tried to switch from one factory to another.

Every detail of the pay system itself was designed to maximize the power of the employers. The whole relationship between employer and worker was presented as one of benevolence, under which the employer "gave" a livelihood to his employees. Remuneration in the sense of pay was not seen as a worker's right (he had no rights). Cash payment was presented almost as a bonus on what the employer was giving—housing and other "services." Frequently, wages were paid only once every three or six months, often in arrears, thus aggravating indebtedness. When it came, pay was often in "tickets" which could be used only in company stores and were worthless if the company went bankrupt (which frequently happened in mining, especially, in the early days). Companies also deducted money from wages as forced savings, which were not refunded if the worker left the company or was dismissed. In addition, pay was broken down into many different units, of which the base pay might be only a very small part, the rest being allotted according to criteria assessed by management on the basis of data (or alleged data) not available to the employees.

Business also fostered straight anti-union work. Unions were stigmatized as being "un-Japanese," something only workers in the West needed.[30] Where unions were formed, employers frequently smashed them with physical violence and dismissed the key workers involved. In other cases, employers sought to undermine the unions, which were never strong, by providing the sort of services which the unions had been promoting or suggesting. The constellation of "amenities" sometimes associated with Japanese business grew up as part of the overall business fight to secure and keep labour on terms maximally advantageous to capital, which included weakening the workers' own organizations.

This all-embracing machine of repression was not the work of "fascism," but of Japanese capitalism. Capitalism's responsibility for the system has been masked both by crude Western descriptions of Japan and by Japanese industrialists' shrewd manipulation of "traditional" ideology. This ideology was extremely functional in every way. In liaison with the official state ideology being inculcated through schooling and other means, it undermined the possibility of *class* solidarity. Language and concepts can be powerful instruments of oppression, and the stress on harmony and loyalty made it much more difficult for the workers to express their demands in terms of rights. The model of the family, a hierarchical and repressive institution, served the interests of oppression and exploitation superbly.[31] In spite of heroic efforts, the Japanese working class, always a minority of the population, never succeeded in breaking through the barriers which were, of course, physical and institutional as well as purely ideological.

It is quite wrong to describe the situation, as George Totten, for example, does by saying that "neither the form nor the content of Japanese working conditions was rationalized."[32] Both the actual organization of work and the wage system were rationalized—in the interests of capital. Low (or zero) remuneration speeded up the accumulation of capital. The seniority wage system forced the workers to depend on the company and was the key to both enterprise-consciousness and the company union.[33]

In September 1880, Gotō Shōjirō, the politician, who had been managing the Takashima coal mine, wrote to J. Keswick of Jardine Matheson, who were trying to get the mine back from him, explaining why he was not paying the miners any wages at all: "Those miners are not the people to be looked at in the same light as ordinary mankind, as they are animals like beasts or birds which . . . know today but not tomorrow; and therefore if they were paid as their works were done . . . , they would have one by one ran away and most probably you would not have been able to find Takashima in the present flourishing state."[34]

CONTESTATION

All this added up to a horrific existence. Nor was there much hope of liberation in sight. As in the West, the introduction of electric light (in the 1870s and 1880s), far from ameliorating working conditions, led employers to lengthen the working day. "It was a commonplace in Nagano Prefecture around 1890 for girl workers at silk reeling plants to work for 15 or 16 hours daily."[35] A survey by the Cotton Spinners' Association in

1897 showed that 84 per cent of all girls working in the industry were "sick or suffering from injuries."[36] Industry's relentless campaign against any lessening of exploitation is concisely revealed in the struggle against legislation to improve or even standardize working conditions in factories. Early moves for some kind of factory legislation were simply squashed in the 1890s. When the first Factory Act was finally passed in 1911, it allowed employers fifteen years' grace to carry out its provisions. Even then they were hedged around with numerous pro-employer qualifications. The meagre restrictions on night work and allowances for holidays, for example, did not apply to men. The mining companies, which enforced the most horrible conditions, were allowed until 1933 to let boys under sixteen and women have two days' rest a month.[37]

The depth of feeling among the workers is shown in a particularly moving account of an early rally organized by the Jiyūtō (the Liberal Party, founded 1881) against Mitsubishi. The rally was held in a temple, and its purpose was to assault the Sea Monster (Mitsubishi).

Outside several banners with the words, "Hurrah for Freedom, Kill the Sea Monster" were put up and vases filled with flowers were displayed. . . . Moreover, the most spectacular and pleasant feature of the day was the destruction of the Sea Monster. . . . After 6 p.m. there was dragged out, as soon as the speeches were concluded, a black monster more than ten feet high. . . . This monster was tied to a tree in the court yard and several tens of men surrounded it. . . . [After a death sentence was pronounced] the bravos stepped forward and jabbed their bamboo spears into the arms and legs and body of the Sea Monster, shouting all the while in unison. It was a spectacular and pleasant sight to see them rip and tear it apart. By this time there had assembled a great crowd of spectators. . . . Seeing the Sea Monster beautifully demolished, it is said they instinctively sang songs of triumph.[38]

Lenin (in *A Great Beginning*, 1919) and Mao Tsetung (in *Analysis of the Classes in Chinese Society*, 1926)[39] list very similar conditions for the emergence of an organized revolutionary proletariat: both put *concentration* and size as the first factor (and the China Mao was discussing in 1926 had roughly the same national percentage of factory workers as Japan around the beginning of the twentieth century). Exploitation and desperate economic conditions came second.

Although ferocious repression detonated reactions, actual *organization* was extremely difficult. While the first violent reactions came from marginal groups threatened by mechanization, such as rickshawmen (in both Japan and Korea), the first serious working class organizations were in large industry (iron, 1897; railways, 1898).

The first strikes after the Meiji Restoration came in the mines, where conditions were appalling. There were major disputes at the Takashima coal mine in 1870, 1873, 1878, 1880 and 1883—all of them settled by labour-boss intermediaries. But oppression in the mines was so severe that organization was almost impossible. Factory workers, although showing militancy later, became organized earlier. The first factory dispute came in 1885 at a silk yarn manufacturing plant in Kōfu.

The first recorded trade union was formed by the rickshawmen in 1883 against horse-drawn carriages. In 1884 a printers' union was set up. But the first concerted attempts at unionization were made in 1897–1900. The textile industry remained impervious. Repression was immediately launched against the nascent unions. From this first period, two factors may be noted. First, an acute awareness of the dangers of foreign capitalist penetration of Japan. This is clearly evidenced in the first major proletarian document, *A Summons to the Workers* (1897), which warned Japanese workers against the increased exploitation likely to result from the time the revised treaties came into effect in 1899.[40] Second, the early appearance of a "social" strike, by engineers at the Nippon Tetsudō (Railway) Company in 1898, which was for better status rather than just higher wages.[41]

It was against the threat of organized proletarian action that the idea of a Factory Act was first mooted. Prepared in late 1897, it was put before the Diet in 1898 and swiftly rejected. But in 1900, after more shop-floor militancy, a new and revised Public Peace Preservation Law was put through which banned all trade union activities, although not (formally) the actual bodies themselves. Until after World War I such groups could function only as "mutual benefit" societies.[42] Censorship was severe on translation: translation into Japanese of such writers as Sombart, Zola, Blatchford, Marx, Engels, Tolstoy and Kropotkin was banned until 1914 —though their works were admitted in foreign languages.[43]

The early years of the century were fairly tranquil for the ruling class. But Japan's success in the war against Russia in 1905 contributed to two new kinds of challenge. First, there were the major riots in Tokyo in early September 1905. These grew out of a demonstration originally called in Hibiya Park to protest the terms of the Portsmouth agreement between Japan and Russia. After what was in effect a police riot against the demonstrators, predominantly working class crowds all over the capital began attacking the police and their installations. Although there were no recorded dead on the police side, over 70 per cent of the police-boxes in the Tokyo area were destroyed. At least seventeen civilians were killed and many more—perhaps two thousand—were wounded, mostly by police swords. For the first time since the Meiji Restoration, martial law was declared because of a domestic political upheaval. After some manoeuvring between Premier Katsura and those directly in charge of the Tokyo police, the Katsura government fell in January 1906 and was replaced with one headed by Prince Saionji.[44]

Much more important, although it did not bring down the government, was the long series of strikes which began in the Ishikawajima Shipyard in

February 1906; spread to Kure Naval Arsenal and then to the Tokyo Military Arsenal in August; thence to the Osaka Arsenal (December 1906), the Nagasaki Shipyard (February 1907) and the Yokosuka Naval Dockyard (May 1907). Overlapping these developments in the arsenals and shipyards was a succession of uprisings in 1907 in the mines: at Ashio copper mine (February), Horonai coal mine (April), Besshi copper mine (June) and the Ikuno silver mine (July). At Ashio it took three infantry companies to suppress the workers, and the army also had to be called in at Besshi (in Shikoku).[45] These strikes were extremely menacing for the ruling class, for they came in the key sectors of the economy—the heavy military industries and mining—which had just had a boom during the war against Russia.[46] The regime responded on two fronts: the reorganization of industrial relations mentioned above, and ferocious repression, particularly against the copper miners. When Katsura returned to power in July 1908[47] repression became even more brutal. The 1907 depression, which started in America, soon hit Japan and greatly contributed to working class misery. Katsura decided to exploit the aftermath of bourgeois fear to eliminate the militant left. A High Treason Trial was staged in 1910–11 at which Kōtoku Shūsui, a leading figure on the left, and twenty-three other socialists were given death sentences (of which twelve were subsequently commuted) on charges of planning to kill the Emperor. The trial, and particularly the sentencing, were staged in such a way as to produce the maximum terror among opponents of the regime. The decision to convict and execute Kōtoku, who was certainly not guilty of the crime as charged, was a political one.[48] The Treason Trial and the assassination of Kōtoku left Katayama, a Japanese socialist leader, and the moderates room to reshape the disoriented proletarian movement. With no let-up in government repression, Katayama decided to leave Japan in 1914 and never returned. Subsequently installed in an honoured position in Moscow, he continued to dispense rather cautious advice on the struggle in Japan until his death in 1933.[49] In Japan itself reformism flourished in the organized working class movement: the Yūai-kai was AFL-oriented and its successor, Sōdōmei, in spite of a brief left stretch in the early 1920s, was also reformist.[50] The biggest challenges to the regime were to come from a different quarter.

In July 1918, with the price of rice soaring, a group of women at the port of Uotsu in Toyama Prefecture refused to load rice onto the grain ships. The news spread, causing demonstrations against officials and merchants elsewhere in the same prefecture. In early August the news hit the national press, and on August 10 there was a major revolt in Kyoto. The army was called out. A strike ensued at the Mitsubishi shipyards at Kobe (near Kyoto) and was met with extreme violence. After this the uprising became more generalized—and urbanized. In cities like Kyoto and Osaka the outcaste *burakumin* took the most militant role.[51] In Kobe slum-dwellers attacked the headquarters of a property company which had just raised slum rents. In the countryside peasants revolted against their landlords, with land tenure and share-cropping contracts the number one issue. On August 17 the miners in the town of Ube (Yamaguchi Prefecture) went on strike, whereupon the entire town rose. The army came in and killed thirteen people; sixteen others were seriously wounded. The same day a revolt started in the mines at Fukuoka in Kyushu and lasted for a full month. This initiated a series of revolts in the mining areas, which went on until mid-October. Eventually these were suppressed by the military and the police.

Altogether some ten million people took part in the events; uprisings occurred at 636 points, mainly in western Japan, and particularly in the rice-*producing* areas. There were 107 interventions by the army, from Hokkaido to Kyushu, in places including Tokyo, Osaka and Kyoto as well as thirty-eight prefectures. The total number of victims is not known. One source gives 8,185 arrests, of whom 94 per cent were indicted and 5,112 found guilty (including 7 given life sentences). Another gives 8,253 judgments found, including 71 confirmed verdicts of ten or more years imprisonment.[52]

What were the causes of this enormous upheaval, lasting two months? In spite of a nearly 500 per cent increase in production in the country's major industries during World War I, real wages fell drastically. Taking 1914 as the base (100), the fall was to 74 in 1916 and to 61 in 1918. The number of factory employees more than doubled—from 854,000 (in 1914) to 1,817,000 (in 1919). Precise data on the cost of living are lacking, but the whole development in the period 1914–18 had created the conditions for an explosion. A sudden jump in the price of rice (by about 50 per cent, varying locally a great deal) between 1917 and 1918 dislocated all strata. In fact, apart from the *burakumin,* the most active sectors in the 1918 upheavals seem to have been agricultural workers and workers in backward industry. The actual origins of the movement are significant. Rice was the occasion, but the system of land ownership and the cost of living were the underlying causes.[53] A further contributory factor to the later developments was the announcement on August 3, 1918, that Japan was sending a military force to Siberia against the Bolshevik Revolution.

The Rice "Riots" toppled the government. General Terauchi was forced out by the upheaval, and replaced by Hara Kei. This represented a real shift in ruling class *tactics* (from "classic" right to "enlightened" bourgeois right)—but Hara did nothing about either the system of land tenure or the price of rice, which rose vertiginously in 1918–19.

The 1918 riots also stimulated the regime to promote both Korea and Taiwan as major rice producers and suppliers to Japan. "The 'rice revolt' assumes the proportion of an epochal turning point in the development of Japanese agriculture."[54] But to be fully understood, the Rice "Riots" must be set in the general context of the great revolts which occurred immediately after the Russian Revolution and in connection with the end of the First World War. In Asia, the Japanese events can not be dissociated from those in Korea and China in 1919.

Although there was no immediate working class follow-up to the 1918 events, they (together with the Bolshevik Revolution) had a big effect on the students. Students at both the Imperial University of Kyoto and the Imperial University of Tokyo, and at Waseda University (in Tokyo) set up special student-worker bodies (in November 1918, December 1918 and 1919 respectively). Many students, including much of the future leadership of the Japanese left (Nosaka Sanzō, Asanuma Inejirō, Akamatsu Katsumaro, Aso Hisashi and Sanō Manabu among them), went out to work with the proletariat.[55]

Further proletarian action soon ensued. In 1920 more than 20,000 workers went on strike at the government-controlled Yawata Iron Works. And in 1921, 35,000 at the Mitsubishi and Kawasaki dockyards at Kobe struck, and launched for the first time the system known as "production control," taking over and running the dockyards.[56] Again, as with the Russo-Japanese War, the Siberian adventure had promoted militancy among the key industrial workers. Once again, the army was sent in to suppress the workers. At the same time, there was a sharp increase in tenancy disputes, which led to permanent tension in the countryside. Women's organizations got a big boost from the 1918 events. And the burakumin had made a striking demonstration of their wretched condition.

The ruling class appeared to waver for a while. Hara was assassinated in 1921, and the Washington Conference and its aftermath greatly engaged the attention of the regime. In 1923 the Tokyo-Yokohama area was hit by a huge earthquake. Exact figures are not known, but this would appear to have been among the most lethal earthquakes in recorded human history. About 100,000 people were killed, and virtually the entire Tokyo-Yokohama area was flattened or burnt in the great fire which raged after the earthquake itself. The conflagration was accompanied by a terrible pogrom in which many thousand Koreans, outcastes and Chinese were slaughtered. The police took the occasion to murder nine Japanese labor militants, as well as Ōsugi Sakae, the only figure comparable to Kōtoku, who was assassinated along with his wife and nephew at Military Police Headquarters.[57]

Much Western writing on the early part of the century, particularly on the Taishō years (1912–26), concentrates on the theme of the development of democracy during this period, a theme summed up in the phrase "Taishō Democracy."[58] But "Taishō Democracy" was severely limited, even by the standards of bourgeois democracy. The real theme of the period is acute class struggle, which culminated in a decisive victory for the bourgeoisie in 1925 when the draconian Peace Preservation Law and the so-called Universal (male) Suffrage Law were simultaneously introduced.

The Hibiya Riots of 1905 had shown two things: that there was a large, inflammable anti-regime potential among the working masses and that officially-sponsored "nationalism" and chauvinism had sunk deep roots among the people. On the one hand, Hibiya signalled to numerous imperialists and militarists the existence of a reservoir of popular right-wing feeling, available for anti-regime activity, if necessary. On the other, it alerted the regime to the need to develop local and grass-roots organizations to canalize popular resentments. A corollary to this, naturally, was the violent suppression of all socialist movements. As Herbert Bix has strikingly put it: "In fact, it is not concern with reform, but the passion for finding a peacetime equivalent for war, for recreating, that is, the wartime atmosphere of total sacrifice for the nation, which dominates Japan's leaders in their relationship with the disfranchised and the poor in the years before World War I."[59]

The 1918 Rice "Riots" shook the regime to its foundations, and political developments from then on must be seen as a direct response to the threat of revolution. The aftermath of the 1923 earthquake showed not only racism but also the violence and volatility of the masses. The real achievement of "Taishō Democracy" is the 1925 Peace Preservation Law, the key instrument of political repression for the next two decades.

THE COMPONENTS OF THE LEFT

The timing at which various ideological trends influenced Japan is important, and sets it off from other societies. The initial external wave of politicization came from Japanese who had been in America and contained two strands. One was Christian humanism (five of the six founding members of the Social Democratic Party in 1901 were Christians). The second was the ideology loosely associated with the name of the American trade union leader Samuel Gompers, a profoundly un-Marxist trend with no concept of the political party or its relationship with the trade union movement.

A third ingredient was anarchism, a term used sometimes to cover all forms of militant, extra-parliamentary action in the period before the Bolshevik Revolution. Political organization was then very difficult and Marxism had yet strongly to influence the Japanese left.[60]

Chronologically, the fourth element was Marxism. The timing of the introduction of Marxism was important in three ways. First, Marxism became a force because of the victory of the Russian Revolution; it was thus a science tied directly to an actual historical achievement.[61] Second, its impact was greatly facilitated because Japan was going through a period of relative liberalization, and third, the Marxism that burst upon Japan was not the victim of decades of exhausting logomachy with revisionism. It was fresh and vital. One bookshop in Tokyo almost immediately sold 300,000 copies of the first translation of *Das Kapital*. Apart from Katayama's Lassallian views,[62] revisionism in its European forms was absent.

In most other industrialized countries, communist parties were breakaways from existing socialist movements on the basis of the Comintern conditions. But in Japan it was a question of setting up a party, if not *ex nihilo*, at least without having to fight a wearing struggle against the Hyndmans and Nennis who plagued the Western proletariats. Very crudely, it could be said that the usual order was reversed. In Japan social democracy was a reaction to communism; in Europe communism was a transcending of social democracy. In Japan Marxism captured the left both organizationally and as a theory.

While Marxism came in on the wave of a victorious revolution, it was not associated with the negative aspects of later communist practice in Europe (at least until 1945). By the time of the mid-twenties, Japan was once again sealed off from the outside world. Marxism was established as a science independent of the subsequent deviations within and from communism which took place in Europe. And historically the record of communism in China, Korea, Mongolia and Vietnam is strikingly better than that of European communism. The police repression which beat down on all left organizations (and primarily on the young Communist Party, the JCP) from the 1920s onwards virtually isolated them from the outside world. Marxism and the ideals of communism were thus never incarnated exclusively in any one movement. As in Italy, there were non-communist Marxists, with their own autonomous relationship with both the local party and international centres. This has been most important in the post–World War II period since all the established left parties have gone through fairly abrupt shifts of position, but Marxism, which has been concretized in both the JCP and in the Socialist Party (JSP), and outside both, has not been vulnerable to attack through exclusive identification with any one organized group. Today, Marxism is firmly established as the dominant science in Japan, and more firmly so than in any other capitalist or industrialized country.

THE JAPANESE COMMUNIST PARTY— AND THE COMINTERN

Since the founding of the JCP was so integrally connected with the Comintern, it is convenient to look at both together.[63]

Having been invaded in 1918 and occupied by Japanese troops, the new Soviet regime was acutely aware of Japan's existence and role. It had no illusions about Japan's unscrupulousness. The 1916 Russo-Japanese secret treaty was revealed and denounced by the new regime. Lenin was not fooled by any talk about "liberalism" in Japan, with the Japanese army lodged in Siberia, and even defying the pressures of its imperialist allies to leave.

On the one hand, then, communications with Japan were almost impossible while Siberia was still occupied—and this must have weighed in the decision to invite Katayama to come and live in Moscow and work on Far Eastern affairs for the Comintern.[64] At the same time, the Soviet leaders were alert to the dangers of both collaboration and rivalry between the imperialists in the Pacific, and to their fervent anti-Bolshevism. When the news of the convocation of the Washington Conference reached Moscow during the Third Congress of the International in 1921, it was immediately decided to counter this by convening a Congress of Toilers of the Far East. As Vilensky wrote: "The intentions of the imperialists should be met with organized resistance by the peoples of the Far East. We believe that now is the time to raise the question of convening an East Asian Conference . . . which should advance the interests of these peoples to counteract the interests of the vultures who are now planning a conference in Washington."[65] The invitation was drafted by Chang T'ai-lei (one of the organizers of the great Hong Kong strike of 1925–26 and the leader of the Canton Commune in 1927, where he was killed):

Comrades of Korea, China, Japan and Mongolia! The last word is with you. . . . On November 11, 1921, a surgical operation over the peoples of the Far East, known as the Washington Conference, will be performed. It is on that day that we convene a congress of the Toilers of the Far East in Irkutsk, the purpose of which is to unite the toilers of the East in the face of a new danger. Our slogans are: Peace and independence of the country. Land to those who till it. Factories to the workers.[66]

Zinoviev and others had frequently referred in an anguished way to the lack of contact with Japan, so Chang T'ai-lei was sent to Japan to locate suitable delegates for the Irkutsk congress. Among those chosen were Tokuda Kyūichi, the future head of the JCP, and Suzuki Mosaburō, the future head of the Japanese Socialists. Stopping off en route in Shanghai, where they conferred with the Dutch revolutionary, Maring (Sneevliet), they eventually reached Irkutsk for the preliminary conference. Although Japan was considered the most important country represented (as evidenced in, for example, Zinoviev's address), it had the smallest contingent: a mere eleven delegates, compared with eighteen from Mongolia, thirty-nine from Korea and fifty-four from China. The conclusions of the conference, as expressed by different speakers, can be summed up as follows.

First, the Washington Conference is an attempt to settle inter-imperialist contradictions in the Pacific and East Asia after the upheavals particularly during the First World War. It is therefore dangerous, even though it cannot succeed, and it is likely to provoke a renewed round of the arms race, and greater belligerency after an as yet unknown period of time.

Second, the two main forces in the Pacific are Japan and America: America has agreed to leave Japan a free hand in Korea, Manchuria and Siberia in return for the "Open Door" in China—this means a concerted American attempt to build up a capitalist China as an anti-Japanese bastion; America therefore is unlikely to attack Japan until China is duly fortified; in addition, of course, this process could boomerang on the Americans, and slow them down.

Third, the only way to prevent a new war is through an international proletarian alliance.

Fourth, Japan is the key, precisely because it is the East Asian imperialist power.[67]

Yet while the key, Japan was also the problem: an imperialist country, and yet with an internal condition which in many ways approximated a colonized country, rather than a developed metropolis. So there was a straightforward problem of organization; more a question of actually *creating* a communist movement than of separating the left from the right. And, of equal importance, there was the question of deciding what *kind* of movement there should be, the kind of revolution to be aimed at. And from the answers to such basic questions as the nature of Japanese society and the Japanese state would flow the correct strategy and tactics. Yet all levels of practice, including theoretical analysis, were extremely difficult, and this is reflected both in the upheavals surrounding the beginnings of the JCP and in the fluctuating interpretations of the nature of Japanese capitalism and imperialism.[68]

When Zinoviev addressed the Second Session of the Congress of the Toilers of the Far East on January 23, 1922, he aligned Japan both externally and internally with the other major imperialist powers. What was needed, he argued, was a proletarian revolutionary movement to stage a full-scale socialist revolution. The delegates to this conference returned to Japan, and in July 1922[69] the JCP was officially established, with a Central Committee of seven (Yamakawa, Arahata, Takase, Hashiura, Yoshikawa, Tokuda and, at its head, Sakai Toshihiko).[70] At the Fourth Congress of the International later that year, the Japanese delegates met with Bukharin, who was to handle Japanese affairs until his decline, and prepared a draft programme. Like the Theses on the Eastern Problem produced at the same time, this text was a step backwards compared with Zinoviev's earlier position. The Comintern Theses emphasized "the hopeless internal crisis of Japanese imperialism, which is rapidly creating the conditions for a bourgeois-democratic revolution in that country, and conditions for the passing of the Japanese proletariat to an independent class struggle."[71] The 1922 Theses took a contradictory stance:

> Japanese capitalism continues to display even today signs of old feudalistic practices. . . . While the remnants of the feudal group continue to hold high positions in the state administration, the reins of government are now

held by a bloc of landowners and commercial and industrial bourgeoisie. The semifeudal nature of the sovereign state is revealed very sharply by the fact that Japanese aristocracy is assigned leading positions by the Japanese constitution. Under these circumstances the forces opposing the present authority of the state come not only from the laboring class, the peasants, and the petty bourgeoisie, but from a wide range of the so-called liberal bourgeoisie as well.[72]

The document saw the development of capitalism making class contradictions more acute, yet it also called for a *tactical* alliance of the broadest possible sector of the social spectrum to overthrow the existing imperial system. At the same time the party's list of demands apparently included an armed workers' militia![73] The theses got a fairly critical reception in Japan. There were two problems. One was whether or not it was a good idea to try to have a legal party, given the conditions prevailing in Japan. The second concerned the class composition of the party. The inescapable fact was that the party set up in 1922 was overwhelmingly an intellectuals' grouping. A wave of arrests in 1923 decimated the JCP leadership. A powerful group in the party, led by the able theoretician, Yamakawa Hitoshi, argued that the existing body should be dissolved and a new start made on a *mass* basis.

After the rather negative response in Japan to the 1922 Theses, one of the leaders, Arahata, had returned to Russia, and at the June 1923 Third Enlarged Plenum of the Executive Committee of the Communist International (ECCI) argued against trying to perpetuate a legal party in such a hostile environment. Zinoviev, on the curious analogy of America, argued that a legal party was best. While Arahata argued that political education was needed before forming a party, Zinoviev claimed that the mass movements were already there and only needed to be guided by a legal party. However, in May (1923) the Japanese police had decided to smash the JCP, and then in the wake of the great earthquake there was a further round of arrests. When Arahata returned he found a majority of the party leadership in favour of dissolution. Yamakawa in fact left the JCP before the formal dissolution, but it was his followers who got the dissolution formalized (March 1924).

The Comintern was displeased. In May 1924 an appeal was issued for the formation of a new party, and just before the Fifth Congress of the Comintern opened (June 1924) a special committee was set up to deal with the emergency. The result was that in January 1925 a meeting was held in Shanghai, attended by a number of delegates from Japan, and a group from Moscow, including Voitinsky and, possibly, Heller, the head of the Far Eastern section of the Profintern (the Comintern trade union federation). Voitinsky prepared a draft, known as the January Theses, the upshot of which was that the party should be re-formed immediately with more stress on working class membership.[74] Though this was approved unanimously (not surprising in view of the revolutionary situation in Shanghai at the time), it was difficult to put into effect back in Japan, especially after the government in early 1925 enacted the notorious Peace Preservation Law. The January Theses were supplemented by another document along the same lines, also prepared in Shanghai, known as the May Theses, and largely involving the trade unions.[75]

Shortly afterwards Stalin accorded an interview to the correspondent of the Japanese newspaper, the *Nichi-Nichi,* who had once interviewed Lenin. This is a very formal interview, with Stalin carefully rephrasing questions into his well-known "You ask me . . ." formula. The only text of its kind, it betrays all the ambiguity of Russia's position at the time. Essentially, Stalin is saying: Japan is an imperialist country, but at the same time it is in contradiction with the Anglo-Saxons and is interested in "freeing" their colonies. While making a special pitch to Japanese youth, he refuses to consider collaboration with the Japanese government against Western imperialism without a change of regime in Tokyo.[76] The interview should be seen as a follow-up to the treaty signed between Russia and Japan in January that year, terminating the Japanese occupation of north Sakhalin and agreeing to a system of fishing concessions, etc. Much of the groundwork for this treaty had been laid by Joffe during a long stay in Tokyo in 1923.[77]

The year 1926 saw yet another attempt to analyze Japan. Again the draft was prepared by Voitinsky, and approved by M. N. Roy, Tokuda and Katayama. The 1926 (Moscow) Theses marked an advance: "In the course of the European war, Japanese capitalism developed so rapidly that the government of the 'landlord-capitalist bloc,' heretofore under the control of the landlords, has now fallen entirely into the hands of the bourgeoisie." But after pointing out that the way the economic crises had been handled had pushed many members of the petit bourgeoisie down to the condition of the proletariat, the document went on to argue once again for a two-stage revolution, even while admitting that the bourgeois revolution "will necessarily be carried out by the proletariat and the peasants" and should be rapidly transformed into a proletarian revolution.[78]

Meanwhile, another major difference of opinion had occurred in Japan. Once again, a wave of arrests had left the party in the hands of a small group of intellectuals. The main influence in the party was now Fukumoto Kazuo, who held that Japanese capitalism had already entered the advanced stage which characterized "the declining and disintegrating capitalistic societies of the West."[79] This clashed with the Comintern position, which Tokuda relayed to Japan. However, along with almost all the other leaders, Tokuda was arrested before the Third Convention of the JCP held at Goshiki in December 1926, where Fukumoto won the day. A few weeks after the Goshiki meeting, the JCP leaders were released, and they found themselves in disagreement with the official "local" organization. A new special committee was set up by the Comintern, headed by Bukharin, which duly produced the July (1927) Theses, adopted by the ECCI: "Japan is now governed . . . by a bloc of the bourgeoisie and landlords, with the bourgeoisie in command. This being so, the hope that the bourgeoisie can in any way be utilized as a primary revolutionary factor, even during the first stages of the bourgeois-democratic revolution, must be abandoned now."[80] The 1927 Theses rejected both Yamakawaism (for refusing to accept party discipline) and Fukumotoism (for going too far in the opposite direction and exposing the party to the danger of isolation from the masses).

Whether this diagnosis was correct was never put to the test. After the surprisingly powerful showing of the proletarian parties in the elections on February 20, 1928 (the total left vote was about 470,000, or 4.95 per cent of the poll), the police proceeded to yet another round-up of left-wing leaders on March 15: over 1,500 people were jailed, although most of the key Communist leaders (except Shiga, Nosaka and Tokuda) evaded arrest. However, from then on repression was not to let up. Later in 1928, the new secretary general, Watanabe, was picked up off a boat in Taiwan and was either murdered or committed suicide. There was a brief left turn in December that year after Watanabe's death. Less attention was given to legal "front" organizations, which had not paid off, and more to work inside the unions. A new union federation, Zenkyō, was set up successfully on December 25, 1928.[81]

The decline of Bukharin and the shift brought about by the Sixth Congress of the Comintern in 1928 necessitated some revision of the 1927 ECCI Theses on Japan, which started to come under heavy fire in 1929. A new critique was not developed until 1931, and was relayed to Japan by Kazama Jōkichi, who reconstituted a new Central Committee after the Tanaka debacle.[82] Kazama wrote up the new line from memory into a thirty-page document, *The JCP's Political Thesis—A Draft*.[83] This adopted the position that Japan was a monopoly capitalist country, and advocated an immediate proletarian revolution. But, as was so often the case, this approach never had time to prove itself. In March 1931 Nosaka made his way to Moscow, where he at once became installed as Katayama's number one aide. He authored a completely new text, the 1932 Theses, which reversed the Kazama document and went back to the earlier stress on feudalism, the monarchy, etc. (*The Situation in Japan and the Tasks of the JCP*).[84] To a large extent this text was a response to Japanese foreign policy of the moment. In autumn 1931 Japan had seized the capital of Manchuria, and then Japanese troops had passed over the Russian-controlled Chinese Eastern Railway. In February 1932 "Manchukuo" had proclaimed its independence. Like Tagliatti at the comparable period in Italy. Nosaka felt constrained to adopt a rightist line and call for a bourgeois-democratic revolution. This thesis remained in force until 1950.

SUMMARY

The history of the left throughout the 1930s and up to 1945 is one of incessant repression, culminating in the last round of mass arrests on May 3, 1933. In November 1933 Katayama died and was accorded a grandiose funeral before his ashes were immured in the Kremlin walls. Nosaka took over his functions, if not his prestige. In Japan itself successive leaders of the party, including Miyamoto, one of the present heads of the JCP, were arrested and imprisoned.

The trade union movement formally fared slightly better, but at the price of rightism. Membership in trade unions never exceeded 7 per cent of the work force.[85] More than one-third of the unionized workers were seamen, who were a very weak group because of the fragmentation imposed by their work. Most of the others were workers in small and medium enterprises. The maximum figure for unionization in coal mining (reached in 1931) was less than 4 per cent of the work force. As elsewhere, this surely exaggerates the reality. That some 5 per cent of the industrial labour force was formally unionized anyway means very little. Many of these unions were mere props for capitalism. Throughout the 1930s Sōdōmei, the largest federation, pursued a solidly rightist line, and in 1937 formally renounced resort to strike action. In 1940 it cooperated in sinking the remnants of the union movement in the government-sponsored Sangyō Hōkoku Kai (Patriotic Industrial Association—usually abbreviated to Sampō). Sampō's slogan was *Jigyō Ikka* ("Enterprise Family"). Modelled on the Nazi Arbeitsfront, it originated from local police officers and worked to sabotage the interests of the proletariat.

However, in spite of constant repression, the period saw an amazing flowering of Marxist theory and study. Non-party forms of organization also flourished for a time. The remarkably powerful Proletarian Cultural Federation, which was set up by a well-known writer, Kurahara, grouped together twelve different organizations made up of writers, cineasts, atheists, birth control supporters and others.[86]

But it was the great debate on the nature of Japanese society, usually known as the Rōnō-Kōza controversy, which was the outstanding theoretical contribution of the epoch. Although these schools were directly connected with the variant Comintern Theses, after the virtual liquidation of the JCP in 1928 the argument raged at its own autonomous level. The material has not been translated into Western languages and is virtually ignored by Western writers.[87] But the vast work of research accomplished by the Rōnō and Kōza groups both laid the foundations for the scientific study of the Meiji Restoration and of Japanese capitalism, and provided the material basis for the sweeping victory of Marxism in the post-1945 period among university and academic cadres.[88]

In many ways the most striking aspect of the period is this wide gap between the quality of the theoretical production and the level of political leadership. The initial Comintern impetus petered out in the face of repression in Japan and the sheer difficulty of political organization. The failure to produce an agreed scientific analysis of the development of Japanese capitalism and of Japanese "fascism," which caused five or six sharp changes in policy in one decade, was a major contribution to the political disorientation *in situ*. The militancy of the Japanese proletariat in conditions of extreme political, social and physical oppression was not matched by the correct line and consistent leadership most essential at such a time.

3.
Japanese Imperialism to the Washington Conference of 1921–22

At the time of the Restoration in 1868, most of the major European powers were already present in the Far East: the British in Hong Kong, the Dutch in the East Indies, the Portuguese in Macao and Timor, the Spaniards in the Philippines, and the French in the Pacific Islands. In 1867 the United States bought Alaska and the Aleutians, and acquired Midway.[1]

Although the United States is usually associated with the "opening" of Japan, Britain and Russia were actually the biggest threats in the early Meiji period. In 1858, while China was being attacked by France and Britain, Russia seized all the territory north of the Amur River through the Treaty of Aigun. In 1859 Russia occupied the maritime province of Manchuria. In the 1870s Russia moved into northern Sakhalin, just off Japan's north coast, and came into direct conflict with Japan. The Trans-Siberian Railway was mostly constructed during the 1890s, bringing Russian power to the Pacific. Up until the Russo-Japanese War of 1904–5, Japan was incessantly occupied with countering the Russians in Sakhalin, Manchuria and Korea.

Towards Britain, on the other hand, Japan adopted a different attitude. Britain, with the most powerful naval force in the world, was well entrenched in China by the time Japan could move into China itself. Japan therefore decided, at least from the time of the Sino-Japanese War (1894–95), to come to terms with Britain. This also suited London, which shared Japanese hostility to Russia, and it coincided nicely with Britain's newly enfeebled military position, due to such involvements as the Boer War (started 1899).

For most of the nineteenth century, after America's initial probes before the Meiji Restoration, Japan had to deal with only two (external) factors: the peoples of Asia, under mainly incompetent governments, and the old

European imperialists. In 1898, however, the United States crossed the Pacific and invaded the Philippines, en route to China. At about the same time, America launched the slogan of the "Open Door"—and the *new* imperialist policy that lay behind these words. This new policy was particularly worrying to Tokyo, since it threatened to undermine the whole basis on which Japan was planning to build its imperialist position—and, indeed, the "Open Door" was one of the main factors contributing to the Pacific War forty years later.

Between 1868 and 1922 enormous changes took place in the Far East. Apart from the arrival in force of the United States, two imperialist powers, Britain and France, considerably increased their holdings. In 1884 France occupied Annam and blockaded Taiwan. The following year Britain annexed Burma and the Berlin Conference settled the carve-up of Africa. European eyes increasingly focused on East Asia, the last major area of the globe not yet entirely grabbed.[2] During this period (1868–1922), three imperialist powers also disappeared from the scene: Spain at the end of the nineteenth century with the loss of the Philippines; Germany at the start of World War I; and Tsarist Russia with the victory of the Bolshevik Revolution. Portugal and Holland remained in the area, but without engaging in conflict with Japan.

Throughout these years Japan manoeuvred with considerable success on two fronts. Vis-à-vis the other imperialist powers, to secure its own independence, first by negotiating an end to the unequal treaties and extraterritoriality, and then by getting itself accepted as a member of the imperialist club. At the same time, Japan moved to acquire as strong a position as possible in Asia, at the expense of the local inhabitants. Its manoeuvrings combined initial patience with, subsequently, victorious wars against weaker rivals (first China and then Russia), cautious grabs for territory (in China and Korea), and judicious alliances (especially that with Britain). Through such policies Japan had, by the end of the First World War, become one of the four imperialist powers that ruled East Asia and the Pacific.

"SEIKAN RON":[3] THE DEBATE OVER INVADING KOREA IN 1873—AND ITS PROLONGATIONS

The last overseas venture of pre-Tokugawa Japan was an unsuccessful attempt by Hideyoshi to invade Korea in 1593, and it is no accident that Korea, Japan's nearest geographical neighbour, was the first object of Meiji Japan's expansionism. The new Japanese government sent a special mission there to explain the change of regime and why Japan had permitted the Western imperialists to "open up" the country, as well as to try to renew diplomatic relations with Korea. The Koreans turned down the Japanese proposals, preferring to maintain their isolation, vis-à-vis which they saw both Japan's moves towards Korea and Japan's relations with the West as threats.

This rebuff from Korea coincided with the already analyzed developments surrounding the opposition to the new conscription law. Though a broad spectrum of opinion backed an invasion of Korea, one key factor was a wish to protect the position of the samurai.[4] Even those who opposed an invasion tended to see Japan as the only possible source of help for an East Asia open to Western imperialist exploitation. "Japan is a doctor," wrote Fukuzawa Yukichi, "responsible as a teacher of civilization. Korea is like a sick person whose limbs are paralysed. Japanese interference in Korea should not be made in a retiring manner, but strongly and swiftly to bring Korean entrance into civilization."[5]

For a time the supporters of invasion seemed to have the upper hand within the government, but no actions were undertaken since a commitment had been given not to engage in any fundamental changes of policy during the absence of Iwakura and his mission, which included Kido Kōin (Takayoshi), Itō Hirobumi and Ōkubo Toshimichi. These four returned in 1873 and gradually reversed the earlier trend. The key element in this crucial decision was the October 1873 "memorial" by Ōkubo.[6] Though the "pragmatists" carried the day, Ōkubo, now the most powerful man in the government, decided to appease his opponents among the southwestern samurai by sending an expedition to Taiwan, ostensibly in retaliation for the murder there a few years earlier of some fishermen from the Ryukyus. Ōkubo skilfully placed the expedition under Saigō Tsugumichi, the younger brother of Saigō Takamori. Ōkubo also made strenuous efforts to involve Westerners, particularly Americans, in the venture.[7]

The Japanese invasion of the southern part of Taiwan was brief. The expedition almost collapsed when British and American ships refused to ferry Japanese troops in the middle of the operation, an event which led Ōkubo to pour government money into Mitsubishi, which got its big break in shipping at this point.[8] China refused to abandon sovereignty over any part of Taiwan and in the autumn of 1874 Ōkubo headed a Japanese mission to Peking to settle the whole business. Japan still did not have enough power to engage in foreign aggression, except on sufferance from the West. Taiwan remained with China until the Sino-Japanese War.

THE SINO-JAPANESE WAR AND THE TRIPLE INTERVENTION

In 1871 Japan signed a treaty of friendship with China, as an alliance against the eastern advance of Western power.[9] But over the next decade and a half both China and Japan tried to strengthen their positions against each other in a technically still independent Korea. A first major crisis between Chinese and Japanese occurred in 1884–85. Tokyo decided to avoid conflict with China, because of its own military weakness,[10] and instead signed the Treaty of Tientsin (1885) with China, under which each party promised not to intervene directly in Korea without informing the other. Immediately after this, Japan took the decision to build a fleet which could control the China Sea.[11]

The Treaty of Tientsin was signed in the same year that the Berlin Conference took place. The Berlin "settlement" of Africa freed imperialist energies, which now began to focus on Korea, and that country became not only the centre of Sino-Japanese rivalry, but also an important area of Anglo-Russian competition, as well as the first Asian territory to experience a concerted American drive for influence.

The Sino-Japanese War was triggered by China's proposal for setting up a Chinese "supervisor" over the Korean royal family.[12] When Japan decided to go to war in 1894, it was a much stronger military power than it had been in 1884–85. China, on the other hand, had done little to prepare itself for battle; right into the late 1880s the examination for entrance into the officer corps included archery as the main item of artillery. Japan won a series of resounding military victories and quickly smashed the Chinese armies. Most of the fighting took place in Korea, although Japan's main strategic objective was control over the Liaotung Peninsula, with Taiwan as a secondary goal.

The Treaty of Shimonoseki (1895) gave Japan a greatly enhanced position in Korea, which remained formally in the same state as before, in Taiwan, a relatively rich island, and in the Liaotung Peninsula, strategically placed vis-à-vis both Korea and North China. There was also a huge indemnity of ¥360 million from China which was of crucial importance. The war had been very expensive for Japan, costing about ¥200 million, or three times the annual government expenditure.[13] While Japan was still on the silver standard it was difficult to raise foreign loans, and the big reparations payment was needed to help put Japan on the gold standard.

The repercussions of Japan's victory were even wider. Just before the outbreak of the war against China, Japan had signed with Britain the first equal treaty with a Western power (signed 1894 to go into effect in 1899). Under the terms of Shimonoseki, China was forced to "open up" several ports on the Upper Yangtse and allow foreigners to set up industrial concerns in China. Tanin and Yohan see these terms as part of a pay-off to the British in a strategy of including Japan in the leading imperialist group.[14] Certainly China's economic concessions were of the greatest benefit to Britain. In addition, the indemnity Japan extracted was so huge that it both blocked China's chances of economic recovery after the war, and forced the Chinese government into ruinous borrowing abroad, ultimately obliging it to cede territory to raise the money, and thus further enfeebling its defences.[15] After Japan's victory Britain turned from its policy of trying to build up China as a bastion against Russia to straightforward acquisition of leases and exploitable assets. In the words of Lord

Rosebery: "There we have a sick man worth many Turkeys, of more value to us as a people than all the Armenians that ever walked the earth; as a commercial inheritance priceless, beyond all the ivory and peacocks that ever came out of Africa."[16]

These British and Japanese moves alarmed other European powers limbering up for their share of the booty. Russia and Germany in particular had been manoeuvring more or less in concert. Russia's Trans-Siberian Railway was under construction, but far from completion, and a consolidated Japanese presence in southern Manchuria was something to be blocked, if at all possible. Germany, too, was extremely anxious to strengthen its position in the area. The result was the Triple Intervention, or Triplice (Russia, Germany and France), only five days after the signing of the Treaty of Shimonoseki, forcing Japan to abandon the Liaotung Peninsula in return for a further indemnity from the Manchus. Russia now moved into the Liaotung Peninsula.[17]

The Sino-Japanese War was thus not wholly favourable to Japan. Japan's main gains on the mainland were immediately confiscated by a group of European powers. By 1899 Britain had seized the "New Territories" on the mainland of China opposite Hong Kong, as well as Weihaiwei, the island guarding the sea lanes to Peking (as "recompense" for organizing a loan to cover the last third of China's indemnity to Japan), and had monopolized the Yangtse Valley; Russia had seized Port Arthur and Talienwan (Dairen/Dalny) and was encroaching upon Manchuria and Mongolia; Germany had seized Kiaochow Bay and had placed Shantung Province under its control; France had forced China to agree to its special privileges and interests in Yunnan Province and in certain parts of Kwangtung and Kwangsi Provinces, and had also "leased" Kwangchow Bay. Japan had surprised the Western powers—and also split them into a pro-Japanese group (the Anglo-Saxons) and an anti-Japanese group (the Three). It had entered the imperialist club and won Taiwan. The war had been brief and the indemnity large. But the *lesson* was that without a countervailing alliance other imperialist powers would tend to sabotage any Japanese successes. These considerations led to the signature of he alliance with Britain in 1902. In addition, the desire for greater military strength led to a decision in 1896 to sanction the doubling of the standing army and the fleet.[18]

THE ANNEXATION OF TAIWAN

The transfer of Taiwan to Japan occurred *at sea,* since neither Chinese nor Japanese officials dared to set foot on the island, which was in a state of upheaval. When the announcement of the transfer of the island to Japan was made, the local population and the administration decided to resist the cession and on May 23, 1895, the Taiwan Republic was proclaimed. Only by fighting a long and cruel war against guerrillas and widespread popular opposition did Japan impose its control. A Japanese chronicler, Dietman Takekoshi, writes: "Whenever our troops were defeated, the inhabitants of the surrounding villages instantly became our enemies, every one, even the young women arming themselves and joining the ranks with shouts of defiance. Our opponents were very stubborn and not at all afraid of death."[19] The capital was only taken on November 18, 1895, six months after the Republic had been proclaimed, and a further four to six years were needed to subdue the guerrillas entirely.

There were frequent uprisings—the Peipu Rebellion (1907), the Liuchi Rebellion (1912), and a revolt at Hsilaian (1915). Petitioners for a local Diet in 1923 were arrested and killed. The Marxist groups which appeared from 1926 onwards were systematically harassed. Unlike in Korea, where some Korean-language papers were permitted, in Taiwan the Japanese did not allow any Chinese-language newspapers to appear. Since only about 10 per cent of the non-Japanese population of the island could understand Japanese as late as 1930, the policy was one of political repression and gross cultural deprivation.[20] Tokyo similarly rejected any assimilation, which was pushed for a time by Itagaki Taisuke—that might have meant a degree of equality.

Taiwan was a profitable enterprise for the Japanese, and a place where a sizeable number of Japanese could live in colonial comfort. It was the only "overseas" territory to which the Japanese moved with alacrity, and was seen as their "colonization university," as Gotō Shimpei, the Chief of Civil Administration on the island, called it. In propaganda, it was used to demonstrate that Japan was the equal of foreign imperialists, because it owned a colony; and more than the equal, because the Japanese also claimed to be promoting the economic welfare of the territory. Takekoshi, dividing European colonialism into three stages—the first or Spanish stage (primitive exploitation and extraction), the second or French stage (as in Indochina), and the final or English stage (high investment in a colony to produce a high return for the metropolitan country)—proclaims: "I cannot but rejoice that we, Japanese, have passed our first examination as a colonizing nation so creditably."[21]

AMERICAN EXPANSION IN THE PACIFIC

American expansion in the Pacific can be divided into two processes. First came the acquisition of coaling stations en route to China after the purchase of Oregon in 1846, which led to the American expeditions to Japan in the early 1850s. Japan then was envisaged primarily as a possible refuelling point on the route to Shanghai.

The second is more complex, and involves simultaneously two phenomena: "classic" colonialism (in the Philippines) and "new" imperialism (in and towards China). These two are fused in time since the grabbing of the China market was the principal reason behind the Spanish-American War (the seizure of the Philippines took priority over the seizure of Cuba). The "Open Door" policy was specifically designed to privilege American economic superiority as against classic imperialism in China. While it had been adumbrated earlier, it became the core of American international policy only under the dual impetus of the domestic economic depression of 1893 (which, following on the "long depression" of the 1870s and '80s, led American business to think there was serious over-production) and the accelerated scramble among the European powers for acquisitions in China after the Sino-Japanese War.[22]

The "new" policy brought some "old" in its wake. The "Open Door" led to the seizure of the intermediate islands: "Hawaii, Wake, Guam and the Philippines . . . were obtained largely in an eclectic effort to construct a system of coaling, cable and naval stations into an integrated trade route which could facilitate realization of America's one overriding ambition in the Pacific—the penetration and, ultimately, the domination of the fabled China market."[23] Thenceforth, the United States confronted Japan both as a competitor in China and as a classically imperialist power acquiring territory in the Pacific.

America's main acquisition was the Philippines. Particularly after Japan's take-over of Taiwan, developments in the Philippines touched closely on Tokyo's interests.

There had been upheavals in the Philippines in 1868, at the time of the Spanish revolution of that year, which coincided with the Meiji Restoration. Some Filipinos had looked to Japan for contact, but at the time the Japanese leaders were preoccupied with their own problems and with territories nearer home. When the revolution broke out in August 1896, many Filipino nationalists looked to Japan for concrete aid. The Japanese government decided on an official "hands off" policy,[24] but part of Japanese business, as well as groups in the military, pushed for a more active approach, and Japan, largely through Sun Yat-sen, became the main base for arms shipments to the Filipino insurgents.[25] With America then visibly joining the other Western imperialists, some Japanese saw the possibility of expansion based on anti-Western local nationalism. Some Japanese interests were prepared to back Asian nationalist movements across much of the spectrum: Sun Yat-sen was a relatively cautious republican; Emilio Aguinaldo, the Filipino leader, was initially a fairly radical nationalist.[26] The extremely bloody suppression by the Americans of the Filipino revolution helped to solidify anti-Western sentiment in Japan—even though Japan was at the same time itself engaged in suppressing the resistance movement on Taiwan.

American intervention in the Philippines and threats to Japan's position in China coincided almost exactly with the nadir of relations between Japanese and Americans in Hawaii. By 1896 there were 24,407 Japanese in Hawaii, the second largest ethnic group after the Hawaiians themselves.[27] In 1896 and 1897 the white settler group in power took two major anti-Japanese initiatives which effectively meant blocking further Japanese emigration to Hawaii, as well as stepping up economic discrimination against Japanese already there. The following year the United States unilaterally annexed Hawaii, and with it the largest "overseas" Japanese population.[28] Naturally, none of this increased Japanese affection for the United States.

THE COLLECTIVE IMPERIALIST INTERVENTION IN CHINA (1900)

From Japan's point of view, two events of momentous consequence occurred between the start of the Sino-Japanese War in 1894 and the end of the century: a group of European powers had shown that they could intervene with superior force to confiscate any unilateral gains by Japan; and the United States had crossed the Pacific in force, occupied Hawaii, Wake, Guam and the Philippines, and was laying siege to the China market.

It was in this *new* political situation that the Yi Ho Tuan movement burst onto the national scene in China.[29] By May 1900 it virtually controlled Peking and Tientsin. An international imperialist coalition was swiftly formed to suppress the movement and "relieve" the foreign legations in Peking—an objective accomplished in an extremely bloody manner. Kaiser Wilhelm delivered a harangue to his departing troops which well resumes the spirit of the enterprise: "Let all who fall into your hands be at your mercy. Just as the Huns a thousand years ago, under the leadership of Attila, gained a reputation by virtue of which they still live in historical tradition, so may the name of Germany become known in such a manner in China that no Chinese will ever again even dare to look askance at a German."[30] Britain, too, pushed intervention vigorously but, seriously hampered by its involvement in the Boer War, London needed the collaboration of other powers. Frightened of Russia, Britain turned to Japan, which "only after strong persuasion from Britain . . . finally agreed to send 8,000 men."[31] Under a Christian European commander, the Japanese provided almost half the total force of some 18,000 and, in the words of the official report of the U.S. War Department, "did about all the fighting."[32] The Japanese were the most, indeed the only, disciplined troops.

Japan's strategic concern throughout the intervention was to prevent Russia taking advantage of the situation. The Yi Ho Tuan had been especially active in Manchuria, where there had been full-scale fighting between them and the Russian army.[33] Russia defeated the Yi Ho Tuan and then occupied the whole of Manchuria. The two imperialists who objected most strongly to this were Britain and Japan.

THE ANGLO-JAPANESE ALLIANCE (1902)

Japan's decision to challenge Russia led directly to the alliance with Britain. Britain, too, actively sought Japan's friendship. Japan was particularly worried by the construction of the Trans-Siberian Railway. Britain was worried by the possibility of Russian encroachment in the Middle East and India. There was talk of a Russian railway through Persia down to Bandar Abbas. This common desire to limit Russia in Asia formed the basis for the alliance. Throughout the period up to the First World War, London went out of its way to conciliate Tokyo, even cancelling private British concessions in China to tranquillize the Japanese. The alliance emboldened Japan to take a more aggressive stance in Korea and launch the war against Russia in 1904. Indeed, although the alliance was never fully operationalized on the battlefield, there were tangible mutual benefits: Britain gave valuable cover and endorsement to the Japanese annexation of Korea, and the Japanese performed such chores for British imperialism as putting down a mutiny of Indian troops in Malaya during the First World War.[34]

THE RUSSO-JAPANESE WAR AND THE PORTSMOUTH SETTLEMENT

Even before the occupation of Manchuria in the 1900 intervention, Russia had skilfully used its railway plans to encroach on Chinese territory. Proceeding from the policy that Manchuria should be a Russian "zone of security" for the Amur River frontier, Witte, the Russian Minister of Finance, backed Russia loans to China after the Sino-Japanese War and organized a major Russian intervention through the Russo-Chinese Bank. China agreed to let Russia build a direct railway line across northern Manchuria to Vladivostok, the Chinese Eastern Railway (or CER). Two years later, in 1898, China agreed to let Russia build a branch line off the CER to connect up with Port Arthur and Talienwan, the South Manchuria Railway (SMR).[35]

Starting with the second Tonghak Rebellion in 1894, Russia also began to meddle in Korea. Japan managed to keep the upper hand and the Nishi-Rosen Convention of April 1898 recognized Japan's special interest in the Korean economy.[36] However, after Russia's utilization of the aftermath of the Yi Ho Tuan uprising to lodge its forces throughout Manchuria, Japan became even more alarmed. About New Year 1901 Japan and Russia began tentative and inconclusive discussions on delimiting their respective spheres of influence. Pressure built up in Japan for decisive action against Russia.

Russia reluctantly agreed to negotiate with China about the situation in

Manchuria, and the Manchurian Convention of April 8, 1902, committed Russia to pulling out in three stages within eighteen months.[37] Russia carried out the first stage, but not the second (April 1903) largely because of internal political shifts in Russia (the ouster of Witte by Bezobrazov and his group).[38] Russia, economically in a fairly weak position with the railway system not proving a commercial success, tried to extract further concessions from China (the "Seven Demands"). These were rejected in April 1903.

It was clear to both Russia and Japan that some solution would rapidly have to be found to the incompatibility of their respective positions. The two countries opened negotiations on August 12, 1903, and these continued right up to the outbreak of the war in February 1904. The Japanese side suggested Russia recognize that Korea was outside its sphere of interest in return for Japan recognizing that Manchuria was Russia's preserve.[39] When Russia turned down this proposal, war was inevitable.

Japan went into the war in a bad financial and military condition. The army calculated its chances of winning at no better than 50–50.[40] In fact, Japan did win the Battle of Mukden (February–March 1905) on land, and the battle in the Straits of Tsushima, in May 1905, when the Russian Baltic fleet was virtually destroyed.[41] Although Japan technically won the war militarily, it was exhausted by the effort, and the oligarchy adroitly switched to the political front at the crucial moment, after Mukden. By early June 1905 the war was terminated.

Of the war's many effects the most important was its demoralization of the Russian military and the undermining of the Tsarist regime. "Internal psychological epidemics may develop," wrote Witte nervously.[42] The Tsar had hoped that a victorious campaign would help to bolster his regime, but "Tsarism miscalculated—and the Russo-Japanese war led to the first Russian revolution."[43]

The victory also raised Japan's prestige in Asia enormously. This was the first time in centuries that a non-European country had defeated a Caucasian imperialist army.[44] Thus, although the *political* effects of the 1905 Russian Revolution were slight in Japan itself, the combination of this revolution (the fight against autocracy) and of Japan's victory (Asia defeats Europe) were colossal throughout the Third World, where the two moments could be psychologically and politically fused.[45] The number of Chinese students in Japan, the beneficiaries of a new policy promoted after the 1900 intervention, a mere 500 in 1902, 1,500 in 1904 and 8,000 in 1905, totalled 13,000 by 1906.[46] These students were to play a crucial role in laying the foundations of the Chinese Revolution. Much more consistent and ardent support for Sun Yat-sen was now forthcoming from Japan. A victorious revolution in China, it was calculated, would leave a big gap in Manchuria which Japan could move into without much competition from Russia.

Japan had attacked Russia first, with an unannounced assault on Port

Arthur, but both sides had been preparing for war, and Russia in fact rather preferred that Japan should fire the first shot. On the day that Japan had taken the final decision for war, Itō Hirobumi had taken the far-sighted step of sending Kaneko Kentarō, a Harvard-educated friend of Theodore Roosevelt, to the United States to promote good relations there during the war.[47] Both Russia and Japan agreed that the peace talks should be held in America, the first international diplomatic conference ever to be held there. With energetic assistance from Roosevelt, anxious to promote himself on the world scene, the conference was convened at Portsmouth, New Hampshire, in August 1905.[48] The Japanese side was led by Foreign Minister Komura; the Russian side by Witte, the more able negotiator, and with a power to act autonomously which enabled him to maximize Russia's recoupment at the talks.

Witte was not unaware of Japan's attenuated position. On the ground in Manchuria, Russia was now in a far superior military position. Consequently Japan quickly lowered its demands once it got to the peace table. Having originally sought the whole of the island of Sakhalin plus an indemnity from Russia, Japan finally settled for just the southern half of Sakhalin and no indemnity. The war and the Portsmouth agreement did, however, greatly strengthen Japan's position on the Asian mainland vis-à-vis Russia. Japan won Russia's acquiescence to a Japanese "protectorate" over Korea, and Russia transferred to Japan its "rights" on the Liaotung Peninsula and in southern Manchuria.

Roosevelt won a Nobel Prize for his organization of the talks. But in Japan the terms were heavily criticized in the press, and big demonstrations only initially inspired by hostility to the peace terms occurred against the government of Premier Katsura. The ruling oligarchy, however, was unanimous in its realistic backing of the terms.[49] Opposition to the peace terms as such was relatively short-lived, and the original Hibiya demonstration against Portsmouth swiftly turned into a proletarian uprising against the government and its domestic policies.

Japan soon signed a new Trade Agreement with Russia in 1907, to consolidate the two countries' holdings in China against American pressure. In the same year Japan negotiated the renewal of the Anglo-Japanese Alliance, thus "accepting the role of reinforcing British rule over India,"[50] and signed the Franco-Japanese Trade Agreement, in which it promised to respect French control over Indochina. Through all these steps Japan solidified its ties with the Western imperialists against the peoples of Asia.

THE SEIZURE OF KOREA

Japan's gradual seizure of Korea has become one of the most contentious political issues in the study of modern Japan. About the only fact not in dispute is that Japan did actually seize Korea.

Japan had four opponents in Korea: the Korean people, and three foreign powers, China, Russia and America. Japan eliminated its rivals one by one: China with its victory in 1895, Russia in 1905. With the signing of the Anglo-Japanese Alliance, Britain fully endorsed Japan's take-over. America also was an economic presence in Korea, and U.S. interests acquired the lease on the most valuable concession in Korea, the Ulsan gold mines, which they retained until 1939.

William W. Rockhill, an architect of Theodore Roosevelt's Asian policy, remarked, "Korea is the place . . . there you will see diplomacy in the raw; diplomacy without gloves, perfume or phrases."[51] In an exemplary case of U.S.-Japanese trade rivalry, the agile missionary, Horace N. Allen, who doubled as U.S. consul in Seoul, persuaded the Korean government to introduce the death penalty for any Japanese copying an American trade-mark. Likewise, when rickshawmen tried to combat American trolley bus interests, the Americans deployed squads of thugs and then installed a cinema at the out-of-town end of the trolley line.

Korea itself, of course, was no threat to Japan. But Tokyo argued that if Korea fell into the hands of one of its powerful rivals this would constitute a threat to Japan. Naturally, there was an autonomous imperialist dynamic to Japan's action, too. The Japanese government intrigued incessantly from the mid-1880s onwards, but its policy rested on a very insecure political and economic base. Japan was never able to fabricate a pro-Japanese Korean regime, nor to build up a foundation of economic interests which would give it automatic priority in Korea. By the turn of the century, Japan had come to play an important part in Korea's foreign trade, three-quarters of which was accounted for by Japanese tonnage.[52] But actual Japanese economic interests on the ground in Korea were relatively weak. Japan proceeded by eliminating its rivals militarily, and got British and American endorsement for doing what it wanted in Korea. Britain was Japan's ally against Russian interests, and the United States had swung its interest towards the race for concessions in China and the war in the Philippines.

Japan annexed Korea in 1910, a year after the assassination in Harbin by a Korean revolutionary of Itō Hirobumi, then Japan's resident-general of Korea. Itō, no anti-imperialist, had been pursuing a policy of gradual integration-assimilation, a merely tactical variant within the general line of annexation.[53] With his death, outright annexation was swiftly implemented by Tokyo.

There was very little protest from outside Korea.[54] But inside the country a major resistance movement developed, which twice exploded into major popular uprisings, in 1907–8 and 1919. Official Japanese figures, which probably are too low, give 17,779 Koreans killed and 3,706 wounded in the years 1906–10.[55] Gradually, through "search and destroy" operations, the resistance movement, led by the *Uibyong* or Righteous Army, was virtually liquidated. But in 1919, aided by the dual impetus of the Bolshevik Revolution and the "spirit" of Woodrow Wilson and Versailles, a new, originally peaceful upheaval took place. The Korean masses taking part in this anti-colonial movement were not aware that none of the great powers would come to their assistance. The Japanese army again intervened, killing at least 7,500 people.[56] Korea was not even discussed at the Washington Conference in 1921–22, which agreed to deal only with matters agreed on by all the participants.

WORLD WAR I AND THE TWENTY-ONE DEMANDS

Japan probably benefitted more from the 1914–18 war than any other country in the world. With all the Western powers tied down in Europe, Japan had a virtually free hand in China. And with the possibility of taking sides without having to make much effort, Japan had its first chance to grab a bit of European-held territory. It wisely chose Germany's.

It has been argued that the situation in 1914–15 parallels in some ways that in the late 1930s: that Japan *over*-accelerated carefully prepared plans when presented with the attractive spectacle of the Western imperialists ensnared in war in Europe.[57] On the contrary, Japan moved with care and skill. First it identified the right enemy, Germany, and promptly declared war on it (August 23, 1914). It then mooted the idea of sending an expeditionary force to help its allies, but wisely sent only a token force to participate in anti-submarine naval action in the Mediterranean, apart from convoying some British Empire troops through the Indian Ocean. Instead, it seized the German islands in the Pacific north of the Equator and Germany's possessions in Shantung. Japan took over Germany's trading posts in China. German prisoners of war were transported to Japan and put to work making beer (the origin of Asahi beer). Munitions sales, particularly to Russia, boomed, as did sales of naval and transportation equipment.

In spite of this easy success, however, Japan's position in China was riddled with weaknesses. As in Korea, Japan was economically not in a position to impose itself without using (or threatening) governmental-military power. The Twenty-one Demands reflected this structural weakness.

The background to the Demands is complex, but essentially Japan was concerned that the leases on its Manchurian possessions had only a relatively short time to run. The lease on the Kwantung territory (acquired from Russia), including Port Arthur and Dairen, was due to expire in 1923, at which date Japan was also scheduled to sell back to China the Antung Railway. The resale of the South Manchuria Railway was due to be completed by 1940. Acquisition of Germany's Shantung holding was especially useful to Japan since it had a very long lease and, it was thought, could be used as a bargaining counter to get the Manchurian leases extended. Consolidating its position in Manchuria also involved negotiations with Russia, which had been going on since the 1907 agreement in the form of a number of secret agreements.[58] Japan, however, was also anxious on this score, since Russia had been making better progress at incorporating its areas of Manchuria than Japan had.

In January 1915, only a few months after Japan had occupied Shantung, China requested all foreign troops to withdraw from its soil. Within days Japan presented to the Chinese government its Twenty-one Demands. These were in five groups. The main Japanese demands were exclusive and expanded privileges in Shantung; the Manchurian leases to be extended to ninety-nine years plus rights of land ownership; rights to mining and railway enterprises in South Manchuria and eastern Inner Mongolia; joint ownership of the Hanyehping Iron Co. on the Yangtse plus exclusive rights to the iron deposits near Hankow; a ban on China ceding any harbour or island along its coast. The fifth group of demands was for further exclusive rights for Japan, including joint administration of the police force, further railway rights and a pledge from China that it would purchase at least half its munitions from Japan.[59]

The Chinese government under Yuan Shih-k'ai naturally resisted the Japanese ultimatum, and some of Japan's Western allies also showed some concern about the publicly known demands. After several months of negotiation, Japan dropped the fifth group of seven exclusive demands, and China acceded. In May 1915 the two countries signed a treaty under which Japan got most of what it had demanded. The upshot of the Twenty-one Demands was to give Japan an absolutely dominant position in China. As well as crippling China, the move also enabled Japan to recover some of the advantages which America had been squeezing it out of, as in the Root-Takahira Agreement of 1908. Second only to the Chinese, the Americans were extremely angered by the Twenty-one Demands. Reinsch, the U.S. Minister at Peking, lamented that they "deeply affected American prospects and enterprise in China."[60]

In fact during the First World War the United States made important gains in China, mainly in oil, railways and dockyards.[61] These American gains helped push Japan toward solidifying its relationship with Russia to ensure itself against later trouble in the Manchuria area. Yamagata was particularly keen to cement Japan's position by balancing an alliance with Russia against Japan's alliance with Britain.[62] The Russo-Japanese Alliance, signed in July 1916, had two parts: a public part which reaffirmed the two countries' mutual support for their imperialist positions in the Far East; and a secret section which stated their joint intention to prevent China falling under the domination of any third power. The alliance was to remain operative so long as the Anglo-Japanese Alliance was in force.

In order further to consolidate its postwar position, Japan signed secret agreements with four of the European imperialist countries (Britain, France, Russia and Italy) during February and March 1917. These agreements greatly conditioned the discussions concerning China at the Versailles Conference. China declared war on the Central Powers in August 1917, and came to Versailles expecting to be given a fair hearing. The Western imperialists, however, declined to support China against Japan, and Japan emerged from Versailles with its China gains undented. This had been the aim of its careful diplomatic policy towards the end of the war, a policy especially remarkable in the light of the fact that much of the Japanese military had for some time thought that Germany would win the war. Japan also acquired America's endorsement of its advances in China, through the Lansing-Ishii agreement (technically only an "exchange of notes") in November 1917. Though America had been disconcerted by Japan's gains in China, two factors seem to have brought about a change in Washington's position—America's entry into the First World War, in which all her allies had signed agreements with Japan, itself formally an ally; and the Bolshevik Revolution, which acted as a powerful stimulant to imperialist unity. Japan had chosen a good moment. At the end of the war the horizon looked clear. Japan had chosen the winning side; it had kept its alliance with Britain; Russia was hardly a threat in Manchuria any longer; Japan had concentrated on a declining imperialist power (Germany) and a tottering colonized empire (China), now in a state of semi-disintegration. Its position in East Asia looked solid.

THE INTERVENTION IN SIBERIA

The Bolshevik Revolution detonated class fear and hatred throughout the bourgeoisies and aristocracies of the world, and an international capitalist coalition was swiftly formed to invade Russia to try to overthrow the Bolsheviks. Japan joined this invasion to obtain material advantages for itself while trying to keep others' to a minimum, and to consolidate its position as a member of the imperialist group, as it had done in the 1900 intervention in China. Tokyo also sought to counter local revolutionary activity on the Asian mainland, both in Russia and among the nascent revolutionary movements in Mongolia, China and Korea, whose participants were active throughout the area.[63]

The first suggestion from outside Japan that the Japanese might take part in an allied counter-revolutionary intervention probably came from Marshal Foch at the Inter-Allied Conference in Paris (November 29 to December 3, 1917).[64] Utilizing the bogus danger of a German breakthrough to Vladivostok,[65] Foch suggested a joint American-Japanese expedition land at Vladivostok and occupy the Trans-Siberian right through via Harbin to Moscow. At the same time various Japanese groups, including the army and the Foreign Ministry, were making their own plans. Japan sent warships to Vladivostok as early as December 1917. Motono, the Japanese Foreign Minister, presented his case for intervention in very much the same terms as Foch, painting a vision of the Siberian coast occupied by Germans. When Gotō Shimpei moved into the Foreign Ministry on April 23, 1918, he gave a determined shove to the interventionist movement, convinced that the United States was about to make a major move into China as well as Siberia.

Yet in early 1918 the Japanese ruling group was not unanimous about intervening, and it was insistent pressure from the United States which forged a united front.[66] President Wilson wanted Japanese involvement in the operation, but only in a subordinate position. The Japanese government agreed to take part on America's terms, alongside contingents from the French and British Empires (largely Vietnamese and Indian troops, respectively) and the United States. However, once lodged in Siberia, the Japanese built up their forces far beyond the parity which had originally been agreed, eventually reaching the total of 72,000 men, or eight times the total of the second largest force, the American, which had just over 9,000 men.

By 1919 Washington was having second thoughts. The war against Germany was over, and the Allied intervention in European Russia was not going well. There was considerable opposition in America and among American troops in Siberia to the operation. Wilson told Churchill at the Paris Conference that "Conscripts could not be sent and volunteers probably could not be obtained."[67] In this situation, the United States switched to a policy of advocating *collective* withdrawal and pressured Japan to pull out. Wilson put an embargo on cotton sales to Japan and on purchases of silk from Japan, and Washington threatened a total blockade and announced its intention of calling a special Conference in Washington to deal with Japan.[68] Understandably, there was some reluctance in Tokyo about withdrawing. And those who favoured staying could easily point to the opportunist line being laid down by Washington.[69] In addition, Japanese interventionists knew about the poor state of the U.S. army and America's likely withdrawal. On the strength of a Japanese promise to pull out, the United States troops left Siberia in 1920. A Japanese band playing "Hard Times Come Again No More" saw them off from Vladivostok.

The Japanese stayed in Siberia until 1922, and on northern Sakhalin until 1925. Although Japan failed to utilize its occupation to lay down any coherent economic policy in Siberia,[70] it continued to prop up counter-revolution in Vladivostok and other centres under its control right to the end. With Japan's withdrawal, the counter-revolution in Siberia collapsed completely. The Far Eastern Republic, the Soviet buffer state, also came to a natural end when the Japanese left the mainland. Japan held onto Sakhalin, allegedly as "compensation" for the deaths of some Japanese at the town of Nikolayevsk some years earlier.[71] Japan returned northern Sakhalin at the time of the general agreement with the Soviet government in 1925. It retained economic concessions there until 1944.[72]

The expedition was a costly failure for Japan. Tokyo made an enemy out of the new Soviet regime. The intervention had contributed to such enormous upheavals as the 1918 rice riots. It was extremely expensive, costing about ¥900 million, while the total of Japanese loans to the Tsarist and Kerensky governments came to a mere ¥240 million.[73] Apart from the concessions in northern Sakhalin, Tokyo acquired nothing in Siberia and had not markedly improved its position in Manchuria either. The new Soviet government now controlled the Chinese Eastern Railway.

THE VERSAILLES AND WASHINGTON CONFERENCES

The focus of Versailles was on Europe;[74] only two issues discussed— China and racial equality—involved the East. At the time Japan was the ally of America, Britain and France in the Siberian invasion. Its position in China was covered by the Lansing-Ishii agreement. The Chinese, like the Koreans, were under the impression that the Americans meant what they said when they talked about every nation's right to independence and non-interference from others, and asked the Conference to refuse endorsement of Japan's gains. In the negotiations a compromise was reached verbally about Shantung and Tsingtao, but this emerged in a different form in Articles 156 and 157. China protested, but all the other powers signed.

This "success" was soon to boomerang on Japan. Just as in Korea the Versailles Conference had raised hopes, already high as a result of the Russian Revolution, so in China the Western imperialists' refusal to lift a finger to safeguard the interests of the Chinese people contributed to a chain reaction which ultimately led to revolutions in both countries. China's May 4 Movement follows immediately after Korea's March 1 Movement.

The second key issue at Versailles was race. Japan formally tried to get a declaration of racial equality written into the Versailles Treaty. The Japanese won a clear majority in a straight vote, but Woodrow Wilson, as chairman, ruled it out on the grounds that it was not unanimous. In fact Japan was opposed by a solid phalanx of the dominant Anglo-Saxons. The most prominent leader of the racist group was Hughes of Australia, eagerly seconded by Cecil and Balfour of Britain. The Japanese move was particularly threatening to Wilson, as its main purpose was to attack the racist American laws blocking Japanese immigration.[75] In addition, the Americans felt uneasy about the already large Japanese presence in Hawaii.[76] Wilson was certainly less rabid than such Californian pressure groups as the Sons of the Golden West and the American Legion—and Gompers's Federation of Labor.[77] And the Japanese certainly did not stand for racial equality (v. their oppression of the Koreans). What Japan wanted was the free movement of population, especially into colonies. The Japanese government could, of course, easily argue that the white imperialists were racists.

It was widely felt in the West, particularly in America, that Japan had gained too much ground during the World War. This feeling combined with anti-Bolshevism and a more general desire to redefine the imperialist implantation in Pacific Asia to bring about the Washington Conference, held in the Washington Exchange from November 21, 1921 to February 6, 1922. The United States, Britain, France, Italy, Belgium, Holland, Portugal, China and Japan were represented. Russia was not invited because it was not recognized by the United States, and the delegation from the Far Eastern Republic was refused admittance.

Within its overall strategic purpose, which was counter-revolutionary consolidation,[78] the momentum of the Conference was towards liquidating old-style or particularist ventures (hence renewed pressure on Japan to leave Siberia, and the termination of the Anglo-Japanese Alliance). In particular, America's main interest was in keeping the "Open Door" in China.

The first important step was to annul the Anglo-Japanese Alliance through a four-power Pacific Treaty, signed by the United States, Britain, France and Japan on December 13, 1921 (this also recognized each others' possessions in the Pacific). The Conference then turned its attention to China: by the Shantung Treaty (February 4, 1922) Japan was obliged to return Kiaochow to China. Two Nine-Power Treaties of February 6 recognized (with qualifications) the territorial and political independence of China. By these arrangements the United States substantially improved its position at the expense of its capitalist rivals.[79]

The Naval Treaty of the same date, February 6, 1922, attempted to settle inter-imperialist contradictions on the military front by fixing a *ratio* for capital warships (5:5:3—for the United States, Britain and Japan, respectively). By this treaty Japan was obliged to accept, on paper, a permanently subordinate position vis-à-vis the Anglo-Saxons. In fact, because of other conditions (including American non-fortification in the western Pacific), the arrangement gave Japan absolute superiority in the area.[80]

The Conference was an event of major importance. It was the only serious attempt in the first half of the century to settle peacefully inter-imperialist contradictions in the Pacific and East Asia. But, though strategically counter-revolutionary, and in spite of the *de facto* advantages of the Naval Treaty for Japan, the Conference was tactically an anti-Japanese operation devoted to recouping the white imperialists' losses during the war. As one observer has put it, Washington "became an international enquiry probing into Japan's activities on the Chinese continent during the world war."[81] In turn, it helped set up new contradictions which, in part, led to the Pacific War.[82]

THE NATURE OF EARLY JAPANESE IMPERIALISM

Japan wants to become a first-rate imperialist robber, but it lacks capital, it lacks industrial possibilities, it lacks full-blooded capitalist maturity and overmaturity.[83]

G. Safarov, 1933

Japanese imperialism reflects simultaneously both the world context in which it emerged, a context of aggressive white expansionism, and the domestic class struggle. A wealth of evidence from the middle of the nineteenth century shows that the ruling class was terrified that the breaking of Japan's cocoon would detonate uncontrollable class conflict and that the peasantry would turn against their rulers. Nationalism was rapidly promoted by the new Meiji leaders as a means to muffle the class struggle. This was no ordinary "patriotism" or even chauvinism, but a sizeable state-directed movement, conducted with unflagging diligence, to force the entire population to think and act in "national" terms both domestically and abroad. Very soon, as the Hibiya riots showed, imperialism had sunk real roots in Japan.

It is equally important to stress that Japanese imperialism was formed ideologically by the example of the advanced imperialist Western nations, and shaped by the context of active imperialist expansion in the Far East at the end of the nineteenth and the beginning of the twentieth centuries. Most Japanese who wished to "modernize" the country along Western lines accepted the idea of imperialism; Fukuzawa and Itagaki are the clearest exponents of "enlightened" supporters of this trend.[84] Moves outside Japan were justified as necessary to Japan's independence vis-à-vis the West. And when Japan did engage in colonialism, it was often complimented and flattered.[85] The Triple Intervention and the Washington Conference were only adjustments by colleagues who felt Japan had gone slightly too far.

Japan, however, was too backward and poor to engage in full-scale colonialism on equal terms with the great powers. This drove the regime in two directions: heavy borrowing abroad to pay for colonialism, and military pressure to retain Japan's privileges. Japanese capitalism was already "capitalism without capital"[86] and Japanese imperialism was, *a fortiori,* imperialism without capital. This situation was aggravated by the high level of domestic exploitation. Minimal purchasing power at home pushed Japanese capitalism (highly concentrated from the start) into a search for markets abroad. The government sponsored the creation of imperialistic banks. These, however, were permanently short of funds and as a result had to borrow abroad *for use abroad:* 44 per cent of all money borrowed abroad by Japan in this period was used on the continent of Asia.[87] Yet Japan was still unable to compete on equal terms, and therefore applied political pressure on China to borrow European money from Japanese government banks at high interest. This pressure could not be maintained without military pressure, which in turn necessitated ever-increasing expenditure. This military pressure irritated Western imperialists and the expenditure for it irritated sectors of the Japanese bourgeoisie—hence the periodic revolts in the Diet against the budget.[88] Heavier taxes irritated the masses. For a time the bourgeoisie tried to use the pressure of the masses against the military, but then, realizing that its own interests lay with the military, joined with them in expansionism.

Another important aspect of Japanese imperialism is the connection between Japanese industrialization and the need for raw materials. The lack of raw materials in Japan and the pressure applied against Japan by the unequal treaties led to the delay in the development of a heavy industrial base. But as the unequal treaties were revised and Japan engaged in expansion, a heavy industrial base became a vital necessity, particularly to cope with the large military building programme. Clearly, Japan could not continue to have its navy built in England. Initially, some Japanese thought they could gain access to raw materials in other parts of Asia by riding the revolutionary national liberation movement against the West. Business interests, and coal mining concerns in particular, helped to bankroll some of the Asian revolutions against European and American colonialism (e.g., in the Philippines).[89] Much the same policy was essayed in China, by subsidizing Sun Yat-sen. But the ineffectiveness of this anti-Western line was exemplified by the relationship between the Japanese steel industry centered on Yawata, and the Chinese iron ore mines at Tayeh.[90] In 1915 Japan imposed the Twenty-one Demands on China to enforce the commercial and territorial conditions which would enable the Japanese iron and steel industry uninterrupted production. Having failed to achieve their aim through the Chinese revolutionary movement (in this case the bourgeois republicanism of Sun), Japan's business leaders felt obliged to apply diplomatic force to ensure the supply of raw materials. The Yawata-Tayeh connection is paradigmatic.

This does not, of course, explain all of Japan's colonial expansion. The initial moves in the seizure of Korea, for example, were largely *pre*-industrial.[91] Subsequently, Korea became an important market for Japan's cotton textile products. The war against China led to a big increase in Japan's military presence. The Hibiya riots led the government to secure Korea (and Manchuria) in late 1905, and the assassination of Itō in 1909 was utilized to justify formal acquisition in 1910. Later, Korea, already an important source of gold from mines controlled by Americans, became a major source of rice, like Taiwan. Sakhalin and Manchuria were acquired for their raw materials, justified by various geo-political rationalizations, and, in the case of Manchuria, partly as a territory for emigration. What needs to be grasped is the connection between the structure of Japanese industrialization and imperialism—the desire to control sources of raw materials and to secure markets; the relationship between expansion *against* the West and expansion in agreement with the West; the fusion in popular consciousness of national prosperity with imperialism; the coincidence of interests between the military and heavy industry.

It has been argued that Japan in many ways is comparable to pre-1905 Russia, and therefore was driven to seek development "in width," through expansion, rather than "in depth."[92] Leaving aside both the pressure of other imperialisms and the search for raw materials, the nature of the kind of development fostered internally by the ruling bloc precluded any great increase in consumer purchasing power. Politically, the Meiji oligarchs were content with a rural and rural-based policy. The compromise between the feudal lords and the bourgeoisie did not allow the latter to destroy the medieval structure of agriculture. Colonization was one way to reduce the contradictions between industry and the preservation of feudal relics in the economy as a whole—hence development "in width" was politically more attractive than development "in depth." The precise location of Japan in the world economy also made it advantageous to keep a very high rate of exploitation at home. This became such an axiom of ruling-class policy that it was not questioned, except by the exploited masses themselves, until the 1930s, when elements in the army began to challenge it. But the high rate of exploitation meant Japan did not develop a large domestic consumer goods market: consumer goods were manufactured mainly for export, and heavy industry was geared primarily towards military needs. The unequal treaties in themselves would have determined a certain kind of economic evolution; but it would be unwise to lose sight of the implication of the Meiji political compromise.

4.
Politics from the Constitution to the Washington Conference (1890–1922)[1]

By 1890 the political system on which so much care and caution had been lavished was formally rounded off with the establishment of a Constitution and the opening of a Diet. It had two related objectives: internally, to ensure the continuation of ruling class power within the framework of a highly restricted oligarchy; externally, to insert Japan as an equal into the world imperialist system. The central theme of the period is the shaking out and co-ordination of the political system, integrating the contesting instances of power, in the age of imperialism.

THE SYSTEM FORMALIZED BY THE CONSTITUTION

The Constitution of 1889, according to Itō Hirobumi, "sounded the death-knell of reactionary intrigue."[2] Nothing could be further from the truth. The Constitution was designed to consolidate the Emperor's position, to prepare the way for a Diet representing just over 1 per cent of the population, and to provide a façade-cum-framework for the self-contained and self-justifying regime constructed by Itō and his colleagues.[3]

The imperial institution had been considerably strengthened in the late 1880s. A peerage had been created as a prop to the ruling group; the cabinet had been instituted prior to the Diet; and the elections to the Diet were based on a minuscule franchise. Underpinning these different instances were the bureaucracy and the educational system already being crafted and implemented before the 1890 Rescript was issued.

The only possible discordant factors were the political parties and the military. Through active imperialism both of these were eventually, to a large extent, integrated.

THE PROCESS OF INTEGRATION

The Parties

The main instance of protest was originally the political party. The ruling group at first rejected the concept of party, which did not enter into its conception of a political system centred on the Emperor. Then, gradually, the regime took over the party movement in stages. Synchronous with this, the bureaucracy was strengthened and its power over the government increased until ultimately, with the imbrication of government and party, there was a unified government-party-bureaucracy ensemble. On the whole, the system functioned quite efficiently for the oligarchs. It was almost completely irresponsible—cabinets with Diet majorities however large could be easily torpedoed by either the Emperor or the bureaucracy; elections could be called at whim and the entire apparatus of state violence applied in the regime's favour; the masses' possibilities of intervention were minimal. In varying crises, such as 1893, 1908 and 1918, the system showed it could produce pseudo-alternatives with a minimum of upheaval.

After the original Meiji coalition broke up in 1873, the first opposition to the regime among the propertied classes formed round Itagaki Taisuke.[4] On the question of invading Korea, Itagaki sided with Saigō of Satsuma, but after he left the government broke with Saigō and came to represent, roughly, the "outs." However, Itagaki had an extremely restricted view of the franchise right from the start (not to mention his attitude to the Korean people)—only samurai, wealthy farmers and merchants ought, he felt, to qualify for the vote (what one militarist called "Upper Class Democracy").[5]

The position of any political grouping outside the government had already been made difficult in advance by earlier reforms which ruled out the idea of any separation of power in favour of centralized bureaucratic control.[6] The 1870s saw peasant uprisings pass their peak, and a sequence of skirmishes within the ruling clique in which the oppressed classes were ignored. Then in 1881 came the crises which culminated in the departure of Ōkuma from the government and the announcement of a Constitution and Diet. The Hokkaido land scandal of 1881 in particular galvanized opposition forces into action, but already the main differences were ones of power: factions formed along non-ideological lines—for example, Ōkuma (from Hizen) was tied in with Mitsubishi, as was Fukuzawa, while Itō (from Chōshū) lined up with Mitsui.[7]

In 1881 the Jiyūtō was founded, regrouping many elements from an earlier organization, the Aikoku Kōtō.[8] The Jiyūtō, the first real political party in Japan, was based mainly on rural interests. The two key groups behind it were the upper landowning class and the poor peasantry. Although the party was little more than a focus for a number of local groups, a mere collection of factions, it contributed considerably to the consolidation of the power of the landlord class. The Jiyūtō was founded almost contemporaneously with the Emperor's commitment to "constitutional" government. This appeared to provide the parties with a loophole into the system, and acted as a brake on the widely held sentiment that an all-out attack was needed on the whole system as such.[9]

The following year Ōkuma established another party, the Rikken Kaishintō, whose nucleus was former bureaucrats who had left the government with him in 1881. The Kaishintō, backed by urban capitalist interests headed by Mitsubishi, was generally more conservative than the Jiyūtō.[10] Although it had urban industrial backing, the Kaishintō, like the Jiyūtō, was essentially a vehicle for the opinion of groups of rich landlords. The bourgeoisie, in fact, did not begin to organize its class interests coherently until after a balance of power had already been arrived at involving the early (landlord-led) parties, the military and the bureaucracy. Initially, the bourgeoisie advanced its interests through the bureaucracy in a rather non-assertive way. Although elements of big business backed both early parties, businessmen in general seemed less interested than landlords in political power. The integration of landlord-dominated political parties into the "Emperor-system" at a time when the bourgeoisie had not organized its own class interests was an important factor giving the whole parliamentary process in Japan a highly chauvinistic and backward orientation. A further factor, of course, was that landlord domination within the more "progressive" of the parties, the Jiyūtō, effectively prevented the mass of poor peasants articulating and operationalizing their position within it. The Jiyūtō contained a lot of small farmers at the local level, but it never pushed as a party for radical reforms in agriculture. Eventually, the party broke up over peasant discontent with its landlord-imposed policies, although the demise of the organization did not effectively weaken the landlord grip on political power.[11]

The new "constitutional" order greatly disadvantaged the parties; "the constitutional order established in 1889 was a restrictive one for the parties, with the legislative and administrative processes clearly beyond their control."[12] The House of Peers was not elected and could not be dissolved; the Privy Council was mainly made up of imperial appointees; the bureaucracy, both civil and military, was out of reach of the parties; the Lower House, based on a minute franchise, did not control the cabinet— and the premier was chosen by the Emperor on the advice of the genrō, or "elder statesmen," a small extra-constitutional group who by their very position tended to shun party activity.

In addition, a much more fundamental policy had been pushed by Marshal Yamagata, in particular, to undercut the organization of opposition by instituting a Prussian-style system of local government. Along with conscription, this was designed to knock away the ground from under the government's opponents by constructing the kind of intermediate institutions which would ensure safe control from above while satisfying Japanese ideology about "participation" and "the happy family." It was Yamagata's commitment to this method of demobilizing opposition that explains his otherwise apparently curious rearguard hostility to Itō's later attempts to integrate the parties into the existing bureaucratic-parliamentary system.[13]

With all these instruments ready to hand, the ruling group probably felt it had little to worry about when the first Diet convened. Yet the principal problem remained the economy, especially the unequal treaties. These became the key issue on which opposition to the government could be galvanized.[14] The unequal treaties provided perfect terrain for all sectors of opposition opinion to merge. Hostility to *Western* imperialism was mixed up with genuine internationalist anti-imperialism, and parts of the "left" and "right" found it easy to collaborate, as they had done in 1873.[15]

When the first Diet convened, the parties immediately attacked the government's budget, particularly over the high payments to the bureaucracy. These attacks were met by a witheringly arrogant speech from Yamagata, who informed the parties that they should mind their own business and not interfere with things like the budget. The government then dissolved the Diet and, when the opposition continued to attack the new cabinet in the second Diet, repeated the dissolution manoeuvre. This second dissolution was followed by an election campaign—"the most brutal in Japanese history"[16]—in which murder and bribery were extensively employed. The third Diet which emerged from these elections soon passed a vote of no-confidence in the government, and a similar vote was passed by the House of Peers. Yet, even in these circumstances, the government refused to resign. An attempt to call in the Emperor was defeated by three votes "because of the gravity of troubling the Emperor's mind."[17] It became obvious that the system was not functioning quite as hoped.

At this point Itō began a sustained manoeuvre to integrate the discordant elements. His first (secret) suggestion was that the Emperor issue a Rescript "admonishing the people." Then he told the Emperor directly that the best solution would be to set up a government party (early 1892). Itō's plan was to install a government party united with the throne to reduce "instability," but the move was premature.[18]

Although apparently unsuccessful, Itō had in fact made the Meiji leaders consider the idea of integrating the parties into the system and of tying them up with the Emperor. And so it was that in 1893, when Itō formed a new cabinet, he was able to involve the Emperor directly in a political dispute, which was solved by an imperial appeal for national unity in the interests of imperialism (the dispute had been over warship construction estimates). A party dispute with the cabinet and the bureaucracy, located in the Diet, was solved by an Imperial Rescript.[19]

This was in many ways an exemplary episode, sharply illuminating the limits of party action in the face of what was conceived of as the "national" interest. The military forces, whose leaders were frequently in top government posts, pushed relentlessly for increases in the army and navy budgets.[20] The parties, representing civilian interests hostile to increased taxation, naturally tended to oppose the escalating military appropriations. Fights between the parties and the government over the military budget became a feature of the early Diet.

This early period, up to the war with China, was one of trying out the system and floating trial balloons such as a government party and the more direct involvement of the Emperor—both with the purpose of creating a more refined version of the system, still apparently hinged on the Diet, but *de facto* simply using the Diet as a tool. Itō was searching for more authority and for more exible and functional intermediate instruments.

The Sino-Japanese War of 1894–95 proved a windfall. The war was extremely popular in Japan. Japan's swift victory, apparently almost painless, coming so shortly after the successful negotiations on the unequal treaties, had an electrifying effect. The successful war was disastrous to the popular rights movement, and entrenched nationalist-imperialist sentiment.[21] From 1895 only the socialist forces could offer any opposition to the regime.

Perhaps the most important consequence of the war was not the fact that the parties capitulated to the government, but that the bureaucracy began to develop a more positive attitude to the political parties. During the period 1895–1900 the landlord-dominated parties and the bureaucracy worked out a new, integrated relationship.[22] This process was not without contradictions, expressed in apparent zigzags and government crises, but by 1900 Itō Hirobumi had successfully manoeuvred to have himself invited to become leader of the main political party, the Kenseitō, in place of Itagaki.[23] Itō insisted on a number of changes, and the new name of the organization—Friends of Constitutional Government Association—is a fair index of its role and orientation. This marked the culmination of Itō's programme: "it reflected adjustment by a party to the constitutional order . . . it meant acceptance of gradual expansion within the system."[24] In other words, it meant the victory of the system over the parties, for what they were worth.

The Military

In domestic politics the military, and particularly the army, headed by Marshal Yamagata, had been pursuing a rather different path. Yamagata's main objective was to consolidate bureaucratic power and keep as much as possible of the central government system out of the reach of the parties and the Diet. From the start of the Meiji period, the military was at the centre of the state and bureaucratic apparatus. Although it had its own specific autonomy, it was not separate from the "political."[25] Indeed, military men played a very important role in Japanese cabinets from the inauguration of the cabinet system in 1885 to the surrender in 1945: fifteen of the thirty Prime Ministers during this period were military leaders, as were many Home and Foreign Ministers, and the military portfolios were always held by ranking officers.[26]

Yamagata continued to oppose Itō's method of coping with opposition throughout the 1890s, and when Yamagata got into power after toppling the Ōkuma-Itagaki cabinet in 1898 he hastened to put through two measures, one of which profoundly affected the future of Japanese political life. The first put all official positions except the premiership and cabinet posts (ministers), but including vice-ministers, under the civil service examination and thus took patronage out of the reach of the parties, until this was reversed in 1913.[27]

The second bill gave the armed forces veto powers over the military ministers in the cabinet. Thus even though a government could line up a majority in the Diet, the bureaucracy and elsewhere, it would be utterly hamstrung without military support. It could not even take office. In 1913 Admiral Yamamoto, then Prime Minister (representing *anti*-army forces), managed to get this modified to allow *retired* generals and admirals to serve, but this had little effect, as retired officers lacked the power needed to control the armed forces.[28]

The beginning of the century saw power oscillating at the summit between Yamagata's stand-in, General Katsura, and Itō's stand-in, Prince Saionji.[29] After Itō's withdrawal in 1901, and his decision to throw the Seiyūkai party behind Katsura's policy in 1902, the struggle was basically an anachronism. On the one hand, neither the Diet nor the parties established their autonomous legitimacy. On the other hand, imperialism and the economic expansion connected with it provided the terrain for the new bourgeois forces to find a satisfactory compromise with both the military and the pre-bourgeois political forces enshrined in the Constitution.

INTEGRATION PERFECTED: BUREAUCRACY, IDEOLOGY AND IMPERIALISM

Thus, while the visible skirmishing was between two cliques, the Itō-Saionji group and the Yamagata-Katsura group, the two underlying trends of the period were the drive to fuse the parties and the bureaucracy internally and the drive to build a co-ordinated political ruling group integrating both the military and the bourgeoisie on the basis of imperialist expansion.

In this light, the intricate political moves up until just after the end of the

First World War can be summarized. Katsura held power after Itō's resignation (in 1901) until he was toppled by the demonstrations after the Portsmouth Treaty. Saionji took over office, but had to resign two months later because of hostility from the bureaucracy. The office of Prime Minister moved between the two groups for several years. In 1912 Saionji was ousted once again, for blocking the army's budget requests, and was replaced by a navy figure, ex-Admiral Yamamoto. At this point Katsura decided that the discordance associated with government had gone on long enough, and capitulated to the idea of a government party. The establishment of the Rikken Dōshikai in 1913 marks the complete conversion of all the ruling elements to Itō's basic plan.

In 1913 the fundamental relationship between the bureaucracy and the parties was also definitively resolved. The chief agent in this was Hara Kei (Takashi), a political figure who had from the start committed himself to merging bureaucracy and the parties. Hara, who cultivated a "commoner" image, was no democrat. In essence, his position was close to Katsura's. To both "a political party was no more than a device to run the Diet smoothly,"[30] though Hara's way of doing this was to try and draw the ruling cliques towards the parties, and thus overcome the House of Peers, while Katsura wanted to try and draw the parties towards the ruling cliques, and thus overcome the Lower House.[31] In 1911 Hara and the party men floated the idea of changing the 1899 law channeling top jobs via the civil service examination. They proposed a reform opening top jobs to "free appointment" (to cover vice-ministers, chief secretaries, ministry councillors, etc.). Yamagata naturally opposed the reform, as did the Privy Council, but in 1913 it went through.

The reform forced leading bureaucrats to join parties. Within three months seven bureaucrats of vice-ministerial rank had joined the Seiyūkai, and the possibility of cadres being drafted from outside put the pressure on the lower echelons to join as well. In fact, the reform did not cause a large infiltration of party men into the top ranks of the civil service, but rather pushed the top civil servants into joining the parties. With the virtually complete imbrication of bureaucracy and parties, the main elements of the Japanese political system were in place.

This process took place against a background of enormous domestic changes and considerable overseas action by the Japanese state. Industrialization brought about major changes in both civil and military life. Throughout the nineteenth century the agrarian propertied groups maintained their pre-eminent position in the political parties, but as Japan began to develop big industries, located predominantly in urban areas, the new bourgeoisie began to fight for more political power. After 1900, immediately after the bureaucracy and the landlord-dominated parties had worked out the balance of power between them, the big and middle bourgeoisie began to get active in the parties, particularly in the Seiyūkai, led by Itō. Big businesses like Mitsui and Mitsubishi pushed for stronger political representation, especially after the victory against China. The relationship between Japan's nascent iron and steel industry and the location of the required raw materials exemplifies this new situation. While Itō was premier, the Yawata works were begun, and it was Itō's friend, Inoue Kaoru, closely linked with Mitsui, who was the main middleman in the operation.[32] Itō's agreement to take over the Seiyūkai in 1900 was a decisive moment of integration, occurring in the same year as the collective imperialist intervention in China which united behind it all sectors of the old ruling group and the new bourgeoisie.

Japan's accelerated overseas activity after 1894 worked as a powerful cement on national integration. Ever since the irruption of the Western powers in the middle of the nineteenth century, economic enterprise had been validated by reference to the "national" interest. The role of the military was seen, by both the armed forces themselves and the civilian rulers, in essentially the same terms. The strategic security of the nation was a concept which covered both military and business activities.

An all-embracing ideological apparatus was gradually developed to extend the early Meiji "familial" ideology of Emperor-loyalty (essentially a *domestic* project) to the wider area of overseas expansion by equating Emperor-loyalty with patriotism. This extension was one of the main elements in a series of textbooks issued by the Ministry of Education in 1910 which revised the teaching of ethics, history and language, tightening up the whole system.[33]

Interestingly, the full development of the concept of "patriotism" accompanied Japan's aggression against its neighbours, rather than the defence of its own shores. Similar ideological displacements were operated in other fields. The most striking of these was the development of the "idea" of the businessman as warrior.[34] This involved quite a sharp rupture with the Tokugawa world: the Meiji entrepreneur was portrayed as a member of a totally different species. Here the key element, paralleling the state's success in "elevating" the family system to a national level, was to claim that Meiji businessmen were serving the nation, whereas their predecessors had been operating with motives of personal greed. It is indisputable that this ideological subterfuge was (and still is) extraordinarily successful. Like all ideology, it was a mixture of illusion and reality: people did go into business to get personally rich, and many became wealthy and powerful, but it is also true that business was a central agent in making Japan a great power—"rich country, strong army." A Meiji banker well summed up his class's position: "After all, from the point of view of rendering service to the country, is there really any difference . . . between taking part in the government as an official and enriching the nation by devoting one's efforts to business?"[35] As overseas expansion went ahead, the role of the military grew, as did its traditionally great prestige. Businessmen therefore tried to raise their own status "by claiming that their contribution to the nation's welfare was of a similar nature to that of the fighting man. Businessmen exhorted one another to greater efforts 'in the competition of foreign trade, which is peacetime war.' "[36]

By the end of the Meiji period, therefore, the bourgeoisie had been successfully integrated into the revamped Emperor-system, which had itself been remodelled to accentuate imperialism, and thus operate even more oppressively as the hegemonizing, mediating and unifying instrument. Businessmen had successfully established themselves *as* "warriors." Far from this in any way weakening the military by diluting the concept of the warrior, it probably strengthened the military by endorsing it as a social ideal.

Meantime, the military had strengthened itself successfully in other ways. Apart from the Takebashi Mutiny in 1878, the army was loyal to the state, and this loyalty was reinsured by the gendarmerie, set up in 1883 to ferret out dissidents in the army.[37] The war against China, followed by the Triple Intervention, led to a big increase in the military budget, which jumped from 10 to over 52 million yen, making the army's share of the national budget over 30 per cent (up from 10.5 per cent). This was to cover an increase of six divisions and four brigades in the army, and a comparable increase in the navy.[38] Further large increases followed as Japan's colonial role expanded. The 1898 budget, for example, called for large sums of money to be spent on Taiwan. Similarly, the 1902 budget planned to allocate greatly increased sums to the navy, in line with the arrangements made with Britain during the negotiations for the Anglo-Japanese Alliance that Japan would build up naval strength greater than that of any other power in the Far East except Britain. The 1908 budget crisis was caused directly by the government's attempts to find extra money to pay for military costs and new expenditures in Korea and Manchuria. The Taishō crisis (1912–13) was directly caused by the army's attempts to get a two-division increase sanctioned by the Diet, over and above the two new divisions which had been formed since 1907.[39] It was easy for the Army Minister to argue that Japan's interests in Manchuria and Korea required more military power.

While the successful wars against China (1894–95) and Russia (1904–5) enhanced the military's prestige, the acquisition of a colonial empire gave it permanent military tasks and bases from which to increase its political weight. The military involvement in the actual acquisition of territories such as Korea and Taiwan inevitably reinforced the chances of a big role for the military in the subsequent colonial administration of the areas, and Japan had no traditional civilian civil service, as Britain had. In Korea, for example, the army had been building up its forces long before the definitive acquisition in 1910 and, indeed, the failure of Itō's assimilationist policy strengthened the hand of the military backers of annexation. Similarly in Taiwan, the need to conduct a full-scale war against the guerrillas enabled the military to stake its claim to control of the colonial administration. The situation in Manchuria was more complex. Under the inter-imperialist rules of operation laid down by the Portsmouth and Peking Treaties, Japan had to conduct its rule in an indirect way through a commercial organization, the South Manchuria Railway Company (SMRC, or Mantetsu).⁴⁰ This was allegedly a civilian organization, although it had a strong military flavour to it, and it was originally set up on the initiative of the army, modelled on the East India Company. Its first head was army general Kodama, and it remained solidly under army hegemony. In addition to the SMRC, which developed fully only after the major concessions extracted at the time of the Twenty-one Demands, the Japanese established a number of other colonial agencies in Manchuria: the Kwantung Civil Government, and Foreign Ministry consulates on the non-military level; while the Kwantung Army functioned as an occupation force, later assisted by the para-military "police" forces of the SMRC.

Overall, the military (particularly the army) was in a curious position. Although predominantly a rural force, the army was greatly involved in the expansion of heavy industry. Although imperialist activity introduced serious contradictions (such as the urbanization of Japan, which the military appears to have genuinely regretted),⁴¹ it also provided the machinery to link military and business activities.⁴² The army's ideal was expansion and industrialization *abroad*. And it is notable that in the key colonial area, Manchuria, despite much rhetoric about the small businessman and certain attempts to block zaibatsu involvement in the 1930s, the Manchurian army never moved to block the implantation of big Japanese business. In fact, the Manchurian colonial economy had much the same structure as the metropolis, with the Mantetsu and Mitsui on top, and a lot of much smaller companies underneath.⁴³ Japanese colonialism was the joint work of the military and business.

By the beginning of the twentieth century Japan had acquired a quite extensive colonial empire administered overtly or covertly via military control. The acquisition and retention of this empire necessitated major military operations, especially against the anti-colonial liberation forces in the colonial areas, and this continued colonial activity, plus Japan's new place in the world imperialist group (participation in collective intervention in China, the alliance with Britain) provided the grounds for the military to push for repeated increases in the armed forces. A specific ideology of empire developed in a form which allowed it to be promoted just as well in peacetime as in time of war. The big financial-industrial combines were formed and consolidated (1900–10) and, on this basis, the big bourgeoisie was able to enter into the landlord-dominated political parties, which thus accommodated themselves to the needs of the economic base.

These changes around the turn of the century are not so much due to the establishment of the Constitution and the Diet, which were relatively marginal, as to Japan's changed place in the world system. The Diet was marked above all by two features: pre-modern authoritarianism and imperialism. From 1895 onwards it is the latter which dominates. The critical period was the decade between the wars against China and Russia (1895–1905) when "the character of the running of Japanese parliamentary politics was formed, the Industrial Revolution was carried out, and the capitalist economy was firmly established."[44]

The rejection by the Diet of the government's budget in 1908 is directly attributable to the insoluble contradiction in which the bourgeoisie was placed. Backing expansion, it still balked at the cost. And while the bourgeoisie was enriched by war, the military also had its prestige strengthened. The recurrent political oscillations which marked Japanese politics until World War II (and which distinguished the Japanese experience from fascism in both Germany and Italy) are a reflection of these contradictions: between the political necessity of repression and the economic necessity of expansion; between the bourgeoisie's desire to expand and the high cost in taxation and social upheaval which accompanied it; between which clique could best further given interests with which instruments (a military group running, a virtually irresponsible cabinet with the aid of a reactionary bureaucracy and the Emperor; or a bourgeois group backed by big business trying to manoeuvre a perhaps slightly wider-based regime).

And beneath these elite manoeuvres for position and power was an impressive series of internal upheavals: the great demonstration and strikes just after the Russo-Japanese War, the 1913 demonstrations and the 1918 riots. The period is actually called the *chinsen ki* or "period of submersion."[45] The great proletarian protests can all the more easily be ignored because bourgeois scholarship has tended to concentrate on a less crucial protest movement, embodied in the Campaign Against the Peace Terms of the Russo-Japanese War in 1905, and subsequently in the two Campaigns for the Defence of the Constitution (1913, 1925). These certainly were important movements. "The existence of nation-wide campaigns among the common people demanding democracy was the fundamental characteristic of the period [1905–25]."[46] But the Campaign Against the Peace Terms embodied the classic dichotomy—a democratic moment (the wish to overthrow a non-constitutional cabinet) plus an imperialist moment (opposition to the peace terms), fused by hostility to the high taxation imposed by the war, without any apparent recompense (the absence of an indemnity); the drive for "constitutionalism" at home (whatever that might be worth)[47] *never* detached itself from the imperialist aspect. The campaigns, moreover, were vehicles for dissident bourgeois opinion, not for the interests of the masses. This is clearly shown by the First Campaign for the Defence of the Constitution in 1913: this was promoted for a very precise *and limited* objective. When the Emperor Meiji died in 1912, the old guard, headed by the military traditionalists, toppled the second Saionji cabinet and restored Katsura to office for the third time—with the wider aim of reorganizing the political system to fend off change. It was against this, which amounted to a regression, that part of the smaller capitalist and urban middle classes mobilized in the campaign.[48] Katsura was soon ousted by a combination of overt pressure and internal compromise, and replaced by Admiral Yamamoto.

The process now repeated itself. The bourgeois parties, which had not originally promoted any of the campaigns, now exploited them, and while appearing to oppose them (and actually opposing them *as such*), proceeded to work on winning over and integrating factions of the opposition: "party political organization was the result of a reorganization of the ruling class against these campaigns."[49] Meanwhile the military abandoned its ousted representative, Katsura, who died later in 1913, and began to promote a new figure, General Terauchi Masatake from Chōshū, as its part of the overall reorganization. A new fusion was greatly aided by renewed overseas activity during the First World War. Business opposition (expressed in part in the 1913 campaign against taxation, particularly against the business tax) was demobilized by the rapid expansion which accompanied the war. At the same time, the war strengthened the old military right. Two divisions were added to the army, the Twenty-one Demands were aggressively pushed by the military, bourgeois democrats were suppressed. In all this the military had the support of the Seiyūkai. Indeed, the war and the community of military and business interests in China helped to bring about the change of government at the end of 1916. Ōkuma, who had been in power since 1914—and since 1915 with a solid Diet majority behind him—was forced to resign,[50] and was replaced by Terauchi, Yamagata's new right-hand man, who served to balance power at the top until he himself was toppled by the great popular uprisings of 1918.

The bourgeoisie as a whole had been greatly strengthened by the economic boom which accompanied the war. There had been very large sales of arms to Russia and a shipping boom, and Japan had encroached sizeably on traditional Western markets in Africa and the Far East.[51] "Nominally on the side of the Allies, Japan was, in fact, given the opportunity to sit on the sidelines of the actual conflict while making huge export profits."[52] Between the end of the war with Russia and the end of the First World War (thirteen years) the number of factories in Japan had increased 2.3 times, and factories equipped with motors nearly 3.6 times. During the war itself the number of factory employees rose from 854,000 (in 1914) to 1,817,000 (in 1919).[53] But, as indicated elsewhere, real wages fell by two-fifths between 1914 and 1918, and the bourgeoisie was eager to implement its comprehensive scheme for disciplining the labour force: the life employment system, which had been advanced around 1910 but wrecked by the First World War boom, now became imperative.[54]

For all these reasons, Hara, the head of the Seiyūkai, and the most far-sighted conservative since Itō, was installed as premier in 1918, and held down the job until he was assassinated in 1921. Hara was the bureaucrat par excellence, and above all the bureaucrat who had fused bureaucracy and party. He was also the agent of big business which was riding high on the wartime boom—and this in spite of the 1918 riots; exploitation had been so severe that even these did not yet dent the boom. Hara held power at a very favourable moment. Japan had done very well out of the First World War, business and military interests coincided in the exploitation of China, and Japan's "case" was accepted at Versailles. There was real disagreement about the wisdom of the Siberian adventure, though this was not a straight civilian-military split, but rather a split within different sectors of each group (thus General Tanaka was against it inside the army, but did not dare to speak his mind).[55] However, on the whole, participation in the counter-revolution in Siberia initially appeared to promise the advantages which co-operation in the 1900 adventure in China had brought: winning friends among the imperialists and eliminating a dangerous political force on Japan's doorstep, with the added bonus this time of blocking the possibility of an American monopoly in Siberia. Yet the Siberian episode (which had been launched just before Hara became premier) was disastrous for the Japanese rulers: it was very costly, and alienated the other leading imperialists (not to mention the Bolsheviks). By 1920 Japan was headed into economic trouble. Hara made a start to a more intelligent policy. While reorganizing the system of industrial exploitation, he also moved to ease the franchise law. Had he lived, he might well have hastened along the changes which came several years later. A first serious attempt at bourgeois government *in relatively favourable conditions* was suddenly terminated. The next try was in a much less suitable situation, after the Western powers had resystematized the balance of forces in Asia at Washington.

5.
From the Washington Conference to the Pacific War (1922–41)

This chapter has two theses. First, that in the 1920s and 1930s Japan did not undergo a basic change of political regime, much less degenerate from "democracy" to "fascism," as some would have it. Second, that there was fundamental agreement between business and the military on an imperialist policy—although there were conflicting viewpoints within both groups. In general, the chapter attempts to explain the breakdown of the world imperialist system in Asia by synthesizing the specific internal features of Japanese society (the depression, the ambivalent nature of the army) and the main elements of the clash between the group of Western powers and Japan's more backward imperialist system.

THE BREAKDOWN OF THE WASHINGTON ARRANGEMENT

The imperialist powers who gathered at Washington all agreed on one thing: that they should continue to plunder China and exploit the Chinese people. In Saitō's words, the arrangement "which emerged from the Washington Conference could be said to be based on a new form of suppressing China."[1]

This arrangement, while apparently coherent, was rather shortsighted, as it left out of consideration a number of important factors: above all, the Chinese masses, aroused to new heights of political activism by the May 4 Movement. It also ignored the dynamism of the Comintern.[2] The powers which met at Washington refused to accord full sovereign status to China. They insisted on their "rights" to intervene, but left a whole number of issues vague. They wanted to keep China as a preserve, but failed to define their own interests among themselves and their interests as a group against China. As a result, they were soon confronted with new Chinese initiatives, the Northern Expedition by the Nationalists in the summer of 1926 and the drive for treaty revision, which upset the internal balance of power. The unilateral Japanese moves which soon followed led to renewed contradictions among the imperialist powers. The Peking Tariff Conference (1925–26) was "the last occasion where the Washington powers tried, unsuccessfully, to give concrete content to their definition of a new order."[3]

The Washington settlement was exploded by Chiang's anti-communist coup in 1927, which caused the Western imperialists to break ranks and swing from the straightforward old policy of opposing all Chinese forces to backing Chiang and the Chinese bourgeoisie. The Western powers, economically more advanced and self-confident, decided to combat the Chinese Revolution by allying with Chiang and the comprador bourgeoisie. Japan, more backward, poorer and immediately threatened by the loss of exclusive control over Manchuria and North China, and by expanding Chinese textile production, felt obliged to fight not only the Chinese Revolution as such, but even the Kuomintang (KMT). It was Japan's war with the Kuomintang that caused Tokyo to be exiled from the Washington group.

To a large extent this was inherent in the Washington settlement, which was constructed to favour the Western powers in China. In Crowley's words, Japan

> alone of the Washington Treaty powers . . . had continental possessions in Northeast Asia (Korea); alone of these powers, it had "semicolonial" rights in China (South Manchuria) that were the key to its overseas investments; of these powers, only Japan was non-Caucasian; and only Japan was singled out by the other sea powers as a potential threat to their economic interests in China.[4]

Initially, it appeared Japan might be able to cope with the combined hostility of the Chinese people and the pressures from the Western powers. Japan's "semicolonial" position in Manchuria was generally tolerated by the West. And Japan continued to take part in the exploitation of the rest of China alongside the Western imperialists. Shanghai was the centre of foreign capital in China; indeed, Japanese investments increased faster, proportionately, in Shanghai between 1914 and 1930 than in Manchuria.[5]

The Japanese rulers disagreed about how to deal with the "China problem." A number of proposals were put forth at various stages, including the possibility of supporting a *strong* Chinese government—for example, under Chang Tso-lin[6] and Wu P'ei-fu in 1926. The "positive policy" of Premier Baron General Tanaka Giichi in 1927–28 involved supporting both Chang Tso-lin and Chiang Kai-shek and playing one off against the other. Most Japanese governmental opinion at this time was for maintaining the status quo, with forceful measures to be used only as a last resort "and then only to protect Japan's rights in Manchuria and not to bring about a drastic change in its political status."[7] In May 1928 the situation got temporarily out of hand when Japanese troops, at the instigation of Japanese army officers, against the advice of Tanaka's government, clashed with Chiang Kai-shek's forces at the town of Tsinan (the "Tsinan Incident"). But the clash was brief. Since 1928 brought an end to a short-lived Sino-Japanese amity, the murder of Chang Tso-lin by Kwantung Army officers, and the Kwantung Army's initial preparations for possible conflict with Chinese forces, it is important to ask why there was no "Manchurian Incident" or complete take-over of Manchuria until 1931.[8]

After the Tsinan Incident and the assassination of Chang Tso-lin, the Tanaka (Seiyūkai) cabinet fell and was replaced by a Minseitō party government with a so-called "soft-line" China policy.

The army was still in some public disrepute over Japan's first undeclared war, and a public consensus had not been developed on the necessity of taking over Manchuria by force, given the international and local complications that were likely to ensue from such action. Nor was Japan's actual domination in Manchuria yet fundamentally threatened. This "soft line" dampened down militant feeling to some extent until the London Naval Conference in 1930, the aftermath of which toppled the Minseitō cabinet.

The events of the late 1920s, however, were extremely important, particularly in building up resentment in the Japanese army, and a combination of this and other elements produced the Mukden Incident in late 1931 and the take-over of Manchuria. The Tokyo regime successfully silenced left and liberal opposition criticism on China policy. The military involved itself more effectively in the political process, not only in the government, but also in the area of political propaganda and "opinion moulding." The London Conference and its aftermath caused a major political crisis. And the depression built up explosive potential in both Japan and its colonies, which became linked in the economic crisis.

DOMESTIC POLITICAL CHANGES AFTER THE FIRST WORLD WAR

Premier Hara's period in office (1918–21) was distinguished by two features: the consolidation of bureaucratic rule and failure to deal with the basic economic and political structural contradictions of the society.

The bureaucracy had changed considerably since the early Meiji period, and grown enormously bloated. By 1922 it had five and a half times more members than in 1890 when the Diet was first convened.[9] Within it, the biggest change was the growing preponderance of Tokyo University graduates in key positions. A study of the situation in eight prefectures shows that fifty-eight of the seventy-one Governors of these prefectures from 1905 to 1925 were Tokyo University graduates. These graduates, moreover, represented a much more diversified class and geographical body than in 1890 when 90 per cent of Tokyo University had come from the samurai class, especially from Chōshū and Satsuma.[10] This proliferation of bureaucrats did not promote democracy or even parliamentarism, but the consolidation of a governmental apparatus with close links to business and the military.[11] Working behind the scenes, its only immutable characteristic was isolation from and hostility to the masses.

Hara had been lifted into office as the representative of the industrial bourgeoisie to cope with the problems which were drastically revealed by the 1918 uprisings. He responded to the pressure of the masses by marginally easing the franchise law and allowing greater freedom of expression. But he failed to deal with the key structural problems, particularly the bottlenecks in agriculture. He promoted a policy for increasing rice production in Korea and Taiwan which later had a catastrophic effect on rural Japan itself. He thus failed to eliminate the *internal* contradiction which subsequently underlay many of the autonomous initiatives of the reforming elements in the army.[12]

After Hara was assassinated in 1921, these internal problems became even more acute. His party, the Seiyūkai, started pushing repressive legislation in 1922 to undermine the left. This trend culminated in the enactment of the 1925 Peace Preservation Law ("the law against dangerous ideas") which, along with the new tenant laws, made the new suffrage bill safe and acceptable. Once again repression and "liberalization" went hand in hand. Indeed the so-called Universal Suffrage Law not only excluded all women outright, but also those who "received public or private relief or help for a living on account of poverty."[13] The bill raised the number of those who could vote from about 3 million to 12.5 million. "Home Minister Wakatsuki felt obliged to assure the Diet that the suffrage bill was not designed to promote democracy."[14]

The government which put through the set of measures in 1925 was headed by Count Katō Takaaki.[15] Katō Takaaki and his successor, Wakatsuki Reijirō, represent a synthesis of old and new bourgeoisie, encompassing the successful second-generation samurai plus the war profiteers from both the Russo-Japanese War and the World War, the bankers who rode high through the 1920 bank failures, and the construction millionaires from the aftermath of the 1923 earthquake (soon to be joined by some spectacular winners from the 1927 financial crisis). The Katō (Takaaki) cabinet was a bourgeois government in the sense that Mitsubishi men held the key positions of power, but the *system* of government remained the same as before. The bourgeoisie had had a great boost from imperialism and a couple of easy wars; but it continued to support the existing forms of oligarchic and autocratic rule (the bureaucracy, rather than absolutism). Although it often differed about the leaders best suited to execute policy, and sometimes about which tactics were correct, the aims of the bourgeoisie coincided very closely with those of the old Meiji ruling class. Katō and Wakatsuki were most successful in promoting the political integration of old and new bourgeoisie and the Meiji aristocracy, while integrating and demobilizing working class pressure. However, their failure to deal with renewed pressure from the Western imperialists abroad, and with the severe contradictions in the land-holding system at home, brought about some violent reactions among the military. In 1927, on the crest of a financial crisis, General Tanaka became premier.

The way in which the Wakatsuki cabinet fell and Tanaka came to power is symbolic of the state of Japanese politics at the time. The system itself was so constructed as to be virtually irresponsive to any outside control, and Tanaka did not even have to stage a putsch to get into power. He simply bribed his way in as the leader of one of the two major established parties, the Seiyūkai, and became premier via the Diet and its traditional procedures.

The instruments of power, while at one level highly functional to the ruling strata, at another level were still to an extraordinary extent unintegrated—hence the widespread existence of bribery, which is functional mainly at a certain point in the development of a capitalist state. Just as Tanaka became premier via the Diet and one of the major parties, using bribery, so Wakatsuki fell after a conflict with the Privy Council over granting government aid to the bankrupt Bank of Taiwan, a typical new imperial operation (though his position was already weakened by a more traditional scandal involving brothel concessions and land in Osaka).[16]

The industrial bourgeoisie, in short, did not stake out a new political position for itself. As a class, it both repressed the left and failed to undertake any basic reform of the political system. This failure can not be reduced to a preference for undercover dealings and behind-the-scenes operations,[17] for Japanese politics in the age of industrial capitalism hewed very close to the lines laid down in the nineteenth century. The bourgeoisie had a structural interest in behaving as it did; because of its historical imbrication with other groups arising out of the Meiji compromise, its interests coincided largely with those of the previous ruling strata.[18] And it is this historical compromise-cum-imbrication which explains the relationship between bourgeoisie and military in the years up to 1945.

THE ARMY AND THE DEPRESSION

Since Tanaka's assumption of the premiership in 1927 can fairly be taken as marking the advance of the military, it is important to set out a few of the latter's salient characteristics. The army and the navy were relatively distinct and autonomous forces. The original clan division of

Meiji times had been considerably broken down by the late 1920s, but the different traditions of Chōshū (army) and Satsuma (navy) lingered on. As is the case virtually everywhere, the navy was less involved in politics than the army. Indeed, the various admirals who rotated as premiers (Yamamoto, Katō Tomosaburō, Saitō, Okada Keisuke and Yonai Mitsumasa) were more in the nature of compromise candidates between the army and the civil bureaucracy than representatives of the military. Yet it was to be the navy which was affected most by the international agreements of Washington and London. Between 1914 and 1921 the naval budget had risen from ¥83 million to ¥483.5 million, but the pace was greatly slowed down by the Washington agreements. Similarly, the 1930 London Naval Conference, which was signed by the Hamaguchi Yūkō government, hit hardest at the navy. There was no separate air force.[19]

In very general terms, the most important distinction between the army and the navy was their different estimate of the optimum imperialist strategy. The army saw Russia as the number one enemy and fought for expansion on the continent of Asia. The navy, more concerned with the United States of America as the number one enemy, wanted to secure Japan's oil supplies, and argued for a southern strategy.

Because of the wartime experience, the Japanese army has usually been written off in the West as an undifferentiated mass of cruel automata.[20] But a more scientific analysis is needed of its composition and objectives.[21]

The Japanese army was overwhelmingly of rural origin. While overall a profoundly counter-revolutionary force, in the conditions of the great depression which hit hardest at the rural areas, it was domestically partly a reforming force. Many of its actions in the later 1920s and 1930s were directed against both the Chinese Revolution *and* a corrupt and sectarian regime at home. Unless this double and simultaneous thrust is grasped, much of the army's activity remains unintelligible. It was both a classic imperialist army (led by the country's elite, scornful of the interests of the peoples whose territory it might be in—particularly in Korea, Russia and China—and counter-revolutionary at home) and rather similar to a reforming army in some of the Third World countries today (bureaucratic, granted, but with genuine links to the rural masses, and containing elements hostile to big business and particularly to foreign big business).

Moreover, the army leadership itself was not of one mind. Two main groups have to be distinguished: those from the Military Academy and those from the War College.[22] The chain of assassinations in the 1930s which became the most spectacular feature of Japanese politics was the work of the first group (from the Academy). These assassinations were not an integral part of the army authorities' attempt to impose their views on the government, and were only indirectly related to the Manchurian problem. They were mainly connected to the depression and to internal social and economic conditions. The real policy-makers in the army were invariably from the War College, did not engage in assassination, and imposed their views by working successfully within the existing political system. This is the crucial distinction, although it was criss-crossed through with several other distinctive contradictions.[23] Yet while there were important differences of opinion within the Japanese ruling strata, these differences cannot be broken down into a civil/military split. At perhaps the most critical juncture of all, in late 1937, it was the government in Tokyo which pushed for an "ultra" policy towards Chiang against the advice and wishes of General Tada Shun and other army leaders.[24]

THE GREAT DEPRESSION AND ITS POLITICAL EFFECTS

Though Japanese agriculture had been languishing in something of a crisis since shortly after the First World War, the full blast of depression hit Japan only in 1927. The crisis which engulfed the country then can be compared to that which hit the United States several years later. This internal depression coincided with Japan's increased problems in China and with General Tanaka's advent to power.

Tanaka's two years in office, from April 1927 to the midsummer of 1929, were ones of considerable chaos at home and incompetence abroad. Japan landed troops in China at Tsingtao, pressured Chang Tso-lin into a railway deal, and had to withdraw from Shantung. The domestic economy underwent extensive concentration.[25] Business profits rose, real wages (as well as employment) fell; banks and businesses went through a spate of mergers. This irritated the strata who had recently been accorded the vote, and although some of the aggrieved sentiment of the petit bourgeoisie could be deflected against the West, a good deal of it rebounded onto the government.[26] It is as much in the catastrophic effects of the depression as in the more visible and spectacular activities in China that the real degeneration in Japan's political life in the 1930s must be sought. Indeed, the events in China largely reflect the domestic effects of the crisis. Western accounts of Japan's behaviour at the time tend to concentrate on the military and on Japan's moves in China. But by so doing they usually ignore or underestimate how Japan, from a decidedly disadvantageous position, was to deal with the negative effects of the world capitalist system in a time of crisis. Participation in the Western-dominated system set up intolerable contradictions for Japan and accounted for much of the violent oscillation in Japanese economic and monetary policy between 1929 and 1931. After futile attempts at conciliation,[27] Japan accepted the contradiction as antagonistic and launched an assault first on many of the West's private markets, and subsequently on sources of vital raw materials.

In this highly contradictory and chaotic setting, Japan moved into the thirties and eventually war with the West. Hamaguchi, who replaced Tanaka as premier in July 1929, got off to a disastrous start, since his

Finance Minister, Inoue Junnosuke, decided to return Japan to the gold standard on the eve of the collapse of the system. On top of this came the London Naval Conference (1930) which was a further attempt by the Western powers, particularly the United States, to upset the relatively acceptable naval balance established by the earlier Washington Conference.[28] Controversy over the government signing the agreement led to a critical clash in Tokyo: the cabinet found itself to a large extent isolated, with the parties and popular opinion supporting the navy in its opposition to Hamaguchi. In the depths of the depression, Hamaguchi and the civilian politicians round him seemed to public opinion to have betrayed Japan's vital interests—and, incidentally, to have infringed the Constitution.[29] Hamaguchi was shot in Tokyo station on November 14, 1930. His successor was Wakatsuki, premier in 1926–27.

Japan was also dealt a heavy economic blow by the introduction of the Smoot-Hawley Tariff in June 1930 which raised the import duty on Japanese goods entering the United States by an average of 23 per cent.[30] Japan's exports to China also suffered at the same time and in 1931 the United States overtook Japan to become the leading exporter to China. Japan made a vain effort to get an international agreement to settle China's debt problem in order to get credit going again, but London's unwillingness to see debts owed Britain by China treated on an equal footing with debts owned by China to other countries stoked up ill feeling in Japan. The Mukden Incident in September 1931, which started Japan's main drive to take over the whole of China, was executed at the precise moment when the West was most preoccupied with the British financial crisis.

THE MUKDEN INCIDENT AND THE ATTACK ON CHINA

The famous Incident at Mukden (now Shenyang) was arranged by a group in the Kwantung Army[31] in Manchuria to provide an excuse for the army to take over Manchuria. In fact, the Kwantung Army was not able to seize all of Manchuria immediately after the Mukden Incident. While it took South Manchuria, the Tokyo government under Wakatsuki blocked its attempts to move into North Manchuria as well. The move up to the Great Wall went ahead only after the Wakatsuki cabinet had fallen in December 1931 and been replaced by one under Seiyūkai leader Inukai Tsuyoshi.[32] The Kwantung Army entered Harbin on February 5, 1932. The state of "Manchukuo" was formally set up in March 1932.[33]

Shortly afterwards the Japanese began encroaching further on North China; they moved into Jehol once it was clear that the League of Nations Lytton Commission would recommend non-recognition of "Manchukuo." By the terms of the Tangku Truce of May 1933 between the Kwantung Army and local Chinese officials, Manchukuo's borders were extended up to the Great Wall. In December 1934, after the decision to abrogate both the Washington and London naval agreements, Tokyo sanctioned a policy of fostering regional governments in North China as "buffers" between Manchukuo and the Nationalists. In June 1935, two Chinese provinces— Hopei and Chahar—became client regimes (by the so-called Ho-Umezu and Ching-Doihara agreements, respectively). These regimes, the East Hopei Autonomous Council and the Hopei-Chahar Political Council, excluded the Kuomintang and the Nationalist Army from their territories.

Until 1931 Japan refrained from a direct political clash with the Western imperialists. As at the Washington and London conferences, it had always compromised under pressure. The take-over of Manchuria was the first time Japan directly refused to accept the West's definition of what imperialism should be in East Asia. The events in Manchuria, coming on top of other things, irritated the Western powers sufficiently for them to mobilize the League of Nations against Japan's new moves. This did not mean that the West was pro-Chinese or fundamentally anti-Japanese. All the Western powers were hostile to the Chinese people. But there were important differences, especially between Britain and the United States, as regards the Kuomintang. The United States had close ties with Chiang and the Kuomintang and wanted to strengthen this regime; Washington did not feel that Japan's case in China should be supported. London, on the other hand, was still pro-Japanese (in spite of the economic threat from Japan), was not close to Chiang, and pressured the Nationalist regime to accept Tokyo's terms.[34] Both Britain and the United States wanted Japan to have a place in China, but they both wanted to use the League "to keep Japan in her place."

The West's mobilization of the League had important effects inside Japan. The government was toppled partly because of this, and the unpopularity of the Western powers increased greatly. Tokyo eventually withdrew from the League. In China the mobilization of the League was clearly perceived as part of inter-imperialist machinations against the Chinese people. The Report of the 1932 Lytton Commission made clear the basic complicity among the imperialist powers over the dismemberment of China.[35] As the Chinese saw, the Manchurian crisis did not definitively rupture the West's solidarity with Japan. None of the Western powers went to war with Japan over events in China. Japan was allowed to advance all the way from Mukden to Indochina over a period of ten years with hardly a finger being lifted by the West. It was only when Japan attacked the colonies of Europe and the United States, and Hawaii, that the Pacific War started.

Internally the political changes were towards *decentralization*.

Beginning in 1932, Japan witnessed a style of cabinet politics and policy-making in which the ministers of state were little more than spokesmen for their respective ministries. The premier became, in the process, an arbitrator between the competing demands of his ministers. . . . Parallel with this development, there appeared the embryonic forms of most of the administrative and policy-making agencies and procedures which eventually matured in the late 1930's. . . . Essentially, with the "whole nation" cabinet of Admiral Saitō, there occurred a shift to a highly bureaucratic system which was characterized by a remarkable decentralization of power among the respective ministers of state. This pattern of policy-making, not the programs and actions of the ultra-nationalistic groups, the political parties, and army factionalism, would determine the foreign policies of the Japanese government after 1932.[36]

The widespread belief in the West that the Japanese regime became more centralized and "totalitarian" in the thirties is false. What is true is that the existing bureaucratic structure both allowed a definite "militarization" of the regime and provided the conditions whereby a decentralized regime could survive. The government became a conglomeration of relatively autonomous bureaucracies among which the premier attempted to operate as arbitrator. The statutory independence of the military as enshrined in the autonomy of the army and navy ministers in the cabinet provided *carte blanche* for increased decentralization.

The extent to which civil and military authorities agreed on imperialist policy in China and to which the main conflicts within the military were in Tokyo rather than between Tokyo and Manchuria is apparent both in the case of Nagata and the sequel to the Marco Polo Bridge Incident. Major General Nagata Tetsuzan was an army officer who had spent ten years in Europe (1913–23) and had been appointed chief of the Bureau of Military Affairs by General Hayashi Senjurō after the resignation of General Araki Sadao. His specific task was to reorganize the top echelons of the army with War College graduates, accelerate the introduction of advanced military technology, and institute economic planning. Nagata's appointment marked a general shift to a wholesale professionalization of the army via the War College, eliminating the more traditional products of the Military Academy, and causing widespread friction among the old-style military leaders. It was in reaction to this trend that Lieutenant Colonel Aizawa Saburō murdered Nagata on August 12, 1935.[37] The supporters of Aizawa's action, led by General Yanagawa Heisuke, decided to use the trial of Aizawa to stir up opinion in their favour. They chose the judges, the procurator and the location of the trial, as well as making the decision that the trial be held in public and "be conducted in a manner that would enable the public to understand the complex motives underlying the assassination of General Nagata."[38] At the melodramatic trial, Aizawa's defence team, which included Dr. Uzawa, the president of Meiji University, was allowed to present Aizawa's motives and the proceedings were turned into an assault on the government. The trial was accompanied by further steps towards military reorganization, and it was out of this atmosphere of tension that there came the rebellion of February 26, 1936 (the "February

Incident")—the nearest thing to a real military coup d'état. Even here there was no coup d'état, for when the Emperor ordered the rebellious troops to surrender after a three-day stand-off in central Tokyo, his order was obeyed. Not even the wildest elements dared oppose the Emperor, although they could squabble among themselves about policy.[39]

Shortly after the February Incident, there is some indication that a more moderate North China policy was developing within the ruling circles in Japan, one which aimed to avoid friction with the Kuomintang, Britain, the United States and the Soviet Union, but not the Chinese Communists. The corollary of this new consensus was to shift priority towards the South Seas.[40]

However, this consensus did not last long. On the night of July 7, 1937, came the Marco Polo Bridge (Lukou Ch'iao) Incident.[41] The proposals put forward by the Tokyo government were rejected by Chiang Kai-shek, and on August 14 Nationalist planes bombed Japanese naval installations at Shanghai. Japan wavered. The vice-chief of the general staff, General Tada backed a policy of caution, but this was decisively repudiated on December 1, 1937, by the Tokyo government and the Emperor, with their decision to march on Nanking and apply the "Policy of Annihilation." Thereafter came the Rape of Nanking and all-out war against both the Communists and the Kuomintang, more or less.

Particularly after events like the Asian and Pacific Wars, it is not easy to review history and realize that although there were elements in Japan, such as the right-wing ideologue Kita Ikki, who were planning for war from way back, this was not true of the leadership of the state as a whole. Although the objectives of the leadership were reprehensible, many of the leaders were also confused. Some were against war; others saw events overtake them (often at least in part due to their own complicity). Until 1931 Japan's leaders, both civil and military, followed a general policy of working together and compromising with the Western imperialists. The combination of army moves in Manchuria and the effects of the economic depression, however, caused Japan to articulate a new, autonomous set of policies, in which the commitment to build the state of Manchukuo was central. The new policy, defined as "an Asiatic Monroe Doctrine," involved three basic characteristics: enlarging the army to protect Manchukuo against both the Soviet Union and Nationalist China as well as the people of "Manchukuo" itself; strengthening the navy to guarantee the security of the empire against the U.S. and British fleets; getting Nationalist China to recognize "Manchukuo," cut its dependence on the Western powers and cooperate with Japan.[42]

This policy was supported by almost all the Japanese leaders in the mid-1930s, although it was opposed by fringe groups in the military and certain sectors of "public opinion." Until 1937 this policy was backed by both the Foreign Ministry and the General Staff. But after the Sian Incident in December 1936, the Chinese Nationalists could no longer tolerate

Japanese imperialism in North China, and with the minor incident at the Marco Polo Bridge the accumulated momentum for a more aggressive policy towards China came into its own in Japan. As in 1931, the support for the two policies was rather evenly balanced and the struggle for supremacy in Tokyo raged until mid-January 1938, when the Konoe government announced it would annihilate the Kuomintang regime. It is important to stress that the General Staff of planners and strategists in Tokyo, among whom the key figure was General Tada, were hostile to this new war with China. The field commanders argued that they could wipe out the Kuomintang armies. But Tada and the strategists at the centre saw a China war as a deviation into a swamp: China was not the main enemy; the Soviet Union was building up its strength in the Far East. A China war was the wrong war in the wrong place at the wrong time.

ECONOMIC FACTORS

The depression greatly promoted concentration in the domestic economy through bankruptcies, take-overs and mergers. The structure of the Japanese economy, with its proliferation of "small and medium enterprises," was a big obstacle to the efficiency needed in time of war. From 1932 onwards, in the wake of the depression concentrations, the state laid out heavy subsidies for further mergers. Car firms had to stop taking private orders in 1933.[43] Export guilds (*yūshutsu kumiai*) were promoted to accelerate a process of concentration which in some sectors was already fairly well advanced.[44] Centralization of control in the crucial area of banking and credit increased, especially after 1937 when the war with China forced big rises in military expenditure.[45]

The military also increased its role within the economy. The military's role in Manchukuo and Korea, as well as the growing importance of munitions and other military hardware in industrial production, naturally helped this trend along. The aggravated contradiction between big spending on "security" and the neglect of domestic welfare and social services led some elements in the military to voice criticisms of big business. A number of new companies emerged during this period which were particularly closely linked to the military, the "new" zaibatsu (*shinkō zaibatsu*). Though some of these undoubtedly made quick killings in the colonies or in arms production, on the whole the big contracts connected with Japan's expansion went to the old zaibatsu, headed by the big four (Mitsubishi, Mitsui, Sumitomo and Yasuda).[46]

The government also moved to restrict foreign capital in Japan, which was quite powerful in some sectors. In 1936 Ford and General Motors together accounted for about three-quarters of the total output of motor vehicles in Japan.[47] About half of the foreign capital in the country was in joint concessions, particularly in the electrical goods and heavy engineering industries. There had been a big rise in Western companies' penetration after the First World War, and in Japan's borrowing from the West, particularly between 1924 (after the earthquake) and 1930. The latter year also saw the peak of foreign investment—¥2,466 million.[48] From this point the figure falls, as Japan tried to bring key sectors back under national control. In general, in spite of the depression and Inoue's gold standard blunder, Japan developed a strong external position during the 1930s. "In 1938 Japan's debt to the West was smaller than it had been in 1914; *per capita,* it was the lowest in the world next to China. With the exception of Turkey, Japan was the only important Asian country to reduce its indebtedness to the West between 1914 and 1938."[49] In the 1930s Japan was the only non-Western net creditor nation, though its attempts at setting up a yen bloc economy independent of the West were not a great success.

Moderate restrictions on foreign capital inside Japan were not particularly irritating to the Western powers. What did infuriate them was Japan's astounding export boom into hitherto reserved territories. The depression had something of the same medium-term advantageous effect as the First World War. Japan seized upon the breakdown *in the West* again. When Britain devalued the pound, Japan devalued the yen even more.[50] The thirties saw Japan leaping forward from the advanced positions conquered during the World War, when it had consolidated its grip on Eastern markets. Now it expanded into the next ring of countries—India, the Dutch Indies and the British colonies in East Asia. While Britain's share of India's cotton cloth market fell from 97.1 per cent in 1913–14 to 47.3 per cent in 1935, Japan's share rose from 0.3 per cent (1913–14) to 50.9 per cent (1935)—taking over the entire British loss.[51] Many of these countries retaliated with quotas and tariffs in the years 1933–34,[52] whereupon Japan moved into Latin America. Exports to Central America increased from ¥3 million in 1931 to ¥41 million in 1936, and to South America from ¥10 million to ¥69 million in the same period.[53] Britain's share of the South American cotton piece-goods market fell from 53.2 per cent in 1929 to 46.4 per cent in 1935, and Japan's rose from 4.5 per cent in 1929 to 38.6 per cent in 1935 (the share of Italy and the United States combined in the same period fell from 42.3 per cent to 15 per cent).[54] The speed of the take-over terrified complacent Western bourgeoisies. For example, from virtually zero in 1931, Japan became the second largest exporter to Morocco by 1934, preceded only by France.[55] The mere possibility of *an alternative* for the first time introduced a whole syndrome of previously ignored options for local traders in countries as diverse as Tanganyika and Palestine. Even where Japan did not take over a market, the high price of British exports often stimulated the growth of local production, as in Egypt. Moreover, as a percentage of Japan's exports, semi-manufactures (including raw silk) fell from 51.8 per cent of the total in 1914 to 26.4 per cent in 1937; and between 1934 and 1936 the percentage of Japan's exports which went to free markets rose from 56 to 65 per cent.[56]

This economic threat led Western business into startling revelations about factory conditions in Japan, particularly in Britain, which in 1929 had still been labouring under the hangover of the Anglo-Japanese Alliance.[57] Books attacking working conditions in Japan began to appear.[58] As well as the League of Nations, the International Labour Organisation (ILO) was mobilized in a particularly hypocritical campaign since Britain and France had expressly prevented ILO stipulations being applied to their sweat-shops in China when the organization was originally founded.[59] What incensed the Western powers more than anything was Japan's refusal to kowtow to unilateral imperialist self-righteousness: Japanese delegates would turn up at international conferences and harangue the delegates with the history of the extermination of the American Indians or the development of the Lancashire textile industry, or contemporary colonialism in Hong Kong. It was Japan's insistence on denouncing *inequality among imperialists* which angered the West—not least because it was a line to which there was no ready answer. Ordinary imperialists were no problem; anti-imperialists could be written off as terrorists or demagogues; but a fellow imperialist who both refused to abide by the rules and in practice caused grave economic trouble was more than could be tolerated.

Finally, Japanese imperialism should be set in its comparative context. Japan greatly oppressed all the peoples it colonized, particularly the peoples of Korea and China. But Japanese colonialism was economically no worse than that of the Western powers. In 1940 Elizabeth Schumpeter wrote that "Japan has been more successful in increasing the purchasing power of these regions [Manchukuo and China] than all the outside powers there have ever been in China."[60] Most of Japan's empire was acquired and held during wartime. But it is interesting that in areas where a peacetime comparison is possible, Japan emerges no worse than the white imperialists. Surveys indicate that in both early postwar south Korea and late-sixties Micronesia a majority of the inhabitants polled stated a preference for a return to Japanese rule over continued American occupation.[61]

The existence of this empire naturally raises the questions: Who was in favour of expansion? Whom did it benefit? And what is the relationship between Japan's justifications for expansion and the general problem of economic development in a world dominated by imperialism?

The justifications advanced by Japan were multiple: the protection of interests acquired fighting Russia in 1904–5; the need to have access to raw materials which would otherwise be looted by Western capitalists; the need to protect investments (and, later, citizens, in the well-known extension); access to markets, and their protection; the desire for a "Japanese sphere of influence," which was easy to argue since Japan's expansion, unlike that of the European and U.S. imperialists, was limited to geographically adjacent areas; geo-political arguments, much used vis-à-vis the U.S.S.R., first over the invasion of Siberia, and later in Korea and China; general statements about the need to control Manchuria and Korea, sometimes combined with a plea that Japan was actually improving the territory; solidarity with the non-white peoples of Asia against the Caucasians; population pressure.[62]

The population question merits a brief examination. In 1930 the population of Japan proper was 64,448,000 (71,253,000 by 1937). The density per square mile was 437 (468 in Great Britain, 670 in Belgium, 324 in Germany). Density in relation to arable land, however, was 2,774 per square mile (2,170 for Great Britain, 1,709 for Belgium, 806 for Germany). The productive agricultural area of Japan proper was about the same as the area of West Virginia.[63] Japan, therefore, was densely populated. Yet very few Japanese emigrated to the colonies or anywhere else. Whereas between 1910 and 1930 about 20 million Chinese moved into Manchuria, by 1929 there were only about 215,000 Japanese there—and 97 per cent of these lived in Kwantung, the Railway Zone and the Consular Jurisdiction areas: these were almost all administrative staff and suchlike, not settlers. In almost exactly the same period (up to 1928), more than four times as many Koreans had moved, usually as a result of either physical or financial force, into Manchuria.[64] Similarly, after more than thirty years of colonization, there were only just over 200,000 Japanese in Taiwan (though this figure rose to some 300,000 by about 1940).[65] The only other area where there was sizeable Japanese emigration was Brazil, which was not a colony: some 200,000 Japanese moved there between 1908 and 1940.[66] Prior to the war, only a little over one million Japanese moved out of Japan to settle or reside abroad. Obviously, climate and housing, as well as lack of adaptability, played their part. Migration to Hokkaido, Japan's Scotland rather than its golden West, was also very low.[67] Japanese preferred to move to balmier climes like Hawaii; many would probably have chosen the United States if it had been possible. Taiwan was clearly more attractive than Manchuria.

The more general question of capitalist development in a world dominated by imperialism is more problematic. The experience of the last century indicates that there is no such thing as peaceful co-existence with imperialism. A non-socialist state has only a choice between attempting to combat other imperialist powers or forming an alliance with one or more of them (usually the most powerful). Japan was not the equal of the other powers in capital, and this plus Japan's relative lateness explains much of the recourse to military actions. There are no examples of non-socialist industrializing countries with Japan's lack of capital and lack of raw materials making their way in the modern world without using force overseas.[68] Apart from capital, raw materials were Japan's biggest problem. After the Second World War, "pure" investment imperialism in other conservative countries became possible (e.g., Japanese investment in Australia, Kuwait, Alaska)—although this phase may itself now be drawing to a close. But before the war, Japan had good reason to think that major investment in Manchuria, Malaya, Indonesia and elsewhere could not be made and protected without some military presence. The type of imperialism Japan "required," investment imperialism, did not become "acceptable" until after the Pacific War.[69]

What were Japan's requirements? Contrary to widespread opinion, Japan was broadly self-sufficient in food in the thirties—execpt for sugar which largely came from Taiwan.[70] But Japan's farms were very dependent on fertilizers. In 1936 some 30 per cent of all commercial fertilizers were imported, about half from Manchuria. Japan had no phosphates at all. Other imported raw materials included bauxite, nickel and crude rubber (100 per cent for all three) and coal (10.8 per cent). A Brookings Institution report concluded that "Japan's military power is fundamentally dependent upon control of, or free access to, colonial and foreign sources of supply."[71] In the imperialist jungle of the thirties, there was no such thing as "free access" without control. Japan's military force was, of course, less needed to cope with its imperialist rivals than to oppress the peoples of Asia.

FROM THE AMUR TO PEARL HARBOR

In the years 1937–39 Japan fought a series of brief but extremely costly encounters with the Soviet army. A large part of the Japanese army considered the Soviet Union to be its number one enemy, and Japanese encroachment and probing along the Soviet frontier from the Pacific to Mongolia, an independent socialist republic under Soviet "protection," had created the conditions for a serious clash. The first major outbreak of fighting came on the Amur River in 1937; the second at Changkufeng (Lake Khasan) in the summer of 1938; and the third, and largest, at Khalkhin Gol (Nomonhan) in 1939, where Japan suffered a major defeat of considerable strategic importance.[72] The signing of the German-Soviet Pact brought the Nomonhan fighting to a halt.

Since Japan was informally allied with Germany, the German-Soviet Pact naturally inclined the Soviet Union to a similar arrangement with Tokyo. As the war progressed in Europe and Germany overran two of the key colonial powers with possessions in Southeast Asia, France and Holland, Japan shifted its attention more and more southwards. Germany's victories in Europe were followed shortly afterwards by the signing of a Tripartite Pact between itself, Italy and Japan (September 27, 1940). In early 1941 Japan's Foreign Minister, Matsuoka Yōsuke, visited Berlin and, on his way back, Moscow, where he signed a non-aggression agreement with the Soviet government. This agreement, which infuriated the Germans, who were about to attack the U.S.S.R., was highly advantageous to both Moscow and Tokyo.[73] The Japanese, although in alliance with Germany, scrupulously respected the non-aggression treaty with Moscow throughout the war, thus ensuring that the Soviet Union would not have to face a war on two fronts. The treaty was similarly advantageous for Tokyo, since it meant that it could concentrate on Southeast Asia without having to fight Russia at the same time.

The history of Japan's dealings with Russia, including the defeat at Nomonhan, are part of the background to Japan's entry into war with the West. In many ways, however, this was a prolongation of the war Japan was already fighting in China. In Japan the war is called "the fifteen years [i.e., 1931–45] war." And to a large extent Japan's attack on Southeast Asia and Pearl Harbor grew directly out of its activities in China.

The question of whether or not war (usually meaning war between Japan and the Western powers) could have been avoided is a highly vexed one, which is the subject of many extensive works.[74] Schroeder, for example, argues that it could at least have been postponed. In an elegant excursus on American moralism, he stresses the extent to which U.S. policy was "designed to uphold principle and to punish the aggressor, but not to save the victim." The emphasis was on "meting out justice rather than doing good."[75] America, he argues, went to war *over* China, but essentially to punish Japan. In a major piece of new research, Jonathan Marshall argues instead that "the United States and Japan fought over Southeast Asia, until then an 'obscure' corner of the world."[76] Recent research and the loosening of wartime prejudice have led to renewed consideration of the operation of Japanese diplomacy and the extent to which Japan was prepared to compromise with the Western powers, and vice versa—against the peoples of Asia. The Brussels Conference of 1937 showed the Western powers profoundly divided on Far Eastern policy, as they continued to be throughout the Second World War.[77] Britain, among others, was anxious to appease Japan, and in September 1940 it agreed to close the Burma Road, the lifeline to the Kuomintang, at Japan's request. France agreed to let Japanese troops be stationed in Northern Indochina to complete the blockade of the Nationalists.[78]

Although most of Southeast Asia was in the hands of European powers, Japan's key negotiations were with the United States. This was not primarily because of America's colonial possession in Asia, the Philippines, but because of America's key role in Japan's trade, particularly in strategic raw materials.[79] The United States began seriously to squeeze Japan in July 1940 when it introduced a licensing system for certain U.S. exports to that country. The two crucial items, crude oil and scrap iron, were added to the list after Japan occupied Northern Indochina in September 1940. A full embargo followed on July 26, 1941.

The American embargo, particularly on oil, severely limited Japan's ability to manoeuvre. Much of Japanese diplomacy prior to December 1941 was taken up with trying to secure supplies of oil: the long negotiations with the Dutch colonial regime in Batavia and Matsuoka's dealings with the Soviet Union whose oil, close to Japan's shores, was less vulnerable to attack during trans-shipment than that from the South Seas. Prior to Pearl Harbor, Japan had only about eighteen months' supply.

Without going into the details of the negotiations between Tokyo and Washington, or into the wider political issues, it is well to remember that the clash between the West and Japan was the result not only of Japanese aggression against Asia, but also of the Western imperialists' refusal to accept Japan as an equal partner. In November 1941, when the talks with Washington were already well advanced, Japan proposed universal non-discrimination in commercial relations in the Pacific area, including China, if this principle were adopted throughout the world.[80] To the United States (and presumably the other Western capitalist powers) this was "unthinkable."[81] Japan was, on the whole, eager to reach a settlement and offered considerable concessions to this end. America could certainly have reached a temporary settlement within the framework of an imperialist carve-up which gave Japan slightly more than it had been granted at Washington in 1921–22. It was America which turned down the Japanese proposal for a summit meeting between Premier Konoe and Roosevelt in autumn 1941. And it was Secretary of State Cordell Hull's outright rejection of Japan's proposals of November 7, 1941 which brought negotiations to a halt.[82]

It was Japan, of course, which attacked—not just at Pearl Harbor, but almost simultaneously throughout much of Southeast Asia.[83] The skeleton of the Japanese plan was to incapacitate the American fleet long enough to enable Japan to take over Southeast Asia—the whole of which, with the exception of Thailand, whose regime was pro-Japanese, was a colonized area. All the colonial powers except the United States were either occupied by Japan's allies (Holland), or subordinated (Vichy France), or direly threatened (Britain), or just plain inoffensive (Portugal). It is also important to remember that when the attack was launched on Pearl Harbor and Southeast Asia, most of the Japanese leaders, while hoping to achieve *some* gains from going to war, did not believe that they could defeat the United States. At the Liaison Conference on November 1, 1941, "the only thing the chiefs of staff of both branches, in spite of their strong stand, assured to the conferees was that Japan could keep on fighting favorably for two years, but the outlook after that was bleak."[84]

THE QUESTION OF JAPANESE "FASCISM"

Most Western writers on Japan accept the applicability of the term "fascist" to Japan for varying periods between some time in the later 1920s and 1945.[85] The term is also used by Japanese Marxists.

The differences over dating immediately signal one obvious difficulty: if Japan had a fascist *regime,* what was its starting date? If Japan did not have a fascist regime, then what is the meaning of defining it as a fascist country? It is not enough to claim that there was a fascist *movement*. After all, there was a fascist movement in Britain in the 1930s, without Britain being a fascist country.

The term fascism raises some problems. Fascism as a political phenomenon is mainly associated with Europe, and particularly with Italy in the years 1922–1943/45 and Germany in 1933–45. It is a phenomenon which has not only political and ideological features, but also economic ones. While there is no universally accepted definition of fascism (one of the few terms used equally by Marxists and non-Marxists), it is generally agreed that the *minimum* characteristics involve the following: "the total, systematic suppression of every form of autonomous organization of the [working] masses";[86] some form of mass petit bourgeois movement; rural discontent. While there is a wide measure of agreement over what constitutes fascist ideology, there is severe disagreement over two key questions: can fascism be produced by capitalism only at one stage of the latter's development? And can one talk of a fascist regime without either a recognizable fascist party or similar organization wielding state power?

As Togliatti and others warned during the fascist period in Europe, trying to over-generalize is pointless. If every form of reaction can be termed "fascism," the word loses its meaning. Fascism can be only a *specific* form of reaction.[87] It seems an open question whether the most valuable approach is indeed to try to compare Japan with the European fascist states. While certain elements in Japan called themselves fascists and were purposefully imitating European fascism, and the Tokyo government was in *political* alliance with Berlin and Rome, posing the question "what was the nature of the Japanese regime?" exclusively in terms of "fascism" may be a Eurocentric approach which obscures the specific features of the Japanese regime.[88]

Unlike the European fascist states, Japan had no successful coup d'état or putsch, such as the March on Rome in 1922 or Hitler's seizure of power in 1933. Equally, there was no violent or abrupt *end* to the wartime regime, which also raises questions about its nature.[89] And there was no mass fascist party in Japan. Indeed, there was a degree of continuity in Japan, at least at the formal institutional level, which was quite unknown in Italy, Germany or Spain.

It is worth looking briefly at the arguments put forward by those who contend that Japan had a fascist state, and at the criteria adopted for this judgement. The only substantial Marxist work in English on Japanese fascism is the book by O. Tanin and E. Yohan, *Militarism and Fascism in Japan,* completed in early 1933.[90] Tanin and Yohan follow the Kōza line and are cautious about applying the label "fascist" to the Japanese *regime.* Their book has an introduction by one of the Comintern's leading theoreticians, Karl Radek, specifically criticizing their theses from the standpoint of the Rōnō faction, which coincided with the then official Comintern line.

The difference between these two (the Tanin and Yohan text and the Radek introduction) illuminates some of the issues.

Tanin and Yohan ask if "the whole reactionary chauvinist movement" can be called "fascist" in the West European sense of the word and answer "no." First,

> West European fascism is primarily an instrument of finance capital, while the Japanese reactionary chauvinist movement, taken as a whole, is the instrument not only of finance capital but also of the Japanese monarchy which represents a *bloc* of two class forces: finance capital and semi-feudal landowners, and besides this possesses the logic of its own development, represented by the army and monarchist bureaucracy whose oppression has an independent significance. That is why at the center of the Japanese reactionary chauvinist movement we find principally the same people who head the system of Japanese military-feudal imperialism. Hence, the role of the army as the backbone of the reactionary chauvinist movement taken as a whole.
>
> The second distinguishing trait of the Japanese reactionary chauvinist movement, characteristic of the most important and so far the most influential wing of it, follows from this. It is the limited use of social demagogy by the reactionary chauvinist movement as a whole.
>
> . . . these peculiarities of the Japanese reactionary chauvinist movement as a whole, distinguishing it from West European fascism, are closely interwoven with the peculiarities of the social structure and the peculiar historical development of Japanese military-feudal imperialism.[91]

Radek takes issue with Tanin and Yohan on both points. On the first aspect, though, the difference is really about what stage Japanese capitalism has reached in its development. Discussing European fascism, Radek states that it "develops on the economic basis of the domination of monopoly capital, which . . . [inter alia] is feeling the approach of the social revolution."[92] Radek asserts that fascism can exist only in a country which is dominated by finance capital. In a country not dominated by finance capital, reaction might share many features with fascism but would not be "homogeneous with fascism."[93] Radek criticizes Tanin and Yohan on the grounds that they overrate the importance of the survivals of feudalism.[94] Japan, he insists, is dominated by finance capital and has reached the stage of monopoly capital. As regards the economic base, therefore, Japan has reached the requisite stage to have a full, "classic" fascist regime. He does not say when the regime first qualified as fascist.

This disagreement among Marxists involves not the question "how reactionary was the Japanese regime?" but "had Japan reached the stage of development where the form of reaction could be qualified as fascist?" Radek says yes. Tanin and Yohan give a qualified no.

Another disagreement concerns not so much the nature of the state apparatus as such, but rather the relationship between the regime and the petit bourgeois masses. Tanin and Yohan go at great length into the many organizations which fall into what they call the "reactionary chauvinist movement." These they divide into two streams: the reactionary organizations of the privileged classes and reactionary organizations among the intermediate social strata.[95] The latter stream is much closer to Western European fascism in its ideology but, though useful for the ruling group, it is also very doubtful that it will attain power. Tanin and Yohan conclude that although there are a lot of fascist or quasi-fascist organizations in Japan, one cannot (1932–33) talk of a fascist party in the same way as in Germany or Italy.

Radek retorts that an actual fascist party is not a prerequisite. "The point is not whether the Japanese fascists have millions of adherents, united into special fascist organizations of a general patriotic nature, created by the bureaucrats and militarists. The decisive question is whether those people who control these mass organizations, although officially non-fascist, serve fascism or not, and what kind of ideas they propound in these organizations."[96] The Japanese regime, he claims, *is* like those in Germany and Italy, in its "search for a bulwark among the broad petty bourgeois masses."[97]

Radek asserts that there are no "primary" differences between European fascism and what he calls Japanese fascism, only "secondary" differences: first and most important, the role of the army as "organizer and leader of the fascist movement"; second, the role of landlords in organizing Japanese fascism in the spirit of the legends of the Middle Ages.[98]

While Radek states that he is interested in both *"the resemblance and differences between Japanese and European fascism,"*[99] the eminent Japanese political scientist, Maruyama Masao, on the other hand, has acknowledged that he is more interested in seeking out the differences between the Japanese and European experiences.[100] Others have suggested that, while it is fair enough to attempt a comparison, an *exclusive* comparison with the West may be misleading. Japan might fruitfully be compared also with some contemporary Third World countries, and its political leadership to a *collective* form of modern nationalist movements.[101]

Yet if Japan became a fascist country, then it must be possible to locate the transition, if not to one exact day, week or month, at least to some definable period. But this turns out to be very difficult. Where could the transition be located? Several liberal observers stress that "party cabinets" came to an end with the assassination of Premier Inukai in 1932. But these "party cabinets" can not be considered the *determinant* of a putative "democracy" as opposed to "fascism." Barrington Moore, seeking to locate the beginning of a "fascist" regime, acknowledges that these assassinations only "inaugurated a period of semimilitary dictatorship rather than of outright fascism."[102] Nor can one go by elections. In his discussion of periodization, Moore appears to adopt the 1932 election in Germany as a criterion for dating what he calls "a . . . distinction between a democratic and a totalitarian phase."[103] But in Japan the 1936 election appears to have been relatively free, and even in the 1942 election opponents of the regime were elected (something impossible at that stage in Italy or Germany). It cannot, therefore, be said that there was a change in the political *system*.[104] Paradoxically, proof of this lies not only in the absence of change on the way into the alleged "fascist" period, but also in the absence of change in the structures of the state in 1945.[105]

In spite of what Radek and others have claimed, the Japanese state was a very different state from those in Germany and Italy. Both the monarchy and the military clearly played completely different roles.[106] The survival of the monarchy as a locus of *real* power is part and parcel of the lack of change needed in the regime as a whole. The system has been described as "imperial absolutism," a reference not to the specific acts of the individual emperor, but to the place of the imperial institution in the structure of the state. The position of the imperial institution had important effects both on the forms of political organization selected by the ruling group, and on the absence of any figure comparable to Hitler or Mussolini.[107]

Bourgeois democracy in Japan was much weaker than in either Germany or Italy, and the left-wing movement was not comparable either. The ruling group in Japan found it fairly easy to consolidate round the throne, and it did not need to develop a mass movement to achieve its ends. Indeed, consolidation round the throne was, in a way, the *opposite* of any form of political expression. The Imperial Rule Assistance Association, formally organized in October 1940 after all the political parties in the Diet had been dissolved, was the culmination of a process—the elimination of contesting organizations disturbing the nation's "harmony"—not an instrument of real mass mobilization.

In addition, the system of imperial absolutism led to definite limitations on those who were fascists. So powerful were both the ideology of the Emperor-system and the state structure that Japanese fascists could attack only the opposition. Otherwise they might "endanger" the Emperor himself. As was clearly shown in February 1936, the Emperor was literally unassailable. Thus, changes could only be brought about *through* the system, and the key problematic area is really the extent to which those with fascist ideas and objectives actually managed to get them implemented through the existing state personnel and machinery.

To decide this involves an evaluation of the role of the military, especially the army. The army certainly was more important politically in Japan than in Germany, Italy or even Spain, but it is by no means clear that it was qualitatively more important than it had been in the 1920s or even in the Meiji period.[108] The army was important in Japanese expansionism in the 1930s and 1940s, but it had been important in moves overseas earlier. And, although expansion overseas was a central feature of the regime in the years 1931–42, expansionism and colonialism are not defining features of fascism. There can be non-expansionist fascism and non-fascist expansionism. What the military did was not simply to play a leading role in overseas expansion, but, while increasingly forming an alliance with the bureaucracy, simultaneously to nudge the regime farther towards the right through the actions of its fascist individuals and groups. In addition, the military played an important role in ideology and "culture." The military were an "elite," fostering an ideology of "heroism." Together with that of Emperor-worship (or state-worship), this ideology helped create the conditions where a mass movement was neither needed nor wanted.[109] In recent years there has been a major reassessment of the role of the Japanese military in the 1930s, and much emphasis has been placed on the fact that the military did not "succeed" in seizing power. This is technically correct. But there was also an element of "success through failure."[110] The violence of the years 1931–36 was disorganized and did not represent the mainstream of the army, as Crowley stresses. On the other hand, there was extensive "seepage," not only of ideas, but also of personnel. The "wild" elements in the army *did* influence policy enormously, even if not in immediately visible ways.

The main proponent of the thesis that there was a specific Japanese fascism radically different from European fascism is Maruyama Masao. Maruyama, while accepting the applicability of the term "fascism," also tends to stress the "uniqueness" of the Japanese case, and lays considerable emphasis on the aspects of "drift," particularly in foreign policy. Yet this somewhat neglects the remarkably direct and linear progression of Japanese foreign policy. Unlike in Germany and Italy, this can not easily be attributed to one man, but this does not mean it was not the result of identifiable class forces. Maruyama tends to base his acceptance of the term "fascism" on similarities in ideology between Japan and Europe, while playing down the dissimilarities of social and political structures.[111]

In "The Ideology and Dynamics of Japanese Fascism" Maruyama singles out three specific features of the fascist movement in Japan: its family-system tendency; agrarianism; and the ideal of the emancipation of the peoples of Asia from European colonialism. The first is a permanent characteristic of Japanese society as a whole—it differentiates Japan as a whole from Europe; the last also marks off much of the Japanese political spectrum from comparable sectors in Europe though it hardly defines Japan in the 1930s as "fascist." The second feature, agrarianism, is more complex. Its potent ideological force is vividly shown by Tōjō's "anxious and pitiful" answer to a question from a Dietman in 1943, who had asked: "Are not the villages of Imperial Japan being endangered by the absorption of their labour power in the armament industries?" Tōjō answered:

This is a point that truly worries me. On the one hand, I want at all costs to maintain the population of the villages at forty per cent of the total population. I believe that the foundation of Japan lies in giving importance to agriculture. On the other hand, it is undeniable that industry is being expanded, chiefly because of the war. It is extremely hard to reconcile these two factors. However difficult it may be, I am determined to maintain the population of the villages at forty per cent. But production must be increased. A harmony must be created by degrees between the two requirements. But, in creating this harmony, care must be taken to avoid making havoc of the Japanese family system. I must confess that things are not proceeding at present in an ideal manner. In the need for a rapid expansion of production large factories have been set up in various places; their workers have to be hired from among farmers. . . . Although things are not proceeding ideally, I still believe that a method can and will be found to establish a proper harmony in the Japanese manner.[112]

Yet while Tōjō's remarks indicate that agrarianism as an ideological element had great potency, in practice "the agrarian current of traditionalist patriotism, expressed in such movements as *Nōhon-shugi,* was mainly a town and landlord affair, directed *against* peasant interests and aiming to keep the peasant frugal and contented—in a word in his place."[113] Agrarianism was never powerful enough materially to alter the chosen orientation of business either at home or abroad. As far as can be seen, it only marginally influenced the process of accumulation and investment. As for imperialism overseas, although the movement animated by Ishihara Kanji for agrarian colonies in Manchuria was active by the mid-twenties, the contours of Japan's imperialism were fundamentally unaffected by agrarianism as an ideology. On the contrary, the regime was swift to excise any threat from those who seemed to want to put a really radical right-wing programme through. Kita Ikki, the most famous exponent of aggressive expansion in Asia and a degree of internal "renovation," was executed, along with his main aide, Nishida Zei, on apparently trumped-up charges after the February 26th [1936] Incident.[114] At home big business dominated policy.

The trouble with the term "fascism" is that it forces any examination of Japan into a Eurocentric category. It is virtually impossible to examine the phenomenon without constructing such an examination in terms of comparisons with Germany, Italy and Spain. Moreover, most of the criteria used to categorize Japan as fascist in, say, 1940 or thereabouts do not define specifically new phenomena within Japan. Maruyama is right to assert that the regime under Tōjō in 1942 was not qualitatively different from that under Inukai in 1932. This is why Japan could move *out* of "fascism" in 1945 as easily as it was able to move into it. Moore is correct to stress the unbroken dominance of big business, with agrarianism functioning at a purely ideological level; "big business needed fascism, patriotism, Emperor worship, and the military."[115] Tanin and Yohan are correct to talk of imperial absolutism. If these factors are kept in mind, the others fall into place: the absence of a mass party, the role of the military, the continued importance of the Emperor, the absence of a Führer or Duce.

Did the Pacific War itself have some effect? Japan was a violent and aggressive country in Asia well before Pearl Harbor (1941) or the Mukden Incident (1931). The oppression of the working classes and political repression against proletarian militancy had been highly developed at least since the turn of the century.[116] If Japan was "fascist" in 1941, it perhaps should be called "fascist" in 1915. There was a definite stepping up of the campaign to smash all autonomous organizations of the working class in the later 1930s, but this was not on the scale of the actions in Germany or Italy.

Although I would reject the term "fascist" for the regime, it is true that there was a fascist *movement* in Japan from the 1920s to 1945 in the sense that fascist *forces* were at work, and were effective, even if their relationship to state power did not take the same form as in Germany and Italy.

6.
The Pacific War

The Pacific War has been the main occasion of mass contact between the Japanese and Western peoples; no other experience has been so influential in forming general ideas in the West about Japan. It is also probably the single major historical event whose general *image* has been overwhelmingly determined by the cinema. And although America followed a consistent "Hitler first" policy,[1] in American mythology the Pacific War is, to a very large extent, the Second World War. For the British there is always *The Bridge on the River Kwai*.[2] For British and Americans, French and Dutch, the films reflect the extent to which the whole war has become shrouded in a fog of mythology and lies. What follows is only a brief attempt to present key political effects of the war on the Asian nationalist and revolutionary movements on the one hand, and on the imperialist countries on the other.

THE EVENTS

Fantasizing in 1935, one writer noted that "to students of war the physical conditions likely to govern an armed conflict in the Pacific present a fascinating field for exploration. At the outset we are confronted by an arena so vast as almost to defy conception."[3] Japan's gains at the beginning of the war against the West lived up to the fantasy. Between December 1941 and March 1942, with only 15,000 of their own troops killed, the Japanese pulled about 500 million people into their empire. The war theatre extended 8,100 by 6,250 miles. It was by far the biggest acquisition of territory (even allowing for all the water) ever made at that speed in history. "The picture, cherished in England and Australia at the time, of ant-like hordes was quite misleading. On land they [the Japanese] committed only some eleven divisions, considerably less than 200,000 men in all, to the conquest of the Philippines, Malaya, Burma and the Dutch

East Indies."[4] The story of Pearl Harbor is quite well known. Less well known are the events surrounding the Japanese capture of the Philippines, Malaya and Burma, their most brilliant campaigns. The key defences in Hong Kong, expected by the British to hold for seven to ten days, were taken in three hours in "a brilliant assault."[5] Hong Kong itself (Victoria Island) was taken with the assistance of "fifth columnists"—i.e., local help. Guam, the first U.S. territory to be taken, fell in twenty-five minutes.

American and British attitudes were mainly determined by one shattering defeat each: the Philippines and Singapore. At Pearl Harbor, unlike in the Philippines, there was no actual land fighting between Americans and Japanese. The Japanese attack on Pearl Harbor was traumatic (witness, for example, the recurrent use of the radio announcement in John Ford's films),[6] but it was only "treacherous." The important categorization of the Japanese as "brutal" and "savage" came after Bataan and Singapore, not after Nanking.

For the Americans, the Philippines was of special concern. America, and Douglas MacArthur in particular, had invested great psychological capital in the country. MacArthur had withdrawn there after retiring as Chief of Staff of the U.S. Army, and had made himself responsible for the country's defence, with disastrous results, since he grossly miscalculated the Japanese offensive capacity (like nearly all Caucasians in Asia). For the Japanese, it was a relatively low priority. Their commander, Homma Masaharu, belonged to the "liberal" wing of the army, and was considered to be dangerously pro-British. He had been appointed to the Philippines command because Tōjō considered it relatively unimportant; yet, despite being deprived of sizeable quantities of air and ground forces at crucial moments, Homma took Bataan three weeks ahead of schedule against a much larger defending force than he had calculated. Numerous Filipinos whom MacArthur assumed would fight for U.S. imperialism simply deserted or failed to fire a shot. MacArthur falsified his reports to try to conceal the size of the defeat. The outright military defeat, plus the widespread defection of their assumed "allies," shook the American military. To cope with this, a major psychological displacement came into operation. The straightforward defeat at Bataan was combined with features from a subsequent event: Japanese treatment of the prisoners from Bataan —especially the famous Bataan "death march," on which a large number of Americans and Filipinos died en route to camps in the interior.[7] These two episodes were conflated to "fix" the nature of the whole war for the American public. Japanese harshness was transmogrified into savagery, and displaced from treatment of POWs to the actual fighting. This image was particularly powerful because America's mythological vision of the land fighting in the Pacific consisted largely of the Philippines (evident from films like *Bataan* and *Back to Bataan*). MacArthur's forces spending half the war bogged down in New Guinea (Irian) is just ignored. Similarly,

America has never faced up to widespread Filipino loathing of U.S. imperialism and all that that involves.[8]

The British defeat in Malaya and Singapore has been virtually suppressed. If asked what has been "the worst disaster and largest capitulation in British history" (Churchill on Singapore), how many people could give a correct answer? Even fewer could indicate how this occurred. The Malayan campaign exemplifies two important features of the whole Southeast Asian war: Japan's vast *fighting* superiority and the disintegration of the European colonial systems. British troops in Malaya consistently outnumbered the Japanese. The Japanese proved far superior in skill and use of the terrain. As in Burma, their use of guerrilla tactics and their ability to fight in the jungle, off the roads, gave them an invincible advantage. In addition, they were aided by the local population and by sizeable numbers of defectors from the British side.[9]

The British have never published a full account of the disintegration of their army in Malaya, but relations between British officers and Indian mercenaries were clearly extremely bad. Far from being, as a recent British history would have it, "one of the happiest armies of all time,"[10] the Indian Army was a miserable shambles of oppression and contradictions. Shortly before the Japanese invasion of Malaya, the Hyderabads mutinied and had to be broken up and spread among other units. There had also been trouble among the Bhawalpures.[11] British policy of enrolling a combination of ethnic and religious minorities resulted in deep-rooted Gurkha-Sikh hostility within the army, and deep loathing among the oppressed troops for their largely racist officers. Even the account by Winston Churchill makes it clear that morale slumped badly and that, in essence, the British Army turned and ran in front of the Japanese, while the Indian mercenaries either did the same or deserted.[12] Before the Japanese reached Singapore, the first nuclei of anti-British Indians from the British Army had been organized, and these crossed over to Singapore Island with the first wave of Japanese troops on February 8/9, 1942.

For a Western readership subjected for decades to imperialist history, emphasis must be put on the extent to which the rapid disintegration of colonial rule in both Malaya and Singapore as well as Burma was due to the nature of British government. The case of the State of Kedah in Malaya is exemplary. With the approach of the Japanese, the masses rose up against the Sultan, who fled into hiding. The Sultan's son, Tengku Abdul Rahman, later Prime Minister of Malaya and Malaysia, kidnapped his father, presented himself to the Japanese and offered his services to them to broadcast a radio appeal to the population to assist the Japanese. Abdul Rahman felt obliged to co-operate actively with the Japanese to protect his family's feudal position and try to prevent a popular uprising, which was already under way as the British retreated.[13]

An even more advanced situation existed in Singapore. This city had been turned into the centre of colonial trade and commercial usury in the area. The Chinese population, vigorously anti-Japanese and extremely alarmed by what had happened in China, asked to be armed. The request was refused by the colonial authorities, who were afraid that it might shift the balance of commercial power away from the main allies of the British, the Malays.[14] Having refused to allow the Chinese to protect themselves, the British regime subsequently ordered a "scorched earth" policy— allegedly to deny facilities and goods to the enemy. The local traders and bourgeoisie naturally objected, and many of them hired gangs of armed deserters, often Australian and drunk, to protect their property and fight off official troops coming to burn down their warehouses, factories and shops. The authorities poured out propaganda about the situation, impeding both defence and flight. After all but complete military incapacity on the part of the local commander, General Arthur Percival (the commander of an equally unsuccessful campaign to repress the Irish revolutionaries in Munster twenty years earlier), and the area commander, General Sir Archibald Wavell, Singapore fell—thirty days ahead of the Japanese schedule. British losses totalled 138,708, of whom more than 130,000 were taken prisoner.[15]

With possession of Indochina and the Malayan Peninsula, and a close alliance with a nominally independent and *de facto* pro-Tokyo Thailand, Japan was able to sweep all over Southeast Asia and up to the Indian frontier. Eventually, on land, the Japanese were held on New Guinea and Guadalcanal by the Americans and Australians. The British were actually pushed back into India towards the end of the war, eventually recovering slightly and advancing into Burma before the surrender. But the Japanese kept up a formidable pace elsewhere, winning their major victories in Southwest China during the final autumn of the war.

Though the strategy of the war is fairly familiar, it needs to be stressed that Japan was fighting a war on two fronts. United States and European accounts of the Asian war concentrate on Southeast Asia and the Pacific area. But throughout the war the bulk of the Japanese army was stationed in China and Manchuria. These troops were not "tied down" in some abstract way. They were in China fighting the People's Liberation Army and the Chinese people—Japan's main enemy. A sizeable part of the Japanese army, too, was stationed along the Soviet frontier.

Even at the end of the war, in 1945, the number of Japanese troops engaged in fighting all the white imperialists together amounted to con- siderably less than half the Japanese forces outside Japan itself.[16]

Japan's strategy against the Western powers was determined by the problem of China. To succeed, Japan had to knock out America long enough to be able to seize the whole of Southeast Asia.[17] Neither Japan's economy, nor its political thinking, was geared to the possibility of a long war. To some extent the wish was father to the thought: since Japan could win only if the war was short, a "short war psychology" dominated the conduct of the war. But this wishful thinking was in turn determined by the social and economic conditions of Japan itself. At the time when Japan went into war against a group of the most advanced nations on earth (when it was already at war with the most populous nation on earth, China), its economy was no match for that of the major industrial powers it was fighting, especially the United States. This was true both of Japan's specific vulnerability through dependence on imported raw materials and of the internal structure of production. Although investment in heavy industry, particularly war-related heavy industry, was high relative to investment in light industry, industry as a whole still played a much smaller part in the economy than it did in any of the Western industrialized nations. And, paradoxically, in spite of their commitment to the *aims* of the war, the evidence is that Japan's wartime (1941–45) and prewar governments had not adequately prepared the country for the *economic* struggle that lay ahead. Amazingly, over the period 1940–44 Japan had a faster growth rate than Britain (and Germany), yet in 1942 it was devoting less of its GNP (30 per cent) to war expenditures than was the United States (44 per cent). The extent of the Japanese leadership's miscalculation of the overall situation can be gauged from the fact that in 1942 Japan actually *relaxed* its war effort. The "limited programme" approach was dropped only in winter 1942–43, after the setback on Guadalcanal.[18]

The Japanese fought a brilliant war in Southeast Asia, as is recognized by all military experts. They smashed the colonial armies and the British, French and Dutch empires in the area. The only white army that beat them in a straight fight was the Soviet army (in both 1939 and 1945). Eventually, the Japanese were defeated by a combination of the Chinese People's Liberation Army (PLA), local national liberation movements (such as that in the Philippines) and American technology. The Japanese were not defeated by American military prowess, as is often alleged. In fact, the Americans did relatively little actual fighting against Japanese troops. Total U.S. battle deaths for the entire Pacific War were "roughly 50,000."[19] After the experience of *fighting* the Japanese at Tarawa (a small atoll in the Pacific) in November 1943, the Americans decided to confine the war on their side as far as possible to machines.[20] The war became much more a navy than an army war, and the chief architect of American success was Admiral Chester W. Nimitz, rather than General MacArthur.[21] Thus MacArthur's Bataan fetish is only one of a coherent string of such phenomena, which includes the virtual suppression of the New Guinea fighting (as well as the role of the PLA), the re-posing of the flag-planting on Iwo Jima (because the real flag was too small for a good photograph), and the falsification of the Battle of Leyte Gulf. And the vindictiveness which lay at the root of America's moralistic entry into war with Japan resurfaced not only in MacArthur's vendettas against Homma and Yamashita, but also in the American decision to "save up" entire tracts of urban Japan on which to use the first atom bombs.[22]

JAPAN AND THE NATIONAL LIBERATION
MOVEMENTS IN ASIA: THE DISINTEGRATION
OF THE EUROPEAN EMPIRES

The ideal of emancipating the Asian peoples from European colonialism is one of the three distinguishing features of Japanese "fascism" which Maruyama identifies.[23] From the time of the Meiji Restoration, Japan's Asia policy had been a fluctuating combination of anti-Westernism and expansionism. A list of the protégés of Tōyama Mitsuru, founder of the ultra-patriotic Amur River Society, embodies the range of the contradictions in Japan's role: Sun Yat-sen, Chiang Kai-shek, Wang Ching-wei, Emilio Aguinaldo, Ras [or Rash] Behari Bose, Kourbangalieff, the Ataman Semyonov, Mahendra Pratap.[24] Except for the occupation of some of Germany's former possessions, Japan was not able to intervene directly against the European imperialist systems until the late 1930s. But it had planned for an active role in "liberating" East Asia. And Japan was seen by many in Rangoon, Bangkok, Djakarta and Hanoi as indeed "the light of Asia."[25]

Japan's main aim was indisputably to tie militarily and economically strategic areas into the "Greater East Asian Co-Prosperity Sphere," a grandiose scheme designed to remove East and Southeast Asia from U.S.-European colonial control and switch it to the job of servicing the Japanese economy. Japan's intentions were themselves quite mixed; the actual attempt to implement policy was riddled with further difficulties; and the effects of Japan's actions outstripped Japan's own intentions. But the main thrust of Japanese policy was clear—to destroy the European and American empires in order to construct an imperial system of its own. While little suggests that economic exploitation of the area, given an extended period of peacetime, would have been any less severe than that by the Caucasian imperialists, Japan did begin to implement important schemes such as the Thai-Burma railroad to redirect and stimulate local commerce. Yet though Japanese rule was marked by racism in Korea in the same way that Caucasian rule was racist everywhere, Japan also adopted a qualitatively different racial attitude to most other Southeast Asian peoples from that of the white colonialists: this fact is attested to by numerous sources, and its importance cannot be underestimated.[26]

Any estimate of Japan's effects on Southeast Asia must take into account a number of other factors. First, Japan's presence in most of the area was very brief, three and a half years at the most (except for China and Korea). Second, there were big problems of language and a shortage of trained personnel. Third, there were such cultural problems as Japanese insistence on Emperor-worship, and face-slapping, which was considered deeply insulting by most Southeast Asian peoples. Fourth, there were real differences of opinion among the Japanese leaders themselves about policy towards the "liberated" areas based on irreconcilable conflict between Japan's economic demands and the political desires of some of its cadres. Wartime Burmese Premier Ba Maw's account of his dealings with Japan reveals a complex situation involving three basic groups. At the centre was the Tokyo government; regionally, there was the Southeast Asia Supreme Command based on Singapore; locally, there were military and political operatives, sometimes acting with considerable autonomy.[27] In Ba Maw's account the Tokyo government was very "Asian-conscious," but the wishes of the leaders were frequently obstructed by bureaucrats and militarists at lower echelons of the administration. The Southeast Asia Supreme Command was basically concerned with military security and therefore was not keen on promoting local political autonomy. The local operatives could vary from dedicated progressive cadres working for Burmese independence to insensitive militarists devoted only to the Japanese empire. In addition, there were army/navy variations and numerous splits between civilians and military and within civil and military bureaucracies.

The effects of Japan's actions are of prime political importance, for they contributed significantly to the structuring of the Southeast Asian scene as it is today. Even if Japan's intentions were obscure and contradictory (as well as oppressive), the mere presence of a powerful voice disputing the position of the U.S.-European powers gave heart to nationalists throughout Asia.

In the Philippines, Japan had a tradition of deep anti-Americanism to build on, and the support of some of the leaders of the original revolutionary uprising, particularly Emilio Aguinaldo and Artemio Ricarte, who returned to Manila from Japan.[28] Japan's experience in the Philippines exemplifies most of the contradictory features of the whole occupation-liberation nexus. In the first place, Japan's military victories and superior strategy wrecked the myth of American superiority and might have destroyed MacArthur's reputation had his incompetence been more widely known. As American power and mass acceptance of American rule crumbled, the U.S. authorities were confronted with large-scale desertions among their Filipino mercenaries. Secondly, the Japanese took a number of steps to win local support. Tagalog became one of the two official languages (along with Japanese). They also brought in a lot of Catholic priests and made a strong appeal to Catholic sentiment.[29] The Japanese administration actively worked on humiliating Americans in front of Filipinos (and indeed this is part of the explanation of the Bataan "Death March" and other incidents). And the Japanese also made an ideological and socio-economic appeal for Philippine support by setting out a critique of U.S. colonial rule and the reasons for Philippine subservience to the Americans. Frugality was identified as the key Japanese quality and the one which would enable the Philippines to liberate itself from the effects of U.S. colonialism.[30]

This interesting effort was, to be sure, undermined from the start by the fact that Japan, short of personnel and time, opted for a form of rule in the Philippines which was essentially based on the very same class American colonial rule had been based on—the oligarchy.[31] The entire Philippines oligarchy collaborated with the Japanese, without great difficulty. There is no evidence that the Japanese, although they advanced the date of independence, had any desire to attack the existing class structure of the country.

The community of *class* interests between Japanese and U.S. imperialisms was swiftly shown when the United States reoccupied its colony in 1945. Behind a smokescreen of highly selective and discriminatory charges of "collaboration," MacArthur engineered the appointment of Manuel Roxas, who had been the top rice collector for the Japanese occupation, as the first President of the formally independent Philippines in 1946. The restoration of the compromised oligarchy was deemed essential in view of the imperialist interests of the United States and the new threat of a powerful armed opposition which had greatly developed during the Japanese occupation—the Anti-Japanese People's Army, or Hukbalahap (Huks), set up in March 1942 under communist leadership.[32]

In the Dutch East Indies, some serious preparation had been put in, particularly in fostering Muslim hostility to the Dutch.[33] In 1938 the Japanese Islamic Association, which had been set up in the mid-1930s, sponsored an Islamic World Conference in Tokyo, which was well attended by Indonesian Muslims.

Once in the Dutch East Indies, the Japanese tried to build up Islam as a counter to the Western-oriented culture of the existing nationalist leaders (in spite of major obstacles such as Emperor-worship). The entire generation of postwar Indonesian leaders, from Mohammed Hatta and Sukarno through to Suharto and the group of generals at present in power in Djakarta, was either trained or at least promoted by the Japanese. Contemporary Western texts usually referred to Sukarno and others by terms such as "the Javanese quisling leader,"[34] but whatever assessment one may make of Sukarno, Hatta or Suharto, it is clear that some differentiated approach is needed to nationalist "collaborationism" here, as in Burma, the Philippines and elsewhere. Japan's mere presence in Indonesia had a startling effect on the Dutch. On December 6, 1942, Queen Wilhelmina announced a wholesale revision of Holland's postwar relations with its colonies. At the time some observers grasped the significance of the changes Japan had brought about; one over-optimistic one wrote: "When their former Dutch governors return, they will come with contrition in their hearts and with a spirit of democracy not previously shown this colonial race. Certainly the success of Japanese expansion alone is responsible for the suddenness of this creditable development in attitude toward the Far East."[35] On the one hand, then, Japan greatly stimulated the power of Islam with critical effect on post-independence Indonesia; on the other hand, in the closing days of the war the Japanese not only granted Indonesia independence as a deliberately anti-Dutch measure, but even armed the Indonesians against the Dutch.[36] When the first Western imperialists, who were the British, returned to Indonesia, they organized the rearming of the Japanese military and led a joint Anglo-Japanese operation against the Indonesian nationalists. As in Korea and Vietnam, this had a searing effect in demonstrating the essential community of interests between Western and Japanese imperialism when faced with the peoples of Asia. Those who had perhaps fallen for Western propaganda against the Japanese were confronted with the inescapable evidence that in the West's struggle to oppress the peoples of the world, the Japanese were the West's ally, not its enemy.

"Burma," wrote J. S. Furnivall, "was not a human society but a business concern."[37] A completely mythological picture of British rule in Burma still prevails in the West, partly due to the assiduous work of mystification perpetrated by Lord Louis Mountbatten. For the British, Burma was simply a territory to be plundered. There was no popular base for British imperialism. Once again, the mere arrival of the Japanese detonated the contradictions. The British had attempted to rationalize their presence with slogans about "protecting the Burmese." But such justifications were proven not only hypocritical but false when the British forces were overwhelmingly defeated by the Japanese in another brilliant campaign. Burmese who had been enrolled by the British deserted. Even the Governor's elite Karen bodyguard, drawn from the Burma Military Police, deserted him as he was scuttling from Government House to Rangoon airport. Even before the Japanese got to Rangoon, British rule had, as in Singapore, taken a severe battering as mass looting, including some by the military, broke out. Some extraordinary scenes of broken-down British imperial masochism took place, like the last dinner at Government House, when the guests repaired to the billiard room after dinner in drunken condition and smashed the portraits of the past governors on the walls by throwing billiard balls at them. As in Indonesia, the Japanese promoted a Burmese regime in which genuine nationalist—and in this case revolutionary—leaders took part. Burma represents the most advanced case in the area, where a group headed by Aung San revolted against the Japanese before the latter were ready to grant independence, and fought against the Japanese for a revolutionary independent Burma. This project was sabotaged by the postwar Labour government, and Aung San was murdered. But equally what Furnivall calls the "attempt to reconquer Burma for capitalism" was doomed. Britain was never able to settle back into its prewar position, despite the prodigious efforts of Lord Louis Mountbatten. The change is strikingly symbolized by the fact that when Sir Reginald Dorman-Smith, the prewar governor, went on a tour to the north, he found himself sitting down to dinner at Myitkyina with the local Kachin chief, who was wearing the dinner jacket which Dorman-Smith had abandoned in his flight three and a half years before. It was very hard to stage a come-back in such conditions.[38]

The Japanese did not plan to try and invade the whole of India at any stage of the war; rather they hoped to win over the large number of Indians in Southeast Asia (2.5–3 million), build up an anti-British army of Indians and stimulate the internal breakdown of British rule. This was a mammoth task. Japan only had a few years in which to initiate it, yet (in admittedly excellent conditions) a great deal was accomplished.

It is obvious from Churchill's narrative that his chief concern in the early stages of the war in Asia was British rule in the colonies, particularly India. His memo to General Ismay of February 2, 1942 reads: "The reinforcement of India has become most urgent. I am deeply concerned with the reactions from Japanese victories throughout Asia. It will be necessary to have an additional number of British troops in India. These need not be fully formed divisions, as they are for internal security against revolt."[39]

What were the conditions which made Japan's task so easy? First, there was the general anti-Western solidarity, which worked in Japan's favour everywhere.[40] Secondly, there was the long history of British oppression, repression and exploitation of India. Within India itself, the British had conducted a mass incarceration of political elements in July 1940. Among those locked up was Subhas Chandra Bose, who had been President of the Congress Party in 1938–39, and had won re-election to this post in 1939 against Gandhi's nominee, but had then been ousted when incapacitated by illness. Bose managed to get himself released by the British after staging a hunger strike, and in January 1941 made an escape to Berlin via Afghanistan and the Soviet Union. In Germany he worked at winning over the Indian POWs who had been captured—with considerable success, since these naturally resented having been dragooned, without being consulted, into an alien war in adverse climatic and political conditions. In 1943 Bose travelled by submarine from Hamburg to Japan, and in July 1943 was installed in Singapore.

Among Tōyama Mitsuru's protégés had been Ras Behari Bose, who had carried out a bomb attack on the British Viceroy, Lord Hardinge, in 1912. In 1915 he had fled to Japan and attached himself to Tōyama. At the beginning of the war he had set up as head of the Indian Independence League based in Bangkok, with Mahendra Pratap heading a branch in Shanghai. As the Japanese armies advanced they encountered a generally warm welcome from the Indian population in Hong Kong, Malaya and Singapore. It was among the Indian mercenaries of the British that they found their most valuable support.[41] The Indian National Army (INA), which was set up based on Singapore, was made up of Indian troops who had been sent to East Asia by the British at the beginning of the war, and who had rallied (as in the Malayan campaign) to the Japanese "side."[42] After Subhas Chandra Bose had made his spectacular journey from Germany, he was elected head of the INA and head of the Provisional Government of Free India at a mass meeting in Singapore on July 4, 1943 (Ras Behari Bose having stood down as leader when Subhas Chandra Bose appeared). In November 1943 Japan convened a major conference of its Asian allies in Tokyo, the Greater East Asia Conference,[43] which Bose (Subhas Chandra) attended as an observer. At this meeting Tōjō announced that Japan was handing over the Andaman and Nicobar Islands to the Provisional Government of Free India, which renamed the islands Shaheed (Martyr) and Swaraj (Independence) Islands.[44] The INA fought on the Burma-India frontier, and in the battles around Imphal and Kohima, but the period in India was too brief and confined to too small a space (mainly in Nagaland) to provide adequate evidence of the size of popular support.[45] What was important, though, was the formation of military and political cadres who contributed to the devastating mutiny in the Indian Navy after the end of the war; and the famous Red Fort trial (of INA leaders after the war) served as a powerful political catalyst to Indian independence.[46] Subsequently many of the INA cadres were integrated (at lower echelon) into the new Indian Army, which remained essentially a Sandhurst-based outfit. The story and achievements of the INA have, like other such phenomena, been virtually suppressed by British historians. When the British reoccupied Malaya, one of their first actions was to wreck the war memorial to the INA dead at Singapore.[47]

In the other countries of Asia, Japan's effect was less the result of deliberate action. In China, Japan's presence induced the British and Americans to relinquish most special rights (January 11, 1943). Reciprocally, this gesture led the Japanese into greater flexibility towards Japanese-occupied China, and in March 1943 Tōjō had to visit China to calm down irate Japanese business interests there.[48] All this had a gradual snowballing effect. In India, two of Churchill's formal allies, America and the Kuomintang, were constantly pressuring Britain to carry out a few reforms in India's putrid colonial regime. Though these suggestions were blandly ignored,[49] they provided an excuse for different imperialists to meddle in hitherto private preserves.[50] And the knowledge that the ruling power was being criticized by an ally to whom some political appeal could be made emboldened Indian demands regardless of the actual nature of the regimes involved. Similarly, Roosevelt thought the war should be used to terminate French rule in Indochina; and if his motives were worthless, the effect was beneficial. Again, in Indochina, towards the end of the war, the Japanese started to release large numbers of political prisoners who had been incarcerated by the French; some of these held positions of power in the closing months of the war.[51]

In some countries at the end of the war there was a revolutionary uprising (Burma), in others a radical utilization of Japanese concessions (Indonesia). But, whether the Japanese granted independence to frustrate the Western imperialists or whether the revolutionary forces seized power on their own initiative, the consequences for Western power were enormous. But perhaps the factor which contributed so much to the arousal of the peoples of Asia was Japanese participation, after promoting the liberation movements, in the suppression of these same movements alongside a colonial army. For the masses in Indonesia, Vietnam and Korea this was an experience comparable in some respects to what the use of German troops to suppress the Partisans in Yugoslavia after the German surrender would have been. The actors in such events do not often commit themselves to print, but the main agent of the new Anglo-Japanese alliance in Indonesia in 1945, Laurens Van Der Post, did later recount his role, suitably buried at the end of a folklorish article in a Sunday newspaper colour supplement.

> I was sent by Lord Mountbatten to the Japanese general commanding the Japanese army in Java to order him to take up arms against the forces of Nationalism he had helped to provoke. . . . [After some initial reluctance] he went straight away to order his Chief of Staff to tell his troops to do whatever I wanted, and *if it had not been for the way the Japanese fought with us, their old enemies, at places like Bandoeng and Semerang* [*sic*] thereafter, there could have been terrible massacres of Europeans. . . .[52]

It should be emphasized that Japanese participation in these episodes mainly strengthened awareness of the reactionary and racist nature of *Western* imperialism, just as had the forcible British *racist* induction of India and Burma into the European war in 1939.

The widely held Euro-American view of Japan's role in Asia in the years 1941–45 as identical to that of Germany in Europe is incorrect. In China and Korea the Japanese behaved very like the European imperialists. But the Japan-Asia and Germany-Europe cases are not comparable because the specific nature of the contradictions between Japanese imperialism and established Western imperialism provided real, if limited, space for nationalist and revolutionary forces in Southeast Asia to promote the struggle for independence. It was the existence of this "space" which led many political groups and individuals to work "with" the Japanese against the European-American imperialist coalition. An awareness of the concrete conditions for this "collaboration"[53] is needed to understand both the speed of the collapse of the white empires and the strength of Japan's grip on Southeast Asia today (which goes hand-in-hand with strong anti-Japanese feeling).

WORLD WAR II AND GUERRILLA WARFARE

One aspect of the Pacific War that merits further study is the guerrilla fighting. The effects of Japan's occupation of China have been well studied[54] and are relatively clear. But a great deal of the fighting by the mass of the Japanese army throughout Asia had "guerrilla" aspects. The big campaigns in Malaya and Burma against the British were won mainly through Japan's superior utilization of the jungle. On the other side, the Philippines and Burma saw the first large-scale development of Western guerrilla units, first with the Americans in the Philippines, and subsequently in Burma. British guerrillas were first organized by the maverick Orde Wingate, who had previously operated in Palestine aiding the Zionists and then in Ethiopia. Wingate had no interest in Burma and the Burmese as such. When he was killed, the operation virtually evaporated. However, he had caught the imagination of American military fantasists and of Roosevelt, and it was the Wingate experience that led to the setting up of Merrill's Marauders in Burma to try to keep open the Burma Road to China. These operations were a failure. There was negligible Burmese support.[55] Merrill's Marauders in particular were very poorly supplied. And the Japanese knocked out the U.S.-Kuomintang position in Southwest China, thus making the venture pointless. But the experience incubated and eventually bore disease in America's counter-insurgency in the Philippines, Vietnam, Laos, Cambodia and Thailand.

THE POLITICS OF THE WAR

Most Western writing on the Pacific War obscures both the nature of the Caucasian colonial regimes in the area and the real complexity of Japan's relationship with the Southeast Asian nations. It is not surprising, therefore, that the politics of the war, as opposed to the disembodied military tactics, are largely suppressed. Gabriel Kolko's major study, *The Politics of War,* demolishes the prevalent mystifications in masterly fashion.[56]

The attitude of the British, the main colonial power in the area, was, in Kolko's words, "entirely political." Unlike Holland and France, which were effectively eliminated from the zone, Britain was able to hang on to the edge of the battle area, in India and Ceylon. Britain's objectives were simple: to hold onto India, repress political opposition there, and reconstitute its own and the other European empires in Asia as fast as possible before the Japanese, with American and KMT help, had completely eroded the bases on which these empires rested. Churchill was acutely aware of the political dangers released by Japan's victories: his voluminous writings on Asia talk of little but the restoration of British colonial power, by which he meant that Britain must show itself to be *powerful*. He tried frantically to get British troops into the fighting outside the Burma theatre, especially in order to be able to recapture former British colonies like Hong Kong by force.[57]

American strategy was more complex. America had two leading allies in Asia: its colony, the Philippines (in this case synonymous with the quasi-autonomous MacArthur), and the Kuomintang headed by Chiang Kai-shek. The United States was well aware of the dangers of getting embroiled in a land war in China, and although China remained its number one political concern in Asia (subordinate to the overall "Europe first" strategy), Washington's entire war policy was premised on actually staying away from China. At the same time, Roosevelt was not keen on the restoration of the European empires. American strategy, therefore, was cautiously to approach Japan from the Pacific Islands, avoiding land fighting, with the single exception of the Philippines, as much as possible. This "island approach" also allowed the United States to consolidate its position in the Pacific, using the islands as a means of making the ocean an American lake.[58] Along with the island approach, America made sure that Britain and other Europeans kept out of the Southeast Asian fighting altogether; and, because of the inestimable worth to the United States of having half the Japanese army tied down in China, Washington actively tried to promote Russian entry into the war on the Asian mainland, making political concessions to Stalin to secure this commitment, at least until spring 1945.

In many ways, therefore, America's political aims and harsh reality were in conflict. America wanted to "save" China, yet did not want to get involved in fighting there. This contradiction was often repressed in official thinking, which shows strong elements of drift and inertia. In addition, while Washington put China among its main Asian preoccupations, America's operative on the spot, MacArthur, was more concerned with the Philippines. MacArthur, too, fought strenuously against the "Europe first" strategy, on the prescient (if confusedly expressed) grounds that America's political future was more bound up with Asia than with Europe. Moreover, as the war neared its close, the United States became more aware of the contradictory results of its own approach. If indeed Russia did enter the war against Japan, it would be in Manchuria and China, with inevitable political consequences. The prospect of a strong Chinese communist movement, a Soviet presence in China and a thoroughly debilitated Kuomintang left little room for a China that could be America's main Asian ally. Attention naturally swung to the possibility of Japan returning to its place in the world imperialist camp. This option was argued for vigorously by Under Secretary of State (and former Ambassador in Tokyo) Joseph Grew, who held that a Japan somehow purged of its "militarists" could become the United States' number one ally in Asia; indeed, America, he argued, had a greater identity of interests and outlook with Japan than it did with Germany.

Japan also had a highly political attitude towards the war. However, hard economic aims (access to raw materials) and strategic objectives (fighting on every front) almost always pushed its political goals into the background. Although Japanese strategy effectively locked the British out of the war for almost its entire duration, the attack on Pearl Harbor was not the knockout blow that had been hoped for. And in China, neither Japan's political nor its military strategy was effective.

As the cases of Burma, Indonesia and the Philippines show, Japan wanted to promote *political* alliances within an overall strategic vision of a Japanese empire (the Greater East Asia Co-Prosperity Sphere). Tokyo also played with the idea of "independent" states as buffers between itself and the other great powers. Finally, as the war neared its end, Japan both tried to promote Asian nationalist movements to positions of power and manoeuvred to reinsert itself back into alliance with the Western powers. The decisions to fight alongside the British, French and Americans in Vietnam, Indonesia and Korea were part of a coherent outlook (not a plan) which naturally envisaged rejoining the imperialist group.

JAPAN'S RELATIONSHIP WITH GERMANY

In spite of their formal alliance, Japan and Germany were never able to carry out any kind of joint operation during the war. Indeed, Japan was responsible for bringing the United States into the war against Germany, by attacking Pearl Harbor. Hitler wanted Japan to attack Vladivostok, Singapore and the Dutch colonies, not America. Japan's best contribution, in German eyes, would be to tie America down short of war.[59] Once the Japanese entered the war, the most important fact was that they were not at war with Germany's main enemy, the U.S.S.R. Hitler himself may have been partly to blame for this, since he refused to let Matsuoka in on his plans during the latter's visit to Berlin in early 1941. Had he done so, the Japanese might not have signed the pact with the U.S.S.R. which staved off war between them until 1945.

Germany and Japan were too far apart geographically, given the technology of the epoch. When Subhas Chandra Bose travelled from Berlin to Japan in early 1943, it took him three months to make the journey by submarine. Policy differences between the two allies were negligible, since they were operating virtually independently—although it is interesting to note that Hitler opposed the desire of the Japanese military political agents for a formal declaration of Indian independence.[60] Neither Germany nor Japan had trouble modifying its racial policy to make the other an "honorary" member of the ruling race.[61]

THE JAPANESE ECONOMY DURING THE WAR

During the Pacific War, Western preconceptions about Japan led many observers to claim a degree of efficiency and central planning for the Japanese economy which simply did not exist at any level—economic, bureaucratic or political.[62]

While it is easy to state the economic reasons for Japan engaging in war (the drive to secure raw materials in Southeast Asia, for example, is a much clearer economic "motive" than, say, any economic gains Germany could derive from Poland), the Japanese government itself had no comprehensive plan for the war. In fact Japan's economic aims at the start of the war were curiously limited. Just as militarily Japan was geared up for only a short war, so economically it aimed just at the acquisition of strategic raw materials, not at expanding the base of its own industrial machine.[63] There was no plan to try to increase total output, which was pathetically inadequate compared with that of the United States. Japanese munitions output was never more than one-tenth that of the United States, and coal and steel production one-thirteenth. Fifty per cent of the population was involved in agriculture and fisheries, and even so between 20 and 25 per cent of the rice consumption had to be imported—to provide a standard of living where the average caloric intake in 1941 was only 6.4 per cent above subsistence level.[64] Japan lived on a razor's edge, where loss of either raw materials, fishing grounds, transportation, fertilizer production or manpower would quickly drive the whole economy to collapse. In addition, although on the surface Japan had a large reserve labour force, in fact there was a dire shortage of skilled workers. Japan took virtually none of the elementary steps needed to build up the economic base for a long war.

Equally astounding was the very narrow vision of a "war economy." Unlike the United States, which expanded its entire economy to fight the war, Japan merely tried to shift resources from non-military to war-related sectors, without expanding the economy as a whole. Whereas the U.S. economy expanded by about two-thirds from 1940 to 1944, that of Japan grew only one-quarter. After Japanese reverses on Guadalcanal, Tokyo took its first really drastic steps to put the whole economy on a war footing (November 1942).

By that time, it was too late. The Japanese economy was wholly dependent on imported raw materials and the U.S. blockade had already begun to strangle the country. A high percentage of Japanese shipping was sunk (over half by U.S. submarines), and industry ground to a halt. Planning for shipping was highly over-optimistic as regards construction estimates, likely losses and the need for protection.

In addition to these purely economic factors, the Japanese regime was not *organized,* or even easily adaptable, to the kind of centralized planning needed to fight a major war. Both the Prime Minister and the Cabinet (which technically had no constitutional existence at all) had little organized power.[65] Several attempts were made to overhaul the administrative and decision-making structure during the war, but most of these came too late. By the time they were made, shortages of all kinds of goods made army-navy squabbling virtually impossible to conciliate within a context where the entire economy was short of everything it needed. Technically, a number of these reorganization measures functioned quite efficiently, but always within a context of impossible scarcity. Reorganization took place on two levels: governmental and business. In November 1942 Tōjō initiated a number of changes which culminated in November 1943 with the abolition of both the Cabinet Planning Board (hitherto dominated by the army) and the Ministry of Commerce and Industry (dominated by big business) and their replacement by a Ministry of Munitions to govern overall economic policy. This new Ministry was formally headed by Tōjō, but in fact was run by Vice Minister Kishi Nobusuke, an old comrade of Tōjō's from Manchuria, and later Prime Minister (1957–60).

Business reorganization mainly took the form of streamlining cartel arrangements and facilitating mergers. As already noted, the "big four" zaibatsu increased their strength both absolutely and relatively during the war years.

Kishi played a crucial role in overseeing mergers in the big business and banking fields.[66] But, although the reorganization was technically quite sound in the abstract, from the point of view of promoting production, actual output fell drastically, particularly from mid-1944 onwards, due to the American blockade. In addition, Japan developed no dispersal plans, and tried to disperse industry only in the final year of the war when it was already vulnerable to bombing. When finally enacted, the dispersal measures probably aggravated the industrial chaos.

By early 1945 Japan had been blockaded to its knees. This was true of both food and raw materials. Oil imports had ceased completely by the end of the war, and refining was down to less than 15 per cent of the 1943 output. The merchant fleet was just over 12 per cent the tonnage Japan had started the war with. Similar statistics prevailed in every sector of the economy. Even where productive capacity had actually been raised in the latter years of the war, production itself was everywhere down due to lack of materials.

The Japanese political system changed remarkably little during the war years. With the notable exception of Dietman Saitō, who so eloquently criticized the Greater East Asian Co-Prosperity Sphere,[67] most prewar politicians, sometimes slightly muted, were able to continue in activity. The Imperial Rule Assistance Association provided an umbrella under which many political elements could shelter, and since it never became an efficient party along Nazi or Italian Fascist lines, most people, including some prominent members of the prewar social democratic left, managed to stay there.

From 1937 on it is impossible to speak of any organized resistance to the regime from the left. The figures for those arrested on charges of having "relations" with the Communist Party tell their own story:[68]

Years	Number of Arrests
1931–33	45,722
1934–36	9,229
1937–39	2,165
1940–42	1,895
1943–45	518

But, though there was no organized resistance, there was considerable "negative" resistance from the proletariat, especially from requisitioned workers. A secret 1942 Home Ministry document speaks of an

aggravation of the feelings of hostility felt [towards the regime] by a large number of workers. The trend towards desertion, absenteeism, sabotage and moonlighting has spread to the whole country; collective violence is frequent; the number of bad workers is increasing. We find criminal acts of positive opposition, such as the destruction of military equipment, or products deliberately made defective. The development of such a situation among the workers during the second half of the year must rightly be feared by the authorities . . . especially as this activity, which formerly was subterranean, has now become positive and aggressive.[69]

Thus, as the same document notes, although the number of strikes fell, there was no real decline in work *conflicts* as a whole, since the number of work stoppages due to sabotage grew by about as much as the strikes fell.[70] In addition, as noted above, the increased exploitation of the masses through obligatory labour, often in very bad conditions, on inadequate rations, led to both absenteeism and other forms of dissidence. Most of the wartime disputes were over food, price increases and bad conditions.

The regime, although active in repressing any opposition, and though treating its political opponents of the far left with cruelty, did not execute any of them, with the exception of convicted spies.[71] This is in marked contrast to both Germany and Italy. In addition, although freedom of speech in general was severely restricted, newspapers were able to criticize the government right up to the end (from a bourgeois standpoint) in a way unthinkable in either Nazi Germany or Fascist Italy on such topics as government organization.

The war was an unmitigated disaster for the Japanese people. Conscription, economic mobilization, food shortages and, later, bombing caused terrible hardships. Exploitation of imported Korean workers plumbed new depths during the war. Apart from the many Koreans literally worked to death in the mines, it seems certain that many others were secretly killed after being used to construct underground military installations.[72]

But if Japan changed itself surprisingly little during the war, it completely altered the face of Southeast Asia. It redrew colonial boundaries, changed the language and culture systems of much of the area,[73] devastated the myths of white colonial supremacy, and, perhaps most important of all, mobilized much of the youth of Southeast Asia.[74]

In the words of one Western commentator: "The Japanese ensured that the old order of Western political domination could never return. But they did more than this. They attacked not only Western rule in Asia, but the whole Occidental way of life."[75]

In the words of Ba Maw:

> The case of Japan is indeed tragic. Looking at it historically, no nation has done so much to liberate Asia from white domination. . . . Had her Asian instincts been true, had she only been faithful to the concept of Asia for the Asians that she herself had proclaimed at the beginning of the war, Japan's fate would have been very different. No military defeat could then have robbed her of the trust and gratitude of half of Asia or even more, and that would have mattered a great deal in finding for her a new, great, and abiding place in a postwar world in which Asia was coming into her own. Even now, even as things actually are, nothing can ever obliterate the role Japan has played in bringing liberation to countless colonial peoples. The phenomenal Japanese victories in the Pacific and in Southeast Asia which really marked the beginning of the end of all imperialism and colonialism, the national armies Japan helped to create during the war which in their turn created a new spirit and will in a large part of Asia, the independent states she set up in several Southeast Asian countries as well as her recognition of the provisional government of Free India at a time when not a single other belligerent power permitted even the talk of independence within its own dominations, and finally a demonstration by the entire Japanese people of the invincibility of the Asian spirit when they rose out of the ashes to a new greatness, these will outlive all the passing wartime strains and passions and betrayals in the final summing-up of history.[76]

7.

Japan Under American Occupation (1945–52): "Interlude" and Reorganization

The blockade of Japan had virtually strangled the country by the beginning of 1945, to the extent that the government decided to reserve the little available shipping space for food, at the expense of raw materials.[1] Not only was the economy crippled, but the population was facing starvation.

In the spring of 1945 the new Prime Minister, Suzuki Kantarō, commissioned a special study from the Chief Cabinet Secretary, Sakomizu Hisatsune, on the overall economic situation. Sakomizu's report stated flatly that the entire economic basis for continuing war had been destroyed. Further, if the Okinawa campaign then at its height turned out badly for Japan, it would become impossible to keep communications open with the continent of Asia, where over half the armed forces were stationed.[2]

There was thus a solid economic impulse towards ending the war. By 1945 Japan was smashed in the economic sphere. But it was relatively intact politically.[3]

Most Western accounts of Japan's decision to surrender concentrate on the technical-military aspect of the question,[4] which is undoubtedly important. But there was also the underlying manoeuvring by big capital. Control over access to raw materials had been crucial in causing the Pacific War. And big business had strengthened its position within the economy during the war years. It would, therefore, have been surprising if it had not made its voice heard during the critical discussions on how to preserve capitalism in conditions of military defeat.

Corwin D. Edwards, the head of the U.S. Mission on Japanese Combines in January 1946, noted that only three days after Pearl Harbor, on December 10, 1941, Baron Iwasaki Koyata, the head of the Mitsubishi combine, addressed the Mitsubishi Inter-Company Conference and already looked forward to the restoration of the U.S.-Japanese capitalist alliance:

Our American and English friends have up until present been sharing with us the same enterprise and interests thereof as good friends and partners. Unfortunately divided, we now belong to two warring groups of nations. The State may have to take lawful steps on their properties, but our old friendship must never be affected accordingly. So within the limits of the law, it will be the humane responsibility with us Japanese who are essentially bent on fair play to offer protection wherever possible to their persons and rights. If and when peace comes, they will again prove to be our worthy partners in the same manner as they were our good friends in the past. . . .[5]

Even if not publicly voiced often during the war, this sentiment was shared by many of the more far-sighted among the Japanese ruling group.

The statistics on the growth of zaibatsu power during the war are eloquent testimony to business's power. It is also possible to detect the strength of big business in the way it lobbied the later wartime governments to carry out extensive nationalizations, which amounted to state insurance for private enterprise.[6] When the time came for Japan to surrender, two Japanese bankers working with the Bank for International Settlements in Switzerland played a key role in the negotiations with Allen Dulles's OSS, via Per Jacobsson, the Swedish director of the bank.[7] As in Germany, a central concern of the ruling class in Japan was to make sure that when surrender came, the country would be occupied by its capitalist opponents rather than its socialist enemies. Fujiyama Aiichirō, a big businessman who later became Foreign Minister, recorded that: "When it was learned that the occupying power would be the U.S. . . . many industrialists uncorked their champagne bottles and toasted the coming of a new 'industrialists'' era."[8]

In considering the Occupation of Japan, two methodological points need to be made. First, most Western sources concentrate on U.S. policies and tend to ignore what the Japanese rulers were doing, downplaying the autonomous undercurrent of Japanese political goals and portraying the situation simply as one where the United States imposed its reforms.[9] Second, as Iwasaki foresaw in 1941, the end of the war was bound to lead to some kind of restoration of the world capitalist alliance. And, as Fujiyama's friends envisaged, an occupation by U.S. capitalism could not but have favourable results for Japanese capitalism, in the long run. Put another way, the character of the U.S. Occupation was defined by the nature of U.S. imperialism. While it is correct to recognize the contradictions and fluctuations within U.S. policy in the early years of the Occupation, the emphasis given in most Western sources to alleged "switches" in policy tends to obscure the *structural unity* behind American actions.

THE POLITICS OF SURRENDER

Nineteen forty-five marks the second great moment of transition in modern Japanese history, more clearly defined than the Meiji Restoration of 1868. The year of the war's end did not mark a transition in terms of a change in the mode of production, but it was a transition from seeking autonomous imperialism to accepting subordinate imperialism in a reorganized world in which the United States guaranteed Japanese capitalism the essential medium- to long-term conditions under which it could prosper. And precisely because there was no change in the mode of production, there was no change in the ruling class.

Though the details of Japan's decision to surrender are fairly well known,[10] the resolute manoeuvring by the Japanese leadership to prepare for the American Occupation is shrouded in secrecy. Of prime importance was the role of the royal family which intervened publicly in a major way to bring about the surrender. The Emperor made an unprecedented radio broadcast announcing the surrender, while leading members of the royal family were dispatched to the forces overseas to ensure compliance with the surrender decision.[11]

The cabinet which held office over the surrender period, moreover, was headed by the Emperor's uncle, Prince Higashikuni Naruhiko, the first member of the royal family to hold this office.[12] This cabinet, which was carefully manufactured for the occasion, oversaw the very delicate transition from autonomy to acceptance of a foreign occupation force on Japanese soil. It supervised the surrender and co-ordinated the cessation of military activities while continuing the reactionary domestic policies of its predecessors (for example, it made no move to release left-wing opponents of the regime until ordered to do so by the Occupation).[13] Most important of all, it supervised a gigantic redistribution of assets which greatly assisted the ruling class in "sitting out" the lean first years of the Occupation. Much of this operation was carried out during the two and a half weeks between the agreement to surrender and the actual surrender, though this period probably more accurately ran from the time when Japan's leaders *knew* they were going to surrender to the time when the Occupation (SCAP—Supreme Commander for the Allied Powers) was able to institute rudimentary checks. Even then the lack of U.S. planning for actual occupation work and a critical lack of interpreters and skilled personnel gave the Japanese plenty of leeway. Estimates of the quantities of money, supplies (including military hardware), food and industrial equipment distributed during this period vary greatly, but the total was probably worth around $10 billion. The goods officially looted would probably have made a stockpile large enough to supply Japan's peacetime economy for some four years.[14] These goods went almost exclusively to big business supporters of the regime, and the profits from them were redistributed to consolidate the power of the ruling class, including lavish donations to the political parties in power. The Japanese ruling class probably understood the nature of the U.S. Occupation far better than the latter understood the former. The Japanese exploited American attitudes in order to preserve the Emperor, their political regime and the core of the "national polity" (*kokutai*), while anticipating the punitive aspect of the Occupation, which they met by making an apparently straightforward 100 per cent capitulation on the purely military front, as on the judicial front, along with successful subterfuge on the economic front.

THE ATTEMPTED U.S. INTEGRATION OF JAPAN

In spite of America's imperialist record in the Philippines, its active efforts to restore capitalism in Europe, and its colonialist behaviour in Korea, few in the West saw the United States as an imperialist power in Japan in 1945 and the following years. Moreover, both reactionaries and liberals have traditionally been rather successful in putting over the idea that it is only the left which has plans and "plots," while countries like the United States and Britain just "muddle along." Thus, it is hardly surprising that nearly thirty years after Japan's surrender there is still no full-length study of America's attempted integration of Japan into its new empire.

There was a dual impetus to the U.S. Occupation of Japan. On the one hand, the momentum of America's war with Japan naturally carried on after the war's end into policies for the demilitarization of Japan, the punishment of those held to be responsible for the war, and into the more nebulous areas of "justice" and "democratization." On the other hand, U.S. capitalism had its own specific objectives which operated with *relative* autonomy from the military-related objectives: the integration and subordination of Japanese capitalism.

A number of points need to be made here on this contentious issue. First, within *overall* agreement on objectives, there were real differences of opinion within the U.S. ruling class about the new relationship with Japan. Second (and one of the reasons for these differences of opinion), America's project was for a *new* type of integrated world imperialist coalition, dominated by the United States, but with *relatively* autonomous sections under U.S. hegemony. Third, policy did evolve and change significantly; yet, from a structural point of view, these changes can be seen as *stages* in a single process: from destruction to restriction, to stabilization, to promotion. Moreover, policy moved at different speeds in different fields, and there is a real problem about periodizing the *transition* from the dominance of the war-related aspect to the "postwar" aspect, particularly in the economic domain. But the contradictions within U.S. capitalism and, at the superstructural level, between different sectors of the U.S. administration, were only contradictions within a general line or strategy. Thus, the periodization implied by the widely used term "the reverse course" may, unless qualified and set in context, mislead.[15] There was no basic change in the *nature* of the U.S. Occupation regime, which reflected and mediated the interests of U.S. imperialism and its overall strategy.

Personnel and Policies

During the war the United States set up a training programme both to study wartime Japan and to prepare personnel for administering the country after its surrender. By the end of 1942 the project was already under fire for its conservative policies, which included the retention of local laws and insititutions, including government officials and police.[16] Among the social scientists and others working on these plans for reforms of industry, agriculture and ideology were Ruth Benedict, Talcott Parsons and Robert King Hall.[17] This group, however, was to have little impact on actual policy. While the war was still on, policy was set by the politicians in Washington, who had a lackadaisical relationship with their scholars. The war, ending sooner than expected, caught the planners and scholars unprepared. Most important, General MacArthur, appointed Supreme Commander from the time of the surrender, established an administration which largely excluded the scholars and other Stateside personnel.

Although planning for Japan was less extensive than for Germany, the general principles of U.S. planning apply as much to Japan as to Germany.[18] As Kolko puts it:

> The major premise of the unusually sophisticated planning that went into United States economic peace aims was that World War II was an exceptional incident in the history of world capitalism, and not the beginning of its end after two suicidal conflagrations. The political assumption was that the great capitalist states and their prewar spheres of influence would re-emerge from the war as powers America could control and reform, and not that the war had irrevocably weakened the prewar order. The Americans envisaged these states, primarily Great Britain and Germany, as economic competitors but ideological allies. . . .[19]

One reason that U.S. planning for Japan may have been so much less perfected than that for Germany was that the United States knew it had many less problems on its hands in Japan. From the time U.S. policy began to be specifically spelt out in the first half of 1944, Washington made it clear that there would not be occupation zones for the different powers as there would be in Germany and that the Occupation would use "much of the Japanese administrative machinery."[20] Under the general guidance of Joseph Grew, Director of the Office of Far Eastern Affairs in the Department of State (May to December 1944), Washington explicitly indicated that it felt it had a lot in common with the Japanese ruling class and could work with its "liberal" sector after the end of the war. This policy, Kolko notes,

> was extremely lenient, and it reflected American priorities and definitions of the causes of the war. To Hull the emphasis on economic factors was critical, for he was sure that the United States could reintegrate Japan into a liberal world economy and that its reasons for imperialism in Asia would be eliminated as a by-product of the attainment of American economic war aims. Unlike Germany, they could identify cordial groups with whom to work.[21]

This solidarity between the ruling classes in the two countries naturally involved a common hostility to the proletariat and to revolution. U.S. planners were well aware of the revolutionary dangers of defeat. World War I had released a torrent of revolutionary élan which had been only partially contained at Versailles and by military interventions across the Eurasian land mass from Munich to Vladivostok.[22] Washington's attitude towards the end of the war and towards the *form* of Japan's surrender was conditioned by fear of the revolutionary potential of the Japanese masses. This was a major factor in the U.S. attitude towards both the U.S.S.R. and the Japanese ruling class. The only problematic element in the class equation was the Emperor. In spite of Grew's efforts to make it clear that it was not U.S. policy definitely to get rid of the Emperor, policy on this one aspect remained fluid, partly due to America's commitment to unconditional surrender. In the end, after the two atom bombs and Soviet entry into the war, the issue of the Emperor was circumvented rather than solved, but in such a way that it was fairly clear to both Japanese and Allies that he would not be removed.[23]

The initial decision to retain the Emperor was not an aberration, for it fitted coherently with earlier decisions on retaining the bureaucracy and working with "liberal" elements in business and even in the police and armed forces. Nor was America alone in pursuing this line. As a volume issued by the quasi-official British Royal Institute of International Affairs (Chatham House) in 1945 stated:

> Notwithstanding the insubordination and terrorism for which the military and naval officers were responsible between 1932 and 1936, it remains true that in internal emergencies, the armed forces have shown themselves to be a stable element in the State. . . . This may prove to be the case also in the internal crises which will follow defeat, provided there is acceptable national leadership. . . . If the Japanese are not to be deprived in the stress of defeat of the qualities of stability and discipline which the armed forces alone may prove to possess, . . . success may lie along some intermediate path between [an] uncompromising attitude and a toleration of their hitherto exaggerated influence.[24]

Although later moves were not necessarily tied by formulations of policy made before the start of the Occupation, it is well to remember, in considering the development of post-surrender policy, the extent to which the outlines of the policy and its class character had already been spelt out.

U.S. Manoeuvring to Monopolize the Occupation

As the whole conduct of the Pacific War showed, the United States was determined to acquire a position of outright dominance in the control of post-surrender Japan. This involved making sure that none of its allies was in a position, militarily or politically, to participate in the real decisions about Japan both during and after the war.

The United States very much wanted the Soviet Union to join in the war against Japan, at least until the explosion of the first atom bomb and the Potsdam Conference (mid-July 1945).[25] After some wavering at Potsdam, partly under the influence of the ultra-reactionary Churchill, Truman pushed ahead with the original idea of getting Russia into the fighting in the Far East. At Potsdam the United States, Britain and China issued the Potsdam Proclamation, which outlined the terms on which Japan was to surrender.[26] The Proclamation did not mention the Emperor and made only one mention of unconditional surrender. It stated that the Allies would welcome Japan back into the world economy, minus its imperial conquests, on the principle of equal access of all nations to raw materials. As a non-belligerent, Russia did not sign the Potsdam document, although it later adhered to the terms.

Prior to Potsdam the (U.S.) State-War Navy Coordinating Committee (SWNCC) had set out a clear directive on post-surrender policy which allowed the other belligerents little voice in formulating policy. The United States was to have "control over implementation of these policies"; government was to be centralized without any occupation zones. "The major share of the responsibility for military government and the preponderance of forces used in occupation should be American, and the designated Commander of all occupational forces . . . and the principal subordinate Commanders should be American."[27] With Truman's support, this outline was followed.

Russia, like the other Allies, was allowed a purely token role. A Soviet representative signed the formal surrender document on the *Missouri* on September 2, 1945, and the Russians sat on the International Military Tribunal for the Far East (IMTFE), which tried leading Japanese accused of war crimes. But Stalin was refused a token separate surrender, which he requested on the northern island of Hokkaido.[28] The Russians recovered their pre-1905 territory, south Sakhalin and the Kuriles. On the mainland of Asia, Stalin fell in with Truman's unilateral disposition, even where, as in Korea, Soviet troops held unchallenged pre-eminence.[29] The Soviet

Union had a seat on the main inter-Allied bodies set up to deal with post-surrender Japan, the Allied Council for Japan (AC) and the Far Eastern Commission (FEC), but these bodies came into operation very late, after some nine months of even formally untrammeled U.S. power over Occupation policy and were allotted very limited authority.

The American attitude to its capitalist and satellite allies was basically rather similar and, in this respect, post-surrender policy was simply a continuation of the wartime approach delineated above. Britain and its Empire (the Commonwealth) were given much the same formal rights as the U.S.S.R.—seats on the Allied Council and the Far Eastern Commission, participation in the surrender ceremony on the *Missouri* and on the War Crimes Tribunal. Other combatants were given seats on the FEC and on the Tribunal. But right from its inception, the Occupation was fundamentally an American enterprise.

Ensuring Japanese Collaboration

Throughout the war, the U.S. administration signalled that what it wanted after the surrender was a stable Japanese regime, purged of its more "militaristic" elements. Most of all, it did not want a revolution. Former Ambassador to Tokyo Joseph Grew was the main proponent of this line and, though his views were not supported by all those responsible for formulating policy, his was a dominant voice at crucial stages. Grew made it clear that Washington would not treat Japan like Germany or even Italy; Japan's leadership was one with which the United States could get along. Tokyo responded by making clear its determination to collaborate in blocking any attempt at revolutionary upheaval and signalled back that the key element in ensuring such a policy was retention of the Emperor, the linch-pin of the class system.

This mutual understanding (in which, of course, there were elements of uncertainty) allowed the Japanese ruling class to plan for the U.S. Occupation with a fairly high degree of assurance. This planning on Tokyo's part in turn conditioned the Occupation: the United States was delighted to find "democratic" alternative personnel and a vigorously counter-revolutionary ruling group when it arrived in Japan to begin the Occupation. Whatever doubts and differences there may have been about the "Grew line" were conjured away by Japanese actions to make sure that that policy was implemented.[30]

The Administrative Structure of the Occupation

The Occupation of Japan was very different from that of either Germany or Italy. In Germany the wartime regime was disbanded, and the country both reduced in size and divided up into occupation zones. In Italy, there was relative continuity of government, but originally under Allied Military Government (AMG), in which power was shared between Britain and the United States. In Japan the American government unilaterally designated an American general, Douglas MacArthur, as Supreme Commander (formally for the Allied Powers). MacArthur was given considerable autonomy, subject only to ultimate supervision by the U.S. President. He was not responsible to any of the other Allies.[31]

Apart from the exclusion of the Allies from any effective say in Occupation policy, the United States took two other key, and complementary, decisions right from the start: to maintain the Japanese system of government, including Emperor, cabinet, and bureaucracy; and to reject military government. Although the United States ultimately built up a large bureaucracy of its own in Japan, SCAP did not become the government of Japan. It transmitted orders to the existing Japanese government, which was usually in charge of implementing them.

The character and outlook of MacArthur himself were quite important in determining the form of the Occupation regime. MacArthur was extremely vain and enjoyed a hermetic existence, surrounded by his wartime cronies, most of them belonging, like himself, in the far right section of the political spectrum. MacArthur's vanity made him very vulnerable to flattery by Japanese political, economic and journalistic figures, and as a result he was quite often charmed, or conned, into accepting Japanese hypocrisies for facts.[32] It also made him exceptionally eager to claim credit for all SCAP's actions. He fortified his claims by subsidizing a large propaganda machine, accompanied by rigid censorship, including the expulsion from Japan of unwelcome newspapermen from the United States and other countries. Indeed, during the early postwar years, when Japanese could not leave Japan and no one could enter the country without special permission, MacArthur often manipulated the news to his own ends.[33]

MacArthur's rejection of military government had an excellent rationale behind it. Military government in Italy was very brief, and was expected to last only three years if instituted in Japan.[34] By rejecting it, MacArthur secured a uniquely long Occupation, with himself as Supreme Commander for five and a half years.[35] In addition, by circumventing military government MacArthur made it possible to set up a personal regime in Tokyo which cut out the trained personnel prepared by the military bureaucracy in the United States. MacArthur also moved resolutely to exclude or downgrade civilian personnel prepared by the State Department.[36]

The result was a curious set-up, with the general lines of policy being laid down in Washington, SCAP making many of the day-to-day decisions, and the existing Japanese regime left with considerable *de facto* power and initiative. Inadequate preparations for Japan's surrender plus MacArthur's extensive exclusion of Stateside personnel meant that the power of the Japanese bureaucracy was virtually untouched.[37] In many essential ways, especially in the immediate day-to-day events that dominate people's lives—jobs, credit, housing, police harassment and suchlike—Japan continued to be governed very much by a Japanese government which was a direct continuation of the pre-surrender regime.[38]

SCAP itself had two major divisions: the General Staff, which dealt with military matters; and a number of Special Staff sections, which dealt with non-military matters. SCAP issued directives to the Japanese government through a body called the Central Liaison Office, which was manned largely by former officials of the Japanese Foreign Office.[39] The heads of both key sections of GHQ, SCAP, were old cronies of MacArthur. Brigadier General Courtney Whitney headed the Government Section and Major General Charles Willoughby headed the Public Safety Division and Military Intelligence (G–2). Both Whitney and Willoughby were extremely conservative, though Whitney, like MacArthur himself, was eager to support certain reforms which were designed to stabilize the Japanese capitalist system. Willoughby was a reactionary whose chief concern as early as December 1945 was reported to be the strengthening of Japan as an ally of the United States in "the coming war with Russia."[40]

While MacArthur dominated the local scene in Japan, the U.S. government intervened in a number of ways through its own personnel and a succession of special missions. These special missions were mainly to deal with the complex economic situation in Japan, which SCAP was poorly equipped to handle. Most of the important missions were sponsored by the military, not by the civil sections of the American government. Indeed, although the State Department maintained a representative in Tokyo (William Sebald) for much of the time, the first important State Department official to visit Japan was George Kennan—in March 1948, two and a half years after the start of the Occupation.[41] Through these missions and envoys Washington could check on MacArthur's actions, give him "advice" or obtain direct on-the-spot reports on the basis of which the President or senior officials could issue new orders to SCAP. Though MacArthur did not operate with complete autonomy, there was real devolution of power to SCAP. Particularly in the later years of the Occupation, there were splits within SCAP and between sections of SCAP and sections of the Washington bureaucracies which had an appreciable effect on policy, especially in the economic field.

Given what amounted to a unilateral American domination of the Occupation, it is hardly to be expected that all Washington's allies would accept the situation lying down. Having secured *de facto* U.S. control of the Occupation, Washington suggested the setting up of a powerless Far Eastern Advisory Commission, to sit in Washington. In spite of protests, which were stronger from America's Western allies than from the Soviet Union, this Commission was duly set up and undertook a trip to Japan in late 1945.[42] While it was there, the Moscow Conference of Foreign Ministers in December 1945 decided to establish two new bodies which superseded the FEAC: the eleven-power Far Eastern Commission, which would meet in Washington, and the four-power Allied Council for Japan, which would meet in Tokyo.[43] In spite of surface appearances, neither of these bodies was endowed with the kind of power which could in any way impede American control of the Occupation. Both the FEC and the AC had to respect the existing control machinery and the existing chain of command. Furthermore, the U.S. government could issue so-called interim directives on any issue, without FEC or AC right of intervention. Of perhaps even greater importance was the fact that the machinery was not set up until after many months of the Occupation had gone by. The Allied Council in Tokyo met for the first time on April 3, 1946, nine months after the surrender ceremony on the *Missouri*. Neither the FEC nor the AC had the power even to review past Occupation policy, whose essential framework was already established. MacArthur made it quite clear at the Allied Council's opening meeting that he would not tolerate any real interference in SCAP's activities and at the second meeting of the Council he deputed his aide General Whitney to spend three hours answering a question from the Soviet representative. In the words of the Commonwealth representative on the Council, "General Whitney's performance was a gross and ill-mannered affront to every member of the Council."[44] Where necessary, SCAP either interpreted the powers of the FEC and the AC in a unilateral manner or simply violated their principles, as in the case of MacArthur's moves against Japanese workers' organizations in 1948.[45] Important FEC recommendations, such as that the first general election be delayed until the purge had safely eliminated the far right, were simply ignored.[46] When the occasion suited, however, MacArthur was not averse to falling back on the FEC as a subterfuge to avoid taking action, claiming that he was not empowered to move without FEC approval.[47]

The Reform Programme

POLITICAL REFORM

Though Western accounts of the Occupation usually present its objectives as being demilitarization plus democratization,[48] the real objective was the restoration of Japanese capitalism via an induced "cleansing" operation, which involved attempts at both the subordination and the integration of Japan into the American empire. This partly explains why America's political reforms were carried out with so little trouble. The *structural* scope of the reforms was extremely limited and did not affect the system of government. Numerous key individuals in virtually every field except the military were left in effective power. The Occupation regime itself often proved incapable of pushing its own reforms, leading to considerable devolution of authority to Japanese officials. The Japanese leadership acutely understood the ideological confusions and limitations in the American programme. Finally the vagueness of some of the key initial directives to SCAP left both MacArthur and the Japanese leaders considerable room for manoeuvre and interpretation.[49]

The Occupation started out by freeing all political prisoners under a Civil Liberties Directive of October 4, 1945: 439 "thought offenders" imprisoned under the 1925 Peace Preservation Law; 17 persons under preventive detention; 39 spy suspects; plus 2,016 persons under "protection and surveillance."[50] The Japan Communist Party and other left organizations were legalized, to the annoyance of much of the Japanese right, which was unused to the concept of countervailing power.

The two main elements in the political reform were the introduction of a new Constitution and a purge. In fact, SCAP was given no formal directive about a new Constitution and simply interpreted the Potsdam Proclamation to the effect that there should be one.[51] The Constitution was drafted by MacArthur's staff in haste, largely in order to obviate Allied intervention, through the FEC or other channels. This Constitution was produced in February 1946 and enacted in 1947. The FEC was distressed: "The members of the Commission doubted that the pending draft Constitution expressed the free will of the Japanese people . . . they were apprehensive that it would be pushed through the Diet without adequate time for consideration."[52] This is in fact what happened, causing a feeling of hostility to the Constitution, because of both its contents and the way it was imposed, which lasts to this day.[53]

With one exception, Article 9, the Constitution was in fact a fairly innocuous document, embodying American-style "civil rights." The new Constitution calls the Emperor a "symbol of the State and of the unity of the people," deriving his position "from the will of the people with whom resides sovereign power" (Article 1). It established the principle of legislative supremacy and made the judiciary legally independent.[54]

The most important, and contentious, clause was Article 9:

> Aspiring sincerely to an international peace based on justice and order, the Japanese people forever renounce war as a sovereign right of the nation and the threat or use of force as a means of settling international disputes.
>
> In order to accomplish the aim of the preceding paragraph, land, sea and air forces, as well as other war potential, will never be maintained. The right of belligerency of the state will not be recognized.

This clause was apparently insisted on by MacArthur himself, and represents perhaps more his own personal attitude than the policy of the U.S. regime, although it *reflects* the "demilitarizing" facet of the latter's policy at a transitory moment.[55]

In effect, both SCAP and the Japanese right, as well as the left, overestimated the importance of the new Constitution. The institution of universal suffrage, the location of sovereignty in the people and suchlike steps did not alter the basic political texture of Japan.[56] The real situation was vividly shown in 1950 when MacArthur authorized the official breaking of the law of the Constitution. It could even be argued, too, that the Japanese right is pursuing a pointless path in urging constitutional revision, since the arbitrariness of bourgeois law makes it available for virtually any manipulation by the ruling class.

The second key area of political reform was a purge of Japanese officials, accompanied in certain cases by legal prosecution. The purge, technically "The Removal and Exclusion of Undesirable Personnel from Public Office," was ostensibly a purely bureaucratic operation decided on wholly formal criteria. Actually, it formed part of a general manoeuvre, not always perfectly co-ordinated, to eliminate the kind of right wing which in the short run might stand in the way of integration, and to try to bring about a realignment of political groups to assist absorption. In Baerwald's words, the purge "was the Occupation's principal tool for transforming Japan's political leadership."[57]

The first wave of the purge, in 1946, "all but extinguished the Progressive Party"[58] and removed virtually the entire Liberal Party leadership from office. The Liberal leadership was further weeded out in the second stage of the 1946 purging (the re-screening of Dietmen elected in the 1946 election). The second wave of purging came in early 1947 and mainly affected local party organizations. Aside from the fact that in Japan the purge was almost exclusively directed against military personnel, it was a very sketchy affair.[59] Compared with Germany, where 2.5 per cent of the population was removed or suspended from office in the U.S. Zone, the figure for Japan was only 0.29 per cent. The differences bore "no relation to national social structures."[60] The German purge was also more efficient: 16.47 persons screened by each examiner, compared with 769.6 in Japan, where an average of less than one minute was devoted to each local screening, and over 99 per cent of the persons screened were exonerated. Between February 20 and March 15, 1947, the national screening board processed more than 900 candidates a day, with predictable results.

On top of this, the government of Japan was a direct emanation of the system which was allegedly being purged. "A serious aspect of the operation of the purge was its control by a highly conservative cabinet which could, by judicious timing, affect the political prospects of opposing political leaders."[61] One such case was the destruction of the opposition Minshutō [Democratic Party] a few days before the April 1947 general election: "It seems highly unlikely that this opportune emasculation of the Democratic party was purely coincidental."[62] The Japanese leaders also manipulated the purge to settle personal vendettas: a most revealing and obnoxious case involved Matsumoto Jiichirō, an outstanding *buraku* leader, who became Vice-President of the Upper House of the Diet in 1947 and the first outcaste to enter the Emperor's presence. At the formal opening of the Diet in 1948 Matsumoto refused to bow in the traditional kotow to the Emperor. The Japanese leaders successfully got Matsumoto's name put on a purge list "which included the leaders of the Japanese war effort who were held responsible in war crimes trials."[63] Premier Yoshida even insisted on having Matsumoto kept on the purge list at a time when general de-purging was taking place. He was reinstated only in August 1951.

As Table 1 shows, the military was the group most affected by the purge.

TABLE 1

PURGEES BY CATEGORIES

Category	Number	Per cent
Military elite	167,035	79.6
Bureaucratic elite	1,809	0.9
Political elite	34,892	16.5
Ultranationalistic elite	3,438	1.6
Business elite	1,898	0.9
Information media elite	1,216	0.5
Total	210,288	100.0

SOURCE: Baerwald, *The Purge of Japanese Leaders*, p. 80.

On the whole, the Japanese military was fairly extensively purged, in the sense that the armed forces were rendered temporarily inoperative. The purge did not, however, fulfil the clause in the Potsdam Proclamation calling for the causes of Japanese aggression to be eradicated "for all time." And a special nucleus of the Japanese armed forces was preserved by MacArthur's Intelligence chief, General Willoughby.

> Willoughby from the beginning opposed a hard policy toward Japan and in particular succeeded in freeing from the purge certain key officers of the former Imperial Army and Navy. If Willoughby's plans had carried through, these men—approximately fifteen in number—would have become the nucleus of the general staff of Japan's future military establishment. They formed several noteworthy groups. Intelligence personnel headed by Lt. General Seizo Arisue, former Chief of Military Intelligence for the General Staff, were incorporated into G-2's historical section; they were key sources of intelligence concerning Russian military dispositions in the Soviet Far East. A second group headed by Colonel Takushiro Hattori, Tojo's former secretary and Chief of the First Section of the General Staff's Operations Division, managed the Demobilization Boards through which some four million Japanese servicemen were returned to civilian life.[64]

As Dower notes, the potential influence of these Boards was enormous. "By virtue of their position they maintained up-to-date files on the whereabouts of some 70,000 former career officers: the clerical work for demobilization could obviously function equally well for remobilization. . . . In 1950, when the decision was made to rebuild a Japanese army, Willoughby very nearly succeeded in having Hattori made its chief of staff."[65]

Although the military was the group most obviously hit by the purge, the most important political effect of the purge as a whole was its promotion of the bureaucracy. As Table 1 above shows, bureaucrats made up less than 1 per cent of all purgees. Of the 1,809 bureaucrats designated, only 830 were actually fired as a result of the purge; the rest either resigned or retired. "The purge," writes Baerwald, "left the bureaucracy almost unchanged in the composition of its personnel."[66] In fact, only 1.9 per cent of the bureaucrats screened were actually removed from their jobs. The Americans apparently decided that more visible personnel, such as members of the Diet or the armed forces, were automatically more "guilty" than members of the bureaucracy.[67] Yet nothing was further from the truth. The bureaucracy was closely involved with the military-industrial complex and with Japanese militarism and expansion. It was in many ways the core of the Japanese governmental system: "More than any other organized group in contemporary Japan it [the bureaucracy] is rooted in Japan's pre-surrender past."[68] Even within the restricted terms of the SCAP purge, the bureaucracy was a highly reactionary body; it played a key role in sabotaging reformist measures such as the 1947 National Public Service Bill.

MacArthur's decision to govern through the Japanese regime enormously strengthened the bureaucracy. His method of rule "would have been impossible without the wholehearted cooperation of the Japanese bureaucracy, the only group capable of running the government."[69] This may be only another way of saying that this is how MacArthur and the Japanese *chose* to run the country.[70] The relatively much heavier purging of the party politicians greatly promoted the bureaucracy, bringing about a big increase in civil servants among Dietmen, suggesting to one American ideologue "the possibility that actual power may not have been located where it nominally reposed."[71] Forty-two of the fifty-five bureaucrats elected to the 1949 Diet, for example, were assigned important party posts, including eight cabinet seats.

In summarizing the political and military results of the purge, it should be stressed that the purge was fairly inefficient and also rather selective. Leading reactionary politicians like Yoshida who inescapably fell under the *formal* purge directives were simply allowed to escape because they were useful to SCAP. The purge was thus technically "unjust" as well as inefficient. Visible targets were not always those most responsible. And the formal nature of the criteria often allowed those designated to continue to exercise real power. When SCAP overruled the FEC recommendation that the first general election (in 1946) be postponed until the purge was completed, the old reactionary politicians were able to get themselves elected and then, when purged, name their own replacements. What power SCAP delegated ended up with the old guard.

Although, as Table 1 above shows, the purge also applied to other fields, one area of activity about which SCAP did very little was organized crime. As in the United States, big crime was an integral part of politics. Wartime destruction had created enormous distribution and marketing problems, aggravated by the wholesale looting carried out under the government's auspices at the end of the war. The black market was controlled by a coalition of police and gangsters, in league with city bosses. Feeble SCAP attempts to crack down on some of this activity simply produced charades where gangs would hold formal dissolution ceremonies and convert themselves into such things as democratic co-operatives.[72]

The most important postwar trial was the International Military Tribunal for the Far East (IMTFE), which sat in Tokyo for almost two and a half years, from June 1946 to November 1948. It tried a selection of Japan's leaders, including Tōjō Hideki, Prime Minister for much of the period during which Japan was fighting the West, but not the Emperor. Yet no proof has ever been produced to exonerate the Emperor of *responsibility* for those things of which the Western powers complained. The whole Japanese system of government and decision-making is irrefutable proof of the Emperor's responsibility, as was clearly stated by, for example, ex-Prime Minister Tōjō in his testimony on December 31, 1947, and, even more important, by the Emperor himself at his first meeting with General MacArthur.[73] "The decision not to accept the emperor's assessment of his role in the war effort of Japan, regardless of the motivations which induced him to make it, fundamentally compromised the whole effort of removing those who had deceived and misled the Japanese people."[74] The Japanese were aware of this, too, and the trials and executions were understood as largely token gestures. There were two reasons for this. First, the absence of the Emperor meant there was at least a missing link in the chain of responsibility. Secondly, it was apparent that vindictiveness was a major element in some of the trials and that this factor often outweighed considerations of justice. Churchill, among others, objected to the execution of Tōjō since, as he pointed out to U.S. Secretary of Defense James Forrestal, "On the same theory, both Roosevelt and himself would have been executed if the Allies had lost the war."[75] MacArthur had the two generals who had humiliated him in the Philippines, Homma and Yamashita, executed after staged trials.[76] In addition, the Japanese can hardly have failed to observe that in spite of the moralism in the West's attitude towards Japan, the predominantly Western powers prosecuting Japanese defendants tried almost solely Japanese accused of offences against Western victims, who represented less than one-tenth of the victims of Japanese aggression.

ECONOMIC POLICY AND REFORMS

American economic policy towards Japan during the Occupation period, while filled with contradictions and modifications in the programme, is notable for a constant trend towards *control* of the Japanese economy.[77] The word "reform" may be misleading, for the American project might better be designated as an attempt to "re-form" or reorganize the Japanese economy so as to ensure its ultimate integration, with relative autonomy, within the U.S. empire. Apart from the relatively brief period of restrictive economic policies, U.S. activities were always predicated upon rebuilding Japanese capitalism, whose re-promotion was the constant principal feature of the control which U.S. imperialism attempted to institute. Furthermore, as with the political reforms, most Western accounts tend to exaggerate the Occupation's success in applying its programme, while rather underestimating the ability of the Japanese conservatives success-fully to block economic programmes uncongenial to them.[78]

INDUSTRIAL POLICY

At Cairo Japan's opponents agreed that Japan should be deprived of its empire, which it had acquired by "greed." The Potsdam definition of "unjust" acquisitions could have been applied equally to both the United Kingdom and the United States, which underlines the structural limitations on post-surrender economic policy.

Reparations

The first aspect of Occupation policy in the economic field was to *limit* Japan and oblige it to make reparations to the countries it had damaged. The programme for this was set out in a report prepared by a delegation headed by Ambassador for Reparations Edwin W. Pauley which visited Japan in November–December 1945.[79] The Pauley Report is extremely interesting not only for its wide-ranging critique of Japanese big business, but even more so for its attempt to assess Japanese economic development as fundamentally an anomaly in East Asia. Pauley's plan for reparations was set out as part of a larger scheme for a general restructuring of the whole economy of East Asia.[80] In the Asian context, Japan's develop-ment, according to Pauley, had been too unequal compared with that of its neighbours. Japan, therefore, should not simply pay reparations but send part of its industrial equipment to the other East Asian countries, thus both building them up to the same economic level as Japan[81] and preventing Japan using reparations payments to consolidate its economic superiority over its neighbours. In Pauley's view, the existing industrial capacity of Japan in 1945 was more than enough for peaceful production, since in spite of the wartime destruction, so much of the economy had been devoted to war-related production.

By the time Pauley had prepared his report, SCAP had realized that implementation of his recommendations would make the Occupation's task more expensive and more difficult. By the time the United States had submitted Pauley's recommendations to the FEC, Washington had revised its policy on the subject. Ultimately, rather less than 30 per cent of the industrial facilities declared surplus by the FEC were dismantled and transferred to other countries, with more than half the equipment going to China.[82] Later on, Japan developed a highly sophisticated "reparations" programme of the kind Pauley had explicitly warned against, and these second-stage reparations became a key element both in Japan's economic recovery and in the reconstruction of its economic empire in Asia.[83]

Restructuring Japanese Industry

American moves to restructure the domestic economy covered a wide field. The best known element, although ultimately of minor importance, was the zaibatsu dissolution programme. But the United States also intervened in other important fields—in foreign investment (in Japan), in key sectors like oil, in the trade and transportation fields, and in patents and licensing (later of crucial importance over computers, for example).

The Zaibatsu Dissolution Programme

There is no single statement of official U.S. capitalist policy towards Japanese big business which can fairly be taken as representing "American" policy throughout the early part of the Occupation. In essence, though, the U.S. position was that the Japanese zaibatsu (sometimes just the very big zaibatsu) were (*a*) monopolistic and (*b*) militaristic and, therefore, should be broken up.[84]

The U.S. Initial Post-Surrender Policy for Japan, made public in late September 1945, announced that SCAP would "favor a program for the dissolution of the large industrial and banking combines which have exercised control over a great part of Japan's trade and industry."[85] Dissolution of the combines was put forward as part of a wider programme towards greater equality of income and ownership and to encourage forms of economic activity and ownership which "are deemed likely to strengthen the peaceful disposition of the Japanese people and to make it difficult to command or direct economic activity in support of military ends." According to Corwin D. Edwards, head of the U.S. Mission on Japanese Combines (January 1946), "The purpose is not to reform the Japanese social system in the light of American economic preferences, nor even in the interest of the Japanese people themselves; it is to bring about a psychological and institutional demilitarization. The thought is that the Zaibatsu have been instruments of war and that a dispersed control of business would be more consistent with peace."[86]

Edwards, moreover, gives what is probably the most lucid formulation of the U.S. regime's initial position:

The responsibility of the Zaibatsu for Japanese aggression is primarily institutional rather than personal. Whether or not individual Zaibatsu were warmongers is relatively unimportant; what matters is that the Zaibatsu system has provided a setting favorable to military aggression.

Japan's industry has been under the control of a few great combines, supported and strengthened by the Japanese government. The concentration of control has encouraged the persistence of semi-feudal relations between employer and employee, held down wages, and blocked the development of labor unions. It has discouraged the launching of independent business ventures and thereby retarded the rise of a Japanese middle class. In the absence of such groups there has been no economic basis for independence in politics nor much development of the conflicting interests and democratic and humanitarian sentiments which elsewhere serve as counterweights to military designs. Moreover, the low wages and concentrated profits of the Zaibatsu system have limited the domestic market and intensified the importance of exports, and thus have given incentive to Japanese imperialism. The combines have been so dependent upon government favor that . . . they necessarily became instruments of their government in international politics. They necessarily served its purpose in order to be loyal not only to Japan but to their own profits.

To break the system which produces such results and to create the groups which in democratic countries provide resistance to the capture of government by military zealots are the central purposes of American policy toward the Zaibatsu.[87]

This is only an interpretation of a programme, not a description of applied policy. But it does set out succinctly the overall social and political objectives of American economic ideas for Japan at the early stage of the Occupation. The Pauley programme summarized one aspect: depriving Japan of its empire (and thus the zaibatsu of some of their assets); removing part of Japanese industry and transferring it to its neighbours; maintaining the Japanese standard of living at a fairly low level. The Edwards programme meshes with Parsons' thesis, that is reorganize the domestic economy to bring about social and political changes which will make it easier to control Japan. But already it is possible to detect at least one major unexpressed contradiction between the Pauley and Edwards programmes: Pauley suggests virtually *de-industrializing* Japan, taking it out of the group of advanced capitalist powers, so as permanently to reduce it again to the same status as the other countries of East Asia. Edwards is suggesting a programme of internal change which, from a capitalist point of view, would be likely to promote a kind of economic growth which would make it impossible to apply the Pauley proposals in full.

In spite of the directives in the Initial Post-Surrender Policy concerning the combines, SCAP in the early stages had neither the personnel nor the ability to accomplish much. Recognizing the possibilities of intervention, one of the big four zaibatsu, Yasuda, came up with a "voluntary" dissolution plan in October 1945, which was approved by MacArthur in early

November. The Yasuda Plan, evolved in co-ordination among the big four zaibatsu (Mitsui, Mitsubishi, Sumitomo and Yasuda),[88] proposed the dissolution of the central holding company, and the sale of all their stock by the controlling family in each zaibatsu, as well as by the holding company and the zaibatsu banks. As the Kolkos have pointed out, dissolution along the lines proposed under the Yasuda Plan would hardly be dissolution at all, since no one but the zaibatsu had the funds to purchase the divested stock. Yet MacArthur, lulled as ever by this apparent co-operation, not only endorsed the plan but apparently considered it adequate for the time being. This view was not shared by the textile millionaire who was U.S. Under Secretary of State at the time, William Clayton, who got the Justice Department to dispatch a mission of anti-trust experts, under Corwin Edwards, to Japan.[89]

The Edwards mission reported to the State-War-Navy Coordinating Committee (SWNCC) which later, after extended discussions between Washington and Tokyo, drew up the final U.S. policy on the deconcentration of industry, usually referred to as FEC–230.[90] At the same time as this SWNCC document was submitted to the FEC, it was sent to SCAP as a directive for immediate implementation. In November 1946 SCAP directed that all zaibatsu assets be converted into non-negotiable government bonds. And in January 1947 a purge of business leaders was officially launched.

Table 1 above shows that the business elite accounted for less than 1 per cent of all purgees. In fact, only 468 people in private economic enterprises were designated after screening.[91] In Baerwald's words, "it is fallacious to believe that the purge substantially altered the composition of Japan's leadership in these fields of endeavor."[92] The long delay in implementing the purge gave businessmen plenty of time to prepare replacements, in the few cases where this was even necessary. In addition, only certain enterprises fell under the directive, so that purgees could simply transfer to other businesses. Moreover, the business purge lasted a very short time, being operative really for less than two years.

FEC–230, however, proposed a rather more radical intervention. It recommended "Dissolution of all excessive concentrations of economic power" defined as:

> any private enterprise conducted for profit . . . which, by reason of its size in any line or the cumulative power of its position in many lines, restricts competition or impairs the opportunity for others to engage in business independently, in any important segment of business.
>
> . . . any private enterprise or combination operated for profit is an excessive concentration of economic power if its asset value is very large; or if its working force . . . is very large; or if, though somewhat smaller in assets or working force, it is engaged in business in various unrelated fields, or if it controls substantial financial institutions and/or substantial industrial or commercial ones . . . or if it produces, sells or distributes a

large proportion of the total supply of the products of a major industry.
. . . It is desired to eliminate not only monopolies but also aggregations
of capital under the control of a given enterprise which are so large as to
constitute a material potential threat to competitive enterprise.[93]

FEC–230 recommended that sales of divested holdings go ahead as soon
as possible.

A decided purchase preference, and the technical and financial aid necessary to take advantage of that preference, should be furnished to such
persons as small or medium entrepreneurs and investors, and to such
groups as agricultural or consumer cooperatives and trade unions, whose
ownership of these holdings would contribute to the democratization of
the Japanese economy. . . . In the case of negotiated sale, prices should
be fixed with special reference to such purchasers' ability to pay. . . .[94]

This was an exceptionally radical programme. That it was ever suggested is much more surprising than its subsequent abandonment.

At this point it may be convenient to look briefly at the state of the
Japanese economy before returning to U.S. policy and its vicissitudes.

First, the central and dominating role of the zaibatsu in the economy was
undisputed. In 1946 the big four accounted for just under 25 per cent of
total paid-up capital of all incorporated businesses in Japan proper; but
they accounted for 49.7 per cent of finance and 32.4 per cent of heavy
industry. A further 16.6 per cent of heavy industry was accounted for by
"the Other Six."[95]

Secondly, the zaibatsu were integrally interlocked with the state and with
the imperial family; this was particularly true of banking and heavy industry. The Imperial Household owned about 25 per cent of the stock of the
Bank of Japan and was a major shareholder in many of the biggest zaibatsu
enterprises, including the South Manchuria Railway Co.[96] As Pauley put
it: "Japan's Zaibatsu . . . throughout the modern history of Japan have
controlled not only finance, industry and commerce, but also the government."[97]

In dealing with foreign assets, Pauley concluded, "the Zaibatsu investments are in the same category as the Japanese Government investments.
. . . Moreover the Zaibatsu during these periods had immense profits
returned to themselves, and by virtue of grants, subsidies, and tax exemptions and manipulations which are reported, the money they used would
seem to be the money of the Japanese people."[98] Even more than
monopolies in the Western sense (production and markets), the zaibatsu
were, in Shibagaki's phrase, "monopolies of capital as such"—and this
monopoly position in finance and credit was the key element in the state-
zaibatsu tie-up.

Third, the zaibatsu were heavily involved in Japanese expansion, and aggression.

> They [the zaibatsu] are the greatest war potential of Japan. It was they who made possible all Japan's conquests and aggressions, from the Sino-Japanese War of 1894–95 on through the Russo-Japanese War, the Korean and Manchurian depredations and the war on China down to the war which began on 7 December 1941.
> Not only were the Zaibatsu as responsible for Japan's militarism as the militarists themselves, but they profited immensely by it.[99]

The involvement of the zaibatsu was hotly contested by leading members of the Japanese ruling class, particularly by then Foreign Minister Yoshida in a speech in October 1945, in which he tried to argue that it was only the new (*shinkō*) zaibatsu who had been militarist, while the old established combines had been anti-militarist.[100] In fact, the big four doubled their position in the economy in the years 1941–45.[101] The zaibatsu-militarism tie-up was so undeniable that it still formed part of the official American thesis even at the time when U.S. policy was being reversed. In a key speech announcing the reversal on January 6, 1948, U.S. Secretary of the Army Kenneth Royall stated that: "the Zaibatsu . . . dominated completely and ruthlessly the Japanese economy. . . . The influence over the Japanese Government of these and other monopolies was almost unbounded, and they were linked inseparably with the militarists. . . ."[102]

Fourth, as stated by Pauley, Edwards and other observers, the zaibatsu's position depended on a high degree of exploitation both at home and abroad. Depriving Japan of its empire might eliminate overseas exploitation, but the zaibatsu, whose money, in Pauley's words, "would seem to be the money of the Japanese people," were still in a position to exploit and rob the domestic proletariat—not just by paying low wages, but through the extensive looting and stockpiling which took place at the end of the war, followed by control of the black market, manipulation of taxation and, indeed, every sector of government through to the police.[103]

The U.S. proposals for dealing with this situation were hopelessly inadequate right from the start. Indeed, as Pauley noted, the zaibatsu strengthened their position between the end of the war and the time when he conducted his investigations, and this consolidation went on for the long period until SCAP began to take its first actions. In 1947 the two most important bills were passed, the Deconcentration Law and the Anti-Monopoly Law (nos. 207 and 54, 1947), the latter to be supervised by a Fair Trade Commission (FTC) of five members.[104] By this time opposition to the zaibatsu dissolution programme was strong in the United States, as well as in Japan, and the Deconcentration Law, in particular, was seized on by opponents of the whole programme as an issue on which to fight for a reversal of the policy. SCAP pushed ahead with the programme for a time, for reasons outlined by MacArthur in a letter to U.S. Senator Brien McMahon which was read into the *Congressional Record:*

> . . . the tearing down of the traditional pyramid of economic power [is] the first essential step to the establishment here of an economic system based on free private competitive enterprise. . . . [A]part from our desire to reshape Japanese life towards a capitalistic economy, if this concentration of economic power is not torn down and redistributed peacefully . . . there is no slightest doubt that its cleansing will eventually occur through a blood bath of revolutionary violence.[105]

However, in spite of MacArthur's commitment to this policy, Washington soon imposed a halt to deconcentration. On April 27, 1948, after a brief visit by a high-powered group from Washington, MacArthur announced the establishment of a five-man Review Board to function as a front for halting deconcentration. By the time the programme was finally brought to a full stop, the original list of twelve hundred firms had been whittled down to nineteen, of which a mere nine had been dealt with.[106]

Though the entire programme, on which so much thought, time and energy had been lavished, came to naught, it is worth looking briefly at how and why it was halted and why new policies were introduced.

The reasons for the programme not being carried through can conveniently be grouped under four headings: first, the actions of the Japanese leadership; second, the structural limitations on the critique of Japanese capitalism carried out by U.S. capitalists; third, the direct opposition of a powerful group of American business interests right from the start of the Occupation; and, fourth, the changing international political climate of the Cold War.

Japanese actions can not be reduced simply to the category of "sabotage." The Japanese did fool, charm and con SCAP and the Americans in many ways. But when U.S. authorities accepted a Japanese regime which was an undiluted continuation of earlier capitalist governments, they had made the fundamental decision from which so much else followed. "No commentary is more telling than the fact that the government through which we now promote reform is one of the most thorough zaibatsu Cabinets in Japan's history."[107] Apart from the government being headed by two men closely tied to the zaibatsu, Shidehara and Yoshida, the Finance Minister supposedly in charge of breaking up the zaibatsu at the time (March 1946) was Viscount Shibusawa Keizō, head of a zaibatsu supposedly scheduled for extinction. The Yasuda Plan, prepared before any coherent U.S. document, skilfully pre-empted deconcentration action to a very large extent. In addition, the Japanese regime successfully kept control of credit and capital so that the Occupation, whatever its subjective proclivities, was not able to construct any alternative system.[108]

The structural limitations on the U.S. programme were quite simply due to the fact that the United States, a capitalist power, was only trying to carry out a remoulding of another capitalism, not trying to destroy it. Limited American understanding of the nature of Japanese capitalism was partly instrumental in the failure of American reforms to attack the banking and credit system, which was central to the power of the zaibatsu and to the relationship between economic and state power.[109] Moreover, the Occupation plans failed to deal with wealth in actual resources, or with the effects of inflation. In a context of economic stagnation and high unemployment, the results were thoroughly predictable. "No redistribution of wealth was evident during the occupation that could have created a firmer base for a free enterprise economy."[110] Finally, the United States completely failed to create or foster the political and economic conditions which would have allowed for some real shift in power.[111] Major U.S. economic interests were actively hostile to the programme. FEC–230 was scheduled to apply to American property in Japan, as well as to Japanese holdings. The United States had been by far the largest foreign investor in Japan before the Pacific War, with over 80 per cent of all the foreign capital in the country.[112] The largest single U.S. investment in Japan was that of General Electric, which held 16 per cent of the paid-up capital of Tokyo-Shibaura Electric (Toshiba). Other U.S. companies with major investments included Associated Oil (in Mitsubishi Petroleum); Westinghouse (in Mitsubishi Electric); Owens-Libby (in Japan Sheet Glass [Sumitomo]); American Can (in Oriental Can [Mitsui]); and Goodrich (in Yokohama Rubber [Furukawa]). These companies, which had flourished in alliance with the Japanese zaibatsu, lobbied vigorously against deconcentration.

This group of American interests was opposed by an equally strong group which had not benefited from Japanese economic growth: textile manufacturers, rayon and ceramics producers, and almost all traders. At first, this group tended to dominate, in line with official U.S. policy, and the first head of the Economic and Scientific Section (ESS) of SCAP was a textile merchant and industrialist, Colonel Robert C. Kramer.[113] However, the anti-deconcentration (and therefore anti-restrictive) group played an important role in pressuring both SCAP in Tokyo and the U.S. government in Washington to abandon the early programme. In this way, U.S. interests were able not only to restore their pre–Pearl Harbor ties, but also to obtain a commanding position in some of the key sectors of the Japanese economy, including the crucial sector, oil.[114]

The final reason can be summarized under the term, the Cold War. It is impossible to date exactly the moment when the full-scale restoration of Japan became *de facto* U.S. policy. But from the moment when the United States decided to build up Japan as a major ally in East Asia, the move to restoration became logical. Although MacArthur continued to support the official anti-zaibatsu line until the winter of 1947–48, he was anxious to revive Japanese industry from at least as early as mid-summer 1946.[115] The big public debate promoted on the question of rebuilding Japan in the winter of 1947–48 tended to concentrate on the cost to the U.S. taxpayer of going on subsidizing Japan at the relatively low level of economic production which continuation of the restrictive economic policy would entail. But, in fact, the sums of money involved, several hundred million dollars per annum, were paltry, and this "cost to the taxpayer" line needs to be set within the essentially Cold War decision to build Japan back up as an anti-communist ally. Politically, too, the United States realized that it might be easier to control Japan if it assisted the restoration of a stronger capitalist regime, especially in the face of the strength of the left which, MacArthur argued, was thriving on economic hardship.

The Rebuilding of Japanese Capitalism

The Japanese ruling class had well prepared itself to sit out the restrictive period of U.S. economic policy. While the capitalist class was cushioned from hardship, the vast mass of the Japanese people barely survived. In these conditions, Japan was, technically, a "burden" on the United States. The swift deterioration of the U.S.-KMT position in China and the desire to strengthen the entire anti-Soviet alliance also played their part in promoting the decision to restore the Japanese economy.[116] With leading figures like MacArthur and Forrestal already discussing the need for Japanese industry to revive in early July 1946, it is not surprising to find concrete steps in this direction soon following.

The first step was to halt the reparations and removal programme. Early in 1947 Washington sent out to Japan a commission of executives, headed by Clifford Strike. In February R. M. Cheseldine, the representative of Assistant Secretary of War William Draper, reported that: "The Congress will not permit the present heavy cost of the occupation to continue very long and failure . . . to reduce expense can result in a sudden decision to withdraw from Japan, thereby losing all previous investment and endangering the future."[117] Cheseldine recommended a new economic policy.

The Strike Commission's report, issued in April, "rejected all but a minor $79 million in reparations payments. It called for the complete rehabilitation of the very industries that the Pauley Commission had recommended be totally dismantled. And, most critically for future policy, the commission criticized all the democratic reforms as adding '. . . additional difficulties in the process of quickly achieving self-sufficiency.' "[118] In May MacArthur ordered all interim reparations stopped; the issue was postponed until the San Francisco Peace Treaty in 1951.

This initial step, halting removals and reparations, was much the simplest and was accomplished without difficulty, in spite of vigorous protests from the FEC. The next stage, the actual rebuilding of the economy, was more complex. This part of the programme was developed over a period of some two years, 1947–49, by a series of mainly army missions from the United States.[119] SCAP itself, the FEC and the Allies played virtually no role in drawing up policy.

These new policies faced two major problems, the Japanese masses and America's allies. The Americans involved in the programme were well aware that it would probably provoke widespread unrest. In his conversation with President Truman before travelling to Japan, Joseph M. Dodge, the conservative Detroit banker who planned the crucial final stage of the programme, raised this possibility with the President. "I said I believed that if what I thought might be necessary action was taken, probably there would be created internal difficulties, perhaps serious ones. Mr. Truman said that was recognized and they were prepared to meet it."[120] The wide range of measures to suppress the left and weaken the working classes through layoffs and police actions are detailed in the next chapter.[121]

The restoration of Japan also angered the United States's wartime allies, especially the U.S.S.R. and Britain. Britain, in particular, wanted to keep the Japanese economy operating at a low level in order to preserve its own markets in the Far East. Britain's frequent objections to U.S. policies were regularly overwhelmed by superior U.S. power. The equally vigorous protests of the Soviet Union, and of East Asian countries such as the Philippines and China, were ignored or brushed off as hysteria.[122]

Externally, Japan's geo-political situation was very much changed from the prewar period. Not only had it lost its empire, from which it had imported large quantities of raw materials and foodstuffs, but it was cut off from normal foreign trade by the Occupation. By the time the United States came to promote the restoration of the economy, not only had half Korea joined the socialist camp, but the rest of Korea and the whole of China, including Taiwan, were in a state of revolutionary upheaval. The United States was present as official or unofficial occupying power in all the other areas nearest Japan: Okinawa, southern Korea, Taiwan and the Philippines. The United States took a political decision to try to cut Japan off from socialist Asia, which meant *relocating* it in a relatively new Asian context. The commission which visited Japan in February 1948, usually known as the Johnston Committee, issued recommendations which provided a systematic framework for the reintegration of Japan into the world economy. It recommended "a guarantee of raw materials for Japan, a shift of exports from dollar to sterling and Far East markets, and the reestablishment of Japanese shipping to cut down on the foreign exchange drain."[123]

The United States had its own specific economic interests in all this. These covered both trade and investment, which interlocked. George Kennan neatly outlined the complex area of political-economic action in 1949:

. . . you have the terrific problem of how the Japanese are going to get along unless they again reopen some sort of empire toward the south. Clearly we have got, if we are going to retain any hope of having healthy, stable civilization in Japan in this coming period, to achieve opening up of trade possibilities, commercial possibilities for Japan on a scale very far greater than anything Japan knew before. . . .

. . . it seems to me absolutely inevitable that we must keep completely the maritime and air controls as a means of . . . keeping control of the situation with respect to Japanese in all eventualities.

. . . [it is] imperative that we retain the ability to control their situation by controlling the overseas sources of supply and the naval power and the air power without which it cannot become again aggressive, that is, without challenging which it cannot become aggressive.

MR. LATTIMORE: I think it remains today [as at the time of Theodore Roosevelt] that Japan is a valuable new power from the standpoint of whoever controls the seas and the air today in the Pacific region, and there are raw materials . . . on which she will be vitally dependent. If we really in the Western world could work out controls . . . fool-proof enough and cleverly enough exercised really to have power over what Japan imports in the way of oil and such other things as she has got to get from overseas, we could have a veto power on what she does need in the military and industrial field as great as that, I think that is not incorrect.[124]

In fact, this is very much what happened. Although the U.S. companies with prewar investments in Japan fought energetically to get curbs on foreign investment in Japan eased, Japan proper did not become a big investment area for U.S. capital. On the other hand, the United States came to exercise overall control over the supply of oil to Japan without which, as Lattimore stressed, neither military nor industry can function.[125] This control continues to the present day, and it seems impossible that Japan, in spite of considerable efforts, can expect to alter the situation qualitatively within this decade.

The United States, during the early postwar period, provided nearly two-thirds of all Japan's imports, while taking less than a quarter of Japan's exports.[126] Japan became a major captive market for the United States, something of particular importance for America's large agricultural surplus. But, in relocating Japan in its new anti-communist East Asian structure, the United States, as outlined in the Johnston report, also set it in a complex new triangular system, whereby the United States would sell, say, cotton, to Japan to be made into textiles, which Japan would then export to the East Indies, from which the United States would then purchase tin and other raw materials. Where necessary, Washington would provide the loans to lubricate such triangular operations.[127] These loans came both directly from the United States and through the various "international" bodies dominated by it, such as the World Bank, which was tightly controlled by the same group of oil company lawyers and bankers who were connected to the biggest U.S. economic interests in and around Japan and who also managed most of American foreign policy towards the Far East.[128] With total control over the Occupation, the United States was able to take any measures it wanted in restoring Japan as a trading power in this new triangular system. This was particularly unwelcome in Britain, whose position in the Far East was declining significantly at this time. In October 1949 SCAP removed the price floors on Japanese exports. The Japanese, in the middle of a general worldwide recession, could thus "dump" goods at any price they wished. These economic contradictions played a major part in the disputes over the Japanese Peace Treaty since Britain desperately wanted Japan not to be cut off from China, a market which, London hoped, might divert Japanese exports from British preserves in Southeast Asia.[129]

This rebuilding programme was, naturally, not carried out overnight, or without fairly large problems. A brief survey of the various missions and stages involved may help to draw together the policy, along with the obstacles it encountered inside Japan, from the Japanese masses, from SCAP and, to some extent, from the Japanese regime itself.

After the Strike visit in early 1947, the first public outcry against the overall economic reforms came from an American lawyer, James Lee Kauffman, who represented U.S. investment interests in Japan and who himself had extensive prewar interests there.[130] After a visit to Tokyo in summer 1947, Kauffman launched a vigorous attack on the whole programme, concentrating on the need to make Japan an "attractive prospect for American industry." This could be done, he argued, if the United States would scrap its "economic experiment" and "replace the theorists now there [in Japan] with men of ability and experience who can restore Japan's economy."[131] This view was shared by leading officials in Washington, but not yet by MacArthur, who wished to stick by the deconcentration and reform programme. But by November 1947 the U.S. government had drawn up a comprehensive statement of policy embodying the changes MacArthur opposed.

> The U.S. Government . . . considers that the Japanese Government must devise and develop plans under SCAP supervision for the economic recovery of Japan to the end that the Japanese economy will be balanced at the earliest possible time. . . . Not only is a self-sustaining . . . economy necessary to the early achievement of political stability in Japan, but the U.S. people cannot be expected indefinitely to subsidize the economy of Japan. . . .[132]

George Kennan, head of the planning staff which prepared the Marshall Plan, was sent to Japan, the first important State Department figure yet to go there, to swing MacArthur round. Kennan outlined the new situation: "The changes in occupation policy that were now required were ones relating to an objective—namely, the economic rehabilitation of Japan and the restoration of her ability to contribute constructively to the stability and prosperity of the Far Eastern region. . . ."[133] According to Kennan, MacArthur expressed concern about the opposition these changes would meet in the FEC, and Kennan convinced him that he had already carried out the terms of the Potsdam Proclamation, to which the FEC was linked, and that MacArthur could proceed without worrying about the Allies from there on. MacArthur was pleased to hear this.[134] Kennan toured Japan and came away stressing the danger of internal upheavals. In his view, therefore, Japan was not nearly ready for independence, as MacArthur had been arguing. Rather, according to Kennan, there was an urgent need to build up the police, boost the position of the Japanese capitalist class and consolidate Japan as a firm ally of America before there could be a peace treaty and independence.

Kennan's visit had followed immediately after the whirlwind trip by the Draper-Johnston group, which set out the new trading structure for Japan and the conditions necessary for accelerated domestic capital accumulation: stronger forces of repression; direct measures to weaken the trade unions and the left-wing parties; aid to Japanese capitalism in reconstituting and stabilizing the old system of exploitation, including the low-wage structure and company unions. The Draper-Johnston group only outlined this part of the programme, and when Draper returned to Washington he asked Joseph Dodge to follow up with a visit to Japan to draw up specific recommendations. Since Dodge declined to go at that time, another commission was sent in May 1948 under Ralph Young, a member of the Federal Reserve Board. Its recommendations were subsequently embodied in a nine-point stabilization programme issued by SCAP in December 1948.[135]

The nine-point programme included "balancing the budget, strengthening the tax collection system, wage, price and trade controls, an improved system of allocating raw materials in order to increase exports, increased production of raw materials and manufactures, and more effective means for bringing food from the countryside into the cities."[136] The Japanese government, now once again in the hands of the conservatives, headed by Yoshida, was glad to co-operate. Already in July 1948, SCAP had ordered a major series of anti–working class steps, including depriving all government employees of the right to strike, or even to engage in collective bargaining. The nine-point programme called not only for "fixed wages," but also for longer hours, and mass layoffs. The Yoshida government found it easy, with active SCAP assistance, to use the layoffs to attack the positions of the left.

Just about the time the nine-point programme was issued, Dodge, after careful preparation, was persuaded by Truman to visit Japan on his postponed trip. He was accompanied on the early stages by Secretary of the Army Kenneth Royall, who had already played an important part in the new economic course with his much-quoted speech in San Francisco on January 6, 1948. The Royall-Dodge mission reached Tokyo on February 1, 1949, when the nine-point programme had had time to sink in. Dodge worked on formulating the nine-point programme into budget terms.[137]

The Dodge programme, or Dodge line, as it is often called, is usually referred to as a "stabilization" plan. But in fact, it had a dual aspect: it was both deflationary (to produce capitalist stability) and designed to fix the Japanese economy into an integrated U.S.-dominated network.[138] The "deflationary" aspect involved huge cuts in certain areas of government expenditure, including elimination of all funds for school building and dismantling unemployment payments; at the same time, measures were introduced to channel capital into export-oriented production. This control of capital involved tightening up tax collecting, altering the taxation system and the price system (by removing subsidies), and controlling bank credit. Dodge had no illusions about the implications of his programme. In a private memo he wrote, "it is important to realize that the problem of too little production, which immediately followed the war, is passing"; the patriotic momentum of wartime needs to be replaced with "the incentive of retainable profit." "A mild increase in unemployment will . . . lead to increased efficiency of labor and a greater production and productivity which makes possible continued volume production at lower prices." "There should be no fear of mass unemployment. But there should be a move away from over employment [sic] to a reasonably defined full employment." "The first use [of income from cut government expenditures] should be to cover the cost in revenues from reducing taxes which are a deterrent to capital formation."[139] Dodge zeroed in ruthlessly on the central issue of capital accumulation. When SCAP's labour adviser pointed out in a budget meeting in March that "we must consider political implications of any policy which will depress the standard of living of the Japanese worker," Dodge replied, "standard of living has probably been permitted to go too high—cannot increase further—we cannot give them everything they want."[140] Later on, in a memo to the chief of the Economic and Scientific Section of SCAP, Dodge, emphasizing once again the need to concentrate on promoting export industries, suggested a "more liberal depreciation policy directly related to our needs and objectives in Japan" to stimulate investment.[141] A few months later in a memo to the same official, when his "Plan" had already brought about untold misery for the people of Japan, Dodge remarked, apropos of public works expenditures: "It is a tough job to halt a Santa Claus economy."[142]

Dodge rode roughshod over objections from both the labour division of SCAP and the Japanese government, which argued that some of the provisions (particularly the sales tax, but also the elimination of the public works programme and the cuts in the education budget) would help the left.[143]

As well as a barrage of internal austerity measures, the April 1949 budget presented by Finance Minister Ikeda Hayato (later Prime Minister in the years 1960–64) contained a new mechanism which was of great importance in cementing Japan into the American economic empire: the "U.S. counterpart fund special account."[144] This, in theory, allowed Japan to pay for imports from the United States without having to expend its minute or non-existent foreign exchange reserves. It functioned as a kind of massive tied loan, except that repayment was to be more or less instantaneous with the loan. From the U.S. point of view it provided a mechanism whereby the United States could be reimbursed for its surplus agricultural products, which it was unloading on Japan. The Japanese payments could be used either in acquiring assets in Japan, or in paying for direct or indirect military assistance from the Japanese, which took the form of both production of goods and provision of services. In effect, the tied loan was paid for by the Japanese taxpayer.

It was only after this apparatus of control was in place that the United States restored the yen's convertibility. In April 1949 the yen, which up till the Dodge visit had not had a fixed exchange rate, was set at 360 to the U.S. dollar (a rate held until 1971). Prior to this date it had been extremely difficult for Japan to engage in foreign trade with any country, and Japanese traders were accepted only in America. The yen was fixed artificially low in order to give Japan a competitive edge in exports. This delighted a surprised Japanese business community, further consolidated the U.S.-Japan relationship, and angered America's capitalist allies.

In addition, the lack of an internationally accepted exchange rate for the yen had (along with other factors) helped to impede foreign investment in Japan. In June 1949 Draper was at work trying to set up a small group, including Dodge (now back in the United States), to develop a plan for foreign investment in Japan "at least to selected industries."[145] In June 1950 the Japanese government enacted a Foreign Investment Law. Since that time the United States has been responsible for about two-thirds all the foreign investment entering Japan.[146]

AGRICULTURAL POLICY

The lack of a land reform in the Meiji period led to a grave structural bottleneck and contradictions in the 1920s and 1930s.[147] The agricultural depression in Japan lasted more or less uninterruptedly from 1920 to about 1936, and during this period tenancy disputes seriously threatened the existing system. The government was obliged to intervene in favour of the small farmers with a semi-reform.

Most Western writers have tended to underestimate the structural changes which occurred in landholding during the depression. Yet as a Japanese authority wrote in 1967, "The cornerstone of the present agricultural structure, which consists primarily of small-scale owner-farmers, was laid during the period of the Agricultural Depression, although its superstructure remained to be built through the agonies of the Second World War and the dictum of the post-war land reform."[148] In addition to the changes brought about as a result of the depression, wartime mobilization, by reducing available manpower, had strengthened the position of the *kosaku* vis-à-vis their landlords. Official statistics for 1941, which may understate the case, show 3,308 disputes with more than 30,000 *kosaku* involved.[149] Such structural pressure forced the changes in the 1930s and, as Takahashi writes, "it goes without saying that this [the postwar] agrarian reform was necessitated by the structural contradiction inherent in the *jinushi* system specific to Japanese capitalism."[150]

With the loss of its empire in 1945, Japan also lost access to assured supplies of certain key foodstuffs. And, in spite of severe wartime losses, the population was about to increase, with the scheduled return of about 6.5 million Japanese from overseas—the largest single such population movement in history.

American action was therefore geared towards two goals: first, to further the process of structural change in agrarian relations—"unlocking the land"[151]—in order to reduce revolutionary potential; second, to make sure that Japan filled the gap in its agricultural imports by taking part of the United States's agricultural surplus. The two goals are not entirely unconnected.

Agrarian Reform

The lessons of agrarian reforms after the First World War were unambiguous: in societies as different as the Baltic States and Rumania reforms had indisputably helped to demobilize radical movements. The planners in the United States were well aware of this. An important text by Talcott Parsons, written before the surrender, envisaged a potential Japanese revolution as predominantly rural.[152] A land reform therefore was thought necessary if Japan was to be made safe for capitalism. A seminal influence on the whole American agrarian reform programme was the Russian émigré, Wolf Ladejinsky, a classic combination of "virulent anti-communism and New Deal reformist idealism," who had been studying the structural problems of Japanese agriculture since the 1930s.[153] The general project, as outlined by Parsons, combined demobilizing the domestic revolution and reinserting Japan into the imperialist world order. Japan's landholding problems, it was argued, could be solved only if there were substantially fewer people on the land, since the land itself, with the exception of the northern island of Hokkaido, could not be developed much further without a great deal of time and considerable difficulty. There was only one possible solution, within a capitalist optic, urbanization and industrialization. This project meshed automatically with the rebuilding of the Japanese economy.

The first version of a land reform bill was produced by the Japanese Ministry of Agriculture, at MacArthur's request, and passed by the Diet in

December 1945. This was a very cautious project: a non-absentee landlord could hold up to 5 *chō* (1 *chō:* 2.45 acres), which meant that only about 900,000 *chō* would be transferred at most, and the number of landlords *affected* (the crucial political calculation) a mere 100,000. MacArthur, on Ladejinsky's advice, rejected the bill, which also came under severe criticism from the Allied Council.[154]

This first version represented a traditional Japanese conservative approach. Rural interests were heavily over-represented in the Diet (as they still are) and to them the rural population, far from being the revolutionary force Parsons and others feared, was the lifeblood of stability and reaction. An agrarian reform which both altered the structures of landholding, and thus landlord-tenant relationships, and changed the social structure of the country by driving people into the cities might easily, it was thought, undermine the right's electoral base.

The second bill, passed in October 1946, was essentially the product of Ladejinsky and the Commonwealth representative on the Allied Council, Macmahon Ball, with amendments by the Japanese Ministry of Agriculture.[155] The main provisions of the bill required that absentee landlords sell all their land; non-operating landlords living in the local community had to sell all land in excess of one *chō;* farmers working their own land could own three *chō* plus the one *chō* allowed non-operating landlords; land was to be bought at a fixed price, with tenants being allowed to pay in instalments over thirty years, at 3.2 per cent interest. The purchase, sale and policy-making were entrusted to a three-tiered land commission, composed of five tenant representatives, two owner-farmer delegates and three landlords.[156]

The actual redistribution of land took place in 1947–48. The percentage of owner-operated land rose from 54 per cent of all cultivated land in 1947 to 90 per cent in 1950. Owner-farmers increased from 38 per cent to 70 per cent, and farmers renting more than half their land fell from 39 per cent to 6 per cent.[157] These impressive statistics have tended to dominate discussion of the land reform. But, although the percentage of land under the tenant system may be small, the number of people involved in tenant *relationships* was still very large even after the land redistribution. For example, after the reform, in one village where the total area of tenanted land was slightly less than the 10 per cent national average, out of 733 households, 134 landlords were leasing some land to 335 different tenants.[158] In 1949, 43 per cent of all farm households in the country owned less than half a hectare, while the minimum necessary to keep a farm family was one hectare (2.47 acres).[159] This meant both the perpetuation of traditional power relationships in the village, since a farmer obliged to lease even 10 per cent of the land he needs is in a dependent class position, and the expulsion of more and more people to the cities.[160]

The reform left untouched forest land, which amounts to two-thirds of the whole country. Forestry directly affects the lives of almost the entire rural population of Japan, particularly in mountainous areas, where lumbering is frequently the main economic activity. Large forest-owners were thus able to perpetuate their power in many areas.[161] These crucial relationships of class and power are masked in many accounts, including R. P. Dore's *Land Reform in Japan,* which tries to reduce class relations of employer to employed to pre-capitalist relations of "obligation" and "personal" dependence.[162]

The results of the land reform have certainly been extensive. First, millions of people have been shifted into the cities: in the decade 1950–60 the active agricultural population fell from 16 to 12 million, and by 1970 the government's White Paper on Agriculture estimated that there were only 6.76 million people employed in agriculture and fisheries. Between 1960 and 1970 no less than 8.13 million people left farming for other occupations.[163] Second, the reform helped bring about a very swift rise in the rural standard of living: taking 1934 as the base (100), the figure for the average rural standard of living in 1954 was 136.4, whereas it was only 94.1 for urban areas at the same time. [164] Third, there has been a big rise in agricultural production, partly due to increased use of fertilizer and other "improvements," but partly attributable to the land reform. Besides rice output, animal husbandry and fruit production, for example, have grown enormously.[165] Fourth, the reform, along with other measures, helped disarm rural protest and kept the countryside relatively conservative.[166]

These last two points need amplifying. The agrarian reform, like the Meiji settlement, merely *froze* the situation at a stage suited to a few years ahead *then,* and many years ago now; it locked agriculture in an intermediate position, with a built-in impediment to further expansion. Further increases in agricultural productivity were long ago seen to depend on increasing the size of the holdings, but this raises intractable political contradictions for the ruling Liberal Democratic Party, whose base is in the countryside and whose ideology (even more than Christianity) has fostered the preservation of the family. Change may come with the demise of the current generation of elderly farmers, whose sons have left. In spite of such measures as the 1961 Fundamental Law on Agriculture, which envisaged reducing the number of farming households to 2–3 million (there were still nearly 5.5 million in 1970),[167] the LDP has opted instead for a ruinous policy of agricultural subsidies which lurks beneath the title of the Food Control Programme. Not only is this programme extremely costly (1.2 per cent of GNP in 1967), but the policy of guaranteeing to buy all rice produced has fostered conservatism and hindered switching to other crops. The subsidy system has produced a sizeable rice surplus which Japan has attempted to sell off to Southeast Asian countries in competition with Third World countries and with the United States.[168] In addition to the permanent subsidy system, the LDP decided in 1965 to pay a "reward" in the form of government bonds to ex-landlords for their "co-operation" in the land reform—in other words, belated compensation.[169] The government's indebtedness to its rural supporters is such that it is engaged in an almost absurdly counter-productive operation. The huge rice surplus it has accumulated is impossible to sell, and the price of fresh rice has escalated vertiginously on the black market. Thus, a vast intertwined double contradiction has emerged: the agricultural system is structurally locked in a stage already outmoded, and the ruling LDP is electorally committed for its own survival in power to a disastrous subsidy policy. The urban population has to pay for this not only in taxes and increased food costs, but also in what amounts to political disfranchisement.[170]

The overall results of the agrarian reform and subsequent changes represent something of a compromise between the interests of the American and Japanese ruling classes. On the one hand, the U.S.-imposed reform, by demobilizing the structural contradictions unsolved in the 1930s, greatly strengthened Japanese conservatism as a whole.[171] By actively promoting the urbanization of the population, the reform (and later events) strengthened the Japanese industrial bourgeoisie by fostering the social and economic restructuring which was needed to reinsert Japan into the new world imperialist system. And, while reinforcing the dominance of the industrial bourgeoisie,[172] the United States allowed the Japanese ruling group to operate an electoral-constitutional subterfuge under which, by maintaining the constituencies on the basis of the 1950 population figures, the LDP has been able to perpetuate a Diet which is essentially a reflection of the pre-industrial era. The reform, in short, accelerated industrialization and at the same time allowed the political effects of the industrialization process to be largely avoided.

Japan as the Principal Market for the U.S. Agricultural Surplus

The United States systematized the unloading of part of its surplus on Japan in a complex series of deals concluded in March 1954. The core of the combination was the Mutual Defense Assistance Agreement, signed in Tokyo on March 8. At the same time the two countries signed an agreement under which Japan would import surplus American agricultural products, as well as guaranteeing U.S. investments in Japan.[173] Boiled down to its essentials, what this deal meant was that the United States and Japan would strengthen their military alliance beyond the terms of the 1951 Security Treaty, with the United States further backing Japanese rearmament by helping to finance Japan's arms industry with "counterpart funds." The Japanese guarantees to the United States were quite explicit: guaranteed purchase of farm surpluses plus guaranteed insurance on U.S. investments. "The 'counterpart funds' formula thus functioned after the Korean War to convert surplus U.S. grain into Japanese war potential."[174] Three further agreements were concluded under U.S. Public Law 480 (PL 480—the Agricultural Trade Development and Assistance Act). As Bix stresses: "Apart from their crucial military value, these four agreements reflected the growing compatibility of U.S. and Japanese mercantilist trade policies during these years. They also confirmed that postwar Japanese capitalism, no less than the prewar variety, intended to cannibalize the countryside for the development of an urban industrial Japan."[175]

A second stage in the U.S. export drive began in the early 1960s after the European Economic Community (EEC) common agricultural policy began to function in 1962 and common protective barriers began to come into effect. An upsurge in exports to Japan contributed directly to the decline of Japan's production of wheat, barley, soybeans and rapeseed. Output of wheat had dropped by 1969 to 750,000 tons, compared with 1.78 million tons in 1961. By 1971, 85 per cent of the wheat consumed in Japan and 93 per cent of the soybeans were imported from the United States. Between 1965 and 1971 the United States accounted for at least 70 per cent of Japan's agricultural imports, and Japan had become not only the biggest importer of U.S. agricultural goods (about twice India's annual total), but the biggest foreign market ever for U.S. farm produce.[176] With food becoming a larger and larger item in the family budget, and the price of the key commodities such as wheat, soybeans and meat rocketing, the importance of this food tie-up (emblematically fused with the 1954 military agreement) should not be underestimated.[177] It is today intricately interwoven with such developments as the American onslaughts on the Japanese retailing system and Washington's drive to accelerate Japanese economic "liberalization."[178]

Subordinate Independence, 1952

Japan recovered its formal independence in April 1952, on the basis of a U.S.-drafted Peace Treaty and a linked U.S.-Japan Security Treaty signed simultaneously on September 8, 1951 in San Francisco. These two treaties tied Japan's independence into the Western alliance, and codified Japan's relations with world imperialism in the essential form in which they have since survived.

In 1947 MacArthur first publicly suggested that Japan might be ready for a peace treaty. This proposal was apparently made entirely on his own initiative, and was swiftly suppressed by Washington.[179] Apart from such predictable effects as angering some of America's World War II allies, it also stimulated the Tokyo government into formulating, for the first time since 1945, its own ideas about Japan's military policy.[180]

Early the following year, George Kennan's trip to Japan spurred a systematization of the conditions under which the United States would return sovereignty to the Japanese, and why this should not be done at once. In the Kennan scheme, several preconditions needed to be filled: the left should be thoroughly straightjacketed; the restoration of capitalism, including Japan's international trading position, should be consolidated; Japan should build up a "reinforced and re-equipped" police establishment, to which should be added "a strong, efficient coast guard and maritime police force."[181] In order words, a start should be made on the remilitarization of Japan.

The suppression of the militant left went hand in hand with the full-scale restoration of the capitalist economy, as sketched out not only by Kennan from a political point of view, but also by Dodge and others from a more purely economic standpoint. There had, of course, been moves against the left (as well as in its favour) as early as 1946; and throughout 1947 and 1948 severe restrictions were placed on workers' rights as regards both organization and strikes (see chapter 8). But it was in 1949, coinciding with the Dodge visit, that SCAP took its biggest *political* counter-offensive against the left. In January 1949 the drive against the left in universities went into high gear when a leading SCAP official stated that all communist teachers should be automatically excluded from universities and all student strikes banned.[182] In April SCAP ordered all left-wing groups to register on the basis of Category C of the original purge, and both government and private industry began to fire large numbers of employees under this directive.[183] The main Korean organizations in Japan, where the Korean population was overwhelmingly left-wing, were also ordered to dissolve in 1949. And the next year, before the start of the Korean War, MacArthur ordered Yoshida to purge the entire Central Committee of the Communist Party and seventeen editors of the party daily, *Akahata* (*Red Flag*).[184] In August, the left-wing trade union federation, the Zenrōren, was forcibly disbanded. The Communist Party was never formally banned as an organization, but *de facto* life was made impossible for it, and its cadres were obliged either to go underground or to emigrate to China. The severe repression of the left was maintained right through the period of the Korean War up to 1955.

Prior to the outbreak of the Korean War, the deflationary aspects of the Dodge Plan seemed to be working out more effectively than those designed to foster capital accumulation and investment. However, the outbreak of the war gave a huge boost to the Japanese economy. From July 1950 the United States began a special procurements programme, which was crucial in the re-expansion of the economy, particularly in machinery, metals, chemicals and the armaments sector.[185] Helped along by active intervention by the Yoshida regime in manipulating credit and other facilities, this swift expansion greatly assisted the reconcentration of economic power. Yet however important the Korean War was in restimulating the arms industry and turning Japan into America's active partner, the outlines of the plan had already been laid down before the Korean War started. As the total collapse of the Kuomintang in China came nearer, the United States had moved to build up Japan as an industrial and strategic ally in the Far East.[186] As Dodge told the U.S. Congress in April 1950:

I would ask that in the future America should continue to pay close attention to Japan as the focal point of the rights and interests which she has
established in the Far East. In the past year, and in particular as a result
of the events which have taken place in the Far East, we have been made
painfully aware of the necessity of strengthening the position of these
rights and interests in Japan. It may be that in the future, as America's
Far East policy unfolds, the time will come when a call will be made for
Japan to be used as a spring-board for America, and as a country supplying the material goods required for American aid to the Far East.[187]

This is exactly what happened. Japan was turned into what Yanaga calls
"the Far Eastern arsenal of the Free World."[188] In September 1951
Dodge returned to Japan at the request of MacArthur's successor, Matthew
Ridgway, to oversee the finalization of Japanese economic planning in
connection with U.S. strategy.[189] The six-man Japanese delegation which
almost simultaneously travelled to San Francisco to sign the Peace Treaty
contained two top economic figures: Finance Minister Ikeda and the
Governor of the Bank of Japan, Ichimada Hisato. "It was clear that
organized business had played an important part in presenting to American
policy-makers its ideas regarding the kind of peace settlement that would
be most effective in making Japan—the workshop of Asia—a reliable ally
and a bastion against Communism in the Far East. Organized business
knew that its day had arrived."[190]

The remilitarization of the economy was matched both by a lesser, but
significant restoration of the Japanese military, and by U.S. military
entrenchment in Okinawa and in Japan proper. The U.S. decision to remain
in Japan for a long stretch predates the Korean War. A National Security
Council draft of December 1949 quoted in the *Pentagon Papers* sets out
the overall strategic considerations (primarily anti-Soviet at the time)
behind this decision.[191] In October 1949, at the moment of the victory of
the Revolution in China, the U.S. Congress voted $58 million for military
construction work on Okinawa.[192] This U.S. build-up was directly connected both with events in China and with the partial U.S. withdrawal of
forces from southern Korea at the time. As of late 1949 and early 1950
Washington had apparently not decided to try to hold Taiwan for Chiang
Kai-shek. The island was politically insecure for Chiang, who had been
hard pressed to put down a major uprising there in 1947.[193] But the
partial American retreat in the area betrayed signs of the aggressive retrenchment characteristic of America's East Asian policy.[194]

Moreover, U.S. economic policy for Japan directly gave an impetus to
remilitarization. Draper, one of the architects of the restoration, was a
major exponent of Japanese rearmament. In early 1949 General Robert L.
Eichelberger, commander of the Eighth Army in Japan, voiced the views of
many when he said that "dollar for dollar there is no cheaper fighting man
in the world than the Japanese. He is already a veteran. His food is simple.
His uniform can be manufactured in Japan. . . . This man, if armed,

could defend his country from internal uprisings or in the last analysis his country from invasion. . . . Japanese soldiers would be a commander's dream. They are the kind who stay on a ridge-top until they die."[195] Eichelberger, one of the top military men in SCAP, knew what he was talking about since he had fought not only against the Japanese, but alongside them in Siberia in 1920, and retained close contacts from that old counter-revolutionary enterprise. He had played a central role in promoting ideas of rearmament as early as 1947.[196]

On June 24/25 the fighting in Korea escalated into full-scale war. Earlier, on April 2, 1950, the U.S. Assistant Secretary of the Army, Tracy Voorhees, announced the indefinite occupation of Okinawa, and this in turn led to a call for "defence in depth" in Japan proper.[197] Thus, when the war in Korea escalated, the United States was able to move on both fronts: to dig in further in Japan, and to move Japan's rearmament into higher gear, on pre-existing foundations. The core of intelligence experts and the navy had been preserved; the demob bureaucracy was staffed solidly with veterans of the Imperial Army; the *kempeitai* (secret police) had been reactivated earlier to grill Japanese POWs returning from the Soviet Union.[198] Now, on the pretext that the war in Korea would remove or tie down all available U.S. troops in Japan, a 75,000-man National Police Reserve (i.e., army), the Keisatsu Yobitai, was set up, equipped with mortars, machine-guns and tanks, directly under the control of the Prime Minister. A top-secret Basic Plan, probably dating from the first week of July, made clear that the Police Reserve was to be the nucleus of a revived army.[199]

The systematic recommendations articulated by Kennan were gradually incorporated into National Security Council (NSC) policy documents. This Kennan-NSC position formed the basis for the settlement ultimately crafted by John Foster Dulles.[200] After the domestic ruckus in the United States over Far Eastern policy, and the "loss" of China in particular, Dulles, a Republican, was appointed Foreign Policy Adviser to the Secretary of State on April 6, 1950 as a "bipartisan" move. On May 18 he was assigned to handle the treaty with Japan, with full autonomy. He visited Korea and Japan from June 14 to 29. On June 24/25 the Korean War erupted.[201]

Dulles had been on the U.S. delegation at Versailles, and was deeply marked by the experience. His concept of a peace treaty was a unilateral counter-revolutionary charter rigorously excluding both Russia and China, and fully codifying the complete rehabilitation and integration of Japan as America's principal ally in East Asia in all fields. His main aide on the project was Dean Rusk, later Secretary of State under Kennedy and Johnson.

Dulles and the U.S. military, who were heavily involved in the preparations for Japan recovering its independence, had to manoeuvre on several fronts to bring about the right conditions. They had to ensure the muzzling of the Japanese left, which was effectively achieved by the time the Korean War broke out. But they also had to cope with certain resistances from both Premier Yoshida and Douglas MacArthur. In addition, the United States had to convert or subvert its various allies who had a claim to a say in the peace terms.

While MacArthur was actually removed from his several offices, including that of SCAP, only in April 1951, because of Korean policy, considerable opposition had already built up against him in Tokyo, Washington, London, and other capitals for his actions in Japan. He was four years past retirement age, and had stolidly ignored open hints that he should withdraw. Averell Harriman, for example, had urged that MacArthur be fired in 1949 because of his opposition to U.S. economic policy for Japan. MacArthur had even refused to visit the United States to discuss the issue, and Royall had had to be sent out to Tokyo to bring him into line.[202] Dulles wanted him out of the way, and Yoshida implies in his *Memoirs* that this was also a simple way of reducing pressure from some of the United States's Western allies.[203] As soon as MacArthur was out of the way, Dulles and Rusk began secret negotiations on the treaty in Paris and London.

Dulles had already begun trying to soften up the Japanese regime during his trip in June 1950. Before the start of the Korean War, he had tried to pressure Yoshida into a rearmament programme, and into allowing the United States to keep bases in Japan.[204] Simultaneously a top-level U.S. military delegation headed by Secretary of Defense Louis Johnson, accompanied by Chairman of the Joint Chiefs of Staff Omar Bradley, visited Japan, arguing vigorously for retention of America's military position in post-treaty Japan. The Korean War provided an excellent excuse for the United States to push ahead on both issues—retention of U.S. bases under privileged conditions, and Japanese rearmament. The Japanese regime had little option but to capitulate, since Washington made these two issues preconditions for the restoration of sovereignty.

In January 1951 Dulles returned to Japan for an eighteen-day visit, during which he pressured Yoshida to increase the army from 75,000 to 300,000–350,000 men.[205] Apart from cost and other factors (the United States apparently offered to cover the costs), Yoshida was concerned that the Americans would use such an increased force to help them in Korea. In fact, the U.S.-U.N. side did use Japanese in Korea, although this was repeatedly denied. According to Robert Murphy, the first postwar U.S. Ambassador to Japan: "The Japanese were not asked or permitted to recruit soldiers to help us, but Japanese shipping and railroad experts worked in Korea with their own well-trained crews under American and United Nations commands. This was top-secret, but the Allied forces would have had difficulty remaining in Korea without this assistance from thousands of Japanese specialists who were familiar with that country."[206] Allowing for a degree of censorship on Murphy's part, what this implies is that the United States was using former Japanese troops as military engineers in Korea. Japanese ships, too, were used *in combat operations* (minesweeping Wonsan) in October–December 1950: this, too, was covered up at the time.[207]

The re-establishment of an armed force only five years after the surrender on the *Missouri* naturally meant that there was considerable continuity in personnel. A largely formal ban on recruiting former officers of the Imperial Armed Forces was dropped about late summer 1951.[208] From this point on the number and influence of former officers of the Imperial Army and Navy grew, so that by 1970 about 80 per cent of the top personnel in the three services came from the pre-1945 military.[209] In the early period, before the full restoration of these former military, power was shared with civilians, who were mainly ex-bureaucrats from the Ministry of Home Affairs, including many police officials. At no stage have the Japanese armed forces ever been removed from the control of those who ran the military and police machine up to 1945.

Dulles knew perfectly well what was involved in this restoration, and so did America's allies. The projected treaty was extremely unpopular in virtually every country in the world. The British, after much protestation, based largely on fears for their own rickety economy, surrendered to American pressure. Australia, New Zealand and the Philippines had to be mollified with special new military agreements established at the same time as the U.S.-Japan Treaty—specifically to guarantee these countries against attack *by Japan*.[210] The settlement was opposed by India, Burma and Indonesia.

It was also vigorously opposed by the Soviet Union and the People's Republic of China. A Soviet aide-mémoire of November 20, 1950 summarized in seven points Moscow's objections. The aide-mémoire reminded the United States that there was a wartime commitment that none of the Allies would make a separate peace with Japan. Furthermore, on the important territorial question, the Soviet note pointed out that the Yalta Agreement specifically returned south Sakhalin and the Kurile Islands to the U.S.S.R., whereas under the Dulles-authored treaty, the status of these was left to be determined, thus leaving open a dangerous and irritating problem for the future.[211]

China had even more cause to object, since the American plan involved, as an integral element, cutting Japan off from virtually all contact with the People's Republic, a refusal to make any compensation to the Chinese people for the colossal harm done to them over previous decades, and the total exclusion of China from the scheduled Peace Conference at San Francisco. Yoshida apparently objected strongly to Dulles' line on this and attempted to avoid the 100 per cent anti-China thrust which the settlement imposed. However, the Japanese government, outgunned and outmanoeuvred, eventually conceded, when the United States made it clear that Congress would not ratify the agreement unless Tokyo agreed to support the Kuomintang. As John Dower notes: "That so virulent an anti-communist as Yoshida had to be pressured into taking this position indicates how widely divergent the two countries were . . . in their evaluation of the situation in Asia."[212]

In fact, it seems very clear that there was not a majority in Japan in favour of the settlement as it was imposed.[213] A representative poll in Japan at the time (*Yomiuri* poll, August 15, 1951) showed only 18.3 per cent of those questioned positively supporting the retention of U.S. military bases in Japan, with 29 per cent against, with the rest either "don't knows" or "felt they could not be helped."[214] Even pro-governmental U.S. sources barely try to conceal that the San Francisco settlement was "pushed through" (Murphy's words) against worldwide opposition.

Though it is quite incorrect to argue, as Yanaga does, that "the event that impelled the United States to build Japan into an ally of the Free World and a bastion against Communism was the outbreak of the Korean War . . . ,"[215] the Korean War *was* extremely important. It placed Japan in the front line. U.S. planes took off on bombing raids direct for both Korea and, later, Indochina, from Japan: "When it was decided that the 7th Fleet should be based on Sasebo [a port in southwest Japan] for the defence of America, Japan became a forward military base for intervention in the Chinese Communist Revolution. The influence of the Korean War on Japan was epoch-making . . . [it] made Japan into a counter-revolutionary base in all senses of that expression."[216] The majority of the Japanese people were aware then and have been ever since that the whole treaty settlement formed part of America's counter-revolutionary crusade in East Asia, and this is one reason why the mass struggles against the treaty and its later revisions have been so closely tied to the anti-imperialist movements on the Asian continent.

Moreover, the timing of the San Francisco meeting was integrally connected to America's machinations in Korea. As I. F. Stone has argued, the United States stalled the Korean peace talks in order, *inter alia,* to get the Japan Treaty through first. If the Korean talks had started before the Japan Treaty was signed, this would greatly have strengthened the position of both the U.S.S.R. and the P.R.C. (Chinese delegates were still attending the U.N. at this time), and perhaps have forced America to admit China to the San Francisco Conference.[217]

On September 8, 1951, the Peace Treaty was ready for signature in San Francisco. The Conference was formally convened jointly by the United States and the United Kingdom and was carefully stage-managed to avoid any chance of real debate on the treaty. To Washington's surprise, the U.S.S.R. attended, but could only register its opposition with a no vote (along with Poland and Czechoslovakia). Forty-nine countries signed the treaty, and on the same day Yoshida and U.S. Secretary of State Dean Acheson signed a parallel military treaty, the United States–Japan Security Treaty. In effect, as Dower puts it, "the peace treaty . . . had no separate existence of its own, but rather was contingent upon Japan's agreeing to a military alliance with America: magnanimity under lock and key."[218] The Security Treaty was opposed by conspicuously more members of the Japanese House of Representatives than was the Peace Treaty when they were both approved in October 1951. As well as being a thoroughly unequal treaty, the San Francisco settlement specifically violated Article 9 of the Japanese Constitution. Moreover, crucial decisions in the settlement were spelled out in such texts as the "administrative agreement" of February 1952, which was not subject to approval by either the Diet or the U.S. Senate.[219]

Apart from directly contravening Japan's Constitution, the San Francisco Treaty broke both the Cairo and Yalta Agreements by endorsing the U.S. seizure of the Ryukyus and other smaller islands, and by refusing to endorse the return of Sakhalin and the Kuriles to the U.S.S.R. At the same time the United States forced Japan away from the contact it desired with its largest neighbour, China, even going so far as to push through a uniquely tough embargo on Japanese trade with the P.R.C.[220] It embroiled Japan in the Korean civil war on the side of reaction. It made Japan's recovery of independence subject to the willingness of a conservative government to accept an open-ended military agreement with the United States, under which America would both occupy part of Japan indefinitely and hold an undefined—and largely uncontrollable—number of military installations in the country.

The extent of Japanese oppositions to the whole U.S. treaty complex, and the extent to which Dulles had to force the settlement upon Japan is rarely stressed in the West. In effect, the San Francisco treaties form part of the continental counter-revolution most clearly articulated in Truman's message of June 27, 1950, announcing that the United States would intervene in force in Korea to block the victory of the Revolution there; simultaneously interpose the Seventh Fleet between Taiwan and the rest of China; and qualitatively step up its intervention against the popular struggles in Indochina and the Philippines. The founding moment is always crucial and in Japan's case its postwar independence was founded upon imposed semi-occupation which has never had the support of the Japanese people.

The situation bequeathed by the American coup is vividly illustrated by a member of the Diet from the ruling Liberal Democratic Party (LDP):

> The worst thing possible about Japanese politics today is the fact that the same class of people who led and guided the mistaken war policies of Japan from the start of the Showa period [1926 on] still continue in positions of power—overbearing in their arrogance and stubborn in their refusal to reflect upon their past. Like the suppurating roots of carious teeth, these people exude an offensive stench. They have debased diplomacy into an instrument for the furtherance of their own interests, they have created

a weird atmosphere in which political acumen is measured by the ability of politicians to tell falsehoods to the people and to indulge in sophistries in fudging on their political responsibilities. The stench of these rotting teeth rises to the high heavens. . . .

The Far East military policy of the United States . . . was begun openly at a certain stage in the post-war period in order to utilize the defeated militarists and the totalitarian bureaucrats of Japan. From the depth of their lamentations, these men, eyes glistening with joy, rallied to this call and continue, to this day, in craven flattery and subservience to this policy.[221]

8.
Proletariat versus Capital Since 1945

Since the wartime Japanese regime was not a startling departure from the established order, it was simultaneously more challenged and less threatened by defeat than the German and Italian regimes. The government's performance could not be palmed off on leaders like Hitler and Mussolini. The whole system was called into question. Initially this gave the left a great deal of room in which to operate, as well as a major claim to authority. But at the same time, the absorption of Japan into the American empire and the reconsolidation of capitalist rule were facilitated by the fact that there was no abrupt break between the pre- and post-surrender regimes. MacArthur's rejection of military government, which preserved continuity, made this much simpler.

Western writing on the postwar period usually stresses SCAP's actions in favour of the Japanese working classes. But these actions need to be set firmly in context. SCAP made no attempt to weaken conservative rule in Japan: indeed, it oversaw the reconsolidation of political power in the hands of the capitalist class. Furthermore, SCAP's establishment of certain elementary bourgeois democratic rights, such as the right to strike or the right to set up trade unions, was both limited *and conditional*. SCAP did not break the power of the right. The ruling class remained very much in control of such vital areas as the police, property, the accumulation and investment of capital, and employment.

At the time of the surrender in 1945 conditions were hardly favourable to the left. The working class had never been as well organized or as strong as it had been in pre-fascist Germany and Italy. Thus the early post-surrender period found the Japanese proletariat surfacing from a longer period of repression than in either of those two countries; Japan occupied by a capitalist power willing to establish *limited* democratic rights; continuity of capitalist rule at the political level (no coalition with left-wing parties, as in Italy, or military government to make a possible break with the past); and a breakdown of industrial production, but not of the economic system as a whole (banking, ownership of the means of production, etc.).

Both right and left in the West have their mythologies about the Japanese left. The Western right, including much of the United States academic establishment, often repeats Japanese conservative propaganda about "subversive minorities" threatening the system.[1] On the other side, much of the Western left, particularly the student movements in Europe, has had an exaggerated impression of the strength of the Japanese opposition. The Japanese left is not poised to seize power and establish the dictatorship of the proletariat. The organized strength of the working class is relatively *weak* compared with most of the Western capitalist countries; its militant and combative stance on anti-imperialist issues, such as U.S. bases in Japan and the Indochina war, is far ahead of its strength on domestic issue. The student movement is both imaginative and combative, but is certainly no substitute for the working class as the vanguard of the revolution.

THE UNION MOVEMENT AND THE ORGANIZATION OF THE WORK FORCE

There is a great political difference between the revolutionary overthrow of a capitalist ruling class and the surrender of one conservative regime to another. The Japanese government only surrendered in 1945, it did not collapse. Much less did the structure of capitalism disintegrate. While the Occupation altered the laws on political activity, the oppressive system of industrial and social relations continued with some modifications. The development of both political parties and unions was conditioned by this.

All union movements reflect the capitalist system under which they function.[2] Japanese industrialization produced unions which reflected the ideology and interests of the ruling class. In spite of heroic efforts, the Japanese working class was unable to exploit the limited hiatus which accompanied the surrender in 1945 to bring about any lasting restructuring of relations between capital and labour. After a period of initial upheaval, the ruling class, with crucial assistance from SCAP, was able largely to reconstruct the pre-surrender system of employer-employee relationships in spite of both the disintegration of *kokutai* ideology and a large expansion of unionization. The key elements of the old system were re-established: enterprise unions[3] (for that minority of workers who were unionized), and a discriminatory wage policy.

The Post-Surrender Explosion

The end of the war was greeted with relief by the Japanese people as a whole. Although there had been no organized resistance movement, quite significant sections of the population were opposed to the policies of the wartime regime.[4] This opposition soon took the form of mass support for the Communist Party. Most Western accounts of the Occupation period tend to portray the situation as one where SCAP simply "bestowed" rights and freedoms on the Japanese people. Yet it would be more correct to see the situation as one where SCAP removed some of the restrictions blocking the Japanese masses from expressing their wishes and, to a lesser extent, putting them into action.[5] It is impossible to appreciate the actions of the Japanese masses in the post-surrender period unless their autonomous impetus is recognized. Indeed, such actions would be incomprehensible if seen simply as the result of an American "grant." However, SCAP's actions set part of the context within which the left had to act, and so it is necessary to look briefly at the Occupation's initial acts on the political and labour fronts.

Elementary rights introduced by SCAP at the beginning of the Occupation included the right to form trade unions and political parties, as well as the enfranchisement of women for the first time. Political prisoners were released from prison. There were political restrictions on criticism of the U.S. Occupation, however, for which offenders could be given severe sentences.[6]

As early as October 16, 1945, barely one week after SCAP's proclamation of the new rights, a big march was organized by the left calling on MacArthur to ensure distribution of the food which the government had hoarded and demanding the resignation of both the cabinet and the Emperor. MacArthur did not openly react against this demonstration, but as popular opposition continued against both SCAP's economic policies and the cabinets supported by MacArthur, the alliance between United States and Japanese reaction swiftly consolidated. The Japanese police, too, began to recover their anti-proletarian morale.[7] By April 1946 a mass demonstration outside the premier's residence against the Shidehara government was fired on by police. Demonstrations continued against this cabinet and its successor, the first Yoshida cabinet, almost non-stop. Alarmed by the strength of the left, MacArthur was already travestying the situation by May 1946, on the occasion of the first May Day parade for several decades.[8]

With the lifting of the ban on organizing a union, there was a phenomenal upsurge both in the number of unions and in overall membership (see table on p. 207).[9] This is perhaps the most startling expansion of unionization ever seen, and the strengths and limitations of the process merit some attention.

Date	Number of unions	Membership
January 1946	1,179	900,000
End 1946	17,000	4,800,000
June 1948	33,900	6,668,000
June 1949	34,688	6,655,483

The peak prewar union membership was a mere 420,589, in 1936.[10] In the opinion of one Japanese authority, the labour movement "as an organized activity was wiped out [from] 1937."[11] What unions remained formally dissolved themselves in 1939 into the Sampō, or Industrial Patriotic Society,[12] a government-sponsored formation for fostering class collaboration. The main objective of Sampō's activities was to minimize the possibilities of autonomous working class action by making it even more difficult than before to stage a strike or a slowdown, or for workers to change jobs.[13]

It has been argued that, quite apart from the ideology of "collaboration" deliberately fostered by the regime to damp down class conflict, the Sampō period produced a genuine democratization of relations within individual plants since wartime scarcities and hardship brought everyone within the plant closer together into something resembling a co-operative organization.[14] It seems questionable to what extent such genuine feelings of solidarity as did undoubtedly exist during the war may be attributed to the Sampō as such. However, one result of the wartime experience was a consolidation of intra-plant collaboration between workers and management.[15]

SCAP dissolved Sampō on September 30, 1945. But the same conditions which had fostered class collaboration during the war continued to prevail. Apart from a terrible shortage of food, there was high inflation, almost no materials were being delivered to factories either because there were none in the country or because of looting and stockpiling, and there was a virtual strike by capital. In most places the plant-level units which had made up Sampō simply continued, now under the guise of enterprise unions. Such unions tended to contain everyone working in the plant, with the exception of the president. These unions more closely approximated collective self-preservation societies than what is called a trade union in the West. In the early postwar months and years the Japanese workers had to concentrate on the central issue of simply staying alive. This involved focusing union demands on job security, guaranteeing production and a *living* wage. The early union agreements, which set the pattern for years to come, reflect these basic demands.[16]

In spite of meagre documentation, it is clear that the Japanese working class staged a major challenge to capitalist rule in the months immediately after the surrender, and that this challenge was staved off only by the joint action of SCAP and the Japanese conservative regime. The specific details of SCAP's interventions on behalf of Japanese capitalism have been particularly obfuscated in Western accounts. These sources also tend to place too much emphasis on the role of the right-wing union federation, Sōdōmei, and indeed, altogether, on the formal, institutional aspects of the working class struggle, rather than on the class struggle itself.

At the time of the surrender Japanese business staged a virtual strike of capital. Business's straight refusal to invest, or often even to keep production going, was accompanied by massive government protection for looting and stockpiling, a form of long-term retrenchment in favour of private interests which was particularly deleterious to the working population. The initially restrictive U.S. economic policy for Japan, of course, played a part in fostering such moves. Under these circumstances of capitalist sabotage and extreme scarcity, the Japanese workers perceived the top priorities to be both employment and production.

It was these twin priorities which determined the form of class struggle in the early post-surrender period. The most advanced tactic to emerge was the work-in, which was widely adopted in many sectors of the economy.[17] The first big worker take-over came at one of the national newspapers, the *Yomiuri*. This was explicitly undertaken by the newspaper employees as a move to change the policy of the paper which had hitherto been controlled by the publisher, Shōriki Matsutarō. Shōriki had been a key figure in the suppression of the left in the early 1920s, a former chief of the criminal section of the Metropolitan Police Board and sponsor of the Imperial Rule Assistance Association. Before and during the war his paper had pursued a reactionary and militarist line. The workers forced Shōriki to resign and took over and, for a time, ran the paper successfully.[18] Shōriki was imprisoned.

"Production control" was also instituted in a number of major industrial enterprises. At Mitsui's Bibai coal mine in Hokkaido, workers increased production from 250 to over 650 tons per day, while cutting the working day from twelve to eight hours. The workers also set up a People's Court and arraigned the management of the mine before a ten-hour People's Trial which reverberated around the country.[19] In the Keisei Electric Railway Company the workers took over, speeded up repair work three and a half times, worked Sundays and holidays and let the public travel free, thus *actively* pressuring management into conceding their demands. Likewise, during the big demonstrations in May 1946 against the formation of the first Yoshida cabinet, workers in the National Railways (JNR) let demonstrators travel free. These moves enabled the workers to exert maximum pressure on management and the government, win allies among all strata of the population, and solidify political self-confidence and technical know-how among workers who had been living under heavy oppression for decades.

The importance of "production control" was clear to all involved. As Reubens put it, "it challenges the traditional concepts of industrial relations and the institution of private property."[20] It also transcended the usual "negativity" of industrial action under capitalism and subverted the hierarchical despotism of both industry and society as a whole. The work-ins were swiftly caricatured by the conservative press and presented as a menace to the nation's economy. Yet as Miriam Farley records, "an abundance of reliable testimony confirms the fact that in many cases output was greatly expanded, not only because the employees worked harder under their own leaders—this nearly always happened—but because they introduced administrative improvements."[21] These striking gains by the working class forced the capitalist class to abandon to some extent, with SCAP assistance, its previous stance of sabotage by withdrawal. Beginning in the spring of 1946, a more active policy of intervention against the unions emerged, with concerted efforts to discipline the working class and reconstruct the old oppressive wage and employment systems.

Although Sampō was formally dissolved, many plant-level Sampō units continued to survive as unions combining both blue- and white-collar workers, including managerial staff. In the weeks after the formal ban on Sampō, both wings of the prewar union movement began to reorganize themselves. In August 1946, after the failure of talks to form a joint federation, two separate federations emerged: the Sanbetsu Kaigi on the left, and the Sōdōmei on the right.[22] Among all these groups, it was only the Sanbetsu which tried to create a really new policy and fight against the reconstruction of the old capitalist system. The Sōdōmei, representing pre-Sampō policies and personnel, adopted capitulationist policies which essentially coincided with those pursued by the plant-level "unions" which emerged from Sampō.[23]

A number of observers have asked how the system survived. Why was it not swept away in 1945? In a sense, it *was* temporarily swept away (Kishimoto, for example, talks of a situation where "labour's power had overwhelmed management"),[24] but was then quickly reconstructed by the Japanese ruling class with vital help from SCAP. Indeed, the survival of the system is really less surprising than the strength of the challenge brought against it.[25]

It was the desperate situation of the mass of workers which allowed capital to reimpose a modified version of the old wage and employment system. Throughout the winter of 1945–46 demonstrations took place against the reactionary regime which SCAP was keeping in power, and especially against food hoarding. May Day 1946, the first May Day since the surrender, was the occasion of particularly impressive mass action against the regime and against the first Yoshida cabinet, then being formed after the April general elections. On May 19 about one-quarter-million people staged another food rally in Tokyo and a group of militants, led by the head of the Communist Party, Tokuda Kyūichi, invaded the Emperor's kitchens.[26]

The next day MacArthur warned that: "If minor elements of Japanese society are unable to exercise . . . self-restraint . . . I shall be forced to take the necessary steps to control and remedy such a deplorable situation."[27] Although MacArthur did not at this stage explicitly condemn other militant actions, such as "production control," the new Yoshida government equated the work-ins with the actions which MacArthur had warned against and issued a blanket condemnation of all militant activity. In spite of this, "production control" continued. Later at the ninth session of the Allied Council, the Soviet delegate, Lieutenant General Kuzmo Derevyanko, submitted twenty-two recommendations on labour issues, including one to endorse the workers' right to take over an enterprise if it was closed without paying dismissal allowances. SCAP retaliated against this proposal with a 100 per cent endorsement of the sanctity of private property.[28]

As the new Yoshida government was proving unable to break the militancy of the proletariat, in spite of increased police violence and other measures, SCAP began to move towards new legislation during the summer of 1946. In August both Sōdōmei and Sanbetsu Kaigi were formally reconstituted. Sanbetsu, with 1,500,000 members, dominated the labour movement, both by its militant stance, and by the key roles played by its members in the economy and administration. Against hunger and continued inflation the labour movement was pressing hard for a new kind of guaranteed wage and employment system from capital, which the Japanese ruling group bitterly opposed. In addition, both the Japanese government and SCAP were greatly concerned over the strength of Sanbetsu among government workers and public employees.[29]

In September, therefore, SCAP put through a new bill, the Labor Relations Adjustment Law, which contained three key anti-union provisions: a ban on both strikes and the formation of unions among policemen, firemen and prison guards; a ban on strikes (but not unions) among general government employees; and enforced "arbitration" procedures with a mandatory thirty-day moratorium on strikes among public utility workers, plus a clause allowing the government to designate as a "public utility" any enterprise it desired.[30] This bill was partly a reaction to "production control" and other industrial advances by the proletariat. But it was also designed *directly* to weaken the Sanbetsu, which both SCAP and Yoshida saw as the number one enemy. The legislation, like the subsequent anti-union bills, was wholly unjustified on the grounds of lost production. It was a political reaction to working class *strength,* not an "economic" measure to ensure the well-being of the nation. Man-hours lost through strikes for the entire period from September 1945 to June 1948 were extremely low.[31] "Production control," as noted, generally seems to have raised output. Government employees, who came under a total strike ban, included most railway workers, telephone, telegraph and postal workers, public school teachers, tobacco workers and most of those in the salt industry. These groups were the mainstay of the Sanbetsu.

The Sanbetsu responded on two fronts: with demonstrations and mass actions against the new law, and against the reactionary Yoshida government which was implementing it with a vengeance; and on the industrial front, where crucial disputes were taking place in labour's struggle to survive and tilt the balance of power between itself and capital.

The Densan Wage System

The desperate economic conditions at the end of the war fostered the maintenance of plant unions. As Iida puts it, "The first phase of the postwar Japanese labour movement was characterized by the reconstruction of an enterprise by . . . co-operation between employers and employees, and by the betterment of . . . working conditions within the logic of capitalism."[32] The shortage of jobs put employers in an overwhelmingly dominant position, and the plant-level unions, which had very poor national co-ordination, or none at all, found themselves forced to make major concessions to management in return for job security and a living wage. The industrial disputes of the first year after the surrender focused on these two issues, which came to a head in a major dispute lasting fifty-four days in autumn 1946. The settlement reached in this case, on November 30, 1946, is usually referred to as the Densan wage system, after the union federation involved, the Council of Electric Power Industry Workers' Unions. This was:

> . . . a seniority wage system which was to guarantee the minimum standard of living and which was made up of the minimum wage by age group, family allowance, service-length allowance, and pay according to ability.
> The Densan wage system which arose out of the demand to "Pay us the minimum wage based on the cost of living," put a stress on the "basic wage." . . .[33]

This agreement was epoch-making in several ways, particularly in the way it purported to relate pay *inside* the factory to the needs of a given worker in society (i.e., size of family, inflation, etc.). But the Densan system went against what Kishimoto calls

> . . . the fundamental principle that wages were to correspond to the quality and quantity of labour, as long as the wage system guaranteed the minimum standard of living by *age*. . . . Though it contained pay according to ability which was to "be based on a certain standard of assessment in respect to the technique, ability, experience, and knowledge of a worker," it only offered additional pay of less than ¥800 and the method of assessment was solely dependent on the management. In this sense pay according to ability was not part of the wages which corresponded to the quality of labour. . . . The Densan wage system was nothing but a rearranged seniority-wage system, a capitalistic system of wages.[34]

The objective of business was to secure itself skilled labour on terms which would allow the reconstruction of the enterprise through self-financing via capital accumulation based on low wages. The employers controlled the assessment of labour, and also succeeded in forming intra-enterprise agreements, rather than unified collective agreements covering a whole industry.[35]

Kishimoto, one of the most intelligent commentators on this era, identifies this settlement as the key to labour's failure to turn the tables on capital. In particular, he argues, it was the acceptance of wages being determined allegedly according to the criterion of a "living" wage, a criterion not directly related to *work* (and whose assessment was anyway left to management), rather than fighting for equal pay for equal work, which weakened the Japanese union movement and the whole working class right at the outset.[36]

It is not hard to see how the unions and management met on this common ground. To the reasons already ascribed to management, some others should be added. First, the extensive war damage meant that equipment was usually quite particularized to a given plant, and management therefore became even more eager than before to retain workers familiar with a given capital stock. Second, the reconstruction of the permanent/temporary categories meant that management could tie down employees at a time when rapid technological change was in the offing. Third, by fostering the maintenance of enterprise unions, many of which were already fairly right-wing, employers "lessened the chance that the enterprise union would become overly concerned with conditions in the subcontracting plants and in other medium and small enterprises which produced parts or subassemblies."[37] In brief, by guaranteeing employment (to some workers), employers were able to buy guaranteed labour at sufficiently low cost to ensure the revival of capital accumulation. And, by exploiting the conditions of extreme hardship, they were able to reconstruct the old system of discriminatory wages and employment, thus weakening the chances of united industrial action.

It was precisely against this which the Sanbetsu and the Communist Party struggled so hard through the winter of 1946–47, the second winter of cold, hunger and privation since the surrender. In the face of SCAP's increasingly anti-proletarian measures, the indifference of the Yoshida government and growing police repression, the left, led by the Sanbetsu, decided to call a general strike for February 1, 1947. The strike plan included government employees, and MacArthur formally intervened on January 31 to ban the strike. Although his action was of the utmost importance, in Iida's words "a turning point in the course of the Japanese labour movement,"[38] it was not the complete departure from previous policy that it is often made out to be. Under the catch-all rubric of preventing anything which, in its own opinion, would make its task more difficult, SCAP had already been banning strikes locally well before this, and passively allowing the Japanese police to break up workers' demonstrations. Government employees, of whom some 2.6 million were unionized by then, were in the vanguard of the planned general strike movement, although formally banned from such action by the September 1946 legislation. Moreover, too much emphasis on MacArthur's ban on the February 1 planned strike may obscure his anti-union attitudes from much earlier on.

Yet even so, it is impossible to overstate the importance of the February 1 ban and its devastating effects on the Sanbetsu, and on the union struggle. What is rarely stressed in Western accounts is that the planned general strike was to be the culminating point in a whole programme of mass action, carried on inside and outside the Diet, against the entire economic programme of the Yoshida government. The Sanbetsu, although a minority of the organized union movement, had won itself its dominant position through its militant actions on behalf of the working masses. It was striving not just to bring down the existing government, but to bring about a complete change in economic priorities, ranging from the release of stockpiled food for the hungry to a reversal of economic goals to bring about social reconstruction rather than restore capitalism. The intervention by SCAP on January 31 crippled the Sanbetsu at the crucial moment when it was trying to build up a mass movement to provide the political and organizational strength to restructure the relationship between labour and capital.[39]

However, the planned general strike showed the strength of anti-government feeling. Purely negative moves attacking the proletariat, like the ban on the strike, could not in themselves produce results within the context of SCAP's economic policy and the Yoshida regime's reactionary line. Immediately after banning the February 1 strike, MacArthur wrote to Yoshida calling for new general elections to be held in April.[40]

The Socialists in Government, 1947–48[41]

The Socialists emerged from these elections as the single largest party in the country, winning 143 seats in the House of Representatives, slightly more than either the Liberals (132 seats) or the Democrats (126), with the People's Cooperative Party getting 31 seats and the Communist Party 4. The conservatives thus had a solid majority, producing a situation in which SCAP and the more far-sighted elements of Japanese capital could embroil the parliamentary leaders of the centre-left in a reactionary coalition government.[42] The Socialists entered a government which they headed only formally, based on a Diet where they were in an overwhelming minority, under an Occupation regime dedicated to the reconsolidation of capitalism. In addition, the Socialist Party lacked trained personnel, was strongly opposed by the bureaucracy, and lacked the political will, the

214 A POLITICAL HISTORY OF JAPANESE CAPITALISM

party programme and the class orientation to operate in the interests of the working masses.

The willingness of SCAP and of some of the Japanese right to promote a coalition with some Socialists is in no way surprising. SCAP had long sought to demobilize revolutionary opposition, and the disastrous economic policies of the Occupation and of the Shidehara and Yoshida governments had brought the working class to a dangerous pitch of hostility. By lumbering the Socialists with responsibility for a new government they could not really control, SCAP ensured both that working class pressure would be eased temporarily and that a large segment of the political representation of the working class would be discredited in the long run.

The Socialist Party made a major blunder in accepting participation in the government in such adverse circumstances. Quite apart from SCAP's economic policies, the Socialists from the start knew they could not command a majority in the Diet. They also failed to exact anything but a purely nominal commitment in the form of a joint programme from the coalition partners, the Democrats and the People's Cooperative Party. The Socialists made by far the biggest concessions, including a commitment to exclude their own left wing from all cabinet posts, the sacrifice of their entire anti-inflation programme, the dilution of their coal nationalization policy and a promise not to reveal any "state secrets." The masses, in short, would not be taken into their confidence on such issues as capitalist sabotage, SCAP interventions, budget funds, etc.

The Katayama government presided over the highest rate of inflation in postwar Japan. At a time when average income compared to real costs was about one-third what it had been in 1935, Katayama's government gave crucial assistance to business by fixing a flat base monthly wage in manufacturing (¥1,800). This "horrible low-wage policy," as it has been vividly called,[43] directly sacrificed the working class and aided oligopolistic capital. Katayama's mild state interventionism functioned in effect to channel public money into subsidizing private capital. Its emphasis on reviving basic industries "gave industrial management and capital a breathing spell, and also restrained the demands and pressures of trade unions."[44] Black markets prospered. "Taxes rose, unemployment spread, and scarcity prevailed."[45] Socialist inexperience strengthened the entrenched bureaucracy, on which it was forced to rely. On top of all this, the right-wing Socialists held office at a time when SCAP was pursuing policies which made enactment of the party's programme an impossibility. In particular, SCAP forced a last-minute change in the planned tax reform. Under the heading "Japan Will Place Tax Onus on Poor," the *New York Times* wrote that MacArthur's measures were "designed to place the bulk of the burden upon the poor."[46]

It is very important to stress that the Katayama government, which lasted eight months, was by no stretch of the imagination a left-wing government. On the contrary, it was virulently anti-communist in the classic Social Democratic manner. The Katayama regime was integrally tied to Sōdōmei and thus to the fight against the Sanbetsu Kaigi and the communist-led militant left.[47] In the crucial area of union activity and capital's attempts to reimpose its wage and employment system, Katayama worked actively to cripple the militant left and assist the restoration of industrial relations and agreements which were of the greatest harm in the long run to the Japanese workers.[48]

The government fell early in 1948, partly as a result of internal dissension within the JSP. In spite of the ban on the February 1, 1947 general strike, and repeated interventions by SCAP, the Japanese right and the Katayama regime to hobble the Sanbetsu, the militant left remained fairly strong, and its pressure for a reallocation of budget resources, and specifically, for revised wage standards for government workers, formed the background to both the demise of the Katayama cabinet and the formation of its successor. This new government, headed by Ashida Hitoshi, the leader of the Democratic Party (Minshutō), contained some members of both the right and the left of the JSP. The coalition adopted a joint programme which was slightly more specific than that adopted by the Katayama government, but was crucially vague on some key issues such as interest payments on war bonds,[49] which affected a large part of the population. The Ashida cabinet was more openly cautious than was Katayama's.

Immediately, the Sanbetsu and the public employees' unions announced their intention of staging a general strike, largely to back up their demands for new wage standards and also to prevent the retrogressive revision of the labour laws and the further strangulation of the militant unions. After the *Densan* settlement in late 1946, and particularly MacArthur's ban on the February 1, 1947 general strike, business went on the offensive throughout the land. Where unions had managed to extract real concessions in the immediate post-surrender period, management was now counter-attacking, changing these agreements into seniority-wage ones, and trying to break ties between trans-enterprise unions to facilitate the reconstruction of the intra-enterprise system. This meant that there would be no industry-wide negotiating by any category of workers and that management would retain control over the actual distribution of the total sum of wages agreed on in any enterprise negotiation. It is this context which reveals the importance of the general strike to the struggle led by the Sanbetsu: it was only through a general strike that business's machinations to break class solidarity could be blocked. The Sanbetsu saw a general strike as a means to concretize solidarity across enterprise lines: business, the Ashida government and SCAP were determined to prevent this. Business's aim was not only to reconstruct the seniority-wage system, but, even more important, to smash the industry-wide organizations, build up enterprise unions and force the working class back to a position of vulnerable dependency within the individual enterprise.

SCAP duly banned the planned March strike. About the same time, management took a further step to demobilize the left by putting forward proposals for modifying the wage system which on the surface appeared to be a major concession to the militant unions: viz., "pay for the job."[50] Yet this "new" arrangement was merely a remodelling of the existing system: "pay for the job" assessed by management, based on seniority, while maintaining low base pay at a time of high inflation. Once again, the working class saw their hard-won gains being wrecked by inflation and a government-backed wages policy. The left-wing unions decided to call another major strike for August 7 over both the wage system and the labour laws.

On July 22, 1948, MacArthur sent Ashida an open letter ordering him to extend the ban on strikes among government employees to a wider ban on collective bargaining of any kind. The Ashida government used the letter to revoke its contracts with public employees. Local authorities often went even further and introduced tighter restrictions on the holding of meetings and demonstrations. This further move by SCAP was directly linked to the renewed union offensive. By giving the Ashida government virtually dictatorial powers over all public employees, who were in the vanguard of the union struggle, SCAP assisted the Japanese regime and big business in smashing the workers' offensive on the wages and employment issues.[51]

SCAP's actions were of doubtful legality. A complaint by the Soviet delegate at the Allied Council that MacArthur's July 22 letter and the ensuing Ashida ordinance of July 31 contravened the Potsdam Proclamation was brushed aside. These SCAP actions, however, were not solely anti-union, for they covered all areas of political activity. There were severe limitations on political proselytizing and electioneering. One prominent (and non-communist) Japanese official is quoted to the effect that it was more difficult in 1948 to hold a public meeting than it was under Tōjō.[52] House-to-house canvassing for votes, which is always more important for poorer parties, which have less access to the media, was made illegal for the 1949 election.

In October 1948 the Ashida cabinet resigned after a major scandal involving leading members of the government.[53]

The period 1947–48 is the only time that any political representatives using the title "Socialist" have participated in a Japanese cabinet. Most assessments of the JSP tend to emphasize the Katayama episode as determinant in the party's life—that the decision to head a coalition cabinet in adverse conditions was what kept the party in a state of permanent minority in Japanese society and out of participation in central government power ever since. This fiasco *was* important, yet there is little evidence that the Katayama episode *per se* was the make-or-break factor. By revealing its own weakness so starkly, the party definitely lost electoral support. But the JSP's behaviour in 1947–48 was only an index of its nature, not a startling departure from its previous performance. It seems extremely unlikely that the JSP, had it declined to participate in a coalition government, would have had the political capacity to turn itself into a serious threat to the conservatives' organized control of power. To have achieved this the JSP would have needed a revolutionary programme, something it simply did not have. It is doubly illusory to think that the JSP could have joined a coalition and somehow persuaded its partners and the hostile Diet majority to legislate through a socialist programme. Such considerations simply do not touch on the key issue: the leadership and much of the membership of the party were hostile to revolutionary action and dedicated to destroying the communist movement which at the time was leading the militant struggle at both the political and the union level.

The Destruction of the Sanbetsu Kaigi and the Formation of Sōhyō

With the collapse of the Ashida cabinet, a caretaker government was formed under Yoshida, who quickly called a new general election to capitalize on the Socialists' disarray. The election on January 24, 1949, shattered the Socialist Party, whose seats fell from 143 to 48 in the Lower House, while the Communist Party was enormously strengthened, winning 35 seats and nearly 10 per cent of the vote. The overall result, however, was a swing to the right and Yoshida became premier of the new post-election government, a post he was to hold for nearly six years. Yoshida, with SCAP backing, now moved the anti-union struggle into higher gear. This took the form of a linked attack on two fronts: extensive subversion of left-wing unions from within, via so-called "democratization leagues" or *mindō*;[54] and an "anti-inflationary" policy, one of whose chief features was retrenchment and wholesale dismissals of militant workers.

As early as the end of 1946, a concerted effort began to weaken the Sanbetsu and the left-wing unions by forming right-wing cells within them. The main element in this tactic was an appeal to anti-communism, a slogan which had several components: on the one hand, it was alleged that the Communist Party was somehow manipulating the unions, turning their struggle into a "political" one; further, the JCP was alleged to be subservient to Moscow. SCAP's Labor Section took an active role in promoting the *mindō*, part of a global struggle to split the world union movement which had recently united under left-wing leadership in the World Federation of Trade Unions.[55] SCAP was aided by Japanese police intimidation and open intervention on the shop floor,[56] as well as by management and government pressures of dismissal, pay and promotion. Special efforts were made to split the National Railway Workers' Union, one of the key militant organizations, in which over 100,000 workers were later fired, and in the All Communications Employees' Union. Estimates vary of the number of workers who joined *mindō,* but there is no doubt that the leagues, in conjunction with deflation, mass layoffs and repression, were an important instrument in weakening the left. Sōhyō, the biggest union federation in Japan for more than the past twenty years, was originally founded as part of the anti-communist drive which began with the *mindō.*

Even before the Dodge Plan, Ashida had carried out a major round of dismissals after the events in July 1948. But it was the implementation of the Dodge proposals which led to firings and layoffs on a really large scale. This retrenchment programme, again, is often presented under the technical guise of a "deflationary" policy. But it was much more than this, for it was specifically designed to eliminate a large sector of the militant left, and to reorganize and strengthen oligopoly capital.[57] In 1949 alone, 435,465 workers were dismissed from their jobs, and the figure for the whole 1949–50 retrenchment was about 700,000. Although, on the whole, the Dodge programme involved expanding big industry[58] and therefore employment in big industry, the reorganization was used carefully to weed out militant workers in these expanding sectors, and to weaken the union movement overall by cutting total employment.[59] In roughly the same period as 700,000 workers lost their jobs, the number of unions fell by more than 5,500 and union membership by 880,000.[60] The government purges were accompanied by direct promotion of the anti-communist *mindō,* which were thus enabled to take over the union leadership through this double-barrelled operation.

This retrenchment was extremely important in assisting management to consolidate its dominant position over the working class. The many dismissals naturally made employees more desperate to hold on to their jobs. The figures on the disappearance of unions and the precipitous fall in union membership cover a multiplicity of personal tragedies among the proletariat. As jobs became more and more scarce, and unions which would back the workers' interests weaker and weaker, the pressures to compromise with management by acceding to the latter's version of the enterprise union became stronger and stronger. Whereas in the early postwar period an enterprise union had usually contained all the employees in a plant, management now seized the initiative and demanded that the union grant membership only to a limited number of the enterprise's employees—viz., usually the *minimum* work force which the company would want to employ at the period of maximum retrenchment. Workers, desperate to keep their jobs, were obliged to go along with this definition of the union, which thus became limited to so-called "permanent" workers. Correspondingly, there was now a re-expansion of the number of "temporary" workers, as there had been in the 1930s, on similarly disadvantageous conditions.[61]

As Taira has shown, the inordinately large wage differentials between big and smaller industry which have been specific to Japan developed very quickly in the years 1945–51, in spite of high inflation during most of the period.[62] He ascribes this to the strength of the enterprise unions in the early period. What is surprising is that the tendency accelerated during the period of deflation. The upshot of the growth in wage differentials, however, was a counter-offensive by management, paradoxically. By restricting membership of the enterprise unions during the Dodge Line period, business both cut down the number of employees who had a (relatively) high guaranteed wage, and correspondingly increased its own chances of exploiting "temporary" and other non-"permanent" labour, and of devolving work to subcontracting firms, where unions were much weaker, or non-existent, and wages far lower.[63] This constellation of factors had very important effects on the structure of postwar Japanese industrialization, since labour costs, unionization and company size all formed a nexus determining the structure of investments and work allocations. In brief, in return for guaranteeing a relatively high wage to a limited number of workers, protected by a union and a negotiated agreement, business ensured itself a much larger pool of labour ("temporary," casual, subcontracted, etc.) which was almost wholly un-unionized, employed in small and medium enterprises, and heavily discriminated against. Business's main goals included not simply cheap labour, but also *weak* labour. The discriminatory wage *and union* system, which was largely the work of management, ensured both these, but also involved business in the apparently curious situation of securing its own expansion by maintaining an archaic industrial structure, with a relatively small number of large enterprises, with high unionization and high wages, while the large majority of workers continued to be employed in very small factories, almost wholly un-unionized, and with much lower wage levels. The success of business's low-wage, anti-union policy has been a major element in Japan's postwar expansion, and in the right's retention of political power at the centre.

The assault on the militant working class on the shop floor was accompanied by action at other levels: in education, where a major purge had been launched by SCAP and the Yoshida regime from the beginning of 1949 (see chapter 9), in the media, and at the party political level. In May–June 1950, before the outbreak of the Korean War, MacArthur launched a direct attack on the leadership of the Communist Party and on its newspaper, *Akahata* (*Red Flag*). This purge of political leaders on the left started well before the outbreak of the Korean War, and it was a direct continuation of the dismissals of militant workers which had marked the overall drive to cripple the left.

MacArthur's announcement on May 3, 1950 of a stepped-up drive to root out "destructive communist elements,"[64] often referred to as the "Red Purge," took on the proportions of a nationwide witchhunt. Though this phase of the operation tends to be better known than others because it hit prominent political and media figures, the really crucial part of crippling

the left was the destruction of Sanbetsu and Zenrōren, the wholesale wrecking of the militant unions and the dismissal of hundreds of thousands of
workers who were the backbone of the struggle.[65] As the Sanbetsu and the
left were being gravely weakened, the Yoshida government, the Employers'
Federation (Nikkeiren)[66] and SCAP worked towards a new union coalition based largely on the *mindō*. The new federation, Sōhyō, was founded
in July 1950, immediately after the purge of the JCP and the start of the
Korean War. As the head of Sōhyō wrote to George Meany in 1965: "the
history of the foundation of Sohyo is closely connected with the fight
against the domination of the Japanese trade unions by the Communist
Party."[67] Just after the formation of Sōhyō, Sanbetsu membership dropped
to 47,000, and in 1953 it went down to 13,000. The Federation was dissolved on February 15, 1958.

Although Sōhyō moved to the left on a number of issues connected with
foreign policy and U.S. imperialism shortly after it was founded, it retained a cautious position on domestic matters related to industrial relations.[68] Sōhyō's domestic platform and the wrecking of the Sanbetsu
were a big victory for business in imposing the seniority-wage system and
intra-enterprise unions, which Sōhyō began to challenge only in the mid-
fifties.[69] However, on other questions Sōhyō took up a fairly militant
stance. It opposed the terms of the San Francisco Treaty and the Security
Treaty. It also opposed attempts to force it into the anti-communist International Confederation of Free Trade Unions, which had recently seceded
from the World Federation of Trade Unions. Sōhyō lined up with the JCP
and the left of the JSP in opposing the terms under which the United States
conceded formal independence, and this experience determined the outlook
of the federation in the years ahead. Sōhyō, for example, took a leading
part in the 1959–60 struggles against revision of the Security Treaty with
the United States.

The Union Movement Since Formal Independence (1952)

Although business succeeded in re-establishing its dominant position
after the immediate post-surrender period, this dominance has not gone
unchallenged, and important changes have taken place both in the methods
of struggle and in the balance of power between labour and capital since
that early period. The Korean War brought about a large upsurge in
employment and in output.[70] In many cases this involved reactivating old
equipment in conditions where employers felt unsure of the future. Business insisted that many of the workers taken on be employed on a "temporary" basis, since, it claimed, it could not guarantee the regular employment
which the unions were demanding. Business continued to use much the
same arguments against the unions in the years after 1955 when a new

wave of "temporary" employees was hired in the wake of technological innovations.[71] At this stage the unions were too conservative, and too much on the defensive, to react.

Taira, following Magota, periodizes the history of the Japanese unions so that the postwar enterprise unionism forms a unit with the wartime Sampō;[72] and this stage interpenetrates from the mid-1950s with a new stage—that of the "spring offensive" or Shuntō,[73] which is now the main feature of Japanese union activity. Shuntō is a peculiarly Japanese phenomenon. It can be explained as a means to counter the weakness of the enterprise system. Since individual enterprise unions had such difficulty organizing across enterprise lines, a group of Sōhyō leaders took the initiative, in 1955, of trying to organize a joint offensive rather than a lasting federation. This offensive has been repeated every spring and began to show results about 1960. Each year the Shuntō organizers, Sōhyō and the Chūritsurōren,[74] choose a lead-off union, one which is in a particularly strong bargaining position either because of its internal strength or because of its crucial place in the economy. The Private Railway Workers' Union and the Iron and Steel Workers' Union have most often been chosen to "go first."[75] The settlement achieved by this union, which is backed up by other unions, tends to set the standard for agreements between management and the other unions involved in the Shuntō: average wage increases achieved in this way rose steadily from 1965 to hit 17 per cent in 1970, falling to around 15 per cent in 1971 and 1972, but going back up to almost 20 per cent in 1973.[76] Clearly the acute labour shortage from the late 1960s was an important factor in increasing wages.[77] But there are a number of other factors specific to Japan which explain the Shuntō's success.

Because of the high ratio of credit financing on which Japanese companies tend to operate, plus the crucial importance of maintaining a given market share, Japanese firms are very badly placed to survive a long strike.[78] This strengthens the position of the unions who, through the "spring offensive," have been able not just to win an increase for one union, but by the mechanism of trans-enterprise solidarity, persuade other firms to make quick settlements along the lines achieved by the lead union. In fact, the average length of strikes in the Shuntō has been only between 2.0 and 3.3 days.[79] In theory, of course, any individual union could win a big wage increase by striking against a firm which could not afford a long strike, but it has been precisely the element of solidarity which has given the Shuntō its strength.

To a Western observer, the curious factor is probably why the unions strike *before* negotiations, or at any rate before a stalemate has been reached.[80] There may be an element of ceremony here, but there is also an important economic-cultural factor at work. Fundamentally, Japanese business has still not accepted a union's right to speak for its members.[81]

In innumerable ways a union is still treated as a body which is sabotaging the enterprise's harmony and the "beautiful" relations between exploiters and exploited. Because of the broad gamut of discriminations against unions, they more or less have to prove each year that they do represent the workers they claim to represent, and that these workers are united behind a given goal. Through the Shuntō the unions try to tell management that they do represent the workers; management then has only a short time, usually, to come to a settlement.

Japanese unionism is in a transitional stage. Enterprise unions still are the dominant form of union; but at the same time the Shuntō provides a solid form of multi-union coalition which can be mobilized annually, even if it is not an all-year institution like a union confederation in the Western countries. In some ways, the Shuntō is clearly stronger than most Western confederations.

But the relative success of the Shuntō needs to be set in perspective. First, labour's share of gross value added.[82] Over the entire period of the postwar boom as a whole, wages have risen considerably more slowly than productivity; moreover, wages have moved across a much narrower band than productivity. The crucial fact is that labour's share of gross value added has been falling constantly—whereas it has risen in all the other major capitalist countries. Labour's share in Japan fell from 39.6 per cent in 1953 to 33.8 per cent in 1966, and an estimated 33.7 in 1970. This compares with figures of over 50 per cent for Canada, Sweden, Holland and the United Kingdom. Thus, not only is labour's share of gross value added much lower than in comparable capitalist countries, but this share is falling constantly. The gap between the rich and the poor, in spite of government rhetoric, is constantly growing.[83]

In addition, Japanese workers as of 1970 had, on average, the longest working week of any of the advanced capitalist countries: 43.1 hours (45.0 in an ordinary week), compared with 39.1 hours in West Germany, and 37.5 in the United States.[84] For this they were paid less, absolutely, than workers in these other countries.[85]

As of 1970, only about 35 per cent of all industrial workers were unionized (the U.K. figure is about 40 per cent).[86] Of unionized workers, some one-third did not then belong to any of the four main federations. Unionization still depends very much on the size of the plant: 63 per cent of companies employing more than 500 people had unions; one-third of those employing 100–500 had unions; but less than 10 per cent of those employing 30–100 workers had a union, and for smaller companies the figure was 4 per cent. In the same year (1970), 58,000 unions were organized on an enterprise basis, though the number of unions combining blue- and white-collar workers had fallen considerably, to below half.[87]

There is, therefore, a direct correlation between company size, degree of unionization, wage levels and employment systems. In fact, in the context of the government's overall economic policy, and business's decisions about investment, it is clear that unionization is only a partial index of the strength of the working class. Indeed, it is fair to say that formal unionization does not represent the fully autonomous aspirations of the working class, but rather the common ground between labour and capital, and that within the total context of Japanese industrialization the unions represent instruments of conciliation, in the last instance, between the two sides.[88]

The Weakness of Sōhyō

Although Sōhyō has moved quite a long way from its starting point in 1950, it has never fully escaped from the limitations which marked its inception or formed a really cohesive central organization. Thus in the 1960s when big business launched a major subversive drive against it, business was able to undermine the federation by setting up new "democratization leagues," which soon combined to form a new, more right-wing federation, the Dōmei-kaigi (reorganized in November 1964 as Dōmei), which soon became the second biggest in the country. By mid-1971 Dōmei had well over two million members and, what is more important, overtook Sōhyō in private industry in 1967.[89] In 1970 Sōhyō had only 39 per cent of its members in private industry, while Dōmei had no less than 93 per cent, being especially strong in the electronic, automobile and textile industries. Thus, although Sōhyō has been responsible for a very high proportion of the registered strikes and other industrial disputes,[90] it has not mounted any major challenge to capital.

On the contrary, Sōhyō has pursued a centrist and essentially collaborationist policy on the shop floor. It has refused, or been unable, to make the leap across such capitalist-imposed barriers as those dividing "permanent" from "temporary" and other workers. Sōhyō-affiliated unions have supinely accepted management directives to exclude "temporary" workers from membership, even in the stage of high growth, and consequent labour shortage. Sōhyō's role in the key sector of steel is exemplary. The Yawata-Fuji (re-)merger produced the biggest steel firm in the world, Nippon Steel. The local union at Yawata, affiliated to the Federation of Steel Workers' Union (which is in Sōhyō), was completely debilitated from within by the company, which systematically isolated the militant members. At the time of the re-merger, the union was entirely in the hands of the company's representatives, and yet was still accepted by Sōhyō.[91]

Sōhyō went along with the JSP and the JCP in excluding members of the militant workers' group, the Hansen Seinen Iinkai,[92] from its ranks. It also cut its ties with Beheiren, the loose-knit, but dynamic and influential anti-imperialist movement that grew up at the time of the Vietnam War.[93] As one observer recently stated, Sōhyō has aided the integration of the working class into capitalism: "real disruption would be more likely without this organization."[94]

THE MECHANISMS OF CAPITALIST CONTROL

The Exploitation of Women

The exploitation of women has been absolutely central to the whole development of Japanese capitalism: low-wage female labour has been a key factor in the accumulation of capital since the beginning of industry in Japan. Moreover, discrimination against women in wages, terms of employment and pensions is still qualitatively more severe in Japan than in the other advanced capitalist societies.

First, there is the whole area of housework and other completely unpaid labour. In the late 1960s only 63 per cent of the employed labour force were actually classed as employees at all, and about 17 per cent of the employed were unpaid family workers (including some 8 per cent of those employed outside agriculture and forestry).[95] A high proportion of these can reasonably be assumed to be women. Moreover, it is impossible even to know how many women are *unemployed,* since government statistics describe most people who are not working as "without occupation" rather than "unemployed." A 1969 survey found that nearly one-quarter of those women classified as "without occupation" wanted "employment."[96]

But it is in factory work that women play the biggest role. In 1972 women accounted for 32.4 per cent of all employed workers in the economy as a whole (11.2 million out of 34.52 million), but they accounted for no less than 57.5 per cent of all factory workers—and 46.8 per cent of all office workers, the next biggest area.[97] The importance of the exploitation of women can be seen from the fact that, while they provide well over half the factory workers in Japan, the average woman's wage is only 48.2 per cent of the average man's wage.[98] Moreover, women are excluded from the *nenkō* system and are forced into *formal* retirement much earlier than men—often being statutorily dismissed at the age of thirty, or at marriage.[99] By firing women so early, and by excluding them from any system of guaranteed wage increases, business can then rehire them cheaply after marriage or in old age at particularly low rates, a practice which became increasingly common as the labour shortage became more acute.[100] This barrage of discriminatory measures against women not only helps management keep their wages down, but also has aided management in preserving sexist exclusionism in the unions, which have been appallingly passive on this issue. Organized action against this system is now beginning, with attention focused on the early obligatory "retirement," but this action is largely taking place outside the established union framework.[101] Further, as Kaji Etsuko trenchantly notes, both sexist ideology and the whole "division of labour" between the state and private industry stand in the way of any major improvement in women's lot: "in Japan, the strength of the sexist ideology is reflected in an appalling lack of social services for children to make women *prefer* grossly underpaid jobs as temporary workers, because this is the only way they can combine work with childcare"—which the ideology promotes as their main function.[102]

General Mechanisms for Weakening the Proletariat: The Organization of the Work Force

One of the most striking features of the Japanese economy is that although in terms of GNP it is the third largest in the world, as of the late 1960s two-thirds of all employees in manufacturing were still employed in small and medium enterprises. This is partly the result of the historical formation of Japanese industry, with many plants sited in rural areas,[103] with only limited labour and raw materials available, very bad transportation, and, until recently, very few people in urban areas. But it also represents a deliberate option by capitalism, since the smaller the enterprise the lower the wages which employers have had to pay (although productivity has also been lower).[104] Smaller enterprises, being proportionately less unionized, have also allowed management greater freedom of action in reducing wages and firing workers, as well as sources for cheap labour which can be used in subcontracting outside *and inside* bigger plants. There are also other economic factors connected to credit and cash-flow which have made it advantageous for big business to maintain smaller, subordinate companies.[105]

Even with this advantageous big/small industry division, business has worked to maintain the key elements in its wage and employment system: the special discrimination against women, the division of workers into "permanent" and others, and the division of pay into "basic" and other. In this way, *pace* Abegglen, both labour force and wages have been kept variable, at management's wishes, providing a *double* cushion.[106]

Outside the core of "permanent" employees, business has developed a flexible band of non-"permanent" workers. These are: "temporary" workers, some of whom are *permanent* temporary workers; day-labourers and casual workers; *shagaikō* (extra workers); and subcontractors. There is not universal agreement on how many people are covered by the guaranteed employment system. According to one source, in the early 1960s it covered only one-fifth of all wage-earners in manufacturing. Another source, referring to the late 1960s, states that it covers "perhaps not even a majority" of Japanese workers.[107] Those who are covered by it include most regular workers in large corporations, governmental employees, including those in governmental corporations, and university employees. Those excluded are all temporary employees of large corporations, day-labourers, and most employees of medium and small industry. Probably nearly all the long-term employees in big private industry are covered by some kind of guarantee system. But conditions vary enormously in small and medium plants, where it would seem that firms subcontracting to bigger enterprises, or otherwise closely subordinate to them, tend not to have a *nenkō*-type system, whereas independent smaller industries do.

This cushioning system is almost invulnerable. The stipulation that unions may usually only enrol permanent workers[108] in effect enlists the unions' aid in perpetuating the discriminations, and in fragmenting the working class.

The use of "temporary," subcontracted and other types of labour at much lower wages varies greatly between different sectors of industry, and by size of enterprise. The highest number of temporary workers is employed in *big* industry, where the "saving" tends to be highest.[109] The car industry has had a particularly high proportion of "temporary" workers, an average of 19 per cent for the whole sector in 1957, with Toyota showing the staggering figure of 52 per cent of all employees being "temporary" in 1961.[110] Business also invented the category of "permanent temporary" workers, who were just kept on low pay in spite of being employed for very long periods by one enterprise. The number of "temporary" and day workers reportedly dropped towards the mid-1960s, amounting to 5 per cent of all employees in private establishments as of mid-1966.[111]

Probably more important than the "temporary" worker ploy is the extensive use of subcontracting.[112] This involves not only putting work out to smaller enterprises which pay lower wages, but also using workers from these smaller plants *in* the "parent" plant, where they are paid less than the big enterprise's permanent workers for exactly the same job. This practice appears to be particularly prevalent in the shipbuilding and construction industries, although it is impossible to get precise figures on "internal subcontracting." By paying all these non-"permanent" workers considerably less, and by keeping them in a situation where there is no job guarantee, business protects itself against recessions, as well as against other troubles such as strikes, allowing it to "adjust" at its discretion.[113]

The other key element in this is the structure of wages. For male permanent workers, management makes a calculation which in essence boils down to this: we will pay you x amount of money for the "lifetime" you spend with us (i.e., from hiring date to compulsory retirement date),[114] but we will pay it out to you at our own rate, which *starts* very low, but will rise fairly steadily to about age 40–44 and then fall again gradually until retirement in the mid- to late 50s (and very steeply after that).[115] In this way, business, holding out the carrot of "fair" wages only in return for a long-term commitment by a worker, secures a cheap labour force. Moreover, as well as usually being the most productive, younger workers are often the most militant, and the seniority-wage system, on the whole, strengthens the position of older employees.[116] The Shuntō and other actions seem in the context of a growing labour shortage to have had a good deal of effect on the gap in *starting* wages between big and small industry, but not on the *internal* pay differentiations in either big or small enterprises, which have stayed very much the same. Starting wages for all sizes of enterprises are now much closer to each other, but wages in big industries rise much more steeply.[117]

But the pay system is not simply an automatic one. It is important not to overemphasize either age, or even years of service, as the criteria either for wage increases or for promotion.[118] Recently, non-*nenkō* factors have been becoming more and more important in wage assessments. This has not necessarily weakened management's power, since a system of wage fragmentation has been devised to maximize control. In one of the factories that Robert Cole studied, wages in the late 1960s were made up of fourteen different components: six of the standard wage, and eight of the supplementary wage.[119] This fragmentation of pay makes it very much more difficult for any workers, whether unionized or not, to bargain effectively over wages, since management has so many categories with which to juggle.[120] In addition, the supplementary wage sector can be manipulated either to repress a combative work force or to increase capital accumulation through lower wages.

A word should be said about management's ability to "adjust," particularly as this is a subject which has been rather obfuscated in many Western sources.[121] There is no evidence that Japanese business has had difficulty dealing with recessions or other questions (such as accelerating capital accumulation) through manipulating the labour force. In the 1962 slump employers used a whole gamut of measures ranging from shortening working hours, via curtailment of external employment and reallocation of ordinary employees, to straight dismissals. The restricted dimensions of the *nenkō* and "life employment" (*shūshin koyō*) systems give an indication of the extent of the protective cushioning which business has established. Of course, there are compromises in the set-up. In some cases, for example, an employer will keep *some* employees on something around 60–70 per cent of *basic* pay over a relatively long layoff (say, six months);[122] but there is no reason to think this may not be a self-protective measure against the next wave of the boom.

The idea, too, that there is no mobility of labour in Japan is a myth. The seniority-wage system and other devices[123] have definitely served to restrict labour mobility by Western standards. But there is fairly high mobility among young workers, both male and female, with low mobility among experienced workers. Roughly half the labour force changes jobs at least once in a decade, with about half these moves involving inter-industry mobility. Thus, in Evans's words, "it would appear that the elasticity of labour supply has been quite extensive."[124] Mobility has been growing very fast in the last decade or so, particularly among blue-collar workers. Government policy, aimed at countering the effects of the labour shortage, has been designed to promote mobility among certain categories of workers in the interests of big business.[125] Since the various guarantee systems cover at most half the labour force, and probably much less, these requirements are by no means in conflict with each other.

To sum up: as Kaji so correctly emphasizes in her discussion of the capitalist exploitation of women, the wage and employment systems are integrally tied to ruling class ideology and to the Japanese social system itself. Unless these are changed, although there will probably be a gradual trend towards less inequality, an increase in job-related factors in assessing pay, and more mobility, the system is likely to remain an adjusted mix of *nenkō,* personal and job factors.[126]

The Context of Opposition: The Division of Repression Between Government and Business

The system of capitalist rule does not, of course, depend only on these relatively "technical" mechanisms. It rests on class struggle—class struggle in which the ruling class wages an unrelenting battle against the working masses at every level, with ideology, law, physical repression and straight exploitation. The legal system has failed to support the idea of a contract; and official ideology fosters the idea that employers have rights over their employees, but not vice versa, and that these rights are open-ended, while employees have only duties towards their employers.[127]

It is in this context that one should consider the high degree of repression and exploitation in Japanese industry. Japanese factories have an extremely high number of supervisory staff.[128] Repression inside the plant is sustained through constant espionage on militant workers and the sabotage of contesting workers' organizations—such as splitting a combative union or forming a subsidized "second" union[129] to bribe or terrorize away wavering workers from the militant line—and also through the constant "family-like" interference in workers' everyday lives. In many cases companies hire gangsters and goon squads, which operate off the shop floor as well as on it. Terror in and around the plant by private companies is complemented by massive police repression against militants in society in general.[130]

The working conditions of the most exploited workers in postwar Japan are rarely reported in detail in the West. An account of the life of coal-miners in Kyushu in the late 1950s describes how the most dangerous work in the mines was done by "temporary" workers employed by a gang-boss hired by the company. These workers were paid at most half the regular wage, sometimes getting only a small bag of rice for an entire month's work; when factory inspectors visited the mine, these workers were sealed into remote areas of the pits for the duration of the visit. They were housed in hovels patrolled by armed guards, and visitors were rigidly excluded. The union refused to intervene.[131]

Again, much has been written in the West about air and sea pollution in Japan, but little about "pollution" and danger *inside* the factories and mines where most workers spend half of their waking life. A 1968 government survey (which may understate the case) showed nervous fatigue in 80–96 per cent of all workers; "great fatigue" after each day's work in some 80 per cent; fatigue frequently lasting over till the next day in well over half.[132] Over 6,000 people were killed in industrial accidents in 1968, and 6,200 in 1969.[133] Compensation for death at a big company like Nissan at the time could be a mere ¥50,000 (£50 at that date).[134]

As the study of the Hitachi mine cited above showed, old workers and members of the families of workers injured frequently have to take up badly paid work to make ends meet. But the statistics on fatigue indicate that nervous troubles extend right through the work force. Japanese capitalism is well aware of this, as is shown by the case of Matsushita Kōnosuke and the "self-control room" he has set up in one of his factories. This room, the approach to which is lined with distorting mirrors "to help workers relax and perhaps even laugh at themselves" (in the words of *Time*),[135] contains a stuffed dummy of Matsushita himself on which workers can unleash aggression with bamboo staves provided by the company. At another level, such institutions as the obligatory singing of the company song and physical exercise, far from being the expression of "harmony," are management-imposed devices to facilitate exploitation by creating a climate of bogus enterprise solidarity where dissidence and revolt are made difficult.[136]

As in the Meiji era, business continues to talk about "serving the nation," claims to eschew profit (and the profit motive), and veils exploitation in a vocabulary of "harmony" and "love." Yet the facts tell a different story. The labour share is the lowest in any of the advanced capitalist countries, the rate of capital accumulation is the highest and, contrary to widely accepted belief, the real rate of after-tax profits is about the same as in the other major capitalist economies.[137]

An important element in the preservation of this situation has been the ruling class's success in establishing the ideology of Japan as a "classless" society. It must be emphasized that this denial of class is in a qualitatively different league from the efforts in the same direction undertaken by the Western bourgeoisies and their ideologists.

An exceptionally sophisticated expression of this ideology has been provided by the sociologist Nakane in *Japanese Society:*

> The overall picture of society . . . is not that of horizontal stratification by class or caste but of vertical stratification by institution or group of institutions. . . . Even if social classes like those in Europe can be detected in Japan, and even if something vaguely resembling those classes that are illustrated in the textbooks of western sociology can also be found in Japan, the point is that in actual society this stratification is unlikely to

function and that it does not really reflect the social structure. In Japanese society it is really not a matter of workers struggling against capitalists or managers but of Company A ranged against Company B. The protagonists do not stand in vertical relationship to each other but instead rub elbows from parallel positions. . . . The antagonism and wrangling between management and labour in Japan is unquestionably a "household" problem, and though their basic divergence is the same as it is the world over, the reason it cannot develop in Japan into a problem intimately and powerfully affecting society as a whole is to be found in the group structure and the nature of total Japanese society.[138]

The plain fact is that while the workers in a factory are *subjected* to this ideology, management shows no "enterprise solidarity." The simplest evidence of this is the superb trans-enterprise organization of Japanese big business, which has the most powerful federations in the capitalist world. Group solidarity is an ideological weapon, where the capitalist class operates class solidarity within itself and fragmentation among the working class. Nakane shows that this condition is brought about and maintained by violence: "each member [of a group] is shaped to more or less the same mould, and forced to undergo the kneading effects of group interaction whether he likes it or not. The individual Japanese has little opportunity to learn sociability. Whatever security he feels is derived from aligning and matching himself with group purpose and plan."[139] As Nakane notes later, "there is a cruelly heavy handicap against the powerless and the socially inferior."[140]

The government fosters the preservation of these conditions not only by promoting such ideology in schools, but by directly and indirectly creating the conditions where business can continue to exploit the working masses. Here government action and inaction over the labour laws have both been extremely important.

Under the Occupation, the Japanese regime was able both to enact anti-working class legislation and to refuse to apply SCAP laws of which it disapproved. The Labour Standards Law of 1947, for example, which included equal pay for equal work, was almost completely ignored. In 1949 alone, according to Premier Yoshida, there were 1,200,000 violations of the law brought before the authorities, of which only a derisory number were actually proceeded upon.[141] After independence the government revised the labour laws in an anti–working class direction and made particularly extensive use of MacArthur's measures depriving public employees of the right to strike. Until 1965 the government refused to ratify ILO Convention 87, which calls for unrestricted rights for all workers to organize and bargain, including the designation of bargaining representatives. The government finally ratified the Convention and then simply refused to apply it.[142] The Ministry of Labour has played the lead, along with the Ministry of International Trade and Industry, in these machinations, which have been accompanied by much rhetoric about aiding labour and management to meet on an equal basis to solve labour problems.[143]

On a wider scale, too, the state, by keeping down spending on social services, has actively fostered the conditions under which business has been able to seize and hold labour;[144] protecting insecurity outside the enterprise, it enhanced the appeal of such company services as housing.[145] In more complex ways, too, the state has played an active role, particularly over pensions.[146] By refusing to provide care for the aged, the state has not simply strengthened the appeal of private companies' pension schemes, but also worked to force more older people back into jobs after the statutory retirement age (and therefore on much lower pay).[147] Further, by keeping the prospect of a poverty-stricken old age ever-present, the regime stimulated the highest savings rates in the world, double those (proportionate to earnings) in any other advanced capitalist country, among all income groups. The vast majority of these savings have gone not into assets, but straight to the banks whence they have been redirected largely to favoured private industry rather than towards public services.[148] In 1964, for example, government outlay on social services per capita was about the same as in Tunisia or Sri Lanka.[149]

It is important to realize that this situation represents a consistent long-term policy for a specific form of high capital accumulation based on low wages and a rigidly controlled work force. But, though control of the work force has been largely achieved, the economic options of the ruling class and the state have themselves created acute new contradictions, particularly at the social level, which have given political struggle in Japan its unique configuration.

The neglect of social services and assistance has had striking effects in Japan. The refusal to allocate money for such things as sewers and urban improvements has made many working class areas in the cities into slums or quasi-slums. A 1969 survey showed that only 9.2 per cent of Japanese houses had flush toilets (98.2 per cent in the United Kingdom); the sewer service saturation rate was only 17 per cent (90 per cent in the United Kingdom); the percentage of roads paved was a mere 10.8 per cent. There were only 0.9 square meters of park per urban citizen (compared with 19 in the United States).[150] Swift economic "growth" partly masked this situation and the dire poverty in which many Japanese have been living during the so-called miracle. A 1963 Ministry of Welfare publication showed that 20 per cent of all households were living below the officially-defined poverty line (defined as an income of about the then equivalent of 45 U.S. cents per person per day).[151] In one *burakumin* village studied, not only was the population density ten times that of its non-*burakumin* neighbouring village, but the average income of the *burakumin* village was one-twentieth that in the village next door. Moreover, in the early 1960s about 60 per cent of all the fully unemployed persons in Japan were *burakumin*.[152]

Alongside this failure to reallocate the fruits of economic growth, the government has assisted capital accumulation by allowing industry to use maximally untrammeled methods in its operations. It is important to stress that a very large part of Japan's overall "pollution" problems are the direct result of a chosen policy for capital accumulation and not the unavoidable "by-products" of development, as they are frequently presented.[153] This contradiction has now reached acute political proportions, with pollution in Japan now worse than anywhere else in the world except the Seoul area of south Korea. The crucial political factor is that the noxious effects of big business's "high growth" policies have spilled over from the shop floor and the mines into society as a whole, and this has had important effects on the class struggle. Government attempts to defuse mass opposition to its economic policies by spreading pollution under the guise of decentralization have been dismal failures.[154]

The ruling class's economic policies have increasingly blighted much of Japan and increasingly *destroyed* the livelihood of many Japanese—for example, those who lived off fishing. Several of the biggest struggles of recent years have been against "development" plans which threatened to wreck local communities. The most famous was the struggle against the new Tokyo airport at Narita,[155] which lasted several years. This struggle is particularly important both because of the high level of combativity and because it fused the domestic fight against Japanese capitalism with the fight against U.S. imperialism.

With the escalation of U.S. aggression against the peoples of Indochina, Tokyo's main airport, Haneda, became overloaded. This was because between one-third and half of the traffic there was made up of U.S. military charter and other related flights tied to the war against Indochina. The "need" for a new airport was thus a direct result of U.S. imperialism's activities and the Tokyo government's relationship to the United States.

In July 1966 the Satō government, without consulting the local inhabitants, decided to put a new airport at Sanrizuka, a small village about forty miles north of Tokyo. One reason Sanrizuka was chosen was that the Emperor owned 500 hectares there and the authorities would have the Emperor's land as a secure base from which to start.[156] The fight against the construction of the new airport was waged for over five years on the interconnected issues of the farmers' determination not to be evicted from their rich farmland and the popular rejection of a new airport designed largely to assist U.S. aggression.

After a first attempt to seize the land, in which the police terrorized the local population and beat up the farmers' elderly leader, Tomura Issaku, the farmers organized local defences and publicized their struggle, which became a national issue. Support flooded in from thousands of workers and students from all over the country, and a solid farmer-worker-student alliance was formed. The defenders built an extensive system of trenches and interconnecting tunnels, guarded by watch-towers, palisades and blockhouses, protected by cadres armed with grenades and staves. A survey team which tried to penetrate the area on February 19, 1970 had to be accompanied by three thousand armed riot police (Kidōtai) and plainclothesmen, yet was still held off by the farmers and their supporters. In February 1971 the government decided to launch a full-scale attack to carry out further expropriations: four thousand Kidōtai assaulted the farmers with water-cannon, bulldozers and baton-charges. Fourteen hundred people were injured, at least two hundred seriously. Goon squads employed by the construction companies also went on the rampage at the same time, unwisely beating up two JSP Dietmen. In September 1971, after a further police attack on the area, three policemen were killed. More than one year after that, several years behind schedule, the last farmers were finally evicted.[157]

The portrayal of events at Sanrizuka as a rearguard fight by backward peasants against innocent progress is a classic travesty of the struggle, which was a vanguard struggle on a highly political issue.[158] The struggle aroused an unprecedented wave of mass support throughout the country: it showed that the regime's alliance with U.S. imperialism meant literally the destruction of people's livelihood and of the Japanese countryside. Particularly terrifying to the regime was the fact that the high level of militancy shown by the defenders at Sanrizuka found such a widespread echo in the society at large.

Another big struggle surged up over plans to build a new industrial area at Rokkasho in the far north of Honshu Island. Again issues of "pollution" enter into the struggle, but it is basically one by the local inhabitants against exploitation of their land, their labour and their lives.[159] Many of the big struggles against the U.S. presence in Japan and on Okinawa have been against both the U.S. exploitation of Japan for its imperialist activities and the appalling effects of the U.S. bases and personnel on life in Japan itself.[160]

The Japanese left has consistently been able to mount extensive demonstrations and active interventions against U.S. and Japanese imperialism: strikes among the base workers on Okinawa and at the big U.S. bases in Japan proper; actions by railway workers to block the transportation of U.S. military equipment, including petrol and armaments for use in Indochina; actions by local government authorities to prevent the transit of tanks for the Saigon regime in 1972;[161] attacks on U.S. bases, including the destruction of American military equipment in the bases and of U.S. property outside, as well as attacks on U.S. military personnel.[162] On the occasion of Premier Satō's departure for a trip to the United States, the government had to mobilize 75,000 armed police to ensure his passage to Tokyo airport—five times the total number of British troops in Northern Ireland.

Yet this strength on issues of imperialism goes together with considerable isolation. Some of this isolation is due to problems of distance and language. But more important, and little appreciated outside Japan, are the systematic government efforts to isolate the Japanese left from contact with progressive forces in the rest of the world, particularly in East Asia, and to prevent militants from other countries getting into Japan. The new Immigration (Control) Bill, which the LDP government has in draft form, is designed to make it very hard for anyone the Japanese government does not like to enter Japan. It lays down extremely strict conditions for being in Japan, combined with a degree of vagueness so that almost anyone can be deported. The Japanese police have been particularly diligent in rounding up critics from south Vietnam, south Korea and Taiwan. There is no recognized legal redress against being held in one of the two detention centres (Omura in Nagasaki, and Yokohama), or against deportation.[163]

THE POLITICAL PARTIES

The political party in Japan has not, on the whole, been a successful organizational form in any sector of the political spectrum, and the difficulties facing any left-wing organization in Japan are especially acute. The society has built innumerable barriers against trans-group organization and the notion of class solidarity is resolutely discouraged by every instance of power, from the family to the state to the school.

The Japan Socialist Party (JSP)

The JSP has been the largest opposition party in Japan since the war in terms of votes, but has never been able to build up an organized base and a mass membership. By 1972 party membership had fallen from a peak of about 50,000 to some 37,000, whereas the party's vote in both the 1969 and 1972 general elections came to around 10 million. Admittedly, 1969 was the nadir of the party's fortunes since 1949, immediately after the Katayama fiasco. In the December 1972 election the party's fortunes improved, and it won 118 seats in the Lower House—28 more than its 1969 total of 90. But this was achieved not by any comparable upsurge in support for the party, but mainly by cutting the number of JSP candidates standing in the same constituencies.[164] The JSP's percentage of the poll in 1972 (21.9) was well below that in 1967 (27.9). These fluctuations, largely unrelated to real, active political support, highlight the party's structural problems: it exists primarily as a Diet group; outside the Diet it relies overwhelmingly on Sōhyō for organizational support. In the early 1960s, for example, 80 per cent of JSP members were members of Sōhyō-affiliated unions; half the JSP Dietmen came from Sōhyō; and all JSP candidates depended on Sōhyō support at election time.[165] This unsatisfactry relationship between parliament, party and unions is much more of a problem than factionalism.

The JSP, like all the opposition parties, is seriously disadvantaged because voting constituencies are multi-member, and the system is weighted in the LDP's favour. In addition, both the multiplicity of social classes, involving the proliferation of different relationships to the productive process, and the pace of technological change have made its task more difficult. The JSP has not been able to develop a hegemonizing ideology to embrace a situation where two-thirds of the industrial labour force has been employed in small, despotic plants, where the ruling party has carried out a vast campaign of bribery and mystification to secure rural votes, and where the traditional fragmenting operations of ruling-class ideology are still effective.

Furthermore, the changes which have been taking place in Japanese society have been bewildering to all the parties. Over the period 1947–58 the JSP vote (and the JCP vote) was directly correlated with the degree of urbanization; yet in the 1967 election, for example, the JSP's percentage of the votes decreased in urban-type constituencies and increased in rural-type ones. On the whole, the JSP has benefitted from urbanization:[166] its main areas of strength are in the big cities and on the islands of Hokkaido and Okinawa. In 1960, for example, 45 per cent of the JSP vote came from the cities of Tokyo, Osaka, and Kyoto plus Hokkaido and the prefectures of Kanagawa, Aichi, Hyogo and Fukuoka in which are to be found, respectively, the big cities of Yokohama, Nagoya, Kobe and Fukuoka. The JSP is a key force in the anti-LDP coalitions which govern many of Japan's major cities, including Tokyo, Yokohama, Nagoya and Kyoto, as well as the Ryukyus.

So far the JSP has not capitalized on these areas of strength to undermine the LDP in a major way. Nor has the party developed any of the attributes of a real grass-roots force. Apart from its very low membership, the party also has a very feeble press—in striking contrast to the JCP. The JSP has been supinely negligent on the crucial issue of the rice subsidy, an area where an imaginative proposal could have a real restructuring effect on the society. Nor has it been able to transcend the corporativist limitations which it shares with Sōhyō. Just as Sōhyō fails to extend its cover to any but "permanent" workers, so the JSP fails to attract much support from the poorest and most discriminated against in Japanese society. In 1958, for example, the two classes from which it got least support were the upper and the lower—16 and 17 per cent, respectively.[167]

The JSP has been important in some areas of foreign policy. It has fought against the maintenance of Ampo, the Security Treaty with the United States. It also championed good relations with China, and played an important part in forcing a change in government policy on this issue. But, although it contains within itself a Marxist component, comparable in this way to the pre-1963 Italian Socialist Party, it has never developed a thorough critique which could put it on top of the changes in Japanese society. As in the case of the rice subsidy programme, it has been tailist.

And, more recently, in the crucial field of relations with the new left militant groups outside the "established" framework, such as the Hansen Seinen Iinkai, the JSP has adopted an exclusionist attitude.

The Japan Communist Party (JCP)

The only party in Japan (with the exception of the maverick Kōmeitō)[168] which has built up a sizeable membership and organization in the post-war period is the Communist Party. From a base of virtually nothing in 1945, party membership expanded rapidly in the late 1940s, particularly among the working class. By the party's XI Congress in July 1970, membership totalled 300,000—up from 45,000 in 1958 and 140,000 in 1964.[169] The JCP claimed that 59 per cent of its members then were manual or clerical workers.[170] In addition to this solid party organization, the JCP has a very powerful press, probably the strongest of any communist movement in a capitalist country. The circulation of the party newspaper, *Akahata,* rose from 74,000 in 1960 to 400,000 in 1970, and 550,000 by 1973 for weekdays; and from 99,000 to 1,420,000 and 1,950,000 on Sundays.[171]

Until the end of the 1960s the JCP was in many ways the inverse of the JSP. In spite of its real party strength, it failed to exercise anything like the same influence on national politics as the JSP. This can not be ascribed solely to its conservative line (which, after all, is shared by the JSP). Moreover, the JCP has failed to make inroads into the unions commensurate with its party and electoral strength.

In the December 1972 general election the JCP got 10.5 per cent of the 52 million votes cast, giving the party 38 seats, three more than it had after the 1949 election (its previous peak). In terms of Diet strength, this made the JCP the third largest party in the Lower House, entitling it to seats on the important committees which prepare legislation. The JCP is also a major force in the left coalitions which rule most of Japan's major cities and control local government for more than one-third of the country's population.[172]

The JCP is in many ways similar to the French and Italian Communist Parties, an essentially reformist organization dedicated mainly to improving the working and living conditions of its members and of the working and middle classes, rather than to the revolutionary overthrow of capitalism and the installation of the dictatorship of the proletariat. This is not too surprising, considering that this has been the general tendency in all the advanced capitalist countries in the period since 1945, and that the pressures in Japan from a combination of local capitalists and Washington-led imperialism have been fairly like those in comparable countries, such as France.

However, in Japan's case, there are two special features that might have been expected to alter the picture somewhat. The first is that Japan had no legacy of a direct colonial kind after 1945; indeed, Japan itself was occupied by an alien power. Second, Japan is the capitalist country closest in geography and culture to China. In addition, many of the JCP's leaders lived for long periods of time in China and worked with Mao Tsetung and other Chinese Communist Party (CCP) leaders. The most famous of these is Nosaka Sanzō, who spent the war years at Yenan, where he published a book entitled *The Establishment of a Democratic Japan*,[173] which was fundamentally an attempt to apply to Japan Mao's theses on "New Democracy."

On his return to Japan, Nosaka hailed MacArthur as a "liberator" and went so far as to claim that a revolution could be carried out under the U.S. Occupation. In spite of the JCP leaders' close ideological and personal ties with the CCP leaders, the JCP pursued an ultra-right line in the period 1945–January 1950. Given that U.S. imperialism was engaged in trying to smash the Chinese Revolution during this period, the JCP's right line calls for some interpretation.

First, the relative *and sudden* freedom after decades of fierce repression was obviously a startling novelty to the party and seems to have significantly affected its political judgement. Second, the party's real weakness in terms of lack of a mass organization, very few trained cadres and no experience such as the Resistance in Europe, pushed it towards caution. Third, it may be that the party made an over-optimistic reading of Truman's Post-Surrender Directive to MacArthur, which explicitly ordered MacArthur not to intervene in Japan's domestic politics and *apparently* allowed for the use of force by Japanese political groups to bring about political change.[174] The party followed what came to be known as the "lovable party line," which involved participation in official bodies such as the Labour Legislation Council. At the same time, the JCP led the militant struggle inside the unions against the reconsolidation of capitalism and against the Emperor-system.

In spite of increasing repression by SCAP and the Japanese police, the JCP followed this line until January 1950. In that month the Cominform launched an unprecedented attack on the JCP, criticizing it for complacency vis-à-vis the Occupation regime and for being over-committed to peaceful methods.[175] This attack has since been attributed to Stalin personally.[176] The attack came during Mao Tsetung's prolonged stay in the Soviet Union during the winter of 1949–50 immediately after the proclamation of the People's Republic of China. The attack would seem to have had two main reasons behind it. First, there was Soviet (and perhaps Chinese) concern over the Japanese left's failure to impede the consolidation of U.S. imperialism in Japan, including the establishment of long-term military installations and the integration of Japan into the American anti-communist alliance. Second, Stalin was agitated about the effects of Mao's victory in China. Japan was not only a major ally of the United

States; its Communist Party was one of the most prestigious which had openly praised Mao and the CCP, and was the only communist party in an industrialized capitalist country which had proclaimed that it was following the "Chinese" road.[177] The JCP at first tried to stave off implementation of the Cominform critique until the CCP intervened later in January with an editorial in the *People's Daily* backing up the Cominform criticism, in rather more nuanced and principled language than the original. Even then, the JCP handled the attack in a relatively autonomous manner and, above all, refused to engage in the kind of hatcheting and exclusions which marked the upheavals in the European communist parties at the time. Shortly after this, just prior to the outbreak of the Korean War, SCAP ordered the purging of a large part of the party leadership. Most of the rest of the top cadres went underground or escaped once again to China.

During the Korean War the party followed an ultra-left line, including the endorsement of guerrilla warfare in Japan.[178] This met with little response, in spite of the fact that the JCP had received the support of 9.7 per cent of the voters in the 1949 general election. And the failure of ultra-leftism, combined with the renewed repression during the Korean War, caused a general swing inside the party towards the right which became clear later.[179] The party's caution was most clearly shown during the mass struggles against the renewal of the Security Treaty in 1959–60, when the JCP was severely attacked and condemned for its rightist line. The JCP has continued to follow an essentially rightist line in all the major disputes, including those of 1964–65 against the "normalization" treaty between Tokyo and Seoul, the demonstrations in 1969–70 against the further renewal of the Security Treaty and all the struggles against the terms of Okinawa's reversion. The JCP has rigorously excluded the militant Hansen Seinen Iinkai, although it has been prepared to collaborate with the Kō-meitō and even the extremely conservative Democratic Socialist Party (DSP) on certain issues in the Diet and in local government.

Externally, the JCP has followed a curious zigzag course. By 1961 it had lined up clearly alongside the CCP in the international dispute, but without any repercussions on its domestic policy. It vigorously opposed the Moscow Partial Nuclear Test Ban Treaty, which it denounced as a fraud.[180] This issue was used by the Russians to bring about a tiny pro-Soviet splinter movement, led by Shiga Yoshio, the head of the JCP Diet group.

Then, in 1966, after the Secretary General of the party, Miyamoto Kenji,[181] had made an extensive trip to Vietnam, Korea and China, the JCP broke with the CCP—apparently largely over strategy in Japan, with the Indonesian debacle and Vietnam as perhaps additional issues.[182] After a period of attempted "neutrality," during which it maintained good relations with both the Vietnamese and the Korean communist movements, the JCP began to drift closer to the CPSU, with which it had much more in common politically and ideologically than it had with the CCP. In 1971 it sent a delegation to the XXIV Congress of the CPSU. Throughout this period the JCP was roundly denounced by the CCP as "the Miyamoto revisionist clique" and one of the "four enemies" of the Japanese people, as designated by Mao himself.[183] China insisted that the JCP be kept out of any organization working for the restoration of Japan-China relations, and Chou En-lai denounced the JCP to James Reston: "The JCP," he said, "is supporting Prime Minister Satō in his efforts to revive Japanese militarism."

The party, pursuing a line of nationalism and class collaboration, in conditions very different from those prevailing in other East Asian countries, has tended to become more and more isolated from the Asian revolutionary movement as a whole. In 1971, when it was announced that Nixon would be visiting China, the JCP openly attacked both the visit itself, and the Chinese and North Korean assessment of its significance. In appearance, this attack came from the left. It may well have been motivated not only by basic disagreements with the CCP, but also by extrapolation from the particular Japanese situation where the fight to prevent any American President entering the country has been one of the central points of left-wing activity since the war. But the upshot of the JCP's move was to cause a rupture with the Korean Workers' Party, which was aggravated when the JCP refused to go along with the Workers' Party assessment of the July 4, 1972 North-South Communiqué. The JCP insisted on remaining sceptical, on the grounds that the reactionary Japanese government was pleased with the North-South Korean talks.[184] The overall result has been the virtually complete isolation of the JCP from the Asian revolutions (except for Indochina), and a further swing towards a "national" and nationalistic policy, involving both an endorsement of armed forces for Japan "for defence," and a "welfare" approach whose logic is to protect the standard of "well-being" of the Japanese people at the expense of Japan's exploited neighbours.[185]

ELECTORALISM AND THE CLASS STRUGGLE

The history of postwar Japan can not be understood without reference to the working masses. The class struggle is the key factor in the whole history of the past thirty years. Studies which ignore this and glamourize businessmen as the "makers" of postwar Japan render Japan's history incomprehensible.

It is fashionable in the U.S. academic establishment and its penumbra to criticize the Japanese left as obstructionist, without much time being spent detailing the thoroughly reactionary nature of capitalist rule in Japan.[186] The left is also frequently criticized as "a failure." But it is vital to transcend this kind of ideological critique. This involves identifying the nature of capitalist rule in Japan, in the first place, and what the left has been trying to obstruct and change since 1945. It can then be seen that, although the proletariat has not seized power in Japan, in one vital sense the left has been successful, inasmuch as it has prevented the reconsolidation of a regime on the same basis as that which prevailed from the Meiji Restoration until 1945. Although the Japanese regime *is* extremely reactionary, the left has at least kept the situation open, and has prevented the restoration of a consensus favouring militarism and imperialism.

Yet it must also be acknowledged that in spite of the masses' heroic record on anti-imperialist issues, and their combativity in actual struggle, ruling class control is probably tighter in Japan than in other industrialized capitalist countries. Hundreds of thousands of people can be mobilized for mass actions against the LDP government's alliance with U.S. imperialism, yet *organized* proletarian opposition against the core of capitalism, on the shop floor and at the centre of the productive process, as well as on the political front, is relatively weak.

There is, besides, a left and a "left." The establishment left (JCP and JSP + Sōhyō), in spite of the strength of Marxism in Japan and in spite of the combativity of the masses, is consolidating a purely electoralist, vote-catching strategy. The 1972 general election and subsequent local elections indicate a solid and increasing JCP-cum-JSP vote, which has put JCP-JSP-backed municipal councils into power,[187] allowed the formation of something like a joint opposition front in the Lower House, and threatens the LDP's majority in the Upper House—for the first time. This constitutes a real advance. But, in spite of the LDP's heavy-handed reaction to these gains,[188] there is little reason to think that Japanese capitalism can not contain the kind of parliamentarism and reformism which has been integrated in Italy, where capitalism originally reacted in a similar manner.

In the meantime, the Japanese ruling class has succeeded in making a sharp distinction between the JCP and the militant left.[189] Through the careful application of violence and terror against the latter, the ruling class has exercised pressure on the JCP and the JSP to dampen down their support for real struggles, whether they be against capitalism itself, pollution, the military, or the LDP regime. The JCP and the JSP, engaged on the electoralist road towards a "democratic coalition government," have multiplied their denunciations of the militant left. In effect, much the same situation as that in Italy or France is coming into being: electorally powerful reformist parties edging towards governmental power (in coalitions), while a grass-roots militant movement grows up outside the parliamentary, electoralist framework.

9.
Education
and the Student Movement

The relationship between education and the state has been the main determinant of student and teacher reaction in the postwar period. A distinction should be made, however, between reactions against the American role in education in the period 1945–52 and reactions against the specifically Japanese (right-wing) system. Although only recently has the essential connection between education and capitalist rule been widely understood in the West, in Japan education since the Meiji Restoration has been seen and recognized as essentially a state system.[1] Education was the linch-pin in the life employment system, for it was via examinations that one's position was irrevocably fixed for life. Education was thus not only a system of oppression, but the organizer and reorganizer of social life— geared to the interests of the state, and inculcating such alleged virtues as loyalty and piety.

U.S. REFORMS

Educational Reform

Well before the end of the Second World War a special committee was set up at the University of Chicago to formulate educational policies for post-surrender Japan.[2] American efforts were directed particularly towards the "moral" aspect of Japanese education (evident in the work of Ruth Benedict). During the Occupation years (1945–52) educational reform was an almost exclusively U.S.-Japanese operation. As in the economic field, policy on education was laid down by a section of SCAP, the Education Division of the Civil Information and Education Section of General Headquarters, SCAP—Education Division of CI&ES, GHQ, SCAP. It was advised by two quasi-independent U.S. Education Missions (one in 1946 and one in 1950). The policy was then largely implemented through the Japanese Ministry of Education (*Mombushō*). Quite apart from the politics of U.S. educational reforms, the fact that they were channelled via the Japanese Ministry, which remained extremely conservative, was of considerable importance throughout the period.[3]

The U.S. reforms dealt with both the structure and the content of education. Prior to the surrender Japan had a centralized educational system, modelled on the French system, while the universities were mainly modelled on the German pattern. The pre-1945 system was basically a 6–2 system (six years of primary school, followed by two years in an upper primary school). Coeducation existed only in elementary school. Compulsory education covered only six years. Under the 6–2 system, education was divided into an elite and a mass sector, with only 14.3 per cent of the population reaching secondary and higher education in 1940.[4]

The Occupation made all education coeducational; compulsory schooling was extended from six to nine years. And the 6–2 pattern was changed to a 6–3–3–4 system (six years' elementary school; three years' lower secondary [roughly equivalent to junior high school in the United States]; three years' upper secondary [senior high school in the United States]; and four years' university). This relatively straightforward structural reorganization was carried through without much opposition. Coeducation, however, never functioned on a basis of real equality.[5] Recently the actual 6–3–3 structure has come under increased fire (see below).

The first U.S. Education Mission, which came to Japan in March 1946, also recommended changes in the administration of education. Most of its recommendations were embodied in the 1947 Fundamental Law of Education,[6] and such subsequent legislation as the 1949 law on the organization of the Ministry of Education. The administrative reform decentralized power, transferring it from the Ministry in Tokyo to prefectural and municipal authorities. Local elective boards of education were established. Each prefecture was to set up its own university, and the status required for an institution to call itself a university was altered. The Occupation did not radically overhaul the Ministry of Education itself. Nor did it fundamentally alter the financing of education, particularly that of universities. The real *power* of the key universities, especially Tokyo University and Kyoto University, was unaffected.[7]

In addition to these structural reforms, there was a concomitant attempt at an overhaul of the content of education. This was a staggered process involving first the attempted abolition of the existing "moral" education and then its replacement with a different curriculum. The abolition directives came directly from SCAP and were not open to question by the Japanese government. The fourth SCAP directive on education (December 31, 1945) suspended courses in morals, Japanese history and geography.[8] This blocked the further use of most of the key ideological texts, the *Shūshin* texts, the 1937 *Kokutai no Hongi* and the 1941 *Shinmin no Michi*, which were all issued by the Ministry of Education.[9] But SCAP did not repeal the fundamental document, the 1890 Imperial Rescript on Education. This document, heavy with prestige and repression, was central to the whole Japanese *political* system, and failure to repeal it explicitly gave rise to important discussions and machinations which say a good deal about early postwar Japan. Immediately after the surrender, indeed, on October 15 and 16, 1945, the Ministry of Education convened a meeting for principals of teacher-training colleges. The Minister, Maeda Tamon, "urged the necessity of seeking spiritual composure by reading the Imperial Rescript on Education at student assemblies. He urged that a Japanese democracy be established by seeking out those democratic qualities latent in the national polity of Japan."[10] The Rescript was to be a valuable weapon in shoring up the repressive order.

When the ethics course was removed from the curriculum, the Rescript remained officially in force, while SCAP dithered over whether to get a new one, formally abolish the old one or leave it as it was. In 1946 the Japanese Educational Reform Council[11] voted to replace the Rescript with something more in keeping with the times, but this decision was not put into effect. Finally, in 1948, a resolution was passed by both Houses of the Diet rescinding the Rescript in fairly vague language.[12] No substitute as such was issued. Meanwhile, the ethics course was replaced by a social studies course covering the old history and geography courses as well as elementary economics and civics. The teaching of history and geography had been particularly marked by racism, mythology and imperialism and, given this framework, the U.S.-instigated "democratization" sank few roots, least of all in the Ministry of Education bureaucracy. Thus, in spite of real changes, the fact that the United States failed to get to the bottom of the relationship between the state and the educational system, and that it failed to undo the link between the examination ordeal and the employment system left education, though modified, still very much an instrument of Japanese capitalism.

The Americans also made a number of abortive moves to reform the Japanese language and script, which were perceived to be obstacles to education and to communication between Japan and most other countries.[13] These moves were unsuccessful.

Occupation Repression in the Educational Field

Since the Occupation's objective was the "cleansing" of Japanese capitalism, the initial moves towards "democratization" were quickly accompanied by an assault on the left as soon as the latter showed its strength in the area of education. In spite of the right-wing bureaucracy in the Ministry of Education, the Japanese intelligentsia and the teaching corps had been one of the bastions of anti-regime thinking, and the teachers were recognized by SCAP as the most enthusiastic supporters of thorough reform in the early postwar period.[14] However, with the wider assaults on left-wing movements, from 1948 onwards, all students were banned from belonging to political organizations on campus. From mid-1949 teachers were also ordered not to engage in any political activity on the grounds that they should immure themselves in the "pure" work of on-campus education. The Occupation authorities also began to let the Japanese police launch their own raids into university campuses. On October 7, 1949, the *New York Times* reported that "Japanese official agencies [were] quietly purging university professors, school teachers, and administrative assistants *suspected* of being members of the Communist Party or of harboring Communist *or radical* sympathies."[15]

Assessment of the U.S. Role

An assessment of U.S. educational reforms in Japan can only be incomplete. The effects of the reforms are still being worked out, and the reforms themselves are still being revised. The most common criticism voiced by Americans is of the kind by Robert K. Hall: "It is readily apparent that the greatest mistake was that of confusing punitive action with implementation of the democratic philosophy."[16] Another similar criticism is that "the American educational reforms failed whenever they confused the word 'American' with the word 'democratic' "—a failure particularly serious where the prefectural universities were concerned. "The impression is unmistakable that the occupying Americans never quite penetrated the Japanese ivory tower. It is true they did extensive remodeling on the outside . . . but the essentially Japanese interior remains."[17] These criticisms are basically about America's failure to remould Japanese education into the American pattern.

The U.S. Education Missions' reports also reveal the difficulties of adjusting Japanese education to an American pattern. The first Mission descended on a nation still in a state of shock only a few months after the end of the war. The second Mission, in 1950, betrays no coherent understanding of the role of education in a capitalist society. The section of its *Report* on "Moral and Spiritual Education" is completely vacuous.[18] Initial projects to tackle the roots of the "problem" were soon shelved when it was discovered, *mirabile dictu,* that the roots of the "problem" were such things as patriotism, hard work, self-sacrifice and the other ingredients of American capitalist mythology. The Emperor, the linch-pin of the whole system, was kept in place. The family was heavily endorsed. Only perhaps at the level of the individual did SCAP promote a new policy, but it may reasonably be doubted that this sank in to any great extent. What one ideologue refers to as the lack of revolutionary "ideals" on the part of the Americans in fact masks the close similarity between American and Japanese capitalist ideology, and the extent to which the "positive" aspects were inextricable from the "negative" ones. Even to attack such an apparently fundamental aspect as "militarism" was difficult. The U.S. Occupation was partly dressed in military garb, and the whole American position was based on having had a stronger military force than the Japanese.[19] Nor was it too easy to knock "nationalism"—another allegedly essential ingredient of pre-1945 ideology, yet equally necessary in holding the society together without revolution after 1945.[20]

JAPANESE REPRESSION AND THE "REVERSE COURSE"

This discussion needs to be divided into two: anti-left measures, which started well before the end of the Occupation, supported and often promoted by SCAP; and the steps taken first to block and then to roll back the U.S. reforms.

Moves against the left started well before the outbreak of the Korean War. The open call by a SCAP official for the exclusion of communist professors from universities came as early as January 1949.[21] From at least this time on the Japanese police were allowed to operate freely on campuses against the left. The new U.S. reforms provided no protection for left-wing teachers, professors or students. Instead, the American advocacy of personal "freedom" was used to justify the dismissal of left-wing persons on the grounds that they were a threat to "freedom." The Japanese authorities gladly fell in with this approach.[22] Equally useful for repression was the new liberal political line of "keeping politics out of education."

In the early years of the Occupation, the Ministry of Education bureaucracy's opposition to some SCAP reforms took the form of subtle obstruction rather than open hostility, especially in such areas as the Imperial Rescript and a possible substitute, the teaching of ethics and morals, and textbook certification.

Towards the end of the Occupation, however, the Japanese right began to be much more vociferous about what it alleged was a general decline in Japanese morality, particularly in the state of the family. This was largely ascribed to the postwar American reforms. The issue of the Rescript was more or less settled by the 1948 Diet resolution. And so conservative pressure was brought to bear mainly on the possibility of introducing a new morals course. In 1951 the Minister of Education, Amano Teiyū, produced a text of a moral code to be used after the recovery of independence, in which "the basic pattern of social relationship was that of hierarchy rather than equality."[23] The text appeared in one of the national dailies and caused a big stir. The document was strongly traditional, and left the definite impression that Amano would like a return to the pre-1945 situation, with only slight modification. It rejected equality between men and women, and put the family, not the individual, as the basic component of the state. Freedom was characterized solely in terms of restraint; and the text contained a veiled assertion of racial uniqueness. Due to the outcry, and to Amano's subsequent inept handling of the affair, the "Outline" was not implemented.

However, the drive to reinstitute a separate morals course by breaking up the new social studies curriculum went ahead. In late 1952 the Ministry of Education officially began to advocate restoring the pre-1945 division between the morals and ethics course on the one hand and geography and history on the other. The Ministry decided to implement this change in 1956.[24]

Shortly after the end of the Occupation, the government also began to attack the new administrative structure of education. The first key move in this area was the reorganization of the local education boards. In 1954 a bill was put through the Diet which made the boards nominated instead of elected bodies on the grounds that the elective system had made it impossible to maintian political neutrality. Actually, the government felt obliged to move against this system because the majority of the people was to the left of the education policies the regime desired.[25] The bill also greatly strengthened the power of the central Ministry to interfere in every facet of local education.

Textbooks also came under strong attack. In 1956 the government, utilizing a SCAP reform originally aimed at eliminating "nationalistic and militaristic indoctrination," tried to get the Diet to pass a bill changing the manner of selecting textbooks.[26] But even though the bill failed, the government still restored central control over school textbooks, thus both standardizing education to its own satisfaction, and weeding out any textbooks it disliked. This struggle has been raging ever since, with the teachers' union, the opposition parties and most of the press ranged against the government. In 1970 a leading Japanese historian Ienaga Saburō, won an appeal against a Ministry of Education rejection of his book as a textbook in a landmark case which was immediately appealed by the Ministry—which then ordered schools and universities to continue ignoring the court's decision.[27] Along with the exclusion of progressive textbooks, there has been a major resurgence of right-wing material used in education, particularly in the teaching of history.[28]

The government also moved directly against the teachers. Apart from dismissals in the "Red Purge" period, the government passed a bill to prevent teachers joining political parties, and prohibiting Nikkyōso, the teachers' federation set up in 1947, from disseminating "political" literature and campaigning against government policy. The regime also introduced a merit-rating system making teachers liable to discipline on political and other grounds.[29] Since 1959 individual teachers have been prevented from choosing their own curricula to suit local circumstances.[30]

Throughout the 1950s top government officials, headed by the Minister of Education, gradually restored most of the prewar system. In February 1953 Minister Okano Kiyohide (Kiyotake) became the first top government official to voice the old theory of Japan's racial superiority in the Diet.[31] In 1956 the Minister, Kiyose Ichirō, launched the first open attack on the 1947 Fundamental Law of Education.[32] The following year, the Minister of Education in the second Kishi cabinet, Matsunaga Tō, denounced SCAP policies on education as having been aimed at "the weakening of the Japanese race."[33] The rewriting of the history of World War II, as outlined by Okano in 1953, is well advanced.

The central government's means of applying pressure have been enormous. Where formal legal measures have not been successful (as originally over the certification of textbooks), fiscal and other means have usually been effective. Education has consistently been the field on which maximum political, economic, "moral" and other force has been brought to bear. Student militancy has been greeted with a wave of recidivist moralizing, appeals to Confucius, petitions to restore militarist and jingoist textbooks, and the like.

In June 1970 the Central Education Council (CEC) submitted the Third Educational Reform Plan to the Minister of Education. This formally proposed scrapping the 6–3–3 system, and replacing it with a 4–4–6 system, starting at the age of four instead of six. The CEC also proposed reviving the pre-1945 division of education into "elite" and "non-elite" sections, with much quicker promotion for "precocious" children, and less education for the others. These proposals would not only give Japan an unparalleledly low school starting age, but would also greatly strengthen the position of the rich; above all, they would radically restructure education along the lines desired by industry.[34] The proposals have been vigorously opposed by Japanese teachers. Along with this proposed restructuring, the government put forward plans to accentuate the oppression in girls' education, restoring the full sexist impetus of the prewar curriculum, and to reintroduce compulsory training in the so-called martial "arts."[35]

THE BACKGROUND TO RADICALISM

"Education," writes Dore, "seems to have become the major mechanism of social selection at an earlier stage of industrialization in Japan than in Western countries. Learning was the royal road not only to the professions and to government, but also to business as well."[36] Business and the bureaucracy both laid enormous emphasis on formal educational qualifications, yet education did not by any means work against the class *hierarchy*. It filtered opportunity into a prearranged hierarchy, and although formally available to all as a route to the top it was primarily the weeding-out mechanism within the ruling class.[37] As an integral part of the existing hierarchical system, it was designed to help defuse possible class pressures with the ethics course playing the central role. Within education itself obsequiousness and grovelling were carefully preserved and institution-alized.[38]

Access to educational institutions is extremely closely controlled via a murderous examination system—commonly referred to as "entrance ex-amination hell."[39] Since many people's positions are fixed when they enter the bureaucracy or business, their educational status is absolutely deter-minant. And this status is entirely decided by examinations and university rating. A survey by the Japan Federation of Employers' Associations (Nikkeiren) showed that about 96 per cent of the people they took on (presumably in upper echelon posts) in one year, 1957, came from government universities which had operated as colleges or universities under the old (imperial) educational system.[40] Thus, the extent status is attached by business to a person's school makes the entrance exam a pivotal point in an individual's life.[41] Because their whole life depends on it, students will go on trying again and again to get into a maximally prestigious state (old imperial) university. In 1957, of the 2,000-odd students who gained admittance to Tokyo University, only 554 were recent high school graduates; 930 hab been *rōnin* for one year, 363 for two years, and 157 for three or more years. In other words, only just over one-quarter of those who got in came straight from school.[42] Only 12 per cent of the year's high school graduates who took the Tokyo University exams passed, whereas 21 per cent of the one-year *rōnin* applicants passed, and 15 per cent of the two-year *rōnin* applicants. The percentage of *rōnin* entering Tokyo University in 1966 was 49.7 in the liberal arts and 32.7 in sciences; and 55.4 and 47.0 per cent respectively in 1967.

The effects of this system include a proliferation of expensive crammers, and the sprouting of magazines designed to help students to pass exams by remembering by rote. The extra years of study involve major expenditures, and thus a further weeding out of the rich from the poor. "Upper class families are able to send their children to private universities . . . lower class families do not have the financial ability to send their children to any university at all."[43] This amounts to a system whereby youth, in Gregory Bateson's phrase, is kept on ice: a large sector of the intelligent youth is just knocked out of circulation for one or more years. Higher education remains largely the prerogative of the rich (the private universities which can be entered only by the children of the wealthy always being there as a fallback if needed). The most formal qualifications of an incredibly antique and often reactionary kind are perpetuated and there is a high incidence of serious neurosis. The main difference between the suicide graphs of Japan and other countries is that Japan's rate is spectacularly high in the 15–30 age group (while not particularly high in the other age groups). In this age group suicide is the number one cause of death.[44] "The typical prospective examinee has come to be close-minded, selfish and lonely. Even his parents tend to become nervous and be on edge. In short, the situation has become tragic."[45]

Once a student enters a university, things are not much better. Until recently, obsequiousness and servility have been very much the order of the day. Grants have been quite inadequate. In 1959 nearly two-thirds (63 per cent) of all students at Tokyo University were moonlighting—23 per cent out of "absolute necessity." The figure was 70–80 per cent for other, minor universities in the mid-fifties.[46] The 1956 government White Paper on Education stated that 30–40 per cent of the students who were working in their extra time were seriously ill with respiratory troubles alone. The average student expenditure on recreation of all kinds was approximately one U.S. dollar per month.

Even so, it might be thought, once into a university and with some hard work, one could get out comfortably at the far end. Even this is not true: the reason for the original upheaval at Tokyo University in early 1968 among the medical students, who started the great wave of militant action, was that medical graduates were having to put in one year's unpaid work as menials for the older staff.[47] Further, in many cases individual applications to a company from students are simply not accepted. A student has to be recommended by his university supervisors before the company will even consider him for a job.[48]

Education is thus the process of institutionalizing obedience and rank through formal qualifications and the pressures on anyone who wants to attain them. The May 1968 Paris slogan, "Examination = Servility, Social Climbing, Hierarchical Society," applies better to Japan than to any other country. The neuroses attendant on exams spread throughout the family—and the emotional and financial strain is made even more acute by the fact that since the retirement age for most employees in Japan has been fifty-five, this often coincides with the period when the child of a retiring worker might be just about to take the examination. Since welfare facilities and old-age pensions are so inadequate, the coincidence of the parent's retirement with the child's examination can create an intolerable crisis.

NIKKYŌSO

Japan's surrender in 1945 produced an ideological vacuum; with the old ruling class ideology in forced disfavour, only two forces openly disputed the field—Marxism and liberalism. Given the base Marxism had laid down in the 1920s and early 1930s and the prestige of the Japanese communist movement, as the only political force untainted by co-operation and compromise with the pre-surrender regime, Marxism easily carried the day within significant sectors of the labour movement and intelligentsia. Furthermore, the generation of teachers approaching senior rank in the immediate postwar period contained many radicals who had trained in

Germany during the days of the Weimar Republic, a Germany far removed from the old Germany of the Kaiser and Bismarck so dear to the Meiji oligarchs.

Since no such teachers' body has ever existed in any of the Western capitalist societies, it is important to stress the role played by Nikkyōso in the postwar period. Founded in 1947, at its peak it included more than 90 per cent of all primary and junior high school teachers in Japan.[49] A militant Marxist organization, it introduced a powerful element of contestation right into the heart of the society in the early period. In conjunction with a university teaching corps which was overwhelmingly Marxist or Marxist-oriented, this gave everybody who went through the Japanese system at least an acquaintance with left-wing ideas.[50]

Nikkyōso, which included some teachers who were only superficially reconstructed elements from the wartime period,[51] radicalized markedly in the years 1949–51, when the climax of American oppression coincided with the upsurge in Japanese political repression. With the collective imperialist invasion of Korea in 1950 and the unveiling of America's plans for the rigged "independence" of Japan, Nikkyōso stood alongside Sōhyō and the mass left-wing movement. This position, embodied in the Nikkyōso Code of Ethics first published in 1951 and officially adopted in June 1952, grew directly out of the union's support for Sōhyō's Four Principles of Peace. The Code gives an idea of the atmosphere in the teaching body at the time:

> Upon our shoulders have been laid the historical tasks of protecting peace . . . and realizing a society free from exploitation, poverty and unemployment. . . . The youth of the country must be raised and educated to become capable workers who will give themselves . . . to the accomplishment of these tasks. . . . Teachers shall live and work with the youth. . . . Each teacher shall make an intensive critical examination of himself and shall study and make efforts to prepare himself for his new role in education.
>
> Teachers are labourers whose workshops are the schools. Teachers, in the knowledge that labour is the foundation of everything in society, shall be proud of the fact that they themselves are labourers. At the present stage of history, the realization of a new society . . . is possible only through the power of the working masses whose nucleus is the labouring class. Teachers shall be aware of their position as labourers, shall live forcefully believing in the historical progress of man and shall consider all stagnation and reaction as their enemies.
>
> There is no other way today in which the teacher can establish himself as an individual except through unity of action. The teachers of Japan, through the labour movement, shall unite with the teachers of the world, and shall join hands with all labourers. Unity is the highest ethic of the teacher.[52]

Although Nikkyōso began a decline almost immediately after its 1952 convention, the government still felt the need to launch a systematic campaign against it, particularly through the imposition of the Teachers' Efficiency Rating System, and by instituting the appointive system for boards of education (October 1956). From 1953 on, Nikkyōso began to lose sizeable numbers of its membership. The government and ruling party blatantly manipulated financial strings to force left-wing teachers out of positions of responsibility throughout Japan.[53] Nikkyōso is now completely debilitated, and came out (relatively cautiously) against the big secondary school protests in 1968.[54] But the development of the student movement, and indeed the whole implantation of Marxism in the culture, becomes incomprehensible without some understanding of the exceptional role played by the vast majority of Japanese teachers, through their union, linked to the proletarian masses at the critical juncture of postwar Japan's history.

THE STUDENT MOVEMENT

The Zengakuren

The vacuum existing in Japan after the end of the war in educational institutions is starkly revealed by the speed with which students all over the country moved to set up their own organizations, so-called self-governing associations. The first of these was inaugurated at Kyoto University in November 1945, the Kyōto Gakusei Renmei (Kyoto Federation of Students). In September 1948, 300,000 students from 145 universities joined together to form the National Federation of Students' Self-Governing Associations, the Zengakuren.[55] From the start the Federation adopted a militant platform, calling for "opposition to any new attempts to utilize education to further fascism and colonialism." It took an active part in all the big political struggles of the early fifties: against MacArthur's "Red Purge" in 1950, against the Subversive Activities Prevention Law in 1952, and in the 1953 general election campaign, where the main issue was rearmament.

Throughout this period the Federation tended to back the JCP's policy, which was ultra-leftist. But when the JCP resurfaced into legality in 1955 under its new, post-Tokuda leadership, it opted for a more cautious domestic line of peaceful coexistence. Disoriented by this shift, the student movement began to dissociate from the JCP; in 1958, at the tenth Plenary Conference, the left won control of the Federation. The JCP expelled members of the new "mainstream" faction, and the new Zengakuren leadership retaliated with a critique of the JCP as opportunist.

One of the main peculiarities of Japanese politics is the planned and phased long-term struggle for or against some specific objective. Parties tend to schedule their gains in Diet seats over periods of twenty-five years. And the struggle against the renewal or revision of the U.S.-Japan Security Treaty likewise tended (at least till 1970) to be scheduled over a multi-annual period. The victory of the left within the Zengakuren in 1958 was directly linked to the preparations for the 1960 struggle against the renewal of the pact.

Two other organizations were founded in 1958 which were to exercise considerable influence on the student movement. The Kakukyōdō (Kaku-meiteki Kyōsan Shugi Dōmei, or League of Revolutionary Communism) was not a purely student organization, though it attracted a great number of students to it (until they broke away from it in 1960 to set up a separate student organization, the Marugakudō).[56] In May 1958 a new, specifically student body called the Shagakudō (Shakai Shugi Gakusei Dōmei, or League of Socialist Students) was set up which in effect joined with another group, the Kyōsandō (Kyōsan Shugisha Dōmei, or League of Communists) which was well to the left of the JCP. With the aid of the Kyōsandō, the Shagakudō built itself up into the best organized student body in the country, and in the tumultuous events of 1960 played the leading role.[57]

Prior to 1960 a People's Council for the Prevention of the Revision of the Security Pact, a joint front centred on the JCP and the JSP, had been set up. There were profound differences, both organizational and political, within the Council, and these were exposed by the first great demonstration of the anti-treaty campaign—the "invasion" of the Diet grounds on November 27, 1959. This "invasion"-cum-reclamation occurred during a demonstration sponsored by Sōhyō, the JSP and Zengakuren, but was held to be the exclusive work of the students. As a result, Zengakuren was temporarily expelled from the People's Council. The students felt that the official parties (and unions) were not being militant enough, and they themselves had understood the huge potential of student and student-led action:

> As was the case during our struggle against the Red Purge in 1950, we students were able to put up quite a struggle by ourselves [in breaking into the Diet compound]. Thus, we believed that if we students put up a bitter struggle to the end, even if we had to do it all by ourselves, we would be able to prevent for certain the signing of the Security Pact. This was the line we took in our appeal to the students.[58]

The 1960 events put the Japanese students into the world headlines for the first time, but they were only a part (sometimes the spearhead but not the vanguard) of a mass popular movement against the treaty with the United States, and the whole nature and structure of Japan's relations with the United States.[59] The kind of political issues on which the students have mobilized in Japan since the war have found a much greater echo in the society than has been the case in almost any other country (the few exceptions would include Korea, Thailand and the Indochina issue in the United States). No European country has had atom bombs dropped on it; none of America's wartime enemies and later allies in Europe had a sizeable part of its territory occupied by the United States for twenty-seven years; none of the NATO countries has actually served as a bombing base for a "hot" war. The presence of nuclear weapons and the visits of nuclear-powered ships, the occupation and degradation of Okinawa, the use of Japanese airfields as bases for direct attacks first on Korea and then on Indochina—all these issues stirred profound feelings throughout the Japanese population.[60] Thus, to say that Japanese students are highly political is only part of the truth: the crucial fact is that their politics have consistently to a very large extent represented the politics of the society. It is this which explains their role in the great upheaval of 1960, as in more recent actions, such as those at Narita (Sanrizuka) and at Ōji Hospital.

The background to the 1960 upheaval was the long-standing *mass* hostility to the treaty, and to two aspects in particular: the presence of U.S. bases containing nuclear weapons aimed at the continent of Asia, and the remilitarization of Japan itself being carried out under cover of the treaty. At the time of the original arrangement, in 1951, the percentage of Japanese who positively supported the presence of U.S. bases in Japan was less than one-fifth.[61] Further, the premier in the years 1957–60, Kishi Nobusuke, who had been a key minister under Tōjō, was widely loathed for his high-handed behaviour in the Diet, and his barely concealed scorn for bourgeois democracy.

The attempt to "reclaim" the Diet, although condemned by the People's Council for the Prevention of the Revision of the Security Pact, certainly had considerable popular support and was hardly the "wild" gesture often depicted in the Western media. This first action at the Diet (November 27, 1959) was followed by a major demonstration at Tokyo's airport, Haneda, against Kishi's visit to Washington to discuss the revision and renewal of the treaty (January 16, 1960). The "mainstream" Zengakuren faction, who argued that the left should concentrate its fire on Kishi, as the representative of Japanese monopoly capitalism, which in their view was the number one enemy, took part in this demonstration. The more famous second demonstration at Haneda, on June 10, 1960, when Eisenhower's Press Secretary, Jim Hagerty, was surrounded—but not attacked—in his car, and was lifted out by helicopter, was supported by the anti-mainstream faction, which held that U.S. imperialism was the number one enemy.[62] Although Hagerty was not molested, Eisenhower had to cancel his projected visit to Japan. Finally came the (unsuccessful) storming of the Diet on June 15, 1960, when a girl student, Kamba Michiko, secretary of the League of Communists (the Bundō) was killed.

Alongside these actions, and more problematic, was student involvement in connection with the National Railway Workers' Union strike called as part of a general Sōhyō-affiliated protest movement against the Security Pact on June 4. In conception, the strike was one of sympathy, a *gesture* of solidarity rather than a strategical operation aimed at interrupting communications. Some students, however, felt that it should be turned into the latter, and therefore invaded stations and staged sit-downs, blocking many trains. This was not always a politically remunerative move, although, again, readers accustomed to "legalistic" action in the West should remember that the question of intervention is very different in Japan: there have been successful strikes by communication workers and the masses to block the U.S. military. A call for such action does not have the same quotient of voluntarism as it would in a Western capitalist society. The Pact had gone through. On the other hand, Kishi had been forced to resign (although his policies were not disowned), and Eisenhower had had to cancel his planned visit. The students and militant workers had shown there was a mass potential for extra-parliamentary action, and even more important, that it was possible to envisage "reclaiming" the Diet, since *extra*-parliamentary action had directly affected *intra*-parliamentary practice. But, at the same time, the student movement emerged from the experience organizationally disoriented, and thoroughly disillusioned about the possibility of any systematic relationship to existing political parties (the JCP had distinguished itself during the events by the vigour of its denunciations of the mainstream).

In the aftermath, the movement broke up. The leading force, the Shagakudō, split into three, and then virtually disintegrated. As always in such circumstances, there was a strong swing towards theory, led by the Marugakudō. Of the two main parties, the JCP emerged from the 1960 upheaval much more damaged than the JSP.

The JCP, although heavily criticized by the activist majority during the 1960 events, did manage to rebuild its position again in the years 1962–64. As of winter 1970–71 the JCP group, the Minsei (Democratic Youth League, sometimes referred to as the JCP-Zengakuren) controlled the allegiance of a slightly larger number of the *politically active* students than did the radical, non-JCP left: about 453,000 to 440,000.[63] Two qualifications need to be made, however. First, students join their local association *automatically* (in some cases their membership fees are actually deducted by the university authorities themselves and paid into the self-governing association's coffers). Like many students, these associations are not all by any means particularly militant: the emphasis is frequently on improving conditions (often extremely bad)—for example, getting more showers installed for students, obtaining better library facilities and suchlike. The Minsei's emphasis on these mundane issues led to their policy being named "the toilet-paper line." Second, affiliation does not necessarily entail total control. Since the Minsei has the support of many "floating," or "civic-minded" students, its units can often be swayed by activists. This occurred at Kyushu University in early 1968. When the JCP-Zengakuren Dormitory Committee decided not to let members of the Sampa Zengakuren[64] sleep on the campus before the Sasebo demonstrations, a general meeting of all Kyushu students reversed the decision by a four to one majority. Thus on a specific issue such as demonstrating against a visit by the U.S. nuclear aircraft carrier, *Enterprise,* the mass of students, although "affiliated" to the Minsei, overwhelmingly supported a group which the JCP had branded as "ultra-leftist counter-revolutionary elements."[65]

There was a sizeable resurgence of the student left in 1964–65 at the time of the Tokyo-Seoul "normalization" treaty, but organizationally the main product of this was the AWYC (Anti-War Youth Committee, or Hansen Seinen Iinkai—see chapter 8), a non-student formation. In 1969, however, there occurred an event of some importance and novelty—the formation of Zenkyōtō (Zenkoku Kyōtō Kaigi Rengō, or National Union of Struggle Councils).[66] This was formed at a meeting in Hibiya Park on September 5, 1969, attended by 26,000 participants from 178 universities of whom two-thirds were non-sectarian. It grouped together in a united front the struggle councils of all the universities, the strike committees, and the post-graduate struggle councils. Zenkyōtō emerged as almost the polar opposite of Zengakuren; organizationally highly decentralized, it "arose in the course of the struggle and reflects very clearly the anti-authoritarian, anti-bureaucratic, egalitarian camaraderie of the world behind the barricades in which it was conceived."[67] Although the 1970 struggle against renewal of the Security Treaty was no more successful than that in 1960,[68] there was not a comparable collapse in opposition militancy to the pro-imperialist policies of the LDP as there was ten years before.

Some Important Struggles

One of the differences between Japan and the West is the absence of anti-student feeling among the working class. This is due less to the class origins of the students than to the much more standardized culture of Japan as compared to the West. Many of the major events in which students have played a big part have involved issues which did not *directly* affect students as such. The big upheavals of 1959–60 and 1964–65 (against the treaty with Seoul) were not directly tied to educational questions. There have been several major actions in which students played a big part which say much about their role in Japanese society. One of these was the struggle at Sanrizuka. Two others may be briefly mentioned.

SASEBO, JANUARY 1968

During the Vietnam War, Sasebo was converted into a gigantic U.S. base for aggression against the Asian continent. It was chosen as the port for the first visit of a nuclear powered vessel, the U.S.S. *Enterprise,* to Japan. The visit was widely opposed throughout Japan, and particularly by the inhabitants of Sasebo, near Nagasaki (where the second atomic bomb had been dropped). A large number of students travelled to Sasebo to assist the local population in opposing the visit and attempting to occupy the base, which is connected to the town by a bridge, where the students and townspeople fought a prolonged pitched battle with the Japanese police. This action won the students widespread support in the town, and throughout Japan.[69] And support for their action rose when, a few months later, after the visit of the U.S. nuclear submarine *Swordfish,* a check showed a noticeable rise in radioactivity in the water of Sasebo harbour—which temporarily led the United States to call off visits by all nuclear-powered ships to Japan.[70]

UNIVERSITY STRUGGLES

It is, of course, impossible to divide up the student struggles into two utterly separate categories—"university" and "non-university." But it is useful to distinguish, analytically, between the kind of issues which mainly stimulated student activity in 1959–60 (the Security Treaty with the United States) and 1964–65 (the "normalization" of relations with Seoul), on the one hand, and those which increasingly lay at the root of militant student actions in the late 1960s: university fees, corruption, administration reform, curriculum reform, the expulsion of military cadets and the restructuring of the educational system to meet the new needs of capitalism.

The basic distinction to be made about Japanese universities is between state and private establishments. Whereas state universities are fairly well subsidized and maintained, private universities are often run as business concerns, where money tends to be the dominant factor.[71] According to the April 1968 government White Paper on Education, facilities in private universities actually declined from 1955 to 1967, while student fees rose more than three times in the same period. The proportion of teachers per student in private universities is about one-third that in state universities, and their educational experience averages out at about half that of teachers in the state universities.[72] Above all, in state universities, expenditure per student in the late 1960s was almost quadruple that in private universities; and, of course, in private universities, students have to cover a large proportion of the costs of their education through fees.

The much lower costs in state universities have, naturally, contributed to the size of the *rōnin* population, since the children of the poor can not afford private universities. On the whole, the state universities have tended to produce more militant students, partly because only the rich can get into the private universities.[73] But in the wave of student protests which started at Keiō University in 1965, there was considerable dissidence in the private institutions, largely to do with specific issues connected with those institutions' structures.[74]

The issues which have sparked off campus protests have ranged from the presence of military personnel in the university (Tokushima and Toyama), to changing the location of the campus (Niigata, Yokohama and others), to demands for better equipment, changes in the curriculum, and democratization of campus life and better dormitories.[75] Students have mobilized against the whole range of oppression: from the use of universities to assist the remilitarization of Japan[76] to the increasing technologization of education demanded by big business.[77] The case of Nihon University is exemplary. The students discovered that the administration had embezzled £ 2 million of university funds.[78] The president of the university, a friend of Premier Satō, had been using the funds to make donations to the LDP, build himself a mansion and so on. Similarly, the upheaval at Waseda University in 1966, which started over control of a student hall, soon broadened. A study of the Waseda upheaval quotes one girl student as saying: "When I first entered college, my parents told me again and again that I must listen to the teachers and behave myself. The fact is we have no idea what professors are thinking about. What kind of fellow is the head of the university, President Ōhama Nobumoto? We didn't have the slightest idea till we read about him in the newspapers and magazines after the fracas began."[79] In fact President Ōhama was a long-standing liege of the government, had served on a committee of review for the Ministry of Justice, was a specialist in corporation law, and after his resignation as president of Waseda became special adviser to Satō and Chairman of the Council on Okinawa Problems. As at the London School of Economics and elsewhere, the detonation of student action quickly led to the exposure of many "administrative" potentates.

The indisputably impressive actions by hundreds of thousands of Japanese students do, however, need to be put into perspective. The overall context has not been one which has favoured them since, in effect, the government did not mind that many of the country's universities were closed down and that graduation ceremonies (and the issuing of degrees) were suspended. The former head of Tokyo University, Ōkōchi Kazuo, lamented in 1967 that what he called the "passion" for education was causing a serious labour shortage.[80] It was, therefore, in the government's interests to trim the university system and "rationalize" education *as a whole*.[81] This was done both by letting many universities be closed down, thus knocking out, say, two years' quota of graduates, and by "rationalizing" expenditure on university education—a task facilitated by the agreement among both critics and supporters of the existing regime that per capita expenditure needs to be greatly increased. This can most easily be accomplished by cutting down on the total number of university students.

The government has also been able to engage in various forms of direct repression. Already in 1952, during the Korean War and at the height of the persecution of the left, the Yoshida government put through an extremely tough Subversive Activities Prevention Law which to many was reminiscent of the prewar legislation against "dangerous thoughts." Hatoyama Ichirō (premier in 1954–56), likewise, showed little concern for the opinion of those who opposed him, and simply mobilized a force of some 500 policemen to invade the Diet and attack the JSP Dietmen who objected to his forcing the Education Boards through in 1956.[82] In 1968, at the height of the student protests, after two particularly large and relatively violent demonstrations in Tokyo—at Shinjuku Station (October 22) and at Roppongi (against the Defense Agency), the Satō government decided to apply the 1952 Decree for the first time.[83] In 1969 the regime went further: it introduced a Draconian new bill, the Universities Control Bill, to legalize and facilitate police entry onto campuses. The bill permits the direct, and irresponsible, intervention of the Minister of Education in university affairs; it also strengthens the powers of university presidents and deans, as against the powers of faculty meetings and university councils, as well as those of students.[84] The 1969 law formalized the government's control over university education, administratively and legally, as well as financially and curriculum-wise. There was also a sizeable escalation in police violence: at least 8,800 people were arrested during the course of 1969, of whom 70 per cent were imprisoned for several months.[85] Akita Akehiro, one of the leaders of the struggle at Nihon University, spent ten months in solitary confinement before trial. A number of students at Tokyo University were given terms up to thirty-two months hard labour.[86] During the attempts to prevent Satō leaving for the United States in late 1969, over 2,000 arrests were made.

There is a need to correct misapprehensions prevalent in the West about the Japanese student struggle. The fundamental fact is that most of the student struggles have been on popular mass issues connected with Japan's relationship with the United States—nuclear weapons, rearmament, the status of Okinawa, relations with Korea. Other important struggles, such as those at Sasebo, Narita and Ōji, have all been connected with the same issue, if less directly. Second, the media coverage has given only a distorted picture of what is really happening in Japan; the conventional picture of the student movement is that it is (a) isolated, (b) extremely violent and (c) quite effective. Its isolation and effectiveness I have already dealt with. But here a word about violence. The Japanese student movement has been extremely non-violent.[87] Although a girl student was killed (probably by police) during the 1960 upheaval, the very first death of a policeman in a clash with the students did not occur until the autumn of 1968, and that was probably an accident. The apparently "violent" get-up of Japanese students developed only as protection against the violence of the police, who were armed with truncheons, helmets, tear-gas, water cannon, tanks and armoured cars, long before the students, who suffered numerous violent injuries, were able to develop and standardize an effective defence.[88]

There has been a degree of in-fighting among the left-wing groups unparalleled in any other society, and this factional fighting (uchi-geba) has often been more violent and more lethal than the fighting against police repression or against right-wing athletic club violence. Initially, the formation of Zenkyōtō in 1969 damped down *uchi-geba,* but in August 1970 a Kakumaru student was reported killed at the hands of a Chūkaku group (the Kakumaru had stayed out of Zenkyōtō).

Then in 1972 came the news of the internal fighting within the Red Army (Sekigun) in which a dozen members of the group had been killed. Prior to this the police and mass media had disseminated large amounts of propaganda on militant student actions, and the Red Army Incident came as a severe blow to the militant left.[89]

The other factor which needs to be taken into account is the heavy weight of failure, since, on the whole, the student struggles of recent years have not been successful. Certainly, they brought about the resignation of several old reactionaries, but the government responded by systematizing LDP control over the universities and greatly strengthened police powers. A sizeable number of left-wing students ended up in jail, and the university system has been streamlined to cope better with the demands of big capital in the 1970s.

This does not mean there is no positive side to the students' many heroic efforts. The students have helped keep the crucial issues of Japan's external relations in the headlines, through the struggles at Sasebo, Narita, Okinawa, etc. In the universities themselves, they have won some reforms. At Takushoku University, they exposed both President Nakasone personally and the whole structure and ideology of his control of the institution.[90] The appropriation by the students of halls traditionally used for ceremonies, the occupation of administration offices and suchlike measures helped to expose the structures of authority and repression. This type of action reached its highest point with the trials of university authorities and professors before a mass audience of students. Hayashi Kentarō of Tokyo University, for example, was put through 170 hours of grilling by students. At Nihon University, the chancellor, Furuta, was forced into a public self-criticism; "he and the five other directors were forced to bow deeply to the 10,000 students and admit their negligence."[91] The exposure of corruption, injustice, the buying of exam results and places in the university, and administration links with the LDP had a positive echo in the society at large. But it would be wrong to think these are ills which the present ruling group is wholly incapable of remedying.

THE ATTEMPTED OVERHAUL OF CAPITALIST EDUCATION

The relationship between a successful capitalist system and the educational system remains a relatively mysterious one. Some of the mystery is, of course, the work of capitalism itself, which likes to throw a pall of smoke over its role in funding education into specific channels. But this still leaves quite a large area of doubt which is obscure to both the ruling group and its opponents.

The major student upheavals in the late 1960s showed both the strength of student opposition to the reforms which capitalism was trying to put through, and the need for even more radical changes if the educational system was to survive. Between 1969 and the 1971 the Central Education Council (CEC) worked out a tripartite scheme to stabilize the situation.[92] In addition, the Japanese government received the assistance of an exceptionally high-powered study group from the central economic agency of imperialism, the Organisation for Economic Co-operation and Development (OECD).[93] The key CEC recommendation was that universities should be uniformized by eliminating the differences between state and private universities as far as possible, perhaps even liquidating a number of private universities. In this way more students from the non-rich sectors of society could be got into universities, and the currently dysfunctional filtering operated by the top few universities, particularly Tokyo and Kyoto, could be halted. This had become an urgent priority since the criteria for selection and advancement being used by both business and the bureaucracy were hyper-formal, and this was actually accentuating the state/private university split.[94]

The changes recommended involve altering the entire university structure, overhauling university entrance examinations, as well as unifying the content and funding of courses. Curiously, up till now, although overall expenditure on education has been about the same as in comparable capitalist countries, Japan's spending on higher education and research has been relatively low.[95]

The OECD study is particularly interesting, since it reveals some of the dialectic of Japan's increasing integration into the world imperialist system. Strategically, the OECD group clearly went along with Japanese monopoly capitalism's structural reorganization plans.[96] The main area in which obvious differences appeared was over democratization of communications—a prospect stolidly opposed by the Japanese side.[97] The OECD found an "extraordinary blockage in communication," which the Japanese government implicitly acknowledged to be one of the weapons in its system of rule.[98] The OECD study is quite explicit on the educational changes needed to further the integration of Japan into the imperialist group:[99] much more and better teaching of foreign languages for actual use, rather than just for reading literature; sending more Japanese to study abroad; opening up Japanese education to foreigners, perhaps even running university courses in languages other than Japanese; and training Japanese for "a world role." The study also recommends the "Americanization" of educational financing, through the setting up of foundations with tax exemption privileges.[100] The establishment of the Japan Foundation in late 1972, with a large budget and the backing of Tanaka's Foreign Minister, Ōhira Masayoshi, was a key move in this new strategy.[101]

Big business, which, in the last instance, determines educational spending, was particularly dismayed with the feeble performance of university administrations during the late 1960s. Capital, openly frightened at the idea of large numbers of militant students being released into positions of authority in the society, advocated direct police intervention to expel militants forthwith.[102] Rather than try to solve the problems, the regime responded to the crisis by unleashing the Kidōtai (riot police) and forcing the 1969 Universities Control Bill through the Diet. This on-campus repression was accompanied by a marked escalation of surveillance and control in the society as a whole. The experience with the OECD group would indicate that the regime is having increasing trouble coping with the contradictions of an educational policy which is determined by the instrumental needs of big capital. The unflagging opposition to governmental policy from both students and teachers for almost thirty years now is perhaps the most damning indictment, and the most revealing index, of the state of Japanese education.

10.
The Politics
of Japanese Capitalism

THE SITUATION OF THE JAPANESE BOURGEOISIE

The role of the Japanese bourgeoisie in the postwar period can be grasped only by relating it simultaneously to the class struggle at home and to Japan's location within the world imperialist system. At home it has maintained iron control over the state. It has transformed the support of a minority of the population into majority representation in the Diet. Over the period as a whole it sustained the fastest long-term growth rate of any major capitalist country while preserving greater inequalities of income and wealth than any comparable society.

Internationally the Japanese bourgeoisie pulled off an equally remarkable coup. By accepting a subordinate political relationship with the United States it won the political and military context for unparalleled economic growth. Unlike Gaullist France, which fought for a degree of political autonomy but built few economic defences, Japan accepted political and military dependence on the United States while developing some real autonomous economic power. Yet, though the alliance with U.S. imperialism (less a nuclear than a class umbrella) has been important, the core of the Japanese ruling class's strategy has been its political and economic action at home.

The classical theoretical distinctions seem somewhat inadequate when confronted with the complexity of Japan's bourgeoisie, which displays features of both "national" and comprador bourgeoisies; or, to be more precise, *fractions* of the Japanese bourgeoisie have, *at certain times,* displayed "national" or comprador characteristics.[1] Although in 1945 Japan was actually occupied by the United States and the Japanese bourgeoisie *as a whole* entered into close political alliance with the American ruling class, on the economic front the Japanese bourgeoisie resisted foreign encroachment to an extent which no other bourgeoisie achieved or even attempted.

Conventional Western analysis of Japan largely ignores class and the social relations of production. "Japan" is presented as an undifferentiated mass, as a nation with negligible internal divisions and contradictions. In fact, the history of the period has been determined by the inter-related class struggle at home and class alliance internationally. Thus, more important than the ruling party, the LDP, it is the whole apparatus of the state which must be considered; and more important than the factions of the LDP are the fractions of the bourgeoisie.

The Machinery of Bourgeois Rule

The bourgeoisie rules through a constellation of instruments, headed by the state apparatus (bureaucracy, police, etc.), including ideology and economic power (both straight and mediated). Thus, while it is important to assess and criticize both the cabinets (often referred to as "the government") and the ruling party, the LDP, it is even more vital to grasp the machine of class rule as an articulated unit.

The central element is the state apparatus. The class nature of the state is determined not by the class origins of individual members of the different echelons of the state organization, but by which class interests the state as a whole serves. The state need not be (and is not) synonymous with the economic interests of the bourgeoisie or of its dominant fraction. On the contrary, the state bureaucracy has a *relative* autonomy.[2] Thus, although the state does engage in direct intervention on behalf of the economic and political interests of the bourgeoisie,[3] it can not be reduced to a simple "agent" of the bourgeoisie. It also *mediates* the interests of the bourgeoisie, engaging in economic and political compromise and conciliation.

The state also plays a crucial role in the ideological field. Here there are numerous types of intervention: through education; through widespread control over the mass media (censorship, licensing of TV stations, etc.); and especially through the promotion of Tennōism, which is the main specific feature of Japanese bourgeois ideology. As the development of Tennōism during the Meiji period showed, the key feature is not "Emperor-*worship*" as such, but the "validation" of authoritarianism, which in the present stage takes the form of oligarchy. Tennōism arbitrarily "legitimates" the flow of authority from the top. Subordinates must obey their "superiors" without question, and rights are severely circumscribed. Tennōism creates a climate where reason and justice are ostracized; where the term "benevolence" covers a panoply of terror and violence in family, school, army and factory.

Thus, although Tennōism requires an Emperor, it is not an instrument of imperial rule; it is flexible about the Emperor's personal location within the state apparatus.[4] The ideology of Tennōism serves capitalism, and meshes with the attempt to deny the existence of classes in Japan. All being subjects of the Emperor, questions such as one's location in the production process allegedly become irrelevant. Tennōism attempts to eliminate the *right* to stake demands; the denial of class operates to deny the possibility of class interests, and thus the grounds on which demands might be advanced.[5]

The third area which needs to be considered is the general field of violence, which may be both legal and extra-legal, overt and covert.[6] The main legal force of repression is the police. By early 1971 this force numbered 300,000—more than at the height of Japan's wartime mobilization. Like the army, the police are to a large extent an unreconstructed force. Apart from their day-to-day operations of surveillance,[7] the police have been engaged in numerous violent operations against ordinary citizens at Sanrizuka, Sasebo and elsewhere. But the most striking example of the police's role as strongarm men on behalf of the ruling group came in 1960. When Kishi was trying to push revision of the Security Treaty with the United States through the Diet, the government called in the police to remove all the JSP Dietmen from the Chamber *by force*. The vote ratifying the treaty was then put through with less than half the members of the House present.[8]

The events surrounding the revision of the Security Treaty reveal well the relationship between the various instruments of repression, both legal and extra-legal. The government discussed using the army to intervene against the demonstrators. Although the decision went against calling out the troops, the experience was not lost on the regime, and in 1965 it was revealed that at least since 1963 a plan had been in existence for a form of military take-over. This was the Mitsuya Kenkyū, or Three Arrows Plan, drawn up by a group of staff officers (90 per cent of whom were graduates of the Imperial Military Academy).[9] *Inter alia,* the Plan envisaged full-scale mobilization of civilian society, censorship and military control over the Diet. The Plan noted that: "Vulnerability in the strategy for the defence of Japan . . . is found extensively not only in the military field, but in political, economic, social and other general fields."[10] The Plan cited in its "vulnerability" list the "constant threat of socialism because of freedom of political parties."[11]

The Plan was drawn up without reference to the civilian staff in the Defence Agency (interestingly, there is no law for disciplining military officers who violate civilian or Diet control, which was an offence, at least technically, up till 1945). It is not only the "conspiratorial" aspect which needs stressing but that it is functional to the regime to have a military apparatus which openly hints at intervention and thus fosters an authoritarian climate. As in the 1930s, military influence can not be measured solely by whether or not there is a putsch. There is also the erosion effect of feints, scare tactics, trial balloons and suchlike.

A further component, not specific to Japan, is the quasi-political gang. Such groups lie outside the overt, official state apparatus, but are contiguous with it and, on occasion, virtually integrated with it. In 1960 the Kishi government asked Japan's leading rightist, Kodama Yoshio, to mobilize thousands of right-wing thugs to supplement the official police during Eisenhower's planned visit; they were to be given funds, and paramilitary assistance.[12] These groups also provide the personnel for prime ministers' bodyguards and airport welcoming parties for right-wing visitors such as Pak Jung-hi.[13]

The use of such groups in Japan far transcends anything known in the West—and this is true not only of operations in and around the actual government, but equally with regard to the LDP and the organization of business, finance and the distribution trades.[14] *Yakuza* (gangsters) are used extensively in shake-downs, raising funds for the LDP, to terrorize workers on the shop floor and outside the factory precincts, against shareholders at company meetings, and against citizens' organizations such as anti-pollution groups.[15] By their widespread activity, which is promoted by the ruling oligarchy, and by their very visibility they foment fear and subservience. The value of these mobs to the regime is that they enable it to deploy a high level of violence and intimidation while maintaining a relatively "clean" legal force of repression and keep the boundaries of legality fluid.

The Liberal Democratic Party

This control of the state apparatus and of the machinery of ideological and physical repression provides the context within which parliamentary and party activity take place. The LDP is not *the* sole instrument of bourgeois political power, but simply one element. The machinery for preserving the interests of the ruling class involves not only keeping the LDP "in power" but also *subtracting* power from the domain of democratic control[16] as well as the straightforward subversion of democracy itself.[17]

The LDP was formed in 1955 through a merger of the two existing conservative parties, the Liberal Party and the Democratic Party.[18] However, as an American journalist has aptly commented, "The LDP . . . is neither liberal nor democratic nor a party but is a conservative, authoritarian alliance of *habatsu* [factions]."[19] This sentiment was also trenchantly voiced in 1962 by the chairman of the Party Organization Research Council, Kuraishi Tadao: "I say to anybody, whether in the party or outside, that the Liberal Democratic Party hardly deserves to be called a political party."[20] On one thing, though, all are agreed: the LDP is bone-deep corrupt. As the leading Japanese daily, the *Asahi,* put it in late 1966, "The conservative party is rotten through and through and is oozing pus."

The party's official documents vividly express its view of its role. The LDP Mission states: "Our party . . . is firmly determined to fight against the Communists and class-ruling Socialists, both of which aim at nothing but dictatorship."[21] The party Constitution states: "the LDP is . . . a party which is striving strictly for the elimination of the procommunist forces."[22]

Based on the solid majority of the combined Democratic and Liberal Parties, the LDP had till early 1974 retained a majority in both Houses of the Diet since its formation. It achieved this in spite of having virtually no party organization as such. As of the late 1960s it had only about 50,000 dues-paying members, almost all of whom were either Dietmen (420), local politicians (8,600) or legmen in the 2,600-odd party branches. In addition, the party had some 1.9 million purely nominal members and about 10 million people associated with various supporters' associations.[23] But these associations are not integrated into anything which could be called party activity. Local organizations take the form of *kōenkai*, individual Dietmen's support groups, loyal only to their boss.[24]

There are, of course, historical and cultural reasons for this type of organization, where followers pay personal allegiance to a leader in return for favours. The key point here is that this form of organization functions to demobilize political and class interests and thus is an important instrument in LDP rule.

A report of a Dietman's meeting in 1966 gives an idea of the explicit refusal of political discussion fostered by the LDP:

> The scene is a small sea-coast village . . . in Aichi Prefecture. Better than a hundred men and women are gathered in the auditorium of the elementary school. . . . They are clapping their hands and singing.
>
> > "Toughened by the winds of Mount Ibuki,
> > Blossoms the flower of peace of a united Asia.
> > This is the road which Kuno Chūji follows.
> > Firmly treading the red carpets of the Diet,
> > The man Kuno Chūji proceeds in triumph."
>
> Finally, bathed in loud applause, Dietman Kuno Chūji climbs the podium and begins to talk.
> "My friends, politics is not a matter for the head. Let us put aside difficult things like policy debate. Let's be friendly! Let's sing and dance! Let's enjoy ourselves!"
> Once again the chorus starts, "Firmly treading the red carpets . . ." Kuno Chūji has won seven elections and is regarded as a candidate for the next cabinet. He has held "songfests" four times in each of 150 places for a grand total of 600 meetings at which he has "sung and danced" with the 100,000 members of his kōenkai in the past six months.[25]

Given the LDP's lack of an organized base, much of the explanation for its electoral power revolves around the use of money. In Kishi's words, "what controls politics is power, and power lies in money." Money is collected at the centre, mainly from big business, and then distributed as hard cash by faction leaders to their followers, and subsequently by individual Dietmen to district clients and legmen. In 1958, for example, the cost of winning a Diet seat was estimated at ¥5 million, of which the party would raise one million and the individual Dietman the rest (usually from his faction leader). Since then costs have escalated many times. A leading Japanese political scientist writes:

> In plain language, Dietmen directly or indirectly purchase their posts. . . . The high cost of vote-getting . . . makes elections a nursery for corruption. . . . When elections are so dominated by mammon, politicians are enticed to go astray and a distorted stress is put on a candidate's ability to raise money instead of on his political aptitude or his record. Thus the Diet is now filled with men whose singular ability is raising election funds.[26]

Once money is entrenched to this extent, it can be used as a kind of "forward bribe." In the April 1971 election for the post of Governor (Mayor) of Tokyo the LDP candidate was former police chief Hatano Akira. The LDP was extremely keen to oust the popular Socialist incumbent Minobe Ryōkichi and announced that if Hatano was elected the federal government would allot ¥4 trillion (U.S. $11 billion) for the "rehabilitation" of Tokyo.[27] The commitment was not to put up the money for the people of the capital—unless they voted in the LDP's law-and-order candidate.

Money makes its most clamorous appearance with the election for the chairmanship of the LDP, which carries with it automatic installation as Prime Minister. In the hotly contested 1956 election calculations of the candidates' expenditures ranged from ¥120 million to ¥300 million for Kishi Nobusuke, ¥90 million to ¥150 million for Ishibashi Tanzan, and ¥60 million to ¥80 million for Ishii Mitsujirō.[28] Ikeda Hayato's election to the top post in 1960 was reportedly the most corrupt ever. The long-drawn-out struggle to replace Satō as Prime Minister in turn led to unprecedented expenditures: some two years before Satō finally stepped down the then leading contender for his job, Fukuda Takeo, took in almost U.S. $600,000 in one half-year period, while the Satō faction itself raked in half a million dollars over the same period.[29]

This is small change for big business, of course. Yet, although there is no evidence that factions as such have been deleterious to bourgeois rule, business's concern is, naturally, to see that its contributions are well spent, and it has several times thrown its weight behind the "modernization" of the party. Particularly energetic efforts were made in this direction while Ikeda was Prime Minister (1960–64). In March 1961 a new body, the Kokumin Kyōkai or People's Association, was set up. This increasingly became a centralizing fund-raising unit. By the mid-sixties it was reportedly handling a very high percentage of all the funds going to the LDP as a party.[30] The establishment of the Kokumin Kyōkai coincided almost exactly with that of the Party Organization Research Council (PORC), which was supposed to start streamlining the party and minimizing, possibly liquidating, the factions.[31] Such "modernization" would tend to increase the influence of big business on the party as a whole.[32] Yet, though such a move would appear objectively to be in business's interests, and though there have been reports of threats to withhold contributions unless the party "modernizes" itself, all evidence is that business is contributing larger funds than ever to both the LDP central coffers and to individual factions. In 1973 the LDP took in a total of ¥20 billion from big business alone (U.S. $70 million), and the party was reported to have asked for a special additional sum of ¥8 billion to pay for the mid-1974 Upper House election.[33] Leading polluters and hoarders have been prominent in pay-offs to the LDP.

Funds from such sources inevitably raise questions of bribery and corruption. The official bi-annual report covering the period January–June 1970 showed that only 745 out of the 1,495 political associations registered with the government submitted the reports required of them by law. Furthermore, of the funds reported, 70 per cent were unaccounted for.

Sociological studies support the thesis that corruption is not seen as particularly reprehensible. The ruling class, in its turn, while retaining a formal legal sanction against corruption, has managed to digest the phenomenon at its legal-institutional level. In the December 1969 elections about 70 per cent of the Dietmen elected to the Lower House won their seats on the basis of some kind of *legally* recognized fraud.[34] National Police Agency figures gave a total of 7,667 election law violations exposed, involving 13,346 persons; 1,733 people were arrested, of whom 84 per cent were charged with buying votes. Not surprisingly, the figure for successful campaigners was significantly higher than that for losers. Three members of the third Satō cabinet had supporters arrested and campaigners for two other ministers were questioned on suspicion of irregularities. Yet, though the regime maintains a legal definition of corruption, and even proceeds against it by arresting 1,733 people, there is no attempt to go further and question the validity of Diet seats held by people who have secured them illegally.

The methods for staying in power, however, go much wider and deeper than simple vote-buying, corruption and fraud. Legislation discriminates against those out of power and the poorer groups in actual campaigning and political propaganda.[35] Moreover, the LDP government actively fosters a climate of depoliticization to keep down the proportion of the electorate which will go to the polls and to help create a climate inimical to real political discussion.

But the main mechanism for maintaining LDP rule is the loaded voting and constituency system which produces a consistently higher percentage of seats for the LDP than its popular poll (see Appendix II). This has had important political and economic effects, since it has narrowed the area of political conciliation which the LDP has had to manoeuvre in to retain power, and thus lessened the class contradictions facing the party. This, in turn, has made it easier for successive LDP governments to pursue economic policies which furthered the interests of a relatively small segment of the population.[36] The policy of promoting pell-mell industrialization involved increased urbanization. In the "normal" course of events, the LDP would have lost its electoral majority through the economic policies it promoted. But the *real* erosion of its electoral majority was countered by keeping the constituencies heavily loaded in favour of rural areas. However, its position is little short of desperate. In the December 1969 general election its vote was:[37]

Large cities	30.7 per cent (of votes cast)
Cities	47.5 " " " " "
Semi-urban areas	54.1 " " " " "
Semi-rural	52.5 " " " " "
Rural	62.4 " " " " "
Average (nation-wide)	47.6 " " " " "

Furthermore, by the middle of 1973 half the population was living under local administrations in which the JCP and the JSP were the leading parties. This consolidation of anti-LDP administrations in the very nerve-centres of the country is inevitably further undercutting the LDP's national position.

The politico-economic contradictions threatening the LDP affect its base in two ways. First, the coalition of the different factions of the bourgeoisie which held relatively solid for two and a half decades showed signs of splitting under intense pressure from internationalization of the economy about 1971. Nixon's protectionist moves over textiles in 1971 forced the Tokyo regime to axe the domestic textile sector, with drastic results. U.S. penetration of the food distribution and retailing sector has also caused severe fissures within the Japanese bourgeoisie. As internationalization aggravates economic contradictions within the bourgeoisie, it is becoming harder for the LDP to conciliate the resulting political contradictions within this class.

At the same time, the inter-class coalition supporting the LDP is breaking up, partly as a result of the economic pressure from Japan's rivals, but also from the exploding contradictions of the type of economic policy which the LDP fostered. That is, by supporting the *economic* interests of the capitalist class while claiming to support the interests of much wider strata of the population (its political operation) the LDP itself laid the basis for the break-up of its own coalition, since the economic policies of big capital proved irredeemably harmful to many who had given their support to the LDP. A clear example of such a contradiction is the way industrial pollution has led to the virtual destruction of the livelihood of many fishing communities in Japan.[38]

The reaction of the ruling class has taken several forms. There has been a stepped up drive to alter the political climate of the nation, and the general context in which the political struggle is carried on. Emphasis on Tennōism has been increased to its highest pitch since 1945. The purpose of this campaign is to downplay the importance of the people and of democratic activity in general and correspondingly to promote authoritarianism and irresponsible government. The remobilization of the Emperor himself for trips abroad has been an important element in this.[39] The repromotion of the Emperor is the central element in a campaign headed by the National Congress for the Establishment of an Independent Constitution led by former premier Kishi Nobusuke, and supported by many LDP potentates.[40] This body would "clarify" the status of the Emperor by redefining him as *Daihyō* ("Representative" or "Head") of State. The Congress would alter the status of the military under the Constitution and make them official. It would further restrict individual rights under the catch-all rubric of "safeguarding public welfare" and ensuring "social solidarity." Such bodies as this National Congress can be instrumental in nudging petty bourgeois sentiment rightwards as the strength of the left increases. These ideological operations are being cemented by reactionary reforms in the education system.

The regime has also launched a renewed campaign to revise the constituency system.[41] The new proposals would, if enacted, ensure the LDP a Diet majority almost irrespective of its actual vote. Under the proposed system the LDP would have secured 80 per cent of the Diet seats on the basis of its vote in December 1972 of 46.8 per cent.[42] The constituency and voting reform proposals assume that the LDP can not win majority support and that the issue of the people electing their own representatives is something which has to be circumvented.

Precisely the sharpness of class divisions makes normal bourgeois mediation and compromise so difficult for the LDP. The party's economic policies are *absolutely* irreconcilable with the interests of the mass of the population, and with the aggravated contradictions of international capitalism in both markets and supplies of raw materials. The LDP can thus neither really protect the interests of a sufficiently large segment of the population nor delude a sufficiently large proportion of the population into believing that it is looking after their interests.

This is an unprecedented crisis for the LDP, and as the crisis deepens the party is revealing more and more its imbrication with the state. At the same time, the capitalist class is making it clear that it does not intend to allow bourgeois democracy to stand in the way of its control of state power. The revised constituency proposals would produce a displacement of almost two for one. And by early 1973, as the possibility of an opposition coalition became more likely, the party was suggesting that an opposition coalition would be illegal.[43]

THE ECONOMY

The organization of the Japanese economy involves a specific division of labour between the state and a number of powerful business bodies. The close relationship between business and government is frequently noted. Equally important, a large area of activity which in most Western capitalist countries has been assigned to the state, in Japan remains under the direct sway of economic interests. There has been minimal state intervention over wage levels. There has been maximal combined intervention and non-intervention in areas such as taxation and social security, directly influencing the formation and accumulation of capital.[44] And, while the state "neglects" some areas, it is extremely active in others, for example, in providing credit to private businesses. Through bodies like the Ministry of International Trade and Industry (MITI) and the Economic Planning Agency (EPA), the state provides expert services for business.

Business[45] co-ordinates its interests and intervenes in the economic direction of the country through a number of organizations. Throughout much of the postwar period the most important of these was the Keidanren, or Federation of Economic Associations,[46] made up exclusively of members of big business. It is misleading to see the Keidanren as somehow "outside" the government. Though not formally part of the state apparatus, it is certainly an integral part of the ruling class system of domination. As an editorial writer on the big business newspaper, the *Nihon Keizai Shimbun,* put it, the task of the business organizations "is to exercise 'environmental control' to protect the general interests of capital."[47] One of the Keidanren's twenty-one committees is entrusted with "studying how to improve the organization of the government."[48] The second main business organization, the Keizai Doyūkai, or (Japan) Committee for Economic Development, was set up just after the war. Unlike the Keidanren, this includes small and medium businessmen. In some ways, the Keizai Doyūkai has been more aggressive than the Keidanren in areas such as new management techniques and economic planning.[49] The main down-to-earth anti-proletarian role has been played by a third organization, Nikkeiren, or Japan Federation of Employers' Associations.[50] A fourth body, Nisshō, or Japan Chamber of Commerce and Industry (JCCI), has dealt mainly with trade and marketing.[51] In 1966 a completely new body, Sanken, was set up, with tightly restricted membership to co-ordinate business activity even further and, in particular, to plan the streamlining of the economy and assist strategic mergers in the age of "liberalization" and accelerated internationalization. Sanken, with the key leaders of both the Keidanren and the Keizai Doyūkai represented on it (see Table 1), is truly a

TABLE 1

BIG BUSINESS GHQ: THE SANKEN (1971)

The Sanken's 24 members are as follows, listed by group affiliation:

Fuyo Group: Y. Iwasa (president, Fuji Bank); M. Anzai (president, Showa Denko); H. Imazato (president, Nippon Seiko, & director-general, Nikkeiren); T. Sakurada (chairman, Toho Rayon and adviser, Nisshin Spinning, as well as Nikkeiren chief)—in addition to the presidents of Fuyo-kai members Hitachi Ltd. and Nissan Motor, both of which head konzerns.

Mitsubishi Group: F. Kono (chairman, Mitsubishi Heavy Industries); W. Tajitsu (chairman, Mitsubishi Bank); C. Fujino (president, Mitsubishi Shoji).

Sumitomo Group: K. Kobayashi (president, Nippon Electric); N. Hasegawa (president, Sumitomo Chemical); H. Hyuga (president, Sumitomo Metal Industries).

Mitsui Group: S. Tashiro (honorary board chairman, Toray Industries); T. Mizukami (chairman, Mitsui Bussan)—in addition to the president of Tokyo Shibaura Electric, known as an old "Mitsui man."

Other Zaibatsu: M. Segawa (chairman, Nomura Securities, Sanwa Group); T. Taniguchi (chairman, Toyobo, allied with Dai-Ichi Kangyo Group).

Industrial Bank of Japan sphere of influence: S. Nakayama (counsellor to the bank); K. Kikawada (president, Tokyo Electric Power)—in addition to the four executives of konzerns close to the bank, Nippon Steel, Nissan and Hitachi.

Leading Konzerns: S. Nagano & Y. Inayama (chairman and president, respectively, of Nippon Steel); K. Komai (president, Hitachi); T. Doko (president, Tokyo Shibaura Electric, of Toshiba-IHI); K. Kawamata (president, Nissan). Of the six top industrial konzerns, two are not represented (Toyota and Matsushita); interestingly these are the only two of the six where a single family retains a significant degree of control, and where traditions of relative independence remain strong.

Other Sanken Members: K. Uemura (president, Keidanren); M. Minato (ex-president, Nikko Securities); S. Kitano (president, Nippon Rare Metals).

NOTE: The four leading long-established *zaikai** organizations are now all represented on the Sanken. They are (with key officers seated on the Sanken):
—*Keidanren* (Federation of Economic Organizations): K. Uemura, president; T. Doko, F. Kono, Y. Inayama and Y. Iwasa, vice presidents.
—*Keizai Doyukai* (Japan Committee for Economic Development): K. Kikawada, chairman.
—*Nikkeiren* (Japan Federation of Employers' Associations), which deals with labor relations: T. Sakurada, president, and H. Imazato, director-general.
—*Japan Chamber of Commerce & Industry:* S. Nagano, president.

SOURCE: *Pacific Imperialism Notebook,* Vol. 3, No. 1 (December 1971–January 1972), p. 13.

"power above government."[52] It is now *the* voice of big business. These bodies wield considerably more power than even their most powerful counterparts in the West, such as the Confindustria in Italy. As Thayer puts it: "These men do not put pressure on the center of government; they are the center of government."[53]

* See note 45, pp. 418–19, and Glossary.

The Structure of the Economy

The Japanese economy is characterized by a very high degree of concentration. It is dominated by a very small number of giant combines which determine the direction of the entire economy. These combines are surrounded by a proliferation of smaller enterprises which usually depend on them directly or indirectly. They wield relatively little "countervailing" power.

Concentration is the first feature of imperialism.[54] In Japan this takes the form of oligopoly rather than monopoly. The situation, as Rowley puts it, is "one of oligopolistic competition between the *zaibatsu* over a wide range of industries, with a fringe of small, specialised companies (often subcontractors for the *zaibatsu* enterprises) clustered around them."[55]

Six groups qualify as zaibatsu: the Mitsubishi, Mitsui, Sumitomo, Fuyo, Dai-Ichi Kangyo and Sanwa groups.[56] In addition, there are seven other major groups which can conveniently be referred to as konzerns—"mainly non-financial companies characterized by intergrated operations, ususally within a single industry or within several related industries."[57] The seven are: Nippon Steel, Toshiba-IHI, Hitachi, Toyota, Nissan, Matsushita and Tokyu.[58] The konzerns are not purely "industrial" combines, but, unlike the zaibatsu, they do not have a bank or other central financial institution within the group.

In considering the question of ownership and control, several factors must be taken into consideration. First is the overall structure of the economy. In 1970 primary industry (agriculture, fishing, etc.) accounted for only 7.5 per cent of national income, compared with 18.2 per cent in 1940 and 28.7 per cent in 1920. The role of the secondary and tertiary sectors has, therefore, greatly increased. Second is the relationship between paid-up capital and credit. One recent study found that the average percentage of owned capital in Japanese businesses in 1972 was only 16 per cent, compared with 66 per cent before the war.[59] Another recent study found that shareholders accounted for only 9.1 per cent of the total capital used by the big corporations; including other items, these corporations' owned capital came to only 17.3 per cent of their total capital. The rest was borrowed, with banks accounting for 37.6 per cent, inter-business credit 21.1 per cent and debentures 4.7 per cent.[60] Mitsui & Co. Ltd. (Mitsui Bussan) was capitalized at ¥23 billion in 1972, but it had long-term debts of ¥400 billion, nearly twenty times its capitalization, and the grand total of its loans came to ¥1,000 billion—or almost 50 times its capitalization.[61]

These figures indicate the absolutely central role of the banks and credit institutions. Ultimately, credit is determined by the government-controlled Bank of Japan, through a mixture of formal and informal mechanisms.[62] But the zaibatsu banks, which naturally have very close links with the

TABLE 2

HOW BANK RESERVES HAVE BEEN HELD DOWN
HOW MUCH COMPANIES RELY ON THE BANKS

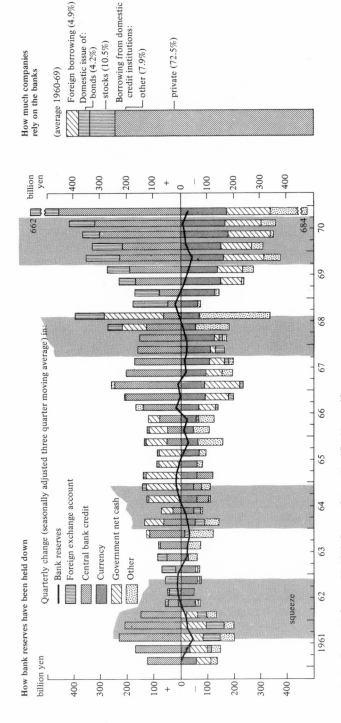

SOURCE: *Economist*, January 27, 1973, Survey: International Banking, p. 45.

Bank of Japan, play a crucial role in determining investment and trade policies. It is credit and turnover rather than capitalization and share ownership which count in Japan. Mitsui Bussan, for example, is paying almost five times its own capitalization value in interest alone each year.[63] In 1966 no less than 41 per cent of total industrial profits were paid to banks as interest.[64]

In finance, zaibatsu firms accounted for half the paid-up capital of fifty-five leading financial institutions, as of the fiscal year ending March 31, 1970. In heavy industry (companies with yearly sales over U.S. $100 million) the thirteen groups (zaibatsu + konzerns) accounted for 92 per cent of the paid-up capital. As of March 1970 the thirteen groups (members + allies) overall accounted for a bare minimum of U.S. $8,149

TABLE 3A

ECONOMIC CONCENTRATION (1970)

The Stake of the 6 Zaibatsu & 7 Konzerns in Mining & Manufacturing

1. Of the top 11 mining & manufacturing firms, with sales over $1 billion—
   The 6 zaibatsu and 7 konzerns account for: 91 per cent of companies
                                               94 per cent of sales.
   Breakdown: Six firms belong to the konzerns, four to zaibatsu, and one is considered independent (Nippon Oil Co.)

2. Of the top 30 firms, with sales over $500 million—
   The 6 zaibatsu and 7 konzerns account for: 87 per cent of companies
                                               90 per cent of sales.
   Breakdown: Nineteen firms are members or allies of zaibatsu, seven belong to the konzerns, and four are considered independent.

3. Of the top 90 firms, with sales over $200 million (comparable to the US top 450 industrials, in terms of sales)—
   The 6 zaibatsu and 7 konzerns account for: 83 per cent of companies
                                               87 per cent of sales.
   Breakdown: Fifty-nine firms are members or allies of zaibatsu, 16 are members or allies of the konzerns, and 15 are considered independent.

4. Of the top 170 firms, with sales over $100 million (comparable to the US top 700 industrials in terms of sales)—
   The 6 zaibatsu and 7 konzerns account for: 70 per cent of companies
                                               over 75 per cent of sales.
   Breakdown: Ninety firms are members or allies of zaibatsu, 28 are members or allies of the konzerns, and 52 are considered independent.

5. Of the top 316 firms, with sales over $50 million—
   The 6 zaibatsu and 7 konzerns account for: 58 per cent of companies
                                               over two-thirds of sales.
   Breakdown: One hundred thirty-five firms are members or allies of zaibatsu, 48 are members or allies of the konzerns, and 133 are considered independent.

SOURCE: *Pacific Imperialism Notebook,* Vol. 3, No. 1 (December 1971–January 1972), p. 9.

TABLE 3B

ECONOMIC CONCENTRATION

The Stake of the 6 Zaibatsu in Other Sectors of the Economy

Finance—Under zaibatsu control are six of the top seven commercial banks; the top five trust & banking companies; six of the top eight life insurance firms; and six of the top eight non-life insurance firms (the other two belong to the Toyota and Nissan konzerns).

General Trading—The top 11 general trading houses (all with over $1 billion in operating revenues) are all members or close allies of the zaibatsu. These are the primary organizers of business activity at home and abroad.

Transport & Storage—Four of the top five transport firms and the top three warehouse firms are zaibatsu-controlled.

Construction—Four of the top five construction companies are members or close allies of the zaibatsu.

Real Estate—The top three real estate companies belong to Mitsui and Mitsubishi zaibatsu and to the Tokyu Konzern.

NOTE: Sales figures for Tables 3A and 3B are for the fiscal year ended March 31, 1970, as cited in President Directory 1971 (figures for independently operating subsidiaries being generally not consolidated). Zaibatsu and konzern listings in this Special Report were used as a basis for the computations.

SOURCE: *Pacific Imperialism Notebook*, Vol. 3, No. 1 (December 1971–January 1972), p. 10.

million in paid-up capital.[65] Details of the financial resources of the zaibatsu and the extent of economic concentration under their control are given in Tables 3A, 3B and 4.

Special mention should be made of the *sōgō shōsha* or giant general trading companies, institutions unique to Japan. These mammoth enterprises act as investment bankers, provide insurance, storage and transportation, as well as dealing in every kind of trade. In 1972 the top ten handled half the country's exports, 62 per cent of its imports and 20 per cent of domestic wholesale transactions.[66] In 1972 the top six had combined sales of £33 billion and accounted for 70 per cent of business transacted by eighty-eight wholesale firms listed on the stock market. The companies command monopoly over 70 per cent of primary wholesale trade. Moreover, according to the Fair Trade Commission, the top six have gradually acquired control over more than half of the 19,000 companies listed on the stock exchange.[67] In 1972 it was estimated that the value of the business transacted by the top ten was twice the national budget and about 30 per cent of GNP. Moreover, to provide a comparison with industry, the annual gross business of the top two trading companies was three times the sales volume of Nippon Steel, the world's largest steelmaker.[68] This concentration of trading and trade-related power is unparal-

TABLE 4

FINANCIAL RESOURCES OF THE ZAIBATSU*

(All figures are in billions of U.S. dollars)

Zaibatsu	Main Bank (assets)	Life & Non-Life Insurance Cos. (assets)	Trust & Banking Co. (funds in trust plus deposits)	Total**
Sumitomo	9.1	1.7	4.5	15.3
Mitsubishi	8.7	1.6	4.8	15.2
Sanwa	8.5	3.2	3.2	14.9
Fuyo	9.3	0.8	3.0	13.2
Dai-Ichi Kangyo***	11.6	1.2	—	12.9
Mitsui	6.2	0.9	3.9	10.9

*   Based on financial reports for year ending March 31, 1970.
**   Figures may not add up to totals due to rounding.
*** Dai-Ichi Kangyo Group Main Bank figure consolidates assets of Dai-Ichi Bank and Nippon Kangyo Bank. Group does not possess a trust and banking house.

A recent report by the *Oriental Economist* provided another index of financial strength. The Tokyo publication surveyed leading Japanese businesses with a view to discovering the leading loan source for each company. Industrial Bank of Japan led in this regard, with 133 firms for which it was the largest supplier of loans, followed by Sumitomo Bank group (121), Mitsubishi Bank group (120), Mitsui Bank group (103), Fuji Bank group (98), Dai-Ichi Kangyo Bank (estimated at 90), Long-Term Credit Bank (79) and Sanwa Bank group (67).

SOURCE: *Pacific Imperialism Notebook,* Vol. 3, No. 1 (December 1971–January 1972), p. 7.

leled elsewhere in the world, and has enormous ramifications, since it puts virtually every firm in Japan in some kind of subordination to the big combines.

As it is, the zaibatsu and their allied konzerns already control virtually every large-scale industry, the key exception being the petroleum sector (both refining and marketing).[69] In the chemical industry, the top five firms are affiliated to the zaibatsu, as are the top five shipbuilders, six of the seven top textile companies, the top seven makers of industrial machinery, the top seven electrical equipment manufacturers, and the leading steel and automobile companies.[70]

There has been considerable discussion over whether concentration now is greater than in the past. Although the old holding companies have disappeared (see chapter 7) and the combines are formally less centrally controlled than before, the groups are still highly co-ordinated, even though this co-ordination frequently takes apparently informal shape.[71] The dissolution of the holding companies and other forms of Occupation intervention helped to foster stronger ties between business and government and increased the role of the banks. Ownership is thus a much less reliable index than in the pre-1945 period. In terms of relations with the state apparatus, facilities from government, credit, turnover and market control, it would seem that concentration (certainly concentration of power) has increased over the pre-1945 era.

The pressures towards concentration were particularly acute from about the mid-sixties. As Table 5 shows, mergers increased in the late 1960s,

TABLE 5

COMPANY MERGERS IN JAPAN, 1951–69

	1951–55	1956–60	1961–64	1965–67	1968	1969
Total (annual average)	345	402	812	933	1,020	1,163
Companies with capitalization value of more than 1 billion yen	4	8	27	35	28	36

SOURCE: OECD, *Economic Survey of Japan,* 1971 (Paris, OECD, June 1971), p. 29.

especially among larger firms. As "liberalization" advanced, so did mergers. With state assistance, the big firms launched a concerted programme to further their vertical integration.[72] Though the essential mergers and take-overs in sectors like the automobile and steel industries were completed before the full impact of foreign competition was felt, further pressure from Japan's rivals and the slowdown in the growth rate are likely to keep the merger rate high. When a leading Japanese newspaper editorialized that the 1970s would see a shift from an era of "competitive oligopoly" to one of "cooperative oligopoly"[73] the situation envisaged was probably not so much one where competition between capitalist companies would vanish, but one where the giant firms would have taken over all their rivals except the other combines.

Recurrent references by Western capitalism to Japan's GNP and its economic "miracle" may easily obscure the extent to which there is indeed room for further concentration and, above all, structural transformation of the economy. Although within industry heavy industry plays the predominant role, and Japan for long now has had the largest proportion of its industrial sector devoted to heavy industry, the economy is still largely made up of very small units of production. In 1971 Japan was only in fifteenth place among OECD countries as regards GNP per head, below countries like Iceland, Austria and the United Kingdom.[74] In 1975, it is estimated, Japan's per capita GNP will still be less than 60 per cent of the U.S. figure.[75] These figures reflect the *structure* of the economy better than those showing Japan's total GNP.

In a way, Japan's economy is top-heavy. Contrary to widely held assumptions in the West, the sectors of industry which have been most vigorously promoted have not been those producing consumer goods, but those in the heavy industrial sector.[76] Japan has the largest steel company in the world, Nippon Steel, which overtook U.S. Steel in 1971. Japan has also achieved a leading position in the heavy chemical industry: already in 1961 this sector accounted for a higher proportion of manufacturing industry as a whole than in any other economy in the world.[77] By about 1965 production of the major heavy and chemical industries far exceeded the level of domestic demand.

This has been achieved through state policies in favour of extremely high rates of capital formation and investment. Gross fixed investment averaged 32.4 per cent of GNP over the years 1960–69, and 36.6 per cent over the years 1966–70 (see Table 6).[78] These rates are far higher than any of

TABLE 6

SAVING AND SPENDING

(1960–69 averages)

Households	*Japan*	*America*	*Germany*	*France*
% of disposable income:				
invested in real assets	7.7	5.5	6.7	5.5
held in financial assets	11.3	4.1	3.6	4.5
saved in total	19.0	9.6	10.3	10.0
Companies				
Internal funds as % of total funds	46.4	67.4	66.4	61.1
Share in GNP (%)				
Consumers' spending	54.8	62.4	56.5	61.0
Government spending	8.7	19.2	15.1	12.7
Gross fixed investment	32.4	16.7	25.1	23.4
Exports	10.6	5.6	20.8	16.2

SOURCE: *Economist,* January 27, 1973, Survey: International Banking, p. 44.

Japan's leading capitalist rivals, and considerably higher than in any other OECD countries. Throughout the postwar period as a whole the rate of capital accumulation has been both high and unstable, while the growth of production has been smoother and steadier than investment.[79] This type of capital formation has been technologically highly progressive and has boosted labour productivity.

Even now, Japan is still largely a production-oriented economy of scarcity. Big industry has not pulled the other sectors of the economy along with it at the same pace as in the more consumer-oriented Western capitalist economies at a comparable stage. Paradoxically, this has accentuated the power of big business, since there are comparatively fewer centres of opposition power and most of the rest of the economy remains vulnerably dependent on the big combines.

Aspects of the Crisis in Japanese Capitalism

In 1973 Japan had a GNP of ¥112,870.8 billion (about $395 billion). The Basic Economic and Social Plan 1973–1977 (drawn up before the 1973 oil crisis) forecast a GNP for the financial year 1977 of ¥182.9 trillion.[80] Even if this figure is not reached, the emergence of this economy, the third largest in the world, in a country with almost no raw materials, has major ramifications for all concerned—the peoples of Southeast Asia, Japan's capitalist rivals and the Japanese people themselves.

DOMESTIC FACTORS

Japan's economy is like a bicycle: if it slows down, it is in danger of toppling over and crashing. The heavy reliance on credit creates a situation where companies are forced to come up with large interest payments at frequent intervals. Such a situation is tolerable during periods of high growth, and over the years 1967–72, for example, when the growth of real GNP averaged 10.9 per cent annually, the state backed this system of reliance on bank credit as an almost automatic mechanism for squeezing out non-profitable companies.[81] But, though Japan weathered the post–"Nixon shock" crisis of 1971–72, the 1973 oil crisis slowed the economy to a much lower growth rate and the indebtedness syndrome began to produce a cascade of bankruptcies, with repercussions throughout the economy.

Two other factors should also be borne in mind. First, there is the over-production in the heavy and chemical industries. Up till now Japan has tended to absorb over-production in increased exports. Although Japan has had a *low* volume of exports compared to its GNP,[82] *increased* exports have been important in solving crises of over-production. Second is Japan's very high rate of inflation. In 1973 it had the highest rates in the advanced capitalist world, with retail prices rising 20.1 per cent in the calendar year.[83] Throughout the 1960s and the beginning of the seventies inflation was absorbed in high growth rates, and high increases in labour productivity kept exports competitive. This equation has now changed radically.

Japanese industrial growth contains within itself contradictions which are already tending to limit its rate of expansion as in the past. As Ui Jun, Japan's leading expert on *kōgai* (all kinds of environmental pollution), has pointed out, certain key sectors of the economy built their postwar position not only on lower labour costs than their competitors, but also on their decisions not to spend capital on anti-pollution and safety devices. On furnaces for steel mills Ui calculates the initial saving at about 30 per cent of the total cost of the furnace.[84] A large number of people have been killed directly by industrial poisoning, and thousands of others maimed and crippled, many of them from birth. Whole industrial areas such as Yokkaichi are blanketed in a pall of smog and poison. Workers there function below the desired level of efficiency from capitalism's point of view.

The strength of the anti-pollution movement is already having a major effect on the economy and on industrial planning. In 1972 only 32 per cent of the planned total work on constructing new electric power plants was completed due to opposition from citizens' groups (compared with 89 per cent in 1971).[85] Thus, quite apart from the oil problem, there are major internal obstacles to continued rapid "growth." The scale of the menace from industrial activity was spelled out by Ui Jun in 1973: "At least 50 per cent of the common people here will die out in 20 years at the present economic growth rate even if all technological anti-pollution measures known at present are applied."[86]

Given such problems the government more than ten years ago adopted the first National Comprehensive Development Programme (Zensō).[87] It was supposed to outline a plan for decentralizing industry and population. The Programme's objectives were not met, and in 1969 it was overhauled as the New National Comprehensive Development Programme (Shin-zensō), which in turn was again overhauled in 1972, about the same time as Premier Tanaka launched his "remodelling the archipelago" scheme.[88] But it is important to recognize that none of these plans has yet been fulfilled nor is likely to be. Even before the autumn 1973 crisis industry itself was divided on the Shinzensō and on Tanaka's "remodelling." In spring 1973 the Industrial Planning Council, a top-level business body, directly challenged many of the assumptions behind the "remodelling" scheme.[89] In an era of increasing scarcity and rapidly shifting terms of trade, the two crucial factors regarding Japanese industry are its very high level of dependence on raw material imports, and the fact that the coeffi-cient of its consumption of natural resources per unit of GNP is the highest of all the advanced capitalist countries.[90] The Industrial Planning Council noted that Japan almost certainly would not be able to go on acquiring the raw materials to continue its present type of growth which, for example, would require importing a projected 600 million tons of petroleum in 1980. The report suggested reducing planned automobile production, and major cutbacks in petroleum refining, petrochemicals, steel, chemical, pulp, electric power generating and other fields.

The logical and rational course for Japanese capitalism would be towards what are termed "knowledge-intensive and low resources-consuming" industries,[91] away from industries which are labour-intensive, highly polluting and consume a very high quantity of natural resources per unit of output towards industries based on high technology and a very high level of education. But it is more than doubtful that such a level of capi-talist rationality is attainable. Moreover, capitalist "decentralization" is inextricable from the destruction of farmland, property speculation and the further spreading of pollution, sickness and death.[92] When it comes to the crunch, Japanese business has shown that rhetoric about serving the nation and contributing to social harmony means very little. Any major switch from growth- and profit-oriented industrialization to a programme placing substantial emphasis on social services seems out of the question under an LDP regime. This is even more the case in a period of high inflation. In the new cabinet formed in December 1973 in the wake of the oil crisis, the Finance Ministry was entrusted to Tanaka's old rival, the ultra-conservative Fukuda Takeo, who explicitly jettisoned the premier's "remodelling" scheme and enunciated a policy which would maintain the present type of growth, at an initially reduced rate.[93]

The development of the economy will also be crucially affected by the situation of the working classes. The key elements here are the labour shortage, the evolution of wages and the organic composition of capital (the ratio of the money laid out on wages of production workers to the money laid out on raw materials and instruments of production). The shortage of labour in the late 1960s and early 1970s certainly helped to drive wages up at an accelerating pace—from 10.3 per cent up in 1966 (over 1965) to 20.1 per cent in 1973 (over 1972).[94] Internal decentralization can have some effect on wage levels, by moving industry to areas where wage levels are lower, and where workers can more easily be prevented from forming a union in a new plant. But short of a major recession and greatly increased unemployment, the labour shortage is likely to persist, and it is not something which can be altered overnight. In 1972 the government did, however, start to reverse its stance, which previously had favoured tight control of the population (currently about 110 million), by suggesting that economic reasons should no longer be considered grounds for abortion. As the women's movement has argued, this seems clearly designed to try to bring about an increase in the ethnic Japanese population.[95]

One solution would be to follow the example of Western Europe and the United States and import labour from poorer countries. But there are major obstacles in the way of such a move, including the opposition of the Japanese unions and petit bourgeois racism, which is hostile to foreigners, particularly Koreans (the most likely candidates). Towards the end of 1973 the government chose Okinawa to test the possibility of bringing in Korean labour to work on a major construction project, the 1975 International Ocean Exposition which was allegedly behind schedule because of shortage of labour.[96]

Another partial solution, already initiated, is to move production abroad. Again, pollution and the opposition it has aroused in Japan are major factors. Already in 1970 the leaders of both the Japan–Republic of China [Taiwan] and the Japan–Republic of [South] Korea Co-operation Committees were proposing the planned export of high-pollutant industries to these two client territories.[97] And in May 1973 the Keidanren issued a major document entitled "Environmental Pollution and Japanese Industry," which, in the words of the *Guardian* correspondent, "sanctioned the sharing of the pollution burden," a "policy of spreading Japanese muck with Japanese money."[98]

But the main reason Japan has to export production facilities derives from relative wage costs and the organic composition of capital. Comparative daily average wage rates in industry at the end of 1971 were estimated as follows:[99]

Country	Amount (U.S. $)
Japan	6.70
Hong Kong	2.80
Taiwan	1.70
South Korea	1.20

Thus, by moving production to nearby dictatorships, Japanese capital can both evade the wrath of its own poisoned citizens by dumping pollution on the peoples of Korea and Taiwan and at the same time increase its own profit margins. But "pure" profit is not the only, or necessarily even the main, reason Japanese firms are moving abroad.[100] The relative costs of increasing productivity in domestic industry (i.e., the capital investment needed to produce a sizeable diminution of the unit cost of a given product) are such in many sectors that moving production out of Japan is an absolute necessity.

This, in turn, has further important economic effects. It ultimately works to keep down labour costs in Japan itself, by lowering the "average" wage in Japanese plants (at home and abroad). It further stimulates Japan's own economy by increasing demand in the periphery. It also allows Japanese firms both to evade the protectionism of its capitalist rivals and to avail themselves of United Nations Conference on Trade and Development (UNCTAD) preference schemes, which give a tariff advantage of 15–20 per cent to developing countries.[101]

JAPAN IN THE WORLD ECONOMY

Strong measures were adopted to defend the domestic economy against foreign interference throughout the postwar period. There were tight restrictions on foreign investment in both manufacturing and distribution, as well as in banking. The result was that, apart from the U.S. stranglehold on the oil sector, foreign investment and control remained comparatively weak (Appendix III). As of the early 1970s total foreign assets in Japan (of which the U.S. share was estimated to be 60–70 per cent) probably accounted for only about 2–3 per cent of total Japanese corporate assets.[102] By keeping foreign capital out of the domestic economy to this unparalleled extent, the Japanese ruling class preserved for itself unique flexibility as regards investment and production decisions and this, in turn, was extremely important in preserving the *political* cohesion of the bourgeoisie as a class. Surprisingly, in view of the furore aroused by the much feebler efforts of Gaullist France, the Japanese regime managed to stick to this position for some twenty-five years, until 1971, before incurring direct U.S. retaliation, either economic or political. This very low level of foreign investment in Japan was an important factor in facilitating Japan's very high growth rates. By opposing foreign investment in Japan, the state succeeded to a large extent in blocking the realization of the tendency towards the international equalization of the rate of profit. This, in turn, of course, favoured Japan's exports.[103] Japan's very high "imports" of foreign technology and payments on patents and licences were a direct alternative to accepting foreign investment—and, in the long term, a much more profitable option.[104]

But in an era of great change across the globe, when many Third World countries are increasingly resisting the looting of their resources by the few rich nations, the crucial aspect of the relationship between Japan's economy and the rest of the world is the import requirements of existing and planned industry in Japan and in the Japanese-dominated periphery. Agricultural imports are also of critical importance.

Prior to 1945 much of Japan's agricultural imports were supplied from colonies like Taiwan, Korea and Manchuria. During the Occupation much of the shortfall between domestic production and consumption was met by imports from the United States, which captured a dominant position in the market. This subordination to the United States was part of a strategic decision, which was matched internally by the sacrifice of much of domestic agriculture to industry. On the one hand, in order to keep the politically important rural population in line, the regime launched a rice subsidy programme which encouraged the decreasing farming population to increase rice production to the point where Japan had a large surplus from the early sixties onwards.[105] On the other hand, the regime decided to sacrifice its national grain economy, which was less productive than the rice sector.[106]

This agricultural policy had several effects. It made Japan dependent on a source of supply which proved to be limited in the early 1970s and, as the U.S. surplus rapidly evaporated, prices rocketed. But by reducing the grain economy and subsidizing rice, Japan also blocked off the possibility of becoming a market for agricultural exports from Southeast Asian countries which had a rice surplus and were running large trading deficits with it.[107] Indeed, Japan has even tried to unload its rice surplus on its Southeast Asian neighbours, thus further aggravating trade imbalances.

With its present population level and economic structure, it is impossible for Japan to be self-sufficient in food. Like Britain, it has followed a path of of economic growth which requires large agricultural imports. The latest move has been towards creating agricultural enclaves, mainly in Third World countries like Indonesia, to supply Japan with foodstuffs. Within the "logic" of Japanese capitalism, this is a development which is likely to increase, given Japan's plans to continue destroying its own countryside and the dwindling surplus in the rich Anglo-Saxon nations.[108]

On the industrial raw materials front the position is one of overwhelming dependence on imports: 100 per cent for nickel, aluminium and uranium; about 99.7 per cent for oil. Japan's long-range position is brought out by a 1972 report from a business study group, the Industrial Planning Conference:

Our country . . . is now importing one quarter of the total exported volume of raw materials of the world. If Japan continues to increase its raw material imports at the past annual tempo of 19 per cent, in 1980 it will be importing 2,100 million tons of raw materials, or 7.4 times more than in 1969. In the meantime, the world will produce 9,400 million tons of raw materials, given the hitherto output growth rate of 5 per cent annually. The volume of exportable raw materials the world over, expected to increase 6 per cent annually, will reach only 2,040 million tons in 1980. That would mean that in that year our country will have to monopolize the whole volume of exportable raw materials in the world.[109]

This poses starkly the issues involved in Japan's development, its relations to the other advanced capitalist countries and its essentially extractive relationship to the Third World producing countries, as well as the nature of the world resources problem as a single, global one. The 1973 oil crisis showed Japan's dependence not only on the producing countries, but also on the giant U.S. and Anglo-Dutch oil companies which control the supplies to Japan. At the end of 1973 Japan was relying on the oil majors for 67 per cent of its supplies and even Japan's "national refiners" (18.9 per cent of Japan's total capacity) rely on the majors for crude.[110] (See Appendix IV.)

This dependence on the oil majors reflects in acute form Japan's general dependence on the established Western capitalist powers, especially the United States. The whole postwar development of the economy has been largely shaped by Japan's subordination to the United States. One aspect of this, mirroring Japan's barriers to foreign investment within the country, has been Japan's very low level of investment overseas—and thus a relatively low level of control over its sources of supply, much smaller than the United States, the United Kingdom, or West Germany, proportionate to GNP. In 1970 only 12 per cent of Japan's imports of the five main metallic raw materials (excluding iron ore) came from enterprises in which Japan had some sort of financial interest.[111] In oil, Japan's dependence on the majors was higher at the end of 1973 than it was four years earlier when it launched an extensive search for independent supplies.[112]

This search highlighted Japan's inability to fashion an independent place for itself. After a few years of desperate attempts at going it alone, Japan was obliged to abandon this approach and acknowledge its subordination to the giant Euro-American companies which control most of the supplies

TABLE 7

EUROPEAN-AMERICAN CAPITAL CONTROL OVER
WORLD MINERAL RESOURCES

Copper	10 companies	70.9% of world production
Nickel	4 "	74.5% " " "
Aluminium refining	6 "	82.8% " " "
Crude oil	8 "	64% " " "

In copper, aluminium and oil, the U.S.A. controls 40 per cent or more of world output.

SOURCE: MITI (Ministry of International Trade and Industry), *Tsūshō Hakusho* [Trade White Paper], *Sōron* [General Considerations], 1971, p. 349.

of key raw materials outside the socialist bloc (see Table 7). After a vigorous drive in Southeast Asia, concentrated on offshore prospecting off Indonesia, Japan moved away from the "develop and import" formula, and towards buying into consortia with the established Euro-American companies (as in the Abu Dhabi formula), and going into large long-term development projects with the Third World countries which export oil to Japan, such as Iran (Japan's number one supplier), Saudi Arabia, Indonesia, Iraq and Algeria, in return for direct deliveries by these states to Japan ("DD," or Direct Deal arrangements). The 1973 crisis pushed the cost of these deals for Japan up to at least one billion dollars each in the cases of Iraq and Iran. This is apart from the quadrupled price of the oil itself.[113]

The oil experience has been repeated in other fields. Virtually everywhere that Japan has envisaged trying to break away from the United States, it has rapidly been brought to heel. This is true of Southeast Asia and Siberia[114] as much as of the Middle East. After initial opposition to U.S. "joint energy" plans from a sector of the ruling class, represented politically by Minister of International Trade and Industry Nakasone, Japan buckled by the time of the February 1974 Washington Conference of leading capitalist importers, where it followed behind the United States.[115]

Thus, although Japan is likely to continue to increase the level of its overseas investment considerably in the years ahead, it seems certain that it will not be able to match the degree of control over its supplies which most of its major capitalist competitors have enjoyed (see Appendix V). Though Japan had the highest rate of increase of overseas investment (32 per cent p.a. over the years 1966–70), its total was well below that of the United Kingdom: to the end of March 1973 it was U.S. $6,773 million—compared with a U.K. total of U.S. $18,700 million at the end of fiscal 1969, and a U.S. figure of U.S. $78,100 million at the end of fiscal 1970.[116]

As can be seen from Appendix V, the main category of Japanese investment overseas has been in the area of securing raw material supplies. But manufacturing investment (28 per cent of the total) also plays a big part;

most of this is in light industry. However, there has been a third sector which should not be ignored: investment in marketing, which has been an essential factor in promoting and sustaining Japanese exports, particularly in other advanced capitalist countries.

Over the period 1951–69 almost half of all Japanese investment in North America went into marketing subsidiaries.[117] The structure of Japan's overseas investment was directly functional to the overall type of economic growth selected. High investment in Japan's main export area directly stimulated domestic production, while relatively low investment in manufacturing overseas during a certain stage (until the end of the sixties) also worked to protect domestic production. Relatively low investment in the sources of raw materials also cut down on multi-national ties both outside and inside Japan and helped ward off foreign pressure to invest in Japan, as well as aiding Tokyo to protect its reserves.

The effectiveness of the investment in marketing in North America was soon proven, perhaps too well. In the early seventies, as soon as Japanese exports to the United States became a threat to domestic U.S. interests, Washington launched a strong counter-offensive. In view of widespread misapprehensions about Japanese exports,[118] especially to the United States, it is worth examining this aspect more closely.

Trade between Japan and the United States is extremely important to both countries. Japan regularly sends about one-third of its exports to the United States. In 1970 these goods accounted for 16 per cent of U.S. imports, up from 10 per cent in 1965.[119] Japan's dependence on the United States as a market is therefore much greater than that of the United States on Japan as a source of imports. This factor is important in considering Japan's attitude towards U.S. restrictions on Japanese exports. In addition, for nineteen years, from 1945 until 1964, Japan had a trading deficit with the United States. Trade was roughly in balance for the next three years, from 1965 to 1967. It was only in 1968 that Japan first ran a sizeable surplus with the United States—U.S. $1.1 million for the year. From 1951 to 1970 total trade between the two countries added up to a deficit on the Japanese side. Only in 1971 did Japan go into overall surplus. Japan's surplus in that year alone was $3,206 million, and the figure was $4,115 million in 1972, accounting for 50 and 60 per cent, respectively, of the total U.S. trade deficits for 1971 and 1972.[120]

In mid-1971 the United States put a 10 per cent surcharge on imports. At the time much play was made about Japan allegedly abusing the principles of free trade. But was this really the case? In 1970, 20 per cent of Japan's exports to the United States were subject to restriction, and this figure had risen to 23 per cent in the first half of 1971. By 1971 the United States had reversed the situation as regards restrictions on imports vis-à-vis Japan (see Table 8). The U.S. also had higher tariff barriers than Japan (or the EEC) (see Table 9).

TABLE 8

NUMBER OF RESTRICTED IMPORT ITEMS OF MAJOR COUNTRIES

Year	U.S.	U.K.	W. Germany	Japan
1963	7	112	87	132
1971	132	69	63	40*

* Reduced to 34 by April 1972.

SOURCE: MITI, *Comparative Data of Economy Between U.S. and Japan* (Tokyo, MITI, 1972), p. 7, cited by Fuse, "Japan's Economy in the 70's," p. 73.

TABLE 9

AVERAGE TARIFF RATES
(arithmetic average)

Subject to Duties

U.S.A.	10.9 per cent
Japan	10.1 per cent
EEC	6.8 per cent

Tariff Rates of over 20 Per Cent on Imports

U.S.A.	12.0 per cent
Japan	4.9 per cent

SOURCE: Shintaro Hayashi, *Japan's Trade and Industrial Policy* (Tokyo, International Economic Affairs Department, Ministry of International Trade and Industry, 1971), p. 18, cited by Fuse, "Japan's Economy in the 70's," p. 74.

In addition to these tariff barriers, there have been major non-tariff impediments, such as the U.S.-imposed "voluntary export quotas." Moreover, Japanese industry is vulnerable to pressure from the U.S. companies which control many of its supplies of raw materials. Other pressures, such as "price cartels," restriction of production, unilateral shifts in the prices of materials or discrimination against Japanese firms in supplies all affect Japan's ability to trade competitively. This is the context for Japan's nervousness about its international trade.

Another factor is that by 1970 the EEC was the biggest trading entity in the world. Its economy was growing faster than that of the United States, and the increase in the EEC's imports was the number one factor in the growth of world trade during this period. Japan thus found itself sending the biggest single proportion of its exports to the number two importing entity whose economy was growing slower than the main world trading bloc, to which Japan was sending a fairly small proportion of its exports, and which was showing increasing signs of restrictive practices towards Japanese goods.[121]

Yet, by far the most important fact about Japan's export trade is not the relatively small effect it is having on the economies of the rich capitalist countries, but the much deeper damage it is inflicting on the countries of Southeast Asia. OECD figures show that the area with which Japan has by far the most favourable unbalanced trade is Southeast Asia. In 1971 Japan's average monthly exports (f.o.b.) to Southeast Asia came to U.S. $403.5 million, while its imports (c.i.f.) from the same area came to only U.S. $232.04 million.[122] Thailand, Taiwan and south Korea, for example, all imported goods from Japan to more than double the value of their exports there.[123] Already by 1968 Japan was accounting for more than 40 per cent of the imports of both Taiwan and south Korea, and over 35 per cent in the case of Thailand.[124] These very high levels of dependency have important strategic, political and social ramifications. Most of these countries have no visible means to right their indebtedness vis-à-vis Japan. Loans and interest payments pile up. Foreign encroachment on the economies increases. Once again, Japan's giant trading companies play an important role. In Taiwan they control over 50 per cent of the territory's foreign trade and much of its internal commerce as well.

IMPERIALISM, MILITARISM AND FOREIGN RELATIONS

The Japan–United States Relationship

Throughout the postwar period Japan has been locked into a subordinate alliance with the world's leading imperialist power, the United States of America. For most of the period this relationship has been very close on all fronts, political, military and economic. At least till 1971 Tokyo trailed along behind Washington on all major international issues. In military affairs Tokyo remains very much a subordinate of the United States. It is at the economic level that contradictions have been most acute.

Analysis of U.S.-Japan relations since 1945 has often been vitiated by economic determinism. But it is important to note that the real economic contradictions between the two countries have not been reflected in an unmediated manner at the political and military levels. To some extent this is because the economic contradictions have not usually been so acute as most observers have thought. But questionable assessments may also spring from a failure to understand the *essence* of the imperialist relationship between the United States and Japan.

The U.S. relationship towards Japan in the postwar period can not be reduced simply to the level of intentions. But it is also vital to balance an assessment of the *strategy* of imperialism with the contradictions which it has detonated.[125] When the United States took the strategic decision to build Japan back up as a major economic bastion in Asia, this was not simply to turn it into a "puppet"; rather it was to create a controlled, but strong, ally whose power and responsibilities would grow as its economy expanded. Utilizing its powerful position as the occupying force, the United States carried out a double-barreled operation. On the one hand, with heavy political support from the State Department, U.S. interests got a stranglehold on Japan's oil system. On the other hand, the U.S. ruling class as a whole strongly encouraged Japan's economic expansion. For the entire postwar period the United States has been engaged in large-scale military and political activities in East Asia which have required sizeable logistic support. The United States actively assisted Japan's economic growth as the *indispensable* source of supplies, initially, and, later, as economic and political ally.[126]

This is the context within which the economic contradictions of the early 1970s must be set. While these economic contradictions have had very little effect at the political and military levels, it is worth looking briefly at the United States's moves to realign its position vis-à-vis Japan in the early 1970s, and the effects of these moves on the political and economic situation of Japan.

It was in 1970–71, as the U.S. economy was moving very slowly compared to both the EEC and Japan, that America began to mount a full-scale campaign. This had several aspects, of which U.S. restrictions on Japanese exports were only the most publicized.[127] The other aspect of the American drive was to force Japan further to "liberalize" its domestic economy. The United States sought a further integration of the two countries' economies and a relative improvement in the position of the U.S. economy compared with that of Japan. Paradoxically, the U.S. moves were designed *both* to slow down the Japanese economy *and* to hitch the United States more closely to Japan's faster growth rate.[128]

Washington demanded that Tokyo make it easier for foreign capital to invest in Japanese manufacturing,[129] and allow greater access to the distribution sector, seen as crucial to bigger sales of American consumer goods, especially agricultural products, foodstuffs and soft drinks.[130] Although foreign capital did not enter the country at anything like the rate some foreign observers expected (partly because it was already there in the key sectors, partly because of skilful blocking by Japanese capital, partly because the big rises in wage costs in Japan diminished the projected relative advantages of moving to Japan), the years 1971–73 saw a definite, if relative, "internal" internationalization of the Japanese economy.

At the same time, Japan was engaged in rapid "external" internationalization. Its greatly increased exports necessitated further major expansion of its marketing, distribution and banking systems overseas.[131] The relatively sudden awareness of Japan's weak position regarding access to raw materials brought about an acceleration in its activities overseas, and further subordinate alliances with the giant trans-national corporations.

The internationalization of the economy was thus a two-sided process. Politically, the combination of increased overseas activity involving the

hitherto "national" Japanese giants in unprecedentedly integrated relationships with the U.S. trans-nationals and the greater power of foreign capital
inside Japan has caused major problems for the ruling class. Fractions of
the bourgeoisie have made politico-economic options on the basis of
inextricable long-term liaisons with non-Japanese interests. The oil crisis
and the subsequent upheavals within the ruling class revealed deep fissures
within the bourgeoisie.[132]

On the economic front, this internationalization will increase Japan's
vulnerability as well as its power. After an initial period when Japan may
be able to make use of its greater dynamism and alacrity, the net effect of
the internationalization of the economy, linking Japan more closely into
the rest of the more sluggish capitalist bloc, is likely to contribute towards
a slowing of Japan's growth rate.[133]

The Japanese Military

After 1945 the United States pressed Japan into its present position as
the Far Eastern arsenal of imperialism and a major supporting military
power. The United States first preserved a core of the military apparatus
and then oversaw the restoration of sizeable armed forces.[134] Japan, for
its part, accepted the American military demands as part of the package
involved in the overall alliance. In many areas, such as Korea, the interests
of Tokyo and Washington have closely coincided. Yet, while part of the
U.S.-led alliance, Japan has also been developing a military capacity
centred on its own specific counter-revolutionary interests. This includes
the ability to suppress domestic revolution; to intervene against revolution
in Korea; and to "show the flag" and meddle in areas of strategic-economic
importance, especially along the oil supply lines to Japan.

The prerequisite for a strong military is a strong economic base with a
large armaments sector. The fact that the United States restored Japanese
industry along heavily military-oriented lines[135] was long masked by several
factors, including misleading economic statistics and the low profile
adopted internationally by the Japanese military. Especially from the 1950s
on, Japan came to serve three interconnected functions in the military
field. It was, first, the major supplier in the Far East for the U.S. armed
forces. Second, it manufactured a very high proportion of the arms and
other goods needed for its own military. Third, it supplied a wide range of
military equipment to America's client regimes in Asia. Japan was forced
into the U.S. "standard gauge" in all the main areas of arms production.
Thus, while Japan became subordinate to U.S. patents and technology, for
which it had to pay heavily, this probably resulted in a net "saving"
compared with the expenses of a go-it-alone weapons system (which could
never have had such a large market). The savings cover not only actual

munitions, but also a wide range of machinery, the chemical industry and electronics. Military research and development costs have thus been low, which has helped to keep the arms budget down.

Measuring the military budget in terms of the GNP is not satisfactory.[136] From a *political* viewpoint, it is the *relative* strength of Japan which affects its Southeast Asian neighbours. Already in 1970 a U.S. Congressional committee estimated the Japanese military establishment as the sixth largest in the world.[137] Its firepower is greater than that of the Imperial Army during the Second World War. It has a high-technology air force and navy and a heavily over-officered ratio in all three services, allowing for rapid expansion. It has reached the threshold of becoming a nuclear power, with a high capacity in rocketry and delivery systems.[138] Several factors demand attention.

The *rate* at which the military budgets have been growing is enormous. The Fourth Defence Build-Up Plan, covering the years 1972–76, stands at ¥4,630 billion formally, but is scheduled to rise to at least ¥5,100 billion with price rises and personnel costs.[139] This figure is over twice the size of the Third Plan (1967–70), ¥2,450 billion. This is a rate of increase unprecedented in any major economy in the world since 1945. The Fifth Plan (1977–81) is likely to run to ¥11,000–12,000 billion, or over double again, and it has been suggested by the authoritative *Oriental Economist* that Japanese military leaders are planning the Fourth and Fifth Plans together.[140] Even this budget probably represents less than half the actual expenditure on military and military-related areas such as airport maintenance, numerous aspects of arms production and suchlike.[141] In addition, over-production in key areas of the economy, in combination with a situation where the military-industrial complex is extremely strong vis-à-vis "civilian" authority[142] is likely to increase pressures from businesses for expanded munitions production, particularly if industrial production is forced to slow down.

The ruling group has also been fostering the restoration of militarism and military thinking.[143] Such activity covers a vast area from censoring schoolbooks to altering the school curriculum, to the campaign to change the Constitution and strengthen Tennōism. Some of these activities, such as moves to change the Constitution or reform the school curriculum, are concrete and easy to pin down. Others are less tangible, but nonetheless real. The regime's moves since the preparation for the Meiji Centenary (in 1968) in every area of culture indicate a drive towards rebuilding a highly authoritarian system. This is especially important since popular opposition to militarism has up to now exercised a restraining influence. Though popular opposition to rearmament has not prevented the regime from breaking Article 9 of the Constitution[144] and restoring the military, domestic as well as foreign opposition has been a restraining factor. Militaristic films, glorification of the Imperial Army and Navy, refurbishing the

Emperor and his ancestors, along with a touch of racism and plenty of reactionary education all contribute to altering the climate.

The possibility of renewed Japanese activity abroad is not a fantasy. There were large-scale Japanese activities during the 1950–53 Korean War and exchange visits and training schemes since then. There were Japanese "observer" missions with U.S. pilots in Vietnam.[145] Calls for military "protection" for Japanese ships and investments have come from the top echelons of both business and government. In autumn 1970 Nakasone Yasuhiro, the author of the Fourth Defence Build-Up Plan and of the 1970 government White Paper on Defence, stated: "Japan will actively invest her capital in Southeast Asia and will own sizeable assets in this area. This will give rise to rights and interests and a vital frontier. In order to defend them, Japan will eventually require military strength."[146] A similar opinion was put, more bluntly, by Herman Kahn: "This is Japan's natural area of expansion. If you have a dynamic country like Japan with an economic backwater area which is relatively primitive and undefended, the idea of taking over is as natural as Americans taking over what is now the western United States. . . . If necessary, with troops."[147]

With strong revolutionary movements in many of Japan's neighbours, and mass hostility to Japanese militarism at home and abroad, the balance of forces in the area is not favourable to a new wave of aggression from Japan. However, the point "is not that Japan is about to launch some military adventure today. Rather, a continuation of developing tendencies means that a broadening of Japan's military role in Asia is an all too likely prospect."[148] Fear of this threat is realistic, and can hardly be dispelled by the combination of authoritarian moves inside Japan, a hugely increased arms budget, and the steep rise in Japanese economic interests in Southeast Asia which, according to Nakasone, give Japan "rights" and which will "eventually require military strength."

Japanese Imperialism and East Asia

As Douglas MacArthur predicted, East Asia has been the main area of politico-military activity by world imperialism since the end of World War II. This is in spite of the greater importance of other areas of the globe from a more strictly economic and profit point of view.[149]

The geo-political situation in East Asia is quite different from that in Europe. Germany, for example, was contiguous to a number of other important capitalist countries with which it could be integrated in many ways; U.S. imperialism did not delegate to Germany anything like the responsibility it delegated to Japan. The relative isolation of Japan from other capitalist countries is one factor. Another, complementary and even more important, is the strength of the revolutionary movement on the continent of Asia, right opposite Japan. Whereas in Europe imperialism was confronted with a weak U.S.S.R., following a very cautious line of self-protection, in Asia the revolutionary movement has been advancing continuously since the end of the Second World War—in China, Korea, Vietnam, Laos and Cambodia, with major episodes of armed revolutionary struggle in Malaya and Malaysia, Thailand and the Philippines.

The U.S.-Japanese alliance represents something new for both Japanese imperialism specifically and world imperialism in general. For Japan, the U.S. umbrella provided the chance to rebuild its economy to the point where it would have a much more powerful economy than its neighbours, the Japanese people would have a very much higher standard of living, and the East Asian countries would be forced back into a position of dependence. But, whereas up to 1945 Japan accomplished this with a combined operation involving investment, trade and military intervention, in the postwar era it has been mainly the United States (along with some of its allies) which provided the military arm and the initial investment money; Japan's imperialist position has rested very much on its dominance in trading relationships, with investment playing a much smaller role, at any rate up to the late 1960s. The form of Japanese imperialism in Asia has been largely conditioned by the role of its guardian, U.S. imperialism.[150]

The situation in much of East Asia can be described as "double colonialism." To varying extents, territories like south Korea, the unliberated areas of south Vietnam, and Okinawa can all be considered "double colonies." In Korea and Vietnam there is a division of labour between the two imperialist powers: the United States has provided the military, while Japan has played the supporting economic role. Okinawa, though formally restored to Japan in 1972, still in effect functions as a joint colony from both economic and military standpoints.[151]

Obviously the Japanese and American bourgeoisies have the same goal—to prevent further revolution in East Asia. And, though they engage in joint measures towards this common goal, it is analytically useful to distinguish Japan's role in support operations for U.S. imperialism from its role as an imperialist power in its own right. For, within the overall context of suppressing revolution, the two bourgeoisies have specific interests of their own.

In the case of Korea, a former colony[152] and the country geographically closest to Japan, Tokyo's intervention against the revolution in the early 1950s mainly took the form of extensive but (with some exceptions) non-combat support for the imperialist forces. As the Japanese military expanded and a pro-Japanese regime was installed in Seoul in 1961 for the first time since the end of World War II, Japan began to develop military plans vis-à-vis Korea in overall liaison with the United States, but carrying their own momentum. Then, as the war in Indochina began to drain the United States more and more, and some 50,000 Korean mercenaries were shipped off to Vietnam, Washington pressured Tokyo into a large-scale and long-term financial role in south Korea—a direct result of the situation in Indochina and of the relative weakness of both the United States and of its Korean satellite army. Some 60,000 U.S. troops were stationed in Korea to ensure "stability." Japanese economic support for the United States in Korea was very valuable to Washington, while Tokyo derived considerable advantage from America's work.[153]

As for the U.S. war against Indochina, Japan served as the base for many operations, ranging from the manufacture of napalm and "smart" bombs to providing repair facilities for vehicles and tanks, and airfields for bombing missions direct to Vietnam, Laos and Cambodia.[154] Japan also intervened more directly by providing at one period most of the crews for the boats ferrying arms and supplies up and down Vietnam at a time when transportation by land was virtually impossible.[155] Japan not only provided munitions to the U.S. forces and its client armies, it also provided the consumer goods and the retailing services which played a major role in consolidating the grander U.S. schemes for demobilizing the revolution through "urbanization." As the Americans bombed more and more people either to their death or out of the rural areas, survivors flooded into the towns where the most conspicuous consumer goods were Japanese transistors and motor bikes. As well as saying that Americans used Japanese to supply them with bombs, one could say Japanese used Americans to drop Japanese bombs, and blast the survivors onto Japanese-made bikes. This was not only good business for Japanese companies; it was politically useful to the United States. Much the same support role of providing the goods to consumerize a newly urbanized population has been played in other countries in the area, such as Thailand and, to a somewhat lesser extent, in the Philippines.[156]

The support role for the United States here clearly overlaps with Japan's activities as an imperialist power in its own right. Japan's strength is powerfully indicated by the trade figures, which show most of the Southeast Asian countries running very large, and growing, trade deficits with Japan. An Asian Development Bank study of 1970 estimated that by 1980, 53 per cent of the exports of nine Southeast Asian countries would be going to Japan.[157] In other words, the area as a whole will be both heavily dependent on Japan as a market, and heavily indebted to it in a long-term bind. Important political and strategic results are likely to flow from such an unbalanced economic relationship. Increased Japanese investment may appear to cause the trading imbalance to be reduced after a time, but this can be accomplished only at the expense of the Southeast Asian countries in the long run.

Japan's largest single investment in Korea is exemplary. The giant Pohang Steel Works will provide Japan with the "industrial capacity both for mercenary operations in other Asian theaters and for waging "limited" warfare against North Korea."[158] The steel works were built in General Pak's political fief, where he is a large landowner and the Pohang project reportedly functions as conduit for funds from Japanese big business to bolster Pak's personal position. In one respect, of course, Pohang will be a "rival" to Japanese industry, since it will mean that steel (and arms) can be manufactured in Korea. But such investments are necessary for both political and economic reasons. Politically, Japan has to seek to strengthen a counter-revolutionary regime in Seoul. Economically, Japanese capitalism has to seek to stimulate capitalism on its periphery and thus enlarge its own markets. Japan's relationship with Southeast Asia bears many of the same features as America's relationship with Japan in the early postwar period.[159]

The nature of Japanese imperialism has been obscured by several factors. One is the U.S. umbrella. After the long war by Japan against the peoples of Asia, both Washington and Tokyo realized it was advisable for the latter to stay in the background playing a support role. Japan was thus able to expand in the shadows. At least up till the "Nixon shocks" of 1971, the Japanese regime generally welcomed this obscurity, which had definite advantages. A second factor was Japan's relatively low level of investment abroad, which was too often equated with a lack of financial and commercial leverage. Externally, the main feature of Japanese imperialism throughout the period up to 1970–71 was trade. And the search for markets must continue at a very high rate. The nature of the regime does not allow it to raise domestic purchasing power beyond a certain pace. In addition, many of the changes which would be required to bring about a really big rise in domestic purchasing would involve such alterations to the society that they cannot reasonably be expected within the next decade, at least under a big business regime. Japan also feels that it is entitled to raise its exports since, relative to GNP, they are low. (Japan's growth has not been export-led, as West Germany's was.) The search for markets will therefore continue as a crucial determinant in Japan's political activities. The situation is especially critical on this front since both the EEC and the United States are toying with various protectionist measures. In the present crisis phase of capitalism it is hard to see either the EEC or the United States endorsing free trade in practice. The two areas where Japan seems likely to try most to increase its exports are the socialist bloc and Southeast Asia.

Although trade seems destined to continue playing the main role, investment is not unimportant. In the late 1960s and early 1970s Japan had a large balance of payments surplus and accumulated reserves which at one point officially totalled almost U.S. $20 billion.[160] With these large reserves and desiring to have some control over its raw material supplies Japan increased its overseas investment very swiftly in the years around 1970. Greatly increased payments for oil imports seem likely to slow down the rate of Japan's investment abroad; nonetheless, Southeast Asia seems likely to remain a leading target area for what investment there is.[161]

Rather than try to survey the whole field, two examples may indicate possible developments. The first concerns Indochina. Especially from the late 1960s on, Japanese interests began preparing detailed studies on investment schemes for the "postwar" period. These preparations bore fruit in summer 1973 when it was announced that the Saigon regime was turning to the Japanese firm of Mitsui to draw up a blueprint for a U.S. $200 million "Japanese-dominated industrial zone" at the former U.S. base at Cam Ranh Bay.[162]

The second involves the island of New Guinea. This vast territory, the second largest island in the world, is divided into two parts: the western half is part of Indonesia (West Irian); the eastern half, Papua New Guinea (P.N.G.), was administered by Australia, obtaining self-government in December 1973. P.N.G. is the largest ungrabbed area in Asia, and surveys indicate it is one of the richest places on the globe. Japan took a keen interest in the colony as independence came nearer. But some of the Japanese suggestions were a bit startling. The president of Mitsui Mining and Smelting suggested that Japan should acquire a fifty-year "development mandate" over the whole island (including the Indonesian half) under which, in return for "developing" the island, Japan would be free to use its raw materials for half a century.[163] Prior to this Nagano Shigeo, chairman of Nippon Steel and a member of Sanken, had proposed that Japan buy P.N.G outright. This suggestion was reportedly vetoed by the Foreign Ministry in Tokyo. The P.N.G. case was perhaps an extreme one. But these proposals give an indication of big business thinking, which is dominated by a desire to have access to raw material supplies with as little interference as possible. The prime goals are very long term deals. More nuanced methods of purchase can be deployed in the ministries and nightclubs of Southeast Asia where Alaska-style bids might be considered rather out of date.

Nagano's blunt suggestion reflects an important weakness in the international strategy of the Japanese bourgeoisie—its lack of an effective diplomacy. Japan's international relations for most of the postwar period reflected the direct economic interests of big business. However the deterioration of the imperialist position in Asia in the late sixties and early seventies pushed Tokyo, like Washington, towards an accommodation with China. Such an accommodation threatened to conflict much more directly with Japanese business interests than it did with American. The 1971 "Nixon shocks" led to Japanese recognition of China in 1972. And, in turn, recognition of China exerted pressure on Tokyo to try to settle relations with the U.S.S.R. This meant renewed attempts to agree on terms for Siberian operations which Moscow has been tying to some settlement of the territorial dispute over what Japan calls "the Northern islands."[164]

While the "Nixon shocks" caused a major spurt of diplomatic activity on Tokyo's part which included some apparent shifts of emphasis, Japanese capital has continued very much on its original course, consolidating its bases in neighbouring countries ruled by conservative regimes, especially

Taiwan and south Korea. Diplomacy operates both as a mask and as a means of seeking out real channels for implementing policies favourable to a nation's ruling class. Diplomatic relations between Tokyo and Peking do not mean the breaking of the economic alliance between the ruling groups in Tokyo and Taipei, even though this alliance may have to take new forms. Likewise, while edging towards an improvement in relations with Pyongyang, the Japanese ruling class was simultaneously working (and paying) to strengthen the Pak dictatorship in Seoul. This was in line with the general policy of consolidating capitalism in south Korea through perpetuating the division of the country (the "two Koreas" policy).

The period since the "Nixon shocks" of mid-1971 has shown that, in spite of the severe buffeting which Washington-Tokyo relations suffered, the essence of the alliance is untouched. What the "Nixon shocks" did to Japan was to galvanize the regime into multilateralizing its international relations. The subsequent flurry of activity produced meagre results. A substantial improvement of relations with China is hard to envisage, since China can not be interested in consolidating the rule of big capital in Tokyo, least of all if a sizeable sector of it continues to support Chiang Kai-shek.[165] Nor can the Soviet Union be expected to take kindly to Japanese revanchism about the "Northern islands." Moreover, Tanaka's trip to Southeast Asia in January 1974 showed, if evidence were needed, that Japanese imperialism was not a popular phenomenon in the area.

Put another way, this reflects the fact that the regime can operate only according to the logic of its own class interests, which necessitate alliances with repressive regimes, most of them outright military or quasi-military dictatorships. Under its present regime, Japan can be expected to reinforce its economic grip on south Korea and Taiwan, while on the diplomatic front it tries to develop a closer liaison with Indonesia and Australia— what has been called the "Pacific maritime triangle."[166] This would seem to be the logical tactic. Indonesia is by far the largest nation in Southeast Asia, with 125 million inhabitants, vast natural resources and a pliable junta. Australia, though having a much smaller population, has large resources (both mineral and agricultural), high domestic purchasing power —and a Caucasian government. The advent of the Tanaka and Whitlam regimes to power in 1972 produced a rapid multiplication of visits between Tokyo, Djakarta and Canberra. This "triangular" tactic would seem to offer the Japanese bourgeoisie better chances than one relying heavily on the smaller and more vulnerable regimes nearer home. To some extent, too, it represents a counter-weight to total reliance on the United States and to concepts such as the "Pacific Rim" strategy which, given U.S. power on *both* sides of the Pacific Ocean, could only perpetuate Japan's sub-ordination.[167]

But closer links with the Suharto dictatorship, like the plans to plunder Papua New Guinea, are a far cry from anything that could be called friendship with the peoples of Asia, Japan's neighbours. The inexorable dynamic of economic and class interests can not simply be conjured away by diplomacy. The type of economic "development" being promoted inside Japan, with its concomitant demands for raw materials and markets, requires a structurally unequal relationship with the Southeast Asian countries, in which the Japanese bourgeoisie must continue to oppose revolutionary change.[168] Unequal development requires imperialism. It is on the common ground of destroying Japanese imperialism that the class struggle inside Japan and the revolutionary struggles in Southeast Asia must one day meet.

APPENDIX I

Some Statistical Data
on Higher Education

TABLE A

GROWTH OF UNIVERSITIES

	No. of universities	Teachers	Students
1873	29	180	4,263
1898	106	2,262	31,341
1923	327	11,223	145,405
1953	461	57,898	536,087
1960	525	74,677	711,618
1967 (May 1)	874	133,464	1,429,171

SOURCE: OECD, *Reviews of National Policies for Education, Japan* (Paris, Organization for Economic Co-operation and Development, 1971) [henceforth: OECD, *Education: Japan,* 1971], p. 69, citing Government of Japan, *Education in 1967, Japan,* 1970.

TABLE B

DISTRIBUTION OF STUDENTS BY TYPE OF UNIVERSITY

	1963	1964	1965	1966	1967
National	27.1	26.4	25.4	24.6	23.7
Public	4.4	4.2	4.1	4.1	3.9
Private	68.5	69.4	70.5	71.6	72.4
Total	100.0	100.0	100.0	100.0*	100.0

* Total in source adds up to more than 100.0.

SOURCE: OECD, *Education: Japan,* 1971, p. 70.

In 1965 Japanese students and their families in private institutions were paying a larger amount for education than their counterparts in Britain or Germany, which then had available double the consumption expenditure per capita (OECD, *Education: Japan,* 1971, p. 159).

TABLE C

HIGHER EDUCATION RECURRENT EXPENDITURE (¥1,000)

	A. Expenditure per student	B. National income per capita	A:B
Japan (1965)	143*	255	.56
U.S.A. (1965)	805	943	.85
U.K. (1965)	818	515	1.60
W. Germany (1959)	338	396	.86

* Average for all universities. The per student figure for national/public universities is four to five times that of private universities.

SOURCE: OECD, *Education: Japan,* 1971, p. 75.

TABLE D

COMPARISON OF NATIONAL, PUBLIC AND PRIVATE UNIVERSITIES

	National	Public	Private
Teachers per student	0.119	0.115	0.039
Teacher salaries per student	127,158	112,404	36,371
Expenditure per student:			
medicine	889		787
languages	156		97
commerce	215		43
Proportion of total annual expenditure:			
a) Recurrent	63%		53%
b) Capital	37%		47%
Fees paid per student, 1965	15,000		77,000
Proportion of recurrent expenditure covered by fees	5%		92%
State and local government support relative to total expenditure	97.2%		2.1%

SOURCE: OECD, *Education: Japan,* 1971, p. 77; cf. Table on Income and Expenditure in Private Institutions 1966–1967, *ibid.,* p. 159.

TABLE E

POSITION OF TOKYO UNIVERSITY (TŌDAI) AND KYOTO UNIVERSITY (KYŌDAI)

University	Percentage of students at national universities	Percentage of budget for national universities
Tokyo	5.7	10.3
Kyoto	4.7	6.1

SOURCE: Adapted from information in OECD, *Education: Japan,* 1971, p. 77.

In addition, at the time, more than 90 per cent of the faculty of Tokyo University was drawn from its own graduates; the figure for Kyoto was 80–90 per cent. Eleven of the eighteen members of the cabinet came from these two universities—six of them from the Law Faculty at Tokyo University (OECD, *Education: Japan,* 1971, pp. 81–82).

The Multi-Member Constituency System and Loaded Votes

For Lower House elections, each constituency returns three, four, or five members, depending (in theory) on population size. This means that, unlike in, say, Britain, where each party can enter one candidate in each constituency, subject (more or less) only to its ability to campaign there without detracting from its national effort, in Japan each party has to calculate fairly exactly its likely strength in any constituency where it is strong. Since each voter only has one vote, two or more candidates from the same party may draw votes away from each other and thus let another party's candidate get in, even though the latter party may have less votes altogether than the party with two candidates who split the party vote. Even the LDP, therefore, runs less candidates than there are seats in the Lower House. The results of the 1972 General Election (Lower House) were as follows:

Party	Candi-dates ad-vanced	Candi-dates elected	Candi-dates elected 1969	Popular vote (%) 1972	1969	Votes per seat	Gain/ loss
LDP	339	271	288	46.8	47.6	90,600	−0.8
JSP	161	118	90	21.9	21.5	97,200	+0.4
JCP	122	38	14	10.5	6.8	144,600	+3.7
Kōmei	59	29	47	8.5	10.9	152,900	−2.4
DSP	65	19	31	7.0	7.7	192,600	−0.7
Others*	149	16	16	5.3	5.5		−0.2
Total	895	491	486	100.0	100.0		

* Mainly "independents" who affiliate with the LDP after the election (if successful).

SOURCE: adapted from Tosh Lee, "A Tenuous Victory," *JI*, Vol. 8, No. 1 (Winter 1973), Table 1, p. 7.

As is obvious from this, the LDP obtains far more seats than its popular vote, proportionately. The disparity in the 1967 and 1969 general elections was as follows:

| | 1967 | | 1969 | |
Party	Vote (%)	Seats (%)	Vote (%)	Seats (%)
LDP	48.8	57.0	47.6	59.2
JSP	27.9	28.8	21.4	18.5
DSP	7.4	6.2	7.7	6.4
Kōmei	5.4	5.1	10.9	9.7
JCP	4.8	1.0	6.8	2.9

The main fact is clear: the LDP has held a majority of seats with a minority of the vote. The main element in this has been the loaded voting. The constituencies were established on the basis of a postwar census. The result is that rural votes are worth much more than urban votes in terms of seats: the spread can be more than 4:1. In other words, an LDP candidate may win a Diet seat from a rural constituency with, say, 30,000 votes, while, say, a JCP or JSP candidate fails to win a seat from an urban constituency where he or she has polled more than four times that number of votes.

APPENDIX III
Foreign Investment in Japan

A firm is designated as foreign-affiliated by the Japanese government when 20 per cent or more of its capital stock is in foreign hands. Statistics on foreign investment in Japan tend to deal only with these firms. The value of this yardstick is severely limited, for the reasons explained in note 102, pages 422–23 below, in particular since owned capital frequently accounts for 20 per cent or less of a company's total assets. Furthermore, as the well-informed John Roberts stresses, both the Japanese government and foreign investors go to great lengths to conceal the real extent of foreign investment.

A June 1972 survey by the Ministry of International Trade and Industry found that of the 1,176 foreign-affiliated companies, 54 per cent were tied up with U.S. firms. The multinationals played a leading role, accounting for 216 of the affiliates. Of the top 200 U.S. mining and manufacturing firms, 94 were represented, as were 15 of the 79 largest non-Japanese firms outside the United States. The 216 affiliates of the multinationals accounted for nearly 80 per cent of the sales of all the foreign-affiliated companies, and the top 15 accounted for 60 per cent of sales and 56 per cent of profits.

Attempting to assess the real extent of foreign capital in Japan, Roberts noted in 1973 that "foreign holdings (including portfolio) of Japanese shares listed on the Tokyo exchanges amount to 3.7% of the total number": if evenly distributed among stock of all price levels, the value of these would then have been about $5.4 billion. But, since foreigners hold a larger proportion of the lending stocks, Roberts calculates that the total value is probably greater.

MITI gives the total assets of foreign-affiliated companies in 1972 as $14.7 billion, of which $11.7 billion was in industry. Including hidden assets and foreign equities in companies which are not listed as "foreign," Roberts gives a qualified total of perhaps as much as $20 billion foreign direct investment ("but this is a very rough guess"). *Survey of Current Business* gives U.S. direct investment as accounting for about one-fifth of total U.S. assets in Japan as of the end of 1970.

The pattern of foreign participation reflects the Japanese regime's long-term concern to keep foreign capital out of certain key sectors. There is very little foreign investment in primary, heavy and strategic industries, or in light industry. Foreign capital does, however, dominate the oil refining industry, with

56 per cent of total sales. Petroleum accounts for 32.5 per cent of all sales by foreign manufacturing firms, with general machinery responsible for 14.2 per cent, electrical machinery 11.9 per cent, rubber 4.8 per cent and non-ferrous metals 4.7 per cent. The U.S. food multinationals have also recently become extremely prominent.

SOURCES: John Roberts, "You Still Can't Have It All," *FEER,* November 25, 1973, pp. 50–54; *ARB,* Vol. 2, No. 3 (August 1972), p. 1106 (a survey of the June 1971 MITI report). Further details in Bix, "Japan: The Roots of Militarism," p. 331 (Table: Foreign Capital Inductions in Japan 1950–1969.)

APPENDIX IV
Japan's Oil and Energy Situation

TABLE A
SUPPLIES OF PRIMARY ENERGY
(in oil equivalents)

	1955	1960	1971
Total (in thousand kilolitres)	56,016	93,749	320,611
Petroleum	11,945	37,422	252,349
Produced in Japan	356	624	867
Imported Crude	9,271	32,879	224,255
Imported Products	2,318	3,919	20,592
Imported LPG*	—	—	3,649

* In thousand tons (LPG: Liquefied Petroleum Gas).

TABLE B
ENERGY SUPPLY
(in percentages)

Source	1955	1960	1971
Petroleum	20.2	37.7	73.5
Coal	49.2	41.5	17.5
Domestic	44.8	34.4	6.3
Imported	4.4	7.1	11.2
Hydro Power	21.2	15.3	6.7
Nuclear Power	—	—	0.6
Others	9.4	5.5	1.7

Table C

JAPAN'S OIL IMPORTS BY AREA AND COUNTRY
OF ORIGIN (1972)
(in percentage of total)

Asian Middle East	80.7	*Africa*	2.4
Iran	37.3	Nigeria	1.7
Saudi Arabia	16.7	Gambia	0.5
Kuwait	8.9	Libya	0.2
Neutral Zone	8.3	*Latin America*	0.3
Abu Dhabi	5.9	Venezuela	0.2
Others	3.6	Others	0.1
Rest of Asia	16.4	*Communist Bloc*	0.2
Indonesia	13.7		
Brunei	2.7		
Others	0.2		

Table D

BREAKDOWN OF JAPAN'S OIL IMPORTS BY SUPPLIER
(second half of 1973)

Source	Percentage	
Caltex	16.9	(Nippon Oil, Koa Oil)
Exxon	13.3	(Toa Nenryo, Kyokuto Oil, General Oil)
Shell	12.1	(Showa Oil, Seibu Oil)
Gulf	9.1	(National Oil Refineries)
Mobil	8.8	
BP	6.7	(National Oil Refineries)
Arabian Oil	5.1	(National Oil Refineries)
Far East Oil	4.5	
CFP*	3.1	(National Oil Refineries)
Abu Dhabi Oil	2.8	
Getty Oil	2.6	(Mitsubishi Oil, Tohoku Oil)
Union Oil	2.5	
Saudi Arabia (DD)†	1.9	
Japan Line	0.7	
U.S.S.R.	0.7	
China	0.7	
Arco	0.5	
Iran (DD)†	0.5	
Occidental	0.4	
Others	7.2	

* CFP: Compagnie Française des Pétroles (holding company of total).

† DD: Direct Deal oil—i.e., purchased directly from producing countries, by-passing the majors' distribution channels.

Source: Yamakawa Akio, "Petroleum and Political Vision: Coming to the Crunch," *Ampo*, No. 19 (Winter 1974). Cf. Muneo Isshiki, "Keeping Pace with Energy Demands," *Investors Chronicle*, September 7, 1973, Supplement, pp. 45–46. Some of Yamakawa's figures for 1971 (see Tables A and B above) do not tally with those given by Isshiki.

APPENDIX V
Japanese Investment Abroad

Like foreign investment in Japan, Japanese investment abroad is not easy to calculate accurately. One reason is the very high percentage which is in the form of loans, which tend to be self-liquidating, unlike equity holdings. Japanese investment in mining in Latin America, for example, was calculated in 1973 to be 95 per cent in the form of loans. A 1972 MITI survey covering data up to the end of 1970 gave loans as accounting for $1,854 million, stock for $1,334 million, direct cash $375 million, and overseas branches for $328 million.

As of late 1973 the total of Japanese overseas investment was calculated at about $7 billion. As of March 31, 1973 the largest share was in resource development (mining, lumber, marine products, etc.): 32.6 per cent of the total. Only 28 per cent went into manufacturing industry, and this was mainly in light industry. Commercial investments accounted for 11.7 per cent of the total, and were mainly in the advanced capitalist countries.

By region, the breakdown was as follows (as of March 31, 1973):

Area	*Percentage of total Japanese investment abroad*
North America	25.5
Asia (excluding Middle East)	23.1
Europe	16.1
Latin America	15.8
South Pacific	8.7
Middle East	8.3
Africa	2.5

As of December 1972 the number of projects per area was as follows:

Area	*Number of Projects*
Asia	2,660
North America	1,695
Latin America	777
Europe	665

In the year to March 31, 1973, the country which attracted the biggest investment from Japan was Britain—$816 million or 34.9 per cent of Japan's total invested abroad in that year. This compares with $356 million in the United

States (15.2 per cent of the total), $218 million in Kuwait, $168 million in Brazil, $147 million in south Korea and $120 million in Indonesia. Estimates of Japan's future investment abroad vary greatly. In the year from March 1972 to March 1973 the figure jumped from less than $4.5 billion to an estimated $7 billion. Estimates compiled before the 1973 crisis generally put forward a figure of $25–30 billion as likely for 1980 (Sebestyen comes down cautiously for about $24–27 billion cumulative total by 1980). In the wake of the 1973 crisis and especially in the light of the dwindling reserves, seriously affected by increased payments for oil and agricultural products, the evidence is that Japan's overseas investment may well slow down, at least for a period.

SOURCES: Charles Sebestyen, *The Outward Urge: Japanese Investment World-Wide* (London, Economist Intelligence Unit, Quarterly Economic Review, Special No. 11 [February 1973]); Y. Kobayashi, "Expanding Investment Overseas," *Investors Chronicle*, September 7, 1973, pp. 11–13; *ARB*, Vol. 2, No. 11 (April 1973); *Observer* (London), March 3, 1974. Further details in Halliday and McCormack, *Japanese Imperialism*, especially chapter 2.

Abbreviations Used in Notes

AAAPSS	*Annals of the American Academy of Political and Social Science*
ACS	*Asian Cultural Studies*
AER	*American Economic Review*
AHA	*Annals of the Hitotsubashi Academy* (from 1960: *Hitotsubashi Journal of Economics*)
AHR	*American Historical Review*
APSR	*American Political Science Review*
ARB	*Asia Research Bulletin*
BCAS	*Bulletin of Concerned Asian Scholars*
CSPSR	*Chinese Social and Political Science Review*
CSSH	*Comparative Studies in Society and History*
DE	*Developing Economies*
EDCC	*Economic Development and Cultural Change*
EEH	*Explorations in Entrepreneurial History*
FA	*Foreign Affairs* (U.S.A.)
FEER	*Far Eastern Economic Review*
FEQ	*Far Eastern Quarterly* (from 1956: *Journal of Asian Studies*)
FES	*Far Eastern Survey*
HJAS	*Harvard Journal of Asiatic Studies*
HJE	*Hitotsubashi Journal of Economics* (formerly: *AHA*)
ISSJ	*International Social Science Journal* (Paris)
JAS	*Journal of Asian Studies* (formerly: *FEQ*)
JCA	*Journal of Contemporary Asia*
JEJ	*Japan Economic Journal*
JHI	*Journal of the History of Ideas*
JI	*Japan Interpreter* (formerly: *Journal of Social and Political Ideas in Japan*)

JLB	*Japan Labor Bulletin*
JMH	*Journal of Modern History*
JQ	*Japan Quarterly*
JSPIJ	*Journal of Social and Political Ideas in Japan* (later: *JI*)
JSR	*Japan Socialist Review*
JWH	*Journal of World History* (*Cahiers d'histoire mondiale*)
KES	*Keio Economic Studies*
KUER	*Kyoto University Economic Review*
MN	*Monumenta Nipponica*
NLR	*New Left Review*
OE	*Oriental Economist*
PA	*Pacific Affairs*
PHR	*Pacific Historical Review*
PIN	*Pacific Imperialism Notebook*
PRJ	*Peace Research in Japan*
RHDGM	*Revue d'histoire de la deuxième guerre mondiale*
S&S	*Science and Society*
SN	*Sohyo News*
TASJ	*Transactions of the Asiatic Society of Japan*
UMOP	*University of Michigan Occasional Papers*
YR	*Yale Review*

Notes

Chapter 1
THE MEIJI STATE

1. Rather than enter in great detail into the controversies about the Meiji Restoration/ Revolution, I have thought it more useful to concentrate on the construction of the Meiji state. It should be said that among Japanese Marxists the "left" tends to stress feudal survivals and argues that there was no bourgeois revolution in the nineteenth century; this group refers to the "Meiji Restoration"; the "right" argues that the Meiji Restoration was a bourgeois revolution which qualifies for the term "Meiji Revolution." The dominant trend in recent Anglo-Saxon scholarship has been the "modernization" line, represented by the Princeton series (see note to John Dower's introduction). The assumptions and methods of this line are criticized and set in context in an excellent brief text by one of Japan's greatest historians, Tōyama Shigeki, in "The Meiji Restoration and the Present Day," *BCAS*, Vol. 2, No. 1 (October 1969), pp. 10–14. Interesting light is also thrown on the "modernization" approach in *JI*, Vol. 6, No. 1 (Spring 1970), a special issue entitled " 'Modern' Man and Modernization."

2. This mission, which contained about half the leading political figures in the new regime, toured America and Europe in the years 1871–73: see Marlene Mayo, "Rationality in the Meiji Restoration: The Iwakura Embassy," in Bernard S. Silberman and H. D. Harootunian, eds., *Modern Japanese Leadership: Transition and Change* (Tucson, University of Arizona Press, 1966); Masakazu Iwata, *Ōkubo Toshimichi: The Bismarck of Japan* (Berkeley and Los Angeles, University of California Press, 1964), pp. 257–58; Sidney Devere Brown, "Ōkubo Toshimichi: His Political and Economic Policies in Early Meiji Japan," *JAS*, Vol. 21, No. 2 (February 1962), p. 190.

3. See Itō's letter of August 11, 1882 to Iwakura in Nobutaka Ike, *The Beginnings of Political Democracy in Japan* (Baltimore, The Johns Hopkins Press, 1950), pp. 175–76. Henceforth: Ike, *Beginnings*.

4. The Tempō period covers 1830–43. The reforms came in the years 1841–43, after a disastrous prolonged famine; the commercial treaties and the convocation of the Diet are discussed below. The dating of the "Restoration" as a whole is controversial; here I am following the suggestion of Toyoda Takeshi ("Revolution française et révolution de Meiji: Etude critique des interprétations de Kosa et de Rono," *Annales Historiques de la Révolution Française*, No. 171 [January–March, 1963], p. 17).

5. For most of the concepts used here a lucid exposition can be found in Nicos Poulantzas, *Political Power and Social Classes* (London, New Left Books, 1973); see also Étienne Balibar, "Self Criticism—An Answer to Questions from 'Theoretical Practice,' " and the exchange round this article (two texts by Antony Cutler) in *Theoretical Practice* (London), No. 7/8 (January 1973); on the transition from feudalism to capitalism (as well as specific texts cited later) see Antony Cutler and John Taylor, "Theoretical Remarks on the Theory of the Transition from Feudalism to Capitalism," *Theoretical Practice*, No. 6 (May 1972)—a review article on Pierre-Philippe Rey,

Sur L'Articulation des Modes de Production (Paris, Centre D'Etudes de Planification Socialiste, Ecole Pratique des Hautes Etudes, 1968).

6. See Glossary.

7. Charles David Sheldon, *The Rise of the Merchant Class in Tokugawa Japan* (Locust Valley, N.Y., J. J. Augustin, 1958), pp. 4–5. Toshio G. Tsukahira, *Feudal Control in Tokugawa Japan: The Sankin Kōtai System* (Cambridge, Mass., Harvard University, East Asian Research Center, 1966), pp. 6–7, details the holdings and major changes; the Tokugawa holdings were mainly in central Honshu along the Pacific coast between Osaka and Mito, but they had some holdings in 48 of the 68 provinces, strategically located to minimize the possibility of an anti-Tokugawa coalition. This core area was either held directly by the Tokugawa family or entrusted to hereditary vassals (*fudai*), the largest of whom became known as *fudai daimyō;* the rest of the country was divided into the realms of the non-Tokugawa lords, usually referred to as the *tozama* or "outside" *daimyō*, concentrated in northern and western Honshu, Shikoku and Kyushu. Note that, contrary to information in some sources, the *tozama daimyō* are not synonymous with the opponents of the Tokugawa at Sekigahara.

8. Tsukahira, *Feudal Control, passim.*

9. Though this interpretation is not universally accepted, it seems to me beyond question that the Tokugawa attempted to protect the dominance of the feudal mode of production. See Kenji Kawano, "Révolution française et Révolution de Meiji: Aspects Economiques et Sociaux," *Annales Historiques de la Révolution Française*, No. 171 (January–March, 1963), p. 4. John Whitney Hall, "The Castle Town and Japan's Modern Urbanization," *FEQ*, Vol. 15, No. 1 (November 1955)—reprinted in John W. Hall and Marius B. Jansen, eds., *Studies in the Institutional History of Early Modern Japan* (Princeton, Princeton University Press, 1968), p. 174—disputes the refeudalization thesis. Information below on the seclusion policy and its antecedents from: Sheldon, *The Rise of the Merchant Class*, chapter 1, especially pp. 21–23; E. Herbert Norman, *Japan's Emergence as a Modern State: Political and Economic Problems of the Meiji Period* (New York, Institute of Pacific Relations, 1940), p. 19; Yosoburo [sic] Takekoshi, *The Economic Aspects of the History of the Civilization of Japan* (London, Allen & Unwin, 1930), Vol. 1, pp. 480–503.

10. Matsuyo Takizawa, *The Penetration of Money Economy in Japan and Its Effects upon Social and Political Institutions* (New York, Columbia University Studies in History, Economics and Law 285, 1927); Sheldon, *Rise of the Merchant Class;* Toyoda Takeshi, *A History of Pre-Meiji Commerce in Japan* (Tokyo, Kokusai Bunka Shinkokai, 1969), esp. chapter 4. For the more general issues of Japanese feudalism, see John Whitney Hall, "Feudalism in Japan—A Reassessment," *CSSH*, Vol. 5, No. 1 (October 1962), reprinted in Hall and Jansen, eds., *Studies in the Institutional History . . .* ; Takeshi Toyoda, "The Character of the Feudal Society in Japan (1)," *AHA*, Vol. 8, No. 1 (October 1957), pp. 29–35.

11. Toyoda, "The Character of the Feudal Society in Japan," p. 31, is good on this (the translation is shaky). For the more general issues concerning the Emperor see Herschel Webb, *The Japanese Imperial Institution in the Tokugawa Period* (New York and London, Columbia University Press, 1968). An extremely stimulating text on the imperial institution, raising numerous themes of ambiguity, myth and manipulation is Masao Yamaguchi, "La structure mythico-théâtrale de la royauté japonaise," *Esprit* (Paris), No. 421 (February 1973), pp. 315–342.

12. On the outcastes, see George De Vos and Hiroshi Wagatsuma, *Japan's Invisible Race: Caste in Culture and Personality* (Berkeley and Los Angeles, University of California Press, 1966). The essays in this volume tend to skate over the Japanese Marxist work on the outcastes and are not politically or theoretically entirely satisfactory; see entry for *burakumin* in Glossary and notes 51 and 57, pp. 334, 335 below. On the general class situation see Barrington Moore, Jr., *Social Origins of Dictatorship and Democracy: Lord and Peasant in the Making of the Modern World* (London, Allen Lane, The Penguin Press, 1967), pp. 230–54; Toyoda, "The Character of the Feudal Society in Japan," pp. 34–35.

13. Ike, *Beginnings*, pp. 12–13.

14. Susan B. Hanley and Kozo Yamamura, "A Quiet Transformation in Tokugawa Economic History," *JAS*, Vol. 30, No. 2 (February 1971), pp. 377–78; Sheldon, *Rise of*

the Merchant Class, p. 5, for population expansion in the period 1600–1730; Yoshi S. Kuno, *Japanese Expansion on the Asiatic Continent* (Berkeley, Northeastern Asia Seminar of the University of California, 1937), Vol. 2, p. 359.

15. Irene B. Taeuber, *The Population of Japan* (Princeton, Princeton University Press, 1958), p. 44, cited by Kazushi Ohkawa and Henry Rosovsky, "A Century of Japanese Economic Growth," in William W. Lockwood, ed., *The State and Economic Enterprise in Japan: Essays in the Political Economy of Growth* (Princeton, Princeton University Press, 1965), p. 54.

16. E. Sydney Crawcour, "The Tokugawa Heritage," in Lockwood, ed., *The State and Economic Enterprise,* p. 25; Crawcour notes that the primary/secondary industry division is certainly unrealistic.

17. Adapated from: Motokazu Kimura, "Fiscal Policy and Industrialization in Japan 1868–1895," *AHA,* Vol. 6, No. 2 (April 1956), p. 13.

18. Norman, *Japan's Emergence,* p. 12.

19. Joseph R. Strayer, "The Tokugawa Period and Japanese Feudalism," in Hall and Jansen, eds., *Studies in the Institutional History . . . ,* p. 6. In addition to the sources cited at note 10 on Japanese feudalism, see also especially E. Herbert Norman, "Andō Shōeki and the Anatomy of Japanese Feudalism," *TASJ,* 3d series, Vol. 2 (December 1949). Andō Shōeki was an early eighteenth-century physician.

20. Hall, "The Castle Town," p. 178. In theory, all land belonged to the Emperor, and was held in trust by the shogun, who parcelled it out among his vassals (Tsukahira, *Feudal Control,* p. 13).

21. Daniel Lloyd Spencer, "Japan's Pre-Perry Preparation for Economic Growth," *American Journal of Economics and Sociology,* Vol. 17, No. 2 (January 1958), p. 197; cf. Sheldon, *Rise of the Merchant Class.*

22. Horie Yasuzo, "The Transformation of the National Economy," *DE,* Vol. 3, No. 4 (December 1965), pp. 416–17; Thomas C. Smith, "Japan's Aristocratic Revolution," *YR,* Vol. 50, No. 3 (Spring 1961), pp. 370–77.

23. Smith, "Japan's Aristocratic Revolution," pp. 373–76; Tsukahira, *Feudal Control,* p. 2; Toyoda, "The Character of the Feudal Society," p. 30.

24. Norman, "Andō Shōeki," p. 113.

25. This is a vast and little studied question. Some elements of analysis on bourgeois culture under the Tokugawa appear in Donald H. Shively, *"Bakufu* versus *Kabuki," HJAS,* Vol. 18, Nos. 3–4 (December 1955) and reprinted in Hall and Jansen, eds., *Studies in the Institutional History . . . ;* Thomas C. Smith, "Old Values and New Techniques in the Modernization of Japan," *FEQ,* Vol. 14, No. 3 (May 1955), pp. 357–58; Howard Hibbett, *The Floating World in Japanese Fiction* (London, Oxford University Press, 1959). Situating remarks on Zen and militarism can be found in D. C. Holtom, *Modern Japan and Shinto Nationalism: A Study of Present-Day Trends in Japanese Religions* (Chicago, University of Chicago Press, 1947, revised ed.), p. 149; Minoru Hashimoto, "Zen Doctrine and Its Influence upon the Samurai Class," *Cultural Nippon* (Tokyo), Vol. 6, No. 1 (March 1938). The post-Restoration cultural rollback is discussed later. One of the most interesting phenomena to appear during the Tokugawa period was the Shingaku movement, which Dore has called "a kind of moral rearmament for adults of the lower classes" (R. P. Dore, *Education in Tokugawa Japan* [London, Routledge & Kegan Paul, 1965], p. 39). The movement is discussed at some length, from a strongly anti-materialist point of view, in Robert N. Bellah, *Tokugawa Religion: The Values of Pre-Industrial Japan* (Glencoe, The Free Press, 1957), pp. 133–77. The Shingaku movement, while strong among the merchant class, and containing *elements* tending to foster bourgeois self-confidence, was essentially a proponent of the "everyone in their place" outlook, exemplified in a statement by Nakazawa Doni: "Crows caw, sparrows chirp, willows are green and cherry blossom pink. Everything is the way it is and the way it should be, and to desire nothing more is the true secret of life" (cited by Dore, *Education in Tokugawa Japan,* p. 238).

26. Albert Craig, "The Restoration Movement in Chōshū," *JAS,* Vol. 18, No. 2 (February 1959), p. 189. Chōshū is in southwest Honshu.

27. The key works are: Albert Craig, *Chōshū in the Meiji Restoration* (Cambridge, Mass., Harvard University Press, 1961); Marius B. Jansen, *Sakamoto Ryōma and the Meiji*

Restoration (Princeton, Princeton University Press, 1961); Yoshio Sakata and John Whitney Hall, "The Motivation of Political Leadership in the Meiji Restoration," *JAS*, Vol. 16, No. 1 (November 1956), pp. 31–50 [Sakata is promoted by Beasley as a kind of exemplar for the anti-Marxists: see W. G. Beasley, *The Meiji Restoration* (Stanford, Stanford University Press and London, Oxford University Press, 1973), pp. 9–10]; on Satsuma, see Robert K. Sakai, "Feudal Society and Modern Leadership in Satsuma-han," *JAS*, Vol. 16, No. 3 (May 1957), pp. 365–76. For the problems of a Marxist definition of a social class, see Poulantzas, *Political Power and Social Classes*, pp. 57–98.

28. *Chōnin* covers both artisans and merchants.
29. Thomas O. Wilkinson, *The Urbanization of Japanese Labor, 1868–1955* (Amherst, University of Massachusetts Press, 1965), p. 28.
30. On the very even development of cities, see Hall, "The Castle Town," pp. 183–84.
31. Yasuzo Horie, "An Outline of the Rise of Modern Capitalism in Japan," *KUER*, Vol. 11, No. 1 (July 1936), p. 101.
32. Crawcour, "The Tokugawa Heritage," p. 41. I am very grateful to Ben Brewster for allowing me to consult his paper, "Pre-Restoration Conditions for Economic Growth in Japan" (manuscript, 1967), which elucidated many issues.
33. E. S. Crawcour, "Changes in Japanese Commerce in the Tokugawa Period," *JAS*, Vol. 22, No. 4 (August 1963), reprinted in Hall and Jansen, eds., *Studies in the Institutional History . . .*, p. 196.
34. Cf. Norman, *Japan's Emergence*, p. 19; Toyoda, *History of Pre-Meiji Commerce*, p. 91.
35. Wilkinson, *Urbanization of Japanese Labor*, p. 32; Norman, *Japan's Emergence*, p. 82; for some qualification, Toyoda, *History of Pre-Meiji Commerce*, p. 91.
36. Arthur T. Von Mehren, "Some Reflections on Japanese Law," *Harvard Law Review*, Vol. 71 (1958), pp. 1486–96; Sheldon, *Rise of the Merchant Class*, pp. 38–39; Poulantzas, *Political Power and Social Classes*, for an excellent exposition of the role of law, a subject inadequately assessed by many Marxists.
37. Ike, *Beginnings*, p. 17; cf. Crawcour, "Changes in Japanese Commerce in the Tokugawa Period," pp. 199–201.
38. Norman, *Japan's Emergence*, p. 50.
39. Sheldon, *Rise of the Merchant Class*, p. 38.
40. Mataji Umemura, "Agriculture and Labour Supply in Japan in the Meiji Era," *DE*, Vol. 3, No. 3 (September 1965), pp. 269–85; reprinted, slightly revised, in Kazushi Ohkawa, Bruce F. Johnston, Hiromitsu Kaneda, eds., *Agriculture and Economic Growth: Japan's Experience* (Tokyo, University Press, 1969).
41. Norman, *Japan's Emergence*, p. 19; Sheldon, *Rise of the Merchant Class*, p. 22. On this, and many other matters, see W. Donald Burton, *The Origins of the Modern Japanese Iron and Steel Industry, with Special Reference to Mito and Kamaishi 1853–1901* (Ph.D. thesis, London University, 1972).
42. Spencer, "Japan's Pre-Perry Preparation for Economic Growth," p. 214.
43. H. K. Takahashi, "Recent Trends of the Studies in Economic History in Japan" (unpublished MS, n.d.), p. 19. Herbert Bix has pointed out to the author how the guild merchant/rural merchant split prefigured the split between privileged and non-privileged merchants that lay at the root of some of the anti-capitalist animus of the later Meiji and early Taishō periods. On the question of absolutism, which crops up at the end of this paragraph, see below.
44. Crawcour, "The Tokugawa Heritage," pp. 36–42, assesses the percentages.
45. Much information on this in Thomas C. Smith, *The Agrarian Origins of Modern Japan* (Stanford, Stanford University Press, 1959); cf. Hanley and Yamamura, "A Quiet Transformation in Tokugawa Economic History." See also below on the Nakamura controversy. Recent Western scholarship has revealed increases in productivity which were not known to earlier writers, and from this have deduced a general improvement in the standard of living of the peasantry as a whole. However, the documentary evidence, such as that assembled by Norman in *Japan's Emergence* and by Borton (Hugh Borton, "Peasant Uprisings in Japan of the Tokugawa Period," *TASJ*, 2d series, Vol. 16 [1938], pp. 1–219), shows that the lot of the peasant was

extremely grim—a fact not revealed by the manipulation of gross economic statistics.

46. Moore, *Social Origins of Dictatorship and Democracy*, p. 255.

47. T. C. Smith, review of Craig, *Chōshū in the Meiji Restoration*, and Jansen, *Sakamoto Ryōma* (see note 27 above), *JAS*, Vol. 21, No. 2 (February 1962), p. 216. Smith's use of the word "journalistic" helps to cover the fact that such a view is "popular" in *political* circles. His conclusion involves a magical approach to history where there are "revolutionary consequences" which are not the product of class struggle.

48. Hideichi Horie, "Revolution and Reform in Meiji Restoration," *KUER*, Vol. 22, No. 1 (April 1952), p. 24; Borton, "Peasant Uprisings." One revolt in 1823, for example, involved 100,000 farmers in one domain—a very large number by any standards.

49. Borton, "Peasant Uprisings," pp. 33–38.

50. *Ibid.*, p. 129; cf. *ibid.*, p. 95.

51. E. Herbert Norman, *Soldier and Peasant in Japan: The Origins of Conscription* (New York, Institute of Pacific Relations, 1943), p. 37. Borton edges close to acknowledging this position when he writes: "Their [the uprisings'] effect upon the downfall of the government had been accumulative during the whole period of the Tokugawa Shoguns" ("Peasant Uprisings," p. 121). In the end, Borton's position boils down to a dismissal of the class character of the uprisings merely on the grounds of the peasantry's consciousness and intentions. But the class nature of events is not determined by subjective criteria such as "consciousness." For some extremely interesting observations on the relationship between "consciousness" and political activism at the time, see E. Herbert Norman, "Mass Hysteria in Japan," *FES*, Vol. 14, No. 6 (March 28, 1945), pp. 65–70. It should be said that some of Norman's conclusions (in *Japan's Emergence* and *Soldier and Peasant*), and the research on which he based them, have since been challenged. Thomas C. Smith, "The Land Tax in the Tokugawa Period," *JAS*, Vol. 18, No. 1 (November 1958), is an example of empirical work which *implicitly* tries to undermine the position exemplified by Norman. Cf. T. C. Smith's review of Craig and Jansen cited at note 47 above.

52. This is largely based on Takahashi, "Recent Trends of the Studies in Economic History in Japan." Takahashi adopts a rather different position on the emergence of wage labour from that set out by T. C. Smith in *The Agrarian Origins* (especially chapter 8).

53. Takahashi, "Recent Trends of the Studies in Economic History in Japan," p. 19.

54. Hideichi Horie, "Revolution and Reform in Meiji Restoration," p. 26.

55. *Ibid.*, p. 28.

56. T. C. Smith's evolutionist account of rural development considers each region as at a more or less developed stage within a general trend. Such an interpretation makes it difficult to understand the role in the Restoration of Satsuma, in particular, which was an extremely "underdeveloped" *han*, where sub-infeudation was maintained until the Restoration (Brewster, "Pre-Restoration Conditions for Economic Growth in Japan").

57. Norman, *Japan's Emergence*, p. 73; cf. Norman, *Soldier and Peasant*, on the urgent need for conscription to build up an army to ensure peasant submission to the new state.

58. Mao Tsetung, "The Bankruptcy of the Idealist Conception of History," *Selected Works of Mao Tsetung* (Peking, Foreign Languages Press, 1967), Vol. 4, p. 455.

59. Sheldon, *Rise of the Merchant Class*, p. 20; G. B. Sansom, *The Western World and Japan: A Study in the Interaction of European and Asiatic Cultures* (London, The Cresset Press, 1950), pp. 177–78; information below from Norman, *Japan's Emergence*, pp. 15–16. Kuno, *Japanese Expansion on the Asiatic Continent*, Vol. 2, covers Japan's contacts during the Tokugawa period.

60. George Alexander Lensen, *The Russian Push Toward Japan: Russo-Japanese Relations, 1697–1875* (Princeton, Princeton University Press, 1959), p. 553.

61. Sansom, *The Western World and Japan*, pp. 212–14, 243–45.

62. Borton, "Peasant Uprisings," p. 86 (apparently referring to the years 1814–36).

63. What is now known as the Ussuri area (Wu-su-li in Chinese) was seized immediately after the Treaty of Aigun. It is these seizures which are at the root of the present Sino-Soviet territorial disputes.

64. William C. Amidon, "The Issue of Sakhalin in Russo-Japanese Relations," *UMOP*, No. 7 (1959).

65. Sansom, *The Western World and Japan*, p. 245.

66. Marius B. Jansen, "Changing Japanese Attitudes Toward Modernization," in Marius B. Jansen, ed., *Changing Japanese Attitudes Toward Modernization* (Princeton, Princeton University Press, 1965), pp. 56–59; R. H. van Gulik, "Kakkaron: A Japanese Echo of the Opium War," *Monumenta Serica*, Vol. 4 (1939), pp. 478–545; C. R. Boxer, *Jan Compagnie in Japan: An Essay on the Cultural, Artistic and Scientific Influence Exercised by the Hollanders in Japan from the Seventeenth to the Nineteenth Century* (The Hague, Martinus Nijhoff, 2d rev. ed., 1950), pp. 185–87 (Appendix V); Hu Sheng, *Imperialism and Chinese Politics* (Peking, Foreign Languages Press, 1955), pp. 14 ff., on the Treaty of Nanking (1842). Cf. Carmen Blacker, *The Japanese Enlightenment: A Study of the Writings of Fukuzawa Yukichi* (Cambridge, Cambridge University Press, 1964), p. 16.

67. As N. I. Konrad has put it, Japan was indebted to the revolutionary spirit of the peoples of China and India, not to Commodore Perry, for aid during the "Meiji Restoration" (N. I. Konrad, "The Centenary of the Japanese Revolution," [Fukuoka, Fukuoka Unesco Association, Third Kyushu International Cultural Conference, 1972], pp. 3–4).

68. "If that double-bolted land, Japan, is ever to become hospitable, it is the whale ship alone to whom the credit will be due" (Herman Melville, *Moby Dick*, Everyman edition, p. 98).

69. See, for example, Sansom, *The Western World and Japan;* it is also covered in the main texts on the Meiji Restoration: see Beasley, *The Meiji Restoration*, pp. 88–98; Paul Akamatsu, *Meiji 1868: Revolution and Counter-Revolution in Japan* (London, Allen & Unwin, 1972), esp. pp. 92–100; on the 1854 Treaty mentioned below, see *ibid.*, pp. 99–100; Sansom, p. 278. There is not space here to go into the specific conjuncture at the time, but it should be noted that the 1858 Treaty signed by Harris was not unconnected with the 1856–58 economic recession in the United States.

70. Akamatsu, *Meiji 1868*, pp. 127–32; John McMaster, "The Japanese Gold Rush of 1859," *JAS*, Vol. 19, No. 3 (May 1960), pp. 273–87.

71. Sansom, *The Western World and Japan*, pp. 279–95; Akamatsu, *Meiji 1868;* H. D. Harootunian, *Toward Restoration: The Growth of Political Consciousness in Tokugawa Japan* (Berkeley, Los Angeles and London, University of California Press, 1970), pp. 38–39.

72. Brewster, "Pre-Restoration Conditions for Economic Growth," p. 15.

73. Thomas C. Smith, "The Introduction of Western Industry to Japan During the Last Years of the Tokugawa Period," *HJAS*, Vol. 11, Nos. 1 and 2 (June 1948), pp. 130–52; cf. Burton, *The Origins of the Modern Japanese Iron and Steel Industry.*

74. Webb, *The Japanese Imperial Institution*, p. 231; the basis on which the Emperor was able to make this intervention, so to speak "out of the past," is examined below.

75. *Ibid.*, pp. 239–47; Herschel Webb, "The Development of an Orthodox Attitude Toward the Imperial Institution in the Nineteenth Century," in Jansen, ed., *Changing Japanese Attitudes Toward Modernization*, p. 178.

76. Akamatsu, *Meiji 1868*, pp. 169–70, for details.

77. See Eijiro Honjo, "Léon Roches and Administrative Reform in the Closing Years of the Tokugawa Regime," *KUER*, Vol. 10, No. 1 (July 1935), pp. 35–53 (Roches was the French envoy). On Chōshū's role, Craig, *Chōshū in the Meiji Restoration;* Roger F. Hackett, *Yamagata Aritomo in the Rise of Modern Japan, 1838–1922* (Cambridge, Mass., Harvard University Press, 1971), pp. 9–49.

78. On the question of absolutism, see A. D. Lublinskaya, "The Contemporary Bourgeois Conception of Absolute Monarchy," *Economy and Society* (London), Vol. 1, No. 1 (February 1972). This is a disputed issue. Many Japanese Marxists use the term "absolutism" or "imperial absolutism" to describe the regime set up after 1868. In such cases, the term is often applied to the regime in existence well into the twentieth century. In my opinion, it is very difficult not to say that at least from about 1900 Japan was a capitalist state, engaged in imperialism—which precludes it being an "absolutist" state. Poulantzas, *Political Power and Social Classes*, pp. 157–67, discusses some of the theoretical questions concerning absolutism as an instrument for handling the transition from feudalism to capitalism in Europe, and denies the term "absolutism" to Bismarckian Germany. A brief comparison between the transitions in Germany and Japan has been adumbrated by Takahashi (H. K. Takahashi, "A

Contribution to the Discussion," in Paul Sweezy et al., eds., *The Transition from Feudalism to Capitalism* (New York, *Science & Society*, 1954), pp. 54–55). Absolutism was used as an instrument to handle the transition in Japan, but this does not make the Meiji state an absolutist one. It was a transitional state with the (imported) features of a capitalist state dominant, using pre-capitalist instruments. On the specific role of the Emperor and of the imperial institution in Japanese "absolutism," see Webb, "The Development of an Orthodox Attitude Toward the Imperial Institution," pp. 188–91, and cf. below.

79. See Craig, *Chōshū in the Meiji Restoration;* Jansen, *Sakamoto Ryōma.*

80. For an excellent theoretical analysis of Gaullism, written right at the start of the Gaullist decade, see Lucio Magri, "Ipotesi sulla dinamica del gollismo," *Nuovi Argomenti* (Rome), Nos. 35–36 (November 1958–February 1959); cf. Moore, *Social Origins of Dictatorship and Democracy, passim;* Poulantzas, *Political Power and Social Classes,* p. 158: "The Structure of the transition in general . . . is specified by a *non-correspondence* between the relation of *property* and the relation of *real appropriation"* (italics in original).

81. As does Thomas C. Smith, "Japan's Aristocratic Revolution."

82. Though the Meiji Restoration was not a straightforward bourgeois revolution, it has some of the characteristics of a bourgeois revolution objectively, since it was a political response to a series of acts by the Western imperialists which thrust Japan into a world economy where the capitalist mode of production was already dominant. Konrad, "The Centenary of the Japanese Revolution," p. 12, sets out some of the domestic reasons why, in his opinion, the Japanese experience qualifies as a "bourgeois revolution." But, as Toyoda stresses, there are several major problems in calling the episode a "bourgeois revolution." Not only was the bourgeoisie relatively inactive in the actual "revolution," but it did not come to power afterwards, except in a long-term coalition with the aristocracy. Moreover, most important, there were no bourgeois assemblies of the kind which appeared during the French Revolution (Toyoda, "Révolution française et révolution de Meiji," p. 21); cf. Norman, *Japan's Emergence,* p. 82.

83. Though, of course, the primary feature of imperialism is the degree of concentration; some observations on this problematic by Ōtsuka Hisao (Ōtsuka Hisao, "Kindai shihonshugi no tokushitsu" [The special characteristics of modern capitalism] in Rekishigaku Kenkyūkai, ed., *Nihon shakai no shiteki kyūmei* [A historical study of Japanese society] [Tokyo, Iwanami Shoten, 1949]) are paraphrased in a review article by John Whitney Hall, *FEQ,* Vol. 11, No. 1 (November 1951), p. 102.

84. James I. Nakamura, *Agricultural Production and the Economic Development of Japan 1873–1922* (Princeton, Princeton University Press, 1966), pp. 15–16.

85. The situation in education and industrial relations is discussed more fully below. The question of cultural hegemony and its role is extremely complex, and inadequately dealt with in most Western sources. Chitoshi Yanaga, "Transition from Military to Bourgeois (Chōnin) Society," *Oriens* (Leiden), Vol. 8, No. 1 (1955), suggests that during the long period of peace under the Tokugawa *chōnin* (bourgeois) ideology largely hegemonized the samurai class. This interpretation is at least open to question. On the whole, it would seem more likely that the aristocracy attempted to repress bourgeois culture—not entirely successfully, of course. When the social fabric began to disintegrate in the middle of the nineteenth century, some of the more repressive components of aristocratic culture, such as the tea ceremony and Nō, became virtually extinct. For a time the cultural situation remained relatively open. Then, as samurai ideology began to be more insistently propagated, particularly in the schools and in the army, and the role of the Emperor became increasingly important, both aristocracy and bourgeoisie began to come to terms on a cultural synthesis for the new ruling bloc—but a synthesis in which samurai culture was clearly dominant. Thus, on the one hand, Smith is correct to note that after the Restoration, as the warriors were not thrown back onto the defensive by another class, they "never felt the need to make a cult of their peculiar style of life" unlike, for example, the British aristocracy, with their gambling, duelling and sexual pursuits (Smith, "Japan's Aristocratic Revolution," pp. 381 ff.). On the other hand, the new bourgeoisie took the lead in resurrecting some of the most oppressive forms of samurai culture, such as the

solipsistic tea ceremony, which was "revitalized" by a special society of businessmen, the Wakeikai or Harmonious Respect Society, restricted to sixteen members, who also disguised themselves as Buddhist monks. Kendō (the way of the sword), too, almost died out, and was kept alive only by a group in the Metropolitan Police Board. In this way, the bourgeoisie took an active part in accepting and perpetuating aristocratic culture in the interests of bolstering the repressive powers of the new ruling bloc. Samurai ideology was subsequently exploited on a massive scale in industry. One of the key Meiji business leaders, Shibusawa Eiichi, stated explicitly that "the spirit of a modern businessman should be Bushidō [the way of the samurai]"; Nakamigawa Hikojirō, the founder of the Mitsui industrial combine, called for a "Bushidō of the *chōnin*" (Kee Il Choi, "Tokugawa Feudalism and the Emergence of the New Leaders of Early Modern Japan," *EEH*, Vol. 9, No. 2 [December 1956], p. 81); on this see also Byron K. Marshall, *Capitalism and Nationalism in Prewar Japan: The Ideology of the Business Elite, 1868–1941* (Stanford, Stanford University Press, 1967), especially chapter 3. On the wider cultural issues, elements for a critique appear in Jintarō Fujii, comp. and ed., *Outline of Japanese History in the Meiji Era,* trans. and adapt. by Hattie K. Colton and Kenneth E. Colton (Tokyo, Ōbunsha, 1958), pp. 416–18.

86. Norman, *Soldier and Peasant,* p. 38.

87. *Ibid.,* pp. 37–41; Norman is one of the very few authors who discusses this crucially important *founding moment* of the new regime; cf. pp. 48–51 on peasant reactions to conscription a few years later and the violence required to suppress them.

88. Horie Yasuzō, "The Transformation of the National Economy," p. 408; the same conclusion is reached in Bernard S. Silberman, *Ministers of Modernization: Elite Mobility in the Meiji Restoration 1868–1873* (Tucson, University of Arizona Press, 1964), p. 108; cf. Silberman, "Criteria for Recruitment and Success in the Japanese Bureaucracy, 1868–1900: 'Traditional' and 'Modern' Criteria in Bureaucratic Development," *EDCC*, Vol. 14, No. 2 (January 1966), pp. 158–73.

89. Beasley, *The Meiji Restoration,* pp. 335–49. George M. Beckmann, *The Making of the Meiji Constitution: The Oligarchs and the Constitutional Development of Japan, 1868–1891* (Lawrence, University of Kansas Press, 1957), p. 40, tends to overestimate the importance of deceit and misunderstanding in the remission. An important role in this episode was played by Kido Kōin (Takayoshi), possibly the most lucid of all the early Meiji leaders (see Sidney D. Brown, "Kido Takayoshi [1833–1877]: Meiji Japan's Cautious Revolutionary," *PHR*, Vol. 25, No. 2 [May 1956]).

90. Norman, *Japan's Emergence,* p. 94 (italics in original); cf. pp. 91–101.

91. *Ibid.,* p. 97.

92. Nakamura, *Agricultural Production and the Economic Development of Japan,* p. 177.

93. Harry D. Harootunian, "The Progress of Japan and the Samurai Class, 1868–1882," *PHR*, Vol. 28, No. 3 (August 1959); Harootunian, "The Economic Rehabilitation of the Samurai in the Early Meiji Period," *JAS*, Vol. 19, No. 4 (August 1960); information below from "The Progress of Japan."

94. Harootunian, "The Economic Rehabilitation of the Samurai." Beasley, *The Meiji Restoration,* pp. 379–90; Yasuzo Horie, "An Outline of the Rise of Modern Capitalism in Japan," p. 105.

95. Harootunian, "The Progress of Japan and the Samurai Class," pp. 264–65.

96. Harootunian, "The Economic Rehabilitation of the Samurai," p. 444.

97. Thomas C. Smith, "Landlords' Sons in the Business Elite," *EDCC*, Vol. 9, No. 1, Part 2 (October 1960); James C. Abegglen and Hiroshi Mannari, "Leaders of Modern Japan: Social Origins and Mobility," *EDCC, ibid.;* Kee Il Choi, "Tokugawa Feudalism and the Emergence of the New Leaders of Early Modern Japan." It should be noted that many samurai also fell by the wayside in the process. In addition, the children, and particularly the daughters of samurai, were systematically recruited for factory work, and this influx of "aristocracy" as workers as well as management had a definite retarding effect on the emergence of a militant proletariat (Yasuzo Horie, "An Outline of the Rise of Modern Capitalism," pp. 107–8).

98. James B. Crowley, "From Closed Door to Empire: The Formation of the Meiji Military Establishment," in Silberman and Harootunian, eds., *Modern Japanese Leadership,* p. 269.

99. Norman, *Soldier and Peasant*, pp. 48–51; Marlene J. Mayo, "The Korean Crisis of 1873 and Early Meiji Foreign Policy," *JAS*, Vol. 31, No. 4 (August 1972), pp. 793–95.

100. Crowley, "From Closed Door to Empire," p. 272; the foreign policy aspects are discussed later, in chapter 3.

101. Part of Ōkubo's memorial is reproduced in Ryusaku Tsunoda, Wm. Theodore de Bary and Donald Keene, eds., *Sources of Japanese Tradition* (New York and London, Columbia University Press, 1964 edition), Vol. 2, pp. 151–55; cf. Iwata, *Ōkubo Toshimichi*; Brown, "Ōkubo Toshimichi"; Mayo, "The Korean Crisis of 1873," pp. 813–14.

102. Hackett, *Yamagata Aritomo*, pp. 71–72. Saigō's departure caused serious dissension among the Imperial Guards, many of whom were Satsuma men. It is an interesting reflection on the feeble position of the Emperor at this stage that, in spite of two personal interventions, in which he misinformed the guards about the reasons for Saigō's departure, he failed to prevent over 100 of them from leaving.

103. The Hizen (or Saga) uprising had external ramifications in helping to pressure the government to go ahead with an attack on Taiwan the same year (1874); see Mayo, "The Korean Crisis of 1873," pp. 817–19, and chapter 3 below.

104. Norman, *Soldier and Peasant*, pp. 43–45; Hackett, *Yamagata Aritomo*, pp. 76–81.

105. Hackett, *Yamagata Aritomo*, pp. 84–85; Norman, *Soldier and Peasant*, pp. 55–56.

106. Norman, *Soldier and Peasant*, pp. 56–57, stresses the *politics* of the alleged "no politics" line (cf. such contemporary slogans as "keeping politics out of sport"); Hackett, *Yamagata Aritomo*, pp. 84–85, tends to take it more at its face value; the man who drafted the Admonition, Nishi Amane, is a particularly representative contradictory figure who both participated in a group of (relatively) enlightened writers, the Meirokusha, along with Fukuzawa Yukichi and others, and worked as a close aide to Yamagata. On Nishi, see Roger F. Hackett, "Nishi Amane—A Tokugawa-Meiji Bureaucrat," *JAS*, Vol. 18, No. 2 (February 1959), pp. 214–55; and Thomas R. H. Havens, *Nishi Amane and Modern Japanese Thought* (Princeton, Princeton University Press, 1970).

107. Hackett, *Yamagata Aritomo*, p. 85.

108. Crowley, "From Closed Door to Empire," p. 276; Hackett, *Yamagata Aritomo*, p. 86; Tsunoda and others, eds., *Sources of Japanese Tradition*, Vol. 2, pp. 198–200; Norman, *Soldier and Peasant*, p. 52.

109. Hackett, *Yamagata Aritomo*, pp. 82–83; cf. below on the position of the Emperor, both institutional and financial.

110. Frank O. Miller, *Minobe Tatsukichi: Interpreter of Constitutionalism in Japan* (Berkeley and Los Angeles, University of California Press, 1965), p. 20.

111. Full text in Tsunoda and others, eds., *Sources of Japanese Tradition*, Vol. 2, p. 137.

112. From Article 11 of the 1868 Constitution: text in full in *ibid.*, pp. 137–39.

113. Joyce Chapman Lebra, "Ōkuma Shigenobu and the 1881 Political Crisis," *JAS*, Vol. 18, No. 4 (August 1959), pp. 475–87; Andrew Fraser, "The Expulsion of Ōkuma from the Government in 1881," *JAS*, Vol. 26, No. 2 (February 1967), pp. 213–36; George Akita, *Foundations of Constitutional Government in Modern Japan 1868–1900* (Cambridge, Mass., Harvard University Press, 1967), chapter 3; Junesay Idditie, *The Life of Marquis Shigenobu Ōkuma: A Biographical Study in the Rise of Democratic Japan* (Tokyo, The Hokuseido Press, 1956); Tsunoda and others, eds., *Sources of Japanese Tradition*, Vol. 2, pp. 183–84, for Ōkuma's suggestions to the Emperor.

114. Cited in full in W. W. McLaren, ed., *Japanese Government Documents*, *TASJ*, Vol. 42, Part 1 (1914), pp. 86–87.

115. Marius B. Jansen, "Ōi Kentarō: Radicalism and Chauvinism," *FEQ*, Vol. 11, No. 3 (May 1952); on the ideology of the *jiyū minken undō*, cf. H. K. Takahashi, "Robespierre et le Jacobinisme dans l'historiographie japonaise," *Actes du Colloque sur Robespierre* (Vienna, Congrès International des Sciences Historiques, 1965); and R. P. Dore, "The Meiji Landlord: Good or Bad?," *JAS*, Vol. 18, No. 3 (May 1959).

116. Cf. John Whitney Hall, review of Maruyama Masao, "Meija kokka no shisō" [The ideology of the Meiji State], in Rekishigaku Kenkyūkai, ed., *Nihon shakai no shiteki kyūmei*, *FEQ*, Vol. 11, No. 1 (November 1951), pp. 102–3.

117. R. P. Dore, "Japan as a Model of Economic Development," *Archives Européenes de Sociologie*, Vol. 5, No. 1 (1964), pp. 143–44.

118. Blacker, *The Japanese Englightenment,* p. 159, cites the recollection of a man from Keiō University: "When Buckle's *Civilization in England* first appeared the whole atmosphere of Keiō Gijuku suddenly changed. People ceased altogether to study the Bible" (quoted from Ōkubo Toshiaki, *Nihon kindai shigakushi,* p. 239). For Kōno's fulguration, see Akita, *Foundations of Constitutional Government,* p. 167. For the anecdote about Smiles' *Self-Help,* Donald H. Shively, "Motoda Eifu: Confucian Lecturer to the Meiji Emperor," in David S. Nivison and Arthur F. Wright, eds., *Confucianism in Action* (Stanford, Stanford University Press, 1959), p. 309. For Kinoshita, Ki Kimura, comp. and ed., and Philip Yampolsky, trans. and adapt., *Japanese Literature, Manners and Customs in the Meiji-Taisho Era* (Tokyo, Ōbunsha, 1957), p. 53. On the dangers of Cromwell's example, cf. Donald H. Shively, "Nishimura Shigeki: A Confucian View of Modernization," in Jansen, ed., *Changing Japanese Atitudes Toward Modernization,* p. 208.

119. J. S. Mill's arguments for representation in taxation were used by the Japanese to plead for tariff autonomy and an end to the unequal treaties (Jansen, "Changing Japanese Attitudes Toward Modernization," p. 67). On protectionism generally, see Frederick Clairmonte, *Economic Liberalism and Underdevelopment—Studies in the Disintegration of an Idea* (London, Asia Publishing House, 1960) and Karl Polanyi, *Origins of Our Time: The Great Transformation* (London, Victor Gollancz, 1945).

120. "The survival of the fittest was a cry that struck a most responsive chord, and its rendering into Japanese, *Yūsho Reppai* (Superior Wins, Inferior Loses), was freely used in political debate" (Sansom, *The Western World and Japan,* p. 433); Michio Nagai, "Herbert Spencer in Early Meiji Japan," *FEQ,* Vol. 14, No. 1 (November 1954). Spencer visited Japan and warmly endorsed the oligarchs—as did former U.S. President Ulysses S. Grant, who urged the formation of a Sino-Japanese alliance against the West.

121. Charles Frederick Remer and Saburō Kawai, *Japanese Economics: A Guide to Japanese Reference and Research Materials* (Ann Arbor, University of Michigan Press [Center for Japanese Studies], 1956), pp. 14 ff.

122. Webb, *The Japanese Imperial Institution,* pp. 133, 136.

123. *Ibid.,* p. 133.

124. *Ibid.,* p. 134; cf. Holtom, *Modern Japan and Shinto Nationalism,* pp. 127–28.

125. Webb, *The Japanese Imperial Institution,* p. 138. In fact, the word "restoration" is a misleading translation; the words used, *fukko* and *chūkō,* mean "return to antiquity" and "regeneration" [sc. of a dynasty]; borrowed from Chinese, they represent concepts of Chinese political ethics.

126. *Ibid.,* pp. 206–9, 214–16.

127. Yamaguchi, "La structure mythico-théâtrale de la royauté japonaise," p. 338; cf. Holtom, *Modern Japan and Shinto Nationalism,* pp. 57–58, on the origin of the mirror as one of the three imperial emblems.

128. Wilbur M. Fridell, " 'Family-State' *(Kazoku-kokka)*: An Imperial Ideology for Meiji Japan," in Harry J. Lamley, ed., *East Asian Occasional Papers (II),* Asian Studies at Hawaii, No. 4 (Honolulu, 1970).

129. *Ibid.,* p. 145; Holtom, *Modern Japan and Shinto Nationalism,* pp. 127–28; information below the strength of Buddhism from Holtom, p. 59.

130. Fridell, " 'Family-State,' " p. 145; the reasons it was less urgent to disentangle it from Confucianism are set out below.

131. On Fukuzawa, see Blacker, *The Japanese Enlightenment;* en passant, it may be noted that Fukuzawa supported an invasion of Korea in the early 1870s.

132. Herbert Passin, *Society and Education in Japan* (New York, Columbia University, Bureau of Publications, Teachers College, and East Asian Institute, 1965), pp. 69–70; the preamble to the Code is reprinted in Passin, pp. 210–11.

133. Blacker, *The Japanese Enlightenment,* p. 122; cf. Passin, *Society and Education,* pp. 62–68, on the early liberal period.

134. R. P. Dore, "Education," in Robert E. Ward and Dankwart Rustow, eds., *Political Modernization in Japan and Turkey* (Princeton, Princeton University Press, 1968 ed.), p. 190.

135. Passin, *Society and Education,* pp. 70–71; strictly speaking, the post of minister did not exist until the cabinet was set up in 1885.

136. Miller, *Minobe Tatsukichi*, p. 18.
137. *Ibid.*, pp. 18–19.
138. Passin, *Society and Education*, p. 82.
139. *Ibid.*, p. 83; the document is reproduced at pp. 227–28.
140. Shively, "Motoda Eifu," p. 328.
141. John Whitney Hall, "Education and Modern National Development," in John Whitney Hall and Richard K. Beardsley, *Twelve Doors to Japan* (New York, McGraw-Hill, 1965), pp. 396–400; Norman, *Japan's Emergence*, p. 186.
142. Quoted by Shively, "Motoda Eifu," p. 328.
143. Quoted in *ibid.*, p. 328.
144. Passin, *Society and Education*, p. 85; these words are Passin's, not Kōno's.
145. Norman, *Japan's Emergence*, p. 186.
146. Quoted by Miller, *Minobe Tatsukichi*, p. 3.
147. Robert M. Spaulding, Jr., *Imperial Japan's Higher Civil Service Examinations* (Princeton, Princeton University Press, 1967), p. 306.
148. Quoted in Ike, *Beginnings*, p. 172 (from *Itō Hirobumi Den* [The Biography of Itō Hirobumi] [Tokyo, Shunbo Ko Tsuisho Kai, 1940], Vol. 2, p. 218). Cf. Robert A. Wilson, *Genesis of the Meiji Government in Japan 1868–1871* (Berkeley and Los Angeles, University of California Press, 1957); Wilson points out how the setting up of a system with eighteen degrees of Court rank (August 1969) allowed the assignation of Court rank to posts in the new government—and subtle class variation in administrative posts (p. 68). The rank system provided class stability by reference to the Emperor at a time of dangerous fluidity.
149. Quoted in Ike, *Beginnings*, pp. 175–76; on Stein, see also Joseph Pittau, S.J., *Political Thought in Early Meiji Japan, 1868–1889* (Cambridge, Mass., Harvard University Press, 1967), chapter 5; Herbert Marcuse, *Reason and Revolution: Hegel and the Rise of Social Theory* (London, Routledge & Kegan Paul, 2d ed., 1955), pp. 374–88; Kaethe Mengelberg, "Lorenz von Stein and His Contribution to Historical Sociology," *JHI*, Vol. 22, No. 2 (April–June 1961), pp. 267–74; and Bela Foeldes, "Bemerkungen zu dem Problem Lorenz von Stein—Karl Marx," *Jahrbücher für Nationalökonomie und Statistik*, Vol. 102 (1914), pp. 289–99; for Mosse (mentioned immediately below) and his importance in planning local government in Japan, see Hackett, *Yamagata Aritomo*, pp. 108–11.
150. Norman, *Japan's Emergence*, p. 187.
151. Beckmann, *The Making of the Meiji Constitution*, p. 75.
152. Passin, *Society and Education*, pp. 86–91.
153. *Ibid.*, pp. 88–89.
154. Toshiaki Okubo, "The Birth of the Modern University in Japan," *JWH*, Vol. 10, No. 4 (1967), p. 776.
155. The regime's wish to bring in more men of talent was, of course, not incompatible with its desire for self-preservation.
156. Miller, *Minobe Tatsukichi*, pp. 16 ff.; the private universities, such as Keiō, were set up by the political opposition; "state" and "private" applied to universities were virtually synonymous with "government" and "opposition," respectively.
157. In effect, this meant the bureaucracy would be limited to career bureaucrats (see Hackett, *Yamagata Aritomo*, p. 199).
158. Extended from information in Masamichi Inoki, "The Civil Bureaucracy," in Rustow and Ward, eds., *Political Modernization in Japan and Turkey*, p. 293.
159. Along with Itō Hirobumi, Itō Miyoji and Kaneko Kentarō (Akita, *Foundations of Constitutional Government*, p. 63); cf. Akita, p. 235, note 35, correcting the error of both Scalapino (Robert A. Scalapino, *Democracy and the Party Movement in Pre-War Japan: The Failure of the First Attempt* [Berkeley and Los Angeles, University of California Press, 1953]) and Ike (*Beginnings*) in confusing Inoue Kaoru and Inoue Kowashi.
160. Johannes Siemes, S.J., "Hermann Roesler's Commentaries on the Meiji Constitution," *MN*, Vol. 17, Nos. 1–4 (1962), pp. 6–7, and cf. references there. The same passage occurs, very slightly modified, in Johannes Siemes, *Hermann Roesler and the Making of the Meiji State: An Examination of His Background and His Influence on the Founders of Modern Japan & The Complete Text of the Meiji Constitution Accom-*

panied by His Personal Commentaries and Notes (Tokyo, Sophia University, in Co-operation with Charles E. Tuttle Co., Tokyo and Rutland, Vt., 1968), pp. 37–38. Roesler's draft for the Constitution was printed by the opposition under the title "Dream Stories of Western Philosophy."

161. The full text of the Rescript is available in several sources, including *JSPIJ*, Vol. 1, No. 3 (December 1963), p. 122. Motoda had argued for the removal of the phrase "respect the Constitution and observe the laws" on the grounds that it detracted from the concentration of all allegiance in the person of the Emperor. The Emperor himself rejected Motoda's suggestion.

162. Webb, "The Development of an Orthodox Attitude Toward the Imperial Institution in the Nineteenth Century," pp. 188–89.

163. Much of the political discussion and manoeuvring discussed here were inextricably bound up with initiatives (and disagreement) about revising the unequal treaties and ending extraterritoriality in Japan.

164. Fridell, " 'Family-State'," pp. 146–47.

165. *Ibid.*, p. 147; Fridell acknowledges his debt to the work of Kawashima Takeyoshi, *Ideorogii Toshite no Kazoku Seido* [The family system as an ideology] (Tokyo, 1963). The strengths and weaknesses of Kawashima's position can be gauged from a synopsis/analysis of an earlier work by him, *Nippon Shakai to Kazokuteki Kosei* [The familial structure of Japanese society] (Tokyo, Nippon Hyoronsha, 1948), in John W. Bennett and Iwao Ishino, *Paternalism in the Japanese Economy: Anthropological Studies of Oyabun-Kobun Patterns* (Minneapolis, University of Minnesota Press, 1963), Appendix B, pp. 260–66.

166. Fridell, " 'Family-State,' " p. 148.

167. *Ibid.*

168. *Ibid.*, p. 149.

169. *Ibid.*, pp. 148–53; this specific aspect is given further treatment in Wilbur M. Fridell, "Government Ethics Textbooks in Late Meiji Japan," *JAS*, Vol. 29, No. 4 (August 1970), pp. 823–33.

170. Crawcour, "The Tokugawa Heritage," pp. 40–41.

171. H. Kohachiro Takahashi, "La Place de la Révolution de Meiji dans l'histoire agraire du Japon," *Revue Historique* (Paris), Vol. 210, No. 2 (October–December 1953), p. 248.

172. Nakamura, *Agricultural Production and the Economic Development of Japan*, p. 7.

173. *Ibid.*, p. 15; the theses expounded by Nakamura have aroused considerable controversy. The upshot of Nakamura's findings is to lower considerably the previously accepted growth rate for both agricultural output and the economy as a whole during the Meiji and most of the Taishō periods. The most substantial attempt to question Nakamura's findings is Henry Rosovsky, "Rumbles in the Ricefields: Professor Nakamura vs. the Official Statistics," *JAS*, Vol. 27, No. 2 (February 1968), pp. 347–60. It may not be accidental that Nakamura sharply criticizes the earlier work of Rosovsky and his colleague Ohkawa Kazushi. A useful brief review of Nakamura's book is that by Koji Taira, *AER*, Vol. 57, No. 4 (September 1967), pp. 941–43. Some of the crucial points raised by Rosovsky (and Ohkawa) are scrutinized and questioned in Kee Il Choi, "Technological Diffusion in Agriculture Under the Bakuhan System," *JAS*, Vol. 30, No. 4 (August 1971), pp. 749–59. A useful summary of the controversy is to be found in Koji Taira, *Economic Development and the Labor Market in Japan* (New York and London, Columbia University Press, 1970), pp. 5–8; Taira assesses the positions of both Nakamura and Rosovsky and the new work done (especially by Shionoya Yūichi) on the revised index of industrial production, synthesizing the findings of the debate for the economy as a whole.

174. I am grateful to Don Burton for supplying me with this information. 1 *chō* = 2.45 acres.

175. Ike, *Beginnings*, p. 173; Ikeda and Sasaki, *Kyōyō-jin no Nihon Shi* [Japanese history for teachers], Vol. 4, pp. 174–75; cf. the Emperor's financial intervention to bring the Imperial Guard back under control in 1873.

176. Takahashi, "La Place de la Révolution de Meiji dans l'histoire agraire du Japon," p. 255.

177. The Emperor's holdings in banks and other public and semi-public enterprises

amounted to 8,600,000 yen in 1890. In 1889 the Emperor had acquired the important Sado gold mines and the Ikuno silver mines. From Ikeda and Sasaki, *Kyōyō-jin no Nihon Shi*, Vol. 4, pp. 174–75; Ōshima Shinzō, comp., *Ōshima Takato Kojitsu* [The achievements of Ōshima Takato] (Tokyo, privately published, 1938), pp. 921–33.

178. Norman, *Japan's Emergence*, pp. 144–45; Ike, *Beginnings*, pp. 139–46. Cf. Norman, pp. 144–53, on the dispossession of the peasantry. Takahashi stresses that the Meiji reform helped only the *jinushi*, not the *kosaku*. The latter even lost rights they had had under the seigneurial system; the annual rent in kind which they had to continue to pay to the *jinushi* sometimes increased, and it took up virtually all the surplus production of the *kosaku*. The Meiji Reform thus, in effect, reorganized and strengthened the *jinushi*, so that the upshot was: the *kosaku* paid rent to the *jinushi* who, in turn, paid part to the state as a land tax in money, keeping the rest. The *jinushi* thus had total control over the transformation of agricultural produce into merchandise, becoming a kind of "landlords-cum-sellers" ("propriétaires-vendeurs"). See H. Kōhachirō Takahashi, "Quelques Remarques sur la Répartition Sociale de la Propriété Foncière au Japon depuis le XVI Siècle," Third International Conference of Economic History (Munich, 1965), especially pp. 424–26.

179. Norman, *Japan's Emergence*, esp. pp. 150–51; the lack of industry can hardly have been the reason, Norman also notes, since when industry did begin to grow it did not draw people away from the land (p. 150); cf. Wilkinson, *The Urbanization of Japanese Labor*, passim.

180. Nakamura, *Agricultural Production and the Economic Development of Japan*, p. 15.

181. The question of the extent to which this terminology is accurate is discussed in chapter 2 below; inasmuch as the family is a basically repressive institution, where relations between members are not founded on the principle of equality, there was a real similarity; on the other hand, industry developed its own *specific* forms of repression as well. Women were particularly vulnerable since they had virtually no rights either in civil society at large, or within the family, or in an institution such as a factory. The extension of some of the methods of male domination prevalent within the family was particularly functional in industry. The subordination of women was given further legal formalization and force by the Civil Code of 1898. In addition, apart from not being allowed to vote in political elections, women were barred from joining unions (cf. chapter 2 below).

182. Norman, *Japan's Emergence*, p. 153.

183. Ōtsuka Hisao, "Modernization Reconsidered—with Special Reference to Industrialization," *DE*, Vol. 3, No. 4 (December 1965), p. 394. This has been called by some "semi-feudal capitalism" (e.g., by Yamada Moritarō, cited by Ōtsuka, *ibid.*), but it seems best to reject this categorization, as it does not recognize the priority of the capitalist mode of production. For an excellent survey of the effects of this rural origin on industrialization and the proletariat, see H. Kōhachirō Takahashi, "Quelques Remarques sur la Formation des Classes Ouvrières Industrielles au Japon," Third International Conference of Economic History (Munich, 1965), pp. 215–25.

184. Norman, *Japan's Emergence*, p. 97.

185. *Ibid.*, p. 98.

186. Takahashi, "La Place de la Révolution de Meiji dans l'histoire agraire du Japon," p. 250. Nakamura calculates that tax as a proportion of total production averaged out at about 8.7 per cent over the period from the quinquennium 1873–77 to the quinquennium 1918–22 (*Agricultural Production and the Economic Development of Japan*, pp. 160–61). The place of the land tax within total taxation is given in Table 2, pp. 48–51. Taxation as a percentage of total revenue rose from 9.5 per cent in 1868 to 12.9 per cent in 1869, 44.5 per cent in 1870 and 88.9 per cent in 1874, falling then slightly to 87.0 per cent by 1877 (Motokazu Kimura, "Fiscal Policy and Industrialization in Japan 1868–1895," pp. 18–19). See also Kunio Niwa, "The Reform of the Land Tax and the Government Programme for the Encouragement of Industry," *DE*, Vol. 4, No. 4 (December 1966), pp. 447–71, esp. 453–64; Harry T. Oshima, "Meiji Fiscal Policy and Economic Progress," in Lockwood, ed., *The State and Economic Enterprise in Japan*, pp. 353–89; G. C. Allen, *A Short Economic History of Modern Japan* (London, George Allen & Unwin, 2d revised ed., 1962), p. 51.

187. Dore, "The Meiji Landlord"; Smith, "Old Values and New Techniques in the

Modernization of Japan," p. 363, has some suggestive observations. "Why," he asks, "did the agrarian sector remain decisive politically when it had ceased to be so economically?" Smith connects this with the dialectic of Japan's expansion *against* the Western imperialist powers: the struggle with the West demanded a docile home base among the peasantry. Smith argues that this is shown *a contrario* by the relaxation of domestic pressure during periods when international tension relaxed, as in the 1920s. The "wild oscillations between uncritical acclaim of the West and xenophobia were not mere fickleness: they were rooted in the real claims of two cultures that could not be reconciled because one was the foundation of a state always imperiled by states built on the other." To this one should add the specific domestic dynamic to ruling class oppression which operated in top gear even during the periods when international tension (in the sense indicated by Smith) relaxed; cf. observations below on the promotion of patriotism.

188. This is discussed in several key sources including O. Tanin and E. Yohan, *Militarism and Fascism in Japan* (New York, International Publishers, and London, Martin Lawrence, 1934); Moore, *Social Origins of Dictatorship and Democracy;* Masao Maruyama, *Thought and Behaviour in Modern Japanese Politics* (London, Oxford University Press, 1963); R. P. Dore and Tsutomu Ōuchi, "Rural Origins of Japanese Fascism," in James William Morley, ed., *Dilemmas of Growth in Prewar Japan* (Princeton, Princeton University Press, 1971), pp. 181–209. Cf. chapter 5 below.

189. Takahashi, "La Place de la Révolution de Meiji dans l'histoire agraire du Japon," pp. 255–56.

190. Cf. note 70 above; and Takekoshi, *The Economic Aspects of the History of . . . Japan,* Vol. 3, chapter 79 ("The Questions of Currency After the Opening of Japan to Foreign Intercourse").

191. Brown, "Ōkubo Toshimichi," p. 185; cf. Horie Yasuzo, "Foreign Trade Policy in the Early Meiji Era," *KUER*, Vol. 22, No. 2 (October 1952).

192. Beckmann, *The Making of the Meiji Constitution,* p. 7; this indebtedness to the bourgeoisie helps to explain the *politics* of the new compromise, as seen, for example, in the Charter Oath of 1868.

193. Article 11 of the Constitution of 1868 states that: "There shall be . . . no private employment of foreigners, and no conclusion of . . . alliances with foreign countries. . . ." (full text in Tsunoda and others, eds., *Sources of Japanese Tradition,* Vol. 2, pp. 137–39).

194. On Ōkubo's programme, see references at note 101 above; on the Taiwan crisis, cf. note 103 above and chapter 3 below.

195. Tōyama Shigeki, "Politics, Economics and the International Environment in the Meiji and Taishō Periods," *DE*, Vol. 4, No. 4 (December 1966), pp. 419–26. China, as Tōyama puts it, was "in the front line." For detailed study of the unequal treaties, see F. C. Jones, *Extraterritoriality in Japan: And the Diplomatic Relations Resulting in Its Abolition 1853–1899* (New Haven, Yale University Press, and London, Humphrey Milford, Oxford University Press, 1931); and Tatsuji Takeuchi, *War and Diplomacy in the Japanese Empire* (Garden City, N.Y., Doubleday, Doran & Co., 1935, and London, Allen & Unwin, 1936), pp. 91–108.

196. Hilary Conroy "Government versus 'Patriot': The Background of Japan's Asiatic Expansion," *PHR*, Vol. 20, No. 1 (February 1951), p. 34.

197. Jones, *Extraterritoriality,* pp. 113–14; Takeuchi, *War and Diplomacy,* p. 96.

198. Takeuchi, *War and Diplomacy,* pp. 101–6.

199. Shibagaki Kazuo, "The Early History of the *Zaibatsu,*" *DE*, Vol. 4, No. 4 (December 1966), p. 549.

200. Shigeto Tsuru, *Essays on Japanese Economy* (Tokyo, Kinokuniya, 1958), p. 142; cf. F. Barret, *L'évolution du capitalisme japonais* (Paris, Editions Sociales, 1946–48), Vol. 3, pp. 17–71.

201. See Andō Yoshio, "The Formation of Heavy Industry—One of the Processes of Industrialization in the Meiji Period," *DE*, Vol. 3, No. 4 (December 1965), pp. 450–70.

202. Around the turn of the century as much as 30–40 per cent of the coal and no less than 80 per cent of all the copper mined in Japan were being exported (Shibagaki, "The Early History of the *Zaibatsu,*" p. 551; cf. below on the zaibatsu).

203. See p. 47 above and note 186 and references there, including Table 2. Ragnar Nurkse,

Problems of Capital Formation in Underdeveloped Countries (Oxford, Basil Blackwell, 1953), pp. 149–50, notes that the land tax in Japan provided about the same percentage of revenue as in Latvia and Poland at comparable stages.

204. G. C. Allen, "Factors in Japan's Economic Growth," in C. D. Cowan, ed., *The Economic Development of China and Japan: Studies in Economic History and Political Economy* (London, Allen & Unwin, 1964), p. 199.

205. Hugh T. Patrick, "Japan, 1868–1914," in Rondo Cameron, ed., *Banking in the Early Stages of Industrialization: A Study in Comparative Economic History* (New York, London and Toronto, Oxford University Press, 1967), pp. 283–84. On the role of the banks (i.e., the state in extracting and recycling the savings of the poor) see note 211 below; the important role of banks in financing business and the central state direction of credit has also been crucial in allowing industry to ride out recessions (cf. Allen, "Factors in Japan's Economic Growth," on this). Under central state control, the Japanese economy has been able to expand *relatively* independent of the short-term rates of capital formation.

206. Takahashi Chotaro, "Capital Accumulation in Early Meiji Era," *Asian Affairs* (Tokyo), Vol. 1, No. 2 (June 1956), Table I, pp. 136–37.

207. Nurkse, *Problems of Capital Formation,* pp. 90–91; William W. Lockwood, *The Economic Development of Japan: Growth and Structural Change 1868–1938* (Princeton, Princeton University Press, 1954), pp. 254–55. Interesting information on the automobile sector is contained in Chō Yukio, "Keeping Step with the Military: The Beginning of the Automobile Age," *JI,* Vol. 7, No. 2 (Spring 1971), esp. pp. 171–75.

208. Herbert Feis, *Europe, the World's Banker 1870–1914: An Account of European Foreign Investment and the Connection of World Finance with Diplomacy Before the War* (New Haven, Yale University Press, and London, Humphrey Milford, Oxford University Press, for the Council on Foreign Relations, 1930), p. 422; Nurkse, *Problems of Capital Formation,* pp. 90–91, for a useful comparison with China; Lockwood, *The Economic Development of Japan,* pp. 254–55, for details on Japan's foreign loans, which became extremely important at the beginning of the twentieth century.

209. Lockwood, *The Economic Development of Japan,* p. 254; Allen, *A Short Economic History,* p. 52.

210. Allen, *A Short Economic History,* chapter 3; Patrick, "Japan, 1868–1914," pp. 250–51.

211. Over the period 1931–37 total real wages of all factory employees declined, although there was a boom from the summer of 1932; women's wages showed the biggest falls (Teijiro Uyeda, *The Small Industries of Japan: Their Growth and Development* [Honolulu, Institute of Pacific Relations, 1938], pp. 304 ff.). Real wages also fell by nearly half between 1914 and 1938, at a time when the economy was booming. Cf. chapter 2 below, and especially the discussions over a Factory Act. Part of Matsukata's programme was specifically to set up banks to mobilize the savings of the poor—terrorized by the lack of social services into saving a large proportion of their earnings (Allen, *A Short Economic History,* pp. 52–53); the situation is starkly revealed by the fact that although over the period 1876–1900 productivity per head was rising steadily, income *spent* per capita fell over the period 1885–1900: this was the source of the savings (Kimura, "Fiscal Policy and Industrialization," p. 26).

212. The weaknesses of this categorization (as of others in current usage) are well identified by Bill Warren, "Imperialism and Capitalist Industrialization," *NLR,* No. 81 (September–October 1973), especially note 1, p. 4. On foreign capital in Japan, see: Nurul Islam, *Foreign Capital and Economic Development: Japan, India and Canada* (Tokyo and Rutland, Vt., Charles E. Tuttle Co., 1960); Edwin P. Reubens, "Foreign Capital and Domestic Development in Japan," in Simon Kuznets, ed., *Economic Growth: Brazil, India, Japan* (Durham, N.C., Duke University Press, 1955); David S. Landes, "Japan and Europe: Contrasts in Industrialization," in Lockwood, ed., *The State and Economic Enterprise in Japan,* pp. 93–100. For a cautious bourgeois statement that Japan was possibly helped by not receiving the other main gift of imperialism, "aid," see Bruce F. Johnston, "The Japanese 'Model' of Agricultural Development: Its Relevance to Developing Nations," in Ohkawa and others, eds., *Agriculture and Economic Growth,* pp. 58–102. On the general problematic, see also André Gunder Frank, "Sociology of Development and Underdevelopment of Sociology," *Catalyst* (Buffalo), Summer 1966, pp. 45 ff.

213. Kamikawa Hikomatsu, ed., and Kimura Michiko, trans., *Japan-American Diplomatic Relations in the Meiji-Taishō Era* (Tokyo, Pan-Pacific Press, 1958), p. 79; Brewster, "Pre-Restoration Conditions for Economic Growth in Japan," pp. 5–6; much of what follows is a paraphrase of Brewster.

214. John W. McMaster, "The Takashima Mine: British Capital and Japanese Industrialization," *Business History Review,* Vol. 37, No. 3 (Autumn 1963), pp. 217–39; Burton, *The Origins of the Modern Japanese Iron and Steel Industry,* pp. 392–93.

215. Lockwood, *The Economic Development of Japan,* p. 253.

216. The old merchants who operated on silver were severely hit by the demonetization of the metal—bimetallism in practice means valuation in terms of the more rapidly rising of the two metals, their ratio rarely being stable for any length of time.

217. There is no such thing as an autonomous consumption pattern. Rosovsky and Ohkawa seem to argue that "stable tastes" kept imports down (Henry Rosovsky and Ohkawa Kazushi, "The Indigenous Components in Modern Japanese Economy," *EDCC,* Vol. 9, No. 3 [April 1961]). But surely the trend is more the other way round: Tokugawa seclusion meant there were virtually no imports; state control of foreign trade in the Meiji period led to concentration on vital industrial imports; low wages, and the absence of government spending on social services and housing, kept incomes so low that "consumers" simply could not afford to buy extra consumer goods. Isolation did, naturally, help to keep people stuck in their ways. But rather than claiming that consumption patterns kept down imports, it would seem more likely that state policy on what goods could come into the country plus state policy in enforcing mass poverty were the main factors in preserving traditional consumption.

218. Horie Yasuzō, "The Transformation of the National Economy," p. 425; Angus Maddison, "Japanese Economic Performance," *Banca Nazionale del Lavoro Quarterly Review* (Rome), No. 75 (December 1965), p. 25.

219. Hirschmeier's attempt to draw a distinction between direct and "indirect" subsidies (claiming the latter were more important) does not strike me as conclusive: see Johannes Hirschmeier, *The Origins of Entrepreneurship in Meiji Japan* (Cambridge, Mass., Harvard University Press, 1964), pp. 240–42. Rosovsky argues that the "effects of direct enterprise have been exaggerated. For long-term growth, the government as an investor—i.e. as a customer of heavy industry—had much more lasting effects" (Henry Rosovsky, *Capital Formation in Japan, 1868–1940* [Glencoe, The Free Press, 1961], p. 36). But if the state is active in promoting and organizing a certain type of economic growth, whether it puts hard cash into the building of a steel mill, or loans an equivalent sum at comfortable rates to private business, or guarantees an assured market does not alter the *character* of the state's role—it merely indicates different points at which it decides to intervene.

220. Islam, *Foreign Capital and Economic Development,* chapter 9; Allen, *A Short Economic History,* p. 91; cf. Hugh Borton, *Japan's Modern Century* (New York, Ronald Press Co., 1955), pp. 271–73; Johannes Hirschmeier, S.V.D., "Shibusawa Eiichi: Industrial Pioneer," in Lockwood, ed., *The State and Economic Enterprise in Japan,* esp. pp. 233–35.

221. On Japan's fuel and energy situation, see Lockwood, *The Economic Development of Japan,* pp. 91–93. In 1936 Japan's raw material dependency was as follows: bauxite—100 per cent; nickel—100 per cent; crude rubber—100 per cent; lead—92 per cent; crude oil—90 per cent; iron ores—87.5 per cent; tin—71.2 per cent; salt—71.0 per cent; zinc—63.0 per cent; copper—38.3 per cent; wood pulp—29.8 per cent; coal—10.8 per cent (Harold G. Moulton and Louis Marlio, *The Control of Germany and Japan* [Washington, D.C., the Brookings Institution, 1944], p. 67).

223. Raw silk was a "God-sent merchandise," which was crucial in the trade balance and was ideally suited to part-time work among farming families: see Horie Yasuzō, "The Transformation of the National Economy," p. 425. Japan was mightily aided by the silk-worm blight in Europe in 1875 which enabled Japan to double its raw silk exports (Miyohei Shinohara, "Economic Development and Foreign Trade in Pre-War Japan," in Cowan, ed., *The Economic Development of China and Japan,* p. 234); Japan's exports also benefited greatly from the Bombay plague.

223. Tanin and Yohan, *Militarism and Fascism in Japan,* pp. 37 ff.

224. Wilkinson, *Urbanization of Japanese Labor*, p. 46; George Oakley Totten III, *The Social Democratic Movement in Prewar Japan* (New Haven and London, Yale University Press, 1966), p. 10. The textile industry in general results in less urban concentration than other forms of industry, and within the textile industry itself, silk was an essentially rural element (Wilkinson, pp. 47, 83, 89): it was only after 1945 that "50 per cent or more of the major urban-oriented employment [was] located within incorporated cities" (Wilkinson, p. 90).

225. Andō, "The Formation of Heavy Industry," is a fundamental text on this; cf. Masao Kihara, "The Militarisation of the Japanese Economy," *KUER*, Vol. 38, No. 2 (October 1968), pp. 26–45.

226. Rosovsky, *Capital Formation in Japan*, pp. 50–51.

227. Andō, "The Formation of Heavy Industry," p. 451. "On grounds of political necessity everything was concentrated in the armaments industries as being typical of modern large-scale industry, or, to express it differently, as being the material backing for the equipment, expansion and strengthening of a huge regular Army and Navy establishment under the Meiji government" (*ibid.*, pp. 466–67); cf. Kihara, "The Militarisation of the Japanese Economy"; on the military budgets, Crowley, "From Closed Door to Empire"; Masazo Ohkawa, "The Armaments Expansion Budgets and the Japanese Economy after the Russo-Japanese War," *HJE*, Vol. 5, No. 2 (January 1965).

228. Cf. the new government's refusal to allow foreign interests to construct part of the new railway system—although Japan did borrow money abroad for this. Rosovsky notes that in the twentieth century, if military investments are counted, "railroads usually accounted for about 25 per cent of total central government investment. If durable military expenditures are excluded, the proportion rises to about 50 per cent" (*Capital Formation in Japan*, p. 31); cf. Nobutaka Ike, "The Pattern of Railway Development in Japan," *FEQ*, Vol. 14, No. 2 (February 1955); Thomas C. Smith, *Political Change and Industrial Development in Japan: Government Enterprise, 1868–1880* (Stanford, Stanford University Press, 1955), *passim*.

229. Andō, "The Formation of Heavy Industry," p. 454. Cf. Tōyama, "Politics, Economics and the International Environment in the Meiji and Taishō Periods." Tōyama remarks that: "The Japanese government, which adopted the policy of 'taking the position of a moved party in the realm of foreign policy and of always being forestalled in the realm of military matters' was especially nimble in making use of the conditions of imperialism" (pp. 433–34); and: "Sustained by this world Imperialist order Japanese militarism rapidly evolved into imperialism" (p. 434).

230. Shibagaki, "The Early History of the *Zaibatsu*"; Shibagaki emphasizes the role of the chronic depression prevailing in Japan prior to World War I and the effect which the process of concentration which accompanied this had on the structure of the zaibatsu.

231. This was in 1880: see Smith, *Political Change and Industrial Development*, chapter 8.

232. Andō, "The Formation of Heavy Industry," p. 451, "political merchants" here being defined as privileged merchants with a special relationship with government leaders; Burton, *The Origins of the Modern Japanese Iron and Steel Industry*, pp. 549–52, for an excellent critique of Smith's position on this (Smith, *Political Change and Industrial Development*, chapters 7 and 8).

233. Shibagaki, "The Early History of the *Zaibatsu*," pp. 537–38.

234. Smith writes that: "it is certain that the better buys went to privileged insiders. And many of the buyers later became dominant figures on the industrial scene"—and then goes on to say: "But until there is evidence for believing otherwise, this must be accepted as an adventitious result of the sale of government enterprises, not its object" (*Political Change and Industrial Development*, p. 100). Apart from both the partial nature of Smith's description, and the plain improbability of the process being a "fluke," this description fails to come to grips with the class nature of the process, which consolidated the class interests of the new ruling bloc.

235. *Ibid.*, pp. 88–89.

236. Burton, *The Origins of the Modern Japanese Iron and Steel Industry*, pp. 551–52.

237. Tanin and Yohan, *Militarism and Fascism in Japan*, pp. 37 ff.

238. Yoshio Ando, "The Evolutionary Process of the Japanee Economy in the Twentieth

Century," *JWH*, Vol. 5, No. 1 (1959), p. 192. This marked a new development in the reorganization of state-private business relations.

239. Shibagaki, "The Early History of the *Zaibatsu*," p. 535; interesting material on the role of the zaibatsu banks in Patrick, "Japan, 1868–1914," pp. 281–87, esp. pp. 286–87.

240. Shipbuilding got off to a very shaky start. The massive naval building programme launched after the Triple Intervention was still mainly carried out in Britain (Ian H. Nish. *The Anglo-Japanese Alliance: The Diplomacy of Two Island Empires, 1894–1907* [London, Athlone Press, 1966], pp. 30 ff.).

241. Shibagaki, "The Early History of the *Zaibatsu*," p. 549.

Chapter 2

THE BEGINNINGS OF THE LEFT

1. Takano Fusatarō, "Typical Japanese Workers," *Far East*, Vol. 2, No. 4 (April 20, 1897), p. 169, cited in Hyman Kublin, ed., *Meiji rōdō undō-shi no hitokoma—Selected works of Takano Fusatarō, a Japanese trade union leader of the Meiji period* (Tokyo, Yūhi-kaku, 1959), p. 31.

2. Umemura, "Agriculture and Labour Supply in Japan in the Meiji Era," pp. 281–82; Totten, *The Social Democratic Movement in Prewar Japan*, p. 10; Marshall, *Capitalism and Nationalism in Prewar Japan*, pp. 63–65; cf. note 224 to chapter 1.

3. Sumiya Mikio, "The Development of Japanese Labour-Relations," *DE*, Vol. 4, No. 4 (December 1966), pp. 500–503 (henceforth: Sumiya, "Labour-Relations"). Elsewhere the same author refers to dormitories as "detention homes" for female labour (Mikio Sumiya, *Social Impact of Industrialization in Japan* [Tokyo, Japanese National Commission for UNESCO, 1963], p. 86). During the year 1900 one large textile mill with over 4,000 employees recruited 6,085 new employees (4,762 female and 1,323 male) and *lost* 7,701 employees; the reasons given for the workers' departures indicate their condition: 82 per cent escaped, 14 per cent were dismissed, 3 per cent left because of illness, and 1 per cent died (M. Y. Yoshino, *Japan's Managerial System: Tradition and Innovation* [Cambridge, Mass., and London, England, M.I.T. Press, 1968], p. 73, citing Hazama Hiroshi, *Nihon teki Keiei no Keifu* [Evolution of Japanese management] [Tokyo, Nihon Nōritsu Kyōkai, 1963], p. 102.) For employees' reactions to mobility of labour, cf. below. Annual turnover at Mitsui's Miike coal mine in 1902 was 163.5 per cent (59.7 per cent in 1930)—from R. N. V. Collick, *Labour and Trades Unionism in the Japanese Coal Mining Industry* (unpublished Ph.D. thesis, Oxford University), pp. 187–89; I am grateful to the author for allowing me to consult the MS of his work. Shop-floor oppression in industry was acute, and very large supervisory staffs were employed to keep the work force in line; see Solomon B. Levine, *Industrial Relations in Postwar Japan* (Urbana, University of Illinois Press, 1958), p. 41.

4. Totten, *The Social Democratic Movement in Prewar Japan*, p. 56. In the Civil Code of 1898 (Article 957), "the wife's right to maintenance from her husband takes third place in the order of priorities, after his parents and his children" (R. P. Dore, *City Life in Japan: A Study of a Tokyo Ward* [London, Routledge & Kegan Paul, 1958], p. 98).

5. On the labour-boss (*oyakata*) system, see Solomon B. Levine, "Labor Markets and Collective Bargaining in Japan," in Lockwood, ed., *The State and Economic Enterprise in Japan*, pp. 642–48; Yoshino, *Japan's Managerial System*, pp. 70–71, 76–77; Bennett and Ishino, *Paternalism in the Japanese Economy, passim,* especially chapter 3. Many of these labour-bosses were (and are) straightforward gangsters (*yakuza*), who recruited members by every means ranging from kidnapping to bribing members of the worker's family (Taira, *Economic Development and the Labor Market*, p. 106). In addition, workers who had contracted voluntarily were frequently deluded as to their destination. Once at their destination, workers often found that their employers paid their wages over to the gang-boss, who had usually already forced his "clients" into debt with real or alleged advances to their families, transportation costs, equipment, and suchlike. Gang-bosses organized the further degradation of their sub-

ordinates by monopolizing control of alcohol and gambling to squeeze out any remaining surplus.

6. As shown below, guaranteed employment for life was nonexistent for women and by no means standard for men.

7. James C. Abegglen, *The Japanese Factory: Aspects of Its Social Organization* (Glencoe, Ill., The Free Press, 1958), although it relied almost entirely on management sources, was a work which for some time exercised wide influence in the West. Abegglen's position has not been conclusively demolished.

   The most extensive refutations of Abegglen are to be found in Taira, *Economic Development and the Labor Market;* Yoshino, *Japan's Managerial System;* Robert E. Cole, *Japanese Blue Collar: The Changing Tradition* (Berkeley and Los Angeles, University of California Press, 1971); briefer, but equally strong refutation in Robert Evans, Jr., *The Labor Economies of Japan and the United States* (New York, Washington and London, Praeger, 1971); cf. Ronald Dore, "Sociology in Japan," *British Journal of Sociology,* Vol. 13 (June 1962); and Kishimoto's study in *KUER* cited below (notes 20 and 28).

8. Taira, *Economic Development and the Labor Market,* p. 127.

9. *Ibid.,* p. 108.

10. *Ibid.,* pp. 110–16.

11. Marshall (*Capitalism and Nationalism,* p. 62) was one of the first Western writers to emphasize that the Japanese themselves did not refer to the system as "paternalism" but as *kazoku shugi* or *onjō shugi* (affection-ism). The term *kazoku shugi* does not mean "paternalism" (even in its nineteenth-century meaning). The best rendering is "family-ism" or "familism" (as suggested by Sumiya, "Labour-Relations," pp. 508–13). Hazama coined the term "management familyism" to cover the whole complex of relationships involved (Evans, *The Labor Economies,* p. 38). Yasuzo Horie, "The Role of the *Ie* (House) in the Economic Modernization of Japan," *KUER,* Vol. 36, No. 1 (April 1966), pp. 1–16, is a useful text on the relationship between the "family" system and industrial organization, though rather complacent about the class issues involved. The Japanese term *ie* means both "house," "dwelling," and the family as an entity extending through past, present and future (cf. the English usage, "The House of Orange"). Bennett and Ishino, *Paternalism in the Japanese Economy: Anthropological Studies of Oyabun-Kobun Patterns,* contains much useful information, presented from a somewhat conservative viewpoint.

12. Taira, *Economic Development and the Labor Market,* pp. 119–26; Yoshino, *Japan's Managerial System,* pp. 65–84.

13. Marshall, *Capitalism and Nationalism,* chapters 4 and 5, *passim;* Taira, *Economic Development and the Labor Market,* p. 100; Dore, "Sociology in Japan," p. 120.

14. Marshall, *Capitalism and Nationalism,* pp. 52 ff.; Yoshino, *Japan's Managerial System,* p. 75.

15. The atmosphere had been prepared for this much earlier by the strong emphasis laid by the state on the "national" and "social" duties of, first, the "model" factories set up after the Restoration and, later, of all economic enterprises (see Yasuzo Horie, "An Outline of the Rise of Modern Capitalism," pp. 107 ff.). It should also be noted that the ideology of "family-ism" provided cultural cover for the imbrication of new and old business enterprises. For example, Mitsui and Mitsubishi, though founded several centuries apart, seemed by the 1920s, say, to be historically and structurally of the same type (Horie, "The Role of the *Ie*," pp. 5–15); see Barret, *L'évolution du capitalisme japonais,* Vol. 1, pp. 66–119, 131–63, for detailed information on the evolution of Mitsui and Mitsubishi.

16. Marshall, *Capitalism and Nationalism,* pp. 57 ff.; R. P. Dore, "The Modernizer as a Special Case: Japanese Factory Legislation, 1882–1911," *CSSH,* Vol. 11, No. 4 (October 1969).

17. Soeda Jūichi, president of the semi-governmental Kōgyō (Industrial) Bank in an interview reported in the *Tōyō Keizai Shimpō,* February 25, 1908, pp. 254–55, cited by Marshall, *Capitalism and Nationalism,* pp. 58, 59.

18. Yoshino, *Japan's Managerial System,* p. 75.

19. *Ibid.,* p. 79; cf. *ibid.,* p. 84. The development of capital-intensive and technically-oriented industry accentuated business's need for a stable labour force. An integral

element in the drive to stabilize the labour force was the qualitative shift by business around the same time towards a long-term liaison with *oyakata* (*ibid.,* pp. 76–77; Sumiya, *Social Impact of Industrialization,* pp. 46 ff.; Taira, *Economic Development and the Labor Market,* p. 124, on the three kinds of recruiter).

20. In the words of Tokonami Takejirō, Home Minister in the early twentieth century, "so long as there are the time-honoured master-servant relations or paternalistic employment relations in Japan, we need not go to the trouble of licking the leavings of Europe and America if we make the clever use of that fine custom" (cited by Eitaro Kishimoto, "The Characteristics of Labour-Management Relations in Japan and Their Historical Formation" (1), *KUER,* Vol. 35, No. 2 [October 1965], p. 55). Cf. the ceremonial propaganda text by Prince Hirobumi Itō, "Some Reminiscences of the Grant of the New Constitution," in Count Shigenobu Ōkuma, comp., *Fifty Years of New Japan* (London, Smith, Elder, & Co., 1909), Vol. 1, esp. pp. 128–29.

21. Taira, *Economic Development and the Labor Market,* p. 134 (and note 13).

22. *Ibid.,* pp. 134–37; cf. below.

23. *Ibid.,* p. 137 (this was not unusual); and p. 142, for the significance of refusing to legislate on a minimum wage. Japan ratified the I.L.O. Conventions on this only in 1971 (*JLB,* Vol. 11, No. 5 [May 1972], p. 10); cf. below.

24. Taira, *Economic Development and the Labor Market,* pp. 110–15, discusses the complicated details of this.

25. *Ibid.,* p. 157; Evans, *The Labor Economies,* pp. 38–44; a fuller term is *nenkō joretsu seido,* which Evans (p. 38) translates as: "age and length of service-based wage system"). Kishimoto, "The Characteristics of Labour-Management Relations," prefers the term "seniority wage system"; on the system in the post-1945 period, cf. R. Cole, *Japanese Blue Collar,* pp. 72–92.

26. Taira, *Economic Development and the Labor Market,* p. 157.

27. Evans, *The Labor Economies,* p. 43.

28. They were also excluded from coverage under the Factory Law and the Health Insurance Law, active inaction by the state (Eitaro Kishimoto, "The Characteristics of Labour-Management Relations in Japan and Their Historical Formation" (2), *KUER,* Vol. 36, No. 1 [April 1966], p. 33).

29. Taira, *Economic Development and the Labor Market,* p. 161 (the 26 per cent includes day labourers).

30. Marshall, *Capitalism and Nationalism,* chapter 5, *passim,* has evocative quotes on this; cf. Tokonami, cited above in note 20; Taira, *Economic Development and the Labor Market,* pp. 160–61; Evans, *The Labor Economies,* p. 43. Management succeeded in blocking almost entirely any moves towards collective bargaining, which still remains a rare phenomenon in Japan today.

31. Cf. note 11 above.

32. Totten, *The Social Democratic Movement in Prewar Japan,* p. 12.

33. Kishimoto, "The Characteristics of Labour-Management Relations," discusses this at length illuminatingly.

34. Gotō Shōjirō to J. Keswick, Sept. 24, 1880, Box Nagasaki, 1880, Jardine, Matheson & Company Archive (University Library, Cambridge), cited in McMaster, "The Takashima Mine: British Capital and Japanese Industrialization," pp. 236–37. A vivid contemporary description of conditions at Takashima, a small island off Nagasaki, can be found cited in Kazuo Okochi, *Labor in Modern Japan* (Tokyo, Science Council of Japan, 1958), p. 37 (note 36); cf. *ibid.,* pp. 20–21.

35. Sumiya, *Social Impact of Industrialization,* p. 41.

36. *Ibid.,* p. 86; since this is an employers' figure it may well be too low. At about the same time, at Osaka, the army was rejecting 94 out of every 100 applicants for enlistment on physical grounds—the result of malnutrition and child labour; yet men were probably better fed than women (Hyman Kublin, "Takano Fusataro: A Study in Early Japanese Trades-Unionism," *Proceedings of the American Philosophical Society,* Vol. 103, No. 4 (August 15, 1959), p. 576.

37. Iwao F. Ayusawa, *A History of Labor in Modern Japan* (Honolulu, East-West Center Press, 1966), pp. 110–11; Hyman Kublin, *Asian Revolutionary: The Life of Sen Katayama* (Princeton, Princeton University Press, 1964), pp. 125 ff.; Taira, *Economic Development and the Labor Market,* pp. 138–42, for a succinct résumé of the provi-

sions of the Factory Act. Although the Act was passed in 1911, the Imperial Ordinance for its implementation was not signed until 1916; revisions of the Act and its related statutes in 1926 prolonged the life of certain key escape clauses—for example, the clause banning the use of women on night shifts was postponed for a further three years (Taira, p. 140).

38. Cited in Ike, *Beginnings*, p. 155. It must be admitted that the motives of the organizers were somewhat suspect, since the Jiyūtō was aiding Mitsui in its struggle against Mitsubishi. Nonetheless, Mitsubishi's encroachment on traditional middleman activities and its high charges on coastal shipping had autonomously stirred up popular rage.

39. V. I. Lenin, "A Great Beginning," in V. I. Lenin, *On Socialist Ideology and Culture* (Moscow, Foreign Languages Publishing House, n.d.), p. 25 [in V. I. Lenin, *Collected Works*, 4th Russian ed., Moscow, Vol. 29]; Mao Tse-tung, "Analysis of the Classes in Chinese Society," in Mao, *Selected Works of Mao Tse-tung*, Vol. 1, p. 18.

40. In full in Tsunoda and others, eds., *Sources of Japanese Tradition*, Vol. 2, pp. 300–303.

41. Sumiya, *Social Impact of Industrialization*, pp. 94–95. One of the first big union victories was in the same year, 1898. The Japan Railway Company Engine-drivers' Union (the "Rectification Society"), by threatening a strike which would have paralyzed the railway system of northern Japan, won a quick and favourable settlement—but the union thereupon rapidly disintegrated. See Collick, *Labour and Trades Unionism in the Japanese Coal Mining Industry*, p. 197.

42. Hence both the name and, to some extent, the outlook of the Yūai-kai (Friendly Love Society), set up in August 1912 under the leadership of Suzuki Bunji, who was associated with the Unitarian Church and the AFL in America (Suzuki was sometimes called *"wa-sei* Gompers" [Japan-made Gompers]). Cf. note 50 below.

43. This list is in Kublin, *Asian Revolutionary*, pp. 179–80. The *Communist Manifesto* was first translated into Japanese in 1904 by, amongst others, Kōtoku Shūsui (see below). The ban on Japanese translations made knowledge of foreign languages very valuable, thus dangerously increasing the importance of intellectuals. As Mao once pungently put it: "Was there ever a cat that did not love fish or a warlord who was not a counter-revolutionary? Intellectuals are three-day revolutionaries whom it is dangerous to recruit" ("On Tactics Against Japanese Imperialism" [December 1935] in *Selected Works of Mao Tse-tung*, Vol. 1, p. 164).

44. Matsuo Takayoshi, "The Development of Democracy in Japan—Taishō Democracy: Its Flowering and Breakdown," *DE*, Vol. 4, No. 4 (December 1966), pp. 618–19, analyzes the Campaign Against the Peace Terms, arguing that the imperialist and democratic moments were intertwined, with the latter dominant. Shumpei Okamoto, *The Japanese Oligarchy and the Russo-Japanese War* (New York and London, Columbia University Press, 1970), chapter 8, provides a useful description of the events, but is weak and even contradictory as far as analysis goes. Okamoto's attacks (pp. 218 ff.) on Japanese Marxist interpretations of the Hibiya Riots seem at variance with the factual evidence presented on the class composition of the riots and their political targets. The crucial long-range political effects of the Hibiya riots are expertly elucidated in Herbert P. Bix, *Japanese Imperialism and Manchuria 1890–1931* (unpublished Ph.D. thesis, Harvard University, 1971), pp. 35 ff. Further major riots, with no imperialist content, occurred in 1913, with extensive attacks on police-boxes (Matsuo, "The Development of Democracy in Japan," p. 622; Tetsuo Najita, *Hara Kei in the Politics of Compromise 1905–1915* [Cambridge, Mass., Harvard University Press, 1967], pp. 160 ff.). For the relative political positions of Katsura and Saionji (the latter being, by and large, more liberal), see chapter 4 below, especially note 29. On the importance of police-boxes, see note 1 to Chapter 10.

45. On the insurrection, see Sumiya, *Social Impact of Industrialization*, pp. 132–33; Ayusawa, *History of Labor*, p. 94. A description of the scene at Ashio is quoted in Sumiya, "Labour-Relations," p. 507. Some background to the February 1907 events at Ashio appears in F. G. Notehelfer, *Kōtoku Shūsui: Portrait of a Japanese Radical* (London, Cambridge University Press, 1971), pp. 65 ff. The copper mine had polluted large areas of farmland, seriously affecting about 300,000 people, both farmers and fishermen. There had been continuous struggle in and around the mine since the end of the nineteenth century. The Ashio case is a striking prefiguration of what is

happening in Japan now. In February 1900 a government stolidly inactive over the pollution since 1891 sprang into action to assault a deputation of farmers trying to reach Tokyo with a petition.

46. Matsuo, "The Development of Democracy in Japan," p. 621. During the war the Japanese rulers had also been confronted with the threat of revolutionary defeatism among the working class for the first time. At the VI Congress of the Second International in Amsterdam in 1904, during the Russo-Japanese War, the Japanese socialist leader Katayama (see below) had publicly shaken hands with Plekhanov, a gesture which became famous round the world overnight. This handshake was a threat to ruling class chauvinism in both Russia and Japan. Cf. Hyman Kublin, "The Japanese Socialists and the Russo-Japanese War," *JMH*, Vol. 22, No. 4 (December 1950), pp. 332–39.

47. The Saionji government had been in office only two months, after winning an easy majority in the May 1908 elections; it still had a comfortable majority in the Diet. But this support was ethereal in the face of bureaucratic and industrial hostility; in particular, the university cliques lodged in the key ministries worked to bring down Saionji. This is one of the clearest cases of the vapidity of Japanese "democracy" (on this episode, see Scalapino, *Democracy and the Party Movement*, p. 189).

48. This is the documented opinion of Notehelfer, *Kōtoku Shūsui*, pp. 141 ff., and seems correct (although Notehelfer's book is, on the whole, rather poor). There was a plot to assassinate the Emperor, and Kōtoku supported assassination in principle, but had dissociated himself from this particular plot towards the end of 1909 (Notehelfer, p. 191). Although later saddled with the label "anarchist," Kōtoku's lasting political contribution was to have exposed sham parliamentarism and advocated all-out direct action. Part of his key text on this, his speech at the Socialist Party Conference in February 1907 (immediately after the outbreak of fighting at Ashio), is reprinted in Tsunoda and others, eds., *Sources of Japanese Tradition*, Vol. 2, pp. 304–7.

49. Kublin's biography of Katayama (*Asian Revolutionary*) is useful for its information, but its orientation is unacceptable. The chapter covering Katayama's later move towards Bolshevism is entitled "The End of Socialism"; so eager is Kublin to negate Katayama's later evolution that he ends up calling him "an uncompromising fanatic." The Sparticists [*sic*] are called "fanatical" (p. 253), etc.

50. Ayusawa, *History of Labor*, pp. 145 ff., esp. p. 152. Recently, there have been several attempts to "rehabilitate" the Yūai-kai as a militant organization—see Kishimoto, "The Characteristics of Labour-Management Relations" (1), pp. 54–55, and especially Stephen S. Large, "The Japanese Labor Movement, 1912–1919: Suzuki Bunji and the Yūaikai," *JAS*, Vol. 29, No. 3 (May 1970), pp. 559–79; doubtless some rectification was needed, but the rehabilitation is not entirely convincing. The interesting and important question of precisely how and why the Japanese trade union movement collapsed has not been adequately studied; some (inadequate) information in Totten, *The Social Democratic Movement in Prewar Japan*, pp. 104, 333–34. Both the nature of the prewar union movement, and the way that movement collapsed into the wartime Sangyō Hōkokukai or Sampō (Industrial Patriotic Association) had important effects on the post-1945 class struggle. Sōdōmei: Japan General Federation of Labour.

51. The *burakumin* (literally, "village people"—see Glossary) are an outcaste *caste* of ethnic Japanese (cf. note 12 to chapter 1). They number somewhere between one and three million—probably about 3 million. Part of the government's role in the general repression of the *burakumin* has been to refuse to find out how many of them there actually are. On the concept of caste and the underlying *class* reality which it masks, see Claude Meillassoux, "Are There Castes in India?," *Economy and Society* (London), Vol. 2, No. 1 (February 1973), pp. 89–111. On the more general question of how much a society reveals of itself by its exclusions, see Michel Foucault's masterly *Madness and Civilization: A History of Insanity in the Age of Reason* (London, Tavistock Publications, 1967; New York, Pantheon Books, 1965).

52. Shiota Shōbei, "The Rice Riots and the Social Problems," *DE*, Vol. 4, No. 4 (December 1966), p. 517; Paul Akamatsu, "Au Japon, les Emeutes du Riz de 1918," *Annales*, Vol. 19, No. 5 (September–October 1964), p. 929. This account is based almost wholly on these two sources. Romein states that there were strikes in government munitions depots and a mutiny among the troops (Jan Romein, *The Asian Century: A History*

of Modern Nationalism in Asia [London, Allen & Unwin, 1962], p. 129). Ōuchi Tsutomu, "Agricultural Depression and Japanese Villages," *DE*, Vol. 5, No. 4 (December 1967), p. 597, notes that speculative cornering by rice merchants was a contributory factor to the riots. It is instructive to notice how little attention is paid to the riots in most Western accounts of the period. Shinobu Seisaburō, an eminent Japanese non-Marxist historian, says flatly that the riots were the most important event in Taishō (1912–26) history (Marius B. Jansen, "From Hatoyama to Hato-yama," *FEQ*, Vol. 14, No. 1 [November 1954], p. 71). Scalapino's large work, al-legedly on the subject of "democracy," has less than one paragraph and no political assessment of the upheaval (*Democracy and the Party Movement*, p. 210). G. C. Allen's standard work, *A Short Economic History of Modern Japan*, p. 100, not only misdates the riots to 1919, but seems also to misinterpret their significance.

53. The fundamental issues were "land, bread and peace" (see Jansen, "From Hatoyama to Hatoyama"). That the system of land ownership was the root cause and seen to be such is confirmed by the location of the uprisings, the majority of which were in rice-producing zones.

54. Kazushi Ohkawa and Henry Rosovsky, "The Role of Agriculture in Modern Japanese Economic Development," *EDCC*, Vol. 9, No. 1, Part 2 (October 1960), p. 56. In 1921, as a belated result of the riots, the government put through a Rice Act (see Teruoka Shūzō, "Japanese Capitalism and Its Agricultural Problems—Culminating in the Rice Riots," *DE*, Vol. 4, No. 4 [December 1966], p. 495). For the effects of the new policy on Korean agriculture, see Andrew J. Grajdanzev, *Modern Korea* (New York, Institute of Pacific Relations, 1944), pp. 105 ff.; and for the boomerang effects of this on Japan see Ōuchi, "Agricultural Depression and Japanese Villages," pp. 610–11. Cf. Y. Yagi, "The Relations Between Japan Proper and Korea as Seen from the Standpoint of the Rice-Supply," *KUER*, Vol. 6, No. 2 (December 1931); Shiota Shōbei, "A 'Ravaged' People: The Koreans in World War II," *JI*, Vol. 7, No. 1 (1971), p. 45. For a good overview: Yujiro Hayami and V. W. Ruttan, "Korean Rice, Taiwan Rice and Japanese Agricultural Stagnation: An Economic Consequence of Colonialism," *Quarterly Journal of Economics*, Vol. 84 (November 1970), pp. 562–89 [Minnesota Agricultural Experiment Station Journal Paper No. 7100].

55. Shiota, "The Rice Riots," p. 525. On the early student movement, see Henry DeWitt Smith II, *Japan's First Student Radicals* (Cambridge, Mass., Harvard University Press, 1972 and London, Oxford University Press, 1973). Two events of importance in the formation of the movement were the drive to provide famine relief for Russia (Smith, pp. 99, 101–2) and support for a big tram-workers' strike in Osaka (Smith, pp. 115–16).

56. The workers operated the yards for 45 days; Tanin and Yohan (*Militarism and Fascism in Japan*, pp. 102–3) give the number of workers participating as 85,000.

57. Quite apart from the specific police usage of the terror and despair created by the earthquake, it is worth reflecting on the racism which could so easily bring about many thousand deaths among non-Japanese and outcastes. Racism was whipped up by the regime to provoke torture and attacks on Koreans in areas hundreds of miles from the earthquake, like Osaka and Nagoya. The few people involved in the killings who were even arrested were mostly released or let off with sentences of 12 to 18 months maximum. Until 1945 the episode was largely buried, which has made an accurate estimate of the number of murdered very difficult. The generally accepted figure is at least 6,000 Koreans and about 600 Chinese (this is the figure given by Kim San to Nym Wales; see Nym Wales and Kim San, *Song of Ariran: A Korean Communist in the Chinese Revolution* [San Francisco, Ramparts Press edition, 1973], p. 94). The standard work on the Koreans in Japan, Richard H. Mitchell, *The Korean Minority in Japan* (Berkeley and Los Angeles, University of California Press, 1967), pp. 38–41, eschews any estimate, merely recording the opinion of Matsuo Takayoshi that *jikeidan* (vigilante corps) killed at least 2,000 Koreans and some Chinese (p. 38). Some Korean sources put the number of dead much higher: Kim Byong Sam, "Homi-cidal Japanese Imperialists Savagely Killed Korean Residents in Japan," *Pyongyang Times*, September 2, 1972, p. 6, puts the Koreans killed at over 23,000. Yamaguchi, "La structure mythico-théâtrale de la royauté japonaise," p. 342, puts the Korean dead at 50,000. It is worth noting that the Japanese government does not acknowledge

Korean deaths from the atomic bombs at Hiroshima and Nagasaki in its statistics (*Rōnin*, No. 7 [1972], p. 17). On Ōsugi see Tatsuo Arima, *The Failure of Freedom: A Portrait of Modern Japanese Intellectuals* (Cambridge, Mass., Harvard University Press, 1969); the limitations on Ōsugi's actions are indicated by the fact that (in his own words) he could feel "neither sympathy nor pity for the miserable life of a worker" (quoted in Arima, p. 59). Ōsugi is the central figure in the film *Eros + Gyakusatsu* (*Eros + Massacre*, Yoshida Yoshishige, 1969).

58. The main example of this trend is Scalapino, *Democracy and the Party Movement in Prewar Japan: The Failure of the First Attempt;* the subtitle sums up this approach. A partial corrective to this view can be found in Matsuo, "The Development of Democracy in Japan." See also the extracts in George O. Totten, ed., *Democracy in Prewar Japan: Groundwork or Façade?* (Lexington, Mass., D. C. Heath and Co., 1965).

59. Bix, *Japanese Imperialism and Manchuria*, p. 41.

60. The question of pre-Marxist political organization is not adequately dealt with in most bourgeois sources. Totten, for example, gives a relatively serious account of why certain forms of proletarian response ("anarcho-syndicalism") appeared in Japan, but fails to describe what "syndicalism" really involved, or what alternatives there were to it in that conjuncture (*The Social Democratic Movement in Prewar Japan*, p. 30).

61. After the 1923 earthquake the Soviet government offered working concessions to the Japanese unions on Soviet territory. This was at a time when Japanese imperialism had concessions on Soviet territory. Clearly, concessions to the Japanese *proletariat* would have been a direct blow at Japanese *imperialism*. The project (to lease concessions to the Japanese unions) was eventually blocked by the opening of official diplomatic relations between Tokyo and Moscow in 1925.

62. Kublin, *Asian Revolutionary*, pp. 71–73. Kublin opined that Katayama was attracted by: (*a*) the comparable experience of German unification; (*b*) Lassalle's dream of an anti-capitalist alliance between proletariat and Junkers; (*c*) romanticism. Katayama wrote a *Life of Lassalle* (1897).

63. Much the best source is George M. Beckmann and Okubo Genji, *The Japanese Communist Party, 1922–1945* (Stanford, Stanford University Press, 1969). Much useful information also in Rodger Swearingen and Paul Langer, *Red Flag in Japan: International Communism in Action 1919–1951* (Cambridge, Mass., Harvard University Press, 1952), with a virulently anti-communist introduction by Edwin O. Reischauer. However, precisely because, as its lurid title proclaims, *Red Flag* pays plenty of attention to the Comintern, it is much more enlightening than the later work by Robert A. Scalapino, *The Japanese Communist Movement, 1920–1966* (Berkeley and Los Angeles, University of California Press, 1967). I have not gone into the complex question of Comintern politics and analyses of the capitalist regimes in detail. Nicos Poulantzas, *Fascisme et dictature: la troisième internationale face au fascisme* (Paris, Maspero, 1970—published in English as *Fascism and Dictatorship* [London, NLB, 1974]), is a stimulating study of the Comintern's analyses of and policies towards Italy and Germany and offers numerous insights into Comintern policy (and lack of policy) towards Japan at the same period, though Poulantzas does not give detailed coverage to Japan. In particular, Poulantzas stresses the Comintern's consistently economic interpretation of imperialism and the lack of a mass line, whether ascribing the emergence of fascim to the fact that capitalism was "weak" (Italy) or "strong" (Germany). Comintern policies did not coincide one to one with the internal policies of the U.S.S.R. In addition, there were serious differences of opinion among the Comintern leaders (e.g., between Zinoviev and Radek at the Fourth Congress). See also chapter 5 below.

64. The difficulty of communication with Japan also led to the expenditure of prodigious energies on Korea during the early years of the Comintern. On the Comintern and the East, see Edward Hallett Carr, *A History of Soviet Russia: The Bolshevik Revolution 1917–1923* (Harmondsworth, Penguin Books, Pelican edition, 1966), Vol. 3, pp. 484 ff.

65. Vl. D. Vilensky in *Izvestiia*, August 2, 1921, quoted in Xenia Joukoff Eudin and

Robert C. North, *Soviet Russia and the East, 1920–1927: A Documentary Survey* (Stanford, Stanford University Press, 1957), p. 145.

66. Eudin and North, *Soviet Russia and the East*, p. 145 (from Boris Zakharievich Shumiatsky in *Revoliutsionnyi Vostok*, Nos. 4–5 [1928], pp. 225–26).

67. Eudin and North, *Soviet Russia and the East*, pp. 222–27.

68. The main documents are: the 1922 JCP Platform; the January (1925) Theses; the May (1925) Theses; the 1926 Theses; the 1927 ECCI Theses; the 1931 Draft Theses; and the 1932 Theses. Full texts of all of these (except the May 1925 Theses) in Beckmann and Okubo, *The Japan Communist Party*, carefully checked against variant versions. The May 1925 (or Heller) Theses are fully discussed in Beckmann and Okubo, pp. 89–92. ECCI: Executive Committee of the Communist International; in fact the 1927 Theses seem to have been almost wholly written by Bukharin (Beckmann and Okubo, p. 119).

69. Swearingen and Langer (*Red Flag in Japan*, p. 14) give July 5 as the official birthday; Scalapino (*The Japanese Communist Movement*, p. 18) and Beckmann and Okubo (*The Japan Communist Party*, p. 49) give July 15, which was the date of the first party convention.

70. Good biographical sketches in Beckmann and Okubo, *The Japan Communist Party*; Yamakawa, Arahata and Tokuda occur below in the text.

71. Theses of the Fourth Congress of the Communist International on the Eastern Problem, cited in Eudin and North, *Soviet Russia and the East*, p. 232.

72. JCP Platform, 1922, cited in *ibid.*, p. 331. The full text is available in a different translation in Beckmann and Okubo, *The Japan Communist Party*, Appendix A. Beckmann and Okubo note that there are two different versions of the text, both published by the JCP (p. 279).

73. Beckmann and Okubo, *The Japan Communist Party*, p. 281; the demand was omitted in some versions.

74. Eudin and North, *Soviet Russia and the East*, p. 334; Beckmann and Okubo, *The Japan Communist Party*, Appendix B.

75. Frequently known as the "Heller Theses"—after the Profintern representative at Shanghai: see Beckmann and Okubo, *The Japan Communist Party*, pp. 89–92.

76. J. V. Stalin, *Collected Works* (in English) (Moscow, Foreign Languages Publishing House, and London, Lawrence and Wishart, 1954), Vol. 7, pp. 231–36; originally in *Pravda*, July 4, 1925.

77. Adolf Abramovich Joffe had handled the peace negotiations with China in Peking in 1922–23. Officially he came to Japan as the guest of the mayor of Tokyo, Viscount Gotō, who invited him there for his health. After six months of intermittent discussion (the intermittence being largely due to Joffe's illness) the negotiations were broken off in August 1923, and resumed in September that year in Peking between Lev Mikhailovich Karakhan and the Japanese ambassador, Yoshizawa. These negotiations were concluded on January 20, 1925. Joffe's account in *Mirovoye Khozyaystvo i Mirovaya Politika*, No. 10–11, 1927. B. Nicolaevsky, "Russia, Japan and the Pan-Asiatic Movement to 1925," *FEQ*, Vol. 8, No. 3 (May 1949), is an interesting, though anti-Soviet article. Nicolaevsky's claim (pp. 289–90) that Moscow wanted to downgrade the JCP seems unjustified.

78. Eudin and North, *Soviet Russia and the East*, p. 337. Full text in Beckmann and Okubo, *The Japan Communist Party*, Appendix C.

79. Fukumoto Kazuo had studied in Germany and had been a member of the German Communist Party, the KPD. There are reflections on him in the various American works on the JCP, which require a critical reading; Beckmann and Okubo, *The Japan Communist Party*, pp. 108 ff., give by far the best account. From a theoretical point of view, one observation should be made: that the correct *analysis* of the condition of Japanese capitalism as advanced capitalism (dominated by monopolies) was accompanied by an incorrect *interpretation*—viz., that this system was about to disintegrate. The correct combination of "advanced" and "robust" was never reached. This error apparently came from an incorrect mechanistic reading of both Hilferding and Lenin (imperialism in its then current form as the highest stage of capitalism *ever*, rather than as the highest stage of capitalism *so far*). Cf. Poulantzas, *Fascism and Dictatorship, passim*.

80. Eudin and North, *Soviet Russia and the East*, p. 338. Full text in Beckmann and Okubo, *The Japan Communist Party*, Appendix D.

81. Nihon Rōdō Kumiai Zenkoku Kyōgikai (National Council of Japanese Labour Unions), a left-wing trade union federation to replace the previous Hyōgikai (Nihon Rōdō Hyōgikai or Labour Union Council of Japan), which had been set up after the left's break from Sōdōmei (Nihon Rōdō Sōdōmei or Japan General Federation of Labour) in 1925, but dissolved in the repression of 1928.

82. Kazama was a young worker who had trained in Moscow earlier. Tanaka Seigen had taken over the party at the age of 23 after the complete elimination of the leadership in 1928–29. He advocated a policy of full violence. He was arrested in July 1930. Like Kazama, he recanted in 1933, and was released in 1941. He was politically active on the right after the war. Good biographies of both in Beckmann and Okubo, *The Japan Communist Party*.

83. *Ibid.*, Appendix E.

84. *Ibid.*, Appendix F.

85. Kishimoto, "The Characteristics of Labour-Management Relations" (2), p. 33, gives peak membership as 420,589, in 1936, equivalent to 6.9 per cent of the labour force; same estimates in Ayusawa, *History of Labour*, pp. 227–28. Figures vary by 50–60,000 in some other sources.

86. Swearingen and Langer, *Red Flag in Japan*, p. 53, for the full list. Cf. Arima, *The Failure of Freedom;* and G. T. Shea, *Leftwing Literature in Japan* (Tokyo, Hōsei University Press, 1964).

87. Rōnō: abbreviation for *Labour-Farmer*, the name of the theoretical magazine of one group, started by Yamakawa Hitoshi. Kōza: literally "studies" or "lectures," from the first key publication of the other group, *Nihon Shihonshugi Hattatsushushi Kōza* [Studies in (or Lectures on) the historical development of capitalism in Japan] (Tokyo, Iwanami Shoten, 1932). The groups are often referred to as the Rōnōha and the Kōzaha (*ha* = "faction"). The main weapons of Western bourgeois scholarship against Japanese Marxism have been neglect and travesty. A partial exception to the general rule is Hilary Conroy, *The Japanese Seizure of Korea: 1868–1910: A Study of Realism and Idealism in International Relations* (Philadelphia, University of Pennsylvania Press, 1960), chapter 9, though even here it is impossible to feel that Conroy's highly critical survey of Japanese Marxist theses on the subject of the seizure of Korea does them justice. Useful information on the Rōnō-Kōza debate in Toyoda, "Révolution française et Révolution de Meiji: Etude Critique des Interpretations de Kosa et de Rono." Much less useful (verging on worthless) are the surveys in English: Saburo Matsukata, "A Historical Study of Capitalism in Japan," *PA*, Vol. 7, No. 1 (March 1934), pp. 71–76—a review of the first four volumes of *Nihon Shihonshugi Hattatsushi Kōza;* Nobutaka Ike, "The Development of Capitalism in Japan," *PA*, Vol. 22, No. 2 (June 1949), pp. 185–90, which purports to spell out the differences between the two schools; John W. Hall, review of Rekishigaku Kenkyūkai, ed., *Nihon Shakai no shiteki kyūmei* (1949), *FEQ*, Vol. 11, No. 1 (November 1951, pp. 97–104; George Beckmann, "Japanese Adaptations of Marx-Leninism," *ACS* (Tokyo), No. 3 (October 1962), pp. 103–14. The important work by Tanin and Yohan, *Militarism and Fascism in Japan*, would merit a separate study on its own. Basically, it partakes of the Kōza outlook—i.e., the official "right" line established by the 1932 Theses (which are themselves out of step with the "left" line prevailing in the Comintern at this period: on this see Poulantzas, *Fascism and Dictatorship*). The interesting introduction to *Militarism and Fascism* by Karl Radek is overly concerned with the theoretical problematic of "finance capital" which seems to prevent Radek from coming to grips with the real issue which he can apparently perceive—viz., the relationship between monopoly and "backwardness." See chapter 5 below for a discussion of Japanese "fascism."

88. However, as in Italy, the fact that major theoretical work was done during a period of extreme repression has had certain negative effects; in particular, the Kōzaha thesis on the need for a two-stage revolution led to a political line advocating a very wide alliance of social strata to "re-establish democracy" rather than bring about a socialist revolution. There has been a similar tendency in both countries, too, to seek

the origins of the contemporary regime in an "incomplete" bourgeois revolution (the Risorgimento, the Meiji Restoration).

Chapter 3
JAPANESE IMPERIALISM TO THE WASHINGTON CONFERENCE OF 1921–22

1. For an excellent outline of the history of Western encroachment on Japan, see William Woodruff, *Impact of Western Man: A Study of Europe's Role in the World Economy 1750–1960* (London, Macmillan & Co., 1966), pp. 29, 35–38.

2. Tōyama Shigeki, "Politics, Economics and the International Environment in the Meiji and Taishō Periods," pp. 432 ff.

3. *"Seikan Ron":* "the argument [*Ron*] over whether Japan should inflict righteous punishment [for the insult] by conquering Korea [*Seikan*]" (Conroy, *The Japanese Seizure of Korea*, p. 18). Takashi Hatada, *A History of Korea* (Santa Barbara, American Bibliographical Center—Clio Press, 1969), p. 92. Hatada's work, originally published in Japanese (Hatada Takashi, *Chōsen-shi* [History of Korea] [Tokyo, Iwanami Shoten, 1951]), is politically sounder than Conroy. The two scholars who translated and edited the American edition of Hatada, Warren W. Smith, Jr., and Benjamin H. Hazard, have seen fit in their translators' preface crudely to attack Hatada's interpretation of events in Korea in the years 1945–50 (p. vii).

4. Crowley, "From Closed Door to Empire," p. 272; Mayo, "The Korean Crisis of 1873." Where Western scholars have attempted to stress the importance of samurai pressure for a samurai army, implicitly downplaying the imperialist aspect, Hatada correctly emphasizes that the Meiji government's foreign policy programme included the idea of attacking weak nations as well as expelling the barbarians and that this programme "was not simply the reactionary expression of a disgruntled military class, but had the general support of the liberals who were promoting the development of Japanese capitalism" (*A History of Korea*, p. 92).

5. Quoted by Hilary Conroy, *"Chōsen Mondai:* The Korean Problem in Meiji Japan," *Proceedings of the American Philosophical Society*, Vol. 100, No. 5 (October 15, 1956), p. 447.

6. Ōkubo's memorial: see note 101 to chapter 1; extracts also in Conroy, *The Japanese Seizure of Korea*, pp. 47–49. Mayo, "The Korean Crisis of 1873," argues against the widely propounded thesis that the Japanese leaders were consciously "postponing" imperialism.

7. Conroy, *The Japanese Seizure of Korea*, pp. 53 ff.; Mayo, "The Korean Crisis of 1873," especially pp. 802–3. The status of the Ryukyu (Liu-ch'iu) Islands was itself subject to dispute at the time.

8. Brown, "Ōkubo Toshimichi," p. 196. Cf. Hirschmeier, *Origins of Entrepreneurship in Meiji Japan*, p. 154.

9. On "the eastern advance of Western power" (*seiryoku tōzen*) see Oka Yoshitake, extracts from "National Independence and the Reason for the State's Existence" (Kokuminteki kokuritsu to kokkai risei) in *Kindai Nihon shisōshi kōza* [Studies in the political thought of modern Japan], Vol. 8 (Tokyo, Chikuma Shobō, 1961) in Marlene J. Mayo, ed., *The Emergence of Imperial Japan: Self-Defense or Calculated Aggression?* (Lexington, Mass., D. C. Heath, 1970), pp. 1–12.

10. Japan had meantime been taking vigorous steps to expand its military forces; see Crowley, "From Closed Door to Empire," pp. 261–87.

11. On the 1884–85 crisis and the Treaty of Tientsin, see Conroy, *The Japanese Seizure of Korea*, chapters 5 and 6; Jansen, "Ōi Kentarō"; Crowley, "From Closed Door to Empire," p. 277.

12. For the background to the war, see Conroy, *The Japanese Seizure of Korea*, esp. pp. 229 ff. Some useful information, poorly presented, appears in T. F. Tsiang, "Sino-Japanese Diplomatic Relations," *CSPSR* (Peking), Vol. 17, No. 1 (April 1933). William L. Langer, *The Diplomacy of Imperialism 1890–1902* (New York, Alfred A. Knopf, 2d ed., 1950) remains a most useful global survey of imperialism manoeuvrings in the period.

13. Kimura, "Fiscal Policy and Industrialization in Japan," p. 24.

14. Tanin and Yohan, *Militarism and Fascism in Japan,* pp. 36–37.

15. Oka, "National Independence," p. 5. Figures for the indemnity vary slightly: Kimura ("Fiscal Policy") gives ¥355,980,000; Lockwood, *The Economic Development of Japan,* p. 254, gives ¥360 million; Allen, *A Short Economic History,* p. 48, has ¥366 million.

16. Quoted by Langer, *Diplomacy of Imperialism,* p. 385.

17. Frank W. Iklé, "The Triple Intervention: Japan's Lesson in the Diplomacy of Imperialism," *MN,* Vol. 22, Nos. 1–2 (1967), pp. 122–30, is a useful recent reassessment of the Triplice, arguing that Germany was the prime mover. On Germany's actions, see also Minge C. Bee, "The Origins of German Far Eastern Policy," *CSPSR,* Vol. 21, No. 1 (April 1937), pp. 65–97 (though Bee's interpretation is faulty in part). Russia's expansion eastwards is dealt with at more length below in the section on the Russo-Japanese War.

18. Crowley, "From Closed Door to Empire," pp. 279 ff.

19. Yosaburo Takekoshi, *Japanese Rule in Formosa* (London, Longmans, Green, & Co., 1907), p. 88. For a good account see Andrew J. Grajdanzev, *Formosa Today* (New York, Institute of Pacific Relations, 1942). A British text of the period had this to say: "Even after the cession, the Japanese had to fight their way mile by mile and it required a campaign of more than one year's duration before the whole island was conquered. Even then disturbances were frequent. . . . Broad-minded as ever, the Japanese recognized the sentiments of the supposedly incorrigible Formosans. Literally the colonization work went on at first within the lines of the Japanese sentries. It was, however, none the less effective and was singularly free from any military tendencies" (Alfred Stead, *Great Japan: A Study of National Efficiency* [London, John Lane, 1905], pp. 407–8—from chapter 18 entitled "Scientific Colonization"). Apart from the absurd internal contradictions in this passage, the thesis that Japanese colonization was free of military tendencies will hardly stand up. On the contrary, the Japanese military used the fact that China refused to acknowledge the loss of Taiwan to impose a (Japanese) military governor general on Taiwan—and this was repeated in all the other Japanese colonies: see Hugh Borton, "War and the Rise of Industrialization in Japan," in Jesse D. Clarkson and Thomas C. Cochran, eds., *War as a Social Institution: The Historian's Perspective* (New York, Columbia University Press, 1941), p. 233. On Japan's policy in Taiwan, Hyman Kublin, "The Evolution of Japanese Colonialism," *CSSH,* Vol. 2, No. 1 (October 1959), pp. 67–84. On the Taiwan resistance to Japan, see Harry J. Lamley, "The 1895 Taiwan War of Resistance: Local Chinese Efforts against a Foreign Power," in Leonard H. D. Gordon, ed., *Taiwan: Studies in Chinese Local History* (New York, Columbia University Press, 1970), pp. 23–76.

20. Grajdanzev, *Formosa Today,* p. 165; for a comparison with Korea, see Edward I-te Chen, "Japanese Colonialism in Korea and Formosa: A Comparison of the System of Political Control," *HJAS,* Vol. 30 (1970), 126–58.

21. Takekoshi, *Japanese Rule in Formosa,* p. 11; cf. pp. 8–10.

22. Walter LaFeber, *The New Empire: An Interpretation of American Expansion 1860–1898* (Ithaca, N.Y., Cornell University Press, 1963), is a superb study of the relationship between the industrial revolution in America and the development of U.S. imperialism. Both LaFeber and Thomas J. McCormick, *China Market: America's Quest for Informal Empire 1893–1901* (Chicago, Quadrangle Books, 1967), amply document the fact that the *policy* of the "Open Door" predates its formal announcement in the first Hay note in 1899. On the whole period, see Marilyn Blatt Young, *The Rhetoric of Empire: American China Policy 1895–1901* (Cambridge, Mass., Harvard University Press, 1968). On the Spanish-American War see also Nance Lenore O'Connor, "The Spanish-American War: A Re-Evaluation of Its Causes," *S&S,* Vol. 22, No. 2 (Spring 1958), pp. 129–43; Timothy McDonald, "McKinley and the Coming of the War with Spain," *Midwest Quarterly,* Vol. 7, No. 3 (April 1966), pp. 225–39; and Philip S. Foner, "Why the United States Went to War with Spain in 1898," *S&S,* Vol. 32, No. 1 (Spring 1968). It should be noted, too, that before the end of the century, the United States was the principal exporter to Manchuria; exports to Japan had also grown considerably, from U.S. $3,900,000 in 1894 to U.S.

$7,600,000 in 1896 and to U.S. $13,000,000 in 1897 (LaFeber, *The New Empire*, p. 301). As Woodruff puts it, "To the Chinese the American policy simply meant that America was able to reap the commercial and financial benefits of western invasion without having fought for them" (*Impact of Western Man*, p. 30).

23. Thomas McCormick, "Insular Imperialism and the Open Door: the China Market and the Spanish-American War," *PHR*, Vol. 32, No. 2 (May 1963), p. 155. That the market was indeed little more than a fable, because of poverty and bad transportation, is the thesis of Paul A. Varg, "The Myth of the China Market, 1890–1914," *AHR*, Vol. 73, No. 3 (February 1968). Many of the same arguments are being rehashed today.

24. The Spanish administration in Manila had rushed to make a deal with Tokyo after Shimonoseki, sensing its need for allies in the area. Japan had reciprocated by *re*-negotiating its *unequal* treaty with Spain in 1896, and even signed a new treaty of amity on January 2, 1897—after the Filipino revolution had started. See Josefa M. Saniel, *Japan and the Philippines* (Quezon City, University of the Philippines, 1962), pp. 269 ff. [*Philippines Social Science and Historical Review*, Vol. 27, Nos. 1–4].

25. Marius B. Jansen, *The Japanese and Sun Yat-sen* (Stanford, Stanford University Press, paperback ed., 1970), pp. 59, 68 ff.

26. On the much-neglected Filipino revolution and its suppression by the United States see Moorfield Storey and Marcial P. Lichauco, *The Conquest of the Philippines by the United States 1898–1925* (London and New York, G. P. Putnam's Sons, 1926); Leon Wolff, *Little Brown Brother: America's Forgotten Bid for Empire Which cost 250,000 Lives* (Garden City, N.Y., Doubleday & Co., 1961); James H. Blount, *The American Occupation of the Philippines 1898–1912* (New York and London, G. P. Putnam's Sons, 1913—reprinted: Quezon City, Malaya Books, 1968, with an introductory essay by Renato Constantino). On the internal history of the Filipino revolution, see two works by Teodoro A. Agoncillo, *The Revolt of the Masses* (Quezon City, University of the Philippines, 1956) and *Malolos: The Crisis of the Republic* (Quezon City, University of the Philippines, 1960)—a two-volume history of Andres Bonifacio and the Katipunan. After the Americans had defeated most of the guerrilla resistance (by about 1901–2), Japan retained the sympathy of some of the Filipino leaders, one of whom, Artemio Ricarte, chose to go into exile in Japan: see Grant K. Goodman, "General Artemio Ricarte and Japan," *Journal of Southeast Asian History*, Vol. 7, No. 2 (September 1966), pp. 48–60. And in 1941–42 Emilio Aguinaldo, still a popular hero to many, backed the Japanese "liberation" of the Philippines from U.S. imperialism (F. C. Jones, *Japan's New Order in East Asia: Its Rise and Fall, 1937–45* [London, Oxford University Press, 1954], p. 359).

27. Hilary Conroy, *The Japanese Frontier in Hawaii, 1868–1898* (Berkeley and Los Angeles, University of California Press, 1953), p. 119.

28. With annexation the white settlers' racist concern about "balancing the races" evaporated and Japanese immigration shot up so that by 1900 there were 61,111 Japanese—more than double the number of any other ethnic group.

29. The Yi Ho Tuan are usually misnamed "Boxers" in imperialist literature. Here only the external, anti-foreign moment is considered. For a more comprehensive view, see Hu Sheng, *Imperialism and Chinese Politics*, pp. 131 ff.; Victor Purcell, *The Boxer Uprising* (Cambridge, the University Press, 1963); Jerome Ch'en, "The Nature and Characteristics of the Boxer Movement—A Morphological Study," *Bulletin of the School of Oriental and African Studies*, Vol. 23 (1960), pp. 287–308; Yuji Muramatsu, " 'I-ho-chuan' Uprising, 1900," *AHA*, Vol. 3, No. 2 (April 1953).

30. Quoted in Langer, *Diplomacy of Imperialism*, p. 699.

31. I. H. Nish, "Japan's Indecision During the Boxer Disturbances," *JAS*, Vol. 20, No. 4 (August 1961), p. 449.

32. Cited in Paul A. Varg, "The Foreign Policy of Japan and the Boxer Revolt," *PHR*, Vol. 14, No. 3 (August 1946), p. 281—referring to Peking (rather than Tientsin).

33. Andrew Malozemoff, *Russian Far Eastern Policy 1881–1904* (Berkeley and Los Angeles, University of California Press, 1958), pp. 135–44.

34. "Nippon helping the British at the time was really God's act" (*Shonan Times*, February 26, 1942—quoted by Jones, *Japan's New Order in East Asia*, p. 386 [Shonan = Singapore]). Yet the racial significance of the alliance was ambiguous; as Ayusawa (*History*

of Labor, p. 89) comments, this was "the first time in modern world history that a Caucasian nation or empire had sought to form a military pact with a non-European and non-Caucasian nation." The alliance was ended by the Washington Conference of 1921–22. One of its main legacies is a pile of delirious imperialist literature. For example, Stead, *Great Japan,* which has an introduction by the Earl of Rosebery which is a virtual plea for dictatorship, plus a chapter on "humane war" which surpasses belief; cf. Colonel A. M. Murray, *Imperial Outposts from a Strategical and Commercial Aspect with Special Reference to the Japanese Alliance* (London, John Murray, 1907), with an introduction by Field-Marshal Earl Roberts pleading for an autonomous military establishment independent of "politicians"; at a less rabid level, Henry Dyer, *Dai Nippon! The Britain of the East* (London, Blackie & Son, 1904). For a general survey of the first period of the alliance, Nish, *The Anglo-Japanese Alliance,* comprehensive, but tedious; Peter Lowe, *Great Britain and Japan 1911–1915: A Study of British Far Eastern Policy* (London, Macmillan & Co., 1969), for the middle years; for the end of the alliance: Ian H. Nish, *Alliance in Decline: A Study in Anglo-Japanese Relations 1908–1923* (London, Athlone Press, 1972) and Malcolm D. Kennedy, *The Estrangement of Great Britain and Japan 1917–1935* (Berkeley and Los Angeles, University of California Press, 1969). There is much interesting information on British (and Empire) attitudes towards ending the alliance in William Roger Louis, *British Strategy in the Far East 1919–1939* (Oxford, Clarendon Press, 1971), chapters 1–3.

35. Malozemoff, *Russian Far Eastern Policy, passim,* esp. pp. 65 ff.

36. *Ibid.,* p. 110.

37. *Ibid.,* pp. 175 ff. Shumpei Okamoto, *The Japanese Oligarchy and the Russo-Japanese War,* pp. 57 ff.

38. Theodore H. Von Laue, *Sergei Witte and the Industrialization of Russia* (New York and London, Columbia University Press, 1963), esp. pp. 239 ff. Sergius Witte, *Memoirs* (London, William Heinemann, 1921), pp. 113 ff. Cf. F. E. White's review of B. A. Romanov, *Ocherki Diplomaticheskoy istorii russko-yaponskoy voyni (1895–1907)* (Moscow, 1947), in *FEQ,* Vol. 11, No. 3 (May 1952), for a useful brief survey of Russian interpretations of the war (including the legacy of Pokrovsky) and the Witte-Bezobrazov split.

39. A policy known as *Mankan Kōkan* (exchange Manchuria and Korea); see Okamoto, *The Japanese Oligarchy,* pp. 69 (on *Man-kan Kōkan*) and 97 ff. (on the actual negotiations); cf. Oka, "National Independence," p. 10.

40. Okamoto, *The Japanese Oligarchy,* p. 101.

41. Richard Hough, *The Fleet That Had To Die* (London, Hamish Hamilton, 1958), is a vivid account of the Russian fleet's voyage and defeat.

42. Witte, *Memoirs,* p. 113. For Japan's attempts to contribute to this state of affairs, see Michael Futrell, "Colonel Akashi and Japanese Contacts with Russian Revolutionaries in 1904–5," in G. F. Hudson, ed., *Far Eastern Affairs Number Four* [St. Antony's Papers Number 20] (London, Oxford University Press, 1967), pp. 7–22.

43. G. Safarov, *The Far East Ablaze* (London, Modern Books, 1933), p. 34 (Safarov was a rather conservative Comintern expert on the East). Witte quotes Plehve, the Tsarist Minister of the Interior, as saying to Kuropatkin: "We need a little victorious war to stem the tide of revolution" (Witte, *Memoirs,* p. 250). Both Lenin and Stalin were greatly excited by the revolutionary implications of the war—see, for example, Lenin's "The Fall of Port Arthur" (January 1, 1905).

44. "The racial theory suffered a terrific defeat on the fields of Manchuria" in the words of Michel Pavlovitch, *The Foundations of Imperialist Policy* (London, Labour Publishing Co., 1922), p. 10; Pavlovitch was a Comintern expert on imperialism; this volume is an excellent course of lectures delivered to the Academy of the General Staff in 1918–19. The wartime Prime Minister of Burma, Ba Maw, records in his memoirs the powerful effect of Japan's victory on children in Burma: at school the children wanted to be the Japanese in war games, and the British fostered this enthusiasm by distributing pro-Japanese pictures (Ba Maw, *Breakthrough in Burma: Memoirs of a Revolution, 1939–1946* [New Haven and London, Yale University Press, 1968], pp. 47–49).

45. On the effects of the 1905 revolution, see Ivar Spector, *The First Russian Revolution:*

Its Impact on Asia (Englewood Cliffs, N.J., Prentice-Hall, 1962), which has chapters on Iran, the Ottoman Empire, China and India—but not Japan. A few Russian socialists moved to Japan.

46. Jansen, *The Japanese and Sun Yat-sen*, p. 112.

47. Okamoto, *The Japanese Oligarchy*, p. 101; and pp. 105–12, on the course of the war.

48. *Ibid.*, pp. 112 ff., for the discussion within Japan on peace terms; pp. 150 ff., on the Portsmouth Conference. On the Conference, see also Witte, *Memoirs*, pp. 134 ff. (readable but one-sided); Raymond A. Esthus, *Theodore Roosevelt and Japan* (Seattle and London, University of Washington Press, 1966), chapters 3–6, useful on American policy; and John Albert White, *The Diplomacy of the Russo-Japanese War* (Princeton, Princeton University Press, 1964).

49. Okamoto, *The Japanese Oligarchy*, pp. 152 ff. The degree of unanimity is strikingly shown by Yamagata's firm backing for the peace terms—see Hackett, *Yamagata Aritomo*, pp. 228 ff.

50. Oka, "National Independence," p. 12.

51. Cited by Fred Harvey Harrington, *God, Mammon and the Japanese. Dr. Horace N. Allen and Korean-American Relations* (Madison, University of Wisconsin Press, 1944); this is a lively work on Korean-American relations between 1884 and 1905.

52. *Ibid.*, p. 305.

53. Hatada, *History of Korea*, pp. 107–11; Conroy, *The Japanese Seizure of Korea*, pp. 330 ff., for Japan's policy from the end of the Sino-Japanese War; pp. 334 ff., for Itō's appointment, and his policy assessed, pp. 379–80. Conroy's assessment of Itō's policy fits in with that given by Crowley of the policy of the Japanese military ("From Closed Door to Empire," p. 282). Whatever nuances scholars may find in Itō's line, the basic fact is that he did not envisage tolerating Korean independence.

Discussion of Japan's seizure of Korea in English language works has tended to oscillate between the false poles of "plot" and "drift." Conroy stresses the "no conspiracy" line. His bourgeois critics tend to emphasize the existence of a Japanese "plot" (see the discussion minutes on Conroy's book, "Japanese Imperialism and Aggression: Reconsiderations I," *JAS*, Vol. 22, No. 4 [August 1963], pp. 469–72). It must be said that Conroy has done a very valuable job of research, clarification and presentation. But he does not present a convincing case against the Japanese Marxists. It is hard to recognize the range and richness of Japanese Marxist thought on the subject in the brief extracts and phrases he reproduces, and several of the examples he chooses do not inspire confidence in his method (for example, his comments on the work of Inoue Kiyoshi at p. 485). Further, although Conroy makes critical use of the terms "idealism" and "realism," he does not satisfactorily answer his own questions about why Itō and his "realist" approach ("realism" here being used as applied to George Kennan) "failed," in Conroy's terminology (p. 499). Also, what bourgeois writers term "plot" and "drift" are not incompatible: American policy in Vietnam combined both for a full decade. What is lacking in the analyses of both Conroy and his critics in the West is a *global structural* analysis. Imperialism, after all, can have *political* objectives. The economy is the dominant only in the last instance—again, compare the relationship between U.S. imperialism and Vietnam (see Poulantzas, *Political Power and Social Classes, passim*, on the articulation of political [and strategical] objectives of a ruling class. It might be added that a group in essential agreement does not have to "plot" to take action; the members of the board of a capitalist enterprise do not "plot" to exploit their workers; they agree on this without having to discuss it. Moreover, a capitalist class is not always aware of its own "best" interests—although this is not absolutely central.). Finally, it is a pity that Conroy did not at least anticipate the longer-term economic advantages to Japan of its exploitation of Korea and the Korean people (particularly the process of reducing the rice intake of the Korean agricultural proletariat to feed Japan's population, and the importation of Koreans into Japan as a sub-proletariat—see Shiota, "A 'Ravaged' People: The Koreans in World War II," pp. 43–45, especially the table at p. 45).

54. America endorsed the take-over both as a quid pro quo for Japan agreeing to leave the Philippines alone, and because it hoped that Korea would provide either a real or a political outlet for Japanese emigration at a time when there was much racist agitation in the United States against Japanese immigration. For the heavy cover

given annexation by Western writers, see George Trumbull Ladd, *In Korea with Marquis Itō* (New York, Charles Scribner's Sons, 1908) and Ladd, "The Annexation of Korea: An Essay in 'Benevolent Assimilation,' " *YR*, Vol. 1, No. 4 (July 1912), pp. 639–656). Payson J. Treat, *The Far East: A Political and Diplomatic History* (London, Harper & Bros., 1928) and P. H. Clyde, *A History of the Modern and Contemporary Far East* (New York, Prentice-Hall, 1937) are well criticized by Grajdanzev, *Modern Korea;* cf. Conroy, "*Chōsen Mondai:* The Korean Problem in Meiji Japan," on Ladd and Treat.

55. C. I. Eugene Kim and Han-kyo Kim, *Korea and the Politics of Imperialism 1876–1910* (Berkeley and Los Angeles, University of California Press, 1967), p. 205.

56. Grajdanzev, *Modern Korea,* gives 7,000; according to George O. Totten, "figures made public" state that 7,509 people were killed (note in Wales and Kim, *Song of Ariran,* p. 332); the figures given by Hatada, *History of Korea,* p. 115, are much lower. Somewhere between half a million and 5 million people (varying estimates) took part in popular demonstrations after the death of the old Emperor of Korea. This uprising forced the temporary lifting of military rule in Korea, and also led to some changes in Japan's colonial policy. After 1919 Japan tried to build up a small intermediate landlord class between itself and the Korean masses: see Hatada, *History of Korea,* pp. 114–118, and L. Kaufman, "Yaponskii imperializm i Koreya," *Novyi Vostok* (Moscow), No. 5 (1924), pp. 86–100, on this shift. It was this stratum which provided continuity between Japanese and American imperialist rule and formed the domestic class basis of the post-1945 Syngman Rhee dictatorship. There appears to be no full account in English of the 1919 uprising; a useful Russian source is F. I. Shabshina, *Narodnoye vosstanie 1919 goda v Koree* (Moscow, Izdatel'stvo Vostochnoy Literaturni, 2d rev. ed., 1958).

57. Mario Toscano, *Guerra diplomatica in Estremo Oriente (1914–1931): I trattati delle ventun domande* (Turin, Giulio Einaudi, 1950); this remains probably the best overall history of the period.

58. Ernest Batson Price, *The Russo-Japanese Treaties of 1907–1916 Concerning Manchuria and Mongolia* (Baltimore, Johns Hopkins University Press, 1933).

59. On the Twenty-one Demands, see Hu Sheng, *Imperialism and Chinese Politics,* p. 209; Toscano, *Guerra diplomatica,* Vol. 1; Jansen, *The Japanese and Sun Yat-sen,* pp. 175 ff.; Jansen, "Yawata, Hanyehping and the Twenty-one Demands," *PHR,* Vol. 23, No. 1 (February 1954), pp. 31–48.

60. Quoted in Victor A. Yakhontoff, *Russia and the Soviet Union in the Far East* (London, Allen & Unwin, 1932), p. 116.

61. *Ibid.,* pp. 118–19.

62. Hackett, *Yamagata Aritomo,* pp. 291 ff.

63. For some information on the Korean diaspora in Manchuria and Siberia and Japanese anti-Korean activities there, see Dae-sook Suh, *The Korean Communist Movement, 1918–1948* (Princeton, Princeton University Press, 1967); Hatada, *History of Korea,* p. 115.

64. James William Morley, *The Japanese Thrust into Siberia, 1918* (New York, Columbia University Press, 1957), pp. 31–32.

65. William A. Williams, "American Intervention in Russia, 1917–1920," in David Horowitz, ed., *Containment and Revolution: Western Policy Towards Social Revolution: 1917 to Vietnam* (London, Anthony Blond, 1967), is excellent on the manipulation of the bogus German threat and completely demolishes the myth of America's alleged reluctance to intervene. The account below is based essentially on Williams and on Chihiro Hosoya, "Origin of the Siberian Intervention, 1917–1918," *AHA,* Vol. 9, No. 1 (October 1958), pp. 91–108.

66. Western historians have gone to great lengths to try to show that their countries' intervention was not against the Revolution and that Japan was the prime culprit in originating the adventure. This traditional U.S. position is repeated in most standard works on America's Far East policy. For example, A. Whitney Griswold, *The Far Eastern Policy of the United States* (New York, 1938; New Haven, Yale University Press, paperback ed., 1962), pp. 226–27, writes: "In the Far East [the U.S.'s] purpose was to resist the Japanese penetration of northern Manchuria and Siberia." Even more absurd positions are sometimes put forward; Richard Pipes (of Harvard) claims

that "the Western Allies saved Eastern Siberia from certain Japanese conquest" (*JAS*, Vol. 16, No. 3 [1957], p. 112). A newer line of defence is exemplified in Morley, *The Japanese Thrust into Siberia,* which essentially argues that a reluctant United States was pushed into Siberia by an aggressive Japan; Hosoya, "Origin of the Siberian Intervention," has some useful criticisms of Morley and is also good on how Hara Kei, soon to be Prime Minister, was brought round to supporting intervention by America's moves.

67. Quoted by Williams, "American Intervention in Russia," p. 55. A description of activity by an American soldier there went as follows: "We went to Siberia with armed forces to help Russia, and did little but talk, nurse the railroad, distribute pamphlets, and show pictures to prove to the Russians what a great nation we were —at home. Among the pamphlets we distributed was one in Russian, entitled: 'If you want a republic we will show you how to build one' " (F. Moore, *Siberia Today* [New York, 1919], p. 327, quoted in Yamato Ichihashi, *The Washington Conference and After: A Historical Survey* [Stanford, Stanford University Press, 1928], p. 319).

68. Chihiro Hosoya, "Japan's Decision for War in 1941," *PRJ* (Tokyo), 1967, pp. 49–51, quoting the Stimson Diary entries for October 4, 1940, where Stimson refers back to this embargo as a successful precedent for the 1940 embargo plans. Hosoya indicates this to be a fundamental element in American miscalculations about Japan in the period prior to Pearl Harbor.

69. In Jansen's words (paraphrasing Shinobu): "American delay in announcing the withdrawal of General Graves' [commander of U.S. forces] forces made it difficult for the Gaimushō [Japanese Foreign Office], which wished to withdraw, to counter the Army, which did not" (Jansen, "From Hatoyama to Hatoyama," p. 74). Shinobu also points out that Tanaka was for withdrawal, but would not come out openly to this effect (*ibid.,* p. 74).

70. On Japan's economic policy, see John Albert White, *The Siberian Intervention* (Princeton, Princeton University Press, 1950), pp. 304 ff.

71. Carr, *The Bolshevik Revolution,* Vol. 3, pp. 360–61, on Nikolayevsk. Japanese policy, in spite of the split referred to above, was largely defined independent of factors such as whether or not the alleged massacre of Japanese had really occurred at Nikolayevsk.

72. On Sakhalin and later events there, see Amidon, "The Issue of Sakhalin."

73. Robert T. Pollard, "The Dynamics of Japanese Imperialism," *PHR*, Vol. 8, No. 1 (February 1939), p. 13.

74. Arno J. Mayer, *Politics and Diplomacy of Peacemaking: Containment and Counter-revolution at Versailles, 1918–1919* (London, Weidenfeld and Nicolson, 1968), brilliantly details the real purpose of Versailles: to construct a water-tight anti-Bolshevik settlement for postwar Europe. Japan was one of the five "Powers with General Interests" but was excluded from the Supreme War Council of Four; when the Council of Ten was reduced to a Council of Four on March 24, 1919, Japan was excluded.

75. The San Francisco school segregation law (1905); the Tokyo "gentleman's agreement" limiting emigrants to the United States (1908); the California law against Japanese acquiring landed property (1913). Restrictions against ethnic Japanese owning property were even tougher than those against blacks.

76. Early *male* migration from the Japanese countryside had been mainly to Hokkaido and Hawaii rather than into the towns of Japan itself. In the early 1880s Kalakaua, the King of Hawaii (still then an independent nation), invited Japan to lead an Asiatic Federation, including Hawaii. Japan refused, in order not to antagonize the West (Conroy, *The Japanese Frontier in Hawaii*, pp. 51–53).

77. Eleanor Tupper and George E. McReynolds, *Japan in American Public Opinion* (New York, Macmillan Co., 1937), p. 53; Gompers accompanied Wilson to France as part of the delegation and helped give the I.L.O., which was set up then, some of its anti-Japanese impetus.

78. See the August 15, 1921, Theses of the ECCI, and the decision to call the First Congress of the Toilers of the Far East as a direct counter to the Conference (Eudin and North, *Soviet Russia and the Far East,* p. 145; cf. chapter 2 above).

79. Before the First World War, in 1912, a "First Consortium" of banks from all the six major imperialist powers had been set up to help finance the exploitation of China. This Consortium included the Hongkong and Shanghai Banking Corporation,

the Banque d'Indochine, the Yokohama Specie Bank, the Russo-Asian Bank, the Deutsche-asiatische Bank and a number of New York banks (Jean Chesneaux, *L'Asie orientale aux XIXᵉ et XXᵉ siècles: Chine- Japon—Inde—Sud-Est asiatique* [Paris, Presses Universitaires de France, 1966], p. 134). Discussions about a new inter-imperialist deal over China had begun before the end of the war (the Lansing-Ishii agreement of November 1917), and the United States had floated the idea of a new banking consortium, to be given a retroactive and current option on all loans to China. Tokyo favoured this idea, and the United States reciprocated by agreeing to exclude some Japanese railways in Manchuria and Eastern Inner Mongolia from the domain of the consortium, while letting Japan in as a partner in the rest of China; see Akira Iriye, *After Imperialism: The Search for a New Order in the Far East 1921–1931* (Cambridge, Mass., Harvard University Press, 1965), pp. 14–15; for British unease, see Louis, *British Strategy in the Far East,* pp. 28 ff.

80. James B. Crowley, "A New Deal for Japan and Asia: One Road to Pearl Harbor," in James B. Crowley, ed., *Modern East Asia: Essays in Interpretation* (New York, Harcourt, Brace and World, 1970), pp. 240, 242–43; Louis, *British Strategy in the Far East,* chapter 3 and pp. 236–37.

81. Saitō Takashi, "Japan's Foreign Policy in the International Environment of the Nineteen-Twenties," *DE,* Vol. 5, No. 4 (December 1967), p. 693; on Japan's position at Washington, cf. Sadao Asada, "Japan's 'Special Interests' and the Washington Conference, 1921–22," *AHR,* Vol. 67, No. 1 (October 1961), pp. 62–70.

82. See Iriye, *After Imperialism,* and James B. Crowley, *Japan's Quest for Autonomy: National Security and Foreign Policy 1930–1938* (Princeton, Princeton University Press, 1966); cf. chapter 2 above.

83. Safarov, *The Far East Ablaze,* p. 15.

84. Fukuzawa: "We cannot wait for our neighbours to become so civilised that all may combine together to make Asia progress. We must rather break out of formation and behave in the same way as the civilised countries of the West are doing. . . . We would do better to treat China and Korea in the same way as do the western nations." Fukuzawa's writings reveal a distinct shift in the mid-1870s from a certain optimism about foreigners (i.e., Western imperialists) to deep pessimism, exemplified by gloomy comments on the extermination of the American Indians, the depopulation of the Sandwich Islands and other contemporary horrors (Blacker, *The Japanese Enlightenment,* pp. 130 ff.)

85. Alfred Stead: "Japan is a colonizing power worthy of study and imitation" (*Great Japan,* p. 426); Lord Rosebery: "Japan is indeed the object-lesson of national efficiency, and happy is the country that learns it. . . . How stands it with us in comparison with these Orientals? . . . We must . . . learn from Japan how to obtain efficiency in spite of the party systems" (foreword to *Great Japan*); Field-Marshal Earl Roberts: "Japan is a brilliant example of a nation in arms. . . . A notable feature of the higher military organization in Japan is the complete separation of questions of defence from politics" (preface to Murray, *Imperial Outposts*).

86. "What we see is capitalism without capital and the capitalist who lacks capital" bringing capitalism to Korea: "the political led the economic" (Shikata Hiroshi, cited in Conroy, *The Japanese Seizure of Korea,* p. 452; cf. Furuya Tetsuo citation in *ibid.,* p. 490).

87. Jansen, "From Hatoyama to Hatoyama," p. 68.

88. Of which the most important was the 1908 rejection of the budget (see *ibid.;* cf. Tōyama, "Politics, Economics and the International Environment," p. 435, on the triangular crisis in 1893, involving the Diet, the bureaucracy and the parties over the government's warship construction estimates, which was solved only by the Emperor's intervention in the form of an Imperial Rescript appealing to national unity and imperialism).

89. Jansen, *The Japanese and Sun Yat-sen,* pp. 84 ff.

90. The Iron and Steel Works at Yawata were begun by the Japanese government in 1896 after the Triple Intervention and the retrocession of the Liaotung Peninsula. A search for iron deposits in Japan in Niigata Prefecture failed, and it became apparent that Yawata was utterly dependent on China. In the face of German competition, Japan arranged to acquire Chinese ore from Tayeh. In 1912 Yawata had to close down as a

result of the fighting in China. See Jansen, "Yawata, Hanyehping and the Twenty-one Demands."

91. Conroy, *The Japanese Seizure of Korea*, chapter 9, discusses some of the Japanese theses on the periodization of imperialism; some ascribe the gradual take-over of Korea to "the absolutist Emperor regime," while later adventures are attributed to "finance capital." What is needed is a clear analytic distinction between the political and economic levels and a theoretical willingness to recognize forms of overseas aggressiveness which predate the dominance of industrial capitalism. A valuable brief text on the issue is Fujii Shoichi, "Capitalism, International Politics and the Emperor System," in Mayo, ed., *The Emergence of Imperial Japan*. Cf. note 53 above.

92. This seems to me correct, in general. It is developed at length by Tanin and Yohan, *Militarism and Fascism in Japan*, and also by Safarov, *The Far East Ablaze*.

Chapter 4

POLITICS FROM THE CONSTITUTION
TO THE WASHINGTON CONFERENCE (1890–1922)

1. This periodization is adopted for the sake of convenience; there was no break in domestic politics in 1922, but it is easier to discuss domestic and foreign events together after Washington. Matsuo ("The Development of Democracy in Japan—Taishō Democracy: Its Flowering and Breakdown," pp. 614–15) discusses variant methods of dating political movements around this time. The use of monarchist dating (Taishō, Shōwa) has no more significance than the use of decades. The personal orientation of the particular Emperor was marginal to political events.

2. In an interview with Colonel Murray (Murray, *Imperial Outposts*, pp. 149 ff.); Murray also asked Itō if the army might not want more wars after the victory over Russia, to which Itō replied: "You may dismiss all fear on this point. Japan wants peace. . . . I know the views of the Emperor, of his Ministers, and of the whole Japanese people. These views may be summed up in two words: 'Peaceful expansion.' "

3. Baron Hozumi, the ex-President of the Privy Council, defined the fundamental principle of the Japanese system as "theocratico-patriarchal-constitutionalism" (Victor A. Yakhontoff, *Eyes on Japan* [London, Williams & Norgate, 1937], p. 79).

4. Itagaki Taisuke came from Tosa, where he had led the advocates of war against the Bakufu. The fact of belonging to a minor *han* put Itagaki outside the central Satsuma-Chōshū nexus in the post-1868 struggle; he thus easily became a focus for dissidents.

5. Quoted in Ike, *Beginnings*, p. 59.

6. "The important reform of 1869 . . . clearly demonstrated the establishment of bureaucratic supremacy based on the premise of Imperial prerogative" (Scalapino, *Democracy and the Party Movement*, p. 54). The new Assembly Chamber (the Shugi-in) retained no legislative powers at all.

7. Ike, *Beginnings*, pp. 94 ff.; on the Hokkaido scandal, Ike, pp. 101 ff.

8. On the Aikoku Kōtō, see Sansom, *The Western World and Japan*, p. 342; the name means "Public Society of Patriots," and it was the first organization of its kind able to evade the accusation of treason (for challenging the competence of the ruler); cf. Scalapino, *Democracy and the Party Movement*, pp. 45 ff. Jiyūtō means Liberty Party, not Liberal Party (its usual translation—cf. the present "Liberal Democratic Party").

9. Scalapino, *Democracy and the Party Movement*, p. 68.

10. *Ibid.*, pp. 77 ff.; Ike, *Beginnings*, pp. 101 ff.

11. Ike, *Beginnings*, p. 190.

12. Tetsuo Najita, *Hara Kei in the Politics of Compromise 1905–1915*, p. 4.

13. On the local government reform, see Hackett, *Yamagata Aritomo*, pp. 107–15; cf. Akita, *Foundations of Constitutional Government in Modern Japan*, pp. 98 ff., on the Yamagata-Itō controversy. Texts by Yamagata are available in English in Alfred Stead, ed., *Japan by the Japanese: A Survey by Its Highest Authorities* (London, William Heinemann, 1904) and in Ōkuma, comp., *Fifty Years of New Japan:* both these texts convey Yamagata's rigidity perhaps more than his real political acumen.

14. The controversy over treaty revision had been the main reason behind the fall of the

Itō cabinet in April 1888, and behind the resignation of Itō's successor, Kuroda, in December that same year: see Jones, *Extraterritoriality in Japan*, pp. 131 ff.

15. "That there was no halting-place mid-way between a conquering and a conquered nation, as far as Japan at any rate was concerned, and that the bitter struggle for national independence logically led to expansionism is strikingly shown by the fact that Japan acquired extraterritorial rights in China before she had shaken herself free of similar foreign privileges on her own land" (Norman, *Japan's Emergence*, pp. 198–99).

16. Scalapino, *Democracy and the Party Movement*, p. 160.

17. Fukaya Hiroji, *Shoki Gikai jōyaku kaisei* [The first Diets: treaty revision] in Kindai Nihon rekishi kōza [Modern Japanese history series] (Tokyo, 1940), p. 255, cited by Scalapino, *Democracy and the Party Movement*, p. 161; cf. Scalapino, pp. 154–63, for a discussion of this period in the Diet.

18. Scalapino, *Democracy and the Party Movement*, pp. 163–65. Itō's brand of manipulative conservatism is succinctly expressed in a phrase from one of his memos (of December 10, 1891): "Our people are still childish and simple; childish, simple people, like white silk, are easy to dye various colours."

19. Tōyama, "Politics, Economics and the International Environment," p. 435.

20. On this, see, for example, Hackett, *Yamagata Aritomo*, pp. 139, 143, 168–69, 195–96, 219 (on the 1890, 1895, 1898 and 1902 budgets); Lockwood, *The Economic Development of Japan*, p. 142, for a general assessment of the effects of the military expenditures, "positive" as well as negative. Lockwood notes that in the interwar periods "direct and indirect outlays for military purposes probably rarely exceeded 10% of national income" but were much larger during war years. Overall, the military establishment absorbed "35 to 50% of national government expenditures from the Sino-Japanese War on."

21. Maruyama's thesis on this would seem to be that until 1881 the drive for popular rights (*minken*) was largely fused with and coterminous with the drive for national rights (*kokken*); with the expulsion of Ōkuma in 1881 and the all-round rollback, the two movements became split; and while liberalism remained jingoistic, "patriotism" was no longer even minimally reformist. Maruyama's position, as expressed in "Meiji kokka no shisō" (see chapter 1, note 116) is discussed by J. W. Hall in *FEQ*, Vol. 11, No. 1, pp. 102–3 and by Joseph Pittau, "The Meiji Political System: Different Interpretations," in Joseph Roggendorf, ed., *Studies in Japanese Culture* (Tokyo, Sophia University, 1963), esp. pp. 118–19. Cf. William H. Brown, S.J., review of Maruyama Masao, *Nihon no Shisō* [Japanese thought] (Tokyo, Iwanami Shoten, 1961) in *MN*, Vol. 16, (1960–61), Nos. 3–4, pp. 231–40/451–60.

22. The role of the civil bureaucracy in the structure of the Meiji state is outlined in chapter 1. In addition to the basic sources cited there (Spaulding, *Japan's Higher Civil Service Examinations;* Inoki, "The Civil Bureaucracy," in Ward and Rustow, eds., *Political Modernization in Japan and Turkey*), there is much useful material in Najita, *Hara Kei*. An outstanding article by Hamza Alavi, "The State in Post-Colonial Societies—Pakistan and Bangladesh," *NLR*, No. 74 (July–August 1972), provides a theoretical framework for consideration of the Japanese bureaucracy, which was not the instrument of any one class, but mediated between the competing interests of the propertied classes, while acting on behalf of them to preserve the social order in which their interests were embedded (Alavi, p. 62; cf. p. 72). It should be added that bourgeois sociology's emphasis on the class *origins* of bureaucracies for assessing the political role of these bureaucracies is quite unsatisfactory. Quite apart from the powerful instruments of transformation in the system (education, but also the military forces), the bureaucracy itself to some extent "transformed" the class outlook of its members: throughout the history of modern Japan it has functioned as the loyal agent of the state, co-ordinating and mediating the interests of the *competing* groups as they coalesced.

23. The Kenseitō was the name of the party (originally the Kenseikai) formed by the merger of the Jiyūtō and the Shimpotō (the successor to the Rikken Kaishintō) in 1898. The main steps in the transformation were: (1) Itō's invitation to Itagaki to join his (Itō's) cabinet when the opposition had plenty of wind in its sails after the government's failure to block the Triple Intervention in 1895; (2) the formation of the first party government (June 1898), on Itō's recommendation. Itagaki rightly

pointed out that "the present Government officials are in their very nature a political party supported by the strong class" (quoted by Scalapino, *Democracy and the Party Movement*, p. 174). Some of the zigzagging was due to bureaucratic (and bureaucratic-military) hostility to the *pace* Itō was setting for the political integration; much of the tacking was due to the colossal corruption virtually endemic in politics; Itagaki and Ōkuma were particularly noted for their venality.

24. Najita, *Hara Kei*, p. 6.
25. On the contrary, political and military leaderships worked extremely closely, and well, together; Crowley remarks that throughout the 1853–1910 period "Japan's military policies were invariably distinguished by the primacy of political leadership and political considerations" ("From Closed Door to Empire," p. 285); he stresses that it is wrong to claim there was anything like a "dual government."
26. Hackett, "The Military," in Ward and Rustow, eds., *Political Modernization in Japan and Turkey*, p. 346, resumes the military role in cabinets during this period.
27. See Inoki, "The Civil Bureaucracy," pp. 209 ff. on the 1889 reform.
28. Najita, *Hara Kei*, pp. 176 ff. Hackett, *Yamagata Aritomo*, pp. 202–3, sets these reforms in their historical perspective; the military first used the threat of not appointing service ministers against a government in 1891 (Akita, *Foundations of Constitutional Government*, p. 92).
29. Katsura Tarō was of rather similar character to Yamagata: somewhat of a heavy and fairly intelligent, but less widely acknowledged than Yamagata. Later on, Katsura tried to break away from Yamagata's influence (Hackett, *Yamagata Aritomo*, p. 258). Prince Saionji was the last of the *genrō;* he had played a "liberal" role in the nineteenth century, and was ideally placed to operate as arch-conciliator.
30. Gotō Shimpei on Katsura, quoted in Najita, *Hara Kei*, p. 124.
31. The background to this is that the parties, particularly through the activities of Hara, had begun to acquire power by doing deals with Katsura at the time of the Portsmouth crisis in 1905.
32. Jansen, "Yawata, Hanyehping and the Twenty-one Demands."
33. Fridell, "Government Ethics Textbooks in Late Meiji Japan."
34. Marshall, *Capitalism and Nationalism*, pp. 46 ff., gives an elegant account of this process; cf. note 85 to chapter 1.
35. Hara Rokurō (as recalled by Kaneko Kentarō), cited by Marshall, *Capitalism and Nationalism*, p. 48.
36. *Ibid.*, p. 47; the quote within the quote is from an interview with Otani Kahei in the *Tōyō Keizai Shimpō*, April 15, 1896, p. 15.
37. Ike, *Beginnings*, p. 92.
38. Hackett, *Yamagata Aritomo*, p. 169.
39. *Ibid.*, pp. 196 (1898), 219 (1902), 239 (1908) and 250 ff. (the Taishō crisis).
40. Herbert P. Bix, "Japanese Imperialism and the Manchurian Economy, 1900–31," *China Quarterly*, Vol. 51 (July–September 1972) [= chapter 4 of Bix's thesis cited at note 44, p. 333 above], is an outstanding text on Japanese rule over Manchuria.
41. See, for example, Tōjō's "anxious and pitiful answer" to a question in the Diet in 1943, quoted in Masao Maruyama, *Thought and Behaviour in Modern Japanese Politics* (London, Oxford University Press, 1963), p. 47.
42. In the 1908 crisis, big business sided with the military in favour of a big budget against the *genrō*.
43. Bix, "Japanese Imperialism and the Manchurian Economy," pp. 437–38.
44. Tōyama, "Politics, Economics, and the International Environment," p. 434.
45. Ayusawa, *History of Labor*, p. 93.
46. Matsuo, "The Development of Democracy in Japan," p. 615. Matsuo's article is a valuable corrective to the picture given by Scalapino: Matsuo's work is self-confessedly instrumental, attempting to recoup and synthesize both the bourgeois liberal tradition and socialism to oppose the renewed authoritarianism of the ruling LDP: the upshot is therefore, as with Scalapino, excessive confidence in the "democratic" ideas of the prewar bourgeoisie.
47. "Constitutionalism" meant only support for partly responsible government, not representative democracy.
48. Here, as so often, the surface contradictions cover yet one more level: the campaign

was financed by Mitsui to counter the tie-up between Katsura and Mitsubishi; it was the creation of business interests (see Najita, *Hara Kei*, note 24, p. 266).

49. Matsuo, "The Development of Democracy in Japan," p. 615.

50. The in-fighting in this period is too complex for any brief explanation. The Yamamoto cabinet fell in March 1914 after a major bribery scandal involving the Siemens company; the peers (lieges of Yamagata) sabotaged the budget; a proposal for a Seiyūkai cabinet (which was backed by Saionji) was vetoed by the other two *genrō;* instead, Ōkuma was allowed to form a cabinet in April 1914, which had Chōshū support, and was designed to cripple the Seiyūkai. Ōkuma then called an election the following year to try to make it easier to run the government: this election was marked by enormous corruption; Ōkuma and his party, the Dōshikai, emerged triumphant; in this way a large number of Ōkuma's men, graduates of Waseda University (one of the original "opposition" universities), were lodged in power, at least for a time (on this see Najita, *Hara Kei*, pp. 189 ff.).

51. Andō, "The Evolutionary Process of the Japanese Economy," pp. 194–98.

52. Rosovsky, *Capital Formation in Japan*, p. 11.

53. Production in what Shiota calls "major industries" increased by nearly five times, and foreign trade grew by four times just during the war years (Shiota, "The Rice Riots and the Social Problems," p. 519).

54. Sumiya, "Labour-Relations," pp. 513–15.

55. The source for this information is Jansen, "From Hatoyama to Hatoyama," p. 74 (based on the work by Shinobu under review by Jansen). On the splits within the Japanese leadership over Siberia, see Hosoya, "Origin of the Siberian Intervention."

Chapter 5

FROM THE WASHINGTON CONFERENCE
TO THE PACIFIC WAR (1922–41)

1. Saitō Takashi, "Japan's Foreign Policy in the International Environment of the Nineteen-Twenties," p. 695.

2. "Between 1922 and 1927 the Soviet Union was the most active agent of change in the Far East" (Iriye, *After Imperialism*, p. 3); on Soviet policy in the East in this early and heroic period, see Eudin and North, *Soviet Russia and the East;* cf. Allen S. Whiting, *Soviet Policies in China, 1917–1924* (Stanford, Stanford University Press, paperback ed., 1968). There was also the evidence of the victorious Mongolian Revolution.

3. Iriye, *After Imperialism*, p. 3.

4. Crowley, "A New Deal for Japan and Asia," p. 240.

5. C. F. Remer, *Foreign Investments in China* (New York, Macmillan Co., 1933), p. 552. Between 1914 and 1930 Japanese investment in Manchuria grew by just over four times (from ¥265.2 million to ¥1,100.4 million), while investment in Shanghai grew over seven times from ¥60 million to ¥430 million (Remer, p. 473). Although these figures are not wholly reliable, the proportions are probably about right. A Japanese source puts Japanese investment in Manchuria "outstanding immediately before the start of the Manchurian Incident" at ¥820 million, substantially below Remer's estimate (*OE* [Tokyo], Vol. 7, No. 3 [March 1940], p. 153). For a useful discussion of these statistics, see Chi-ming Hou, *Foreign Investment and Economic Development in China 1840–1937* (Cambridge, Mass., Harvard University Press, 1965), pp. 10–15, 234–35.

6. Chang Tso-lin was the leading warlord in North China; Japanese ideas for promoting him stretched back as far as 1912. For a definitive study of Chang see Gavan McCormack, *Chang Tso-lin, the Mukden Military Clique and Japan, 1920–1928: The Development and Inter-relationships of Chinese Militarism and Japanese Imperialism in Northeast China* (Ph.D. thesis, London University, 1974).

7. Iriye, *After Imperialism*, p. 207.

8. This issue is dealt with in detail in Bix, *Japanese Imperialism and Manchuria*, pp. 216–23; what follows owes much to Bix.

9. Najita, *Hara Kei*, p. 240.

10. *Ibid.*, p. 33.
11. This was to be particularly important in the 1930s, after the end of the so-called "party governments" in 1932 (see below, and Crowley, *Japan's Quest*, pp. 179–80).
12. The structural contradictions in agriculture are dealt with later under the discussion of the post-1945 land reform. An excellent text on the question is Ōuchi, "Agricultural Depression and Japanese Villages." On the specific connection with the military, see Takehiko Yoshihashi, *Conspiracy at Mukden—The Rise of the Japanese Military* (New Haven and London, Yale University Press, 1963), pp. 107–18.
13. Jansen, "From Hatoyama to Hatoyama," pp. 75–76. Edward G. Griffin, "The Universal Suffrage Issue in Japanese Politics, 1918–1925," *JAS*, Vol. 31, No. 2 (February 1972), pp. 275–90, is a detailed study of this.
14. Jansen, "From Hatoyama to Hatoyama," p. 77; cf. Peter Duus, *Party Rivalry and Political Change in Taishō Japan* (Cambridge, Mass., Harvard University Press, 1968), pp. 199 ff.
15. Katō Takaaki (or Kōmei), to be distinguished from Admiral Katō Tomosaburō, premier from June 1922 to September 1923. Katō Takaaki as Foreign Minister in 1915 had pushed through the Twenty-one Demands, and had also moved to exclude the *genrō* from some of their power by putting an end to the practice of circulating secret documents to them. Katō had worked for Mitsubishi and married the eldest daughter of Iwasaki, the head of the Mitsubishi combine. Shidehara Kijūrō, his Foreign Minister in 1924, was married to another of Iwasaki's daughters (Duus, *Party Rivalry and Political Change*, pp. 54, 191).
16. Duus, *Party Rivalry and Political Change*, pp. 19–24, is useful on corruption. This mention of bribery is not meant to imply that Japan was structurally more corrupt than any other capitalist society (such as the United States, for example).

    On the Bank of Taiwan, see Ōshima Kiyoshi, "The World Economic Crisis and Japan's Foreign Economic Policy," *DE*, Vol. 5, No. 4 (December 1967), p. 631.
17. Scalapino, *Democracy and the Party Movement*, p. 254, appears not to grasp either the relationship between capital and the state or capitalism's need to oppress the proletariat.
18. It is just voluntarist to suggest, as Scalapino does, that capitalism might suddenly have struck out on a different path, or indeed that its chosen instruments, such as Parliament, "remained the chief hope of Japanese democracy" (*ibid.*, p. 220); this immediately after noting that while the Hara cabinet was "probably the most successful since the founding of the Constitution" (p. 212), Hara in office did nothing to lessen the power of the "nonelective forces in Japanese government [and] . . . did as little to build up the power and prestige of the House of Representatives" (p. 218).
19. On the Conference, see Crowley, *Japan's Quest*, pp. 78 ff., and below. The navy was in fact quite badly split into the so-called "shore duty" and "fleet" groups. The former wanted to abide by the London terms; the "fleet" group was for a more activist approach; it was this latter group who assassinated Premier Inukai in 1932 (see Yoshihashi, *Conspiracy at Mukden*, pp. 74–75).
20. This must partly be ascribed to the fact that the main postwar material by which wartime experience and prejudice was felt to be confirmed came from the Tokyo War Crimes Tribunal. Not only was this unreliable because of the vindictiveness involved, but no proper estimate was made of the worth of much testimony. Thus the crude binomic (Kōdōha-Tōseiha) distinction put across by many Japanese witnesses was accepted virtually without question, and later incorporated unchallenged into many books. Cf. note 22 below. Much valuable information on the army is contained in Kazuko Tsurumi, *Social Change and the Individual: Japan Before and After Defeat in World War II* (Princeton, N.J., Princeton University Press, 1970), chapters 2–4.
21. For detailed study of this, see Crowley, *Japan's Quest, passim;* Iriye, *After Imperialism;* Crowley, "Japanese Army Factionalism in the Early Thirties," *JAS*, Vol. 21, No. 3 (May 1962); Crowley, "A New Deal for Japan and Asia"; Saitō Takashi, "Japan's Foreign Policy in the International Environment of the Nineteen-Twenties."
22. Crowley, *Japan's Quest*, is useful in reassessing the major "Incidents" and in reviewing the complex divisions in the army. In general, on the period, David J. Lu, *From*

352

NOTES FOR PAGE 122

the Marco Polo Bridge to Pearl Harbor: Japan's Entry into World War II (Washington, D.C., Public Affairs Press, 1961), is the most sensitive source. See also Richard Storry, *The Double Patriots: A Study of Japanese Nationalism* (London, Chatto & Windus, 1957); Maruyama, *Thought and Behaviour in Modern Japanese Politics.*

23. Thus, for example, the contradictions set up by General Araki Sadao, who was the first non-Chōshū War Minister and (*a*) created a Tosa-Saga clique; (*b*) stimulated a Chōshū revanchist clique; and (*c*) hampered the technological anti-Soviet group inside the army. The most serious attempt at a thorough overhaul of the whole army to introduce an out-and-out technological and anti-Soviet policy was frustrated when the key figure, Nagata Tetsuzan, was murdered by another officer in August 1935.

24. Crowley, *Japan's Quest*, pp. 342 ff. John Hunter Boyle, *China and Japan at War: The Politics of Collaboration* (Stanford, Stanford University Press, 1972), chapter 4.

25. There would appear to be no one single good text on Japan in the great depression. Ōuchi, "Agricultural Depression and Japanese Villages," is excellent on the rural scene; Chō Yukio, "From the Shōwa Economic Crisis to Military Economy—With Special Reference to the Inoue and Takahashi Financial Policies," *DE*, Vol. 5, No. 4 (December 1967), pp. 568–96, and Ōshima Kiyoshi, "The World Economic Crisis and Japan's Foreign Economic Policy," are both most valuable. Tanin and Yohan, *Militarism and Fascism in Japan*, pp. 152 ff., and Maruyama, *Thought and Behaviour in Modern Japanese Politics, passim,* have wide-ranging information on the effects of the depression on ideology, nationalism and the military (cf. section below on Japanese "fascism"). Much useful material, too, exists in James William Morley, ed., *Dilemmas of Growth in Prewar Japan* (Princeton, Princeton University Press, 1971). Allen, *Short Economic History*, pp. 104 ff., has information on concentration (but less on exploitation) accompanying the recession—facilitated by the extended role of credit in the economy. Uyeda, *The Small Industries of Japan*, pp. 304 ff., is useful on the effects of the depression on wages. Robert H. Ferrell, *American Diplomacy in the Great Depression* (New Haven, Yale University Press, 1957), covers 1929–33 competently from a fairly mystified standpoint. Stimulating observations on the effects of the depression on Japan can be found in Geoffrey Barraclough, *New York Review of Books*, Vol. 20, Nos. 9 and 10 (May 31 and June 14, 1973). What is needed is a comprehensive study of the depression *as a breakdown*—the first and only one since Japan entered the capitalist network. While cataclysmic, it also offered *a chance.* Thus the key moves were mainly responses to this: the military acting against suffering and misery at home as well as to exploit the momentary void opened up abroad. Manufacturers rushed to capture textile markets, mainly in what is now called the Third World.

26. The God-Sent Troops Incident of July 1933, for example, was financed by the director of a famous Tokyo department store who had just lost heavily on the stock exchange and planned to repair the loss by administering a shock to the stock market (Toshikazu Kase, *Eclipse of the Rising Sun* [London, Jonathan Cape, 1951], p. 31, published in the United States as *Journey to the* Missouri [New Haven, Yale University Press, 1950]). Kase concludes: "The borderland between crime and passion was indeed narrow."

27. A careful hierarchization of the contradictions is needed. Japan's main contradiction was with the people of China, not with Britain or the United States. But, particularly in the context of the depression, Japan had real secondary contradictions with the Western powers. There is a coherent succession of attempts to settle these contradictions, attempts which often involved sizeable concessions by Japan. This sequence can be followed right from the Washington Conference through the London Conference of 1930, Japan's acceptance of the League of Nations resolution on Manchuria of September 30, 1931, up to the days before Pearl Harbor. These attempts, which reached their apex with the Minseitō cabinet of Hamaguchi and Shidehara, do not represent an anti-imperialist policy which can be *strategically* distinguished from some putative militarist-imperialist approach. Both the policy actually applied by, say, Tanaka Giichi, and that applied by Shidehara when he was Foreign Minister are equally imperialist. Andō ("The Evolutionary Process of the Japanese Economy in the Twentieth Century") is right to see the Hamaguchi-Shidehara cabinet as a "pure"

bourgeois attempt to try and deal with the *results* of the structural contradictions in the economy and to reinsert Japan into the world bourgeois-imperialist system (by lifting the embargo on gold and accepting a bad compromise at London in 1930). But it is incorrect to suggest that someone like Shidehara was qualitatively different from other Japanese imperialists: it was only his willingness to compromise with the Western regimes, not the degree of his determination to exploit the peoples of Asia, that differentiated him from his colleagues. On the diplomacy of Tanaka and Shidehara, cf. the controversial work by Nobuya Bamba, *Japanese Diplomacy in a Dilemma: New Light on Japan's China Policy, 1924–1929* (Kyoto, Minerva Press, 1972; Vancouver, University of British Columbia Press, 1973).

28. In brief the issue was the following: all experts (Japanese and Western) agreed that Japanese supremacy in the area could be maintained if Japan were given a 10:7 ratio in heavy cruisers; the government publicly committed itself to this ratio. At the Conference, however, the United States, with British support, got the Japanese to climb down to a 10:6 ratio. In fact, because of other factors, this ensured Japanese superiority until 1936. On the Conference, see Crowley, *Japan's Quest*, pp. 34 ff.; Louis, *British Strategy in the Far East*, pp. 104–5, 216–17, 236; Crowley, "A New Deal for Japan and Asia," p. 243; Takeuchi, *War and Diplomacy in the Japanese Empire*, pp. 283 ff.

29. Crowley, *Japan's Quest*, pp. 78 ff., on the results of Hamaguchi's acceptance of the agreement. Yoshihashi, *Conspiracy at Mukden*, p. 79.

30. Iriye, *After Imperialism*, pp. 278–85.

31. The Kwantung Army is the name usually given to the Japanese army in South Manchuria (see Glossary).

32. For the slow collapse of the Wakatsuki cabinet see, for example, Richard Storry, *A History of Modern Japan* (Harmondsworth, Penguin Books, 1960), pp. 188–90; Yoshihashi, *Conspiracy at Mukden*, chapter 7.

33. The most detailed source on this period is Sadako N. Ogata, *Defiance in Manchuria: The Making of Japanese Foreign Policy, 1931–32* (Berkeley and Los Angeles, University of California Press, 1964).

34. A good brief text on this is Richard Storry, "The Image of Japan in England, 1870–1970," *Bulletin of the International House of Japan*, Tokyo, No. 25 (April 1970). "All the important London dailies . . . agreed that Japan's cause was just and that she served as the civilizing force in the Far East"; when a Japanese officer, Captain Nakamura, was executed by the Chinese in June 1931 legitimately, the *Times* saw this act "as proof of China's inability to protect foreigners" (Armin Rappaport, *Henry L. Stimson and Japan, 1931–33* [Chicago and London, University of Chicago Press, 1963], p. 18); Rappaport is excellent on Britain's pro-Japan policy at the time.
    A recent work, Christopher Thorne, *The Limits of Foreign Policy: The West, the League and the Far Eastern Crisis of 1931–1933* (London, Hamish Hamilton, 1973), is expertly criticized by John Gittings, *New York Review of Books*, Vol. 20, No. 8 (May 17, 1973). As late as 1935 Winston Churchill was publicly defending Japan's policy in China. British hostility towards Japan developed fully only when Japan's textile exports began to threaten Britain's trading position. The West's use of the League meshed with its unscrupulous and hypocritical use of the I.L.O. against Japan when the latter's exporting capacity became competitive. On U.S.–British differences over China, cf. p. 132 and note 77 below.

35. See *The League of Nations Is a League of Robbers!* (extract from a telegram of the Chinese Soviet Government, dated October 6, 1932, and signed by Mao Tsetung) in Stuart R. Schram. *The Political Thought of Mao Tse-tung* (New York, Praeger, 1965), p. 264. The Marxist critique of the League remains to be written. Essentially the League was an instrument for preserving the imperialist status quo in the Third World, and became active only over *new* imperialist ventures (Japan in China, Italy in Ethiopia). There are some valuable elements for a critique in Jean-Baptiste Mouroux, *Du Bonheur D'Être Suisse sous Hitler* (Paris, Pauvert, 1968).

36. Crowley, *Japan's Quest*, p. 180. "The Saitō cabinet, in effect, marked the appearance of a new form of political oligarchy in which the authority and influence of the political parties, the Emperor's advisers, and the premier would be appreciably altered

—in some instances, almost eradicated" (ibid., pp. 179–80). Saitō Makoto, a former governor-general of Korea, was premier from May 1932 until July 1934.

While Crowley is correct to emphasize decentralization, it is hard to agree that the *pattern* of policy-making *determined* foreign policy, as he claims. Rather, the military and other right-wing elements exploited the existing "pluralism" of the system: see section below on "fascism" and Tetsuo Furuya, "Naissance et développement du fascisme japonais," *RHDGM*, No. 86, 22e année (April 1972), pp. 1–16. Also, the fact that the policies of the far right were *confused* and that those with fascist objectives did not succeed in imposing a unified political leadership does not mean that they were not *consistently* oppressive both at home and abroad.

37. Crowley, *Japan's Quest*, pp. 201 ff., on Araki's resignation; pp. 206 ff. on Hayashi's policies and the appointment of Nagata; and chapter 5 on "Factions, Rebellion, and National Policy." On Nagata, cf. Furuya, "Naissance et développement du fascisme japonais," pp. 7 ff. Also important was the changing social composition of the army: in the period 1920–27, 30 per cent of those entering the cadet corps were from the bourgeoisie and the petit bourgeoisie. And in 1927 the Volunteers Act allowed anyone with a secondary education who could maintain himself for one year in the army to become an officer—i.e., by-passing the military academies.

38. Crowley, *Japan's Quest*, p. 269; after the February 26 [1936] Incident Aizawa was brought before a new court-martial and sentenced to death (Crowley, p. 274).

39. The reasons why this was so are complex and are discussed more fully below in the section on "fascism." In brief, the essence of Japanese "fascism" was the theme of "the association of the Emperor and the people"—hence no one on the right would attack the Emperor directly, only his advisers, the government and others who were allegedly "misleading" him. At the same time, there was unanimous respect on the right for an imperial opinion, even though the Emperor did not himself technically *decide*.

40. Akira Iriye, "Japanese Imperialism and Aggression: Reconsiderations II," *JAS*, Vol. 23, No. 1 (November 1963), pp. 103–13.

41. Japan claimed that Chinese forces fired on Japanese soldiers near this bridge (on the Peking-Tientsin railway).

42. Crowley, "A New Deal for Japan and Asia," pp. 247–48.

43. O. Tanin and E. Yohan, *When Japan Goes to War* (London, Martin Lawrence, 1936), p. 169; Chō, "Keeping Step with the Military."

44. G. C. Allen and Audrey G. Donnithorne, *Western Enterprise in Far Eastern Economic Development: China and Japan* (London, G. Allen & Unwin, 1954), pp. 206–7. In the textile industry, for example, there had been cartels since the nineteenth century.

45. On the militarization of the economy, see Jerome B. Cohen, *Japan's Economy in War and Reconstruction* (Minneapolis, University of Minnesota Press, 1949), pp. 1–47; Chō Yukio, "From the Shōwa Economic Crisis to Military Economy"; Chō, "Keeping Step with the Military"; Takahashi Makoto, "The Development of War-time Economic Controls, *DE*, Vol. 5, No. 4 (December 1967), pp. 648–65; Andō, "The Evolutionary Process of the Japanese Economy," pp. 200–4; Tsuru, *Essays on Japanese Economy*, pp. 154 ff. ("Japan's Economy Under the Strain of the China Incident"); E. B. Schumpeter, "Industrial Development and Government Policy 1936–1940," in E. B. Schumpeter, ed., *The Industrialization of Japan and Manchukuo 1930–1940: Population, Raw Materials and Industry* (New York, Macmillan Co., 1940), esp. pp. 789–96; Kenneth E. Boulding and Alan H. Gleason, "War as an Investment: The Strange Case of Japan," in Kenneth E. Boulding and Tapan Mukherjee, eds., *Economic Imperialism* (Ann Arbor, University of Michigan Press, 1972), pp. 240–61.

46. The relationship between the military and big business is a large and complex question. Basically, Hadley is correct when she writes, "There was no split at all between the older combines and the majority of the senior officers of the army and navy" (Eleanor H. Hadley, *Antitrust in Japan* [Princeton, N.J., Princeton University Press, 1970], p. 40). Hadley also effectively disposes of the thesis that the *shinkō zaibatsu* were in any substantial way more connected with expansionism and colonialism than the old zaibatsu (pp. 40–45). In Manchuria, the key area, Mitsui and Mitsubishi greatly improved their position during the Pacific War. T. A. Bisson (*Zaibatsu Dissolution in Japan* [Berkeley, University of California Press, 1954], p. 14) likewise re-

jects any qualitative distinction between "new" and "old" zaibatsu, and further stresses that: "At all stages of Japan's modern career, the Zaibatsu combines were closely tied to the military-bureaucratic elements that planned and executed the strategic phases of the expansionist program." Curiously, few Western writers have tried to dispute the fact that business and the military worked together in expanding Japan's interests; but the thesis that the old combines were disfavoured by the military, a thesis advanced vigorously and opportunistically by Yoshida in a speech in October 1945 (cited by Bisson, p. 70), is still to be found in several standard works, such as Storry's *History of Modern Japan* ("the economic development of Manchukuo was largely kept out of the hands of the existing *zaibatsu*" [p. 194]). On the whole, there were no *qualitative* changes over time in military-business relations as regards the empire. In some cases (e.g., the Hanyehping mines) business led the overseas drive; in other cases (e.g., at certain stages of the expansion in North China) it was military elements; at other times (e.g., in the exploitation of Korean agriculture) it was the Japanese state. State intervention sometimes took a mediated form through an institution like the Oriental Development Company; sometimes it was direct via the colonial administration. Lastly, in discussing the issue of military-business aggressivity, it should be remembered that the *central* role in Japan's expansion was played by the state, which provided the budgets and credits which permitted both military adventures and capitalist exploitation and looting. See also Itō Mitsuharu, "Munitions Unlimited: The Controlled Economy," *JI*, Vol. 7, Nos. 3–4 (Summer–Autumn 1972), pp. 353–63.

47. Allen and Donnithorne, *Western Enterprise in Far Eastern Economic Development,* p. 231; Chō, "Keeping Step with the Military."
48. Allen and Donnithorne, *Western Enterprise in Far Eastern Economic Development,* p. 264; Chō, "Keeping Step with the Military"; Rosovsky, *Capital Formation in Japan,* pp. 97 ff.; Woodruff, *Impact of Western Man,* pp. 131 ff.
49. Woodruff, *Impact of Western Man,* p. 131.
50. Romein, *Asian Century,* pp. 161–62.
51. Miyohei Shinohara, "Economic Development and Foreign Trade in Pre-War Japan," in Cowan, ed., *The Economic Development of China and Japan,* p. 240.
52. G. E. Hubbard, *Eastern Industrialization and Its Effect on the West, With Special Reference to Great Britain and Japan* (London, Royal Institute of International Affairs, 2d ed., 1938), p. 20, has a table of the month-by-month shift in imports of rayon piece-goods into Jamaica during 1934 (the quota came into operation in June that year). Much of the information below is from Hubbard's excellent and original study.
53. *Ibid.,* p. 25.
54. Shinohara, "Economic Development and Foreign Trade."
55. Hubbard, *Eastern Industrialization,* p. 25, and references there.
56. *Ibid.,* pp. 6, 10. Silk was naturally an immediate casualty of depression.
57. Freda Utley, *Lancashire and the Far East* (London, Allen & Unwin, 1931), chapter 8, compares production costs in Japan and Lancashire.
58. Freda Utley, *Japan's Feet of Clay* (London, Faber & Faber, 2d ed., 1937) is a good example; note also the title of G. C. Allen's work, *Japan: The Hungry Guest* (London, Allen & Unwin, 1938).
59. Jean Chesneaux, *The Chinese Labor Movement 1919–1927* (Stanford, Stanford University Press, 1968), pp. 474–75; for the general use of the ILO, see Ayusawa, *History of Labor, passim.* As of June 1974 Britain was applying to its Asian industrial colony, Hong Kong, less than one-third of the ILO Conventions which it had ratified for the metropolis; see Hong Kong Research Project, *Hong Kong: A Case to Answer* (London, Hong Kong Research Project and Spokesman Books, 1974), p. 25 and Appendix 4.
60. Schumpeter, "Industrial Development and Government Policy 1936–1940," p. 857. This assessment is no more than *relative*—viz., that Japan was no worse than the Caucasian imperialists. Schumpeter is generally far too uncritical on Japanese rule over both Manchuria and Korea; Grajdanzev (*Modern Korea,* pp. 118–19) criticizes her position on Korea.
61. A. Wigfall Green, *Epic of Korea* (Washington, D.C., Public Affairs Press, 1950), p. 95, for the Korean poll.

62. These are summarized in Conroy, "Government versus 'Patriot,' " pp. 36–37.
63. Moulton and Marlio, *The Control of Germany and Japan*, p. 55. On the population question, see Mao Tsetung, "The Bankruptcy of the Idealist Conception of History."
64. Moulton and Marlio, *The Control of Germany and Japan*, pp. 60, 61; cf. Crowley, *Japan's Quest*, p. 104, for Japan's use of bribery to lure Koreans into Manchuria and the resulting tensions: Chinese attacks on Koreans, followed by Korean attacks on Chinese in Korea, followed by the boycott of Japanese goods by the Chinese Chamber of Commerce in Shanghai.
65. The 1928 figure for Taiwan was 211,202 (Moulton and Marlio, *The Control of Germany and Japan*, p. 60); there were 469,043 Japanese living in Korea and 238,235 in Sakhalin at the same time; the later figure for Taiwan is from Grajdanzev, *Formosa Today*, p. 159. For details of Japan's rule over Taiwan, emigration there by Japanese and the contradictions of Japanese economic "policy" towards the island (including the frantic effort to turn Taiwan into a quasi-industrial appendage of Japan), see George W. Barclay, *Colonial Development and Population in Taiwan* (Princeton, Princeton University Press, 1954).
66. Woodruff, *Impact of Western Man*, p. 77; after 1940 quotas were put on Asian immigrants. J. F. Normano, "Japanese Emigration to Brazil," *PA*, Vol. 7, No. 1 (March 1934), pp. 42–61, is an extremely useful text. In 1907 the State of São Paulo signed a deal with a Japanese private company for the import of Japanese; the process later became closely controlled by the Tokyo government; Catholic emigrants were encouraged, while Buddhists and Shintoists were restricted (Normano, p. 48). Emigration rose in the thirties: the 1923 earthquake in Japan, the 1924 Exclusion Act in the United States (and similar policies in Anglo-Saxon countries in the Pacific), and Mussolini's ban on Italians emigrating in 1927 all contributed to this. Some political nationalists in Latin America (though not in Brazil itself) were sympathetic to Japan, as a possible ally against Yankee imperialism (e.g., Manuel Ugarte in Argentina and Juan Merigo in Mexico).
67. Martin Bronfenbrenner, "Some Lessons of Japan's Economic Development, 1853–1938," *PA*, Vol. 34, No. 1 (1961), p. 27, suggests that Hokkaido was Japan's internal "frontier"; there are several possible variants, of which Scotland and California would seem to represent about the extremes. Housing might at first seem an odd deterrent, but the Japanese house is a tropical construction, wholly unsuited to Manchuria—or even to a normal winter on Honshu or Hokkaido.
68. The case of West Germany in the post-1945 world is not comparable because in the competition with socialism the whole of the non-socialist world was converted into a relatively unified protectorate.
69. There was also the question of markets. Bronfenbrenner ("Some Lessons of Japan's Economic Development, 1853–1938"), raising the question of whether Japan was "forced" into imperialism, incorrectly counterposes the search for markets to the search for raw materials: the two were complementary. He is also wrong in his claim to distinguish business from the military: "Insofar as they were interested in 'imperialism' at all, the *zaibatsu* preferred a different form from that which Japanese imperialism finally took—an essentially pacific type of economic penetration whose analogue may be American penetration of the northern half of Latin America" (pp. 21–24). Apart from the claim that America's role in "the northern half of Latin America" (Guyana? Venezuela?) is "essentially pacific," it is pointless to try to argue a civil-military dichotomy abstracted from the specific conditions of inter-imperialist rivalry in a situation of relative inequality.
70. Moulton and Marlio, *The Control of Germany and Japan*, pp. 65 ff.; Japan proper produced about three-quarters of its own admittedly fairly low rice consumption; Shiota, "The Koreans in World War II," p. 45, for Korean rice exports to Japan to 1933.
71. Moulton and Marlio, *The Control of Germany and Japan*, p. 78.
72. Larry W. Moses, "Soviet-Japanese Confrontation in Outer Mongolia: The Battle of Nomonhan-Khalkin Gol," *Journal of Asian History*, Vol. 1, No. 1 (1967), is excellent. The Japanese lost over 50,000 men in the battle, including nearly 25,000 dead—the highest officially acknowledged casualties in any battle between 1931 and the surrender in 1945. These heavy losses were undoubtedly a factor in inclining the

Japanese military and government to turn elsewhere—southwards. The battle plans for Lake Khasan were prepared by the legendary Soviet strategist Blücher (alias Galin). At Khalkhin Gol the Soviet troops were commanded by General Zhukov.

73. Matsuoka's account of his discussion with Stalin leading to the signing of the Pact is hilarious (see Nobutaka Ike, ed., *Japan's Decision for War: Records of the 1941 Policy Conferences* [Stanford, Stanford University Press, 1967], esp. p. 22). Ike's volume gives a vivid idea of the atmosphere in which Japan entered upon the war with the West; cf. Maruyama's brilliant essay, "Thought and Behaviour Patterns of Japan's Wartime Leaders," in Maruyama, *Thought and Behaviour in Modern Japanese Politics*, pp. 84–134. Although Maruyama is the most intellectually exciting source on this, it should be said that both he and Ike tend to mask the hard realities of the situation, and perhaps exaggerate the difference between Japanese decision-making and, say, American decision-making over Vietnam. While Maruyama, in particular, stresses the specificity of Japanese decision-making, it is well to remember that vagueness of language may only mask clarity of intention, and that all ideologies operate as political smokescreens.

74. For a good summing up, see Lu, *From the Marco Polo Bridge*, pp. 238 ff. (the best balanced estimate), particularly useful on the oil question; for the background to Pearl Harbor and the debate about it, also see the extracts in George M. Waller, ed., *Pearl Harbor: Roosevelt and the Coming of War* (Boston, D. C. Heath, 1953) and John McKechney, S.J., "The Pearl Harbor Controversy: A Debate Among Historians," *MN*, Vol. 18, No. 1–4 (1963), pp. 45–88, for a useful overview of the disputed points about immediate responsibility for the starting of the war. See also Roberta Wohlstetter, *Pearl Harbor: Warning and Decision* (Stanford, Stanford University Press, 1962), particularly for the codes and intelligence involved.

75. Paul W. Schroeder, *The Axis Alliance and Japanese-American Relations 1941* (Ithaca, N.Y., Cornell University Press for the American Historical Association, 1958), p. 214.

76. Jonathan Marshall, "Southeast Asia and U.S.-Japan Relations: 1940–1941," *Pacific Research and World Empire Telegram* (East Palo Alto, Calif.), Vol. 4, No. 3 (March–April 1973), p. 1. Marshall states correctly that "Traditional historians have not recognized the role of raw materials in sparking the Pacific war" (p. 1). *Inter alia*, Marshall criticizes Schroeder's line on Cordell Hull's moralism and its effect on U.S. policy (p. 23). Marshall's study* reached me when this manuscript was essentially completed and I have not been able adequately to integrate the results of his original research. (The version in *Pacific Research* is an abbreviated version of a longer text available from Pacific Studies Center, 1963 University Avenue, East Palo Alto, Calif. 94303.)

77. Churchill disagreed with both Roosevelt and Truman on the value of the Kuomintang to the West: see Winston S. Churchill, *The Second World War* (London, Cassell and Co., 2d. paperback ed., 1965), Vol. 7, pp. 119–20. On the Brussels Conference, see note 1 to chapter 6.

78. Storry, *A History of Modern Japan*, p. 208.

79. Jonathan Marshall, "Southeast Asia and U.S.-Japan Relations." Also, if Schroeder is correct, because of America's moralistic "interest" in China (Schroeder, *The Axis Alliance*, p. 200, on American moralism).

80. Schroeder, *The Axis Alliance*, pp. 74–75.

81. Noam Chomsky, "The Revolutionary Pacifism of A. J. Muste: On the Backgrounds of the Pacific War," in Chomsky, *American Power and the New Mandarins* (New York, Pantheon Books, 1969), p. 204.

82. Schroeder, *The Axis Alliance*, pp. 77–81, is excellent on Hull.

83. The attack on Malaya slightly preceded that on Pearl Harbor; the assault on the Philippines, planned to precede that on Hawaii, in fact came after it (see Wohlstetter, *Pearl Harbor*, p. 340). On Japan's relations with Thailand (immediately below), see E. Thadeus Flood, "The 1940 Franco-Thai Border Dispute and Phibuun Sonkhraam's Commitment to Japan," *Journal of Southeast Asian History*, Vol. 10, No. 2 (September 1969), pp. 304–25. On Japan's relations with Portugal in Asia, see Werner Levi, "Portuguese Timor and the War," *FES*, Vol. 15, No. 14 (July 17, 1946), pp. 221–23; initially Australia made an agreement with the Portuguese not to

claim the island—as part of the package under which Britain was granted use of bases on the Azores during the war. The Dutch upset the deal by first invading Timor, followed by the Australians and, finally, by the Japanese, who at first tried to compromise with the Portuguese on the spot. Macao was not invaded.

84. Hosoya, "Japan's Decision for War in 1941," p. 46; Hosoya is good on the psychological factors behind Japan's decision to attack.

85. A notable exception is Norman, *Japan's Emergence as a Modern State*, p. 206.

86. Palmiro Togliatti, "A proposito del fascismo," in Costanzo Casucci, ed., *Il Fascismo* (Bologna, Il Mulino, 1961), p. 285; this text was originally published in 1928 under Togliatti's pseudonym, Ercoli. Togliatti was one of the leaders of the Italian Communist Party in exile and a leading authority on fascism at the time. In 1928 debate on the nature of fascism was still open in the Comintern, but in 1933 Stalin came up with his own definitive formulation which shut off further discussion. In Stalin's definition, fascism was the "open terrorist dictatorship of the most reactionary, most chauvinist, most imperialist elements of finance capital" (Stalin to the XIII plenum of the Executive Committee of the Comintern). One of the most widely used formulations was the expansion of Stalin's definition given by the Bulgarian Communist Dimitrov in his keynote address to the Seventh Congress of the International in 1935: "Fascism is the power of finance capital itself. It is the organization of terrorist vengeance against the working class and the revolutionary section of the peasantry and intelligentsia. In foreign policy, fascism is jingoism in its most brutal form, fomenting bestial hatred of other nations" (in Georgi Dimitrov, *On the Unity of the Workers' and Communist Movement in the Struggle for Peace, Democracy and Socialism* [Sofia, Foreign Languages Press, 1964], p. 117). This speech by Dimitrov officially launched the Comintern's "United Front" policy against fascism; in his long report Dimitrov pays scant attention to Japan.

87. Togliatti, "A proposito del fascismo," pp. 281–82.

88. This point is forcefully made by George Macklin Wilson, "A New Look at the Problem of 'Japanese Fascism,'" *CSSH*, Vol. 10, No. 4 (July 1968), although Wilson tends to ignore the role of capitalism and adopts the unacceptably vague taxonomy of Robert C. Tucker, Friedrich, Brzezinski et al. The fact that certain Japanese were studying and imitating European fascism is of considerable importance and is virtually ignored by Crowley in *Japan's Quest for Autonomy;* for details on the usage and meaning of the term in Japan at the time, see Paul Akamatsu, "L'armée et le prince Konoye," *Annales* (Paris), Vol. 19, No. 1 (January–February 1964), p. 120. Tokyo's international liaison with Berlin and Rome was important, since all three saw each other as allies in a common *political* undertaking (see Z. Vasiljevova, "Le nationalisme japonais et la seconde guerre mondiale," *La Pensée* [Paris], nouvelle série, No. 128 [August 1966], p. 108). On the other hand, the Japanese regime moved ruthlessly against attempts to import what might be called "raw" European fascism: while obliging those with fascist ideas to accommodate them to the existing set-up, the regime also extracted what *it* wanted from fascist ideas and actions.

89. This point is well made by Saito Takashi, "La fin de la deuxième guerre mondiale dans les puissances de l'Axe: Essai de Théorie Comparative," *RHDGM*, No. 89, 23e année (January 1973), pp. 79, 87–88.

90. Tanin and Yohan, *Militarism and Fascism in Japan;* in his introduction (p. 7) Karl Radek identifies the authors as "two Soviet orientalists," but some doubt persists about their identity, particularly since "Tanin" is the Japanese for "another man." One of the many odd aspects of the book (quite apart from the fact that it does not stick to the then orthodox Comintern line) is that there are only two references to Stalin, both perfunctory in the extreme. The Tanin and Yohan book is especially important since all the main Comintern authorities on fascism (Togliatti, Dimitrov, etc.) virtually ignore Japan. This neglect of Japan is also to be found in Nicos Poulantzas' recent study of Comintern policy towards fascism, *Fascisme et dictature* (although this does contain useful elements for evaluating the differences between the three key Soviet figures involved with policy towards Japan: Bukharin, Zinoviev and Radek (see pp. 35 and 43). The most useful texts on Japanese fascism that I have found, apart from Tanin and Yohan's book, are those by Furuya (cited at note 36) and by

Akamatsu and Vasiljevova (cited in note 88) and Kaoru Kataghiri, "Il fascismo nel Giappone degli anni trenta," *Critica marxista* (Rome), anno 7, No. 6 (November–December 1969), pp. 114–29.

91. Tanin and Yohan, *Militarism and Fascism in Japan*, pp. 266–67 (the title of the book indicates the authors' doubts).

92. Radek, "Introduction: Japanese and International Fascism," *ibid.*, pp. 13–14.

93. *Ibid.*, p. 14.

94. *Ibid.*, pp. 21–22; though Radek does recognize the weakness of Japanese monopoly capitalism.

95. Tanin and Yohan, *Militarism and Fascism in Japan*, pp. 266 ff.

96. Radek, "Introduction," *ibid.*, p. 19; cf. pp. 21–22.

97. *Ibid.*, p. 18. The absence of a fascist party obviously is a major difference; at the same time, Radek is on the right track. In Europe fascism had to mobilize vast numbers of *individuals* in fairly atomized societies. In Japan the regime was able both to play on the strong corporativist bonds already existing in the society, and to mobilize the intermediate instances and groups in the area *between* what in the West were individuals and the party (on this, see Vasiljevova, "Le nationalisme japonais," p. 115, and note 113 below; cf. Furuya, "Naissance et développement du fascisme japonais," *passim,* on both the specificity of the "ideal" of the relationship between people and Emperor, and on the mass mobilization projects of the far right. The role of the Emperor was crucial since, in Saitō's words, the Japanese system was "fascism grafted onto the Emperor system" (*Tennō-sei fashisumu*) (Saito Takashi, "La fin de la deuxième guerre mondiale," p. 79).

98. Radek, "Introduction" to *Militarism and Facism in Japan*, p. 20.

99. *Ibid.*, p. 7 (italics in original).

100. Maruyama, *Thought and Behaviour in Modern Japanese Politics*, pp. xiv–xv.

101. Wilson, "A New Look at the Problem of 'Japanese Fascism.' "

102. Moore, *Social Origins of Dictatorship and Democracy*, p. 300. Moore's stimulating book abounds with insights into how Japan's particularly repressive regime came into existence, but he is crucially vague on the terminology and dating of (what he calls) fascism—for example, at pp. 436 (feudal/monarchical confusion) and 447 ("fascism was an attempt to make reaction and conservatism popular and plebeian"). This vagueness is criticized by Wilson, "A New Look at the Problem of Japanese Fascism"; Dore has done two critiques of Moore: one a general assessment (Ronald P. Dore, "Making Sense of History," *Archives européennes de sociologie*, Vol. 10 (1969), pp. 295–305), the other, with Ōuchi Tsutomu, a study specifically devoted to Moore's section on Japan (R. P. Dore and Tsutomu Ōuchi, "Rural Origins of Japanese Fascism," in Morley, ed., *Dilemmas of Growth in Prewar Japan*, pp. 181–209); this latter study is rather disappointing; it is limited to the theme enunciated in the title and begs some of the same questions as does Moore.

103. Moore, *Social Origins of Dictatorship and Democracy*, p. 299; it is not entirely clear what Moore means by the term "totalitarian."

104. Furuya notes that after February 1936: "One can speak of dictatorship to the extent that the opposition was dismantled, but this dictatorship remained weak since it was not able to install a unified political leadership" ("Naissance et développement du fascisme japonais," p. 12); according to Furuya, the political "pluralism" which came out of the Meiji Constitution was not suppressed. Furuya makes the important point that the high degree of what he calls social organization did not produce unity of political leadership (p. 13, referring to the period from summer 1937 on). The army, though holding real power and able to take initiatives, was unable to unify the political leadership since it entered on war against China without coherent plans.

105. Saito, "La fin de la deuxième guerre mondiale," pp. 87–88.

106. On the role of the monarchy, see especially, *ibid.*, pp. 79, 87–88; Furuya, "Naissance et développement du fascisme japonais," esp. pp. 1–5; Tanin and Yohan, *Militarism and Fascism in Japan, passim;* Kataghiri, "Il fascismo nel Giappone," pp. 125–26; Vasiljevova, "Le nationalisme japonais," pp. 109–10. There is a mass of information on the Emperor's role in David Bergamini, *Japan's Imperial Conspiracy* (New York, William Morrow & Co.; London, William Heinemann, 1971). Bergamini has come

in for venomous criticism from part of the Anglo-Saxon academic establishment; it is only fair to praise the book's outstanding merit: it completely succeeds in standing on its head the conventional Western apologetics for the Emperor, which forms an integral part of the imperialist *political* operation which, by exonerating the Emperor personally and labelling his government as "fascist," created the conditions for the devious integration of that same regime into the imperialist camp following the surrender. Further, Bergamini's book, although it subscribes to the "conspiracy" theory (the opposite of a class analysis), provides much information on the Emperor's structural role in the Japanese state system. For the fairest assessments of Bergamini's work, see the reviews by Herbert P. Bix, *JI*, Vol. 8, No. 2 (Spring 1973), and Geoffrey Barraclough, *New York Review of Books*, Vol. 20, No. 9 (May 31, 1973).

107. Thus, the most famous Japanese leader, General Tōjō Hideki, did not become Prime Minister until October 1941, and was fired in mid-1944; the fact that he could be removed without upheaval (and virtually without protest from himself) marks the distance between Tokyo and, say, Berlin; on this, see Richard Storry, "Japanese Fascism in the Thirties," *Wiener Library Bulletin*, Vol. 20, No. 4 (Autumn 1966), pp. 1–2.

108. Robert Guillain sees the events of the late 1920s and 1930s as an army "comeback": the army "had, for all practical purposes, held power up to 1918" ("Government by Assassination: How Japan Went Fascist," *New University Thought* [Detroit], Vol. 3, No. 4 [1963], p. 51). For an explanation of the preponderant role of the army, see Akamatsu, "L'armée et le prince Konoye," pp. 125–26. Education also played a vital role in supporting the existing social structure and in boosting the military's prestige. Tsurumi, *Social Change and the Individual*, chapter 3 ("Socialization for Death: Moral Education at School and in the Army"), is very useful on this. Tsurumi notes that although the army was "a society apart" it was also much *closer* to civilian society than in, say, the United States. In addition, its "moral" status was much higher: in official army terminology (not widely challenged) the army was "the centre" (*chūō*) and civilian society "a province" (*chihō*) (Tsurumi, pp. 88–89).

109. Kataghiri, "Il fascismo nel Giappone," esp. pp. 119–20. Furuya rightly stresses the role of "culture" in the right's mobilization of society. The 1923 earthquake was very important in stimulating military hostility to the "consumer society" (cf. the title of a radio address by Yamakawa Kenjirō, president of the Association of National Culture: "Marxism—A More Redoubtable Enemy than Earthquakes") (Furuya, "Naissance et développement du fascisme japonais," pp. 12–13). In a stimulating text, Robert Paris has noted that a crucial element in European fascism was *de*-culturation through "sport" and other forms of philistine and physical oppression; these forms of oppression were not needed in Japan because culture was integrated with the right already (Robert Paris, "La notion de fascisme," *Partisans* [Paris], No. 6 [September–October 1962]).

110. Kataghiri, "Il fascismo nel Giappone," pp. 123, 124; cf. Guillain, "Government by Assassination," p. 59; and especially Mikio Sumiya, "Les ouvriers japonais pendant la deuxième guerre mondiale," *RHDGM*, No. 89, 23e année (January 1973); Sumiya notes (p. 59) that although the February 1936 coup "failed," it led immediately to both a government ban on all mass demonstrations for the rest of the year from March '36 on the grounds that the people's spirits were "disturbed" and to the forcible dissolution by the army of all unions in enterprises controlled by it.

111. The most succinct statement of Maruyama's position on the similarities in ideology is probably that in the essay, "The Ideology and Dynamics of Japanese Fascism" in Maruyama, *Thought and Behaviour in Modern Japanese Politics*, p. 35; some useful critical ideas on Maruyama in Kentarō Hayashi, "Japan and Germany in the Interwar Period," in Morley, ed., *Dilemmas of Growth in Prewar Japan*, pp. 485–88 (the passage from Maruyama which Hayashi cites at p. 485 is that in *Thought and Behaviour*, p. 35, in a slightly different translation).

112. Quoted in Maruyama, *Thought and Behaviour in Modern Japanese Politics*, p. 47.

113. Moore, *Social Origins of Dictatorship and Democracy*, pp. 307–8; for a definition of *Nōhon-shugi* (literally: "agriculture-is-the-base-ism"), see Moore, p. 295, and R. P. Dore, *Land Reform in Japan* (London, Oxford University Press, 1959), pp. 56–57; Maruyama, more cautiously, writes that "the prominence of agrarian ideology in

Japanese fascism is . . . clearly contradictory to the realistic side of fascism" (*Thought and Behaviour in Modern Japanese Politics,* p. 46); see also Kataghiri, "Il fascismo nel Giappone," pp. 126–28. Moore is absolutely correct in stressing that *Nōhon-shugi,* exactly like fascism, was *an ideology for keeping everyone in their place.* In Europe, fascism saw corporatism as a *new* invention, to close the gap between the state and the individual created by liberalism, to "co-ordinate and sub-ordinate" all groups in society into a "superior unity": "The materialistic conception of democracy identified the will of the people with the *majority* of the people; corporatism overcomes this; corporatism recognizes in the dominion of the majority the old dualism which divides the Nation into governing class and governed class, and asserts the need for the totalitarian State, in which everyone is in their place and from their place can express their will, thus contributing to the government of the whole ssytem" (Ugo Spirito, "Il corporativismo come liberalismo assoluto e socialismo assoluto" [1932], in Casucci, ed., *Il Fascismo,* pp. 64, 65; this text by Spirito, a leading ideologue of Italian fascism, and other texts in the volume edited by Casucci are expertly commented on by Robert Paris in "La notion de fascisme"). Japanese state ideology was already corporativist; everyone was already "in their place" (i.e., as Paris comments, *kept* in their place), and this is one reason why there was no need for the regime to organize a political party. Echoes of this mystification are to be found in the opening passages of Zbigniew Brzezinski's book on Japan, *The Fragile Blossom: Crisis and Change in Japan* (New York, Harper & Row, 1972), where (p. 3) he writes that "most Japanese know their precise place in society"—an unverified and repressive generalization.

114. This is the conclusion of George M. Wilson in his biography of Kita, *Radical Nationalist in Japan: Kita Ikki, 1883–1937* (Cambridge, Mass., Harvard University Press, 1969); this view is not shared by most Japanese Marxists. It should be said that Wilson does not make out his case that Kita was, in the confused terms of Lipset's political map, "more a leftist than a right-winger" (*Radical Nationalist,* p. 90). On Kita, see also Maruyama, *Thought and Behaviour in Modern Japanese Politics,* esp. pp. 67–69; Kōichi Nomura, "Kita Ikki," *DE,* Vol. 4, No. 2 (June 1966), pp. 231–44; Conroy, "Government versus 'Patriot.' " Tsunoda et al. eds., *Sources of Japanese Tradition,* Vol. 2, pp. 266 ff., has extracts from Kita's *An Outline Plan for the Reorganization of Japan.*

115. Moore, *Social Origins of Dictatorship and Democracy,* p. 302.

116. The question of repression is central to the question of reaction, and it is important to recognize that repression in Japan *did* differ from that in Germany (which, in turn, differed greatly from repression in Italy). The key point about Japan is that repression at all levels of society was consistently far heavier than it was in Italy prior to 1922 or Germany prior to 1933; the organized left, too, was much weaker. Thus, there is no sudden phenomenon inside Japan like, say, the appearance of concentration camps. But one reason that the destruction of autonomous militant organizations was comparatively leisurely was that these organizations had already been under constant attack. Police brutality and torture were more or less standard on political prisoners (though the number of political prisoners, as of official executions, was tiny compared with Europe at the same period). Although the regime did gradually move towards the elimination of all unions, the evidence is that this had only marginal effect on the number of working disputes. On this, see chapter 2 above; Sumiya, "Les ouvriers japonais pendant la deuxième guerre mondiale"; and chapter 6 below.

Chapter 6

THE PACIFIC WAR

1. Gabriel Kolko, *The Politics of War: Allied Diplomacy and the World Crisis of 1943–1945* (London, Weidenfeld and Nicolson, 1969), pp. 194–95. The decision was formally agreed by the American and British Joint Chiefs of Staff in March 1941. Before 1939 the United States had shown strong signs of not wanting to get involved in Europe: Herbert Feis ("Europe versus Asia in American Strategy," *YR,* Vol. 43,

No. 3 (Spring 1954), pp. 352–53), notes that at the Brussels Conference of 1937 America tried to get European backing for its interventionist China policy without giving the Europeans any guarantees about Europe; in 1938 Secretary of State Cordell Hull swallowed Munich rather than get involved in Europe. For the political factors involved in the "Europe first" strategy, see Kolko, *The Politics of War*, pp. 194–219— an excellent analysis; also, for U.S.-China relations as affected by this strategy, Shirley Jenkins, *Our Far Eastern Record: The War Years* (Honolulu, American Council, Institute of Pacific Relations, 1946), pp. 75–82. Japan, of course, was able to exploit the "Europe first" outlook of the colonial powers: the original plan for seizing the strategic island of Hainan, one hour's flying time from the Red River delta, had been shelved for fear of political complications with France, but was reactivated in February 1939 during Franco's march on Barcelona when France was preoccupied with the Mediterranean situation.

2. *The Bridge on the River Kwai* has certainly been more important in forming British opinion about the war with the Japanese than any book. A critique of this film by one of the British officers who worked on the railway was shown on British television, entitled *Return to the River Kwai*, from which two factors emerged: first, that the British officers forced a clash with the Japanese command by refusing to go out and work with their own troops on the railway on equal terms; second, that the British officers refused to work on the same conditions as Burmese and Chinese workers. In other words, the Japanese were trying to smash British class barriers and refusing to accept British racism. Australian author Russell Braddon, who was captured by the Japanese and put to work on the Burma railway, describes the situation (in Malaya) in these words: "The Japs made us work for ten cents a day. The officers were separated and paid a living wage for doing nothing. We saw them every day, elegantly clad, playing chess and bridge; they had their amateur theatricals and a jolly debating society. Every day we gazed on the officers, and all we could do was hate their guts" (quoted in the *Sunday Times* [London], September 28, 1969). British accounts rarely indicate the enormous strategic and political implications the railway had for the peoples of Southeast Asia. The imperialist division of the area had isolated each country from its neighbour; communications systems were built to maximize plunder by the colonial power. At the Pan-Asiatic Conference of 1926 in Nagasaki, the construction of a Trans-Asiatic Railway was put forward by the Japanese delegates as their main proposal (Grant K. Goodman, "The Pan-Asiatic Conference of 1926 at Nagasaki," paper delivered at the Third Kyushu International Cultural Conference, August 23, 1972 [Fukuoka Unesco Association, 1972], p. 5). The prewar (1937–39) and wartime (1943–45) Prime Minister of Burma, Ba Maw, writes of the electrifying effect the railway project had on the Burmese, in *Breakthrough in Burma*. Ba Maw gives a very interesting and fair assessment of the building of the railway in the Burma section (pp. 289–97); he notes the huge problems of weather, terrain, etc., and remarks that "Sasaki [the head of the project] and the other top Japanese officers working in the project really did their best for the men" (p. 292) and that, after Burmese complaints, working conditions greatly improved (p. 293). Ba Maw declines comment on conditions on the Thai section.

3. Hector C. Bywater, "Japanese and American Naval Power in the Pacific," *PA*, Vol. 8, No. 2 (June 1935), p. 168.

4. Storry, *A History of Modern Japan*, p. 215.

5. Charles Bateson, *The War With Japan: A Concise History* (London, Barrie & Rockliff, The Cresset Press, 1968), p. 84.

6. Although Ford outdid himself by making his first feature film on the war—in 1945—about MacArthur's defeat at Bataan: *They Were Expendable*.

7. On Homma and the Philippine campaign, see Teodoro A. Agoncillo, *The Fateful Years: Japan's Adventure in the Philippines, 1941–45* (Quezon City, R. P. García Publishing Co., 1965), Vol. 2, pp. 893 ff.; Bateson, *The War With Japan*, pp. 48 ff. It should be noted that most of the deaths on the march were not due to gratuitous cruelty, as the conventional picture would have it. Most of the American deaths were due to fatigue, disease and malnutrition, since the Japanese walked their prisoners through terrain which they themselves had crossed on foot earlier, but to which the U.S. troops were unaccustomed, especially on a poor diet, coming after the long

siege. Also, the fact that the Japanese took Bataan three weeks ahead of schedule meant that they had inadequate transportation available to move the large number of prisoners (which they did not expect). See also Yuji Aida, *Prisoner of the British: A Japanese Soldier's Experience in Burma* (London, The Cresset Press, 1966), which is both enlightening and surprising about the Japanese view of British cruelty and illuminates many other issues, such as the division among the Indian guards in the camps into pro- and anti-British groups.

8. For a good brief description of the years 1941–45 "re-written" from the point of view of the Filipino masses, see Amado Guerrero, *Philippine Society and Revolution* (Hong Kong, Ta Kung Pao, 1971), pp. 53–59.

9. For Indian desertions, see David H. James, *The Rise and Fall of the Japanese Empire* (London, Allen & Unwin, 1951), pp. 211–12. James, who was an officer in the Malaya Command, writes bitterly, but revealingly, that "within a few hours of the unconditional surrender of Singapore thousands of . . . disloyal troops were joining the Indian National Army. They needed no persuasion. . . ." For Indian co-operation with the Japanese during the Malaya campaign (before Singapore), see K. K. Ghosh, *The Indian National Army: Second Front of the Indian Independence Movement* (Meerut, Meenakshi Prakashan, 1969), pp. 22–34. Excellent material in Joyce C. Lebra, *Jungle Alliance: Japan and the Indian National Army* (Singapore, Donald Moore for Asia Pacific Press, 1971).

10. Colonel F. L. Roberts, quoted in the *Times* (London), June 26, 1971; the full quote, which needs no comment: "In its relationship between British officer and native soldier it was one of the happiest armies of all time."

11. Kenneth Attiwill, *The Singapore Story* (London, Muller, 1959), p. 126.

12. Winston S. Churchill, *The Second World War*, Vol. 4, Book I (*The Hinge of Fate*); the section on Malaya and Singapore is in *The Onslaught of Japan* (London, Cassell, paperback ed., 2d ed., Vol. 7, 1965), pp. 31 ff.

13. A valuable text on this is Yoji Akashi, "Japanese Military Administration in Malaya —Its Foundation and Evolution in Reference to the Sultans, the Islamic Religion, and the Moslem-Malays, 1941–1945," *Asian Studies* (Manila), Vol. 7, No. 1 (April, 1969). Akashi points out that Harry Miller's standard biography of the Tengku glosses over all this. When premier, the Tengku invited Kubata Shun, the wartime (1942–43) Japanese governor of Perak, back to Malaya, in 1960; and during his state visit to Japan in 1963 held a reception in Tokyo for the Japanese officials who had participated in the Malaya Military Administration. For the much worse position of the Chinese, see Yoji Akashi, "Japanese Policy Towards the Malayan Chinese 1941–1945," *Journal of Southeast Asian Studies*, Vol. 1, No. 2 (September 1970), pp. 61–81.

14. The Administration were "more interested in pleasing London by getting maximum production of Malayan rubber and tin than they were in defending Malaya. . . . The Governor and his masters in London seemed more afraid of arming the Malayan Asiatics than they were of the menacing Japanese" (Attiwill, *The Singapore Story*, p. 136).

15. On Yamashita, the Japanese general who took Singapore, see A. Frank Reel, *The Case of General Yamashita* (Chicago, University of Chicago Press, 1949). Reel was one of Yamashita's defence counsel at his trial after the Japanese surrender, a trial which was rehearsed like a play (on MacArthur's orders). Like Homma, Yamashita was executed on the grounds of responsibility for crimes by subordinates of which he did not have knowledge; his case later became one of the main historical reference points in discussion of the criminal responsibility of American military such as Westmoreland in Indochina. Reel's book was banned in Japan by MacArthur.

It is extremely illuminating to read Masanobu Tsuji, *Singapore: The Japanese Version* (London, Constable & Co., 1962), which contains in an appendix the text of a Japanese booklet on fighting in Southeast Asia, with political indications on the struggle against European imperialisms. See also Saburo Hayashi (in collaboration with Alvin D. Coox), *Kōgun: The Japanese Army in the Pacific War* (Quantico, Va., Marine Corps Association, 1959).

Tsuji Masanobu was probably the most brilliant strategist in the Imperial Army and played a key role in planning victories in China, the Philippines and Singapore.

At the end of the war he evaded capture and after several years returned to Japan. There, although listed by the British as a war criminal, he was not charged with war crimes; he later became a member of the Diet, joining the ruling Liberal Democratic Party. He disappeared just outside Vientiane, Laos, in 1961, and speculation about his whereabouts has continued rife to this day. Brief biography in I. I. Morris, *Nationalism and the Right Wing in Japan: A Study of Post-war Trends* (London, Oxford University Press, 1960), pp. 450–51; cf. Bergamini, *Japan's Imperial Conspiracy.*

16. James, *The Rise and Fall of the Japanese Empire,* p. 246, for the location of Japanese troops on the day of the surrender.

17. The confusion in Japan's war aims reflects the lack of a unified political leadership. It would seem that there was basic agreement on occupying or controlling the area between, but not including, India and Australia. A document prepared after consultation between the government and the Supreme Command states: "The purposes of war with the United States, Great Britain, and the Netherlands are to expel the influence of these three countries from East Asia, to establish a sphere for the self-defense and self-preservation of our Empire, and to build a New Order in Greater East Asia" (*Reference Materials for Answering Questions at the Imperial Conference on September 6 Regarding "The Essentials for Carrying Out the Empire's Policies,"* cited in Ike, ed., *Japan's Decision for War,* p. 152). The *Draft Proposal for Hastening the End of the War Against the United States, Great Britain, the Netherlands, and Chiang,* approved at the 69th Liaison Conference on November 15, 1941, spells this out: "2. (a) The Empire will adopt the following policies: (1) the connection between Australia and India and the British mother country will be broken by means of political pressure and the destruction of commerce, and their separation will be achieved; (2) the independence of Burma will be promoted, and this will be used to stimulate the independence of India" (cited in Ike, p. 248). Kita Ikki and others had earlier articulated Japan's "right" to engage in international warfare to oust European usurpers from Eastern Siberia, Australia, etc. Kita advanced the concept of Japan as "a revolutionary Empire calling for international justice" (cited by Furuya, "Naissance et développement du fascisme japonais," p. 6).

18. Alfred D. Morgan, "The Japanese Economy: A Review," *FEQ,* Vol. 8, No. 1 (November 1948), p. 67. For excellent overviews of Japan's wartime economy, see Jerome B. Cohen, *Japan's Economy in War and Reconstruction,* pp. 48–109; T. A. Bisson, *Japan's War Economy* (New York, Macmillan Co. for the Institute of Pacific Relations, 1945); and Akira Hara, "L'économie japonaise pendant la deuxième guerre mondiale," *RHDGM,* No. 89, 23e année (January 1973), pp. 33–56; cf. section below on the economy during the war.

19. William L. Neumann, *America Encounters Japan: From Perry to MacArthur* (New York, Harper & Row, 2d ed., 1965), p. 292. The whole question of the psychological factor in America's relationship with Japan would merit deepening: the displacement from Japanese behaviour towards POWs in the camps onto the actual fighting is matched by a vast shift in "public opinion": in 1942 and 1943, in spite of America's very low battle deaths, twice as many people in the United States designated Japan the number one enemy as designated Germany; by 1946 American hostility towards Japan had almost evaporated. In a 1946 poll, Japan rated only fourth most expansionist country—after Russia, Britain (!) and Germany (Neumann, p. 303). The element of racism seems not to have been adequately examined: all Asian opponents of white armies are transformed into "hordes," and are consistently reported, and often believed, to outnumber the Caucasian troops, even where this is not the case: in Malaya in 1941–42, in Korea in 1950, in Vietnam. These "hordes" are also ascribed qualities of "fanaticism" and suchlike which are rarely ascribed to white opponents like Germans and Italians.

Tsurumi (*Social Change and the Individual,* pp. 86–87) provides some interesting background to the great fighting ability of the Japanese soldiers.

20. Five thousand Japanese defenders and over 1,000 U.S. marines died at Tarawa.

21. This was why the Japanese surrender was held at sea, to MacArthur's fury. When the decision was in the balance the navy clinched their point by suggesting the *Missouri,* which won over Harry Truman, who hailed from Independence, Mo. The reasons for

American strategy—attacking Japan via the Pacific Islands—are set out in Kolko, *The Politics of War*, pp. 194–208. Kolko details the connection with both the rotten condition of Kuomintang China and its army, and with the colonial situation of America's allies in Southeast Asia. The United States schemed rigorously to stay away from a land war in Asia, to keep Britain and other colonial powers in a subordinate role, and to try to get the Soviet Union to launch an attack on Japan. Kolko also details U.S. strategy for seizing additional control over the Pacific Islands (pp. 276, 364, 465–66)—a major element in the plan to turn the Pacific into "an American lake." See also John W. Dower, "Occupied Japan and the American Lake, 1945–1950," in Edward Friedman and Mark Selden, eds., *America's Asia: Dissenting Essays on Asian-American Relations* (New York, Vintage Books ed., 1971), esp. pp. 155–59.

22. When the decision was taken to drop the atom bomb on a major war production centre, surrounded by workers' homes, and without warning, Henry Stimson got the B-29 raids eased up "so that unblemished targets would be available when the bomb was ready" (Gar Alperovitz, *Atomic Diplomacy: Hiroshima and Potsdam: The Use of the Atomic Bomb and the American Confrontation with Soviet Power* [London, Secker & Warburg, 1966], p. 116). The ferocity of American bombing can easily be forgotten: the raid on Tokyo on March 10, 1945 was the "greatest single man-made disaster in history" (*ibid.*, p. 106), causing 124,000 casualties; this was the first big napalm raid —on a densely-populated urban area jammed with wooden houses. These casualties are not only much higher than those in either of the A-bomb raids (and just as horrible), but over twice the total U.S. battle dead for the entire Pacific War. Those who have seen pictures of ruined German cities should recall that urban destruction in Japan was two and a half times greater than in Germany. Kolko, *The Politics of War*, pp. 539–43, sets the decision to use the atom bomb in its context.

23. Maruyama, "The Ideology and Dynamics of Japanese Fascism."

24. E. Herbert Norman, "The Genyōsha: A Study in the Origins of Japanese Imperialism," *PA*, Vol. 17, No. 3 (September 1944), p. 273; Jansen, *Sakamoto Ryōma*, p. ix, for the continental repercussions of Japan's earlier actions, regardless of location in the political spectrum; and Jansen, *The Japanese and Sun Yat-sen, passim*. Of the list, Sun and Chiang are familiar. Wang Ching-wei (cf. below) headed what might be called the centre-left of the Kuomintang; in 1927 he had worked with the communists in opposing Chiang Kai-shek, then had a reconciliation with Chiang, and later went over to collaboration with the Japanese. He died in November 1944. Aguinaldo has been discussed (see chapter 3). Ras Behari Bose is discussed in the text below. Kourbangalieff was an important former Russian Muslim leader. Grigorii Mikhailovich Semenov (the Ataman Semyonov) was a far-right maniac supported by Japan after the 1917 Revolution; he was captured by Soviet forces in Manchuria in 1945 and hanged; there is a good description of him in White, *The Siberian Intervention*. Raja Mahendra Pratap was an Indian exile of dubious political colouring, anti-British and anti-monarchist, with a vision of an "Aryan" federation from Iran to Assam.

25. See B. R. O'G. Anderson, "Japan: 'The Light of Asia,' " in Josef Silverstein, ed., *Southeast Asia in World War II: Four Essays* (New Haven, Yale University, Southeast Asia Studies Monograph Series, No. 7, 1966) for an outstanding essay on this. Willard H. Elsbree, *Japan's Role in Southeast Asian Nationalist Movements, 1940 to 1945* (Cambridge, Mass., Harvard University Press, 1953), is an excellent survey of the whole field.

26. Ba Maw, *Breakthrough in Burma*, pp. 34–45, is eloquent on Burmese feeling about this. Britain dragged its colonies into war in 1939 over Poland. The Burmese, Indians and other subjects of Britain saw quite clearly that they were being ordered to fight for the liberty of the Poles, who were white, not for their own liberty. Feelings on the issue were exacerbated when London specifically revoked the Atlantic Charter's applicability to its colonies and when the former cabinet minister, Duff Cooper, told an American audience that "the immediate issue is Poland but, as a matter of fact, the survival of the British Empire has always been the real, the true, issue" (quoted in *ibid.*, p. 43). The postwar trials of some Japanese leaders threw interesting light on one aspect of the racial struggle. Under a rubric entitled "Prisoners of War Humiliated" Japan's leaders were accused of: (1) moving white POWs to Korea and Taiwan; (2) parading them in maximally-populated areas, such as Seoul and Pusan; (3) putting

them under Korean and Taiwanese guards with the specific object of eradicating in the Koreans and Taiwanese attitudes of subservience to the white Anglo-Saxons (as well as to increase their awe of the Japanese for having laid low the Caucasians involved) (International Military Tribunal for the Far East [Tokyo, 1948], *Judgment,* Part B, chapter 8, pp. 431–32). Western accounts, which frequently mention the role of Korean and Taiwanese guards in POW camps, tend to neglect this important "educative" racial role.

27. Ba Maw, *Breakthrough in Burma,* esp. pp. 110–37 (on Col. Suzuki and the experience of the "Thirty Comrades"—among them Ne Win—who went to Hainan for military training with the Japanese), pp. 175–86, 307–47; Ba Maw is particularly interesting on Tōjō and on Count Terauchi Jūichi, the head of the Supreme Command for Southeast Asia.

28. Douglas MacArthur, *Reminiscences* (New York, Crest Books, paperback ed., 1965), p. 145, records that when Aguinaldo broadcast to MacArthur and his troops besieged on Bataan, urging surrender, this "disturbed me greatly" and necessitated immediate consultation with Washington. Aguinaldo's appeal was based not only on a desire to end the fighting and destruction, but on the better *political* conditions Japan was offering than the United States. Cf. note 26 to chapter 3 above.

29. David Joel Steinberg, *Philippine Collaboration in World War II* (Ann Arbor, University of Michigan Press, 1967), pp. 51–53. The task was facilitated by the Vatican's timely diplomatic agreement with Tokyo in March 1942, which allowed Japanese propaganda to invoke the backing of Pope Pius XII "for the cause of peace and the elimination of communism" (Agoncillo, *The Fateful Years: Japan's Adventure in the Philippines,* Vol. 1, pp. 470 ff.).

30. Steinberg, *Philippine Collaboration,* p. 48. Grant K. Goodman, ed., *Four Aspects of Philippine-Japanese Relations, 1930–1940* (New Haven, Yale University Press, 1967), is a valuable collection of background texts. Japan also had the support of Benigno Ramos, the leader of big peasant revolts in the mid-1930s, who had earlier fled to Japan.

31. Steinberg, *Philippine Collaboration,* pp. 60–61, is extremely good on this.

32. Guerrero, *Philippine Society and Revolutions,* pp. 56–63; Steinberg, *Philippine Collaboration,* p. 115. Hector Abaya, *Betrayal in the Philippines* (New York, A. A. Wyn, 1946), is a useful study of the transition back from Japanese to U.S. imperialist rule. The introduction to Abaya's book was written by Harold L. Ickes, U.S. Secretary of the Interior at the time, and is highly critical of MacArthur's role in imposing Roxas. MacArthur's version is in *Reminiscences,* pp. 271–74. There is much interesting information on the guerrilla struggle in Elmer Lear, *The Japanese Occupation of the Philippines, Leyte, 1941–1945* (Ithaca, N.Y., Cornell University Press, 1961), although Lear over-emphasizes the U.S. role in the guerrilla fighting and the extent of Filipino co-operation with U.S. imperialism. Guerrero, *Philippine Society and Revolution,* is a good corrective to this approach. The Hukbalahap, like the Italian Resistance, adopted a basically anti-fascist rather than an anti-imperialist position, and this greatly contributed to their defeat in the political struggle at the end of the Japanese occupation. See also Jonathan Fast, "Imperialism and Bourgeois Dictatorship in the Philippines," *NLR,* No. 78 (March–April 1973), pp. 80–86, and the exchange on this article in *NLR,* No. 81 (September–October 1973). Ba Maw, *Breakthrough in Burma,* pp. 366–67, is revealing on British manoeuvring to turn the anti-colonial resistance movement from an anti-imperialist movement into a purely "anti-fascist" (i.e., anti-Japanese only) resistance; he notes that the communists were particularly responsive to this machination.

33. Harry J. Benda, *The Crescent and the Rising Sun: Indonesian Islam under the Japanese Occupation, 1942–1945* (The Hague, W. Van Hoeve, 1958), is an excellent pioneering work on this. Elsewhere Japan's judgement was not always so good. Tokyo backed all sorts of elements, including groups of worthless White Russians in Manchuria, who were being prepared for an invasion of the U.S.S.R. (see U.S. Department of State, *Trial of Japanese War Criminals* [Washington, D.C., U.S. Government Printing Office, 1946—Far Eastern Series, No. 12], p. 72). Peter De Mendelssohn, *Japan's Political Warfare* (London, Allen & Unwin, 1944), pp. 38 ff., describes the deracinated European drop-outs manning the various sectarian (Vichy, pro-Hitler, pro-Mussolini) fascist radio stations in China under Japanese patronage, broadcasting futilely in Italian,

German and even Hungarian to Southeast Asia.

34. De Mendelssohn, *Japan's Political Warfare*, p. 113.

35. John Goette, *Japan Fights for Asia* (London, Macdonald & Co., 1945). Goette spells out the ambiguity of his title: "As Japan fights for Asia for her own selfish ends, she likewise fights *for* Asia by curbing Western imperialism there" (p. 173; italics in original). His final chapter is an appeal to Washington to recognize the shattering effect of Japanese occupation and refuse to accept the European colonial systems after the war.

36. Jones, *Japan's New Order in East Asia*, pp. 379 ff. Benedict R. O'G. Anderson, *Some Aspects of Indonesian Politics Under the Japanese Occupation: 1944–1945* (Ithaca, N.Y., Cornell University Press, 1961), is an excellent study of the period. On Japan's plan, see also Yoichi Itagaki, "Outlines of Japanese Policy in Indonesia and Malaya During the War," *AHA*, Vol. 2, No. 2 (April 1952).

37. J. S. Furnivall, "Twilight in Burma: Reconquest and After," *PA*, Vol. 22, No. 2 (March 1949), p. 5. Ba Maw, *Breakthrough in Burma*, p. 20: "Burma was regarded as a piece of property within a British-owned empire." Maurice Collis, *Last and First in Burma 1941–1948* (London, Faber & Faber, 1956), p. 81: "The British were hardly tragic protagonists. . . . They had no business to be in Burma, or rather they were in Burma for business. They had deported the Burmese king in 1885 for business reasons. He threatened to do business with the French instead of with them, and had to go."

38. The ludicrous British exile set-up in Simla and the attempt to reconquer Burma for capitalism are well described in Furnivall, *Twilight in Burma*. Collis (*Last and First in Burma*), attempting to rehabilitate Dorman-Smith, has many good anecdotes. Clarence Hendershot, "Role of the Shan States in the Japanese Conquest of Burma," *FEQ*, Vol. 2, No. 3 (May 1943), sheds a light on the conditions which helped the Japanese in one area of Burma. Maung Maung, ed., *Aung San of Burma* (The Hague, Martinus Nijhoff, 1962), is a disappointingly a-political collection of texts, with valuable notes. Dorothy Guyot, "The Burma Independence Army: A Political Movement in Military Garb," in Silverstein, ed., *Southeast Asia in World War II*, is indispensable; see also Dorothy Guyot, "The Uses of Buddhism in Wartime Burma," *Asian Studies* (Manila), Vol. 7, No. 1 (April 1969). Ba Maw, *Breakthrough in Burma*, is invaluable on the whole period 1939–46, particularly on the conditions which produced both mass hatred of British colonialism and good will towards the Japanese. Tsunezo Ohta, "Japanese Military Occupation in Burma—the Dichotomy," *Intisari* (Singapore), Vol. 2, No. 3 n.d. [1966]), is useful.

39. Churchill, *The Second World War*, Vol. 7, Cassell ed. (*The Onslaught of Japan*), p. 85.

40. Churchill saw better than anyone the threat this posed to the British Empire: see, for example, his message to Wavell of January 23, 1942, "And never forget that behind all looms the shadow of Asiatic solidarity, which the numerous disasters and defeats through which we have to plough our way make more menacing" (*ibid.*, pp. 120–21). This was the complex phenomenon with which Stalin also attempted to grapple, from a different point of view, in his *Nichi-Nichi* interview (see note 76 to chapter 2); see also Jean Chesneaux, *L'Asie orientale aux XIXᵉ et XXᵉ siècles* (Paris, Presses Universitaires de France, 1966), pp. 303–4. Kolko, *The Politics of War*, pp. 195–200, 465–66, is excellent in delineating the "entirely political" approach of the British imperialist regime to the war in Asia.

41. Ghosh, *The Indian National Army*, pp. 22–36; S. A. Ayer, *Unto Him a Witness: The Story of Netaji Subhas Chandra Bose in East Asia* (Bombay, Thacker & Co., 1951); James, *The Rise and Fall of the Japanese Empire*, pp. 211–12. The British have consistently exploited, oppressed and mystified soldiers from India in their most repressive operations: against the Taiping Rebellion in China (1850–64); against the Greek Revolution in the late 1940s; compare the use of Nepalese mercenaries in Hong Kong now. British sources tend to smother the fact that many Indians wanted to collaborate with the Japanese.

42. "The history of the I.N.A. is the story of a revolutionary war, set inside a major war between two power blocs" (Ghosh, *The Indian National Army*, p. 252). Forty thousand out of the 55,000 Indian soldiers who were surrendered at Singapore repudiated their allegiance to the British Crown; this included some 400 officers. The British handed their Indian troops over to the Japanese in a separate ceremony from their own

(British) surrender. At its peak the I.N.A. was estimated to contain some 45,000 troops. See also Joyce Lebra, "Japanese Policy and the Indian National Army," *Asian Studies* (Manila), Vol. 7, No. 1 (April 1969); and Joyce C. Lebra, "Japanese and Western Models for the Indian National Army," *JI*, Vol. 7, Nos. 3–4 (Summer–Autumn 1972), pp. 364–75.

43. On the Conference, see Ba Maw, *Breakthrough in Burma*, pp. 336–47; Ba Maw sees the Conference as the direct precursor of Bandung twelve years later; the fifth of the five principles adopted by the Tokyo Conference was to work for the abolition of all racial discrimination. Boyle (*China and Japan at War*, pp. 332–33) minimizes the importance of the meeting.

44. The political-symbolic significance of the transfer far outweighed the islands' value as real estate, since the Andaman Islands had formerly served as the place of exile for Indian political prisoners of the British.

45. In addition, there was a critical political-strategic split between the Japanese army and the I.N.A. which sums up the problems of their alliance. The Japanese army had very *limited* objectives in the campaign—simply to protect its flank; the I.N.A. saw the campaign as the start of a drive to liberate the whole of India. Under these conditions, the two forces could not agree even on basic military issues: see Ghosh, *The Indian National Army*, pp. 169–94, esp., pp. 181–94, and p. 263.

46. Ghosh, *The Indian National Army*, argues convincingly that the work of the I.N.A. and the postwar trials, not the activities of Gandhi, Nehru, etc., were the number one factor in forcing the British to concede postwar independence (pp. 237–43).

47. On hearing of the Japanese surrender, Bose tried to turn to the U.S.S.R. for assistance in liberating India from the north. He was killed when his plane crashed in Taiwan on August 18, 1945, en route from Indochina to Manchuria.

48. Jones, *Japan's New Order in East Asia*, pp. 340–41. Jenkins, *Our Far Eastern Record*, pp. 75–82; the U.S. policy of "Hitler first" produced bitter complaints from Chungking and hints that Chiang might even seek a separate peace with Tokyo. The United States responded to this first with money and then with the rendition of extraterritoriality, which it also got the British to endorse; U.S. "neglect" of China later led to the formal decision to "promote" Chiang by making him one of the Big Four from 1943 onwards; Washington also repealed the Chinese exclusion laws in December 1943. For Japan's overall China policy, Boyle, *China and Japan at War*, is a very thoughtful source; Boyle emphasizes that Wang Ching-wei's failure to secure a more "tolerant" Japanese policy towards his regime in China doomed Japan's whole Pan-Asian policy (p. 338). Wang's failure was, of course, due to the fact that the political opposition to the Japanese was so strong and well organized in China, unlike nearly everywhere else.

49. Jenkins, *Our Far Eastern Record*, pp. 62–67, on U.S. attitudes to India. Roosevelt's personal representative there, William Phillips, urged active American intervention as the only way to turn India into a viable and active ally, since British colonial rule was so oppressive that the Indian forces were little use; Stilwell complained bitterly about the low morale of Britain's Indian mercenaries, particularly among the Indian officers. Washington had to issue a special directive to U.S. troops in India to keep out of Indian politics (August 15, 1942).

50. In line with the agreement on extraterritoriality, the likelihood that Britain might be obliged to return Hong Kong to China was widely discussed and advocated in both Washington and Chungking. Roosevelt had some apparently unthought-out ideas about giving the colony to Chiang in return for him making it a free port (see Barbara W. Tuchman, *Stilwell and the American Experience in China, 1911–45* [New York, Bantam paperback ed., 1972], p. 525). A memo by the leading American political planner, Averell Harriman, dated May 12, 1945, discusses the possibility of obliging the British to hand it over to China as a straightforward policy option (Walter Millis, ed., *The Forrestal Diaries* [New York, Viking Press, 1951], p. 56). In late 1944 the Japanese, who were occupying Hong Kong *as a British colony*, offered to return it to China as part of a package (Boyle, *China and Japan at War*, p. 314). The British appear to have had some difficulty in reimposing colonial rule in 1945; the Japanese surrender was taken by the British, but on behalf jointly of the British government and of Chiang as the Supreme Commander, China Theatre (F. S. V.

Donnison, *British Military Administration in the Far East 1943–46* [London, H.M.S.O., 1956], pp. 151–52): "on every junk and on nearly every house there flew the flag of China" (*ibid.*, p. 202). For an overview of the Japanese occupation, see Henry J. Lethbridge, "Hong Kong Under Japanese Occupation: Changes in Social Structure," in I. C. Jarvie with Joseph Agassi, eds., *Hong Kong: A Society in Transition* (London, Routledge & Kegan Paul, 1969), pp. 77–127. On both the occupation and the British restoration, see Walter Easey, "History of Hong Kong to 1945," in Association for Radical East Asian Studies, *Hong Kong: Britain's Last Colonial Stronghold* (London, A.R.E.A.S., 1972), pp. 22–24.

51. Elsbree, *Japan's Role in Southeast Asian Nationalist Movements*, p. 98: the number of political prisoners released at this time was 8–10,000 (Paul Mus, *Le Viet Nam chez lui* [Paris, Centre d'Etudes de Politique Etrangère, 1946], pp. 14–15, quoted in Elsbree, p. 98). Elsbree remains the outstanding treatise on the subject. He centres on Indonesia, but also deals with Burma, Indochina and Malaya.

52. Laurens Van Der Post, *The Observer* (London), February 23, 1969 (Colour Supplement, p. 61); italics added. This whole aspect is ignored by H. Baudet in his essay "The Dutch Retreat from Empire," in J. S. Bromley and E. H. Kossmann, eds., *Britain and the Netherlands in Europe and Asia; Papers Delivered to the Third Anglo-Dutch Historical Conference* (London, Macmillan & Co., 1968); Baudet appears to imply that Van Der Post was instrumental in persuading Mountbatten to adopt a rather anti-Dutch line (p. 218); be that as it may, what *is* clear is that the Labour government in London was considerably more pro-Dutch colonialism and anti-Indonesian than were the British military on the spot, like Mountbatten and Christison.

   For British use of Japanese troops in Vietnam, see the excellent brief work by George Rosie, *The British in Vietnam: How the Twenty-Five Year War Began* (London, Panther Books, 1970), pp. 77–78, 87–94. Rosie notes that some Japanese "deserters" fought with the Vietminh against the Anglo-French-KMT-Japanese (Imperial Army) coalition (p. 81). Were these Japanese progressives? In Korea the Japanese fought under U.S. control.

53. The text which gives probably the best insight into this is Ba Maw, *Breakthrough in Burma*. Both Steinberg, *Philippine Collaboration*, and Boyle, *China and Japan at War*, are excellent studies of two areas where Japan had very different experiences. Boyle compares Wang's Nanking regime with that at Vichy (pp. 352–58). On the overall political background, Elsbree, *Japan's Role in Southeast Asian Nationalist Movements*, and Anderson, "Japan: 'The Light of Asia.'" The nearest comparison in Europe would be Irish "collaboration" with anti-British forces such as the Boers or Wilhelmine and Nazi Germany.

54. Half of the *Selected Works of Mao Tse-tung* is devoted to the anti-Japanese struggle: viz., part of Vol. 1, and most of Vols. 2 and 3. Useful information on Japan's view of the struggle in Chong-sik Lee, *Counterinsurgency in Manchuria: The Japanese Experience* (Santa Barbara, RAND Corporation, 1967) and Chalmers A. Johnson, *Peasant Nationalism and Communist Power* (Stanford, Stanford University Press, 1966); Johnson's book discusses the relationship between the Japanese occupation and the development of the Chinese communist movement, but he cannot understand this relationship. At p. 238 he writes: "The most important point in any discussion of Maoism is that without the Japanese invasion it would always have remained irrelevant." For an excellent corrective, see Mark Selden, *The Yenan Way in Revolutionary China* (Cambridge, Mass., Harvard University Press, 1971).

55. The key fact that in Burma both British and Americans were just *using* the Burmese to help the KMT, who were nothing but a gang of looters and murderers in both China *and Burma* (see Ba Maw, *Breakthrough in Burma*, p. 272), is ignored by Western sources, such as Frank N. Trager, "The Chindits and Marauders in Wartime Burma," *PA*, Vol. 34, No. 1 (Spring 1961), pp. 62–66; see also Lear, *The Japanese Occupation of the Philippines, passim*, and films: Samuel Fuller's *Merrill's Marauders* (1962) and Fritz Lang's *American Guerrilla in the Philippines* (1950).

56. Most of what follows is based on Kolko, *The Politics of War*, esp. pp. 194–207, 265, 275–76, 364–65, 465–67, 531–47, 550–63.

57. Especially Churchill, *The Second World War*, Vol. 11, Cassell ed., p. 129 (*The Tide*

of Victory): "We had to regain on the battlefield our rightful possessions in the Far East, and not have them handed back to us at the peace table." Cf. Vol. 10, p. 228: "If their [American] plans went well we should not reach Borneo in time to take part even in the assault against Hong Kong, and we should probably find ourselves shut out from the main fighting in the Pacific, in which we were determined to share." On this, cf. Churchill, Vol. 10, chapter 15, *passim*.

58. See Dower, "Occupied Japan and the American Lake," pp. 155–59.
59. H. L. Trefousse, "Germany and Pearl Harbor," *FEQ*, Vol. 11, No. 1 (November 1951). For detailed information on the alliance, see Ernst L. Presseisen, *Germany and Japan: A Study in Totalitarian Diplomacy 1933–1941* (The Hague, Martinus Nijhoff, 1958); Johanna Menzel Meskill, *Hitler and Japan: The Hollow Alliance* (New York, Atherton Press, 1966); Schroeder, *The Axis Alliance and Japanese-American Relations*.
60. Kalyan Kumar Ghosh, "The Indian National Army—Motives, Problems and Significance," *Asian Studies* (Manila), Vol. 7, No. 1 (April 1969), p. 21.
61. See E. L. Presseisen, "Le racisme et les japonais (un dilemme nazi)," *RHDGM*, No. 51, 13e année (July 1963), esp. pp. 4, 9–10.
62. For example, Bisson, *Japan's War Economy*, p. 202: "The chaotic situation which prevailed in the administration of Japan's war economy during 1942–43 was largely rectified [by 1944–45]." Cohen (*Japan's Economy in War and Reconstruction*, pp. 48–49) points out that all American estimates of Japan's capacity before and during the war were wildly high. Ideological blindness, masked under false concepts like "totalitarianism," contributed to American blunders: assuming that Japan was "totalitarian," it must be centrally organized, etc. The uncritical vindictiveness of the postwar trials further contributed to this attitude.
63. Cohen, *Japan's Economy in War and Reconstruction*, p. 51; much of the information below from same, pp. 51–57. The National General Mobilization Law of 1938 contained sweeping control provisions, as did other subsequent laws, but these were essentially only *enabling* acts, whose provisions were not put into effect until much later (Bisson, *Japan's War Economy*, pp. 3–10).
64. For the shifts in manpower during the war, see Hara, "L'économie japonaise pendant la deuxième guerre mondiale," Table 7 ("Mutation de la main-d'oeuvre pendant la guerre"), p. 51; on the food situation, cf. Itō Mitsuharu, "Munitions Unlimited—The Controlled Economy," pp. 359–61; Sumiya ("Les ouvriers japonais pendant la deuxième guerre mondiale," p. 67) notes that by autumn 1943 the regime was only just able to maintain an average diet of 2,100 calories; the resulting hunger led to widespread absenteeism both to find food and because many workers were too weak to work. By autumn 1942 absenteeism was averaging 14.2 per cent of the work force in the main state plants, and it was up to 24.5 per cent of the males in some plants. Food shortages also led to, and fuelled, dissidence (see below).
65. "So nominal was the authority of the Prime Minister that Tojo found it necessary later to have a special act passed empowering him to force the Ministries to carry out his directives" (Cohen, *Japan's Economy in War and Reconstruction*, p. 59).
66. On concentration, see *ibid.*, pp. 100–103; Bisson, *Japan's War Economy*, pp. 79–82, 158–63.
67. In February 1940 Saitō Takao of the Minseitō launched an unprecedented attack on the government, particularly over its China policy. The government, he said, should take another look at Konoe's "New Order in East Asia"; "with its grand talk of a 'holy war,' [it] ignores realities and wilfully conceals from the people the sacrifices which they are forced to make. The government uses phrases like 'international justice,' 'moral diplomacy,' 'co-prosperity,' and 'world peace,' but understanding what these phrases mean is like trying to hold a cloud in your hand" (cited in Usui Katsumi, "Pursuing an Illusion: The New Order in East Asia," *JI*, Vol. 6, No. 3 [Autumn 1970]. See also, Crowley, "A New Deal for Japan and Asia," pp. 256–57).
68. From Sumiya, "Les ouvriers japonais pendant la deuxième guerre mondiale," p. 70 (Table 4).
69. Quoted in *ibid.*, pp. 66–67.
70. *Ibid.*, pp. 68–69; cf. Table 3, *ibid.*, p. 68, for work disputes in the years 1939–44.
71. The most famous spy ring in wartime Japan was that run by Richard Sorge, who

was executed, along with the Japanese communist, Ozako Hotsumi, in 1944. Chalmers Johnson, *An Instance of Treason: The Story of the Tokio Spy Ring* (London, Heinemann, 1965), is a readable but speculative and reactionary account of the Sorge-Ozaki saga. For a different interpretation of Sorge's role, see Bergamini, *Japan's Imperial Conspiracy.*

72. Shiota, "A 'Ravaged' People: The Koreans in World War II," p. 42. Many Chinese were also imported and killed.

73. Japan redivided the Malaya-Indonesia area into three, with Malaya and Sumatra forming a single unit. Japan's language difficulties led them to promote an Indonesian form of Malay, which became the national language of Indonesia vested with powerful nation*list* momentum (Robert Curtis, "Malaysia and Indonesia," *NLR* No. 28 (1964), pp. 10–12). In a different way, the direct Japanese assault on the Chinese population in Malaya led to a mass Chinese exodus to the rural areas where the Chinese organized the widespread guerrilla movement which has continued to this day.

74. John Bastin and Harry J. Benda, *A History of Modern Southeast Asia: Colonialism, Nationalism and Decolonization* (Englewood Cliffs, N.J., Prentice-Hall, 1968), p. 135, write: "The mobilization of youth was without doubt the most radical innovation wrought by the Japanese in wartime Southeast Asia . . . the ranks of the new elite were now thrown open to young people with the right *elan* and daring. . . ."

75. Jones, *Japan's New Order in East Asia*, p. 399. Among other things, the Japanese made a big film in Hong Kong entitled *The Last Days of the British Empire*, using British POWs. The effect in Southeast Asia can be imagined.

76. Ba Maw, *Breakthrough in Burma*, pp. 185–86.

Chapter 7

JAPAN UNDER AMERICAN OCCUPATION (1945–52): "INTERLUDE" AND REORGANIZATION

1. Cohen, *Japan's Economy in War and Reconstruction*, p. 107.

2. *Ibid.*, pp. 107–8; John Toland, *The Rising Sun: The Decline and Fall of the Japanese Empire 1936–1945* (New York, Random House, 1970), pp. 745–46.

3. Cf. Joyce and Gabriel Kolko, *The Limits of Power: The World and United States Foreign Policy, 1945–1954* (New York, Harper & Row, 1972), p. 300: "Japan emerged from World War II crushed as a military power but completely intact as an organized state."

4. For example, such standard works as Robert J. C. Butow, *Japan's Decision to Surrender* (Stanford, Stanford University Press, 1954), or Thomas M. Coffey, *Imperial Tragedy: Japan in World War II: The First Days and the Last* (New York and Cleveland, The World Publishing Co., 1970). There is an interesting *political* discussion of the decision to surrender in Saito Takashi, "La fin de la deuxième guerre mondiale dans les puissances de l'axe," *RHDGM*, No. 89, esp. pp. 87–88; Saito argues that the capitulation decision was mainly due to the political advisers to the throne and very much downplays the role of big capital in pushing for peace.

5. Cited in Corwin D. Edwards, "The Dissolution of the Japanese Combines," *PA*, Vol. 19, No. 3 (September 1946), p. 228.

6. Andrew Roth, *Dilemma in Japan* (London, Victor Gollancz, 1946), p. 70.

7. Toland, *The Rising Sun*, pp. 755–59; Butow, *Japan's Decision to Surrender*, pp. 109–11; Bergamini, *Japan's Imperial Conspiracy*, p. 61, for the importance of the Japanese missions in Switzerland. Japan used other channels, of course, to sound out surrender terms. O.S.S.: Office of Strategic Services, the wartime U.S. intelligence operation which later developed into the CIA.

8. As cited in John D. Montgomery, *Forced To Be Free: The Artifiical Revolution in Germany and Japan* (Chicago, University of Chicago Press, 1957), pp. 106–7.

9. Immediate post-surrender writing in fact stressed the importance of Japanese actions in evading Occupation control: see Roth, *Dilemma in Japan*, and Mark Gayn, *Japan Diary* (New York, William Sloane Associates, 1948), for two excellent examples. Later, partly due to skilful Japanese covering up, but also due to Allied censorship and MacArthur's personal vanity, the Occupation tended to be portrayed from an

exclusively (and mystified) U.S. standpoint. A notable example of re-viewing the period from Japan's point of view is Bergamini, *Japan's Imperial Conspiracy;* J. and G. Kolko, *The Limits of Power,* set the overall Japan–U.S. relationship in its context scientifically; see also Robert E. Ward, "Reflections on the Allied Occupation and Planned Political Change in Japan," in Robert E. Ward, ed., *Political Development in Modern Japan* (Princeton, Princeton University Press, 1968), pp. 494–500, for a fair bourgeois assessment.

10. See references in note 4; also the accounts in Toland, *The Rising Sun,* and Bergamini, *Japan's Imperial Conspiracy;* William Craig, *The Fall of Japan* (London, Weidenfeld and Nicolson, 1968).

11. It is well known that the Emperor, speaking in very remote language and over a radio system giving poor reception in many places, never actually used the word "surrender" but spoke only of "bearing the unbearable"; his most direct reference to the fact that Japan had lost the war was that the war "has not turned out necessarily to Japan's advantage." For the royal princes' visits to the armies, see Toland, *The Rising Sun,* p. 856; Bergamini, *Japan's Imperial Conspiracy,* pp. 151 and 1045; Romein, *The Asian Century,* p. 343.

12. On Higashikuni and his cabinet, see James W. Morley, "The First Seven Weeks," *JI,* Vol. 6, No. 2 (Summer 1970); Bergamini, *Japan's Imperial Conspiracy,* pp. 115–17 and 144–45 (Yoshida Shigeru replaces Shigemitsu Mamoru as Foreign Minister during the cabinet's brief life). The cabinet included Prince Konoe, Prime Minister at the time Japan declared war on China; Ishiwara Kanji, chief theoretician of the colonization of Manchuria; and Yamazaki Iwao, "a long-experienced police official" as Home Minister (Morley, p. 154). The legendary far-right millionaire and gangster Kodama Yoshio served as "adviser" to Higashikuni (Morris, *Nationalism and the Right Wing in Japan,* p. 443).

13. Morley, "The First Seven Weeks," pp. 154–55; Ikeda Daisaku, *The Human Revolution* (Tokyo, Seikyo Press, 1965), Vol. 1, pp. 118–19 [Ikeda is head of the Sōka Gakkai]. It was the death in prison of the famous liberal philosopher Miki Kiyoshi, reported on September 26, which alerted the public to the continued existence of the military security laws. Home Minister Yamazaki endorsed the activity of the Kempeitai (secret police) in arresting opponents of the imperial system. It was after SCAP ordered the government to remove all restrictions on freedom that the Higashikuni cabinet resigned, on the grounds that it could not ensure order if the existing laws were repealed.

14. Ten billion dollars is the figure given by Gayn, *Japan Diary,* p. 496, citing a Diet committee report. The four-year estimate for the stockpile (iron, steel, aluminium, etc.) is from *World Report,* January 6, 1948 (cited in Robert B. Textor, *Failure in Japan, With Keystones for a Positive Policy* [New York, The John Day Co., 1951], p. 48). For the official reports on the looting and redistribution, SCAP, *Political Reorientation of Japan, September 1945 to September 1948* (Washington, D.C., U.S. Government Printing Office, 1949), Vol. 1, pp. 307–13. Ward ("Reflections on the Allied Occupation," p. 500) gives a figure of ¥100 billion (estimated) of public property disposed of just between August 15 and September 2. Further information is to be found in Gayn, *Japan Diary,* pp. 151, 156–57; Bergamini, *Japan's Imperial Conspiracy,* pp. 119, 1068–70; Cohen, *Japan's Economy in War and Reconstruction,* pp. 417–18. Françoise Pons, *Un Cas de Développement sans Inflation: Le Japon* (Paris, Presses Universitaires de France, 1963), p. 57, estimates that the money supply rose 40 per cent in the last two weeks of August as a result of the military disbursing retirement pensions and similar moves. Cohen (*Japan's Economy,* p. 419) states that prices rose 295 per cent "by the time SCAP found out what was happening." Individuals and companies also changed their names during the hiatus.

15. Bix puts the same point another way: "If there was a 'reverse course' in U.S. occupation policy in defeated Japan, then its basis was laid months before the Japanese surrender." (Herbert P. Bix, "Japan: The Roots of Militarism," in Mark Selden, ed., *Remaking Asia: Essays on the American Uses of Power* [New York, Pantheon Books, 1974], p. 320).

16. Kolko, *The Politics of War,* p. 37. The school was located at Charlottesville, Virginia.

17. Benedict's wartime work on Japan was later published in book form as *The Chrysan-*

themum and the Sword: Patterns of Japanese Culture (London, Secker and Warburg, 1947), a book which had an enormous influence on Western thinking about Japan. Parsons's important text, "Population and Social Structure," in Douglas G. Haring, ed., *Japan's Prospect* (Cambridge, Mass., Harvard University Press, 1946), is discussed below in connection with agrarian reform.

18. Kolko, *The Politics of War*, p. 543; a useful brief account of U.S. wartime planning is contained in Frederick S. Dunn, *Peace-Making and the Settlement with Japan* (Princeton, Princeton University Press, 1963), pp. 31–41.

19. Kolko, *The Politics of War*, p. 265.

20. U.S. State Department policy paper cited in *ibid.*, p. 544; the document went on to state that the Occupation would encourage "liberals"—identified as the statesmen prominent in the 1920s—along with Christian leaders and others, and "a considerable sprinkling of business leaders whose prosperity was based on world trade rather than on the greater East Asia prosperity sphere."

21. Kolko, *The Politics of War*, p. 545; Hull is Cordell Hull, U.S. Secretary of State.

22. The efforts of the world capitalist powers to block the revolution after World War I are surveyed in masterly fashion in Mayer, *Politics and Diplomacy of Peacemaking.*

23. Grew's main statements on the issue are given in Joseph C. Grew, *Turbulent Era: A Diplomatic Record of Forty Years 1904–1945* (London, Hammond, Hammond and Co., 1953), pp. 1406–42; Grew's declarations were given added weight by the fact that he explicitly opposed trying to "democratize" Japan (pp. 1420, 1440–41); in addition, he worried about the possibility that the United States might need the Emperor to oblige the Japanese armies in the field to surrender (p. 1420). For a survey of the American positions, see Kolko, *The Politics of War*, pp. 543–63.

24. Royal Institute of International Affairs, *Japan in Defeat* (London, Royal Institute of International Affairs [R.I.I.A.], 1945), pp. 124, 22–23.

25. Potsdam is fully covered in Kolko, *The Politics of War*, pp. 555–63. I have not gone into the absorbing issue of the atomic bomb since, in spite of its general importance, it is only marginal to the questions under discussion here. The basic text on this is Alperovitz, *Atomic Diplomacy: Hiroshima and Potsdam*. An excellent synopsis of the political issues is contained in David Horowitz, *From Yalta to Vietnam: American Foreign Policy in the Cold War* (Harmondsworth, Penguin Books, revised ed., 1967), pp. 52–55.

26. Kolko, *The Politics of War*, p. 565.

27. Cited in *ibid.*, p. 547.

28. *Ibid.*, pp. 598–99.

29. Korea was the one area in Asia where the Red Army, together with the local revolutionary forces, could have liberated the entire territory before the arrival of U.S. troops; yet, even here, Stalin acceded to Truman's unilateral General Order No. 1 of August 14 and accepted Washington's division of the peninsula into two zones (*ibid.*, pp. 600–603).

30. Bergamini, *Japan's Imperial Conspiracy*, esp. pp. 63 ff., is the strongest statement of this position. Whether or not one agrees with Bergamini, he is correct in emphasizing that it was *logical* for Japan to "plot" in its own interests. The burden of proof is on anyone trying to argue the opposite. The United States was signalling its postwar plans and ideas from as early as 1942 (see M. Searle Bates, "How Will the War End for Japan?," *FES*, Vol. 11, No. 14 [July 13, 1942], pp. 155–58, esp. p. 157). The clearest signal possible came in the statement made by Grew at the Senate Foreign Relations Committee hearings on his nomination as Under Secretary of State (December 12, 1944), where he stated that the United States would retain a flexible position and wait to see how the Japanese regime behaved before deciding on its own political line. In other words, it was up to the Japanese (statement in full in Grew, *Turbulent Era*, Vol. 2, pp. 1415–19). Although much of the evidence on this important issue is the subject of bitter contention, it is impossible to over-emphasize the importance of counter-revolutionary class solidarity in the arrangement. Especially contentious is the role of Prince Konoe, and particularly the famous "memorial to the Throne" of February 1945, arguing for surrender to avert revolution. Bergamini (*Conspiracy*, pp. 64–65) treats this as a con. But another interpretation would be that Konoe, the Emperor and the ruling clique were preparing a coherent *class* posi-

tion, and such an interpretation is borne out by Konoe's behaviour after the sur-
render, when he was instrumental in persuading MacArthur to accept the existing
Japanese conservative regime (or perhaps simply reinforcing MacArthur's existing
attitude); on this, see Morley, "The First Seven Weeks," pp. 160–61. Drawing a
parallel with Germany after the First World War, where, he argued, the Social
Democratic Party had been an important stabilizing force, Konoe went on to tell
MacArthur that "in Japan today, the only forces which can serve as the Social
Democratic Party did in Germany, are the feudal forces and the zaibatsu" (quoted
by Morley, p. 161). The key factor in the whole arrangement was, of course, the
retention of the Emperor. Bergamini notes that from 1942 the O.S.S. was pushing an
anti-Tōjō rather than an anti-Emperor line (*Conspiracy*, p. 128; cf. J. and G. Kolko,
The Limits of Power, pp. 301–3). Saitō Takashi stresses the "flawless organization"
by the ruling class in establishing the bases of its postwar political and economic
domination around the time of the surrender ("La fin de la deuxième guerre mondiale," p. 88). Cf. Daniel C. Holton, "The 'New' Emperor," *FES*, Vol. 15, No. 5
(March 13, 1946), pp. 69–71.

31. The key documents are available as appendices in Edwin M. Martin, *The Allied Occupation of Japan* (Stanford, Stanford University Press, and London, Geoffrey Cum-
berlege, Oxford University Press, 1948); cf. J. and G. Kolko, *The Limits of Power*,
pp. 301–6; Dower, "Occupied Japan and the American Lake," pp. 146–47.

32. J. and G. Kolko, *The Limits of Power*, p. 305.

33. A sober account of MacArthur's propaganda machine is contained in W. Macmahon
Ball, *Japan: Enemy or Ally?* (New York: The John Day Co., 1949), pp. 16–19; see
also Gayn, *Japan Diary, passim; en passant,* it may be noted that this censorship
greatly contributed to the folklorish reporting on Japan which came to dominate
Western accounts of events there. Even middle-of-the-road American scholars could
be banned from Japan: Robert King Hall, the author of *Education for a New Japan*,
who had worked in the Charlottesville group, was barred from visiting Japan in
1946 to complete his academic study of Japanese education. The question of precisely
how much policy was decided by, respectively, MacArthur and Washington was a disputed one; overwhelming evidence that Washington in fact dominated is given in
Justin Williams, "Making the Japanese Constitution: A Further Look," *APSR*, Vol.
59, No. 3 (September 1965); cf. George Kennan, *Memoirs 1925–1950* (London,
Hutchinson & Co., 1968), pp. 385–86; J. and G. Kolko, *The Limits of Power*, p. 305.
Williams was an aide to MacArthur during the Occupation, and this text is designed
to counter late anti-MacArthur material by stressing the fact that Washington held
the upper hand. Although Williams is patently pleading a case, there is no reason to
question the facts he presents here.

34. Philip H. Taylor, "The Administration of Occupied Japan," *AAAPSS*, Vol. 267
(January 1950), p. 140.

35. According to Williams, MacArthur wanted an early end to military *occupation* but
did not want to restore full sovereignty to Japan; his original idea was supervision
"for perhaps a generation" (Justin Williams, "Completing Japan's Political Reorientation, 1947–1952: Crucial Phase of the Allied Occupation," *AHR*, Vol. 73, No. 5
[June 1968], p. 1459).

36. Theodore McNelly, "The Japanese Constitution: Child of the Cold War," *Political
Science Quarterly*, Vol. 74, No. 2 (June 1959), pp. 180–81.

37. See John M. Maki, "The Role of the Bureaucracy in Japan," *PA*, Vol. 20, No. 4
(December 1947).

38. In the words of Ball, the Commonwealth (Britain, Australia, India, Burma) representative on the Allied Council: "I have reiterated that the Japanese Government
represents the most conservative forces in Japan, that its pre-surrender outlook is
unchanged, despite its gesture of cooperation with SCAP authority. It is hardly
possible for a Japanese Government of different character to emerge in the near
future. It is my thesis that since the surrender the Japanese Government, in response
to the pressure groups that control it, has sabotaged economic recovery in the effort
to frustrate the Allied aims of 1945, and that it has done this with frivolous indifference to the sufferings it has brought to the mass of the Japanese people. I can
see no grounds for the belief that such a Government will want to use American

aid to construct a welfare economy and enlarge the liberties of the working people. It seems nearly certain that it will try to use its new resources to consolidate the power and privilege of the ruling groups" (*Japan: Enemy or Ally?*, p. 185).

39. Accounts of the set-up in SCAP (literally: GHQ [General Headquarters], SCAP) in *ibid.*, chapter 2; J. and G. Kolko, *The Limits of Power*, p. 306.

40. Gayn, *Japan Diary*, p. 239; Dower, "Occupied Japan and the American Lake," p. 168; Willoughby, the son of a Prussian officer, had highly praised Mussolini in a book published in 1939 (*Maneuver in War* [Harrisburg, Pa., Military Service Publishing Co., 1939], p. 235). Had Willoughby been Japanese, his writings would have qualified him to be purged for racism; after leaving Japan he went to work on Franco's palace guard.

41. Kennan, *Memoirs, 1925–1950*, pp. 368–96; Dower, "Occupied Japan and the American Lake," p. 168.

42. On the FEAC, see Dower, "Occupied Japan and the American Lake," pp. 149–53; Ward, "Reflections on the Allied Occupation," pp. 486–87; E. J. Lewe van Aduard, *Japan: From Surrender to Peace* (The Hague, Martinus Nijhoff, 1953), pp. 19–20.

43. On the FEC and the AC, see especially Dower, "Occupied Japan and the American Lake," pp. 153–55, 183–92; U.S. Department of State, *The Far Eastern Commission: A Study in International Cooperation, 1945–1952* (Washington, D.C., Department of State, Publication 5138, Far Eastern Series 60, 1953); MacArthur, *Reminiscences*, pp. 333–36; J. and G. Kolko, *The Limits of Power*, p. 304; Ward, "Reflections on the Allied Occupation," pp. 479, 488; Lewe van Aduard, *Japan*, pp. 21–25; Ball, *Japan: Enemy or Ally?*, *passim*.

44. Ball, *Japan: Enemy or Ally?*, p. 26. Ball's book is an invaluable account of American machinations in imposing what was, on the whole, policy opposed by all the United States' allies. MacArthur had publicly claimed that Washington had stabbed him in the back by agreeing to the setting up of the FEC and the AC in the first place.

45. Miriam S. Farley, *Aspects of Japan's Labor Problems* (New York, The John Day Co., for the International Secretariat, Institute of Pacific Relations, 1950), p. 197; cf. *ibid.*, pp. 46–48.

46. Taylor, "The Administration of Occupied Japan," p. 147.

47. Williams, "Completing Japan's Political Reorientation," p. 1462.

48. For example, Ward, "Reflections on the Allied Occupation," p. 480.

49. Truman's Initial Post-Surrender Directive to MacArthur called on MacArthur to act only to safeguard his own forces, not to intervene in domestic Japanese affairs even, apparently (from the text), to block a revolution: see Shigeru Yoshida, *The Yoshida Memoirs: The Story of Japan in Crisis* (London, W. Heinemann, 1961), p. 128; this is a self-serving account, of course, but on this point Yoshida is supported by other sources, for example, Textor, *Failure in Japan*, p. 98. Initially, too, SCAP was explicitly directed not to concern itself with Japan's economic condition (Cohen, *Japan's Economy in War and Reconstruction*, pp. 418–19).

50. SCAP Monograph No. 14, "Legal and Judicial Reform," p. 8, as given in Chalmers Johnson, *Conspiracy at Matsukawa* (Berkeley, Los Angeles and London, University of California Press, 1972), p. 15.

51. William Reitzel, Morton A. Kaplan and Constance G. Coblenz, *United States Foreign Policy 1945–1955* (Washington, D.C., Brookings Institution, 1955), p. 170.

52. Department of State, *The Far Eastern Commission*, p. 53, cited in Dower, "Occupied Japan and the American Lake," p. 185. The Constitution was, in McNelly's words, "a child of the Cold War" (McNelly, "The Japanese Constitution," p. 195); on the conditions under which the Constitution was produced, see Dower, "Occupied Japan," pp. 184–85; McNelly, "The Japanese Constitution," pp. 187–88; Ward, "Reflections on the Allied Occupation," pp. 510–13; Yoshida, *Memoirs*, chapters 13 and 14; MacArthur, *Reminiscences*, pp. 342–48; Williams, "Making the Japanese Constitution," for an attempt by MacArthur's aide to pin the responsibility on Washington; "The Story of Article 9," *Newsweek*, October 4, 1971, pp. 13–14.

53. Constitutional revision has been one of the key elements in the right wing's platform; for a useful survey, see Haruhiro Fukui, *Party in Power: The Japanese Liberal-Democrats and Policy-Making* (Berkeley and Los Angeles, University of California Press, 1970), pp. 198–226; Nobusuke Kishi, "Political Movements in Japan," *FA*, Vol. 44,

No. 1 (October 1965), p. 93; Kishi, one of the major wartime leaders, became chair-man of the Liberal Party's Constitution Investigation Committee shortly after Japan regained its independence; his Committee's draft revision of the Constitution, pub-lished on November 5, 1954, put the accent on "filial piety" and stressed that: "Based upon extreme individualism, the existing Constitution and the educational policy based upon it have gone too far in attempting to eradicate the notion of the family" (cited by Takeyoshi Kawashima, "Post-war Democratization in Japan: Law," *ISSJ*, Vol. 13, No. 1 [1961], p. 32).

54. For a run-down of the contents of the Constitution, see Warren M. Tsuneishi, *Japanese Political Style: An Introduction to the Government and Politics of Modern Japan* (New York and London, Harper & Row, 1966), pp. 35–37; Theodore McNelly, *Contemporary Government of Japan* (Boston, Houghton Mifflin Co., 1963), pp. 39–46.

55. It is clear from the text of the Article that the ban on rearmament is absolutely un-conditional and that, therefore, Japan's later rearmament is illegal in terms of the Constitution. What follows from this is a great weakening of the Constitution and of the whole process of law in Japan. The existence of clauses in the Constitution, as of certain laws, is not in itself any guarantee that these stipulations will stay in force. It should be added that, while Article 9 undoubtedly embodies the wishes of the majority of the Japanese people, it does not in itself *necessarily* make respect for the Constitution an effective platform for mobilizing revolutionary forces in Japan. The fact that it can so easily be flouted automatically undermines the Constitution's effectiveness for those seeking to oppose the regime. On the other hand, such victories as the local court ruling in September 1973 that the armed forces were indeed uncon-stitutional can have important, if limited, effects.

There is a valuable discussion of the origins of Article 9, with new information, in James E. Auer, *The Postwar Rearmament of Japanese Maritime Forces, 1945–71* (New York, Praeger, 1973), pp. 43–49.

56. In MacArthur's words, "The new Japanese constitution is really an amendment to the older Meiji one" (*Reminiscences*, p. 345).

57. Hans H. Baerwald, *The Purge of Japanese Leaders Under the Occupation* (Berkeley and Los Angeles, University of California Press, 1959), p. 1. In fact one of the most important effects of the purge was that it accelerated the fusion of the two main right-wing parties (see Kenneth E. Colton, "Pre-War Political Influences in Post-War Conservative Parties," *APSR*, Vol. 42, No. 3 [October 1948], p. 956). It is a striking and little studied fact that in the three major ex-enemy countries, Japan, Germany and Italy, the Western powers manipulated local politics into a mould which pro-duced three very similar long-tenure conservative parties—the Liberal Democratic Party (LDP) (ultimately) in Japan, the Christian Democrat Union (CDU) in Germany and the Christian Democrats (DC) in Italy. Moreover, the moves towards the merger in Japan broadly coincided with upsurges in working class militancy. It should also be noted that it took some time to get the purge under way and that most of it was carried out after SCAP had already designated the left as the main danger: the first public anti-communist statement by a senior SCAP official was made in May 1946 by George Atcheson, head of the Diplomatic Section of GHQ, SCAP and, from April 1946, Chairman of the Allied Council. MacArthur reiterated Atche-son's position later the same month (Yoshida, *Memoirs*, p. 228). Ball (*Japan: Enemy or Ally?*, p. 10) notes that MacArthur formally proclaimed the left the number one enemy in his speech of September 2, 1946 on the first anniversary of the Japanese surrender.

58. Colton, "Pre-War Political Influences in Post-War Conservative Parties, p. 945.

59. Baerwald, *The Purge of Japanese Leaders*, p. 24. Cf. Table 1.

60. Montgomery, *Forced To Be Free*, p. 27; figures from same.

61. Harold S. Quigley and John E. Turner, *The New Japan: Government and Politics* (Minneapolis, University of Minnesota Press, 1956), pp. 108–9.

62. *Ibid.*, p. 109. Yoshida was Prime Minister at the time; his own account (*Memoirs*, chapter 15) is highly disingenuous. Baerwald (*The Purge of Japanese Leaders*, p. 86) notes that Yoshida fell inescapably under the terms of the purge because of his *career;* the only difference between Yoshida and someone like Hatoyama Ichirō (who was purged) was that Yoshida was involved in the 1945 "spring plot"—which Ber-

gamini (*Japan's Imperial Conspiracy*, pp. 64, 144–45) suggests may have been itself a "plot." Whether this is the case or not is anyway not central to the issue, since Yoshida was a trusted representative of the Japanese reactionaries whose pose as a "democrat," which fooled MacArthur, was a gigantic fraud.

63. George A. De Vos, *Japan's Outcastes—the Problem of the Burakumin* (London, Minority Rights Group, 1971), p. 15.

64. John Dower, "The Eye of the Beholder: Background Notes on the U.S.-Japan Military Relationship," *BCAS*, Vol. 2, No. 1 (October 1969), p. 16; Arisue had headed the special team which investigated the first atom bomb attack on Hiroshima, and was the Japanese official who met MacArthur when he landed at Atsugi air base; on Hattori, see also Morris, *Nationalism and the Right Wing in Japan*, pp. 218–22; Auer shows that the navy was never fully disbanded at all, with minesweeping playing the key role in "justifying" its retention (*The Postwar Rearmament of Japanese Maritime Forces*, esp. pp. 4–6, 49–52, 69–72).

65. Dower, "The Eye of the Beholder," pp. 16–17; Auer shows how the Demobilization Bureau was the central body for rearming the maritime forces as early as 1946–47 (*The Postwar Rearmament of Japanese Maritime Forces*, pp. 56–57).

66. Baerwald, *The Purge of Japanese Leaders*, p. 83.

67. "It is a striking fact that nowhere in either American or Allied basic policy for Japan is the bureaucracy as a class mentioned as a target for the reforms necessary to achieve the establishment of a 'peaceful and responsible government' in Japan" (Maki, "The Role of the Bureaucracy," p. 392).

68. *Ibid.*, p. 391.

69. Williams, "Completing Japan's Political Reorientation," p. 1455.

70. Maki, "The Role of the Bureaucracy," p. 397.

71. Montgomery, *Forced To Be Free*, p. 47. On the purge of politicians, see Baerwald, *The Purge of Japanese Leaders*, pp. 83–90.

72. H. E. Wildes, "Underground Politics in Post-War Japan," *APSR*, Vol. 42, No. 6 (December 1948). Bergamini, *Japan's Imperial Conspiracy*, is one of the few works which correctly insists on the key role of gangsterism (i.e., less than fully official violence) in both political and economic life (see esp. pp. 69, 123–24); valuable information in Morris, *Nationalism and the Right Wing in Japan*, on key figures such as Kodama Yoshio; see also Albert Axelbank, *Black Star Over Japan: Rising Forces of Militarism* (New York, Hill & Wang, and London, Allen & Unwin, 1972), especially chapter 5.

73. MacArthur, *Reminiscences*, p. 330.

74. Baerwald, *The Purge of Japanese Leaders*, p. 14 (concerning the purge, but the same applies, obviously, to other measures); cf. *ibid.*, p. 15; Richard H. Minear, *Victors' Justice: The Tokyo War Crimes Trial* (Princeton, Princeton University Press, 1971), pp. 110–17, for an excellent discussion of this question.

75. *Forrestal Diaries*, p. 524.

76. See note 15 to chapter 6. Bergamini, *Japan's Imperial Conspiracy*, p. 1049, suggests that MacArthur's decision to uphold the sentences on Homma and Yamashita was directly connected with the politics of reimposing U.S. imperialist rule on the Philippines, more than with chastising the Japanese.

77. The title of the Brookings Institution study by Moulton and Marlio, *The Control of Germany and Japan*, is the policy; the subordination/integration thesis is argued at more length below.

78. Ball, *Japan: Enemy or Ally?*, p. 185 (quoted at note 38 above); cf. below.

79. Edwin W. Pauley, *Report on Japanese Reparations to the President of the United States* (Washington, D.C., U.S. Department of State, Publication 3174, Far Eastern Series 25, n.d. [released 1948]); Pauley had earlier headed a similar mission on reparations to Germany. J. and G. Kolko, *The Limits of Power*, pp. 322–23; Bruce M. Breun, "United States Reparations Policy Towards Japan, September 1945 to May 1949," *UMOP*, No. 10 (1967), for a conservative retrospective on Pauley.

80. Pauley, *Report*, pp. 6–7. For a statement of the opposite position—that Japan *needs* a degree of economic "room" to expand in East Asia if the West is to have "stability" in the area, see R.I.I.A., *Japan in Defeat*, pp. 93 ff. For a criticism of Pauley on this aspect, see D. S. Holman, "Japan's Position in the Economy of the Far East," *PA*, Vol.

20, No. 4 (December 1947), pp. 371–80. Pauley was a personal friend of President Truman and the head of an oil minor, which explains his rather unorthodox attitude towards the U.S. oil majors as regards Japan (I am indebted to John Dower for this information).

81. Shigeto Tsuru, "Postwar Democratization in Japan: Economics," *ISSJ,* Vol. 13, No. 1 (1961), p. 36, states that Japan's economy was to be reduced to a level *lower* than that of any of the countries it invaded.

82. Cohen, *Japan's Economy in War and Reconstruction,* p. 421. Already in 1946 Edwards was calculating that "reparations will scarcely touch the financial enterprises of the Zaibatsu and will have a relatively limited effect upon other Zaibatsu property" ("The Dissolution of the Japanese Combines," p. 234); Edwards calculated that seizure of overseas assets removed about 14 per cent of the combined holdings of all the zaibatsu together (p. 233). On the negotiations between the U.S. government and the FEC, see J. and G. Kolko, *The Limits of Power,* pp. 322–23.

83. Jon Halliday and Gavan McCormack, *Japanese Imperialism Today: "Co-Prosperity in Greater East Asia"* (Harmondsworth, Penguin Books and New York, Monthly Review Press, 1973), pp. 21–24; Chitoshi Yanaga, *Big Business in Japanese Politics* (New Haven and London, Yale University Press, 1968), pp. 202–28, gives useful information from a conservative point of view.

84. In fact, the zaibatsu were not monopolies in the European or American sense; they were much more like present-day U.S. conglomerates. Anti-monopoly thinking was directed primarily towards breaking the ties within each of the giant conglomerates, rather than towards ending one company's grip on a market: see Hadley, *Antitrust in Japan,* p. 5. A major new study of the zaibatsu policy within U.S. strategy appeared after this manuscript was completed: see Howard B. Schonberger, "Zaibatsu Dissolution and the American Restoration of Japan," *BCAS,* Vol. 5, No. 2 (September 1973), pp. 16–31.

85. *Department of State Bulletin,* September 23, 1945, pp. 423–27.

86. Edwards, "The Dissolution of the Japanese Combines," p. 227. Edwards was a professor of economics at Northwestern University and a consultant on cartels to the State Department. The mission was a joint State-War (Departments) mission.

87. *Ibid.,* pp. 228–29.

88. Bisson, *Zaibatsu Dissolution in Japan,* pp. 68–70 and Appendix 2, pp. 241–43, for the full text of the Plan. Edwards, "The Dissolution of the Japanese Combines," pp. 234–237, esp. p. 237, for a critique of the Plan (Edwards states the Plan was backed by all the big four; Bisson states that it was opposed by Mitsubishi); Gayn, *Japan Diary,* pp. 150–52; J. and G. Kolko, *The Limits of Power,* pp. 320–21; Hadley, *Antitrust, passim,* esp. pp. 86–87, 120.

89. J. and G. Kolko, *The Limits of Power,* pp. 320–21.

90. Hadley, *Antitrust,* pp. 125 ff.; technically, the document was only "FEC–230" when it was before the FEC; the SWNCC text is in Hadley, Appendix 9.

91. Baerwald, *The Purge of Japanese Leaders,* p. 93.

92. *Ibid.,* p. 94.

93. Cited by Hadley, *Antitrust,* pp. 497–98; cf. J. and G. Kolko, *The Limits of Power,* pp. 321–22.

94. Cited by Hadley, *Antitrust,* p. 504 (section 8); cf. section 18 (pp. 511–12).

95. *Ibid.,* pp. 45, 47; further details, pp. 45–57, giving a breakdown of the position of the zaibatsu in 1937, 1941 and 1946. The "Other Six" were: Nissan, Asano, Furukawa, Okura, Nakajima and Nomura. Of these, only two (Nissan and Nakajima) were "new" or *shinkō zaibatsu.* Nakajima (a big aeroplane manufacturer) changed its name to Fuji in the interval between the surrender and the start of the Occupation. Paid-in (or paid-up) capital was chosen by the Holding Company Liquidation Commission as "a measure that would transcend market positions" (Hadley, p. 45); it was also the measure most commonly used in Japan, whereas the Western countries usually measure by assets.

96. Edwin W. Pauley, "Presentation of Interim Program and Policy to the FEC," January 12, 1946, pp. 11–12 (this document is contained in Department of State Publication 3174, cited at note 79). Gayn, *Japan Diary,* pp. 146–48, gives the royal family owning 60 per cent of the Bank of Japan; cf. Bisson, *Japan's War Economy,* p. vii; Bergamini,

Japan's Imperial Conspiracy, pp. 1068–70.

97. Pauley, *Report*, p. 39.

98. Pauley, "Presentation of Interim Program," p. 12.

99. Pauley, *Report*, p. 39.

100. Yoshida, *Memoirs*, pp. 150–51; on this, see Hadley, *Antitrust*, pp. 40–45; Bisson, *Zaibatsu Dissolution*, p. 70; cf. chapter 5 above, note 46. This was also Grew's line.

101. Hadley, *Antitrust*, pp. 45 ff.

102. Cited in *ibid.*, p. 138.

103. Edwards, "The Dissolution of the Japanese Combines," p. 229; Barret, *L'évolution du capitalisme japonais*, Vol. 3, pp. 169–399, for an excellent detailed analysis of the whole structure of exploitation.

104. Hadley, *Antitrust*, especially chapter 6, pp. 107–24; Bisson, *Zaibatsu Dissolution*, esp. pp. 180–88.

105. SCAP, *Political Reorientation of Japan*, p. 783. On the "reversal" see J. and G. Kolko, *The Limits of Power*, chapter 19, and below. Bisson, *Zaibatsu Dissolution*, chapter 6, on the dissolution of the holding companies; Hadley, *Antitrust*, especially chapters 4, 5 and 8.

106. Kazuo Kawai, *Japan's American Interlude* (Chicago, University of Chicago Press, 1960), p. 147.

107. Gayn, *Japan Diary*, p. 151 (entry for March 28, 1946, where he details the zaibatsu figures in key positions).

108. *Ibid.*, p. 151, for a huge "insurance" racket concocted by the regime to keep the zaibatsu afloat with government money during the Occupation; cf. information on looting above.

109. Bisson, *Zaibatsu Dissolution*, pp. 154–56; "The failure to apply Law No. 207 [the Deconcentration Law] to financial institutions and notably to the big Zaibatsu commercial banks represented the most serious omission in the deconcentration program" (p. 154); cf. Hadley, *Antitrust*, chapter 8.

110. Bisson, *Zaibatsu Dissolution*, p. 96.

111. In fact, the Occupation put forward its reforms without taking much account of the immediate needs of the Japanese people: this emerges from accounts such as those of Gayn (*Japan Diary*) and Kawai (*Japan's American Interlude*). This was a major reason for the lack of immediate and active support among any social stratum for the changes which the United States proclaimed it wanted to make (see J. and G. Kolko, *The Limits of Power*, pp. 308, 322).

112. Bisson, *Zaibatsu Dissolution*, p. 96, gives "more than 80 per cent of prewar direct investments in Japanese concerns," and, p. 42, gives "three-fourths of the total foreign capital invested in Japanese industry" (both referenced to *OE*, May 22, 1948, pp. 408–11). The list of U.S. companies is from Bisson, p. 42; cf. *ibid.*, p. 187 and note 15, p. 235, for more details. Lockwood gives the foreign paid-up capital in Japanese companies at the end of 1941 as ¥106 million out of a total (all paid-up capital of all Japanese companies) of ¥30,435 million (Lockwood, *Economic Development of Japan*, p. 260, citing Yasuzo Horie, "Foreign Capital and the Japanese Capitalism after the World War I," *KUER*, Vol. 20, No. 1 [April 1950], pp. 55–56). For the U.S. position in the early automobile industry, see Chō, "Keeping Step with the Military," esp. pp. 172–74.

113. Bisson, *Zaibatsu Dissolution*, pp. 67–68. Many of the U.S. figures involved had economic "interests" directly connected with their work, and a military uniform and rank frequently served as cover for the businessmen involved (see Gayn, *Japan Diary*, pp. 303–6).

114. These U.S. interests formed a Foreign Investment Council which co-ordinated the lobby (Bisson, *Zaibatsu Dissolution*, p. 187). Cf. Williams: "GHQ did indeed ameliorate the severity of the zaibatsu dissolution programme, but not as a cold war measure. . . . This concession resulted directly from opposition of powerful U.S. business interests" ("Completing Japan's Political Reorientation," p. 1468). On the oil question, see further below. It should be said that much more work needs to be done on the U.S. intervention in the Japanese economy during the Occupation. Although certain important aspects of American control in the oil sector, for example,

are fairly clear, several questions remain not fully answered: in particular, why was the U.S. intervention not *larger?* and why did the Americans not use the Occupation to institute a much more extensive take-over?

115. *Forrestal Diaries,* p. 177 (entry for July 10, 1946).

116. Dower, "Occupied Japan and the American Lake," *passim,* for the context of the changes; J. and G. Kolko: "Washington's considerations in Japan were first and foremost economic" (*The Limits of Power,* p. 510).

117. R. M. Cheseldine, "Report on Policy Matters in Connection with Military Government and Civil Affairs Activities for Japan, February 17, 1947," pp. 1–2, cited in J. and G. Kolko, *The Limits of Power,* p. 511.

118. *Newsweek,* March 15, 1948, cited in J. and G. Kolko, *The Limits of Power,* p. 512. Cf. Bix, "Japan: The Roots of Militarism," pp. 321–322.

119. Dower, "Occupied Japan and the American Lake," p. 182.

120. Joseph M. Dodge, memo to Cleveland Thurber and the Board of Directors of the Detroit Bank, December 13, 1948 (Joseph M. Dodge Papers, Detroit Public Library, Japan 1949, box 1; copy in the Gabriel Kolko Papers, London School of Economics and Political Science Library, box 1 [henceforth: Kolko Papers, L.S.E.]; I would like to record here my gratitude to the Kolkos for their making available to others so much of their own prodigious research).

121. On this, see William T. Moran, "Supplement—Japanese Labor: 1949–50," pp. 236–39, in Farley, *Aspects of Japan's Labor Problems;* J. and G. Kolko, *The Limits of Power,* pp. 521–28; Bix, "Japan: The Roots of Militarism," p. 321; Johnson, *Conspiracy at Matsukawa,* pp. 65–70 and ff.

122. Dower, "Occupied Japan and the American Lake," pp. 186–92; Dunn, *Peace-Making and the Settlement with Japan,* esp. pp. 160–63; J. and G. Kolko, *The Limits of Power,* pp. 519, 523, 633; cf. below on the Peace Treaty.

123. J. and G. Kolko, *The Limits of Power,* p. 518; all the key sections of the Report are in Ball, *Japan: Enemy or Ally?,* Appendix II. The Committee was technically headed by Major-General William Draper, advised by a group of big business representatives headed by Percy H. Johnston, chairman of the Chemical Bank and Trust Co.; Draper himself in civilian life was an investment banker with the powerful firm of Dillon Reed, which had interests in Japan. Draper had earlier worked in Germany where he was credited with a major role in halting decartelization and restoring German industry. The Draper-Johnston group, which lacked any detailed knowledge of Japanese affairs, spent only two weeks in the country; its visit may therefore be understood not so much as a tour of analysis as a propaganda visit to signal publicly to SCAP and the world the shift in policy. See Hadley, *Antitrust,* pp. 144–46; Cohen, *Japan's Economy in War and Reconstruction,* pp. 423–26.

124. Typescript, Kolko Papers, L.S.E., box 2; apparently George Kennan addressing the Department of State, Conference on Problems of U.S. Foreign Policy in China, 1949; typescript pp. 25–26; Mr. Lattimore presumably is Owen Lattimore (typescript pp. B-13 and B-14).

125. John G. Roberts, "The American Zaibatsu," *FEER,* No. 30, 1971, pp. 49–51, is an excellent study of this. The Japanese government White Paper on Resources of October 1971 calculated that U.S. capital controlled the supply of 80 per cent of Japan's imports of crude oil (*The Times* [London], October 8, 1971); cf. Halliday and McCormack, *Japanese Imperialism,* pp. 6, 50–51, 59–69; and especially Herbert P. Bix, "Regional Integration: Japan and South Korea in America's Asian Policy," in Frank Baldwin, ed., *Without Parallel: The American-Korean Relationship Since 1945* [New York, Pantheon Books, 1974], p. 190.

126. Warren S. Hunsberger, *Japan and the United States in World Trade* (New York, Harper & Row, 1964), p. 51; cf. Reitzel et al., *United States Foreign Policy,* p. 169; this enormous imbalance needs to be taken into account when considering Japan's later and much briefer trade surplus with the United States, which so agitated Washington; in fact the United States ran a hefty trading surplus with Japan for 19 straight years from 1945 to 1964 (see Toyomasa Fuse, "Japan's Economy in the 70's: Some Problems and Prospects," *Cultures et développement* [Louvain], Vol. 5, No. 1 [1973] [in English]).

127. J. and G. Kolko, *The Limits of Power,* p. 518; cf. Yanaga, *Big Business in Japanese*

Politics, p. 266; Halliday and McCormack, *Japanese Imperialism*, p. 15; Hunsberger, *Japan and the United States in World Trade*, p. 186; and especially John Dower, "The Superdomino in Postwar Asia: Japan in and out of the Pentagon Papers," in Noam Chomsky and Howard Zinn, eds., The Senator Gravel Edition, *The Pentagon Papers* (Boston, Beacon Press, 1972), Vol. 5, pp. 105, 107, on the later period.

128. Roberts, "The American Zaibatsu," on the group; cf. Halliday and McCormack, *Japanese Imperialism*, pp. 14–16, 49–52, on the World Bank.

129. J. and G. Kolko, *The Limits of Power*, p. 523; Dunn, *Peace-Making and the Settlement with Japan*, esp. pp. 150–51, 159–65.

130. Hadley, *Antitrust*, pp. 135–36; Kauffman's report was first leaked by *Newsweek* (December 1, 1947); Hadley analyzes the *Newsweek* story; cf. Bisson, *Zaibatsu Dissolution*, pp. 139–40; J. and G. Kolko, *The Limits of Power*, p. 515.

131. Cited in J. & G. Kolko, *The Limits of Power*, p. 515.

132. "Statement of U.S. Policy Toward Economic Recovery of Japan," November 1947, cited in *ibid.*, p. 516; this document appears to have been drafted by Draper.

133. Kennan, *Memoirs 1925–1950*, p. 386. Cf. J. and G. Kolko, *The Limits of Power*, p. 517; Dower, "Occupied Japan and the American Lake," pp. 178–83; Dower, "The Superdomino," p. 104. Kennan's visit and its consequences are not even mentioned by MacArthur in his *Reminiscences*.

134. Kennan's account (*Memoirs 1925–1950*, pp. 385–86) is not entirely convincing; nothing in the published record indicates that MacArthur was ever really concerned about the opinions of the FEC. MacArthur obviously knew changes were afoot (Kennan notes: "I could see that he [MacArthur] was himself not unaware of some of the dangers that had suggested themselves to us, and that he felt, no less than we did, the need for changing and modifying a number of the occupational policies"); the protestation of concern about the FEC sounds like some kind of feint to draw Kennan out.

135. J. and G. Kolko, *The Limits of Power*, pp. 520, 521.

136. Bix, "Japan: The Roots of Militarism," p. 323.

137. For Royall's January 6, 1948 speech, see Hadley, *Antitrust*, pp. 138–39. Cf. Royall to Stimson, April 21, 1948 (Kolko Papers, L.S.E., box 1).

138. J. and G. Kolko, *The Limits of Power*, pp. 521–24, is a pioneering passage on the Dodge line, whose significance does not emerge from any of the standard Western bourgeois accounts of the Occupation.

139. Kolko Papers, L.S.E., box 2 (n.d. [1949?]); sections also cited in J. and G. Kolko, *The Limits of Power*, p. 522.

140. Minutes of Budget Meeting, March 14, 1949, p. 2 of typescript (Kolko Papers, L.S.E., box 2); also cited in part in J. and G. Kolko, *The Limits of Power*, p. 524.

141. Dodge, memo to Major General W. F. Marquat, June 1, 1949 (Kolko Papers, L.S.E., box 2).

142. Dodge, memo to Marquat, September 16, 1949, p. 2 (Kolko Papers, L.S.E., box 2).

143. Minutes of Budget Meeting, March 14, 1949 (Kolko Papers, L.S.E., box 2); cf. J. and G. Kolko, *The Limits of Power*, p. 524 (the Kolkos are certainly correct in suggesting that much of the government's line about Dodge's measures helping the left was insincere). It is worth quoting in full the final section of the Dodge memo cited in note 139: "Radicals—can make no career for themselves which measures up to own opinion of abilities—seek power and revenge—misfits—thirst for authority over fellows—cant make it in free society."

144. Bix, "Japan: The Roots of Militarism," p. 324; cf. pp. 340–41, re agriculture; Yanaga, *Big Business in Japanese Politics*, pp. 261–62, on the military aspects. The crucial fact that the counterpart fund was designed to *integrate* Japan, which is ignored by most bourgeois economic writers, is flatly stated by Sumiya Mikio: one of the aims of the Dodge Plan, he writes, was "to integrate Japan's economy in the American economic bloc by pooling the money to be paid for aid goods as the counterpart fund of U.S. aid" (*Social Impact of Industrialization in Japan*, p. 223). See also Bix, "Japan and South Korea in America's Asian Policy," p. 191 (and note 27, pp. 221–22).

145. William H. Draper, Jr., letter to Eugene W. Stetson, June 18, 1949 (Kolko Papers, L.S.E., box 2).

146. Compared with the other capitalist allies of the United States, though, the total has been relatively small; the biggest amounts of foreign capital have been imported by the

government, which has preferred loans (better public than private) to equity invest-ment. See Hunsberger, *Japan and the United States in World Trade*, pp. 71, 76ff., 89; for estimates of U.S. capital in Japan as of 1970, Halliday and McCormack, *Japanese Imperialism*, p. 5; cf. chapter 10 below.

147. For my qualifications on the use of the term "fascism," see chapter 5 above. Cf. Dore and Ōuchi, "Rural Origins of Japanese Fascism." See also Morris, *Nationalism and the Right Wing in Japan*, pp. 44–55, on the postwar dispersion of right-wing elements into rural areas.

148. Ōuchi, "Agricultural Depression and Japanese Villages," p. 627. The standard Western work on the land reform is Dore, *Land Reform in Japan;* the best critique of this in English is Minoru Shimazaki, "Some Comments on R. P. Dore's *Land Reform in Japan*," *DE*, Vol. 4, No. 2 (June 1966), pp. 256–63.

149. Commission Internationale d'histoire des Mouvements Sociaux, *Enquête sur "Mouve-ments Paysans et Problèmes Agraires de la fin du 18e Siècle à Nos Jours":* "Mouve-ments paysans et problèmes agraires du Japon de la fin du 18ème siècle à nos jours," by a group under the chairmanship of H. Kōhachirō Takahashi, typescript, n.d., p. 10 (I am grateful to Gavan McCormack for making this text available to me).

150. Takahashi, "La Place de la Révolution de Meiji dans l'histoire agraire du Japon," p. 270; *jinushi* are categorized as "propriétaires fonciers de caractère semi-féodal, sur la base d'une culture minuscule demi-serve" (p. 268). Very useful material on this, too, in Tsutomu Takigawa, "Historical Background of Agricultural Land Reform in Japan," *DE*, Vol. 10, No. 3 (September 1972), pp. 290–310.

151. The phrase is Kelvin Rowley's in Rowley, "Japan: A New Centre of World Imperial-ism," *Intervention* (Carlton, Australia), No. 2 (October 1972), p. 8.

152. Parsons, "Population and Social Structure."

153. Al McCoy, "Land Reform as Counter-Revolution: U.S. Foreign Policy and the Tenant Farmers of Asia," *BCAS*, Vol. 3, No. 1 (Winter-Spring 1971), p. 17. Ladejinsky's influence is noted in Laurence I. Hewes, *Japanese Land Reform Program* (Tokyo, SCAP, Natural Resources Report, No. 127, 1950), p. 15; Ladejinsky's articles on Japan are in *Foreign Agriculture* (a journal of the U.S. Agriculture Department) from 1937 to 1945 (Vols. 1 through 9): cited by McCoy, notes 4, 5, 6 and 8 (p. 45).

154. Ball, *Japan: Enemy or Ally?*, pp. 113–15; McCoy, "Land Reform as Counter-Revolu-tion," p. 17.

155. McCoy, "Land Reform as Counter-Revolution," pp. 17ff.; Ball, *Japan: Enemy or Ally?*, pp. 115–23 (for the programme and the immediate results).

156. Ball, *Japan: Enemy or Ally?*, pp. 120–21; McCoy, "Land Reform as Counter-Revolu-tion," pp. 18–19. On Hokkaido, the northern island, farmers were allowed to retain roughly four times the amount permitted on Honshu, Shikoku and Kyushu.

157. McCoy, "Land Reform as Counter-Revolution," p. 19.

158. Dore, *Land Reform*, p. 371.

159. *Ibid.*, p. 181.

160. Shimazaki, "Some Comments on . . . Dore's *Land Reform*," esp. p. 261, is excellent on this; cf. McCoy, "Land Reform as Counter-Revolution," pp. 19–21.

161. McCoy, "Land Reform as Counter-Revolution," p. 19; cf. Bennett and Ishino, *Pater-nalism in the Japanese Economy*, pp. 135–36.

162. Shimazaki, "Some Comments on . . . Dore's *Land Reform*." Much of Shimazaki's critique is directed towards a new introduction by Dore to the Japanese edition of *Land Reform;* nonetheless, Shimazaki's comments are applicable to the main theses of Dore's capably complacent book.

163. Halliday and McCormack, *Japanese Imperialism*, p. 171; Bix, "Japan: The Roots of Militarism," p. 341. In addition, the specific form of industrialization promoted by the LDP has meant that the majority of people still employed in agriculture and fisheries (4 million out of 6.76 million as of 1970) had to have some kind of regular employ-ment elsewhere. Many of these have had to sign up as "temporary" workers, under very unfavourable conditions (see chapter 8 below). This type of "development" (rural depopulation combined with a large semi-rural proletariat) has been very important in the maintenance of a low-wage system in postwar Japan—as well as in preserving LDP rule.

164. Dore, *Land Reform*, p. 202. Utilization of the black market in food was also crucial

in raising farming incomes, particularly in the immediate postwar period.

165. Tsutomu Ōuchi, "The Japanese Land Reform: Its Efficacy and Limitations," *DE*, Vol. 4, No. 2 (June 1966), pp. 137–38.

166. "We would suggest that the efficacy of the land reform lay in diverting at a stroke into the direction of a tranquil state the farmers' movement which was already fairly well developed before the war and which burst fiercely into flame after the war" (*ibid.*, p. 135). Table 3 in Farley, *Aspects of Japan's Labor Problems*, pp. 67–68, shows the tiny membership of agricultural unions as of June 30, 1948; moreover, agricultural unions had an average of less than 60 members each (higher in forestry).

167. Halliday and McCormack, *Japanese Imperialism*, pp. 170–73; Bix, "Japan: The Roots of Militarism," p. 341; cf. note 163.

168. *The Times* (London), April 29, 1971; *Newsweek*, October 20, 1969, pp. 24–25, for Japanese-U.S. competition in dumping; Bix, "Japan: The Roots of Militarism," p. 341.

169. Ōuchi, "The Japanese Land Reform," p. 132. Fukui, *Party in Power*, chapter 7 (pp. 173–97), is a detailed study of the compensation issue and of the LDP's relationship with its rural backers; cf. Nathaniel B. Thayer, *How the Conservatives Rule Japan* (Princeton, Princeton University Press, 1969), pp. 222ff., on agricultural pressure groups and the LDP.

170. About 50 per cent of Diet members represent (i.e., are voted in by) rural constituencies, while less than 18 per cent of the population is engaged (even part-time) in agriculture; the differential in the weight of rural-urban voting can be more than 4 to 1 —in other words, a Dietman can be elected from a rural constituency with less than one-quarter the votes it may take in an urban constituency (Halliday and McCormack, *Japanese Imperialism*, pp. 170–71, and references there). Cf. Appendix II. The loaded voting is also one of the reasons why the left places so much emphasis on local elections, where it has a better chance to realize its real strength, and why it shows up stronger in local than national elections.

171. Cf. quote at note 166. MacArthur: "[The effect] has been to establish a political segment of society which before was nervous, irritable, exploitable, into one of the most sound conservative elements of the political life in Japan. . . ." (*New York Times*, May 6, 1951, cited in McCoy, "Land Reform as Counter-Revolution," p. 23); cf. Alfred B. Clubok, "Japanese Conservative Politics, 1947–1955," in Robert E. Ward, ed., *Five Studies in Japanese Politics* (Ann Arbor, University of Michigan Press, Center for Japanese Studies, Occasional Papers, No. 7, 1957), pp. 52–53; McCoy, "Land Reform as Counter-Revolution," esp. pp. 19–22, 44–45.

172. J. and G. Kolko, *The Limits of Power*, pp. 316–17, advance an interesting thesis to the effect that "the occupation . . . resulted in a final victory for Japanese industrialism over the landed aristocracy and their military allies" (p. 316). The agrarian reform played its part in this; but the process was complex and, in a way, Janus-faced, since the strengthening of the industrial bourgeoisie via urbanization and industrialization was accompanied by a major "fiddle" whereby electorally the rural bosses retained a disproportionate amount of power in the ruling group.

173. Yanaga, *Big Business in Japanese Politics*, p. 261, and references there; Bix, "Japan: The Roots of Militarism," p. 340.

174. Bix, *ibid.*, p. 340.

175. *Ibid.*, p. 341.

176. *Ibid.*, pp. 342–43; Hunsberger, *Japan and the United States in World Trade*, p. 71, for earlier figures; a large amount of the soybeans come from Arkansas, the home state of Wilbur Mills, the main power on trade in Congress.

177. Ōuchi, "The Japanese Land Reform," pp. 147–48, noted that agricultural imports had placed a heavy strain on Japan's balance of payments ($1.8 billion in 1964 and rising vertiginously then); moreover, Ōuchi correctly foresaw that Japan's continued demand would contribute heavily to putting more strain on world supplies of crucial commodities, leading to scarcities and rising prices. The U.S. ban on soybean sales to Japan in mid-1973 was a traumatic blow.

178. Another vital ramification of the whole nexus is Japan's complicated relationship with the agricultures of the dependent economies of Southeast Asia. This is discussed at length by Bix, "Japan: The Roots of Militarism"; cf. Bix, "Regional Integration: Japan and South Korea in America's Asian Policy"; and chapter 10 below.

The question of the Japanese reform as a "model" for other countries is a fascinating issue which would merit detailed investigation. Suffice it to say here that the Japanese reform is certainly no such model for any poor country; rather, it should be compared with such reforms in relatively advanced countries as the Danish land reform of 1901. However, the Japanese experience has been trumpeted around a great deal in Southeast Asia, and Japan was of central importance as a training ground for the United States's counter-revolutionary agronomists, who fanned out from there to Taiwan, the Philippines, south Vietnam, south Korea, India, Iran and even Szechwan— for a few weeks before liberation: see McCoy, "Land Reform as Counter-Revolution," esp. pp. 24–25 and Table 1.

179. One reason MacArthur may have wanted an early treaty is that it would have allowed him to get back to the U.S. in time for the presidential primaries (at the time he was a leading possibility for the Republican candidate); Howard B. Schonberger, "The General and the Presidency: Douglas MacArthur and the Election of 1948," *Wisconsin Magazine of History*, Vol. 57, No. 3 (Spring 1974), pp. 201–19. I am indebted to John Dower for this reference.

180. Martin E. Weinstein, *Japan's Postwar Defense Policy, 1947–1968* (New York and London, Columbia University Press, 1971), pp. 14–28; Dunn, *Peace-Making and the Settlement with Japan*, pp. 54–70, for the move and its after-effects; Lewe van Aduard, *Japan*, pp. 61–72.

181. Kennan, *Memoirs 1925–1950*, p. 392; the armed forces later masqueraded under titles very similar to those suggested by Kennan; Dower, "Occupied Japan and the American Lake," pp. 178–83.

182. Ōno Tsutomu, "Student Protest in Japan—What It Means to Society," *JSPIJ*, Vol. 5, Nos. 2–3 (December 1967), p. 273.

183. Morris, "Nationalism and the Right Wing in Japan," p. 110ff.; workers who had no job security whatsoever could still be imprisoned for trying to leave their jobs.

184. Bix, "Regional Integration," pp. 20–21; McNelly, *Contemporary Government of Japan*, p. 134; Morris, *Nationalism and the Right Wing in Japan*, p. 111; it is interesting that Kennan records MacArthur emphasizing to him in 1948 that: "The Communists were no menace in Japan" (Kennan, *Memoirs 1925–1950*, p. 384, reporting MacArthur in indirect speech).

185. Yanaga, *Big Business in Japanese Politics*, pp. 254–55; direct U.S. war procurements totalled $145 million in the second half of 1950, $592 million in 1951, $824 million in 1952 and $806 million in 1953; see Kihara, "The Militarisation of the Japanese Economy."

186. Dodge's memo cited at note 120 states that Truman specifically made the connection (to Dodge) at least twice; but it must be emphasized that the U.S. decision, although *influenced* by events in China, was not *determined* by it; in others words, even if Chiang had not collapsed, there is no reason to think the United States would not have moved to restore Japanese capitalism.

187. Cited in Seizaburō Shinobu, "The Korean War as an Epoch of Contemporary History," *DE*, Vol. 4, No. 1 (March 1966), pp. 27–28.

188. Yanaga, *Big Business in Japanese Politics*, p. 255. On the same page Yanaga states that in January 1951, "72 per cent of the nation's [Japan's] production capacity was directly engaged in the manufacture of weapons"; the paragraph in which this occurs is referenced to Takahashi Ryōzō, "Bōei Seisan Keikaku no Zembō," *Chūō Kōron* (April 1953), p. 78. What Takahashi actually says is that postwar reparations confiscations were halted when only 30 per cent of the designated plant had been removed; the greater part of the best plant was left untouched and, in particular, of this unconfiscated plant, 72 per cent was directly related to armaments. In 1951, 80–90 per cent of this productive capacity remained intact. I am grateful to Gavan McCormack for this elucidation of Takahashi's article. Yanaga's error was widely repeated.

189. J. and G. Kolko, *The Limits of Power*, pp. 532–33; cf. *ibid.*, pp. 642–44, on the United States's economic policy immediately prior to independence; Dower, "The Superdomino," p. 106.

190. Yanaga, *Big Business in Japanese Politics*, p. 247. When ambassadors were exchanged the following spring, Japan sent the Governor of the Bank of Japan, Araki, to Washington, while the United States sent the leading diplomatic legman of the military,

Robert Murphy, to Tokyo.

191. Dower, "The Superdomino," pp. 104–5; cf. Dower, "Occupied Japan and the American Lake," pp. 181–82; Dower notes the ultimate political contradictions in the position espoused by Kennan whose "imprint" the NSC document bears; cf. Kennan, *Memoirs 1925–1950*, pp. 393–96.

192. Shinobu, "The Korean War," p. 26.

193. Jack Belden, *China Shakes the World* (Harmondsworth, Penguin Books, 1973 ed.), chapter 53; George H. Kerr, *Formosa Betrayed* (London, Eyre & Spottiswoode, 1966), pp. 187–355, is a very full account of the March 1947 upheavals from a pro-"Taiwan Independence" standpoint.

194. General Dean, who had been military governor of Korea, records that, after he moved from Korea to Japan in January 1949 after the rigged "independence" of southern Korea, he was engaged partly in training south Korean officers with the U.S. 24th Infantry in Kyushu, before the start of the Korean War (William F. Dean, *General Dean's Story* [London, Weidenfeld and Nicolson, 1954], p. 8).

195. Quoted by Textor, *Failure in Japan*, p. 217, from the *Ōsaka Mainichi*, February 12, 1949 and the *New Statesman and Nation*, April 29, 1950.

196. Weinstein, *Japan's Postwar Defense Policy*, pp. 19, 24–25.

197. Shinobu, "The Korean War," p. 27; Dower, "The Eye of the Beholder," p. 20.

198. Ball, *Japan: Enemy or Ally?* p. 96.

199. Dower, "The Eye of the Beholder," p. 21; cf. Shuichi Sugai, "The Japanese Police System," *UMOP*, No. 7 (1957), p. 7. MacArthur justified the NPR on the grounds of guarding against an internal uprising.

200. Dunn, *Peace-Making and the Settlement with Japan*, pp. 98–99; Dower, "The Eye of the Beholder," pp. 21ff.

201. The day the war broke out was June 24 in Korea and June 25 in Washington and New York. Essentially, there was a qualitative escalation of the Korean *revolutionary* struggle to free the southern half of the country from the regime of Syngman Rhee, set up and maintained in power in Seoul by U.S. imperialism. I have tried to argue my interpretation of this contentious issue in "The Korean Revolution," *Socialist Revolution* (San Francisco), Vol. 1, No. 6 (November–December 1970) and (more fully) in *Three Articles on the Korean Revolution 1945–1953* (London, Association for Radical East Asian Studies, 1972).

202. Harry S. Truman, *Years of Trial and Hope, 1946–1953* (London, Hodder & Stoughton, 1956), p. 474.

203. Yoshida, *Memoirs*, p. 57. MacArthur's successor, Ridgway, accelerated the move towards the right within Japan, but his actions may simply have been a reflection of official policy which now had a freer hand with MacArthur off the scene.

204. Dower, "The Eye of the Beholder," p. 21; Weinstein, *Japan's Postwar Defense Policy*, pp. 53 ff.; I. F. Stone, *The Hidden History of the Korean War* (New York and London, Monthly Review Press, 2d ed., 1969), pp. 37–41. It should be said that Yoshida's attitude towards rearmament is not entirely clear. Auer challenges the prevailing view that Yoshida was simply pressured into rearmament by the Americans; on the contrary, Auer argues (with a wealth of inside information), there was a long-standing Japanese design, especially for naval rearmament, and the final Yoshida-Dulles agreement reflects this as much as anything (*The Postwar Rearmament of Japanese Maritime Forces*, pp. 69–89). The key role in this project was played by former Admiral Nomura Kichisaburō, Foreign Minister in 1939–40 and ambassador to Washington from December 1940 until Pearl Harbor, who had extremely close ties to the Americans, as well as very right-wing views (Auer, pp. 69–89, on Nomura's role; cf. Morris, *Nationalism and the Right Wing in Japan*, p. 447; Lewe van Aduard, *Japan*, p. 250). Also important was former Lieutenant General Tatsumi Eiichi/Teruichi, who had been military attaché to Yoshida in the years 1936–38 when the latter was ambassador in London and, according to Weinstein, assisted Yoshida on military matters "in an unofficial capacity throughout the Yoshida era" (*Japan's Postwar Defense Policy*, p. 59, citing Nishimura Kumao; cf. Auer, *Postwar Rearmament*, pp. 72–73); Auer (p. 74) notes the key role, too, of two later prime ministers in rearmament planning—Ikeda Hayato and Satō Eisaku.

205. Dower, "The Eye of the Beholder," p. 22; Weinstein, *Japan's Postwar Defense Policy*,

p. 59.

206. Robert Murphy, *Diplomat Among Warriors* (London, Collins, 1964), p. 424. The fact that Murphy says this was "top-secret" indicates there was plenty to hide; furthermore, if "the Allied forces would have had difficulty remaining in Korea" without assistance from these Japanese personnel, it is clear they were serving a directly *strategic* function. Perhaps they are best compared to the Japanese personnel employed, for example, in North China by the KMT in November 1945 who are referred to as "engineering troops" in a recent authoritative study (David Wilson, "Leathernecks in North China, 1945," *BCAS*, Vol. 4, No. 2 (Summer 1972), p. 34). The presence of the Japanese was no secret to the Korean government, and Murphy records his problems as a result of Rhee arresting some of these Japanese "experts" (*Diplomat*, p. 426). Cf. Mark W. Clark, *From the Danube to the Yalu* (New York, Harper & Bros., 1954), pp. 148–50. Morris, *Nationalism and the Right Wing in Japan*, p. 229, refers to unsuccessful attempts by right-wing Japanese to recruit volunteers for the U.S.-Rhee side, but indicates these failed due to Japanese (right-wing) fears that they would be used as mercenaries by Americans. The Japanese "connection" was particularly important to the Americans for other reasons: most of the top R.O.K. officers were Japanese trainees; the best maps of Korea were available only in Japanese.

207. Auer, *The Postwar Rearmament of Japanese Maritime Forces*, pp. 63–67; one Japanese sailor was killed, and an official from SCAP was deputed to pay off his family (Auer, p. 66).

208. Dower, "The Eye of the Beholder," p. 22; the strongest statements concerning continuity of personnel are to be found in Auer, *The Postwar Rearmament of Japanese Maritime Forces* (p. 5, etc.). Auer was a Lieutenant Commander in the U.S. Navy and political adviser to the Commander of U.S. Naval Forces in Japan; he had the co-operation of numerous top U.S. and Japanese officials in writing his book. Among the many striking features of Auer's work is the fact that he not only goes much further than most left-wing critics of Japanese rearmament in detailing and dating the rearmament process, but he clearly sets out the *structural and political* reasons for the continuity in personnel in the navy. He argues that the Japanese surrender was largely the work of pro-U.S. elements in the Japanese navy (Nomura and others) who argued for surrender *as a political option* to provide the best conditions for continuing the Japanese navy—and that this desire was largely reciprocated by leading elements in the U.S. Navy (Auer, pp. 4–6, 39ff., 49–52, 63ff.).

209. Axelbank, *Black Star Over Japan*, pp. 54–55; for the figures as of 1954, see Morris, *Nationalism and the Right Wing in Japan*, pp. 236–37. Among individuals who returned to the postwar forces were many of Japan's key military strategists, including Genda Minoru, the brain behind the Pearl Harbor plan. Morris (*Nationalism*, p. 237) lists the key figures who had returned as of 1954; Bergamini (*Japan's Imperial Conspiracy*, pp. 113, 1125) notes the presence (in the 1960s) not only of wartime premier Tōjō's son but also of two of the group who allegedly tried to stage a last-minute putsch against the surrender deal in 1945: one heading the Historical Section (i.e., Plans) of the SDF; another running the Self-Defence Staff College. Even if individuals retire, the crucial factor of *continuity* has been assured. Cf. Tsurumi, *Social Change and the Individual*, pp. 80–81; Bix, "Japan: The Roots of Militarism," pp. 306–319.

210. Dower, "The Eye of the Beholder," p. 23; Dower, "Occupied Japan and the American Lake," p. 190.

211. Dunn, *Peace-Making and the Settlement with Japan*, pp. 110–12; India largely agreed with the Russians (Dunn, pp. 113–14); the United States simply ignored the Soviet points. Joseph L. Sutton, "Territorial Claims of Russia and Japan in the Kurile Islands," *UMOP*, No. 1 (1951), is a detailed study, from an anti-Soviet standpoint. Much information on the "Northern Islands" question can be found in Donald C. Hellmann, *Japanese Foreign Policy and Domestic Politics: The Peace Agreement with the Soviet Union* (Berkeley and Los Angeles, University of California Press, 1969), esp. pp. 34, 38, 59, 114, 146 and 163. Hellmann's book is a conservative account of the normalization of relations with the U.S.S.R. under the Hatoyama government (1954–56). The "Northern Islands" question is complicated by a failure to agree on where the southern Kuriles (which Japan agreed to cede) actually end, Tokyo having claimed that the "Northern Islands" are not part of the Kuriles chain.

212. Dower, "The Eye of the Beholder," p. 25; cf. Dower, "The Superdomino," p. 106.
213. Shinobu, "The Korean War," pp. 34–36.
214. Cited in George R. Packard III, *Protest in Tokyo: the Security Treaty Crisis of 1960* (Princeton, Princeton University Press, 1966), p. 12. Packard, a former official of the U.S. Embassy in Tokyo, though mystifying on the origins of the treaty, gives a detailed imperialist account of the Security Treaty issue; cf. Lewe van Aduard, *Japan,* pp. 126–28, 129–36, for a conservative acknowledgement that the Japanese were opposed to a separate treaty.
215. Yanaga, *Big Business in Japanese Politics,* p. 230; although, on the whole, chapter 9 is generally useful for its details.
216. Shinobu, "The Korean War," pp. 32–33. The San Francisco package was in part America's response to Japan's coolness about the Korean crusade. Hugh Borton, a key State Department official who worked on the peace settlement, notes that "the Japanese public reacted to the Communist attack in Korea in an ominous fashion. . . . They failed to accept the thesis that a Communist victory in Korea would be a portentous threat to their own freedom and security" (Borton, *Japan's Modern Century,* p. 435); a careful reading of Borton's passage might lead one to think that the reality was that the Japanese people did not even believe the imperialist version of the origins of the Korean War. McNelly sees the 1951 arrangement as partly a response to "the lack of enthusiasm of the Japanese people for the anti-communist cause in Korea" (McNelly, *Contemporary Government of Japan,* p. 193).
217. I. F. Stone, *Hidden History,* pp. 300–303.
218. Dower, "The Eye of the Beholder," p. 24.
219. *Ibid.;* Yanaga, *Big Business in Japanese Politics,* pp. 249–50; cf. the subsequent expansions of the 1951 Security Treaty.
220. Fukui, *Party in Power,* p. 228.
221. Utsunomiya Tokuma, "On Returning from Santa Barbara: An Attack Against Corruption in Japanese Politics," *Sekai* [*The World*] (Tokyo), April 1969; English translation issued by Utsunomiya's office, pp. 1–2. Cf. Utsunomiya, interview with Fukui, *Party in Power,* p. 257.

Chapter 8
PROLETARIAT VERSUS CAPITAL SINCE 1945

1. Most of the major works in English on the Japanese left are fundamentally hostile to the Japanese masses. This is particularly true of Robert A. Scalapino, *The Japanese Communist Movement, 1920–1966,* and Allan B. Cole, George O. Totten and Cecil H. Uyehara, *Socialist Parties in Postwar Japan* (New Haven and London, Yale University Press, 1966); some of the inadequacies of these two works are criticized, from a liberal standpoint, by J. A. A. Stockwin, "Is Japan a Post-Marxist Society?" *PA,* Vol. 41, No. 2 (Summer 1968), pp. 184–98; J. A. A. Stockwin, *The Japanese Socialist Party and Neutralism: A Study of a Political Party and Its Foreign Policy* (Melbourne, Melbourne University Press, 1968) is a useful brief work. Robert E. Cole, *Japanese Blue Collar: The Changing Tradition,* is an excellent and sensitive study of working class factory life. Johnson, *Conspiracy at Matsukawa,* is extremely useful on the political and trade union situation under the U.S. Occupation.
2. Perry Anderson, "The Limits and Possibilities of Trade Union Action," in Robin Blackburn and Alexander Cockburn, eds., *The Incompatibles: Trade Union Militancy and the Consensus* (Harmondsworth, Penguin Books, 1967), is a very good survey of this field.
3. Although the Japanese enterprise union (*kigyō kumiai*) has some strong similarities with what is called the "company union" in the United States, it seems best to use "enterprise union" to define the Japanese body. An "enterprise union" does not apply to a whole company or firm with several different plants; in each plant there would usually be a separate enterprise union: Evans. *The Labor Economies of Japan and the United States,* p. 49; Taira, *Economic Development and the Labor Market,* pp. 167–72. The term "trade union" is best avoided, although it is used in some quotations reproduced below. There are a few examples of unions with branches in different plants, but this

seems to be a largely formal difference (Ronald Dore, *British Factory—Japanese Factory: The Origins of National Diversity in Industrial Relations* [London, Allen & Unwin, 1973], pp. 324–25).

4. Sumiya, "Les ouvriers japonais pendant la deuxième guerre mondiale," pp. 66–72; cf. chapter 6 above, pp. 158–59.

5. This is a complex and much disputed area. One of the most perceptive of Japanese observers, Iida, pinpoints the extent to which freedoms were granted by SCAP rather than fought for as one of the key reasons behind the collapse of the militant union movement from 1947 (Kanae Iida, "The Origin of the Enterprise Union in the Post-War Labor Movement," *KES*, Vol. 7, No. 1 [1970], p. 62).

6. Farley, *Aspects of Japan's Labor Problems*, p. 109, records the case of a newspaper employee sentenced to four years' imprisonment for allegedly stating in a speech that the Americans were colonizing Japan. In this case the sentence was greatly reduced and the defendant released on bail. Cf. J. and G. Kolko, *The Limits of Power*, p. 309; Johnson, *Conspiracy at Matsukawa*, p. 97.

7. Chalmers Johnson writes that "Police procedure remained almost impervious to change until the 1960s" (*Conspiracy at Matsukawa*, p. 164). Johnson is interesting on both the role of the police and the place of law in the Japanese state. The Japanese police, he notes, see it as their job to exercise *constant* surveillance of the *whole* society (not just to "protect" citizens from "crime," "trouble" and suchlike, as he implies is their function in the West); arrest is seen as a conventional means to grab any and all suspects and *create* the conditions for extracting a confession.

8. Textor, *Failure in Japan*, pp. 99–100. Yoshida, *Memoirs*, p. 76, pictures himself forming a government with the revolution raging outside his window.

9. Kozo Yamamura, *Economic Policy in Postwar Japan: Growth Versus Economic Democracy* (Berkeley and Los Angeles, University of California Press, 1967), p. 17, from SCAP, *Missions and Accomplishments of the Supreme Commander for the Allied Powers in the Economic and Scientific Fields* (Tokyo, 1952), p. 45; cf. Evans, *The Labor Economies*, p. 20; and Eitaro Kishimoto, "Labour-Management Relations and the Trade Unions in Post-War Japan (1)—Revival and Reestablishment of the Labour-Management Relations Based on Seniority," *KUER*, Vol. 38, No. 1 (April 1968), Whole No. 84, p. 2.

10. Ayusawa, *History of Labor in Modern Japan*, p. 227.

11. Iida, "The Origin of the Enterprise Union," p. 62.

12. Sampō is the most common abbreviation for Sangyō Hōkokukai (Industrial Patriotic Society or Patriotic Industrial Association), sometimes also transliterated as Sanpo. Technically Sampō was the organization for promoting the movement calling on Japanese industries to render service to the state (*sangyō hōkokukai undō*), while the state-sponsored movement calling for cooperation between labour and industry was called *rōshi kyōchō undō*, but Sampō in effect covered both areas: see Fukuji Taguchi, "Leadership in the General Council of Japanese Labor Unions," *JSPIJ*, Vol. 3, No. 1 (April 1965), p. 74; Taira, *Economic Development and the Labor Market*, p. 144; cf. chapter 2 above, p. 80.

13. In February 1940 the government stated in the Diet that it "wished the trade-unions to dissolve in the developmental sense" and that "its policy was to spread the Sampō movement so as to remove the need for the trade-union movement" (cited in Ayusawa, *History of Labor in Modern Japan*, p. 229).

14. This thesis is developed by Taira, *Economic Development and the Labor Market*, p. 188, based on Magota Ryōhei, "Senji rōdōron eno gimon" [Doubts about the accepted presumptions about wartime industrial relations] in *Nihon Rōdō Kyōkai Zasshi* [Monthly journal of the Japan Institute of Labor], Vol. 7 (July 1965).

15. Yet Sampō did not reduce the actual number of labour disputes (see Sumiya, "Les ouvriers japonais pendant la deuxième guerre mondiale," pp. 68–69; Ayusawa, *History of Labor in Modern Japan*, Table 27, p. 230.

16. This is basically an attempt to synthesize and reinterpret the material in Taira, *Economic Development and the Labor Market;* Iida, "The Origin of the Enterprise Union"; and Kishimoto, "Labour-Management Relations . . . in Post-War Japan (1)." Cf. Evans, *The Labor Economies*, pp. 19–20.

17. The Japanese term is *seisan kanri* which literally means "production control," but

the experience was the same as what is now called a "work-in." The key text on this is Beatrice G. Reubens, " 'Production Control' in Japan," *FES*, Vol. 15, No. 22 (November 6, 1946), pp. 344–47; see also Farley, *Aspects of Japan's Labor Problems*, pp. 92–95. Ayusawa, *History of Labor in Modern Japan*, p. 261, observes that the Japanese phrase for "collective bargaining" (*dantai kōshō*) also means "mass negotiation."

18. Reubens, " 'Production Control,' " p. 345; Farley, *Aspects of Japan's Labor Problems*, pp. 93–95 and 101–13; Shōriki is one of many unsavoury characters egregiously glamourized by Ralph Hewins in his nauseating and unbelievably bad *The Japanese Miracle Men* (London, Secker & Warburg, 1967).

19. The situation in the coal industry was particularly explosive because of the appalling working conditions imposed on the miners, many of whom were Koreans who had been dragooned into the mines on terms of virtual slavery (see Shiota "A 'Ravaged' People: The Koreans in World War II"). Although production went up in some mines under "production control," in others it fell to as little as 10 per cent of the wartime peak when Korean and Taiwanese miners went on strike as citizens of *independent* countries (Korea and China).

20. Reubens, " 'Production Control,' " p. 344.

21. Farley, *Aspects of Japan's Labor Problems*, pp. 92–93. Reubens (" 'Production Control,' " p. 345) reports a survey by the Coal Control Corporation indicating that the most sensational increases in output came when *unskilled* workers were in charge; these increases are ascribed to the fact that, without managerial supervision, miners ignored safety precautions, but one may doubt this interpretation; capitalism has to travesty and suppress the élan and inventiveness of the working people.

22. Evans, *The Labor Economies*, pp. 19–21; Iida, "The Origin of the Enterprise Union," pp. 47–48; Scalapino, *The Japanese Communist Movement*, pp. 68–69; A. Cole and others, *Socialist Parties in Postwar Japan*, pp. 13–14. Sanbetsu (or Sambetsu): abbreviation for Zenkoku Sangyō-betsu Kumiai Kaigi (National Congress of Industrial Unions).

23. Kishimoto, "Labour-Management Relations . . . in Post-War Japan (1)," p. 3, records that the Communist Party organ *Akahata* was attacking the Sōdōmei leaders as agents of imperialism as early as October 15, 1945; Taguchi, "Leadership in the General Council," is useful on the background of postwar union leaders and the degrees of continuity and non-continuity between pre-Sampō and post-1945 unionism; Taira, *Economic Development and the Labor Market*, pp. 187–88, argues that there was a real caesura.

24. Kishimoto, "Labour-Management Relations . . . in Post-War Japan (1)," p. 8; cf. Iida, "The Origin of the Enterprise Union," p. 53.

25. It has been argued that postwar conditions were highly favourable to the working class. This interpretation relies on an assessment of the economic situation as bad for big capital. Yet, while it is true that there was a kind of economic "collapse," the essence of the situation was a strike by capital against labour. Moreover, conditions of scarcity are not strategically advantageous to the poorest sections of society. At the political level, although *kokutai* ideology was in some disarray, the Emperor remained on the throne, and a conservative regime stayed in power, actively protected by U.S. imperialism.

26. J. and G. Kolko, *The Limits of Power*, p. 313; Yoshida, *Memoirs*, pp. 78, 226–27; Yoshida was particularly incensed by this episode.

27. SCAP, *Political Reorientation of Japan*, p. 356.

28. Reubens, " 'Production Control,' " p. 347.

29. The Sanbetsu was made up of a maximally strategic combination of transportation workers, industrial workers and white-collar government employees. As Evans notes, public employees have played a more important part in the union movement in Japan than in any other country, except possibly Britain. They have been especially important in Japan because their unions, not usually being subject to "enterprise" limitations, have tended to be very large by national standards, and the level of unionization has been about three times the average (three out of every four public employees being unionized, against the national average of about one in three employees)—see Evans, *The Labor Economies*, p. 23.

30. Cohen, *Japan's Economy in War and Reconstruction*, p. 438.
31. Farley, *Aspects of Japan's Labor Problems*, p. 85. Except in October 1946, man-days lost though strikes did not exceed 1 per cent of man-days available; "it would appear that labor disturbances were not a major factor among the many which impeded Japan's industrial revival." Cf. Bix, "The Treaty System and the Japanese Military-Industrial Complex," *BCAS*, Vol. 2, No. 2 (January 1970), pp. 42–47.
32. Iida, "The Origin of the Enterprise Union," p. 52; cf. *ibid.*, p. 63.
33. Kishimoto, "Labour-Management Relations . . . in Post-War Japan (1)," pp. 5 ff.; Iida, "The Origin of the Enterprise Union," pp. 50–52; Taira, *Economic Development and the Labor Market*, pp. 183–87, esp. p. 185.
34. Kishimoto, "Labor-Management Relations . . . in Post-War Japan (1)," pp. 5–6 (italics in original); I would add that I cannot agree with Kishimoto's definition of "the fundamental principle" of wages which is a euphemism for exploitation. On the basic issues involved here, see Gareth Stedman Jones, "The Wage Contract," *7 Days* (London), No. 14 (February 2–8, 1972), p. 18.
35. Kishimoto, "Labour-Management Relations . . . in Post-War Japan (1)," p. 6. Cf. Iida, "The Origin of the Enterprise Union," pp. 50–52. The proportion of the "living wage" component in fact began to decline at once, while that of "pay according to ability" (assessed unilaterally by management) rose correspondingly:

Year	Subsistence Pay	Pay According to Ability
1947	73.5%	26.5%
1951	70.7	29.3
1955	60.9	39.1

SOURCE: adapted from Kishimoto, "Labour-Management Relations . . . in Post-War Japan (1)," p. 6.

Cf. Taira, *Economic Development and the Labor Market*, p. 185, for further ramifications within the "living" wage.
36. Kishimoto, "Labour-Management Relations . . . in Post-War Japan (1)," pp. 8–9. Another factor which has been of vital importance in weakening the working class is that throughout the postwar period management has retained control over the allocation to individual workers of the total sum agreed on in any wage negotiation; even the Sanbetsu and its member unions never succeeded in getting control over the allocation of the total sum of wages agreed on (Kishimoto, pp. 10, 33).
37. Evans, *The Labor Economies*, p. 44, for a good full discussion; cf. Isao Akaoka, "The Development of Trade Unions and the Labour Market," *KUER*, Vol. 40, No. 1 (April 1970), Whole No. 68, p. 78. The importance of subcontracting is discussed below in more detail, along with other aspects of the *nenkō* system (see chapter 2 above, p. 65 and note 25).
38. Iida, "The Origin of the Enterprise Union," p. 47.
39. Kishimoto, "Labour-Management Relations . . . in Post-War Japan (1)"; Iida, "The Origin of the Enterprise Union"; cf. Kihara, "The Militarisation of the Japanese Economy." Much more work is needed on the relationship between SCAP and Japanese capitalism in this period.
40. Although this was definitely a move to break the logjam which he had contributed so much to creating, it is not clear if MacArthur was using the election to put the squeeze on Yoshida. Although MacArthur himself seems to have been amazingly complacent about the social and economic situation, officials in the Government Section of SCAP had begun by the end of 1946 to float the idea of a coalition between the conservatives and the Socialists (J. and G. Kolko, *The Limits of Power*, p. 324; cf. Yoshida, *Memoirs*, p. 79).
41. The party's official name is Nihon Shakaitō (Socialist Party of Japan). The official English "translation" of the party's name, which was adopted in the immediate postwar period to facilitate the party's action under the Occupation, was Social Democratic Party of Japan (thus, for example, A Cole et al., *Socialist Parties in Postwar Japan*, refer to it as the SDP—not to be confused with the DSP, the Democratic Socialist Party [Minshū Shakaitō]). In 1962 the Nihon Shakaitō changed the official

English version of its name to Japan Socialist Party (JSP). I have used this through-out. The party is also frequently referred to as the Japanese Socialist Party—for ex-ample, in the title of Stockwin's book. On the Katayama government, see Farley, *Aspects of Japan's Labor Problems*, pp. 168–88; A. Cole and others, *Socialist Parties in Postwar Japan*, pp. 16–22; *JSR*, Special Issue, October 1, 1964, pp. 11–15.

42. J. and G. Kolko, *The Limits of Power*, p. 514. The Emperor weighed in with an un-usually explicit plea for "harmonious relations between capital and labor" (Farley, *Aspects of Japan's Labor Problems*, p. 172).

43. Kishimoto, "Labour-Management Relations . . . in Post-War Japan (1)," p. 1.

44. A. Cole and others, *Socialist Parties in Postwar Japan*, p. 21.

45. *Ibid.*, p. 22.

46. *New York Times*, November 3, 1947 (cited in Textor, *Failure in Japan*, p. 26).

47. There is much more to be said on this complicated issue. The Sōdōmei was in a federation with the Sanbetsu (the Zenrōren,* with over 5 million claimed members) from immediately after the failure of the planned February 1, 1947 general strike up to June 1948. This was a politically uneasy "alliance" which, among other things, reflected the difficulties of the Socialist leadership in countering the real class solidarity of its own working-class base, which wanted to forge an alliance with the communist and communist-led workers. (Zenrōren: abbreviation for Zenkoku Rōdō Kumiai Renraku Kyōgikai, or National Labour Union Liaison Council.)

48. Kishimoto, "Labour-Management Relations . . . in Post-War Japan (1)," p. 10; cf. *ibid.*, p. 33; this is not explicit in most Western sources. It was of some importance that, whereas the communists had kept up a heroic opposition to the wartime regime, many of the Socialist leaders had actively collaborated with this regime. For example, Kawakami Jōtarō, an important Socialist leader before the war, participated in the founding of the Imperial Rule Assistance Association and, although subse-quently purged after the war, was reinstated in the JSP and became the party presi-dent in 1961. For some suggestions on the reasons for such "collaboration," see Hajime Shinohara, "The Leadership of the Progressive Parties," *JSPIJ*, Vol. 2, No. 3 (December 1964).

49. A. Cole and others, *Socialist Parties in Postwar Japan*, p. 23. On the Ashida govern-ment, *ibid.*, pp. 22–25; *JSR*, October 1, 1964, pp. 15–17.

50. Kishimoto, "Labour-Management Relations . . . in Post-War Japan (1)," pp. 12, 19.

51. *Ibid.*, p. 21. It was under Ashida that the United States began to press hard for the induction of large quantities of foreign (i.e., U.S.) capital, allegedly to help boost the economy (the Ashida government was commonly referred to as "the cabinet for the introduction of foreign capital" [*JSR*, October 1, 1964, p. 16]. Moreover, it was around this time that the United States was considering rebuilding Japan into the arsenal of the Far East. Breaking the working class was a necessary prerequisite for both these moves (see Kihara, "The Militarisation of the Japanese Economy," esp. pp. 32–33, 43).

52. Textor, *Failure in Japan*, p. 115.

53. The key figure involved was the veteran reactionary social democrat, Nishio Suehiro, Ashida's vice-premier. Nishio was ultimately exonerated some ten years later on the grounds that he had received the money "in his private capacity and not as a political leader."

54. *Mindō:* abbreviation for *minshuka dōmei* (which can also be translated as "demo-cratic leagues"); the drive to form anti-communist cells in the Sanbetsu unions dates from the end of 1946 (see Farley, *Aspects of Japan's Labor Problems*, p. 186), though some sources put it rather later—to the end of 1947, or even 1948. Much useful material in *JSPIJ*, Vol. 3, No. 1 (April 1965); Kishimoto, "Labour-Manage-ment Relations . . . in Post-War Japan (1)," p. 32.

55. Bix, "The Security Treaty System," pp. 42–44; Johnson (*Conspiracy at Matsukawa*, p. 24) remarks that SCAP "decimated" union leadership "by prohibiting full-time union officials from receiving salaries or offices from the company. Enterprise unions in small firms could thus no longer afford a full-time union official."

56. Cf. Dore's account of police intervention at Hitachi's Furusato plant slightly later (*British Factory—Japanese Factory*, pp. 118–19).

57. Kishimoto, "Labour-Management Relations . . . in Post-War Japan (1)," pp. 24–27,

is a good account of this.

58. Taira, *Economic Development and the Labor Market*, p. 177.
59. Kishimoto, "Labour-Management Relations . . . in Post-War Japan (1)," pp. 26–27; cf. Yoshida, *Memoirs*, p. 241; Johnson, *Conspiracy at Matsukawa*, p. 23; Farley, *Aspects of Japan's Labor Problems*, pp. 212–41. Speaking of the 1950 phase of the process, A. Cole and others state that: "The process undoubtedly involved widespread disregard of basic civil and human rights" (*Socialist Parties in Postwar Japan*, p. 330).
60. A. Cole and others, *Socialist Parties in Postwar Japan*, p. 331.
61. Taira, *Economic Development and the Labor Market*, pp. 180–87, is excellent on this complex process, which I have somewhat simplified here; in addition, Taira documents the extent to which the unions were gradually pushed out of their earlier involvement in production decisions (p. 180). Information on the different kinds of "temporary" workers (p. 181) and other non-"permanent" workers (subcontractors, extra workers (*shagaikō*) and casual workers [pp. 186–87] is discussed more fully below). Cf. Akaoka, "The Development of Trade Unions and the Labor Market."
62. Taira, *Economic Development and the Labor Market*, p. 175.
63. *Ibid.*, pp. 181–82 (this refers to 1951 onwards); excellent information on this and other matters in Ken'ichi Kobayashi, "The Employment and Wage Systems in Post-war Japan," *DE*, Vol. 7, No. 2 (June 1969), pp. 189–202.
64. Cited in Ōno Tsutomu, "Student Protest in Japan," p. 273.
65. Kishimoto, "Labour-Management Relations . . . in Post-War Japan (1)," p. 31. Dower, "Occupied Japan and the American Lake," p. 204 (note 101), records the view of the eminent Japanese historian Tōyama Shigeki (Tōyama Shigeki et al, *Shōwa-shi* [Tokyo, 1955], p. 274) that the 1950 "Red Purge" is the continuation of the 1949 purge. Western references to the "Red Purge" as something which only started in 1950 (and which is frequently dated, usually by allusion or omission, to *after* the outbreak of the Korean War) obscure the key point that the purges in late 1950 were only the culminating phase of a mass wrecking operation that had already been going on for well over a year.
66. Nikkeiren: Nihon Keieisha Danta Remmei (Japan Federation of Employers' Associations, or JFEA); this has consistently been the most viciously anti-proletarian of all the big business organizations. See A. Cole et al., *Socialist Parties in Postwar Japan*, p. 331; Kishimoto, "Labour-Management Relations . . . in Post-War Japan (1)," p. 32; Bix, "The Security Treaty System," pp. 42–47.
67. Ōta Kaoru in *SN*, No. 246 (April 10, 1965). Sōhyō: Nihon Rōdō Kumiai Sōhyōgikai, or General Council of Japanese Trade Unions. Sōhyō publishes a very useful irregular magazine, *Sohyo News* (hereafter *SN*); the annual special issue of this dated January 15 is an invaluable "White Paper on Wages" which contains much information not easily available otherwise in English. Sōhyō also publishes *This Is Sohyo—Japanese Workers and Their Struggles*. The 1972 edition of this (194 pages) is indispensable. On Sōhyō, apart from the general works cited above (Robert E. Cole, Allan B. Cole et al., Scalapino, etc.), see Bernard Béraud, *La Gauche Révolutionnaire au Japon* Paris, Seuil, 1970), pp. 109–17; Taguchi, "Leadership in the General Council"; David Baker, "The Trade Union Movement in Japan," *International Socialism* (London), No. 23 (Winter 1965–66). Kazuo Ōkōchi, "The General Council of Japanese Labor Unions," *JSPIJ*, Vol. 3, No. 1 (April 1965), is an anti-proletarian account; ditto for Ōkōchi's book, *Labor in Modern Japan*.
68. The question of how and why Sōhyō moved as far left as it did is one of the most complex in postwar Japan. The best source on this is Taguchi, "Leadership in the General Council"; A. Cole et al., *Socialist Parties in Postwar Japan*, deliver the "facts" but so divorced from their real political context that it is hard to follow what was actually happening. How left Sōhyō went is discussed more fully below.
69. Kishimoto, "Labour-Management Relations . . . in Post-War Japan (1)," p. 32.
70. K. Kobayashi, "The Employment and Wage Systems," pp. 194–96.
71. *Ibid.*, where Kobayashi spells out the details of the differences between the two stages; cf. Evans, *The Labor Economies*, pp. 44–47—another excellent account, which deals in full with the accompanying pressures on the *nenkō* system.
72. Taira, *Economic Development and the Labor Market*, p. 189; see note 14 for Magota

source.

73. The Shuntō is also sometimes referred to as the "base up" system. On this, see especially Robert Evans, Jr., "Shuntō: Japanese Labor's Spring Offensive," *Monthly Labor Review* (Washington, D.C.), Vol. 90, No. 10 (October 1967), pp. 23–28; Evans, *The Labor Economies*, pp. 123–30; Haruo Shimada, "Japanese Labor's Spring Wage Offensive and Wage Spillover," *KES*, Vol. 7, No. 2 (1970); Taira, *Economic Development and the Labor Market*, pp. 189–202. Shimada, pp. 34–35, is a very good account of the historical origin of the phenomenon and how it emerged out of debate within the union movement.

74. Chūritsurōren: National Liaison Council of Independent Unions; technically not a union federation but, as its name states, a "liaison council"; for membership, see note 89 below.

75. Shimada, "Japanese Labor's Spring Wage Offensive," pp. 38–41.

76. The extent to which the lead union and the Shuntō in general affect wage increases is discussed in *ibid.*, and in both Evans, *The Labor Economies*, and Taira, *Economic Development and the Labor Market*. Figures for wage increases from: *JLB*, Vol. 11, No. 9 (September 1972), p. 5 (to 1971) and *JLB*, Vol. 11, No. 7 (July 1972), p. 2 (1972: the employers' and unions' estimates vary, the former giving 16 per cent and the latter 15 per cent). The 1973 figure is from the *Guardian* (London), June 5, 1973; cf. the *Economist* (London), May 5, 1973. These figures are for *nominal* increases; real increases are much lower:

WAGE LEVEL INCREASES*

Year	Nominal Wage	Real Wage
1967	11.8	7.6
1969	15.6	9.9
1970	17.0	8.7
1971	14.5	7.9

* Rate of annual increase for the total of cash-paid wages.

SOURCE: *SN*, No. 309 (January 15, 1973), Table 29, p. 104, from Ministry of Labour, *Monthly Labour Statistics*.

It should be noted, though, that most wages are fixed without any collective bargaining at all: less than one-third of all employees have a part in determining the terms at which they sell their labour through "free" collective bargaining (*JLB*, Vol. 11, No. 4 [April 1972], pp. 13–16, and Vol. 11, No. 5 [May 1972], pp. 4, 7–10). Collective bargaining is mainly limited to organized workers in the private sector, and is particularly restricted among blue-collar workers.

77. Both the role of the shortage of labour, and the dating of the shortage are subjects of some dispute. Evans, *The Labor Economies*, pp. 182–84, argues that it is incorrect to talk of a real shortage before about 1968–69 (querying some of Taira's theses in *Economic Development and the Labor Market*); Evans's position is in effect supported by Maekawa for at any rate up to the mid-1960s (Kaichi Maekawa, "Changes of Government Employment Policy in the Face of Economic Growth in Japan since World War II," *KUER*, Vol. 40, No. 2 (October 1970), Whole No. 89, esp. pp. 45–48). What there seems to have been up to about 1970 is an acute shortage in certain sectors, including key sectors of industry, in the context of an overall surplus. To some extent this position is borne out by the "unemployment" figures. What is qualified as full technical unemployment was stabilized at almost exactly 1 per cent from 1969 (Evans, *The Labor Economies*, p. 88); but Japan's economy is one "whose excess demand and supply position may only partly be understood by an examination of the unemployment rate" (*ibid.*, p. 90). This is largely because of the very high number of "underemployed," estimated to total 7,800,000 in 1970, during a full boom period (Tsuji Ken, "Labor," *JQ*, Vol. 17, No. 3 (July–September 1970); cf. Yoshio Kaneko, "Employment and Wages," *DE*, Vol. 8, No. 4 (December 1970), pp. 446–48).

78. Evans, "Shuntō," p. 26; J. C. Abegglen and W. V. Rapp, "Japanese Managerial Behavior and 'Excessive Competition,'" *DE*, Vol. 8, No. 4 (December 1970), esp. p. 430;
cf. note 105 below.

79. Shimada, "Japanese Labor's Spring Offensive," pp. 44–45; Ayusawa, *History of Labor
in Modern Japan,* p. 471. Evans, "Shuntō," pp. 23–24, details the very big fluctuations
in the number of disputes as a result of the Shuntō. On the whole, Japan still has a
relatively *low* level of strikes compared with other advanced capitalist economies:
strikes over wages seem to be about the same level as in the United States, but
strikes over management decisions concerning the work force have been much lower
(Evans, *The Labor Economies,* pp. 29–30; cf. Ayusawa, *History of Labor in Modern
Japan,* p. 350; cf. Arthur M. Whitehill, Jr., and Shin-ichi Takezaw, *The Other
Worker: A Comparative Study of Industrial Relations in the United States and Japan*
[Honolulu, East-West Center Press, 1968], pp. 330–33). For details of disputes, man-
days idle and number of workers involved in recent years, see *JLB,* Vol. 11, No. 11
(November 1972), p. 6. Things may well be changing qualitatively. The period
1972–73 saw two unprecedented strike phenomena for Japan: (*a*) the 1972 seamen's
strike, which lasted from April 14 to July 13, was the longest walkout in the history
of Japanese labour struggles and unparalleled for both the size of the workers' claim
and their militancy during the strike (see *JQ,* Vol. 19, No. 4 [October–December
1972], p. 501; *ARB,* Vol. 2, No. 2 [July 1972], p. 1048; *JLB,* Vol. 11, No. 9 [Sep-
tember 1972], p. 2); and (*b*) the April 26–27, 1973 general strike which was "on a
scale unknown in the history of the Japanese labour movement" (*Peking Review,*
No. 19 [May 11], 1973, p. 17); this was not part of the 1973 Shuntō, but dovetailed
with it, since the central issue in both was the restoration of the right to strike for
public employees.
     The *Japan Labor Bulletin* is a useful source, published by the Ministry of Labour.
It must, however, be treated with caution (see Evans, *The Labor Economies,* p. 39,
for some questionable data advanced in the *JLB* of July 1967). The Ministry of
Labour is virtually the captive of Nikkeiren (this is the opinion of the respected
Japanese expert, Ishida Takeshi, reported by Taira, *Economic Development and the
Labor Market,* p. 230). Most sources, including *Sohyo News,* must to some extent
rely on "official" figures, many of which are probably fabricated by Nikkeiren, directly
or indirectly (see *FEER,* No. 11 [March 13], 1971, p. 13, for an exemplary case in
the late 1960s).

80. Evans, "Shuntō," p. 26.

81. Taira, *Economic Development and the Labor Market,* pp. 227–34; Robert E. Cole,
"Japanese Workers, Unions and the Marxist Appeal," *JI,* Vol. 6, No. 2 (1970), pp.
118–19.

82. Kōtaro Tsujimura, "The Employment Structure and Labor Shares," in Ryūtaro
Komiya, ed., *Postwar Economic Growth in Japan,* is a detailed study; figures below
from *This is Sohyo,* 1972, p. 141; *SN,* No. 303, p. 76; R. Cole, "Japanese Workers,
Unions and the Marxist Appeal," pp. 118–19, gives "labor's relative share of gross
value added" in firms employing more than 10 people as 39.1 per cent in 1965.
JLB, Vol. 11, No. 9 (September 1972), p. 6, asserts that from 1965 wages tended
to grow faster than productivity. Other information from Taira, *Economic Development and the Labor Market,* p. 193; cf. Dore, *British Factory—Japanese Factory,* pp.
330–32.

83. *This is Sohyo,* 1972, p. 141, and *SN,* No. 303, p. 76; *SN,* No. 309, Tables 3 and 4,
pp. 80, 81, and p. 8; cf. Kaneko, "Employment and Wages," p. 466; Yamamura,
Economic Policy, pp. 170–71 (for the period 1952–62).

84. *This is Sohyo,* 1972, p. 145; *SN,* No. 303, p. 96; *SN,* No. 309, p. 110 (which gives
"working hours per week" and "working hours per week for ordinary weeks" for
Japan, but no complete comparison with any single other country); cf. *ibid.,* pp. 43–49.
JLB, Vol. 11, No. 9 (September 1972), puts the working week 2–6 hours above that
in other advanced capitalist countries; cf. *JLB,* Vol. 11, No. 12 (December 1972),
pp. 4, 7–10, for a detailed survey of working hours.

85. *SN,* No. 309, Table 31, p. 105, compares wages in Japan and several other industrial
countries (manufacturing) in 1970, with a "revised" calculation based on the first

yen revaluation (1971); the second yen revaluation put Japanese wages higher in terms of international comparison by roughly the same percentage again, on average.

86. Evans, *The Labor Economies*, p. 191; R. Cole, *Japanese Blue Collar*, pp. 225–29.

87. R. Cole, *Japanese Blue Collar*, pp. 225–27; the 1959 figure of 56.9 per cent of unions (with over 62 per cent of all union members) had fallen to 47 per cent by 1967.

88. There is an excellent political assessment of the current role of the unions in the interview with Higuchi Tokuzō ("Labor Movement in Japan: Its Present and Future"), one of the leaders of Zenrōkatsu, a new national union liaison organization, in *Ampo*, No. 17 (Tokyo, Summer 1973), pp. 27–37.

89. *This Is Sohyo*, 1972, pp. 65–85, for Sōhyō's view of Dōmei. As of June 30, 1971 government statistics gave the following picture:

Total number of workers:	*33,830,000*
Total number of organized workers	*11,798,000*
Rate of organization (Presumed)	*34.9%*
Organizations:	
Sōhyō (General Council of Trade Unions of Japan)	4,245,000
Dōmei (Japanese Confederation of Labour)	2,172,000
Shinsambetsu (National Federation of Industrial Organizations)	76,000
Chūritsurōren (Liaison Council of Independent Unions)	1,350,000
Major Unions Unaffiliated to Above Centres	1,018,000
Others	1,848,000
Unions with No Affiliation	1,108,000

SOURCE: *This Is Sohyo*, 1972, p. iii.

Also of importance in the last decade or so has been the I.M.F.-J.C. (International Metalworkers' Federation—Japan Chapter). This had 1,160,000 members by 1970 and had grown fast in the metallurgical, automobile and electrical industries. It is not a federation, strictly speaking, but groups together unions from other federations— iron and steel from Sōhyō, automobile unions from Dōmei. It is thoroughly collaborationist. Information below from Tsuji Ken, "Labor."

90. In 1968, with about 40 per cent of all unionized workers, Sōhyō unions accounted for 81.6 per cent of all workers "affected" by labour disputes (R. Cole, "Japanese Workers, Unions and the Marxist Appeal," p. 127). For some information on the situation in one car plant of the Nissan empire, see Matsuo Kei, "Nissan Motor: Hell's Battlefield," *Ampo*, No. 20 (Vol. 6, No. 2) (Spring 1974).

91. Interview with Muto Iichiyo, *Ampo*, Nos. 3–4 (March 1970), p. 18. The fusion of Yawata and Fuji was a re-merger, since the two enterprises had formerly been united (prior to 1945). Mergers have been a key device for crippling shop floor workers' organizations, by smashing unions and less formal groups, dismissing militant workers and revamping pay scales downwards.

92. Hansen Seinen Iinkai: Anti-War Youth Committee (AWYC); the key militant working class organization, set up in the mid-sixties: see Béraud, *La Gauche Révolutionnaire*, pp. 117–27; "Street-fighting Workers: Hansen Seinen Iinkai," *Ampo*, No. 6 (1970); Stuart J. Dowsey, ed., *Zengakuren: Japan's Revolutionary Students* (Berkeley, Calif., The Ishi Press, 1970), pp. 263–65; interview with Higuchi Tokuzō, *Ampo*, No. 17; Stefano Bellieni, *Zengakuren Zenkyoto* (Milan, Feltrinelli, 1969), pp. 320–24; Halliday and McCormack, *Japanese Imperialism*, p. 181. A police assessment put AWYC membership at 30,000 as of early 1970.

93. On Beheiren, see Dowsey, ed., *Zengakuren*, pp. 265–67; *Ampo*, No. 1 (n.d.), interview with Oda Makoto. Beheiren is short for "Betonamu ni Heiwa o!" Shimin Rengō (Citizens Alliance for "Peace in Vietnam!").

94. R. Cole, "Japanese Workers, Unions and the Marxist Appeal," p. 128; cf. *ibid.*, p. 117; Evans, *The Labor Economies*, p. 63; hence the active promotion of a Sōhyō-Dōmei merger by the more far-sighted elements in the ruling class.

95. Evans, *The Labor Economies*, p. 89.

96. Kaneko, "Employment and Wages," pp. 455, 461 (useful charts).

97. Kaji Etsuko, "The Invisible Proletariat: Working Women in Japan," *Ampo*, No. 18 (Autumn 1973), pp. 49, 51. This article is an absolutely indispensable text on the

situation of women in Japanese capitalism today.

98. *Ibid.*, pp. 50 ff. for examples. Male/female wage differentials vary greatly according both to the type of industry, and to the size of the enterprise, and age. In general, the wage differences are smaller in larger enterprises and among the younger workers: in 1968 the average earnings of women in the 18–19 age group (all industries) were 79.5 per cent that of men, while in the 40–49 age bracket the figure was only 41.9 per cent (*SN*, No. 293 [January 15, 1971], Table 45, p. 100); cf. Kaji, "The Invisible Proletariat," pp. 51–52, esp. Chart V, p. 52; R. Cole, *Japanese Blue Collar*, pp. 147–48.

99. Kaji, "The Invisible Proletariat," p. 56; Evans, *The Labor Economies*, p. 180.

100. Kaji, "The Invisible Proletariat," pp. 53 ff.; Evans, *The Labor Economies*, pp. 69–71; Kaneko, "Employment and Wages," pp. 457–60; Shigeru Kobayashi, *Creative Management* (n.p., American Management Association, Inc., 1971), pp. 60–66 ("Housewives Prove Their Worth") and pp. 209–10 ("Motivated Women"), for a sexist and exploitative view by the former manager of Sony's Atsugi plant. In addition, many companies make extensive use of female workers employed on side jobs in their homes, and paid piece rates, thus further lowering costs (see Kaji, p. 55).

101. Although women are less unionized than men (29.4 per cent of women workers belonged to a union in 1970 compared with 38 per cent of men workers—see Kaji, "The Invisible Proletariat," p. 51), it is interesting that the evidence assembled by Whitehill and Takezawa shows: (*a*) that women workers are more combative than men vis-à-vis their employers, and (*b*) that women are more in favour of unions and union solidarity than men (*The Other Worker*, Tables 3 ["Subordination"], p. 115, and 28 ["Need for Unions"], p. 327.

102. Kaji, "The Invisible Proletariat," p. 48 (italics in original); cf. *ibid.*, p. 56, on the "my-home-ism" ideology. On *maihōmushugi* [*shugi* = "ism"], see also V. Dixon Morris, "The Idioms of Contemporary Japan III," *JI*, Vol. 7, Nos. 3–4 (Summer–Autumn 1972), pp. 388–90 (entry: "Maihōmushugi"); and, for further background, Frank Baldwin, "The Idioms of Contemporary Japan V," *JI*, Vol. 8, No. 2 (Spring 1973), pp. 237–44 (entry: "Ūman Ribu" [women's lib]). Kaji notes that at Sony and other factories a regular woman worker who has a baby has to become a "temporary" employee if she wants to go on working and use the company nursery or daycare centre; and that mothers who try to keep their regular employment by finding some other way of having their children looked after (for example, by grandparents) "are socially condemned and feel enormous guilt" ("The Invisible Proletariat," p. 55).

103. An excellent study of one typically isolated plant, a Hitachi copper mine in the Kantō plain, is Shizuo Matsushima and Takayoshi Kitagawa, "The Characteristics and Limitations of Labor-Management Policy in Japan," *JSPIJ*, Vol. 3, No. 3 (December 1965); the company's long-range policy, write the authors, was "to make employees and their families completely dependent on the mine for all phases of their livelihood so that they gradually lose all ties with their places of origin and come to look upon the mine as their only home, their only 'native land'" (p. 50). The company provided services from a barber shop to a crematorium. Between 45 and 50 per cent of employees' wages were reabsorbed through company commissaries.

104. Wage disparities by size of enterprise, although decreasing, are still considerable, as the following table shows:

Year	*Enterprise employing:*		
	More than 500 employees	*100–499 employees*	*30–99 employees*
1960	100.00	70.7	58.9
1965	100.00	80.9	71.0
1969	100.00	80.9	69.6
1970	100.00	85.7	70.4
1971	100.00	81.1	71.0

SOURCE: *SN*, No. 309, Table 21, p. 98 (from Ministry of Labour, *Monthly Labour Statistics*).

Note that the progression is by no means linear. Cf. Evans, *The Labor Economies*, pp. 182–88; note 115 below for disparities by age, which criss-cross disparities by enterprise size. These figures are presumably for male workers only.

105. Yamamura, *Economic Policy*, pp. 160–63, discusses the important role of *shiwayose* (delaying payment to subcontractors, often by about 9 months). The latter, being dependent on the big enterprises, are usually reluctant to complain; given the high debt ratios of most businesses, this greatly reduces the interest payments of the big firms, and heightens that of the smaller ones, who tend to take the cost out on their workers; cf. Yamamura, Table 55, p. 164 for the average levels of interest rates by size of firm; Abegglen and Rapp, "Japanese Managerial Behavior," for the wider effects of this practice in assisting big business. Note also the direct correlation between wage costs and growth: a slow-moving company will have a high percentage of older workers (who are relatively highly paid), and vice versa.

106. Taira, *Economic Development and the Labor Market*, pp. 186–87; Evans, *The Labor Economies*, pp. 87–90, both effectively demolish Abegglen (*The Japanese Factory*); see also, K. Kobayashi, "The Employment and Wage Systems," pp. 194–98. Information below from Taira and Evans.

107. The one-fifth estimate is by R. Cole, *Japanese Blue Collar*, p. 115, the higher one from Evans, *The Labor Economies*, p. 38; information immediately below from Evans, pp. 38–39.

108. Dore cites a 1961 survey showing that some 10 per cent of unions admitted temporary workers in practice (*British Factory—Japanese Factory*, p. 325); Kaji notes that part-time contracts usually forbid holders to join the union ("The Invisible Proletariat," p. 54).

109. K. Kobayashi, "The Employment and Wage Systems," p. 197.

110. Evans, *The Labor Economies*, p. 89.

111. *Ibid.*, pp. 88–89; Yamamura, *Economic Policy*, pp. 168–70.

112. Evans, *The Labor Economies*, p. 88; K. Kobayashi, "The Employment and Wage Systems," pp. 198–202; and, especially, interview with Higuchi Tokuzō, *Ampo*, No. 17, p. 31.

113. K. Kobayashi, "The Employment and Wage Systems," pp. 209–10; Taira, *Economic Development and the Labor Market*, pp. 186–87; Evans, *The Labor Economies*, pp. 87–90; cf. note 123 below on mobility.

114. Compulsory early retirement is very important, since it functions as an artificial wage-lowering and de-unionizing device; workers are often rehired after the forced retirement age, on much lower wages: R. Cole, *Japanese Blue Collar*, pp. 84–92, 113–17. Kaneko, "Employment and Wages," pp. 472–73, suggests this may soon have to be changed. The interpretation of wages as a lifetime payment distributed at an artificial rate chosen by management is Evans's (*The Labor Economies*, p. 188).

115. Age-based wage disparities, although declining slightly (for men) are still very high, as the following table shows (this refers only to what is termed the "regular" wage, and only to male workers in manufacturing):

				Age				
Year	Less than 18 years	20–24 years	25–29 years	30–34 years	35–39 years	40–44 years	50–59 years	More than 60 years
1961	54.3	100.00	129.6	160.5	181.5	198.1	175.9	113.6
1964	57.1	100.00	124.9	143.8	158.4	170.4	155.8	107.7
1967	56.8	100.00	126.3	144.5	157.8	168.2	158.8	107.5
1970	58.9	100.00	127.3	143.8	151.3	159.5	148.5	100.0
1971	60.4	100.00	125.2	141.3	147.7	152.3	142.3	99.3

SOURCE: *SN*, No. 309, Table 22, p. 99.

Cf. Dore, *British Factory—Japanese Factory*, p. 313 (Table 12.8); and Ryoshin Minami, "Transformations of the Labor Market in Postwar Japan," *HJE*, Vol. 13, No. 1 (June 1972), pp. 60–65. R. Cole argues that, by and large, "age" and "skill" overlap more than might be assumed at first sight (*Japanese Blue Collar*, pp. 78–79).

116. Evans, *The Labor Economies*, pp. 44–46. R. Cole, "Japanese Workers, Unions and the Marxist Appeal," pp. 114–16, cites the findings of two surveys of two unions in the mid-to-late 1960s which found that workers over 30 were more radical *in their attitudes* than workers under 30, but less radical in their actual behaviour. In the

absence of more detailed work on this, it is difficult to be categorical about age as a factor in radicalism.

117. Evans, *The Labor Economies*, p. 188; this ties up with the fact that the unions have no role in the distribution of the total wage (*ibid.*, p. 191; cf. K. Kobayashi, "The Employment and Wage Systems," p. 213).

118. Evans, *The Labor Economies*, pp. 39–40; information below from *ibid.*, pp. 44–46, esp. pp. 45–46.

119. R. Cole, *Japanese Blue Collar*, pp. 75–78; cf. *ibid.*, pp. 88–92; Evans, *The Labor Economies*, pp. 45–46; Dore, *British Factory—Japanese Factory*, p. 312 (Table 12.7).

120. This is leaving aside the fact that business has not opened the books in Japan, and that the auditing of accounts is in an extremely obnubilated state. In addition, it should be noted that the payment of large "bonuses" (i.e., the *delayed* payment of wages) once or twice a year stimulate a high rate of saving, and thus capital formation (see Kang Chao, "Labor Institutions in Japan and Her Economic Growth," *JAS*, Vol. 28, No. 1 [November 1968], pp. 13–15).

121. But see K. Kobayashi, "The Employment and Wage Systems," pp. 189–202, and esp. pp. 209–10 and Tables 8 and 9; *SN*, No. 309, Figure 5 ("Rates of Different Forms of Employment Adjustment"), p. 126; Taira, *Economic Development and the Labor Market*, p. 187; R. Cole, *Japanese Blue Collar*, pp. 115–22; cf. note 113 above.

122. R. Cole, *Japanese Blue Collar*, p. 122.

123. Including cultural-linguistic mechanisms such as the repressive language used about dismissals: see *ibid.*, pp. 119–20. Chie Nakane, *Japanese Society* (Berkeley and Los Angeles, University of California Press, 1970), pp. 107–8, contributes to the deception by claiming that the definition of changing one's employment as "soiling one's *curriculum vitae* [belongs to a] native moral orientation"; this Abegglenish statement is repeated uncritically by Zbigniew Brzezinski in *The Fragile Blossom*, p. 4; the fact that changing one's job may be "seen" as "soiling one's *curriculum vitae*" only means that this is how it is *made* to "seem."

124. Evans, *The Labor Economies*, p. 81; pp. 76–81, *passim*, and p. 84, for comparison with the United States; R. Cole, *Japanese Blue Collar*, pp. 122–27, 129–31 (the difficulty of switching jobs after the age of 30 for men); *SN*, No. 309, Table 23, p. 100. Much new information appears in Dore, *British Factory—Japanese Factory*, pp. 306–13.

125. Maekawa, "Changes of Government Employment Policy," p. 50; cf. *JLB*, Vol. 11, No. 9 (September 1972), p. 5, for the 1971 White Paper estimates.

126. Kaji, "The Invisible Proletariat," *passim;* Evans, *The Labor Economies*, p. 47; cf. Dore, *British Factory—Japanese Factory*, pp. 335–37; Rowley, "Japan: A New Centre of World Imperialism," pp. 18–20; Kang Chao, "Labor Institutions in Japan and Her Economic Growth," esp. pp. 8–13.

127. Tsurumi, *Social Change and the Individual*, pp. 93–94 on the open-endedness; cf. Uchida Yoshihiko, "Japan Today and *Das Kapital*," *JI*, Vol. 6, No. 1 (Spring 1970), p. 24, for observations on the point that instead of rights, in Japan the state has fostered the "idea" that there are only concessions granted; although these are in fact granted in the interests of the "bestower," they are presented as "benevolence." See Kunihiro Masao, "Indigenous Barriers to Communication," *JI*, Vol. 8, No. 1 (Winter 1973), p. 97, on the weakness of the concept of the contract in Japan.

128. R. Cole reports that there was one member of the supervisory personnel for every 17 subordinates in one of the factories he worked in in 1968 (*Japanese Blue Collar*, p. 106). One shoe factory studied had one supervisor for every 14 workers in the late 1950s.

129. The "second" union is a term adopted to describe management-backed organizations set up to undermine militant unions: this tactic was made famous during the great strike at Miike, a Mitsui-owned coal mine, in the years 1959–60. Cf. Dore, *British Factory—Japanese Factory*, pp. 327–28.

130. See especially the interview with Higuchi Tokuzō, *Ampo*, No. 17, for a striking description of business-state violence against the proletariat; for the concomitant surveillance in society generally, see Muto Ichiyo, "Law & Order, Japanese Style," *Ampo*, No. 12 (March 1972), pp. 3–5; cf. note 72 to chapter 7 and note 86 to chapter 9.

131. Kazué Morisaki, "Dans les souterrains du Japon: la vie des mineurs de Kyushu,"

Les Temps Modernes (Paris), No. 272 (February 1969), pp. 1499–1500. Many of the miners were and are Koreans and *burakumin*. The Mitsui mine at Miike in Kyushu was the site of the biggest strike in postwar Japanese industry, which developed into a mass movement involving an alliance with the local farmers and small traders, whose livelihood was also being threatened by Mitsui's policy of pollution and ecological destruction (see Shinzo Shimizu, "The Labor Movement and the Task of the Democratic Forces," *JSPIJ*, Vol. 3, No. 1 [April 1965]; and Collick, *Labour and Trades Unionism in the Japanese Coal Mining Industry*, pp. 297–306). Gangsters are regularly used at every level of industry, from the coal-face and the shop floor to shareholders' meetings, where they are used to smother protest from opponents of management policy. In the famous Minamata case, the company hired thugs to beat up the crippled villagers from Minamata who were waiting to enter the annual general meeting.

132. Labour Ministry, *Monotonous Labour Survey*, 1968, yuoted in *SN*, No. 293, p. 85.
133. *This Is Sohyo*, 1972, p. 148; *SN*, No. 303, pp. 94–95.
134. Matsuo Kei, "Nissan Capital: the Domination of Workers by Unions and the Formation of Fascism in the Work Place," *Kōzō*, June 1971; I am grateful to Bernard Béraud for making available a French translation of this article. Cf. interview with Higuchi Tokuzō, *Ampo*, No. 17, p. 34.
135. *Time*, October 18, 1971, p. 47.
136. The Matsushita song figures prominently in Herman Kahn's manipulative and ill-informed book, *The Emerging Japanese Superstate: Challenge and Response* (London, André Deutsch, 1971), pp. 110–12. Dore, in a perceptive excursus, adumbrates a comparison between a Japanese company (Hitachi) and the British Army, which bear a very close similarity to each other (*British Factory—Japanese Factory*, pp. 275–76); but neither Kahn nor Dore discusses the systematic manner in which business sets out to break new recruits through mindless drilling and physical exercise. Moreover, some companies actually send their new employees to "breaking-in" courses at Self-Defence Force bases where they "live in army barracks, in an atmosphere of army-style fatigues, and are drilled and exercised by former Imperial Army men now working for the companies" (Max Suich, "A Land Where Workers Salute the Factory Flag," *The Asia Magazine*, October 31, 1971, p. 11).
137. The calculation on after-tax profits is by Abegglen and Rapp, "Japanese Managerial Behavior," p. 428. Yoshino, *Japan's Managerial System*, pp. 101–12, has very interesting observations on the profit motive in Japan; what is most striking is the success of big business, in spite of the evidence of high capital accumulation (which equals future profits), in masking the extent of current after-tax profits. See R. Cole, "Japanese Workers, Unions and the Marxist Appeal," p. 121, for some mystifying managerial slogans.
138. Nakane, *Japanese Society*, p. 87; the same sort of attempts to conjure away the class struggle are to be found in Kahn, Brzezinski, et al.; the most repugnant elucubrations on the subject are those by Brian Beedham, the foreign editor of the *Economist* (see Beedham, "A Special Strength: A Survey of Japan," *Economist*, March 31, 1973, Survey, pp. 8–11).
139. Nakane, *Japanese Society*, p. 131.
140. *Ibid.*, p. 150.
141. Yoshida, *Memoirs*, p. 221. In 1954 working conditions were legally sub-standard in over half the industrial establishments *inspected*, yet only an insignificant number were prosecuted.
142. Alice B. Cook, *An Introduction to Japanese Trade Unionism* (Ithaca, N.Y., Cornell University Press, 1966), p. 16; cf. Taira, *Economic Development and the Labor Market*, pp. 230–34, and Yoshino, *Japan's Managerial System*, chapter 6. *SN*, No. 309, sets out the programme for the 1973 campaign to get the government to recognize the right of public employees to strike and engage in collective bargaining—a campaign which culminated in major demonstrations in the spring of 1973 and a quasi-general strike. It may be noted that by 1972 Japan had actually *signed* only 26 I.L.O. Conventions, far less than any of the other advanced capitalist countries, and considerably less than Algeria or Egypt; Japan had then still refused to sign Convention

No. 1, which stipulated an 8-hour working day (see *The Shinsayoku*, English edition, No. 2 [May 1, 1972], p. 2).

143. On this, see Maekawa, "Changes of Government Employment Policy," p. 53. The main element in the regime's labour policy since the late 1960s has been a drive to force more people into the productive process; as Maekawa makes clear, this was a deliberate pro-business option, taken at the expense of improving social services and easing up on production (Maekawa, pp. 47–48, 51–52; cf. Minami, "Transformations of the Labor Market," pp. 71–72). I have not gone into the fascinating and important subject of new Japanese managerial tactics; those who wish to pursue this may consult Yoshino, *Japan's Managerial System,* esp. pp. 95–117; R. Cole, *Japanese Blue Collar,* pp. 88–92; Ken'ichi Kobayashi, "The Employment and Wage Systems"; Shigeru Kobayashi, *Creative Management, passim;* Evans, *The Labor Economies,* pp. 44–47; Kaneko, "Employment and Wages," pp. 470–73.

144. *SN*, No. 309, Table 40, for an international comparison of welfare costs to cash-paid wages.

145. See Matsushima and Kitagawa, "The Characteristics and Limitations of Labor-Management Policy in Japan"; cf. the widespread employers' practice of intervening in ("patronizing") their employees' marriages. At this level, of course, a Japanese firm really is like a "family."

146. For the dismal pension situation, see R. Cole, *Japanese Blue Collar,* pp. 23, 27–29; for statistics on the condition of the old, see *SN*, No. 303, pp. 88–90. *SN*, No. 309, Table 50, p. 118, gives an international comparison of pension systems: pensions in ratio to national income in Japan in 1970 were less than one-tenth that in the U.K. in 1966, and less than one-twentieth the level in West Germany in 1966, with no sliding scale.

147. See Maekawa, "Changes of Government Employment Policy"; particularly important here is the 5-year gap between forced retirement (at 55) and the age at which government pensions begin (60): see the report by the Manpower and Social Affairs Committee of the Organisation for Economic Co-operation and Development, *OECD Observer,* July 1973, reproduced in the *Quarterly Review of the Anglo-Japanese Economic Institute* (London), No. 48 (October 1973), pp. 16–19. There is an interesting study on Japan's aging labour force in the *Mitsubishi Bank Review,* Vol. 3, No. 12 (December 1972).

148. As well as making a very large amount of workers' *incomes* available for private capital investment, this high savings rate also means that a large amount of money is kept away from consumption: personal consumption in Japan in 1971 accounted for only 50.4 per cent of gross national expenditure, whereas the figures for the U.K., Italy and the United States in 1970 were 63.5, 65.5 and 66.5 per cent, respectively; correlatively, the figure for equipment investment in Japan (1971) was 37.7 per cent, compared with 18.4, 20.1 and 14.4 per cent, respectively, for the same three countries (*SN*, No. 309, Figure 1, p. 122); cf. *Economist,* January 27, 1973, Survey: International Banking, p. 44. Ryūtaro Komiya, "The Supply of Personal Savings," in Komiya, ed., *Postwar Economic Growth in Japan,* is a useful study: see especially Table 8–8, p. 175. Cf. note 120 above (the relationship between "bonuses" and high savings).

149. Yamamura, *Economic Policy,* p. 186. Social security benefits in the years 1963–69 were substantially lower, proportionate to national income, than in the United States, less than half the U.K. level, and one-third those in France and West Germany (*SN,* No. 303, Table 27, p. 100; cf. *ibid.,* p. 104).

150. *This Is Sohyo,* 1972, p. 127. There is much interesting information in Dore, *City Life in Japan: A Study of a Tokyo Ward,* although sizeable changes have occurred since the time Dore did his study.

151. Cited in Yamamura, *Economic Policy,* pp. 166, 168; much information is available in *SN,* Nos. 303, 309, *passim.*

152. De Vos, *Japan's Outcastes,* p. 11; later estimates cited by De Vos put the figure at about 30 per cent, even with high demand for labour. Information on the village (in Wakayama prefecture) cited from Tatsuya Naramoto, "La discrimination des 'Eta,'" *Les Temps Modernes,* No. 272 (February 1969). After the *burakumin,* the Koreans in Japan are in the worst economic plight.

153. The most complete document on the whole subject in English is Jun Ui, ed., *Polluted Japan: Reports by Members of the Jishu-Koza Citizens' Movement* (Tokyo, 1972).

This is an excellent detailed report on all aspects of pollution, including that from fertilizers, drugs, etc., as well as straightforward industrial pollution; it also discusses such matters as the real consequences of "regional development." Available from: Jun Ui, c/o Jishu Koza, Dept. of Urban Engineering, University of Tokyo, Bunkyo-ku, Tokyo, Japan 113. See also *ARB*, Vol. 2, No. 3 (August 1972), pp. 1128–29, for a report on the Government White Paper on Pollution; *Ampo*, Nos. 9–10 (1971), which contains: Ui Jun, "Basic Theory of Kogai" and two texts on Minamata; interview with Ui Jun, "People's Power Is the Only Pollution Countermeasure," *Ampo*, No. 17 (Summer 1973); cf. Halliday and McCormack, *Japanese Imperialism*, pp. 190–95; and the three articles by Hirofumi Uzawa, Jun Ui and Toshirō Saji in *Esprit*, February 1973, pp. 469–93.

The Japanese term *kōgai* (lit.: "public hazard/nuisance") covers straight pollution, noise, vibration, traffic congestion, water shortage, obstruction of sunlight and the whole range of "nuisances." Perhaps the most frightening new discovery is that the high mercury content in Japanese fertilizer is being passed on 100 per cent to new-born children; this is irremovable. Moreover, this danger can not be evaded by leaving an (air-)polluted area, since the fertilizer is now in the soil and the rice throughout Japan.

The legitimate emphasis on *kōgai* can, of course, be a diversion from the central political struggle to overthrow Japanese capitalism. Western reports have been much fuller on pollution than on industrial oppression and exploitation.

154. In 1969 a basic "decentralization" plan was drawn up—the Shinzensō, or New Comprehensive National Development Plan; the scheme in Premier Tanaka Kakuei's book, *Building a New Japan—A Plan for Remodelling the Japanese Archipelago* (Tokyo, The Simul Press, 1973), is basically a variant on this plan. "Decentralization" is both a straightforward economic calculation, and a multi-faceted political calculation, since the LDP's losses in all the big urban centres have threatened its grip on power for the first time. It should also be noted that these schemes are not devised only to "decentralize" pollution, but are also designed to lower wage costs and break up strong unions (which are greatly disadvantaged when a plant is moved) (see *JLB*, Vol. 11, No. 5 [May 1972], p. 10; *SN*, No. 309, p. 74). On the Shinzensō, see Halliday and McCormack, *Japanese Imperialism*, pp. 174, 178. Among other things, the Shinzensō, if put through (even in modified form), will further increase already sky-rocketing land prices. Tanaka himself made his fortune as a property speculator. Tanaka's own version of the Shinzensō should also be seen in connection with his design to "develop" the coast on the Sea of Japan (facing the Asian mainland); Tanaka's constituency is Niigata, the biggest city in this area. The improvement of relations with the U.S.S.R. should also be viewed partly in this light: the opening of a direct Niigata-Siberia air route in spring 1973 lifted property prices in the Niigata area. Another option, of course, is to move high-pollutant industry abroad (on this, see Halliday and McCormack, pp. 155–56). Cf. *Ampo*, No. 11 (n.d.), pp. 21–27 ("Junk-Yard Development"); *SN*, No. 309, pp. 11–13.

155. Also referred to as Sanrizuka; the best account of the struggles there in English is Kitazawa Yoko, "Vietnam in Japan: Sanrizuka," *Ampo*, Nos. 9–10 (1971); see also reports in *Ampo*, Nos. 3–4 (March 1970), No. 5 (1970), No. 11 (n.d.) and No. 15 (December 1972).

156. Takashi Tsumura, "Avatars et aventures du gauchisme japonais," *Esprit*, February 1973, pp. 412–413. Similarly, during the Occupation period, the Americans regularly seized land belonging to *burakumin* as the sites for their bases, using racism to defuse popular hostility to the existence of the bases and prevent solidarity actions against the seizures. (I am indebted to Herbert Bix for this information.)

157. Information from *Ampo* articles cited in note 155; Tsumura, "Avatars et aventures du gauchisme japonais," pp. 412–14; the *Times* (London), February 26, 1971; *Le Monde*, March 5, 1971. It should also be noted that there have been remarkable mass struggles at or near the existing Tokyo airport, Haneda. This fact shows the political and cultural importance of airports in Japan's liaisons with the rest of the world (isolation, relations with imperialism, etc.). For example, in November 1969, attempts to prevent Premier Satō leaving for the United States involved heavy street fighting, accompanied by several assaults on railway stations and an attempt to seize and hold

the Kamata area, on the way to Haneda (*Ampo*, No. 2, 1970, p. 3; Dowsey, ed., *Zengakuren*, pp. 189–90).

158. Tomura Issaku, the farmers' leader, put it thus: "You must understand: our fight is *not a demonstration*, it is *not a protest*. It is a fight for our life" ("A Visit to Sanrizuka," *Ampo*, Nos. 3–4 [March 1970], p. 22 [italics in original]).

159. Halliday and McCormack, *Japanese Imperialism*, pp. 176–78; *Newsweek*, January 29, 1973, p. 13.

160. "Historic Strike—U.S. Okinawan Bases Shaken by Japanese Workers," *Ampo*, Nos. 3–4 (March 1970); Halliday and McCormack, *Japanese Imperialism*, pp. 195–209; Mark Selden, "Okinawa and American Security Imperialism," in Selden, ed., *Remaking Asia*; Kitazawa Yoko, "Okinawa After Reversion," *Ampo*, No. 12 (March 1972); Fukugi Akira, "Struggle Against Military Sharpens," *Ampo*, No. 15 (December 1972).

161. "Thieu's Tanks Stopped: U.S. Taken Aback by New Tactic," *Ampo*, No. 15 (December 1972).

162. This action against U.S. imperialism has gone together with the most militant and best organized programme of assistance and advice to anti-war G.I.s anywhere in the world—far superior to anything mounted by the left in Europe. On G.I. organizing, see *Ampo*, Nos. 3–4 (March 1970), pp. 36–38; Nos. 9–10, pp. 67–71.

163. *Ampo*, Nos. 3–4 (March 1970), Nos. 9–10 and 13–14 (May–July, 1972) for reports on immigration laws; *Gaikokujin Beheiren Bulletin*, No. 1 (Tokyo, n.d.) for suicides by both Korean and Chinese (from Taiwan) detainees; one anti-war soldier from south Korea burnt himself to death in detention at Osaka in December 1968. The basic government position is that no foreigner has a right to be in Japan at all, and if he is there he has no rights anyway: see particularly the exchanges quoted with immigration officials in *Ampo*, Nos. 13–14 (May–July, 1972), pp. 48–49 ("Racism and Japanese Immigration Policy"). At the time of writing, the government had changed the name of its proposed bill from Immigration Control Bill to Immigration Bill, but had not yet passed it into legislation.

164. In 1969 the JSP put up 189 candidates, of whom 53 lost by very small margins. In 1972 the JSP put up only 161 candidates and, with an increase of only 0.4 per cent of the total poll, won 28 more seats than in 1969. See Appendix II for details on the constituency system.

165. Shinohara, "The Leadership of the Progressive Parties," is useful on this. There is no adequate full-length study of the JSP in English. A. Cole and others, *Socialist Parties in Postwar Japan*, is marred by its reactionary outlook; Stockwin, *The Japanese Socialist Party and Neutralism*, is much superior, but brief and on a limited area. The official English-language review of the JSP issued a special number, "A Short History of the Japan Socialist Party," *JSR*, October 1, 1964. This contains many interesting points, but—quite apart from the atrocious translation—the number, like the *JSR* in general, reflects the right wing of the party. A good brief text on the JSP is Hidekazu Kawai, "Parliamentary Democracy in Crisis: An Analysis of the Weakness of the Socialist Party," *JI*, Vol. 6, No. 3 (1970), pp. 266–80.

166. Nobutake Ike, "Urbanization and Political Opposition: The Philippines and Japan," *Asian Studies* (Manila), Vol. 7, No. 2 (August 1969), p. 136; Takeshi Ishida, "Japanese Public Opinion and Foreign Policy," *PRJ*, 1967, pp. 14–18.

167. Robert A. Scalapino and Junnosuke Masumi, *Parties and Politics in Contemporary Japan* (Berkeley and Los Angeles, University of California Press, 1962), p. 177, using a five-class categorization.

168. The Kōmeitō (Clean Government Party) was founded as the political arm of the militant Buddhist organization, the Sōka Gakkai (Value Creation Society), the most powerful of the "new religions" in Japan. Sōka Gakkai springs from the populist (as opposed to the elitist Zen) strand of Buddhism. In the December 1972 elections the Kōmeitō, operating for the first time "disestablished" from the Sōka Gakkai, fell from 47 to 29 seats and from third to fourth place in Diet strength. It still has a strong party organization, however. Its main support comes from disoriented immigrants into the big cities. In foreign policy it advocates a greater distance from the United States and closer relations with China, and it was an important agent in bringing about the establishment of diplomatic relations with

China in 1972. In domestic politics it propagandizes powerfully against corruption and pollution, and has built a devoted following, thanks to its activism. However, it is ideologically highly moralistic and mystifying. Its populism, with heavy emphasis on the "little man," contains many of the elements seen in European fascism. The Kōmeitō has worked in uneasy liaison with the other opposition parties and in 1969 for the first time all four jointly put forward a censure motion on the Satō government over its University Bill (see chapter 9). The Kōmeitō is a thoroughly unreliable and opportunistic grouping. For a statement of the party's position by its current head, see Takeiri Yoshikatsu, "What is True Reformism?," *JI*, Vol. 6, No. 3 (1970), pp. 255–65. Several works in English discuss the Kōmeitō: see, for example, James E. Dator, *Sōka Gakkai, Builder of the Third Civilization, American and Japanese Members* (Seattle and London, University of Washington Press, 1969); James H. White, *The Sokagakkai and Mass Society* (Stanford, Stanford University Press, 1970); both these were written before the Kōmeitō disestablished itself in 1970 and thus treat the party largely with reference to the religious parent.

169. Karl Dixon, "The Growth of a 'Popular' Japanese Communist Party," *PA*, Vol. 45, No. 3 (Fall 1972), pp. 388–89; Paul F. Langer, "The New Posture of the CPJ," *Problems of Communism* (Washington, D.C.), Vol. 20, Nos. 1–2 (January–April 1971), p. 14. Reliable analysis of the JCP is even harder to come by than analysis of the JSP. Writing on the JCP in English has been dominated by anti-communists like Robert Scalapino and Paul F. Langer. The drift of their arguments runs along the lines that: "the JCP is very left-wing and therefore dangerous, but it is also weak and declining because pointless." Stockwin, "Is Japan a Post-Marxist Society?," pp. 184–98, criticizes Scalapino's voluntarism in *The Japanese Communist Movement*. Stockwin's criticism is launched from somewhere well to the right of the JCP itself. A solid critique of the JCP *from the left* in English is Muto Ichiyo, "Vote Without Power—The Communist Party of Japan and Bourgeois Politics," *Ampo*, No. 16 (March 1973). This is an indispensable text. Béraud, *La Gauche Révolutionnaire*, also takes up a critical position from the left. The JCP's English-language *Bulletin* appears irregularly. Some JCP texts have been published in the *World Marxist Review* (and its predecessor) or in Peking when the JCP has been in favour with, respectively, the Soviet and Chinese Communist Parties.

170. Muto, "Vote Without Power," p. 57, suggests that there is at least room for doubt about the class composition of the party, given its weakness among the *organized* working class movement. One remarkable fact about the JCP is that an estimated one-third of its members are women (Dixon, "The Growth of a 'Popular' JCP," p. 394).

171. Muto, "Vote Without Power," p. 56; the Sunday *Akahata* sells about twice as many copies as the next-best-selling weekly; about 40 per cent of the readers are women (Dixon, "The Growth of a 'Popular' JCP," pp. 396–97).

172. The JCP is the number two party in both the Osaka and Nagoya municipal assemblies; in the 1972 general election the JCP won 24.6 per cent of the vote in Kyoto, 21.5 in Osaka and 19.7 in Tokyo. The JCP vote has tended to be concentrated in the same areas as the JSP vote.

173. *Chien-she min-chu ti Jih-pen* (Yenan, 1945), issued under his then pseudonym, Okano. Nosaka had previously been at the London School of Economics, where he had worked under Clement Attlee and had been a founding member of the British Communist Party. He later became closely associated with the Chinese communist leader, Li Li-san. Nosaka reached Yenan in spring 1940, a few weeks after Mao had completed his famous article, "On New Democracy," in January 1940 (Mao Tsetung, *Selected Works*, Vol. 2).

174. Scalapino, *The Japanese Communist Movement*, p. 54, for the JCP's over-optimism about SCAP. Yoshida, *Memoirs*, p. 128, records (not entirely credibly) his fear that MacArthur might not block a revolution.

175. Scalapino, *The Japanese Communist Movement*, pp. 60–67; Swearingen and Langer, *Red Flag in Japan*, pp. 200 ff. There is an interesting discussion of the episode in Kanson Arahata, "Slavery: The Word and the Idea—the Japan Communist Party Lacks Independence," *JSPIJ*, Vol. 3, No. 1 (April 1965), pp. 54–57. This article, by an ex-leader of the communist movement, dates from early 1950.

176. Letter of the CPSU to the JCP, April 18, 1964, cited by Scalapino, *The Japanese Communist Movement*, p. 175.

177. In 1949 Nosaka published a book entitled *The New China and Japan* (*Atarashii Chūkoku to Nihon*) containing passages like the following: "The victory of the Chinese Communists has a deep spiritual and ideological influence upon the Japanese working class. . . . The working people have by their own strength gained a great victory in China—a country which was more reactionary, more feudalistic and more of a colony than Japan. This has given unbounded encouragement to our workers and has inspired them with confidence in victory. Our workers had looked on people's democracy and on socialism as something in far-away Europe, but now it has happened in China, only a sea away, in the country with which we have had the oldest and closest relations. If such was possible in China, why should it not now be possible in Japan?" (quoted in Swearingen and Langer, *Red Flag in Japan*, p. 237). See Shinobu, "The Korean War as an Epoch of Contemporary History," for the U.S. build-up in Japan.

178. There is no adequate study of this period: some elements in Béraud, *La Gauche Révolutionnaire*, pp. 46–48; Scalapino, *The Japanese Communist Movement*, pp. 79–96, is completely unsatisfactory.

179. Scalapino, *The Japanese Communist Movement*, p. 87. It was after the big crackdown on the left that "structural reform" gained ground in Italy (although inherent in the positions of Togliatti and others long before this). For some observations on the transposition of Italian ideas on "structural reform" to Japan, see Paolo Beonio Brocchieri, "I socialisti giapponesi guardano a Togliatti," *Il Filo Rosso* (Milan), No. 3 (June 1963), pp. 21–28; for a critique of the "theory," Jon Halliday, "Structural Reform in Italy—Theory and Practice," *NLR*, No. 50 (July–August 1968).

180. For Kennedy, Japan was one of the three key countries which were to be embroiled in the fraud, along with France and Germany: see the JCP letter to the CPSU, dated August 26, 1964 in *Letters of the Central Committee of the Communist Party of Japan in Reply to the Central Committee of the Communist Party of the Soviet Union* (Peking, Foreign Languages Press, 1965), p. 106.

181. At the XI Congress in July 1970, the hierarchy emerged as follows: Chairman: Nosaka Sanzō (titular head); Presidium Chairman: Miyamoto Kenji (previously Secretary General); Chief of the Party Secretariat: Fuwa Tetsuzō (the first of the postwar generation to reach a top leadership position).

182. There is no adequate full-length explanation of the JCP's break with the CCP. Some elements in J. A. A. Stockwin, "The Communist Party of Japan," *Problems of Communism*, Vol. 16, No. 1 (January–February 1967), pp. 7–10.

183. The "four enemies" of the Japanese people were designated as U.S. imperialism, Soviet revisionism, Japanese militarism, and the JCP ("the Miyamoto revisionist clique").

184. N.a., "Red Jubilee," *JQ*, Vol. 19, No. 4 (October–December 1972), p. 402; Muto, "Vote Without Power," *passim*, especially for a critique of the JCP's isolation.

185. The JCP has also recently taken unprecedented steps to fortify its relationships with the leading revisionist CPs in the West. On the occasion of the party's 50th anniversary, in 1972, it convened an International Conference in Tokyo on the theme "Revolutionary Movements in Advanced Capitalist Countries," with representatives from the French, Italian, British, West German, Australian and Spanish CPs. At the time of the XI Congress, the party conducted a linguistic purge which involved jettisoning the core of Leninist strategy; the dictatorship of the proletariat was officially abandoned as the party's goal, accompanied by tortuous linguistic subterfuges. Two years later, at the time of the 50th anniversary, the party removed the hammer and sickle from its emblem and replaced them with a cogwheel and a stalk of rice (see Muto, "Vote Without Power"; n.a., "Red Jubilee," p. 399; Dixon, "The Growth of a 'Popular' JCP," pp. 391–92, 401).

186. Perhaps the best-known exponent of this view is E. O. Reischauer. Among academics, naturally, much of the criticism is directed towards Japanese intellectuals, who are attacked for opposing the regime. A recent statement of this position can be found in Ivan P. Hall, "Japanese Intellectuals," *Survey*, Vol. 18, No. 4 (Autumn 1972),

pp. 74–94. The whole issue deserves much longer treatment, especially the question to what extent the line I adopt here may constitute an "alibi."

187. It was the election of Minobe Ryōkichi, backed by the JSP and the JCP, as Governor (Mayor) of Tokyo which first helped to smash the "anti-communist" barrier at the local level. From this, the JCP-JSP-backed candidates went on to carry almost all the biggest cities in Japan. JSP-JCP cooperation in the Diet started against the 1969 Universities Bill. In early 1973 all four opposition parties agreed on a joint confrontation vis-à-vis the LDP in parliament, and the JCP and JSP agreed on joint sponsorship of popular mass movements, particularly for local elections (*JEJ*, March 13, 1973; *ARB*, Vol. 2, No. 11 [April 1973], p. 1697). At the same time, the JSP is working to hinder the JCP at the union level: much of the JSP is fostering a Sōhyō-Dōmei merger, which would strengthen JSP-DSP ties, while greatly worsening those between the JSP and the JCP. Likewise, the JSP has been trying to prevent the introduction of a "free vote" in Sōhyō, which might allow the JCP to detach some of the JSP's block support there.

188. This issue is discussed by Muto, "Vote Without Power," p. 59. It is worth resuming the LDP's immediate reaction to the 1972 poll. On January 6, 1973, the LDP Secretary-General, Hashimoto Tomisaburō, announced that if the LDP lost its absolute majority (i.e., of seats) this would be the end of democracy in Japan; the head of the LDP Election Committee, Matsuno Raizō, called for changes in the election rules; the LDP had long been harbouring plans to alter the constituency system for elections to the Lower House, but with Upper House elections scheduled for mid-1974, Matsuno suggested the rules for these should be changed (the LDP in 1973 had a bare majority here: 134 out of 252 seats); the LDP suggested that opposition coalitions should be banned (!); an alarmist Report was issued by the National Police Agency dwelling on the dangers from the left; and both the Director-General of the Defence Agency, Masuhara Keikichi, and a top civil service official in the Agency, Kubō Takuya warned that "in conditions where attacks against public order occur, there is no reason to say they [the troops] won't be used." The Public Security Investigation Agency agitated the old threat that the new strength of the JCP would give rightists "a sense of crisis" and might plunge them into "unlawful action" (*ARB*, Vol. 2, No. 9 (February 1973), pp. 1544–45—based on a UPI report of January 15, 1973).

As of 1973 half the members of the Upper House are chosen from the country at large, which does not disadvantage the opposition; Matsuno suggested that all members should be elected from individual districts by a simple plurality. In May 1973 the opposition brought Diet proceedings to a halt and nation-wide mass demonstrations occurred in protest at the government's attempts to gerrymander the constituency system for the 1974 Upper House election. The government eventually withdrew its proposals (*Times* [London], May 16 and 17, 1973). Cf. Appendix II.

189. I have not gone at length into the state of the militant left. One major problem here is that of sources, which are woefully inadequate. Moreover, any mere listing of membership and suchlike information can not give a correct picture of the militant left, whose strength vis-à-vis both the established left and the government can be seen only in class struggle. Much the most useful source for this is *Ampo* (see especially Muto, "Vote Without Power," *Ampo*, No. 16, and the interview with Higuchi in *Ampo*, No. 17); see also Béraud, *La Gauche Révolutionnaire*, and references in note 92 above on the Hansen. Another issue very much worth studying would be the curious weakness of Maoism in Japan.

Chapter 9

EDUCATION AND THE STUDENT MOVEMENT

1. For some observations on this issue, see R. P. Dore, "Education in Japan's Growth," *PA*, Vol. 37, No. 1 (March 1964); Ryoji Itō, "Education as a Basic Factor in Japan's Economic Growth," *DE*, Vol. 1, No. 1 (January–June 1963), pp. 37–54; Marius B. Jansen and Lawrence Stone, "Education and Modernization in Japan and England," *CSSH*, Vol. 9, No. 2 (January 1967).

2. Masunori Hiratsuka, "World Education and Japan," *JSPIJ*, Vol. 1, No. 3 (December 1963), p. 13. Moves for change were already under way before the arrival of the Americans: "the Ministry of Education resolved *before the end of the war* to extend compulsory education to the secondary level . . . pressures to expand the scope and improve the level of national education originated within Japanese society itself" (Sumiya Mikio, "The Function and Social Structure of Education: Schools and Japanese Society," *JSPIJ*, Vol. 5, Nos. 2–3 [December 1967], p. 121—italics in original). (The last-mentioned is a very valuable special number devoted to the theme "University and Society"; the actual date of printing is March 1969 and the number covers events up to late 1968.)

3. Robert King Hall, *Education for a New Japan* (New Haven, Yale University Press, 1949), p. 82; Tokiomi Kaigo, "A Short History of Postwar Japanese Education," *JSPIJ*, Vol. 1, No. 3 (December 1963), p. 16.

4. Tatsumi Makino, "Japanese Education," *ISSJ* (Paris), Vol. 13, No. 1 (1961), p. 46; Herbert Passin, *Society and Education in Japan*, pp. 108–9.

5. In the early-mid 1960s women held only 13 per cent of all university places, and less than 5 per cent of the places in the leading universities (which dominate even more than Oxbridge or the Ivy League). As in England, women are highly concentrated in certain departments, especially literature and English literature (the literature department in Japanese universities includes philosophy, sociology and history); in "pure" English literature at one university, Gakushuin, in 1962, 96 per cent of the students were women (Passin, *Society and Education*, p. 109); cf. David Riesman and Evelyn Thompson Riesman, *Conversations in Japan: Modernization, Politics, and Culture* (London, Allen Lane, The Penguin Press, 1967), p. 328. See also R. Hall, *Education for a New Japan*, pp. 420–23. Herbert Passin, "Japanese Education: Guide to a Bibliography of Materials in the English Language," *Comparative Education Review*, Vol. 9, No. 1 (February 1965) (also available as a separate pamphlet) has a section of references on women's education.

6. For the text, see General Headquarters, Supreme Commander for the Allied Powers, Civil Information and Education Section, Education Division, *Education in the New Japan* (Tokyo, SCAP, 1948), Vol. 2, pp. 109–11. On the law, see Seiya Munakata, "The Fundamental Law of Education," *JSPIJ*, Vol. 1, No. 3 (December 1963), pp. 54–58.

7. Makino, "Japanese Education," pp. 47–48; Ronald S. Anderson, *Japan: Three Epochs of Modern Education* (Washington, D.C., U.S. Department of Health, Education and Welfare, 1959 [Bulletin 1959, No. 11], p. 57). For the role of Tokyo and Kyoto Universities, see below.

8. Kaigo, "A Short History of Postwar Japanese Education," p. 16.

9. *Shūshin:* morals and/or ethics; *Kokutai no Hongi:* Cardinal principles of the national entity of Japan; *Shinmin no Michi:* The way of the subject (see Robert King Hall, *Shūshin: The Ethics of a Defeated Nation* (New York, Columbia University, Bureau of Publications, Teachers College, 1949), pp. 20–21).

10. Kaigo, "A Short History of Postwar Japanese Education," p. 16.

11. Originally set up to act as the Japanese counterpart to the U.S. Education Mission; it then remained in existence after the U.S. Mission departed.

12. The resolution was only to the effect that because the Basic/Fundamental Law of Education of 1947 and other laws exist, the Rescript and other such documents "have thereby lost their validity"; see R. P. Dore, "The Ethics of the New Japan," *PA*, Vol. 25, No. 2 (June 1952), p. 147; Hall, *Education for a New Japan*, pp. 166–68; the full text of the Diet Resolution is in SCAP, *Political Reorientation of Japan*, Vol. 2, p. 585.

13. R. Hall, *Education for a New Japan*, pp. 293–401; Jean Stoetzel, *Without the Chrysanthemum and the Sword: A Study of the Attitudes of Youth in Post-War Japan* (London, W. Heinemann, 1955), p. 103. There appears to have been some confusion among the first U.S. Education Mission to Japan about the degree of illiteracy or "exclusion" caused by both the Japanese scripts and the forms of the language (see letter from George Sansom in *PA*, Vol. 19, No. 4 [December 1946], pp. 413–15); the U.S. Education Mission appears to have concluded that 90 per cent of the Japanese population was semi-illiterate. For some interesting observations on the abstruseness

of Japanese academic language, see Shunsuke Tsurumi, "Three Ways of Thinking in Contemporary Japanese History," in Hidetoshi Kato, *Japanese Popular Culture* (Tokyo, Charles Tuttle, 1960), pp. 207–208.

14. Marius B. Jansen, "Education, Values and Politics in Japan," *FA*, Vol. 35, No. 4 (July 1957), p. 668.

15. Cited in Textor, *Failure in Japan*, pp. 105–6 (italics added—J.H.); Ōno Tsutomu, "Student Protest in Japan—What It Means to Society," *JSPIJ*, Vol. 5, Nos. 2–3, p. 273. The key SCAP figure in this period was Dr. Walter Crosby Eells of CI&ES, GHQ, SCAP.

16. R. Hall, *Education for a New Japan*, p. 478.

17. Dallas Finn, "Japanese Universities Today," *YR*, Vol. 43, No. 4 (Summer 1954), pp. 571, 561.

18. *Report of the Second United States Education Mission to Japan* (Tokyo, SCAP, September 22, 1950), p. 14. Apart from a mystifying emphasis on the value of religion, it is genuinely difficult to make out what the *Report* is saying.

19. R. Hall, *Education for a New Japan*, pp. 95–103.

20. There was also massive intervention in Japan's educational system by U.S. academics and corporations with both money and ideology: see Bix, "The Security Treaty System and the Japanese Military-Industrial Complex," pp. 46–47. Cf. note 50 below.

21. Ōno, "Student Protest in Japan," p. 273. The term "reverse course" covers both U.S. and Japanese reaction.

22. Jansen, "Education, Values and Politics in Japan," pp. 666–67.

23. Morris, *Nationalism and the Right Wing in Japan*, pp. 154–55. Dore, "The Ethics of the New Japan," gives the full text of the document *An Outline of Ethical Practice for the Japanese People*. Amano deftly exploited the call by the U.S. Education Mission the previous year for a strengthening of "moral" education.

24. Kaigo, "A Short History of Postwar Japanese Education," p. 22; Makino, "Japanese Education," p. 53.

25. Makino, "Japanese Education," pp. 32–33; Eiichi Mochida, 'The Reform of Boards of Education and Its Aftermath," *JSPIJ*, Vol. 1, No. 3 (December 1963).

26. Jansen, "Education, Values and Politics in Japan," pp. 666–67.

27. On the early moves over textbook certification, see *ibid.;* Morris, *Nationalism and the Right Wing in Japan*, pp. 155–57. For later developments, including the Ienaga controversy, see Ienaga Saburo, "The Historical Significance of the Japanese Textbook Lawsuit," *BCAS*, Vol. 2, No. 4 (Fall 1970); R. P. Dore, "Textbook Censorship in Japan: the Ienaga Case," *PA*, Vol. 43, No. 4 (Winter 1970–71); Halliday and McCormack, *Japanese Imperialism*, pp. 187–90.

28. Mitsuo Miyata, "Education for Peace," *PRJ*, 1971, esp. pp. 30–34, for details of the gradual rewriting of history.

29. Kiyoaki Tsuji, "Toward Understanding the Teachers' Efficiency Rating System," *JSPIJ*, Vol. 1, No. 3 (December 1963); the issue is covered in several other articles in the same number.

30. Makino, "Japanese Education," p. 53.

31. Morris, *Nationalism and the Right Wing in Japan*, p. 155; in this speech Okano also used the phrase "the Greater East Asian War" (Dai Tōa Sensō), a formulation which was explicitly banned by SCAP (see SCAP, *Education in the New Japan*, Vol. 2, p. 33). Okano, who was appointed Minister in August 1952, was formerly president of the Sanwa Bank, and the first non-scholar Minister of Education in postwar Japan (Benjamin C. Duke, *Japan's Militant Teachers: A History of the Left-Wing Teachers' Movement* [Honolulu, East-West Center, University Press of Hawaii, 1973], p. 111). Apart from its general effects on education, racism has specifically contributed to poor schooling for both the Ainu and the *burakumin* (De Vos, *Japan's Outcastes*, pp. 8–10). Of course, the ruling class in all the imperialist countries is racist; what is interesting about Japan is that a degree of racialism and a massive dose of mythological history are *official*. For some interesting recent discoveries which threaten the official mythology, see Suzuki Takejuh, "A Blow to Japanese Chauvinism from Ancient Tomb," *Ampo*, Nos. 13–14 (May–July 1972).

32. J. Hall, "Education and Modern National Development," p. 423; Kiyose distinguished himself by proclaiming in the Diet that same year (1956) that Constitution Day

(May 3) was "not a day of glory, but of national humiliation" (quoted in Morris, *Nationalism and the Right Wing in Japan*, p. 21).

33. Morris, *Nationalism and the Right Wing in Japan*, p. 155.

34. N.a., "Education Animal," *JQ*, Vol. 19, No. 1 (January–March 1972), p. 11. Back in 1954 Finn wrote of the coming contradiction: "Sometime soon the Japanese will have to face the problem we overlooked of how 'democratic' you dare be in a country that needs mechanics and grade-school teachers more than it needs a growing intellectual proletariat" ("Japanese Universities Today," p. 572). And, in fact, as Makino records ("Japanese Education," p. 52), it was about this time, in the 1950s, that industry initiated pressure to change the 6–3–3 system. Note also that Japanese schoolchildren currently put in a 6-day week.

35. Halliday and McCormack, *Japanese Imperialism*, p. 190, and references there. SCAP banned several of the more militaristic "sports" such as *kendō* (the "way of the sword") and *judō*, an understandable move which was probably stupidly enacted (see Riesman and Riesman, *Conversations in Japan*, p. 198); R. Hall, *Education for a New Japan*, pp. 78–80. It may be of interest to note that the views of Suzuki Daisetsu, the main purveyor of Zen reaction to the West, were trundled out by the old Japanese right in favour of maintaining *kendō*. Suzuki was also a member of Yoshida's ultra-conservative Education Council (Yoshida, *Memoirs*, p. 172).

36. Dore, *Education in Tokugawa Japan*, p. 293.

37. Sumiya, "The Function and Social Structure of Education," p. 126; cf. Abegglen and Mannari, "Leaders of Modern Japan: Social Origins and Mobility." Passin (*Society and Education*, p. 121) gives the following comparison:

University Students	U.S.S.R.	U.S.A.	Japan
Higher-class origin	50%	63%	73%
Lower-class origin	50%	37%	27%

SOURCE: Mombushō, *Nihon no Seichō to Kyōiku*, Tokyo, 1962, p. 54, and Ministry of Education, *Japan's Growth and Education*, Tokyo, 1963, p. 52 (a slightly revised version of the Japanese document).

Note that the percentage of the total population defined as "higher class" is much higher in Japan (34 per cent) than in the U.S.S.R. (20 per cent); all the same, in Japan the upper one-third has over two-thirds of the university places. Cf. Ronald P. Dore, "The Financing of Higher Education: A Very Tentative Proposal," in OECD, *Reviews of National Policies for Education: Japan* (Paris, Organisation for Economic Co-operation and Development, 1971) [henceforth: OECD, *Education: Japan, 1971*], p. 117, Table 1:

Total Family Income (*thousand yen per annum*)	Per Cent of Total Population in that Bracket	Per Cent of Age Group Entering National Universities	Per Cent of Age Group Entering Private Universities
Less than 575	20	2.8	2.4
575–764	20	2.2	4.9
764–968	20	2.7	7.6
968–1,291	20	4.3	16.7
More than 1,291	20	5.0	37.8
Total	100	3.4	13.7

SOURCE: *Kōsei Hodō*, November 1969 (material refers to 1968).

38. K. Yamagiwa, "Language as an Expression of Japanese Culture," in Hall and Beardsley, *Twelve Doors to Japan*, p. 189: a student talking to his teacher is listed first among "more formal situations" where "niceties of speech and gesture" were retained. On the hierarchical pressures of language, see Hide Shohara, "Honorific

Expressions of Personal Attitudes in Spoken Japanese," *UMOP*, No. 2 (1952); interview with Atsuo Nakamura, *Plain Rapper* (Palo Alto), Vol. 1, No. 7 (October–November 1969): "In Japanese universities the student is nothing. . . . You speak to a professor with a different language, one which shows him great respect. In Japan a professor is revered and you are always in his debt. You would never speak to him in a direct manner. Even if you're right and he's wrong you would never say that to him" (p. 19). Hence the earth-shaking importance of the public "trials" and humiliation of university authorities by students in the late 1960s (see below).

39. Ezra F. Vogel, *Japan's New Middle Class: The Salary Man and His Family in a Tokyo Suburb* (Berkeley and Los Angeles, University of California Press, 1967 paperback ed.), pp. 40–67; and especially Orihara Hiroshi, " 'Test Hell' and Alienation: A Study of Tokyo University Freshmen," *JSPIJ*, Vol. 5, Nos. 2–3—an extremely valuable study based on extensive interviews.

40. Yoshihiro Shimizu, "Entrance Examinations: A Challenge to Equal Opportunity in Education," *JSPIJ*, Vol. 1, No. 3 (December 1963), p. 91.

41. *Ibid.*, p. 89; the fact that the university qualification is largely a *formal* one also means that business tends to plunder the universities for its personnel long before their final examinations, on the basis of teachers' recommendations; final examinations and degree status thus become relatively less important, and this naturally has a back-up effect, contributing to the further deterioration of university work as a whole. For the inevitable corollary, neglect of graduate work, see the section, "The Tragedy of the Graduate School," in Fukuda Kan'ichi, "A Professor's Views on University Education: The Need for a Democratic Policy," *JSPIJ*, Vol. 5, Nos. 2–3, pp. 201–12.

42. For the *rōnin*, see, in particular, Mita Munesuke, "Patterns of Alienation in Contemporary Japan," *JSPIJ*, Vol. 5, Nos. 2–3, p. 175 (note 15); Orihara, " 'Test Hell' and Alienation," p. 248 (note 9); Fukuda, "A Professor's Views on University Education," p. 219 (note 11).

43. Shimizu, "Entrance Examinations," p. 93.

44. Richard K. Beardsley, "Personality Psychology," in Hall and Beardsley, *Twelve Doors to Japan*, pp. 364–65, based on a study by Satō Kōji and Tarō Sonoharo, "A Proposal for an International Study of Suicide," *Psychologia* (Kyoto), Vol. 1 (1957), pp. 71–73. In the list of "objective" factors given, exams come first, then jobs (i.e., closely connected), with marriage third.

45. Shimizu, "Entrance Examinations," p. 89; for the effects on other members of the family, particularly mothers, see Vogel, *Japan's New Middle Class*, pp. 47–52, 54–57. Orihara, " 'Test Hell' and Alienation," gives numerous examples of students wishing ill fortune to their former friends; increasing isolation and misanthropy are instanced as virtually universal effects. It was this downwards pressure which led to the extension of contestation into Japanese schools in the late 1960s (Béraud, *La Gauche Révolutionnaire*, pp. 100–104). The extent to which Japanese society, far from basking in the special "harmony" which the ruling class alleges, is riddled with division and doubt is shown by a 1971 survey conducted among high school students by the Japan Emigration Service: 46 per cent of all the students polled wanted to leave Japan and live abroad—a staggeringly high percentage for a society claiming to provide "security" and a sense of belonging.

46. Fukuda, "A Professor's Views on University Education," p. 220 (note 12); *ibid.*, p. 199, for teachers moonlighting.

47. On this in more detail, see Ōno, "Student Protest in Japan," p. 271 (note 2). Yoko Kitazawa, "Storia della lotta studentesca in Giappone," *Ideologie* (Rome), No. 11 (1970), pp. 131–32; Kitazawa stresses that this initially reformist move swiftly developed into a much wider strike to protest against the government's attempts "further to deform the health service in the interests of monopoly capital." Kitazawa's article, written in 1969, is a rigorous Marxist account of the student movement in the late 1960s.

48. Abegglen, *The Japanese Factory*, p. 24.

49. There is a good deal of information on Nikkyōso in several of the articles in *JSPIJ*, Vol. 1, No. 3 (December 1963)—both for and against. Richard J. Smethurst, "The Origins and Policies of the Japan Teachers' Union, 1945–56," *UMOP*, No. 9 (1965)

is dull and unsympathetic, though it has a useful bibliography. The fullest sources are Benjamin C. Duke, *Japan's Militant Teachers* and Donald R. Thurston, *Teachers and Politics in Japan* (Princeton, Princeton University Press, 1973).

50. There seems to be no study in English of the fascinating question of how Marxism has come to have its deep implantation in Japan. This would involve a major study of the relationship between the class struggle, the social structure and ideology, and might well produce some interesting information applicable to the possibility of revolution in other capitalist societies as well. From time to time more militant crusaders like Reischauer and Scalapino acknowledge the strength of Marxism in Japan in order to attack it. The attack usually takes one of two forms: (*a*) Marxism is there, but it is such an aberration that it cannot be seriously considered (Reischauer); (*b*) it *was* there, but is just about to disappear since it can have no "appeal" in an industrial society (Scalapino). On this, cf. note 20 above and Dower, "The Superdomino," p. 127. There is much useful raw data on the strength of Marxism among students in Tsurumi, *Social Change and the Individual*, Part 3 ("The Student Movement"). Duke, *Japan's Militant Teachers*, chapter 8 ("Militancy: Analysis of the Causes"), pp. 189–203, is disappointing and inadequate.

51. On the internal weakness, see Seiichi Miyahara, "The Japan Teachers' Union and Its Code of Ethics," *JSPIJ*, Vol. 1, No. 3 (December 1963), esp. p. 103.

52. Quoted in full in *JSPIJ*, Vol. 1, No. 3, pp. 129–31, and in Duke, *Japan's Militant Teachers*, pp. 224–27. Sōhyō's Four Principles are detailed in Duke, p. 101.

53. "The Altered Image of Teachers," by the Editorial Staff of the *Asahi Jānaru* [The Asahi journal], *JSPIJ*, Vol. 1, No. 3, pp. 106–12 (pp. 108–11 on the Rating System); Kaigo, "A Short History of Postwar Japanese Education," p. 23.

54. Béraud, *La Gauche Révolutionnaire*, pp. 102–3; cf. Duke, *Japan's Militant Teachers*, pp. 164–86 (covers up to 1967).

55. Useful factual material and a good chart to 1968 in Usami Shō, "Zengakuren," *JQ*, Vol. 15, No. 2 (April–June 1968). See Kitazawa, "Storia della lotta studentesca," Béraud, *La Gauche Révolutionnaire*, *passim*, and Gavan McCormack, "The Student Left in Japan," *NLR*, No. 65 (January–February 1971), for excellent Marxist texts *situating* the student struggles. See also: Dowsey, ed., *Zengakuren;* Jürgen Seiffert, *Zengakuren* (Munich, Trikont Verlag, 1969); *Plain Rapper*, Vol. 1, No. 7; Toyomasa Fuse, "Le radicalisme étudiant au Japon: une 'révolution culturelle'?," *L'Homme et la Société* (Paris), No. 16 (April–June 1970); Tsurumi, *Social Change and the Individual*, Part 3; *JSPIJ*, Vol. 1, No. 3. More specific information on the later period is in sources cited in notes below.

56. Nippon Marukusu Shugi Gakusei Dōmei (League of Japan Marxist Students). See Usami, "Zengakuren," p. 234, for genealogical table and glossary.

57. The fullest account in English of the struggle against revision of the Security Treaty in 1960 is George R. Packard, *Protest in Tokyo: The Security Treaty Crisis of 1960*. Cf. Scalapino and Masumi, *Parties and Politics in Contemporary Japan*, chapter 5. Both these accounts are fundamentally reactionary and fail to understand democracy in terms of the interests of the working masses. Tsurumi, *Social Change and the Individual*, contains useful information as a corrective to the Packard view. One of the leaders of the Bund (Kyōsandō), Shima Shigerō, spoke as follows on the "invasion" of the Diet: "In March 1960 I observed the coal miners' strike in the Miike Mine. I was so deeply impressed by the intense scenes of their valiant fight that I could not get over them. It led me to think that a revolution . . . happens because people are aroused to the occasion by witnessing a heartrending scene. Thus, I thought, what we should do was to present to the public a moving image that would crystallize into one moment the true meaning of the situation. This was why we broke through the Diet gates on November 17 and June 15. It was the most dramatic means of symbolizing the reclamation of the Diet, which had been beyond the reach of the people, on behalf of the people whose representative it should have been" (cited in Tsurumi, p. 333).

58. Karōji Kanetarō, the then chairman of Zengakuren, quoted in Usami, "Zengakuren," p. 239.

59. Kitazawa, "Storia della lotta studentesca," p. 140, for the students' own correct estimate of their role. It must be emphasized that the Japanese government is *not* a

classic bourgeois democratic regime, and that the students are quite right to claim that they *represent* the society's politics at times in a way the government does not. An *Asahi* poll in late May 1960, at the height of the struggle, showed that 78 per cent of those questioned said the Diet did not represent the people (or that they had no opinion of it); only 12 per cent of those polled were in favour of keeping the Kishi cabinet (cited in Edward P. Whittemore, *The Press in Japan Today . . . A Case Study* [Columbia, University of South Carolina Press, 1961], pp. 46–47. This is a valuable study of the 1960 crisis seen through the press).

60. It is enough to note that anti-imperialist actions have had a mass backing in Japan of a kind they have not had in any European country allied to the United States. In May 1957 some 15,000 students demonstrated against Britain's hydrogen bomb tests, carrying slogans like "To Hell with Macmillan!" "Englishmen, why aren't you ashamed of yourselves?" and "British fools!" (Morris, *Nationalism and the Right Wing in Japan*, p. 189).

61. *Yomiuri* poll (August 15, 1951), cited by Packard, *Protest in Tokyo*, p. 12.

62. Whittemore, *The Press in Japan*, pp. 73–76; the vast majority of the demonstrators were militant workers, headed by employees of the Japan Steel Tube Company's Kawasaki plant (p. 73); students made up less than one-quarter of the demonstrators. Roughly speaking, the pro-JCP student movement concentrated its fire on U.S. imperialism; the mainstream (sometimes referred to as "Trotskyite") confined itself to attacking Kishi.

63. McCormack, "The Student Left," p. 42. On the Minsei, cf. Kitazawa, "Storia della lotta studentesca," p. 134, where it is called "a kind of detachment of the police": this is confirmed by Jansen, who records an instance of the Minsei agreeing to take arms from a conservative university administration to oust a Maoist faction from the campus "in the name of university autonomy and academic freedom" (cited by Marius B. Jansen, "The United States and Japan in the 1970's," in Gerald L. Curtis, ed., *Japanese-American Relations in the 1970's* [Washington, D.C., Columbia Books, 1970], p. 44).

64. Sampa Zengakuren: Three-Faction Zengakuren, a coalition of the Chūkaku-ha (Core Faction), the Shagakudō (League of Socialist Students) and the Liberation Faction of the Shaseidō (League of Socialist Youth).

65. As JCP strength increased recently, the Minseidō went into a relative decline: as of December 1971, membership was down to 150,000; JCP-Minsei relations were also strained over the two bodies' different assessments of the Nixon visit to China (n.a., "Red Jubilee," *JQ*, Vol. 20, No. 4 [October–December 1972], p. 402; Dixon, "The Growth of a 'Popular' JCP," p. 389).

66. Béraud, *La Gauche Révolutionnaire*, p. 78; McCormack, "The Student Left," pp. 47–48. The main force which stayed outside the Zenkyoto was the Kakumaru faction.

67. McCormack, "The Student Left," p. 48.

68. A brief comment on the 1970 demonstrations. First, the LDP decided to avoid another 1960 by opting for automatic *renewal,* as opposed to *revision* (the 1960 process). Satō, in order to deny the opposition the use of the Diet as a forum, rushed through his programme and closed down the Diet well before June 1970, so that it was not even in session at the time the treaty was renewed. Second, although the 1970 demonstrations were perhaps not as "spectacular" as those in 1960—partly because the Diet was closed down—many more people took part in the 1970 demonstrations; and on June 23, 1970, 774,000 people demonstrated—more than twice the figure for any single day in 1959–60; the Tokyo demonstrations were, likewise, larger than in 1960. But the atmosphere was indeed rather different. The JSP's severe defeat in the 1969 election greatly weakend the left opposition; the JCP's increased strength only partly compensated for this. On the other hand, it must be noted that by opting for renewal rather than revision, the LDP created a situation where the treaty could be scrapped with one year's notice (cf. the Narita slogan: "Every coming day is another June 23, 1970"): see Ōmori Shigeo, "June 1970," *JQ*, Vol. 17, No. 4 (October–December 1970), pp. 383–92.

69. Usami, "Zengakuren"; inhabitants of Sasebo donated more than a million yen in one day to students' street collections (roughly, £1,000 at the time) (Dowsey, ed., *Zengakuren*, p. 131).

70. This rise in radioactivity caused widespread demonstrations, which expanded greatly after a U.S. Phantom jet crashed on the campus of Kyushu University (after the pilot had bailed out) right next to a building housing enough cobalt to have caused a small atomic explosion (June 2, 1968).

71. The most clamorous case was Nihon University, which had 100,000 students in the late 1960s and was nothing but a degree-producing factory. The discovery that £2 million of funds had been embezzled by the administration led to one of the biggest upheavals of the period (see below). See also Sumiya, "The Function and Social Structure of Education," pp. 135–36; and Appendix XI ("Subsidies and Gifts to Private Colleges"), *ibid.,* p. 305. The increasing indebtedness of the private colleges, where expenditure per student was anyway only about one-quarter that per student in the state universities in the late 1960s, has led to major attempts to squeeze students further. See Appendix I for details.

72. "The average student/teacher ratio at private *daigaku* [universities] is about thirty-seven students to one teacher, though there are often eighty or ninety to one. . . . Statistics on student/teacher ratios are often misleading because they include part-time lecturers who have very little to do with, and may feel no responsibility to, students studying at the site of their moonlighting activity" (Fukuda, "A Professor's Views on University Education," p. 220). Cf. OECD, *Education: Japan,* 1971, p. 76, on moonlighting. The ratio at state universities in 1965 was 11.4 students per teacher (*JSPIJ,* Vol. 5, Nos. 2–3, Appendix X).

73. One aspect that would merit further investigation is: which faculties in which universities produce the most militant students? According to Riesman, in the 1960 struggle it was the faculties of Chinese studies, Classics, Government and Agriculture, while Law, Economics, and Psychology tended to be conservative. This is certainly not the pattern in European universities (Riesman and Riesman, *Conversations in Japan,* p. 347).

74. On the Keiō strike, *JSPIJ,* Vol. 5, Nos. 2–3, Appendix V.

75. *Ibid.,* Appendix VII, for a list of the causes of disputes, and the type of protest involved, up to the summer of 1968. Cf. Fuse, "Le radicalisme étudiant," pp. 248–50; Kitazawa, "Storia della lotta studentesca," *passim.*

76. The highly ideological and thoroughly slovenly reportage of most of the Western bourgeois media on Japan masked this issue. A 1967 Board of Audit investigation into twelve (only) leading universities, released in May 1969, revealed that they had failed to report 279 research projects. Tokyo University headed the list with 87 illegally commissioned items. (Bix, "The Security Treaty System," p. 40). Military personnel studying in universities was a big issue at both Tokyo and Kyoto Universities in 1967. At Kyoto, the Zengakuren triumphed over the university president in an all-night session and got him to exclude SDF personnel. The students were also successful at Tokyo University (*Japan Times,* September 9, 1967). The infiltration of the military onto civilian campuses was accompanied by a drive to militarize civilian education. In December 1967 the Minister of Education, Nadao Hirokichi (who had served under Kishi and led the fight to break Nikkyōso), proposed that primary and junior high school pupils should be taught "defense consciousness" (*New York Times,* December 12, 1967). Likewise, in 1971, Premier Satō is reported to have spoken of the need "to harmonize the strengthening of national defense with future educational policy" (Bix, "Japan: The Roots of Militarism," p. 313; Bix also details SDF interventions in such important education-related areas as the cinema, and the Meiji Centennial celebrations).

77. A policy concretized in the phrase "developing human resources," used during the Ikeda period (1960–64)—see Orihara, " 'Test Hell' and Alienation," pp. 226–27, 246–47 (note 3). Cf. OECD, *Education: Japan,* 1971, for the development of this policy and its contradictions. See also the extracts from Andō Norisuke, *Theory of the Student Revolution,* in Béraud, *La Gauche Révolutionnaire,* pp. 62–66.

78. On Nihon, see *Ampo,* No. 5; Béraud, *La Gauche Révolutionnaire,* pp. 71–73; McCormack, "The Student Left," p. 49.

79. Ōno, "Student Protest in Japan," p. 261; on Waseda, cf. *JSPIJ,* Vol. 5, Nos. 2–3, Appendix VI; Michiya Shimbori, "The Sociology of a Student Movement—A Japanese Case Study," *Daedalus,* Winter 1968, pp. 204–28.

80. Ōkōchi Kazuo, "Japanese University Problems," *JQ,* Vol. 14, No. 4 (October–December 1967), p. 430.
81. This process was under way before the full outburst of student activism: indeed, Kitazawa notes that the student uprising *coincided* with the government's reorganization of higher education ("Storia della lotta studentesca," p. 129). Cf. re the OECD report below.
82. Jansen, "Education, Values and Politics in Japan," p. 667.
83. Fuse, "Le radicalisme étudiant," p. 252.
84. Dowsey, ed., *Zengakuren,* pp. 171 ff.; Fuse, "Le radicalisme étudiant," pp. 288–89, on the earlier decline of the faculties. The 1969 bill was forced through the Diet in a manner comparable to the 1960 treaty revision and the 1965 treaty with Seoul; particularly in the House of Councillors, where the Education Committee passed the bill through without even one minute of debate, and where the President of the House blatantly manipulated procedure, as in 1965 (on this, see Hans H. Baerwald, "An Aspect of Japanese Parliamentary Politics," *JI,* Vol. 6, No. 2 [1970], pp. 196–205; the author's conclusion: "Should the current high-posture tactics of the LDP continue very long into the '70's, it is my belief that the prospects for parliamentarism in Japan are bleak.").
85. Eight thousand is the figure given by Béraud, *La Gauche Révolutionnaire,* p. 133; *Ampo,* No. 2 (n.d.), p. 9, gives 14,202 student arrests for 1969, quoting official police figures.
86. *Ampo,* No. 5, pp. 10, 23. These arrests were the occasion for significant police encroachment on bourgeois democratic rights. Not only were many defendants held months without trial, but, for the first time in modern Japanese history, several hundred arrested persons were sentenced *in absentia,* because they had exercised their constitutional rights to refuse to answer police questions (*Ampo,* No. 2, pp. 5–7). For the severe subsequent erosions of civil liberties, see Muto, "Law & Order, Japanese Style," pp. 3–5. In two weeks in February 1972, 50,000 police checked 240,000 flats; by that date the police claimed to have checked 80 per cent of the 5,300,000 flats on their checking list; 15,000 flats had been placed under constant surveillance as "suspicious" (p. 3). Police posters urging delation on the slightest suspicion were plastered over Tokyo: "Immediately telephone the police if your neighbor has unusually few household articles, if your neighbor has files and rasps . . . or political leaflets, if your neighbor's room gives out unidentified noise or smell, . . . if young men and women visit your neighbor's room frequently . . ." (p. 4).
87. Usami describes the scene at Sasebo: "The students were trapped. . . . The next instant police brutality erupted. The police kept raining blows on the students who, taken by surprise, were running around defenseless, and kept beating the students until they fell unconscious and lay motionless on the ground. Furthermore, even after the order to halt the attack had been given several of the police, as they withdrew from the scene, kept hitting and kicking students lying senseless on the pavement. Despite the fact that over 100 people were injured . . . only a total of 27 persons were arrested. Thus, it can be said the police, completely engrossed in their violence, had forgotten to make arrests" (Usami, "Zengakuren," pp. 235–36). It would seem from the evidence available that the Japanese police have followed the pattern established by their American counterparts: a first stage of massive violence in the streets against demonstrators, concentrating mainly on beating up as many people as possible, followed, when the struggle becomes more politicized, by a second stage concentrating more on strategic arrests, with long-term detention (with or without trial). The 1970 budget showed increased funds for both riot police and security police to improve their equipment and enlarge the personnel. The *Christian Science Monitor,* October 31, 1967, quoted one police official: "We are clamping down where we can. I feel we should arrest hundreds. But because Japan has become so democratic, one has to be careful not to conflict with our criminal laws."
88. Tsurumi, writing about the 1959–60 struggles, puts this bluntly: "It should be noted that not a single politician, authority or policeman was actually killed or injured either by students or by other demonstrators. On the contrary, it was a student who was killed, and students, their professors, and other citizens who were attacked and

wounded" (*Social Change and the Individual*, p. 337). The police attack on the farmers at Sanrizuka resulted in the death of three policemen.

89. Kitazawa Yoko and Muto Ichiyo, "Icarus Falls: History and Ideology of the Red Army," *Ampo*, No. 13–14 (May–July 1972), is an outstanding attempt to fill in the political background to the Red Army incident, and is the best account of the need for revolutionary violence to combat the repressive violence of Japanese capital. Cf. Muto, "Law & Order, Japanese Style." Extremely interesting observations on the issue in Tsumura, "Avatars et aventures du gauchisme japonais," esp. pp. 404–6. Kitazawa and Muto ("Icarus Falls") acknowledge the difficulty of providing an "explanation" for the Red Army incident.

90. McCormack, "The Student Left," pp. 50–51. Nakasone Yasuhiro, the president of Takushoku ("Colonization") University, is a leading figure in the LDP who was head of the Defence Agency (i.e., Minister of Defence) in a crucial period at the end of Satō's term of office, and Minister of International Trade and Industry in the first Tanaka cabinets (see below, chapter 10).

91. *The Times* (London), October 2, 1968.

92. OECD, *Education: Japan*, 1971, p. 13.

93. The main members of the group were: Edgar Faure, former French Prime Minister and Minister of Education and architect of the reorganization of French education; Edwin O. Reischauer, ex-U.S. Ambassador in Tokyo and author of several works on Japan, who has played an active role in attacking Marxism in Japan and in funneling American ideology to Japan; Ronald Dore, perhaps the most intelligent and articulate foreign bourgeois authority on Japan, who has specialized in studying the need for reforms in the society; and Johan Galtung of the International Institute for Peace Research, Oslo.

94. OECD, *Education: Japan*, 1971, pp. 70–71, 93.

95. *Ibid.*, p. 75; in the period prior to the group's visit to Japan in 1970 it was estimated that Japan was the only advanced industrial country in the world where the ratio of public expenditure for education had actually been in decline (*ibid.*, p. 161).

96. Except for Professor Galtung, whose individual contribution, "Social Structure, Education Structure and Life Long Education: The Case of Japan" (*ibid.*, pp. 131–152), pullulates with interesting ideas, and seems to welcome the contribution of revolutionary ideas, if not perhaps revolution itself.

97. *Ibid.*, pp. 33–34; similarly, the advanced bourgeois reformism of Professor Dore, who suggested that the Japanese regime might be wise to come to terms with the broad new centre majority which Dore thought might now exist, and thus eliminate both "extremes," was too precocious for the Japanese side (*ibid.*, pp. 28–31).

98. *Ibid.*, p. 32.

99. *Ibid.*, pp. 43, 109–12.

100. *Ibid.*, p. 78; such reforms had been advocated by numerous American pundits: see, for example, Marshall E. Dimock, *The Japanese Technocracy: Management and Government in Japan* (New York and Tokyo, Walker/Weatherhill, 1968), pp. 175–76.

101. N.a., "Making Friends and Influencing People," *JQ*, Vol. 19, No. 4 (October–December 1972), pp. 387–91. The decision to grant $10 million to U.S. universities to fund Japanese studies, announced in the August 1973 Tanaka-Nixon communiqué, obviously forms part of the same strategy. Interesting information on how Asian students in Japan see the country in Hiroshi Tanaka, "Japan as Asian Students See It," *PRJ*, 1971, pp. 51–61; cf. studies on immigration policy in *Ampo*, Nos. 9–10 (n.d.), pp. 56–63, and *Ampo*, Nos. 13–14 (May–July 1972) ("Racism and Japanese Immigration Policy"), pp. 40–49; see also Hitoshi Hanai, Kazuko Tsurumi and Joji Watanuki, "A Survey of Asian Youth's Expectations of and Attitudes towards Japan— Reflecting Mixed Feelings of Hope and Apprehension," *PRJ*, 1971, pp. 63–70.

102. N.a., "Education Animal," p. 12.

Chapter 10

THE POLITICS OF JAPANESE CAPITALISM

1. Both because of the specific factor of the long postwar Occupation and because of Japan's general location within the world imperialist system, the context for analyzing

Japan's bourgeoisie must be international. For a stimulating critique of the categories of national and comprador bourgeoisies, see Nicos Poulantzas, "L'internationalisation des rapports capitalistes et l'Etat-Nation," *Les Temps Modernes* (Paris), 29ᵉ année, No. 319 (February 1973) (available in English in *Economy and Society*, Vol. 3, No. 2 [May 1974], and in forthcoming NLB volume), esp. pp. 1484 (exposition of conventional definitions) and 1485 ff. (critique, and introduction of the concept of *internal bourgeoisie* [bourgeoisie intérieure]); some of Poulantzas's arguments are criticized in Christian Leucate, 'La contradiction interimpérialiste aujourd'hui," *Critiques de l'économie politique* (Paris), Nos. 13–14 (October–December 1973), pp. 119–50. These questions are discussed more fully towards the end of this chapter.

2. This could be seen, for example, in the debates over "liberalization," where the bureaucracy did not act in simultaneous "harmony" with big business (see M. Y. Yoshino, "Japan as Host to the International Corporation," in Charles P. Kindleberger, ed., *The International Corporation* [Cambridge, Mass., and London, the M.I.T. Press, 1970], pp. 357–59). A valuable survey of "liberalization" up to the end of 1971 can be found in T. F. M. Adams and Iwao Hoshii, *A Financial History of the New Japan* (Tokyo and Palo Alto, Kodansha International Ltd., 1972), pp. 441–536; much unco-ordinated information on business-state relations in Yanaga, *Big Business in Japanese Politics*, passim. Over "liberalization" the task of the bureaucracy was to mediate conflicting economic interests at the political level.

3. As Yanaga puts it, "business [is] the major concern of the government. . . . Today at least 90 per cent of the work of the government's lawmaking body, ministries, and administrative agencies is concerned with problems of business and industry" (*Big Business in Japanese Politics*, p. 3).

4. On the background, see Yamaguchi, "La structure mythico-théâtrale de la royauté japonaise," *Esprit*, No. 421; on the overall trend, Muto Ichiyo, "Mishima and the Transition from Postwar Democracy to Democratic Fascism," *Ampo*, Nos. 9–10 (1971), pp. 34–50; on later moves, Koji Nakamura, "A Cry for the Son of Heaven," *FEER*, June 18, 1973, pp. 12–15, and below.

5. Cf. Nakane, *Japanese Society*, p. 87, and cf. chapter 8, note 138, p. 399.

6. Chapter 1 of Moore's *Social Origins of Dictatorship and Democracy* bears the elegant title: "England and the Contributions of Violence to Gradualism." The degree of overt violence is, of course, an important index of the nature of a bourgeois regime, but it is not the defining feature. Japan presents a combination of a very powerful ideology and relatively powerful overt repressive machinery—a reflection of the acute nature of the class struggle there. The contribution of violence to "harmony" is a major unstudied area of modern Japan; some valuable material and observations on this in Chalmers Johnson, *Conspiracy at Matsukawa;* cf. Textor's description of an attack on the Tōhō film studios—a combined Japanese-U.S. operation during the Occupation (*Failure in Japan*, pp. 136–37).

7. Whereas most Western cities have a number of police *stations*, Japanese cities also have numerous police boxes located at major crossroads and other strategic points; these have detailed building-by-building maps. The importance of these police boxes is enhanced by the fact that Japanese streets do not have names, nor do buildings have numbers; the police box functions as a central information and surveillance point. Cf. Muto, "Law & Order, Japanese Style."

8. On the 1960 events, see Packard, *Protest in Tokyo;* Yanaga, *Big Business in Japanese Politics*, chapter 10. Kishi was obliged to resign immediately after this, partly over his unconstitutional actions as regards the treaty, partly over the humiliation of having to cancel Eisenhower's visit to Japan; but these reasons rested on an existing base of widespread hostility towards him as a result of earlier policies, including his attempts to force through a repressive new police bill in 1958 (see D. C. Sissons, "The Dispute Over Japanese Police Law," *PA*, Vol. 32, No. 1 [March 1959]).

9. Axelbank, *Black Star Over Japan*, pp. 51, 59. The main English language source, Tsukasa Matsueda and George E. Moore, "Japan's Shifting Attitudes Toward the Military: Mitsuya Kenkyu and the Self-Defense Force," *Asian Survey*, Vol. 7, No. 9 (September 1967), pp. 614–25, pulls its punches on the Plan, as does Weinstein, *Japan's Postwar Defense Policy*, which dismisses it in a few lines (on p. 117).

10. Cited by Naitō Isao, defence counsel, in a speech pleading the Eniwa case at Sapporo District Court, January 1967; typescript of English translation, Part 3, p. 27.

11. *Ibid.*, p. 25. The Plan's study documents included a booklet entitled "The Study of Emergency Laws and Regulations," which carried a list of wartime legislation, mainly from 1944–45; it also appended the wartime regime's "Basic Principles for the Empire's National Policies" as (in its own words) "good introductory remarks" (Axelbank, *Black Star Over Japan*, p. 51).

12. Axelbank, *Black Star Over Japan*, pp. 97–99. Packard notes that there was considerable police resentment towards Kishi for creating a political situation which exposed the police to mass popular hostility and "sullied" their postwar reputation (*Protest in Tokyo*, pp. 292–93); a similar situation recurred in 1965 when the National Police Agency protested about the LDP's association with right-wing gangs in the period leading up to "normalization" of relations with Seoul (Axelbank, p. 99).

13. Axelbank, *Black Star Over Japan*, pp. 99–100. There is excellent information on the links between the Japanese right, business and the Seoul dictatorship in Kitazawa Yoko, "Kidnapped: The Kim [Dae Jung] Case and the 'Korean Connection,'" *Ampo*, No. 18 (Autumn 1973).

14. One subject that would merit much further treatment is the relationship between law and crime in Japan. Some observers have adduced a low "crime" rate to support the contention that Japan is a peaceful or harmonious society (see, for example, Beedham, "A Special Strength: A Survey of Japan," p. 27). This is not a very useful index. Law in the Western sense of the term hardly exists in Japan; it exists, of course, as class repression, but not in the "peace-keeping" sense of guaranteeing contracts and suchlike (on this see Johnson, *Conspiracy at Matsukawa*, esp. pp. 396 ff,. for many stimulating observations). The absence of law as (real) protection leads to non-registration of "crime"; moreover because what in the West is called crime is a much more *direct* instrument of the ruling class and the state in Japan, it shows up correspondingly less in official statistics.

15. For information on this, see K. N., "What Is Japan's Underground?," *Mainichi Daily News*, October 15, 1973, for a useful survey, with emphasis on the criminal side; K. Y., "Sasagawa Ryoichi: Impresario of the Japanese Right," *Ampo*, No. 19 (Winter 1974) —a study of one of the biggest far-right backers of the LDP, noting the importance of the right as a source of *economic* support. Much earlier information also appears in Morris, *Nationalism and the Right Wing in Japan, passim*. On violence against the proletariat, see interview with Higuchi Tokuzō, *Ampo*, No. 17; for gangsters at shareholders' meetings, see *International Herald Tribune*, June 8, 1973, which gives a figure of up to ¥300 million (then equal to U.S. $1.4 million) for payments to *sōkaiya* (literally: "general meetings experts") for one company meeting; cf. reports in the *Times* (London), June 5, 1973, and *Time*, February 26, 1973, p. 10B. Violence by gangsters hired by the companies has increased greatly recently since the rise of citizens' welfare and anti-pollution movements.

16. This can also boomerang on the ruling group, since it weakens the mediating institutions of the political system; over an issue like the pollution (i.e., poison) crisis of summer 1973, the government was so out of touch with the masses that it was unable to construct a hegemonizing position and zigzagged frantically from one extreme to another. This lack of channels of communication leads to the kind of lurching seen in both domestic and foreign affairs.

17. See the article, "Why Is the Liberal Democratic Party Which Ignores Public Opinion so Strong?" by Watanuki Jōji, Okabe Keizō and Miyajima Takashi, translated into English as "International Attitudes and Party Support of the Japanese People," *PRJ*, 1968, pp. 1–24; also Ishida Takeshi, "Japanese Public Opinion and Foreign Policy," *PRJ*, 1967, pp. 11–40.

18. On the merger, see Thayer, *How the Conservatives Rule Japan*, pp. 3–4, 10–14; Fukui, *Party in Power*, chapter 2. The fall-out from the manoeuvring around the merger continues to this day and is an important element in alignments within the LDP. The books by Thayer (1969) and Fukui (1970) are the main English-language sources on the LDP: both contain much valuable material, especially on the role of money and

general arm-twisting. On the whole, Fukui's is the better work; Thayer, a former officer in the U.S. Embassy, Tokyo, has added some later thoughts in Nathaniel B. Thayer, "The Stability of Conservative Party Leadership," in James William Morley, ed., *Forecast for Japan: Security in the 1970's* (Princeton, Princeton University Press, 1972), pp. 85–110. Interesting conceptual material appears in Hajime Shinohara, "The Leadership of the Conservative Party," *JSPIJ*, Vol. 2, No. 3 (December 1964), pp. 40–45. Takeshi Ishida, "The Direction of Japanese Political Reorganization," *JSPIJ*, Vol. 2, No. 3, is an outstanding essay on the class machinations and contradictions of the LDP; cf. Ishida, "Japanese Public Opinion and Foreign Policy."

19. Richard Halloran, *Japan: Images and Realities* (New York, Alfred A. Knopf, 1969), p. 116.

20. Cited in Fukui, *Party in Power*, p. 102.

21. *Mission* of the LDP, English-language edition (Tokyo, LDP, 1970), p. 5.

22. *Constitution* of the LDP, English-language edition (Tokyo, LDP, 1967), revised version, preamble.

23. Fukui, *Party in Power*, pp. 74–75, 79; Thayer, *How the Conservatives Rule Japan*, pp. 82 ff.

24. Gerald Curtis, "The Kōenkai and the Liberal Democratic Party," *JI*, Vol. 6, No. 2 (Summer 1970), pp. 206–19; Thayer, *How the Conservatives Rule Japan*, pp. 87–110 (including a detailed study of the *kōenkai* of Nakasone Yasuhiro). There is not space here to go into the question of factions in detail. Clearly, factions relate *both* to interest groups and to "personal" loyalties; like the LDP itself, they *serve* much narrower class interests than their base would initially suggest. Useful observations and bibliographic references exist in J. A. A. Stockwin, "Japanese Politics: Recent Writing and Research in the West," *JI*, Vol. 7, Nos. 3–4 (Summer–Autumn 1972), pp. 409–21.

25. *Mainichi Shimbun*, May 1, 1966, p. 2, cited in Thayer, *How the Conservatives Rule Japan*, pp. 103–4; note the two themes of "a united Asia" and the heavy mystification about the red carpets in the Diet. Kuno subsequently played a leading role in improving relations with the Democratic People's Republic of Korea in the early 1970s.

26. Soma Masao, "The Roots of Political Corruption," *JSPIJ*, Vol. 5, No. 1 (April 1967), p. 5. There is no scientific definition of corruption in either Marxist or bourgeois sociology. Here the term is used simply to denote the use of money outside the framework of the legal system. The Japanese system can be divided into three: a large sector where the use of money to acquire favours is sanctioned; a small sector where it is formally condemned; and a large in-between area where it is actively tolerated. Suggestive indications on corruption can be found in W. F. Wertheim, "Sociological Aspects of Corruption in South-East Asia," in W. F. Wertheim, *East-West Parallels: Sociological Approaches to Modern Asia* (The Hague, W. Van Hoeve, 1964); cf. Alfred W. McCoy with Cathleen B. Read and Leonard P. Adams II, *The Politics of Heroin in Southeast Asia* (New York, Harper & Row, Colophon ed., 1973), pp. 405–7.

27. *Time*, April 12, 1971; on Hatano, cf. N.a., "Police to Play Leading Role in the 1970's?," *Ampo*, Nos. 3–4 (March 1970), p. 41; on Minobe, Crocker Snow, Jr., "Tokyo's Governor Minobe," *JI*, Vol. 8, No. 2 (Spring 1973).

28. Fukui, *Party in Power*, p. 128 (the higher figures are from the *Yomiuri*, the lower from the *Asahi*); cf. Thayer, *How the Conservatives Rule Japan*, chapter 6.

29. Koji Nakamura, "The Golden Egg," *FEER*, No. 2 (January 9), 1971. Both Satō and Fukuda had earlier been heavily involved in major scandals: Satō in a bribery scandal which brought down the Yoshida government in 1954, when Satō was saved from arrest only by special (and probably illegal) government intervention; Fukuda was indicted on major criminal charges; Tanaka, the current Prime Minister, served a prison term in the late 1940s.

30. Fukui, *Party in Power*, pp. 146–151.

31. *Ibid.*, pp. 102 ff.

32. *Ibid.*, p. 169.

33. Koji Nakamura, "Japan: Taking a Breather," *FEER*, February 18, 1974, p. 34.

34. N.a., "70% of Diet Members Elected by Cheating," *Ampo*, Nos. 3–4 (March 1970), p. 43 (i.e., on the basis of campaigns whose activities included actions recognized by Japanese law as legal offences); information below from same.

35. Yoshisato Oka, "Political Parties and Party Government," *JSPIJ*, Vol. 2, No. 3 (December 1964), p. 17.

36. In any society a party which is working to serve the interests of only one class, the bourgeoisie, which is in a minority within the society, has to seek support from outside that class if it is to win a majority of the vote. The loaded voting system in Japan reduces this operation to a minimum. On the general issues raised here, see Ralph Miliband, *The State in Capitalist Society* (London, Weidenfeld and Nicolson, 1969), especially chapters 7 and 8.

37. Sugihara Yasuo, "Shiren ni tatsu gikai sei minshushugi" [Parliamentary democracy on trial], *Sekai* [The world] (Tokyo), January 1973, p. 63; table kindly supplied by Gavan McCormack.

38. Both because pollution has killed off many of the fish, and because it has poisoned the surviving fish to such an extent that they have become a danger if eaten; in mid-1973 Japanese were advised to cut their consumption of fish by about half if they wished to stay alive and reasonably healthy.

39. When the Emperor visited Europe in 1971 those in the West who attacked the trip as a political manoeuvre by the Japanese right were derided. Yet less than two years later the regime had to call off a scheduled visit by the Emperor to the United States in the face of domestic opposition to it as a political scheme (*Time*, May 7, 1973). Clamorous evidence of the Emperor's interference in important political matters came in May 1973 when the Director-General of the Defence Agency, Masuhara Keikichi, was obliged to resign after revealing the content of a conversation with the Emperor about the military budget. According to Masuhara, the Emperor urged him to reincorporate some of the more "meritorious" aspects of the old Imperial Armed Forces, and questioned him as to why the opposition parties were being allowed to fight the vastly increased arms budget in the Diet (*Times* [London], May 30, 1973; Nakamura, "A Cry for the Son of Heaven," p. 12).

40. Nakamura, "A Cry for the Son of Heaven," pp. 13, 15. Apart from Kishi's National Congress, there is an LDP Constitutional Research Committee whose 1972 outline for a revised Constitution, presented by its then chairman, Inaba Osamu (later Tanaka's first Minister of Education), agreed in almost every detail with the Kishi proposals (*ARB*, Vol. 2, No. 1 [June 1972], pp. 937–38).

41. Earlier attempts had been made several times during the postwar period, most notably by Hatoyama Ichirō in 1955–56 (Oka, "Political Parties and Party Government").

42. Up to the early 1970s the focus was on revising the constituency system for the Lower House (see Appendix II). But after the strong showing of the left in the December 1972 general election, the Tanaka government stepped up the campaign for revising the system for both Houses. This was since Tanaka was facing the mid-1974 Upper House elections with a very fragile majority: 134 of the 252 seats (as of early 1974). Mass demonstrations in spring–summer 1973 showed the depth of popular hostility to the reform and staved it off, at least temporarily.

43. *ARB*, Vol. 2, No. 9 (February 1973), pp. 1544–45.

44. On taxation, see Yamamura, *Economic Policy in Postwar Japan*, chapter 8 ("Tax Policy for Economic Growth"); Sei Fujita, "Tax Policy," in Komiya, ed., *Postwar Economic Growth in Japan;* on social security, see chapter 8 above; on fiscal and monetary policy, Adams and Hoshii, *A Financial History of the New Japan*, pp. 285–324; Ryūichiro Tachi, "Fiscal and Monetary Policy," in Komiya, ed., *Postwar Economic Growth in Japan*. A major form of intervention is *non-taxation* in the form of lavish expense account allowances. In 1972 businessmen spent £2,039 million in mostly tax-exempt entertaining—more than the defence budget, and 20 per cent higher than government expenditure on education; corporate entertainment takes about 1.5 per cent of the nation's GNP (*Time*, April 16, 1973, p. 55; the *Times* [London], January 25, 1974). It goes without saying that actual legislation has been overwhelmingly in favour of big business (Yanaga, *Big Business in Japanese Politics*, p. 119).

45. The most common term for big business as a whole is *zaikai*: "Its translation varies from 'financial world' to 'economic circles' but the referent is not necessarily the same as 'economic circles' (*keizaikai*) or 'industrial world' (*jitsugyōkai*). All these terms

include bankers and company executives but *zaikai* has the additional connotation of a smaller group which (1) is in a position to influence national economic policy and (2) can speak from the point of view of business as a whole rather than individual enterprises" (William R. Bryant, "Japanese Businessmen and Private Economic Diplomacy," *JI*, Vol. 6, No. 2 [Summer 1970], p. 230; cf. Yanaga, *Big Business in Japanese Politics*, pp. 32–34). Another term often used to describe the postwar oligopolies is *keiretsu* (see Yanaga, p. 39); this term was introduced to try to avoid the negative connotations attached to the term zaibatsu.

46. Keidanren: abbreviation for Keizai Dantai Rengōkai; on this and the other organizations mentioned immediately below, see Yanaga, *Big Business in Japanese Politics*, pp. 42–52.

47. Suzuki Yukio, *Seiji o Ugokasu Keieisha* [Business executives who move politics] (Tokyo, Nihon Keizai Shimbun-sha, 1965), p. 28, cited in Thayer, *How the Conservatives Rule Japan*, p. 69.

48. Jacqueline Grapin, "Japan and Co.," *Le Monde*, January 7, 1971, p. 24; as Grapin notes, "dont on voit mal, soit dit en passant, qu'il puisse jamais exister en France"— or anywhere except Japan.

49. See especially, Yoshino, *Japan's Managerial System*, chapter 4; cf. Akira Sakaguchi, "The Power of the Financial World in Politics," *JSPIJ*, Vol. 2, No. 3 (December 1964), pp. 115–19.

50. Nikkeiren: abbreviation for Nihon Keieisha Dantai Remmei; cf. chapter 8, note 66.

51. Nisshō: abbreviation for Nihon Shōkō Kaigisho.

52. The title of an article on Sanken by Katō Hidetoshi, *JI*, Vol. 7, No. 1 (Winter 1971); for details on Sanken, see *PIN*, Vol. 3, No. 1 (December 1971–January 1972), special issue: "Who's Who in the Zaibatsu," pp. 11–16; Halliday and McCormack, *Japanese Imperialism*, pp. 131–33, and references there. Sanken: abbreviation for Sangyō Mondai Kenkyūkai (Council on Industrial Policy, or Industrial Problems Study Council).

53. Thayer, *How the Conservatives Rule Japan*, p. 67 (referring to the Japan–Republic of China [Taiwan] Cooperation Committee). Another formulation of the relationship came from Mitsubishi Bank Chairman Tajitsu Wataru after a cabinet-business meeting in February 1974: "We [government and business]," said Tajitsu, "are like man and wife" (quoted by Nakamura, "Japan: Taking a Breather," p. 34).

54. V. I. Lenin, *Imperialism, the Highest Stage of Capitalism*, chapter 1; Rodolfo Banfi, "A proposito di *Imperialismo* di Lenin [On Lenin's *Imperialism*]," *Rivista storica del socialismo* (Milan), No. 23 (1964).

55. Kelvin Rowley, "Japan: A New Centre of World Imperialism," *Intervention* (Carlton, Australia), No. 2 (October 1972), p. 24. Although the term "monopoly" is now widely used to refer to a situation of oligopoly, it seems useful to retain the distinction for Japan since the real monopoly situation which does exist in many sectors in the West does not apply to Japan. It is very rare for one company to dominate a single sector; usually the zaibatsu share out each sector, and this *structural* feature has remained relatively stable throughout the current epoch. For further information on definitions, see Hadley, *Antitrust*, especially chapter 2; Yamamura, *Economic Policy in Postwar Japan*, p. 119. I have not gone at great length into the "miracle" aspects of the Japanese economy, since information on these is widely available elsewhere: in English see, for example, Kahn, *The Emerging Japanese Superstate*, chapter 3; two much better accounts give Hubert Brochier, *Le miracle économique japonais 1950–1970* (Paris, Calmann-Lévy, 1970), and Christian Sautter, *Japon, le prix de la puissance* (Paris, Editions du Seuil, 1973); to set this material in context the two indispensable analytic texts are Rowley, "Japan: A New Centre of World Imperialism," and Anne Vimille, "L'impérialisme japonais," *Critiques de l'économie politique* (Paris), Nos. 13–14 (October–December 1973).

56. *PIN*, Vol. 3, No. 1; later information in *OE*, Nos. 742–745 (August–November 1972), a useful series on "Industrial Groups under Reorganization." Zaibatsu-like groups also exist around the Tōkai Bank (in the Nagoya area) and the Industrial Bank of Japan (*PIN*, Vol. 3, No. 1, p. 3); full descriptions of the six groups in *PIN, ibid.*, pp. 25–59. Yamamura, *Economic Policy in Postwar Japan*, chapter 7 ("The Zaibatsu Ques-

tion"), disputes a number of the positions adopted here; some of Yamamura's arguments, as well as his figures, are challenged in Hadley, *Antitrust,* pp. 253, 324, note 11. Although Yamamura's detailed work on cross-holdings is useful, his general argument is not persuasive.

57. *PIN,* Vol. 3, No. 1, pp. 1, 3. These konzerns are, of course, connected to the zaibatsu.
58. Toshiba-IHI: abbreviation for Tokyo Shibaura Electric Company Ltd., and Ishikawajima-Harima Heavy Industries Company Ltd. (IHI); Tokyu: abbreviation for Tokyo Kyuko Dentetsu (Tokyo Electric Express Railway). For details of the konzerns, see *ibid.,* pp. 60–76.
59. *Japan Times,* November 17, 1973; cf. *Economist,* January 27, 1973, Survey, pp. 44–45; Sautter, *Japon, le prix de la puissance,* p. 173 (Graphique VI.4: La dégradation de la structure du bilan de la grande industrie japonaise); Roger Cukierman, *Le capital dans l'économie japonaise* (Paris, Presses Universitaires de France, 1962), *passim.*
60. N.a., "Just Who Really Rules the Japanese Economy?," *Asahi Evening News,* July 16, 1973 (reporting on Imamura Kōmei, "Those Who Control Japan's Economy," *Chūō Kōron,* August 1973).
61. Kikuiri Ryūsuke, "*Shōsha:* Organizers of the World Economy," *JI,* Vol. 8, No. 3 (Autumn 1973), p. 360.
62. Adams and Hoshii, *A Financial History of the New Japan,* pp. 99–103.
63. Kikuiri, "*Shōsha,*" p. 360.
64. Rowley, "Japan: A New Centre of World Imperialism," p. 25, citing Yoshiro Kimizuka, *Capital Versus Labour Under High Growth* (Tokyo, Science Council of Japan, Division of Economics, Commerce & Business Administration, Economics Series, No. 46, March 1969), pp. 31–32.
65. *PIN,* Vol. 3, No. 1, p. 3, and note 2, p. 19. Note 3, p. 19, indicates the extent to which the figure of U.S. $8,149 million is an understatement.
66. Information from Kikuiri, "*Shōsha,*" p. 354; *OE,* No. 747 (January 1973), pp. 41–57; cf. the *Times* (London), January 23, 1974. For the list of the big ten, see Kikuiri, "*Shōsha,*" p. 373, note 1. The *shōsha* are, naturally, tied in with the zaibatsu and the konzerns, though not always on a 1:1 basis: for details, see *PIN,* Vol. 3, No. 1. The trading companies played a key role in hoarding and stockpiling, especially in land, rice, wool and soybeans, thus contributing to the roaring inflation of 1973 and producing severe shortages: for an excellent account of this, see Frank Baldwin, "The Idioms of Contemporary Japan VI," *JI,* Vol. 8, No. 3 (Autumn 1973), pp. 396–409 (entry: "Kaishime"); cf. *Time,* April 30, 1973, p. 55; John Roberts, "Japan's Wily, Muscular Monsters," *FEER,* No. 37, September 17, 1973, Merchant Banking Focus, pp. 13–16.
67. *Times* (London), January 23, 1974; the top six are Mitsubishi Corporation, Mitsui & Co., Marubeni Corporation, C. Itoh, Sumitomo Shoji Kaisha Ltd., and Nissho Iwai Co.
68. Kikuiri, "*Shōsha,*" p. 354.
69. *PIN,* Vol. 3, No. 1, p. 8, for other important exceptions.
70. *Ibid.*
71. *OE,* No. 744 (October 1972), pp. 15–22; *Newsweek,* April 23, 1973, pp. 30–34 (cover story on Mitsubishi); *PIN,* Vol. 3, No. 1, *passim;* Sautter, *Japon, le prix de la puissance,* pp. 92–98.
72. Yamamura, *Economic Policy,* chapter 7; Rowley, "Japan: A New Centre of World Imperialism," pp. 24–25; *PIN,* Vol. 3, No. 1, pp. 8–11; Vimille, "L'impérialisme japonais," pp. 176–77; Sautter, *Japon, le prix de la puissance,* chapter 7. A crucial role in this has been played by the Ministry of International Trade and Industry (MITI); see Kazushi Ohkawa and Henry Rosovsky, *Japanese Economic Growth: Trend Acceleration in the Twentieth Century* (Stanford, Stanford University Press, and London, Oxford University Press, 1973), pp. 222–24; Yanaga, *Big Business in Japanese Politics,* chapter 6.
73. *Asahi Evening News,* January 11, 1972, cited in *PIN,* Vol. 3, No. 1, p. 11.
74. OECD, *Economic Survey of Japan,* June 1973, table after p. 92 ("Basic Statistics: International Comparisons").
75. James William Morley, "Growth for What? The Issue of the 'Seventies," in Gerald L. Curtis, ed., *Japanese-American Relations in the 1970's* (Washington, D.C., Columbia Books, Inc., 1970), p. 54.

76. See tables in Sautter, *Japon, le prix de la puissance*, pp. 46–50.
77. Kihara, "The Militarisation of the Japanese Economy," pp. 27, 29, 34–35; Kihara emphasizes that the heavy chemical sector is crucial to arms production and that the structure of postwar industrialization, determined by Japan's role as the arsenal for the United States and its clients in East Asia, creates heavy pressure for either a major increase in exports or a bigger military budget. See *ARB*, Vol. 2, No. 11 (April 1973), p. 1718, on proposals to restructure the heavy chemical industry. Cf. *PIN*, Vol. 3, No. 1, pp. 16–19.
78. OECD, *Economic Survey of Japan*, June 1973, table after p. 92 ("Basic Statistics: International Comparisons").
79. Rowley, "Japan: A New Centre of World Imperialism," pp. 20–22; cf. Vimille, "L'impérialisme japonais."
80. EPA calculation, reported in *International Herald Tribune*, March 1, 1974: this represented a 24.5 per cent growth rate over 1972; even after adjustment for inflation, this was well up on the 1972 rate. OECD, *Economic Survey of Japan*, June 1973, p 57; on the Plan, *ibid.*, pp. 52–63, 71–73; figures below from same. In December 1973 the EPA announced that the oil crisis had forced postponement of the formulation of long-term plans for the rest of the century (*Japan Times*, December 7, 1973). There is not space here to deal with all the futurological speculation about Japan's growth. For a good succinct survey of the field, see Fuse, "Japan's Economy in the 70's," pp. 53–61; Fuse concludes that the estimates put forward by observers like Hakan Hedberg (*Japan's Revenge* [London, Pitman, 1972] and Kanamori Hisao ("Japan in 1985," *Economist*, October 19, 1971) assume too high a growth rate; for another sober assessment, see Ohkawa and Rosovsky, *Japanese Economic Growth*, pp. 232–50. In a speech in Tokyo in November 1973 Kahn said he saw no reason to revise his economic predictions about Japan, in spite of the oil crisis and other issues (*Japan Times*, November 21, 1973). In early January 1974 Finance Minister Fukuda Takeo told *Newsweek*: "To contain inflation . . . requires an economic slowdown. . . . Our [growth] target hereafter will be the world average. I predict a growth rate of 2½ per cent next year" (*Newsweek*, January 21, 1974, p. 48).
81. Fuse, "Japan's Economy in the 70's," p. 57. The reason corporations preferred borrowing to equity capital is spelt out by Howard Van Zandt: "the amount they [corporations] must earn to pay the tax-deductible interest is only about two-fifths of what they would have to earn to pay dividends of the same amount" (Howard F. Van Zandt, "Japanese Culture and the Business Boom," *FA*, Vol. 48, No. 2 [January 1970], p. 350). Van Zandt notes that in spite of the role of credit in business financing, the role of credit in society at large is much less than in the West; the relatively small role of hire purchase and of charge accounts in fact serves to stimulate saving, since people have actually to *save* the sum needed for purchases. Despite the high debt ratios of business, both the national debt and individual indebtedness are small compared with the West (*ibid.*, pp. 350–51).
82. Japan exports about 12 per cent of its GNP, compared with a figure of 27 per cent for the U.K. Moreover, Japan has a much lower percentage of its trade with the developed countries than any other advanced capitalist nation. In 1973 *Le Monde* estimated that Japan accounted for only 7.7 per cent of world trade (*Le Monde*, May 13–14, 1973, p. 23); cf. Halliday and McCormack, *Japanese Imperialism*, p. 214.
83. *Time*, February 25, 1974, p. 52.
84. Ui Jun, "Basic Theory of Kogai," pp. 18–19.
85. *Japan Times*, September 26, 1973, citing report on "Japan's Energy Problems" prepared by the Resources and Energy Agency of MITI.
86. Cited by Robert Whymant, the *Guardian*, June 22, 1973; cf. Matsuoka Nobuo, "Pollution Imperialism and People's Struggle," *Ampo*, No. 16 (March 1973).
87. Zensō: abbreviation for Zenkoku Sōgo Kaihatsu Keikaku.
88. Cf. chapter 8; Muto Ichiyo, "Can the Tight Rope Dancer Reach the Other End? Tanaka Kakuei's Politics Analysed," *Ampo*, No. 15 (December 1972), pp. 19–22; Kobayashi Yasuhiro, "Judging Tanaka's 'Remodeling Japan' Theory," in Jon Livingston, Joe Moore and Felicia Oldfather, eds., *The Japan Reader*, Vol. 2, *Postwar Japan 1945 to the Present* (New York, Pantheon Books, 1973), pp. 568–73; Chika-

raishi Sadakazu, "Improving the Remodeling Plan," *JI*, Vol. 8, No. 3 (Autumn 1973).

89. Koji Nakamura, "Japan's Challenge," *FEER*, April 2, 1973, pp. 33, 35.

90. Fuse, "Japan's Economy in the 70's," pp. 72, 83; cf. Shimano Takuji, "Economic Growth and the Rise of Militarism," *JI*, Vol. 8, No. 2 (Spring 1973), p. 205. On Japan's import requirements, cf. below.

91. Fuse, "Japan's Economy in the 70's," pp. 79–89.

92. Since the completion of the postwar land reform successive governments have sacrificed the rural population to a policy of industry-led growth, which has involved moving large numbers of people off the land, the take-over of farmland, and the degradation of rural life. The original Shinzenso called for one-sixth of agricultural land in use in 1969 to be converted to industrial use by 1985; the objective was not only to find more land for industry, but also to squeeze out more labour for industry and facilitate the "rationalization" of agriculture into larger capitalist units of production. The basic issues were starkly posed in *Ampo:* "Should domestic agriculture be exterminated? Should the peasants be discarded? What does it mean to the rest of the world for Japan to rely heavily on imported agricultural products?" (N.a., "Economic Analysis (1): Junk-Yard Development," *Ampo*, No. 11 [n.d.], p. 26). The overall result of economic policy has been an increasingly heavy dependence on agricultural imports. For the effects of this, see Bix, "Japan: The Roots of Militarism"; Rowley, "Japan: A New Centre of World Imperialism," pp. 14–15; Vimille, "L'impérialisme japonais," pp. 156–57; Halliday and McCormack, *Japanese Imperialism*, pp. 170–78; much useful material on the condition of the peasantry and on their struggles is found in *Ampo* texts on Sanrizuka, Kitafuji and the Ryukyus.

93. Fukuda interview, *Newsweek*, January 21, 1974, p. 48: "there is no room left for such a grand program [as Tanaka's 'remodelling' scheme]."

94. *Japan Times*, November 17, 1973; Vimille, "L'impérialisme japonais," *passim*, on the organic composition of capital.

95. Nagano Yoshiko, "Women Fight for Control: Abortion Struggle in Japan," *Ampo*, No. 17 (Summer 1973); Kaji, "The Invisible Proletariat," pp. 57–58; Baldwin, "Idioms of Contemporary Japan V" (entry: "Ūman Ribu," pp. 242–44).

96. *Japan Times*, November 8, 1973. The use of Okinawa (where else?) for this "experiment" needs no comment. The Seoul regime's desire to sell the country's manpower abroad should also be connected to the dire condition of the economy in south Korea: on this, see Bernie Wideman, "The Plight of the South Korean Peasant," in Baldwin, ed., *Without Parallel: The American-Korean Relationship Since 1945;* Hasegawa Kazuto, "Pak Chung Hee vs. the People: The Collision Course in South Korea," *Ampo*, No. 19 (Winter 1974).

97. Halliday and McCormack, *Japanese Imperialism*, pp. 155–56.

98. Cited by Robert Whymant, the *Guardian*, June 22, 1973; Matsuoka, "Pollution Imperialism and People's Struggle."

99. Hong Kong government survey, cited in Charles Sebestyen, *The Outward Urge: Japanese Investment World-Wide* (London, Economist Intelligence Unit, Quarterly Economic Review, Special No. 11, February 1973), p. 9; Vimille, "L'impérialisme japonais," pp. 167 ff.

100. Vimille, "L'impérialisme japonais," p. 169, for more detailed discussion of this.

101. Sebestyen, *The Outward Urge*, p. 49; Kiyoshi Kojima, "Japan's Approach to UNCTAD III," *Hong Kong Economic Papers*, No. 7 (September 1972), pp. 33–44.

102. *FEER*, July 3, 1971, p. 76; *FEER*, November 26, 1973, pp. 50–54; only about one-fifth of the U.S. total was calculated to be in direct investment at the end of 1970; OECD figures indicate that direct investment accounted for a slightly higher proportion of the total in 1970–72 than in 1965–69 (see OECD, *Economic Survey of Japan*, June 1973, Table 12, p. 43); on the other hand, foreign investment as a whole actually fell in Japan in 1972 (*ibid.*, p. 41). Details of foreign investment in Japan in Appendix III.

    Visible direct investment, of course, (even if it can be accurately measured, which is not the case in Japan) is not the sole yardstick for measuring control. Other elements must be taken into consideration. (1) The foreign-controlled capital may be raised locally; (2) it may come in through a third country (Hong Kong, the Philippines, Panama, etc.); (3) control can be exercised with quite a small percentage of the total ownership—often much less than the 25 per cent usually used as a criterion, and less than the 20 per cent which MITI uses as its criterion for "foreign" in Japan; (4) foreign investment is not "indiscriminate"; U.S. investment, in particular, is heavily concentrated in certain key areas, so that an average is not very indicative. More important, the question is not merely one of percentages; it involves American power to impose *worldwide* "standardizations of basic products" and thus, through patents and licences, as well as sheer control of markets, to dominate "national" production. On this, see Poulantzas, "L'internationalisation des rapports capitalistes et l'Etat-Nation," pp. 1470–72, 1479–82; this was the case, for example, with the Japanese arms industry (Kihara, "The Militarisation of the Japanese Economy," p. 32).

103. Vimille, "L'impérialisme japonais," p. 163; on the anti-competitive nature of foreign investment by the trans-national companies, see Stephen Hymer, "The Efficiency (Contradictions) of Multinational Corporations," *AER,* Vol. 60, No. 2 (May 1970), p. 443.

104. Vimille, "L'impérialisme japonais," p. 163; for details, see Bix, "Japan: The Roots of Militarism"; Halliday and McCormack, *Japanese Imperialism,* pp. 12–13.

105. The scheme has spawned a large bureaucratic apparatus: the wages for the 280,000 employees of the Food Control Programme constitute the single largest item in the Programme's budget (N.a., "Junk-Yard Development," p. 25).

106. Bix, "Japan: The Roots of Militarism," p. 342. The 1971 figure for soybeans was 93 per cent. In mid-1973 the United States suddenly introduced severe restrictions on the export of soybeans and other key commodities from America, causing consternation and near-panic in Japan (see, for example, the *Times* [London], July 6, 1973). The quasi-embargo on certain key agricultural exports coincided with a Japanese government report indicating that fish consumption would have to be cut by half because of the danger of poisoning as a result of pollution; since the U.S. restrictions affected mainly animal foodstuffs, this meant it would be difficult for Japan to replace fish with meat. A move to do so would anyway only send meat prices spiralling even higher: in February 1974 beef stood at about £9–40 per pound (lb.) in Tokyo (*Sunday Times* [London], February 24, 1974).

107. On the disappearance of the U.S. surplus, Lawrence A. Mayer, "We Can't Take Food for Granted Anymore," *Fortune,* February 1974. In the period 1965–71 the United States provided about 70 per cent of Japan's agricultural imports, with the rest coming from Australia (14 per cent), Canada (5 per cent), Mexico and Thailand (4 per cent each) (Bix, "Japan: The Roots of Militarism," p. 360, citing Louise Perkens, "Soybeans Spearhead Record U.S. Farm Sales to Japan," *Foreign Agriculture,* August 30, 1971, p. 506). The Southeast Asian total, it may be noted, is a paltry 4 per cent—all accounted for by Thailand.

108. N.a., "Junk-Yard Development," p. 26; a different opinion is conveyed by Kikuiri, "*Shōsha,*" pp. 363–64. Bix, "The Roots of Militarism," p. 344, on the long-term prospects.

109. Cited by Muto, "Can the Tight Rope Dancer Reach the Other End?," p. 22, from the *Yomiuri Shimbun,* October 12, 1972 (translation slightly modified—J.H.); cf. Table 4 in Halliday and McCormack, *Japanese Imperialism,* pp. 18–19, for Japan's dependence on overseas supplies.

110. Yamakawa Akio, "Petroleum and Political Vision: Coming to the Crunch," *Ampo,* No. 19, p. 5. Petroleum plays a bigger role in the energy supply in Japan than in any other country. See also Muneo Isshiki, "Keeping Pace with Energy Demands," *Investors Chronicle* (London), September 7, 1973, Supplement, pp. 45–46; Peter R. Odell, *Oil and World Power: A Geographical Interpretation* (Harmondsworth, Penguin Books, 1970), chapter 6, up to the end of the 1960s. For an excellent up-to-date study of the Middle East oil situation in its political context, see Fred Halliday, *Arabia Without Sultans* (Harmondsworth, Penguin Books, and New York, Random House, 1974). Cf. Appendix IV.

111. The highest was copper: 22 per cent of Japan's imports of this came from enterprises linked with Japanese capital (Sebestyen, *The Outward Urge,* pp. 12–15). The table on p. 424 sets out the relatively low level of Japan's control over its supply sources.

*IMPORTS OF KEY NATURAL RESOURCES
INTO JAPAN, 1970*

	Develop & import	Loan & import	Import	Total imports
Copper ('000 tons)	38	103	510	651
Lead ('000 tons)	7	—	102	109
Zinc ('000 tons)	20	—	369	389
Aluminium ('000 tons)	90	—	889	979
Nickel ('000 tons)	—	9	91	100
Iron ore (mn. tons)	11	2	89	102
Coking coal (mn. tons)	3	1	40	50
Crude oil (mn. kilolitres)	21	—	184	205

SOURCE: Sebestyen, *The Outward Urge*, p. 15.

112. Yamakawa, "Petroleum and Political Vision," p. 5; cf. note 115 below.
113. *ARB*, "Petroleum and Japan," *ARB*, Vol. 2, No. 9 (February 1973), pp. 1570–72; *FEER*, February 25, 1974, p. 58; Yamakawa, "Petroleum and Political Vision," *passim*. The Abu Dhabi formula refers to the breakthrough by Japanese interests at the end of 1972 when a group led by the Overseas Petroleum Development Co. bought a sizeable part of BP's interest in Abu Dhabi Marine Areas Ltd. (ADMA) for U.S. $780 million, giving the Japanese group a 22.5 per cent holding in ADMA. This was the first time a Japanese group had bought into such an international oil operation.
114. On Japan and Siberia, see Halliday and McCormack, *Japanese Imperialism*, pp. 232–237; Kiichi Saeki, "Toward Japanese Cooperation in Siberian Development," *Problems of Communism*, Vol. 21, No. 3 (May–June 1972). In early 1974 the situation began to look somewhat confused: with Japan weakened by the oil crisis and Soviet-American relations turning slightly frosty as Congress continued to block aspects of the Nixon-Brezhnev economic rapprochement, the Soviet regime made moves to attract Japan in, perhaps alone (see Koji Nakamura, "Partners in Siberian Energy," *FEER*, February 25, 1974, pp. 56–57).
115. The American proposals for "joint energy" plans came immediately after Esso, Mobil, Shell and BP had informed the Japanese refiners associated to them that they would be curtailing supplies in the first quarter of 1973. To some Japanese this had an ominous ring. The Japanese bourgeoisie and its political representatives split publicly over the U.S. scheme. Initially MITI head Nakasone went all out to try to consolidate direct deals with the producer countries, but by early 1974 the United States had brought Tokyo back into line. For details, see *International Herald Tribune*, April 25, 1973; *Guardian*, June 8, 1973; Minoru Shimizu, "Nakasone in the Limelight," *Japan Times*, November 29, 1973; *FEER*, February 25, 1974, p. 58. On the question of the fissures within the Japanese bourgeoisie, cf. below.
116. Figures from Y. Kobayashi, "Expanding Investment Overseas," *Investors Chronicle*, September 7, 1973, Supplement, p. 11; cf. JETRO (Japan External Trade Organization), 1973 White Paper on Overseas Investment (November 1973); Sam Jameson, "Japan's Overseas Economic Expansion," *Japan Times*, July 31, 1973. Rates of increase from *ARB*, Vol. 2, No. 9 (February 1973), p. 1582; comparable figures for the same years were 23.3 per cent for West Germany, 9.4 for the United States and 6.0 for the U.K.
117. The figure for marketing investment in these years was $356 million; over the same period only 22 per cent went into manufacturing (and nearly 80 per cent of this was in lumber and pulp)—see Sebestyen, *The Outward Urge*, p. 19; cf. Hymer, "The Efficiency (Contradictions) of Multinational Corporations," p. 445, on the importance of a marketing network; Vimille, "L'impérialisme japonais," *passim*.
118. Fuse, "Japan's Economy in the 70's," p. 57, citing JETRO, *Foreign Trade of Japan 1970* (Tokyo, JETRO, 1971), p. 9. In 1971 Japan stood number 62 among the world's top 76 exporting nations as regards the ratio of its exports to GNP. On Japan's export boom, cf. Sautter, *Japon, le prix de la puissance*, pp. 242–50.

119. Jameson, "Japan's Overseas Economic Expansion," *Japan Times*, July 31, 1973, based on Japan Economic Research Center figures, which predicted that by 1980 about 25 per cent of U.S. imports would come from Japan. Fuse, "Japan's Economy in the 70's," p. 71, on the other hand, considers that Japan "cannot expect much improvement" in the U.S. market "in the near future."

120. Fuse, "Japan's Economy in the 70's," pp. 62–71; *FEER*, May 14, 1973, Supplement, p. 8. In 1973 the United States reduced its deficit with Japan to U.S. $1.3 billion (*International Herald Tribune*, March 1, 1974). Figures below from Fuse, "Japan's Economy."

121. Fuse, "Japan's Economy in the 70's," pp. 59–61.

122. OECD, *Economic Survey of Japan*, June 1973, Table I, p. 88.

123. *FEER*, May 14, 1973, Supplement, pp. 29, 35, 48.

124. Halliday and McCormack, *Japanese Imperialism*, pp. 52–59.

125. This assessment attempts to synthesize the data and ideas in J. and G. Kolko, *The Limits of Power*, with the material in Poulantzas, "L'internationalisation des rapports capitalistes et l'Etat-Nation," Vimille, "L'impérialisme japonais," and Rowley, "Japan: A New Centre of World Imperialism."

126. The modalities of this would merit much more detailed treatment. For example, the relationship between Japan's high growth rate and the relatively low level of foreign capital in the economy. It is clear that *higher* foreign investment would have resulted in *lower* growth rates. The overall strategic-political objective of U.S. imperialism was a stronger Japan. Did the United States therefore *need* to keep down its investment in order to help maintain the growth rates in Japan which it required strategically?

A second vital factor in U.S. policy towards Japan was the very swift militarization of most of the neighbouring economies: this demanded fast growth in certain sectors both in these economies and in Japan. In this respect, the position of Japan is not comparable to that of the West European capitalist economies. Third, there is the much larger question of economic cycles and if and when fast growth in another major capitalist economy "helps" more by stimulating world trade than it hurts by taking a greater share of other countries' export markets.

127. Another factor which deserves scrutiny is the role of currency realignments. In December 1971 the yen was upvalued by 16.88 per cent against the U.S. dollar, giving an exchange rate of ¥308 to the dollar, as compared with ¥360 before. This change was widely interpreted as largely the result of U.S. pressure, to make Japan's exports more expensive. But the exact pressures which caused this realignment, and its effects, remain fairly obscure. In February 1973 the yen was officially floated and by June 1973 had appreciated by as much as a further 18 per cent against the dollar, at ¥258 per dollar, though it was mainly held at about ¥265 per dollar (a 16 per cent upvaluation). A survey of these two quite hefty revaluations conducted in August 1973 found that they had had very little effect on the Japanese economy. Government intervention and Japan's balanced trade undoubtedly helped cushion the effect, but further research on this aspect is needed (see *Japan Times*, August 16 and 17, 1973). What is probably more crucial on the currency front is the fact that Japan has fundamentally worked to prop up the dollar. Even when Japan's reserves were at $20 billion, it bought only $600 million in gold, Tanaka has pointed out. "We bought gold only through the United States Treasury, and it all is deposited in the vaults of U.S. banks. That is symbolic of the fact that the United States and Japan share the same bond of a mutual fate" (Tanaka, cited in *Japan Times*, August 1, 1973).

128. Rowley, "Japan: A New Centre of World Imperialism," on the uneven and combined development of capitalism, in connection with its parasitic character; Hymer, "The Efficiency (Contradictions) of Multinational Corporations"; Poulantzas, "L'internationalisation des rapports capitalistes et l'Etat-Nation"; Vimille, "L'impérialisme japonais." These are fundamental texts for an understanding of the theoretical issues involved in inter-capitalist contradictions today.

It should be added that the United States also deployed political instruments: one of the two "Nixon shocks" was the announcement of Nixon's visit to China in mid-1971. In spite of Kissinger's alleged "neglect" of Japan and disinterest in economic issues, it would be unwise to ignore the important role of diplomacy in its effects on the economic level. The oil crisis greatly strengthened the hand of the United

States, both economically and politically, vis-à-vis its capitalist rivals. And, although U.S. economic policy has at times appeared to be seriously adrift, it is clear that U.S. *political* control of global inter-capitalist economic contradictions is still quite strong.

129. The situation up to the end of the 1960s is surveyed in Yoshino, "Japan as Host to the International Corporation," and to the end of 1971 in Adams and Hoshii, *A Financial History of the New Japan*, pp. 431–536. For subsequent information on specific sectors, see: *ARB*, Vol. 2, No. 4 (September 1972), pp. 1180–82 (the securities market); *ARB*, Vol. 2, No. 6 (November 1972), pp. 1330–31 and *OE*, No. 745 (February 1973) (the internationalization of the banks); *OE*, Nos. 745–48 (November 1972–January 1973) (internationalization of the big business and trading companies); in connection with the latter, cf. the series on the reorganization of big industry, *OE*, Nos. 742–45 (August–November 1972). Pressure on Japan to "liberalize" further was a key element in the 1973 Trade Bill put forward by Nixon; as well as giving the President wide discretionary powers to restrict imports into the United States (aimed mainly at Japanese exports), the bill called for the removal of all restrictions on capital movements out of the United States, a measure which was implemented at the end of January 1974 (*Times* [London], January 30, 1974). As well as freeing capital for investment and loans directly to boost U.S. exports to Japan (v. note 130), this was essential both to expand U.S. income from foreign investment (which shows a higher return than domestic investment*) and, structurally, to lock the United States more closely into the other major world economic centres to try to attenuate the dangers of uneven capitalist development. On the Trade Bill, see the Editors, "The Dollar Crisis: What Next?," *Monthly Review*, Vol. 25, No. 1 (May 1973), pp. 10–14.

The linkage of concessions, and the combination of advantages and contradictions involved in these processes is highly complex: for example, the spring 1973 decision to allow U.S. companies to have their stocks quoted on the Tokyo Stock Exchange meant *both* that U.S. companies could raise hitherto untouchable capital for their own enterprises, *and* that Japanese interests could get a stake in U.S. industry using hitherto inconvertible dollars. Another more subterranean example was raised in spring 1973 when the AFL-CIO attacked the U.S. government, alleging that McDonnell Douglas was exporting an entire missile system to Japan as part of a government-to-government deal which involved Japan allowing investment by U.S. multinationals in the Japanese automobile industry (the deal had allegedly been fixed in 1971). U.S. control in the computer sector has been important in levering Japan into concessions in many areas: see Bix, "Japan: The Roots of Militarism," pp. 336–39.

130. The structure of the retail trade has been particularly important in preserving traditional consumption habits and keeping down imports of non-essential imports. At the end of the 1960s nearly half the wholesaling firms and almost 90 per cent of retailing enterprises in Japan had less than *four* employees (Yoshino, "Japan as Host to the International Corporation," pp. 355–56). For details of later events, see John Roberts, "You Still Can't Have It All," *FEER*, November 26, 1973, pp. 50–54—an excellent survey of "liberalization" and U.S. economic interests in Japan. Cf. Fuse, "Japan's Economy in the 70's," pp. 74–75, for the inroads of U.S. commercial interests in Japan: in October 1971, for example, the United States had 65 per cent of the Japanese soft drinks market.

131. The leading Japanese banks are now organized into two giant international consortia, Associated Bank International and Japan International Bank. Cf. Kikuiri, "*Shōsha,*" on the international role of the big trading companies. Kikuiri states that Mitsui has a better communications network worldwide than either the U.S. State Department or the big networks like AP and UPI, being equalled by only (possibly) the CIA (p. 357).

132. According to a Reuters report, "Economic observers believe the current attacks on big business are the most serious since allied occupation forces broke up the giant combines, or 'zaibatsu,' at the end of World War II" (*International Herald Tribune*,

* On this, see Martin Nicolaus, "The Universal Contradiction," *NLR*, No. 59 (January–February 1970); cf. Ernest Mandel, "The Laws of Uneven Development," *ibid.;* Leucate, "La contradiction interimpérialiste aujourd'hui," p. 136.

February 27, 1974); cf. the *Times* (London), February 26, 1974, for attacks on the leaders of the big trading and oil companies. The background to this can be found in Baldwin, "Idioms of Contemporary Japan VI" (entry: "Kaishime"). The fact that the country's leading firms were stockpiling and inflating prices seems beyond dispute, and should not be surprising. What is important is that these activities created a *political* crisis for the LDP, which is obliged to make concessions to try to retain political power. Ultimately these political concessions are necessitated by the *weakness* of Japanese capitalism internationally faced with the commodities boom. On the commodities boom, see the *Economist*, July 7, 1973, pp. 70–71; Angus Hone, "The Primary Commodities Boom," *NLR*, No. 81 (September–October 1973); Pierre Jalée, "La course aux matières premières," *Le Monde Diplomatique*, No. 238 (January 1974).

133. When Finance Minister Fukuda told *Newsweek* that "our target hereafter will be the world average," it is likely he was simply acknowledging international pressures rather than expressing a desire (*Newsweek*, January 21, 1974, p. 48).

134. Auer, *The Postwar Rearmament of Japanese Maritime Forces*, provides an invaluable survey of this for one arm of the forces; excellent material in Dower, "The Eye of the Beholder"; Dower, "The Superdomino"; Bix, "The Security Treaty System." Less satisfactory information is contained in the three English-language books directly on the postwar Japanese military: Weinstein, *Japan's Postwar Defense Policy, 1947–1968*; Axelbank, *Black Star Over Japan*; John K. Emmerson, *Arms, Yen & Power: The Japanese Dilemma* (New York, Dunellen, 1971). Weinstein and Emmerson are conservative, and the former pretty complacent to boot. Axelbank gives a snappy survey of reactionary moves on the domestic front, but is weak on analysis. Further details in Halliday and McCormack, *Japanese Imperialism*, pp. 77–118.

135. Indispensable on this is Kihara, "The Militarisation of the Japanese Economy," especially pp. 32–35; much information throughout Yanaga, *Big Business in Japanese Politics*.

136. This is decisively demonstrated by Bix, "Japan: The Roots of Militarism," pp. 309–13; cf. Halliday and McCormack, *Japanese Imperialism*, pp. 80–84. Jack D. Salmon, "Japan as a Great Power: The Military Context," *JI*, Vol. 7, Nos. 3–4 (Autumn 1972), pp. 396–408, has useful calculations, but the contention (p. 401) that the Fourth Plan is "clearly defense-oriented" jars with the available information.

137. House Committee on Foreign Relations, *Report of Special Study Mission to Asia* (Washington D.C., 1970), cited by Dower, "The Superdomino," p. 132.

138. On nuclear weapons, see Halliday and McCormack, *Japanese Imperialism*, pp. 93–96; Kunio Muraoka, *Japanese Security and the United States* (London, International Institute for Strategic Studies, Adelphi Paper No. 95, February 1973), pp. 23–28, for a useful technical assessment to date. Apart from the outright infraction of the Constitution, and the conspicuous refusal to ratify the Moscow Partial Nuclear Test Ban Treaty (for the wrong reasons), there are many worrying down-to-earth signs. In late 1972 the Defence Agency reversed an announced decision to "denuclearize" a large number of Nike-Hercules rockets purchased from the United States; this meant that, although the rockets were not supplied with the warheads on them, the *fittings* for nuclear warheads were not removed, as it had previously been stated they would be (*ARB*, Vol. 2, No. 10 [March 1973], p. 1630). On May 31, 1972 the Commander of the Maritime SDF (Navy), Kitamura Kenichi, announced that Japan would have nuclear-powered submarines when it was no longer under the protection of the U.S. Navy; Kitamura was promptly disowned by the Chief of Staff of the MSDF, Uchida Kazutomi (*ARB*, Vol. 2, No. 1 [June 1972], p. 940). Bix argues that, while Japan "will, at the least, retain its nuclear options" over both nuclear-powered submarines and nuclear warheads for its missiles, the U.S. "will oppose a major Japanese effort along these lines because its goal has always been to encourage a dependent military growth in Japan"; Bix, "Japan: The Roots of Militarism," p. 311. In January 1974 the Soviet Union proposed an interesting deal to Tokyo: it offered to supply Japan with uranium and to enrich all the ore Japan could use for the next twenty years— and at cheaper prices than U.S. uranium. The quid pro quo was that Japan should ratify the nuclear non-proliferation treaty and conclude an agreement with Moscow on the peaceful uses of atomic energy. This was a deft manoeuvre to weaken

Japan's relations with both Washington and Peking in the wake of the oil crisis (*Newsweek*, February 4, 1974, p. 35).

139. N.a., "Whither Defense Industry?" *OE*, Vol. 41, No. 748 (February 1973), p. 15. For an excellent study, setting the Plan in the general context of remilitarization, see Fujii Haruo, "Offensive Strategy of 'Defensive Defense': Philosophy and Practice of the Neo-Japanese Military," *Ampo*, No. 12 (March 1972). Cf. Bix, "Japan: The Roots of Militarism," pp. 312–319; Dower, "The Superdomino," pp. 135–36; *ARB*, Vol. 2, No. 6 (November 1972), pp. 1304–5, for a survey of the alarming actions by Tanaka and his government to implement the Plan since they took office in July 1972. Very useful statistical details appear in n.a., "The Evolution of Japan's Defense Plans," *JI*, Vol. 8, No. 2 (Spring 1973), pp. 217–18; cf. Shimano Takuji, "Economic Growth and the Rise of Militarism," *JI, ibid.*, pp. 205–13.

140. *OE*, "Whither Defense Industry?"; cf. Bix, "Japan: The Roots of Militarism."

141. Kihara, "The Militarisation of the Japanese Economy," p. 41; Bix, "Japan: The Roots of Militarism."

142. The weakness of the civilian authorities was strikingly shown by the Three Arrows Plan; Halliday and McCormack, *Japanese Imperialism*, pp. 107–18. Industry tends often to negotiate arms production directly with the military, and the Defence Agency is particularly weak on production planning (*OE*, "Whither Defense Industry?," p. 18). The big unknown here is the extent to which the United States will be able to continue to force Japan to buy roughly the present level of its arms from the United States—a major factor in Tokyo-Washington relations.

143. See especially Bix, "Japan: The Roots of Militarism," pp. 313–19.

144. Article 9 of the Japanese Constitution is a flat and unqualified veto on the maintenance of any armed forces whatsoever; the article contains no sophistry about "offensive" or "defensive" rearmament, the grounds on which the regime has "reinterpreted" the Constitution. On September 7, 1973 a district court on Hokkaido produced the first court decision ruling that the Defence Forces were unconstitutional and therefore illegal. The case had been brought by a group of farmers to block construction of a missile site in a local forest. Although the government was expected to win its appeal to the highly conservative Supreme Court, this process could take many years. Meanwhile opposition to recruitment, military bills and so on will be greatly facilitated (*Japan Times*, September 8, 1973; *Newsweek*, September 17, 1973). *U.S. News & World Report* (September 24, 1973) cited a nameless U.S. official saying: "First we felt it was unthinkable that some kooky decision like that could unravel Japan's defense structure. Now we're not so sure . . ." (p. 78). The Tanaka government's "unified" view on "offensive" weapons was put to the Diet by Premier Tanaka who said that he understood "that 'defensive' weapons [in this case a long-range air-to-ground jet fighter] could be used as 'offensive' ones because of recent progress in technology" (*ARB*, Vol. 2, No. 7 [December 1972], p. 1405). The same line emerged over nuclear weapons: on March 20, 1973 Tanaka told the Upper House: "We are not able to have offensive nuclear weapons. But it is not a question of saying we will have no nuclear weapons at all" (*ARB*, Vol. 2, No. 11 [April 1973], p. 1701).

145. On Japan's military role in Asia, see Halliday and McCormack, *Japanese Imperialism*, pp. 97–107; Dower, "The Superdomino," is an excellent study. For the wider context, particularly as regards U.S. imperialism in Asia, see Virginia Brodine and Mark Selden, eds., *Open Secret: The Kissinger-Nixon Doctrine in Asia* (New York and London, Harper & Row, 1972); and Michael T. Klare, *War Without End: American Planning for the Next Vietnams* (New York, Vintage Books, 1972). A top-ranking mission visited Vietnam in September 1966; the mission included the assistant intelligence chiefs of staff of both the GSDF and the ASDF, General Tabata and Colonel Takeda, respectively (*Mainichi Shimbun*, September 22, 1966).

146. Cited by Edward Friedman, answer to questionnaire on "China's New Diplomacy,"* *Problems of Communism*, Vol. 21, No. 1 (January–February 1972), p. 69, from S. Budkevich and M. Raginsky, "The Tokyo Trials, A Reminder," *International Affairs* (Moscow), No. 8, 1971, p. 74. An outstanding political study of this whole issue is the three-part essay entitled "Economic Analysis" in *Ampo*, Nos. 11, 12 and 13–14;

* Friedman explicitly disowns the title and drift of the questionnaire.

see especially Part 2, "Greater East Asian Co-Prosperity Sphere Once Again," *Ampo*, No. 12 (March 1972), pp. 20–22, and Part 3, "One Drop of Oil, One Drop of Blood: Japanese Imperialism & Oil in Asia," *Ampo*, Nos. 13–14 (May–July 1972), pp. 65–66; both these parts are written by Murata Goro. A concise overview, from a conservative standpoint, is to be found in Richard Ellingworth, *Japanese Economic Policies and Security* (London, International Institute for Strategic Studies, Adelphi Paper, No. 90, October 1972); see also Donald C. Hellmann, *Japan and East Asia: The New International Order* (London, Pall Mall Press, 1972), especially chapters 7 and 8.

147. Interview, *U.S. News & World Report*, February 8, 1971, p. 62, cited by Friedman, contribution on "China's New Diplomacy," p. 69.

148. Friedman, contribution on "China's New Diplomacy," p. 69.

149. Only about 5 per cent of U.S. investment overseas is in East and Southeast Asia (including Japan). Asia, however, shows the fastest rate of profit on investment in manufacturing (16.2 per cent in 1971). Profitability on investment as a whole is higher in the Middle East and Africa, largely because of petroleum (*PIN*, Vol. 4, No. 2 [February 1973], p. 29).

150. A subject which deserves fuller treatment is the relative strength of the United States and Japan in East Asia. This involves calculating both exports from the mother country and the sales of foreign subsidiaries (the U.S. foreign subsidiaries being far more numerous and far stronger than Japan's). Hiroshi Kitamura, "Japan's Economic Policy Towards Southeast Asia," *Asian Affairs* (London), Vol. 59, Part I (February 1972) assessed Japan's overall economic influence in Southeast Asia as only about 60 per cent that of the United States as of late 1969. At the beginning of 1974 Paul Gibson, the Chairman of the Asia-Pacific Council of American Chambers of Commerce announced that his members were gearing themselves up to exploiting the oil crisis to mount a major recouping operation against the Japanese. U.S. exports to Southeast Asia were then estimated at about $4.5 billion, with an equal amount going to Japan, while Japan's exports to the area were $5–6 billion. Total Japanese investments in the area, at about $2 billion, as of the end of 1973 were calculated to be about equal to those of the United States in the region as of March 1973 (*FEER*, February 18, 1974, p. 36).

151. On Okinawa, see note 160, p. 402, and the references there; *ARB*, Vol. 2, No. 1 (June 1972), pp. 922–23, for the situation at the time of reversion. The United States kept some 45,000 soldiers in the Ryukyus after reversion, and still had almost 40,000 military personnel there early in 1974, stationed in 77 military installations, of which only 19 were scheduled to be released by 1978 (*International Herald Tribune*, January 31, 1974). Japan gradually increased the number of troops it said it would send to the archipelago from 3,000 to 6,000 and then 9,000: these troops were ostracized by the local population (*Guardian*, May 24, 1973); cf. Fukugi Akira, "Struggle Against Military Sharpens: Murder on Okinawa Reflects Post-Reversion Tensions," *Ampo*, No. 15 (December 1972), pp. 34–41.

152. Much more work is needed on the relationship between the structures of colonialism in East Asia, "decolonization" and imperialism; on what kind of economic changes took place in countries which had been ruled by France (Indochina), Holland (Indonesia), Britain (Malaya, Singapore, etc.), the United States (Philippines) and Japan (Korea, Taiwan); and on comparing the relationship of colonialism, "decolonization" and imperialism in East Asia with the same relationship in Africa and Latin America. Extremely stimulating observations on this concerning Africa can be found in Giovanni Arrighi, "International Corporations, Labor Aristocracies, and Economic Development in Tropical Africa," in Robert I. Rhodes, ed., *Imperialism and Underdevelopment: A Reader* (New York and London, Monthly Review Press, 1970), esp. pp. 224–25.

153. For excellent surveys of Japan in Korea, see *PIN*, Vol. 4, No. 12 (December 1973), pp. 253–61; and Herbert P. Bix, "Regional Integration: Japan and South Korea in America's Asian Policy," in Frank Baldwin, ed. *Without Parallel: The American-Korean Relationship Since 1945* (New York, Pantheon Books, 1974), pp. 179–232.

154. Halliday and McCormack, *Japanese Imperialism*, p. 104, and references there; Nagano

Yoshiko, "Sony and Those Smart Bombs—An Honest Mistake?," *Ampo,* No. 15 (December 1972), pp. 28–33.

155. *No More Hiroshimas!* (Tokyo), Vol. 16, No. 2 (June 1969), p. 13, citing the *Asahi Shimbun,* April 22, 1967. The Indochina war was also used by the United States to keep its Japanese allies up with the latest techniques. It was discovered that Japanese pilots were flying on combat missions in Vietnam as observers when *Life* published a photograph of one on a raid in 1966. The fundamental text on Japan and Indochina is Dower "The Superdomino."

156. This again raises the fundamental question of the *strategy* of imperialism. Not enough attention has been paid to the key role of "consumerization" as a means to demobolize revolution; in this approach the U.S.-Japan tandem is something new in the history of imperialism; contrast, for example, the British operations in Aden ("pure" repression) with the U.S. operation in Vietnam (killing plus consumer goods). Shortly before the Paris agreements were signed, a leading U.S. banker told *Forbes* magazine why his bank, First National City Bank, was setting up a Saigon branch: "Sure, you'll find a lot of bullets flying around, but there's a lot of money floating around too. . . . Thieu may not last, but that's not as important as whether the infrastructure now developing lasts. We are optimistic that, whatever deal Kissinger makes in Paris, the infrastructure will last, and we'll be able to stay in business" (cited in *PIN,* Vol. 3, No. 11 [November, 1972], p. 299). See Martin Murray, "The United States' Continuing Economic Interests in Vietnam," *Socialist Revolution* (San Francisco), Nos. 13 & 14 (January–April 1973), for a very good survey of the field.

157. Asian Development Bank, *Southeast Asia's Economy in the 1970's* (London, Longman's, 1971); on this, cf. Kitamura, "Japan's Economic Policy Towards Southeast Asia"; Kawata Tadashi, "The Asian Situation and Japan's Economic Relations with the Developing Asian Countries," *DE,* Vol. 9, No. 2 (June 1971); Halliday and McCormack, *Japanese Imperialism,* chapter 2. A sophisticated rationalization for maintaining Japan's dominant position is presented by Kiyoshi Kojima, *Japan and a Pacific Free Trade Area* (London, Macmillan & Co., 1971), especially chapter 2 ("An Approach to Integration: The Gains from Agreed Specialization"); cf. Kiyoshi Kojima, "Reorganisation of North-South Trade: Japan's Foreign Economic Policy for the 1970s," *HJE,* Vol. 13, No. 2 (February 1973). On the more general issues, see Arghiri Emmanuel's stimulating work, *Unequal Exchange: A Study of the Imperialism of Trade* (London, NLB, 1972).

The Asian Development Bank itself may well play a crucial role in bringing this about. The bank has pursued a lending policy designed primarily to assist Japanese and U.S. capital. Less than 13 per cent of its funds have gone to agriculture and less than 1 per cent to education (Peter Hadji-Ristic, "Development Bank to Switch Emphasis to Help Region's Poorest Nations," *Times* [London], February 25, 1974, Banking in Asia Supplement, p. 10).

158. Bix, "Japan: The Roots of Militarism," p. 308. Interesting observations on Japan and Korea in Morton Abramowitz, *Moving the Glacier: The Two Koreas and the Powers* (London, International Institute for Strategic Studies, Adelphi Paper, No. 80, August 1971). Abramowitz, an official of the U.S. State Department, considers that what he calls "the Japanese option," meaning Japanese military substitution for the United States in Korea, "is a real prospect in the second half of the decade [the 1970s]" (p. 20). On Pohang, cf. the *Guardian,* July 4, 1973; Hasegawa, "Pak Chung Hee Vs. the People," *Ampo,* No. 19. By the middle of 1973 Japanese investments (on an approval basis) accounted for $305 million, or 60 per cent of the $513 million total for all foreign investment in southern Korea—a complete turnaround from merely two years earlier when Japan accounted for only 29 per cent, and the United States had 60 per cent of the total (*PIN,* Vol. 4, No. 12 [December 1973], p. 253).

159. These economic projects must be seen in their political context, the key objective being to stabilize right-wing regimes; although new economic contradictions are set up by the process, it does also help to sustain, at least in the short term, types of satellite economies. The deleterious effects of this kind of "growth" seem beyond dispute to all but the Hudson Institute (for Korea's case, see Wideman, "The Plight of the South Korean Peasant"). Moreover, Japan's "reparations" and "aid" policies

have been instrumental in setting up wobbly bicycle-type economies in Southeast Asia, dependent on loans, with high debt-servicing responsibilities. Moreover, economies like that of South Korea which are heavily dependent on petroleum imports for their petrochemical and fertilizer sectors stand to be very hard hit by the increase in oil prices, and this is true of much of the area, which is bound to affect Japan's economic position. South Korea's 1974 oil bill is estimated to hit $1,075 million—nearly as much as India's, and more than twice the total for Pakistan, Bangladesh, Argentina and Ghana together (*Times* [London], January 30, 1974). There appears to have been little application to Southeast Asia of recent theoretical work on the question of peripheric capitalism. Those who wish to pursue this can consult Samir Amin, *Le développement inégal: Essai sur les formations sociales du capitalisme périphérique* (Paris, Editions du Minuit, 1973); Christian Palloix, *L'économie mondiale capitaliste*, Vol. 2: *Le stade monopoliste et l'impérialisme* (Paris, François Maspero, 1971); *Tiers Monde* (Paris), Vol. 13, No. 52 (October–December 1972), special issue on "Le capitalisme périphérique."

160. In calendar 1973 Japan's reserves, virtually none of which are in gold (see note 127) fell $6.2 billion from $18 billion to nearly $12 billion. Japan also has an emergency additional reserve of $10 billion in U.S. Treasury bills and deposited with Japanese foreign exchange banks, but it could be difficult to mobilize the sums held in U.S. Treasury bills.

161. This is the opinion of Sebestyen, *The Outward Urge*, pp. 52–53. For details on this see Appendix V. Preliminary MITI calculations gave the increase in Japan's oil bill for 1974 (over 1973) as $7 billion, giving a total 1974 oil bill of $15 billion. The government estimated that Japan would also have to pay $11.3 billion for imports of agricultural, forestry and marine products in fiscal 1974 (an increase of 68 per cent over the previous year). The annual deficit in invisible trade (shipping, insurance) is about £1.2 billion. Long-term capital outflow in 1973 was about £3.3 billion, which the government hoped to bring down to about £1.85 billion in 1974 by cutting down hard on overseas investment, except in essential raw materials. See the *Times* (London), January 8, 1974; the *Observer*, March 3, 1974.

162. *Newsweek*, July 9, 1973, p. 50 (Cam Ranh was a major Japanese base to 1945 and much of the expansion there in the 1960s was carried out by Japanese construction firms). On the general area, see Banning Garrett, "Post-War Planning for South Vietnam," *Pacific Research and World Empire Telegram*, Vol. 3, No. 5 (July–August 1972); cf. Murray, "The United States' Continuing Economic Interests in Vietnam," esp. pp. 46–55, on Japan and Vietnam—on which see also *PIN*, Vol. 3, No. 7 and No. 11 (July and November 1972) and Vol. 4, No. 6 (June 1973); n.a., "Japanese Investments in South Vietnam," *Ampo*, No. 15 (December 1972); Kaji Etsuko, "Vietnam 'Rehabilitation' Boom Hits Japan," *Ampo*, No. 16 (March, 1973), which details Japan's gains from war procurement and future "aid" projects. One man who played a key role in Japan's economic policy towards Vietnam during the American war on Indochina was Senga Tetsuya, long-time head of the Keidanren's Defence Production Committee. Another was Sejima Ryūzō, former lecturer on military affairs to the Emperor and military expert, now heading a special planning unit in the giant trading company, C. Itoh (Kikuiri, *"Shōsha,"* p. 368).

163. *PIN*, Vol. 3, No. 8 (August 1972), pp. 236–37; information below from same.

164. These are: Iturup (Japanese: Etorofu), Kunashir (Japanese: Kunashiri), Shikotan and the Habomai archipelago off the north of Hokkaido.

165. In early 1974, in the wake of Tanaka's disastrous Southeast Asian tour and as the contradictions in Japan's fence-straddling position between Peking and Taipei became more acute, the right wing of the LDP staged a major attack on the Tanaka-Ōhira foreign policy line. This attack was led by the Seirankai (Young Storm Association), a new grouping of young LDP politicians with close links with Kishi, the gangster-"patriotic" sector, and the Pak and Chiang regimes. See *FEER*, February 25, 1974, pp. 20–24; *Peking Review*, No. 6 (February 8), 1974, pp. 18, 20.

166. Brzezinski, *The Fragile Blossom*, p. 138 (where Brzezinski supports the consolidation of the triangle and urges U.S. backing for it).

167. Peter Wiley, "Vietnam and the Pacific Rim Strategy," *Leviathan* (New York and San

Francisco), Vol. 1, No. 3 (June 1969), was a pioneering study on the "Pacific Rim" policy.

168. More than anyone else in recent years Malcolm Caldwell has insisted on this essential dimension to industrial growth in the advanced capitalist countries—that it is *absolutely* incompatible with the interests of the poorer nations. See, for example, Malcolm Caldwell, "Oil and Imperialism in East Asia," *JCA,* Vol. 1, No. 3 (1971) (now available in revised form as "Oil Imperialism in Southeast Asia" in Selden, ed., *Remaking Asia*), esp. p. 31. It is not a question of singling Japan out for special criticism. The principle is applicable to all the advanced capitalist countries.

Glossary

This glossary provides brief information on names and terms which occur, usually several times, in the text. Most of the entries are more fully explained, in context, at the point where they are first mentioned: this point can be found by looking up the first page given for each item in the index.

Abe Masahirō (1819–57) Daimyō (q.v.) of Fukuyama in Bingo. A member of the shogun's (q.v.) council in 1843, he was *de facto* president of this council and thus in effect "Prime Minister" until his death.

Aikoku Kōtō Public Society of Patriots: the first political association in Meiji (q.v.) Japan, formed 1873.

Ainu Literally, "People" (in Ainu). Now numbering some 50,000, this people were the original, pre-Japanese, occupants of the island of Hokkaido.

Bakufu Literally, "tent government": originally applied to army headquarters in the feudal period and then to the military dictatorship under the Tokugawa (q.v.); means the shogunal (q.v.) government.

Beheiren Abbreviation for "Betonamu ni Heiwa o!" Shimin Rengō (Citizens Alliance for "Peace in Vietnam!"), the main Japanese organization struggling against U.S. aggression in Vietnam and later Indochina.

Burakumin Literally, "village (or hamlet) people." An outcaste group of ethnic Japanese, probably numbering about 3 million (although the government refuses to issue a figure). Concentrated mainly in rural areas round Osaka and in northern Kyushu, this group, though formally enjoying equality, is in fact subjected to severe discrimination. The *burakumin* are still sometimes referred to by the insulting term *Eta* (literally, "full of filth").

Bushi A man of war able to give proof of noble descent.

Bushidō The "way" of the warrior.

Chang Tso-lin Warlord of Manchuria, assassinated by Japanese in 1928.

Charter Oath Document issued in April 1868 in the name of the Emperor Meiji (q.v.); drawn up by lower samurai (q.v.) from the western *han* (q.v.).

Chō Unit of measurement equal to 2.45 acres.

Chokunin Highest rank of official in the Civil Service.

Chōnin Literally, townsmen: generally used to describe merchants and, sometimes, anyone practising trade.

Chōshū The first fief to stand up to the Bakufu (q.v.); situated at the extreme west of the island of Honshu. Continued to dominate the army until well into the twentieth century.

Chūritsurōren National Liaison Council of Independent Unions: a trade union liaison council, roughly equivalent to a federation; had 1,350,000 members in mid-1971.

Cominform Short-lived post–World War II organization of limited number of main European Communist Parties, founded 1947.

Comintern Abbreviation for the Communist International (Third International) (1919–43).

Daimyō Great lord, with a fief of 10,000 *koku* (q.v.) or more; there were 266 daimyō immediately before the Meiji Restoration (q.v.) of 1868.

Densan wage system Wage system named after the Council of Electric Power Industry Workers' Unions, which on November 30, 1946, reached a settlement embodying a new kind of seniority wage system based (roughly) on the cost of living rather than work done.

Deshima Island at the head of Nagasaki Bay where Dutch merchants, the only Europeans in Japan for most of the Tokugawa period, were allowed to reside.

Dōmei The main right-wing union federation, with 2,172,000 members as of mid-1971.

Edo The name of Tokyo prior to 1868.

Emperor See *Tennō*.

Extraterritoriality See *Unequal Treaties*.

Ezo Earlier name for Hokkaido, the most northerly of the four main islands.

Fudai Daimyō (q.v.) who were hereditary vassals of the Tokugawa (q.v.).

"Fukoku kyōhei" "Rich country—strong army" or "Enrich the country, strengthen the army": an early Meiji slogan.

Fukuzawa Yukichi (1834–1901) Leader of the Meiji "enlightenment," author and thinker; also supported early Japanese imperialism.

Genrō Extraconstitutional group of elder statesmen wielding great power.

Han Originally meant "military frontier." Refers to a territorial division, not to a group related by blood; thus, "fief" is better translation than "clan."

Hansen Seinen Iinkai Anti-War Youth Committee (AWYC): militant working class organization set up in mid-1960s.

Hara Kei (Takashi) Seiyūkai (q.v.) Prime Minister 1918–21; far-sighted conservative who played key role in fusing the party system and the bureaucracy. Assassinated 1921.

Hibiya Riots Demonstrations which started out in Hibiya Park, Tokyo, in September 1905 to oppose from the right the settlement reached with Russia at Portsmouth after the Russo-Japanese War; after police riots against the demonstrators, turned into anti-regime riot, leading to martial law.

Hinin Literally, "non-people": ethnic Japanese located below and outside the formal class system under feudalism.

Hirohito See *Tennō*.

Ie House, dwelling, or family as an entity extending through past, present and future (cf. the House of Orange). The character for *ie* is the same as that for the syllable *ka* in *kazoku,* as in *kazoku shugi* (family-ism), *kazoku kokka.*

Imperial Rule Assistance Association (*Taisei Yokusan Kai*) Umbrella political organization founded October 1940 after the dissolution of all political parties in the Diet. Organized from the top, it proved largely ineffective, even though it was joined by most former party leaders of the centre and right.

Itagaki Taisuke (1837–1919) Tosa (q.v.) official, leader of movement for war against the Bakufu (q.v.) in 1867–68. Left the government in 1873 and organized the first attempt at a political alternative to the existing group —the *jiyū minken undō,* or popular rights movement.

Itō Hirobumi (1841–1909) Chōshū official who became the mastermind behind the new Meiji political system. Assassinated by a Korean patriot, 1909.

Iwakura Tomomi (1828–83) Middle-rank Kyoto civil noble who played key role in the coup of January 3, 1868. Chiefly famous because he led an important delegation of government figures to the United States and Europe 1871–73—the Iwakura Embassy or Mission.

Jiyū minken undō See *Itagaki Taisuke.*

Jiyūtō Literally, Liberty Party; usually known as the Liberal Party.

Katayama Sen Christian who became a leader of the moderate left advocating parliamentarism. Left Japan in 1914 and later settled in Moscow, where he died in 1933.

Katsura Tarō Chōshū military figure, protégé of Yamagata (q.v.); military attaché in Berlin; rose to become a general and three times premier between 1901 and 1913. Died 1913. Extremely conservative.

Kazoku shugi See *Ie.*

Keidanren Abbreviation for Keizai Dantai Rengōkai, Federation of Economic Associations: the largest big-business organization.

Keisatsu Yobitai National Police Reserve (i.e., Army), set up mid-1950, with a strength of 75,000.

Keizai Doyūkai (Japan) Committee for Economic Development (JCED): business organization set up after the end of World War II. Unlike Keidanren (q.v.), it includes small and medium businessmen.

Kempeitai Gendarmerie: military police who came to take on many of the functions of a (civilian) secret police.

Kenseitō Literally, Constitutional Party. Formed 1898 through a merger of the Jiyūtō (q.v.) and the Shimpotō (q.v.).

Kido Kōin (*Takayoshi*) (1833–77) Chōshū official who negotiated the Chōshū-Satsuma (qq.vv.) alliance in March 1866, which was the basis for the overthrow of the Bakufu (q.v.). Travelled on Iwakura Mission (q.v.) 1871–73. Very able government leader until sudden death in 1877.

Kidōtai Riot Police (contemporary).

Kishi Nobusuke (*Shunsuke*) (1896–   ) In charge of the economy of Manchuria 1936–39; Minister of Commerce in the Tōjō (q.v.) Cabinet of October 1941; 1943–44, in charge of munitions and the arms industry (the rough equivalent of Speer in Germany); served three years as Class A war criminal 1945–48; LDP (q.v.) Prime Minister 1957–60. Still powerful.

Kita Ikki (1884–1937) Radical right-wing nationalist who exercised enormous influence in 1920s and 1930s. Author of *An Outline Plan for the Reorganization of Japan*. Executed 1937 in the wake of the February [26, 1936] Incident.

Kōenkai Support group for individual members of the Diet (Parliament), working for one person rather than party as a whole.

Kōgai Literally, public hazard or public nuisance. Usually translated as "environmental pollution," but refers to things not covered in English by this term—e.g., factory noise, traffic congestion, obstruction of sunlight, water shortage, vibration, etc.

Koku Unit of measurement, equivalent to about 180 litres; in terms of weight, one *koku* of rice equals about 150 kilograms.

Kokutai National polity, or national entity, a vague and controversial concept used to "define" what was allegedly the unique essence of Japan and the Japanese state.

Kōmeitō Clean Government Party, formed in 1964 by the Sōka Gakkai (q.v.) or Value Creation Society, a militant populist Buddhist group. The Kōmeitō is a vigorous but demagogic organization lying roughly in the centre of the Japanese political spectrum.

Konoe (or *Konoye*) *Fumimaro* (1891–1945) Prince from one of the most famous aristocratic families who was three times premier in the years 1937–41. A weak and conservative man, he committed suicide by poison in 1945 when about to be arrested as a war-crimes suspect.

Kosaku Small dependent peasant-farmers paying rent in kind (rice) to the *jinushi* or large landowners.

Kōtoku Denjirō (pen name *Shūsui*) (1871–1911) Leading left-wing figure before World War I and vigorous opponent of sham parliamentarism. Executed 1911 after a famous show trial (the 1910–11 High Treason Trial) on charges of planning to kill the Emperor.

Kōza Literally, Studies, or Lectures: the name given to one of the two main groups of Japanese Marxists from the title of the group's first key publication, *Nihon Shihonshugi Hattatshushi Kōza* (*Studies in* [or *Lectures on*] *the Historical Development of Capitalism in Japan*), 1932. The work of this group and of the main opposing Marxist group, the Rōnō group (q.v.), continues to influence Japanese Marxism today.

Kwantung Army Japanese army stationed in Manchuria which became a virtually autonomous military force ruling the puppet state of Manchukuo (q.v.). The army was named after the Kwantung area of northeast China, the area which includes the Liaotung Peninsula, on which lay both Port Arthur and Dairen. The army is mistakenly referred to in many English-language works as the Kwangtung Army (Kwangtung being the province in south China in which Canton [Kwangchow] lies).

Liberal Democratic Party (*LDP*) The main conservative organization in contemporary Japan. Formed in 1955 through a merger of the two main right-wing parties, the Liberal and Democratic parties. Though having the support of only a minority of the electorate, the LDP has governed uninterruptedly and alone since its formation. The LDP has a negligible party base, and exists largely thanks to enormous subsidies from big business.

Liberal Party See *Jiyūtō*.

Life employment system A misnomer often applied to the whole of Japanese industry. While some employers do give certain guarantees to their employees in return for commitments, a life-time guarantee or anything like it is virtually nonexistent.

Manchukuo Name of the Japanese puppet state set up in Manchuria in the 1930s.

Manchurian Incident Mystificatory appellation for the definitive take-over of Manchuria by Japanese troops in 1931.

"Mankan-Kokan" Literally, "Exchange Manchuria and Korea." Refers to the terms of a deal which Japan put to Russia before the Russo-Japanese War (1904–5), under which Japan asked Russia to recognize that Korea was Japan's preserve in return for Japan's agreeing to recognize Manchuria as Russia's preserve.

Marco Polo Bridge Incident Incident on the night of July 7, 1937, at Lukou Ch'iao on the Peking-Tientsin railway, when Chinese forces allegedly fired on Japanese troops.

Matsukata Masayoshi (1835–1924) Meiji statesman, and the key figure in determining economic policy in the 1880s especially.

Meiji On October 23, 1868, shortly after the sixteen-year-old Emperor (Mutsuhito) ascended the throne, it was decided that the name of Meiji (Enlightenment) would apply to all the years of this Emperor's reign and that the Emperor would bear this name after his death. The man now known as the Emperor Meiji reigned from 1867/8 to 1912. The Meiji era covers the years 1868–1912.

Mindō Abbreviation for *minshuka dōmei* ("democratization" or "democratic leagues"): anti-communist units formed within the left-wing unions from 1946 onwards with backing from the government and from SCAP (q.v.).

Minseitō One of the two main prewar conservative political parties, founded 1927 as the successor to the Kenseikai. Dissolved 1940. After 1945 many of its members joined the new Shimpotō (q.v.).

Minshutō Democratic Party: a conservative party which existed for a short period in the late 1940s, ultimately becoming part of the Liberal Democratic Party (q.v.).

MITI Ministry of International Trade and Industry, the key ministry coordinating economic policy in postwar Japan.

Mukden Incident Incident staged by the Japanese army on the night of September 18–19, 1931, at Mukden (now Shenyang) in Manchuria to provide an excuse for taking over Manchuria definitively.

Nenkō joretsu seido Age and length of service-based wage system.

Nikkeiren Abbreviation for Nihon Keieisha Danta Remmei (Japan Federation of Employers' Associations, or JFEA): the most reactionary of the main employers' federations; has led the shop-floor struggle against the working class in the postwar period.

Nikkyōso Abbreviation for Nihon Kyōshokuin Kumiai (Japan Teachers' Union, or JTU). Founded 1947; at its peak included more than 90 per cent of all primary and junior high school teachers. Initially adopted militant left-wing positions and played crucial role in liberating young Japanese in the early postwar period. Later, under heavy assault from the government, lost ground and moderated its policies.

Nōhon-shugi Literally, "agriculture-is-the-base-ism": an allegedly agrarian trend which was in fact largely exploited by urban interests and the regime in the pre-1945 period to keep everyone in his or her place.

Ōkubo Toshimichi (1830–78) Satsuma (q.v.) official who played an important role in preparing war against the Bakufu (q.v.) and in the early Meiji regime. Travelled abroad with Iwakura (q.v.) 1871–73; the key figure in opting for consolidation at home in the 1873 debates, and the main author of the centralization of power. Assassinated 1878 after having Satsuma occupied by the Imperial Army after the Satsuma Rebellion.

Ōkuma Shigenobu (1838–1922) Member of the early Meiji government who left it with Saigō (q.v.) and Itagaki (q.v.) in 1873. Keen supporter of parliamentarism. Prime Minister in 1898 and again 1914–16. Founded Waseda University.

Opium Wars The First Opium War (1840–42): Britain attacks China in order to force China to allow British merchants to sell opium in China. Second Opium War (1857–60): joint Anglo-French invasion of China, with Russian and U.S. support. (In some sources, the 1857 fighting is referred to as the Second Opium War, and the 1858–60 hostilities as the Third Opium War.)

Paid-up capital The value of a firm can be assessed in many ways, the most accurate being according to net worth (total assets minus long-term liabilities). Paid-up capital is the amount of money a firm has taken in through selling shares plus issuing bonus shares fully paid and ranking *pari passu* with existing shares. This is usually less than the authorized capital, and much less than the net worth, particularly in Japan, where shares play a relatively small role. The post-1945 assessments of the zaibatsu (q.v.) were thus based on an inaccurate criterion.

"Paternalism" A term often used by apologists for Japanese capitalism to refer to the specific system of exploitation prevailing in Japan.

Portsmouth Agreement Treaty between Japan and Russia signed at Portsmouth, N.H., in 1905 under the auspices of Theodore Roosevelt, settling the Russo-Japanese War of 1904–5. Cf. *Hibiya Riots.*

Profintern Abbreviation for International of Red Trade Unions.

"Red Purge" A purge which threw hundreds of thousands of workers out of their jobs, decimated the media and crippled the top echelons of the Communist Party in the years 1949–50. Contrary to information in many Western sources, the purge started well before the outbreak of the Korean War.

"Reverse Course" A term applied to the alleged shift in U.S. policy towards the Japanese left and right in the mid-to-late 1940s. In fact, the United States was never pro-left, and the so-called reverse course was simply an alteration of emphasis *within* a strategy. Repression of the left began in 1946—long before the "reverse course" is usually acknowledged or claimed to have started.

Rice Riots Riots which swept Japan in the summer of 1918, with some 10 million people taking part in uprisings at 636 points throughout the country. The riots, which started as protests against the high price of rice, soon spread to rice-producing areas and to the big cities. The movement was only put down after 107 interventions by the army.

Rikken Kaishintō Constitutional Progressive Party, founded 1882 under the leadership of Ōkuma (q.v.). Essentially a vehicle for big landlords, with backing from Mitsubishi. On the whole more conservative than the Jiyūtō (q.v.).

Rōnin Usually means masterless samurai (q.v.), but can also mean *bushi* (q.v.) without fiefs or simply out of favour with their lord. In later usage, means students who have failed once or more times to get into university but are still trying (i.e., having already left school).

Rōnō Abbreviation for *Labour-Farmer,* the name of the theoretical magazine of one of the two main Marxist schools in prewar Japan, started by Yamakawa Hitoshi. See also *Kōza.*

Ryukyu Islands Chain of islands, of which the largest is Okinawa, stretching between the south of Kyushu and Taiwan. Occupied by the United States in 1945 and formally restored to Japan in 1972.

Saigō Takamori (1827–77) Satsuma (q.v.) official, one of the authors of alliance with Chōshū (q.v.) in 1866 and organizer of war against the Bakufu (q.v.). The most popular figure in the new government, Saigō fell out with the dominant group over Korea in 1873. Saigō withdrew to Satsuma and in 1877 headed the Satsuma Rebellion against the central government. When defeated, he committed suicide.

Saionji, Prince Kimmochi (1849–1940) The last of the *genrō* (q.v.). A member of the court nobility (*kuge*); twice premier (1906–8 and 1911–12) heading Seiyūkai (q.v.) cabinets. An able conciliator, who affected liberal stances.

Sakamoto Ryōma (1836–67) Official from minor *han* of Tosa (q.v.); son of a sake manufacturer. Played a key role as intermediary in organizing the Satsuma-Chōshū alliance of 1866, which was the prerequisite to toppling the Bakufu. Working on organizing a new regime when assassinated in December 1867.

Sampō (or *Sanpō*) Abbreviation for Sangyō Hōkokukai, Industrial Patriotic Society (or Association): technically, the wartime organization sponsored by the state to promote industry's service to the state; in effect functioned as puppet union federation. Dissolved 1945, but had important effects on postwar unions.

Samurai A term which includes both what are called knights and what are called soldiers in European feudal societies. In other words, all the male aristocracy in feudal Japan below the daimyō (q.v.). Within the samurai themselves there were many internal differentiations.

Sanbetsu (or *Sambetsu*) *Kaigi* Abbreviation for Zenkoku Sangyō-betsu Kumiai Kaigi (National Congress of Industrial Unions): the main left-wing union federation in the early postwar years, with 1.5 million members. Systematically destroyed by right-wing Japanese and U.S. machinations in the late 1940s.

Sanken Abbreviation for Sangyō Mondai Kenkyūkai (Council on Industrial Policy, or Industrial Problems Study Council): a new body set up in

1966 with tightly restricted membership of key top business leaders. The central core of big business.

Sankin kōtai Literally, "alternate attendance": the institutionalized hostage system developed by the Tokugawa (q.v.) to maintain internal control. Under this system all daimyō (q.v.) had to leave their wives and children permanently in the capital, and themselves attend the shogun's (q.v.) court there on alternate years.

Satō Eisaku (1901–) LDP Prime Minister 1964–72. Younger brother of Kishi Nobusuke (q.v.). After starting out as a railways bureaucrat, he rose swiftly to prominence as an aide to postwar premier Yoshida Shigeru (q.v.). Narrowly escaped arrest for bribery after personal intervention of Yoshida. Humourless and reactionary. Wife-beater.

Satsuma Fief in the southern part of Kyushu, the southernmost of the four main islands of Japan. 770,000 *koku* (q.v.). Along with Chōshū (q.v.) played key role in overthrowing the Bakufu (q.v.). Had an unusually high number of samurai (q.v.), who accounted for over one-quarter of the population. Staged the last major revolt against the new Meiji regime in 1877. Provided many of the leaders of the Japanese navy.

SCAP Initials for Supreme Commander for the Allied Powers, the formal title of the head of the Occupation (General Douglas MacArthur for most of the period). The initials now are used to refer to the Occupation regime as a whole.

"Seikan Ron" Literally, "the argument [*Ron*] over whether Japan should inflict righteous punishment [for the insult] by conquering Korea [*Seikan*]": term used for the debate in Japan about whether to invade Korea in 1873 —the debate which split the new ruling group in half, causing Saigō, Itagaki and others to leave the government.

Seiyūkai One of the two main political parties prior to World War II. Founded in 1900 by Itō Hirobumi (q.v.), and largely backed by Mitsui. Full title was Rikken Seiyūkai (literally, Constitutional Political Fraternal Association).

Shi A category of samurai (q.v.) roughly equivalent to the European knight, but with multiple internal differentiations.

Shimonoseki, Treaty of Treaty signed in 1895 between Japan and China after the Sino-Japanese War of 1894–95. Under it Japan acquired Taiwan and the strategic Liaotung Peninsula, plus an indemnity of some ¥360 million. Shimonoseki is a port on the western tip of Honshu, the main island of Japan.

Shimpotō Name of two conservative political parties: one existed from 1896 to 1898, when it merged with the Jiyūtō into the Kenseitō (qq.vv.); the other, the Nippon Shimpotō (1945–47), ultimately became part of the Liberal Democratic Party (q.v.).

Shinkō zaibatsu See *Zaibatsu.*

Shinzensō New National Comprehensive Development Programme; formulated in 1969 as revised version of earlier National Programme (Zensō). Allegedly a plan to decentralize industry and improve transportation and social services, it is in fact more like a plan to spread pollution more widely and turn more agricultural land into building sites. The 1969

Programme was further modified to fit in with Premier Tanaka Kakuei's (q.v.) "remodelling the archipelago" scheme.

Shōgun Short for *sei-i tai shōgun* (literally, "barbarian-subduing generalissimo" or "commander-in-chief against the barbarians"). In theory the office of shogun was that of the Emperor's military deputy, but in fact, as exercised by the Tokugawa (q.v.), it gave the holder virtually total political autonomy. The term "shogunate" refers to the Tokugawa government.

Shōsha (or *sōgō shōsha*) Giant general trading companies which dominate Japan's import and export business and play a major role in insurance, storage, transportation and banking.

Shōwa The name chosen for his reign by the current Emperor (Hirohito), who ascended the throne in 1926. This name, meaning "Peace Made Manifest," is used to date the years of the reign and is also to be applied to the Emperor after his death. The name by which he is known in the West, Hirohito, is his personal name, which is not used in Japan.

Shuntō The "base up" system enshrined in the unions' annual Spring Offensive. Under this system developed from the mid-1950s, the more left-wing unions co-ordinate a national struggle in springtime, with the most powerful union "going first" to try to force a maximally favourable settlement which can then be generalized to other weaker unions.

Shūshin Morals or ethics of a highly reactionary slant embodying hierarchical and repressive ideas. Banned by SCAP (q.v.) from schools in 1945, "ethics" courses were re-inserted into the curriculum after the end of the Occupation.

Sōdōmei Japan General Federation of Labour. The main union federation in prewar Japan; it adopted a cautious and anti-communist line and dissolved itself into Sampō (q.v.) at the end of the 1930s.

Sōhyō Abbreviation for Nihon Rōdō Kumiai Sōhyōgikai (General Council of Japanese Trade Unions). Founded July 1950 as an anti-communist federation, Sōhyō swung left during the Korean War, but has remained essentially a left social democratic body though being the most left-wing of the main union federations, and still the largest such organization in Japan, with 4.25 million members as of mid-1971.

Sōka Gakkai Value Creation Society: populist Buddhist organization which flourished in the postwar period on an anti-corruption "little man" platform. In 1964 founded the Kōmeitō (q.v.).

"Sonnō jōi" "Revere the Emperor and expel the barbarian": one of the key slogans of the anti-Tokugawa activists in the pre-Restoration period. It both galvanized opposition to the shogunate's policy vis-à-vis the Western imperialists, and put forward the alternative of restoring the Emperor.

South Manchuria(n) Railway Co. An allegedly civilian organization, modelled on the old East India Company, which played a leading role in Japanese control of Manchuria. Set up on the army's initiative, it remained under military hegemony in spite of its civilian façade.

Taishō The posthumous name of the Emperor who reigned from 1912 to 1926 (unspoken personal name: Yoshihito), and the name given to the years of his reign. The phrase "Taishō Democracy" is often used to designate the later years of this Emperor's reign, but this is an ideological usage, designed to try to substantiate the impossible claim that there was such a thing as bourgeois democracy in prewar Japan.

Takebashi (or *Takehashi*) *Uprising* Mutiny by the Imperial Guards in 1878 which led to 53 soldiers being executed by firing squad.

Tanaka Giichi, Baron General (1863–1929) After two stretches as War Minister (1918–21, 1923–24), Prime Minister in the years 1925–27. Militarist and important force behind plans for aggression against China.

Tanaka Kakuei (1918–   ) LDP Prime Minister 1972–74. Brash self-made man who became a millionaire in property speculation and construction during the war. Imprisoned when Vice-Minister of Justice, not long after entering politics. Built up position as Secretary General of LDP and Minister of International Trade and Industry. Youngest postwar premier.

Tempō period (1830–43). It was during this period that the great famine known as the Tempō Famine (1841–43) occurred, which was one of the events triggering the anti-Bakufu upheavals.

Tennō The Japanese term for Emperor, and the term by which a current Emperor is usually referred to—the present Emperor, for example, never being referred to as Hirohito, and Shōwa being retained for use after his death. The term *tennō-sei* (Emperor-system) refers to the particular Japanese hierarchical state system, where the Emperor is ultimately irresponsible, and democratic methods for bringing about change thus easily disqualified.

Terauchi Hisaichi, General (later *Marshal* and *Count*) (1879–1946) War Minister March 1936–February 1937; leading militarist. Supreme Commander of the Southern Army during the Pacific War.

Terauchi Masatake, General (1852–1919) Premier October 1916–September 1918. Chōshū man promoted by military as replacement for Katsura (q.v.).

Tōjō Hideki, General (1884–1948). Graduate of the Military Staff College; Chief of Staff of the Kwantung Army (q.v.) in 1937. After a period as War Minister became Prime Minister shortly before the start of the Pacific War and, concurrently, War Minister until 1944, when he resigned after the fall of Saipan. Never the absolute dictator depicted in the West. Hanged 1948.

Tokugawa Daimyō family in what is now the plain of Tokyo. Became the greatest daimyō in 1600, and in 1603 the founder of the dynasty, Ieyasu, was appointed shogun (q.v.). Thereafter until the Meiji Restoration the Tokugawa had a monopoly on the post of shogun (q.v.). The family ruled Japan directly or indirectly for the two-and-a-half centuries prior to the Restoration.

Tosa Minor fief in the south of Shikoku Island which played important intermediary role in the anti-Bakufu (q.v.) movement, especially from 1866 onwards.

Tōsuiken Doctrine of the independence of the supreme command, or prerogative of supreme command. Article 11 of the Meiji Constitution placed control of the armed forces directly in the hands of the Emperor. The military and the Emperor manipulated the prerogative of supreme command both to keep military decisions away from civilian cabinets and to increase the army's control over the affairs of state.

Tozama Literally, "outside": the term used to describe the daimyō (q.v.) who were not members of the Tokugawa family or part of the inner core under close Tokugawa control. The *tozama daimyō* were mainly in northern and western Honshu, Shikoku and Kyushu.

Triple Intervention, or *Triplice* Joint intervention by Russia, Germany and France five days after the signing of the Treaty of Shimonoseki (q.v.) in 1895. The three European powers wanted to weaken Japan after Tokyo's victory over China in the Sino-Japanese War, and the Intervention forced Japan to abandon the Liaotung Peninsula; it also directly strengthened the positions of the three European powers in China.

Tsinan Incident On May 3, 1928, Japanese officers, against the advice of the government in Tokyo, instigated their troops to attack Chiang Kai-shek's army when it entered the city of Tsinan on the Shantung Peninsula.

Twenty-one Demands Group of demands which Japan imposed on China in 1915 to give Japan a dominant position in China; they included exclusive privileges in Shantung, extension of Japan's leases in Manchuria, increased mining and railway rights.

Unequal Treaties Series of "treaties" imposed on Japan by the Western powers in the mid-nineteenth century when the balance of forces was unequal, to Japan's disadvantage. Deprived Japan of control over numerous aspects of its international trade and gave the Western imperialists juridical privileges in Japan. Japan recovered its juridical autonomy only in the 1899 revised treaties, and tariff autonomy in 1911. "Extraterritoriality" is the favoured term in the West to disguise the essence of the operation, which is illegal intervention and infringement of another country's autonomy.

Washington Conference Meeting of the United States, Britain, France and Japan in Washington, 1921–22, to rearrange spheres of influence in East Asia after World War I. Concerted attempt to reorder and co-ordinate inter-imperialist alliance against the peoples of Asia.

Yamagata Aritomo, Marshal (1838–1922) Perhaps the most important single figure in the construction of Meiji Japan. After taking part in the anti-Bakufu movement, he became the key military figure in the new government, establishing Chōshū, whence he came, solidly in charge of the army. Led the then revolutionary campaign to introduce conscription (1872). Later played the leading role in building up the local government system. Twice premier (1889–91, 1898–1900), preferred to exercise power through frontmen. Traditionalist and extremely shrewd. Pen name: "Pure Madness."

Yi Ho Tuan (*I-ho T'uan*) The Band of Right and Harmony: peasant secret society which staged a major uprising (sometimes called "the Boxer Rebellion") in north China in the years 1897–1900. This originally exploded against the Germans in Shantung in 1897, and in 1900 the uprising took Peking and laid siege to the foreign legations—an act which was then seized on as a pretext for the collective intervention by the imperialist powers. Though peasant-based the uprising was directed primarily against foreign encroachment and missions.

Yoshida Shigeru* (1878–1967) Prime Minister May 1946–May 1947 and October 1948–December 1954. Former diplomat (Consul General in Mukden; Ambassador to Italy; Ambassador to Great Britain). Married daughter of Foreign Minister Count Makino Nobuaki; also connected through marriage to powerful coal-mining family, Aso. Put forward as "clean," non-political figure after surrender, Yoshida ingratiated himself with SCAP (q.v.) as a trusty reactionary.

Yūai-kai Friendly Love Society: proto-union organization set up 1912 under the leadership of Suzuki Bunji. The cautious predecessor of Sōdōmei (q.v.).

Yuan Shih-k'ai Former Governor of Shantung Province, where he had led the suppression of the Yi Ho Tuan uprising (q.v.). Briefly became President of China in the turmoil following the 1911 revolution. Died in 1916 shortly after signing the disastrous 1915 agreement with Japan, granting most of the Twenty-one Demands (q.v.).

Zaibatsu Financial-industrial groups; until 1945 organized round holding companies. Reorganized after lying low during the early years of the Occupation, and returned to dominate the Japanese economy once again. Part of zaibatsu cover-up was to pretend there was a sharp distinction between themselves and newer military-related firms known as *shinkō zaibatsu* ("new zaibatsu").

Zaikai The most common term currently in use for big business and finance; the emphasis is on finance rather than industry as such, and the term implies reference to the small group dominating and co-ordinating the financial policy of the capitalist class as a whole.

Zengakuren National Federation of Students' Self-Governing Associations; formed September 1948 with 300,000 members from 145 universities. Militant students' organization which played a major role in the movement to prevent revision of the Security Treaty in 1960.

Zenkyōtō National Union of Struggle Councils (Zenkoku Kyōtō Kaigi Rengō); formed September 1969 as a non-sectarian federation of mainly student and postgraduate groups which largely took over from Zengakuren. Active in the 1970 struggles against the renewal of the Security Treaty.

Zenrōren National Labour Union Liaison Council (Zenkoku Rōdō Kumiai Renraku Kyōgikai): short-lived alliance between the Sōdōmei and the Sanbetsu (qq.vv.) in 1947–48, representing a forced compromise between the demands of the rank and file and the reformist orientation of the Sōdōmei leaders.

---

* NOTE: not to be confused with another Yoshida Shigeru, government minister under Tōjō.

Index

About the Author

Jon Halliday was born in Dublin and studied at Oxford. He is a member of the editorial boards of *New Left Review* and *Screen*, and has written extensively on Japan and Korea. He is the author of *Japanese Imperialism Today* (with Gavan McCormack) and of *Sirk on Sirk*, and co-editor of the forthcoming book *The Psychology of Gambling*.